S0-AWO-655

देवाय तस्मै नमः

A HISTORY OF INDIAN PHILOSOPHY

निखिलमनुजचित्तं ज्ञानसूत्रैर्नवैर्यः
स्रजमिव कुसुमानां कालरन्ध्रैर्विधत्ते।
स लघुमपि ममैतं प्राच्यविज्ञानतन्तुं
उपहृतमतिभक्त्या मोदतां मे गृहीत्वा॥

May He, who links the minds of all people, through the apertures of time, with new threads of knowledge like a garland of flowers, be pleased to accept this my thread of Eastern thought, offered, though it be small, with the greatest devotion.

A HISTORY OF INDIAN PHILOSOPHY

BY THE LATE
SURENDRANATH DASGUPTA

VOLUME I

MOTILAL BANARSIDASS
Delhi :: Varanasi :: Patna

© MOTILAL BANARSIDASS
Indological Publishers and Booksellers
Head Office : BUNGALOW ROAD, JAWAHAR NAGAR, DELHI-7
Branches : 1. CHOWK, VARANASI-1 (U.P.)
2. ASHOK RAJPATH, PATNA-4 (BIHAR)

ISBN 0 8426 0963 6

Reprinted by permission of Cambridge University Press

First Edition : Cambridge, 1922
Reprinted : Cambridge, 1932, 1951, 1957, 1963, 1969, 1973
First Indian Edition : Delhi, 1975

Price Rs. 40.00 (Volume I)
Rs. 200.00 (for 5 Volumes Complete set)

Printed in India
BY SHANTILAL JAIN, AT SHRI JAINENDRA PRESS, A-45, PHASE-I, INDUSTRIAL AREA, NARAINA, NEW DELHI-28 AND PUBLISHED BY SUNDARLAL JAIN OF MOTILAL BANARSIDASS, BUNGALOW ROAD, JAWAHAR NAGAR, DELHI-7

DEDICATION

The work and ambition of a life-time is herein humbly dedicated with supreme reverence to the great sages of India, who, for the first time in history, formulated the true principles of freedom and devoted themselves to the holy quest of truth and the final assessment and discovery of the ultimate spiritual essence of man through their concrete lives, critical thought, dominant will and self-denial.

NOTE ON THE PRONUNCIATION OF TRANSLITERATED SANSKRIT AND PĀLI WORDS

The vowels are pronounced almost in the same way as in Italian, except that the sound of *a* approaches that of *o* in *bond* or *u* in *but*, and *ā* that of *a* as in *army*. The consonants are as in English, except *c*, *ch* in church; *ṭ*, *ḍ*, *ṇ* are cerebrals, to which English *t*, *d*, *n* almost correspond; *t*, *d*, *n* are pure dentals; *kh*, *gh*, *ch*, *jh*, *ṭh*, *ḍh*, *th*, *dh*, *ph*, *bh* are the simple sounds plus an aspiration; *ñ* is the French *gn*; *ṛ* is usually pronounced as *ri*, and *ś*, *ṣ* as *sh*.

PREFACE

THE old civilisation of India was a concrete unity of many-sided developments in art, architecture, literature, religion, morals, and science so far as it was understood in those days. But the most important achievement of Indian thought was philosophy. It was regarded as the goal of all the highest practical and theoretical activities, and it indicated the point of unity amidst all the apparent diversities which the complex growth of culture over a vast area inhabited by different peoples produced. It is not in the history of foreign invasions, in the rise of independent kingdoms at different times, in the empires of this or that great monarch that the unity of India is to be sought. It is essentially one of spiritual aspirations and obedience to the law of the spirit, which were regarded as superior to everything else, and it has outlived all the political changes through which India passed.

The Greeks, the Huns, the Scythians, the Pathans and the Moguls who occupied the land and controlled the political machinery never ruled the minds of the people, for these political events were like hurricanes or the changes of season, mere phenomena of a natural or physical order which never affected the spiritual integrity of Hindu culture. If after a passivity of some centuries India is again going to become creative it is mainly on account of this fundamental unity of her progress and civilisation and not for anything that she may borrow from other countries. It is therefore indispensably necessary for all those who wish to appreciate the significance and potentialities of Indian culture that they should properly understand the history of Indian philosophical thought which is the nucleus round which all that is best and highest in India has grown. Much harm has already been done by the circulation of opinions that the culture and philosophy of India was dreamy and abstract. It is therefore very necessary that Indians as well as other peoples should become more and more acquainted with the true characteristics of the past history of Indian thought and form a correct estimate of its special features.

But it is not only for the sake of the right understanding of

India that Indian philosophy should be read, or only as a record of the past thoughts of India. For most of the problems that are still debated in modern philosophical thought occurred in more or less divergent forms to the philosophers of India. Their discussions, difficulties and solutions when properly grasped in connection with the problems of our own times may throw light on the course of the process of the future reconstruction of modern thought. The discovery of the important features of Indian philosophical thought, and a due appreciation of their full significance, may turn out to be as important to modern philosophy as the discovery of Sanskrit has been to the investigation of modern philological researches. It is unfortunate that the task of re-interpretation and re-valuation of Indian thought has not yet been undertaken on a comprehensive scale. Sanskritists also with very few exceptions have neglected this important field of study, for most of these scholars have been interested more in mythology, philology, and history than in philosophy. Much work however has already been done in the way of the publication of a large number of important texts, and translations of some of them have also been attempted. But owing to the presence of many technical terms in advanced Sanskrit philosophical literature, the translations in most cases are hardly intelligible to those who are not familiar with the texts themselves.

A work containing some general account of the mutual relations of the chief systems is necessary for those who intend to pursue the study of a particular school. This is also necessary for lay readers interested in philosophy and students of Western philosophy who have no inclination or time to specialise in any Indian system, but who are at the same time interested to know what they can about Indian philosophy. In my two books *The Study of Patanjali* and *Yoga Philosophy in relation to other Indian Systems of Thought* I have attempted to interpret the Sāṃkhya and Yoga systems both from their inner point of view and from the point of view of their relation to other Indian systems. The present attempt deals with the important features of these as also of all the other systems and seeks to show some of their inner philosophical relations especially in regard to the history of their development. I have tried to be as faithful to the original texts as I could and have always given the Sanskrit or Pāli technical terms for the help of those who want to make this book a guide for further study. To understand something of these terms is indeed essential for anyone who wishes to be sure that he is following the actual course of the thoughts.

In Sanskrit treatises the style of argument and methods of treating the different topics are altogether different from what we find in any modern work of philosophy. Materials had therefore to be collected from a large number of works on each system and these have been knit together and given a shape which is likely to be more intelligible to people unacquainted with Sanskritic ways of thought. But at the same time I considered it quite undesirable to put any pressure on Indian thoughts in order to make them appear as European. This will explain much of what might appear quaint to a European reader. But while keeping all the thoughts and expressions of the Indian thinkers I have tried to arrange them in a systematic whole in a manner which appeared to me strictly faithful to their clear indications and suggestions. It is only in very few places that I have translated some of the Indian terms by terms of English philosophy, and this I did because it appeared to me that those were approximately the nearest approach to the Indian sense of the term. In all other places I have tried to choose words which have not been made dangerous by the acquirement of technical senses. This however is difficult, for the words which are used in philosophy always acquire some sort of technical sense. I would therefore request my readers to take those words in an unsophisticated sense and associate them with such meanings as are justified by the passages and contexts in which they are used. Some of what will appear as obscure in any system may I hope be removed if it is re-read with care and attention, for unfamiliarity sometimes stands in the way of right comprehension. But I may have also missed giving the proper suggestive links in many places where condensation was inevitable and the systems themselves have also sometimes insoluble difficulties, for no system of philosophy is without its dark and uncomfortable corners.

Though I have begun my work from the Vedic and Brāhmaṇic stage, my treatment of this period has been very slight. The beginnings of the evolution of philosophical thought, though they can be traced in the later Vedic hymns, are neither connected nor systematic.

More is found in the Brāhmaṇas, but I do not think it worth while to elaborate the broken shreds of thought of this epoch. I could have dealt with the Upaniṣad period more fully, but many works on the subject have already been published in Europe and those who wish to go into details will certainly go to them. I have therefore limited myself to the dominant current flowing through the earlier Upaniṣads. Notices of other currents of thought will be given in connection with the treatment of other systems in the second volume with which they are more intimately connected. It will be noticed that my treatment of early Buddhism is in some places of an inconclusive character. This is largely due to the inconclusive character of the texts which were put into writing long after Buddha in the form of dialogues and where the precision and directness required in philosophy were not contemplated. This has given rise to a number of theories about the interpretations of the philosophical problems of early Buddhism among modern Buddhist scholars and it is not always easy to decide one way or the other without running the risk of being dogmatic; and the scope of my work was also too limited to allow me to indulge in very elaborate discussions of textual difficulties. But still I also have in many places formed theories of my own, whether they are right or wrong it will be for scholars to judge. I had no space for entering into any polemic, but it will be found that my interpretations of the systems are different in some cases from those offered by some European scholars who have worked on them and I leave it to those who are acquainted with the literature of the subject to decide which of us may be in the right. I have not dealt elaborately with the new school of Logic (Navya-Nyāya) of Bengal, for the simple reason that most of the contributions of this school consist in the invention of technical expressions and the emphasis put on the necessity of strict exactitude and absolute preciseness of logical definitions and discussions and these are almost untranslatable in intelligible English. I have however incorporated what important differences of philosophical points of view I could find in it. Discussions of a purely technical character could not be very fruitful in a work like this. The bibliography given of the different Indian systems in the last six chapters is not exhaustive but consists mostly of books which have been actually studied or consulted in the writing of those chapters. Exact references to the pages of the texts have generally been given in footnotes in those cases where a difference of interpretation was anticipated or where it was felt that a reference to the text would make the matter clearer, or where the opinions of modern writers have been incorporated.

It gives me the greatest pleasure to acknowledge my deepest gratefulness to the Hon'ble Maharaja Sir Manindrachandra Nundy, K.C.I.E. Kashimbazar, Bengal, who has kindly promised to bear the entire expense of the publication of both volumes of the present work.

The name of this noble man is almost a household word in Bengal for the magnanimous gifts that he has made to educational and other causes. Up till now he has made a total gift of about £300,000, of which those devoted to education come to about £200,000. But the man himself is far above the gifts he has made. His sterling character, universal sympathy and friendship, his kindness and amiability make him a veritable Bodhisattva—one of the noblest of men that I have ever seen. Like many other scholars of Bengal, I am deeply indebted to him for the encouragement that he has given me in the pursuit of my studies and researches, and my feelings of attachment and gratefulness for him are too deep for utterance.

I am much indebted to my esteemed friends Dr E. J. Thomas of the Cambridge University Library and Mr Douglas Ainslie for their kindly revising the proofs of this work, in the course of which they improved my English in many places. To the former I am also indebted for his attention to the transliteration of a large number of Sanskrit words, and also for the whole-hearted sympathy and great friendliness with which he assisted me with his advice on many points of detail, in particular the exposition of the Buddhist doctrine of the cause of rebirth owes something of its treatment to repeated discussions with him.

I also wish to express my gratefulness to my friend Mr N. K. Siddhanta, M.A., late of the Scottish Churches College, and Mademoiselle Paule Povie for the kind assistance they have rendered in preparing the index. My obligations are also due to the Syndics of the Cambridge University Press for the honour they have done me in publishing this work.

To scholars of Indian philosophy who may do me the honour of reading my book and who may be impressed with its inevitable shortcomings and defects, I can only pray in the words of Hemacandra:

Pramāṇasiddhāntaviruddham atra
Yatkiñciduktam matimāndyadoṣāt
Mātsaryyam utsāryya tadāryyacittāḥ
Prasādam ādhāya viśodhayantu[1].

S. D.

TRINITY COLLEGE,
CAMBRIDGE.
February, 1922.

1 May the noble-minded scholars instead of cherishing ill feeling kindly correct whatever errors have been here committed through the dullness of my intellect in the way of wrong interpretations and misstatements.

CONTENTS

CHAPTER I

CHAPTER II

THE VEDAS, BRĀHMAṆAS AND THEIR PHILOSOPHY

CHAPTER III

THE EARLIER UPANIṢADS (700 B.C.—600 B.C.)

CHAPTER IV

GENERAL OBSERVATIONS ON THE SYSTEMS OF INDIAN PHILOSOPHY

CHAPTER V

BUDDHIST PHILOSOPHY

CHAPTER VI

THE JAINA PHILOSOPHY

CHAPTER VII

THE KAPILA AND THE PĀTAÑJALA SĀṂKHYA (YOGA)

CHAPTER VIII

THE NYĀYA-VAIŚEṢIKA PHILOSOPHY

CHAPTER IX

MĪMĀṂSĀ PHILOSOPHY

CHAPTER X

THE ŚAṄKARA SCHOOL OF VEDĀNTA

CHAPTER I

INTRODUCTORY

THE achievements of the ancient Indians in the field of philosophy are but very imperfectly known to the world at large, and it is unfortunate that the condition is no better even in India. There is a small body of Hindu scholars and ascetics living a retired life in solitude, who are well acquainted with the subject, but they do not know English and are not used to modern ways of thinking, and the idea that they ought to write books in vernaculars in order to popularize the subject does not appeal to them. Through the activity of various learned bodies and private individuals both in Europe and in India large numbers of philosophical works in Sanskrit and Pāli have been published, as well as translations of a few of them, but there has been as yet little systematic attempt on the part of scholars to study them and judge their value. There are hundreds of Sanskrit works on most of the systems of Indian thought and scarcely a hundredth part of them has been translated. Indian modes of expression, entailing difficult technical philosophical terms are so different from those of European thought, that they can hardly ever be accurately translated. It is therefore very difficult for a person unacquainted with Sanskrit to understand Indian philosophical thought in its true bearing from translations. Pāli is a much easier language than Sanskrit, but a knowledge of Pāli is helpful in understanding only the earliest school of Buddhism, when it was in its semi-philosophical stage. Sanskrit is generally regarded as a difficult language. But no one from an acquaintance with Vedic or ordinary literary Sanskrit can have any idea of the difficulty of the logical and abstruse parts of Sanskrit philosophical literature. A man who can easily understand the Vedas, the Upaniṣads, the Purāṇas, the Law Books and the literary works, and is also well acquainted with European philosophical thought, may find it literally impossible to understand even small portions of a work of advanced Indian logic, or the dialectical Vedānta. This is due to two reasons, the use of technical terms and of great condensation in expression, and the hidden allusions to doctrines of other systems. The tendency to conceiving philosophical problems in a clear and unambiguous manner is an important feature of Sanskrit thought, but from the ninth century onwards, the habit of using clear, definite, and precise expressions, began to develop in a very striking manner, and as a result of that a large number of technical terms began to be invented. These terms are seldom properly explained, and it is presupposed that the reader who wants to read the works should have a knowledge of them. Any one in olden times who took to the study of any system of philosophy, had to do so with a teacher, who explained those terms to him. The teacher himself had got it from his teacher, and he from his. There was no tendency to popularize philosophy, for the idea then prevalent was that only the chosen few who had otherwise shown their fitness, deserved to become fit students (*adhikārī*) of philosophy, under the direction of a teacher. Only those who had the grit and high moral strength to devote their whole life to the true understanding of philosophy and the rebuilding of life in accordance with the high truths of philosophy were allowed to study it.

Another difficulty which a beginner will meet is this, that sometimes the same technical terms are used in extremely different senses in different systems. The student must know the meaning of each technical term with reference to the system in which it occurs, and no dictionary will enlighten him much about the matter[1]. He will have to pick them up as he advances and finds them used. Allusions to the doctrines of other systems and their refutations during the discussions of similar doctrines in any particular system of thought are often very puzzling even to a well-equipped reader; for he cannot be expected to know all the doctrines of other systems without going through them, and so it often becomes difficult to follow the series of answers and refutations which are poured forth in the course of these discussions. There are two important compendiums in Sanskrit giving a summary of some of the principal systems of Indian thought, viz. the *Sarvadarśanasaṃgraha*, and the *Ṣaḍdarśanasamuccaya* of Haribhadra with the commentary of Guṇaratna; but the former is very sketchy and can throw very little light on the understanding of the ontological or epistemological doctrines of any of the systems. It has been translated by Cowell and Gough, but I

[1] Recently a very able Sanskrit dictionary of technical philosophical terms called Nyāyakośa has been prepared by M. M. Bhīmācārya Jhalkikar, Bombay, Govt. Press.

am afraid the translation may not be found very intelligible. Guṇaratna's commentary is excellent so far as Jainism is concerned, and it sometimes gives interesting information about other systems, and also supplies us with some short bibliographical notices, but it seldom goes on to explain the epistemological or ontological doctrines or discussions which are so necessary for the right understanding of any of the advanced systems of Indian thought. Thus in the absence of a book which could give us in brief the main epistemological, ontological, and psychological positions of the Indian thinkers, it is difficult even for a good Sanskrit scholar to follow the advanced philosophical literature, even though he may be acquainted with many of the technical philosophical terms. I have spoken enough about the difficulties of studying Indian philosophy, but if once a person can get himself used to the technical terms and the general positions of the different Indian thinkers and their modes of expression, he can master the whole by patient toil. The technical terms, which are a source of difficulty at the beginning, are of inestimable value in helping us to understand the precise and definite meaning of the writers who used them, and the chances of misinterpreting or misunderstanding them are reduced to a minimum. It is I think well-known that avoidance of technical terms has often rendered philosophical works unduly verbose, and liable to misinterpretation. The art of clear writing is indeed a rare virtue and every philosopher cannot expect to have it. But when technical expressions are properly formed, even a bad writer can make himself understood. In the early days of Buddhist philosophy in the Pāli literature, this difficulty is greatly felt. There are some technical terms here which are still very elastic and their repetition in different places in more or less different senses heighten the difficulty of understanding the real meaning intended to be conveyed.

But is it necessary that a history of Indian philosophy should be written? There are some people who think that the Indians never rose beyond the stage of simple faith and that therefore they cannot have any philosophy at all in the proper sense of the term. Thus Professor Frank Thilly of the Cornell University says in his *History of Philosophy*[1], "A universal history of philosophy would include the philosophies of all peoples. Not all peoples, however

[1] New York, 1914, p. 3.

have produced real systems of thought, and the speculations of only a few can be said to have had a history. Many do not rise beyond the mythological stage. Even the theories of Oriental peoples, the Hindus, Egyptians, Chinese, consist, in the main, of mythological and ethical doctrines, and are not thoroughgoing systems of thought: they are shot through with poetry and faith. We shall, therefore, limit ourselves to the study of the Western countries, and begin with the philosophy of the ancient Greeks, on whose culture our own civilization in part, rests." There are doubtless many other people who hold such uninformed and untrue beliefs, which only show their ignorance of Indian matters. It is not necessary to say anything in order to refute these views, for what follows will I hope show the falsity of their beliefs. If they are not satisfied, and want to know more definitely and elaborately about the contents of the different systems, I am afraid they will have to go to the originals referred to in the bibliographical notices of the chapters.

There is another opinion, that the time has not yet come for an attempt to write a history of Indian philosophy. Two different reasons are given from two different points of view. It is said that the field of Indian philosophy is so vast, and such a vast literature exists on each of the systems, that it is not possible for anyone to collect his materials directly from the original sources, before separate accounts are prepared by specialists working in each of the particular systems. There is some truth in this objection, but although in some of the important systems the literature that exists is exceedingly vast, yet many of them are more or less repetitions of the same subjects, and a judicious selection of twenty or thirty important works on each of the systems could certainly be made, which would give a fairly correct exposition. In my own undertaking in this direction I have always drawn directly from the original texts, and have always tried to collect my materials from those sources in which they appear at their best. My space has been very limited and I have chosen the features which appeared to me to be the most important. I had to leave out many discussions of difficult problems and diverse important bearings of each of the systems to many interesting aspects of philosophy. This I hope may be excused in a history of philosophy which does not aim at completeness. There are indeed many defects and shortcomings, and these would have been much less in the case of a writer abler than the present one. At any rate it may be hoped that the imperfections of the present attempt will be a stimulus to those whose better and more competent efforts will supersede it. No attempt ought to be called impossible on account of its imperfections.

In the second place it is said that the Indians had no proper and accurate historical records and biographies and it is therefore impossible to write a history of Indian philosophy. This objection is also partially valid. But this defect does not affect us so much as one would at first sight suppose; for, though the dates of the earlier beginnings are very obscure, yet, in later times, we are in a position to affirm some dates and to point out priority and posteriority in the case of other thinkers. As most of the systems developed side by side through many centuries their mutual relations also developed, and these could be well observed. The special nature of this development has been touched on in the fourth chapter. Most of the systems had very early beginnings and a continuous course of development through the succeeding centuries, and it is not possible to take the state of the philosophy of a particular system at a particular time and contrast it with the state of that system at a later time; for the later state did not supersede the previous state, but only showed a more coherent form of it, which was generally true to the original system but was more determinate. Evolution through history has in Western countries often brought forth the development of more coherent types of philosophic thought, but in India, though the types remained the same, their development through history made them more and more coherent and determinate. Most of the parts were probably existent in the earlier stages, but they were in an undifferentiated state; through the criticism and conflict of the different schools existing side by side the parts of each of the systems of thought became more and more differentiated, determinate, and coherent. In some cases this development has been almost imperceptible, and in many cases the earlier forms have been lost, or so inadequately expressed that nothing definite could be made out of them. Wherever such a differentiation could be made in the interests of philosophy, I have tried to do it. But I have never considered it desirable that the philosophical interest should be subordinated to the chronological. It is no doubt true that more definite chronological information would be a very desirable thing, yet I am of opinion that the little chronological data we have give us a fair amount of help in forming a general notion about the growth and development of the different systems by mutual association and conflict. If the condition of the development of philosophy in India had been the same as in Europe, definite chronological knowledge would be considered much more indispensable. For, when one system supersedes another, it is indispensably necessary that we should know which preceded and which succeeded. But when the systems are developing side by side, and when we are getting them in their richer and better forms, the interest with regard to the conditions, nature and environment of their early origin has rather a historical than a philosophical interest. I have tried as best I could to form certain general notions as regards the earlier stages of some of the systems, but though the various features of these systems at these stages in detail may not be ascertainable, yet this, I think, could never be considered as invalidating the whole programme. Moreover, even if we knew definitely the correct dates of the thinkers of the same system we could not treat them separately, as is done in European philosophy, without unnecessarily repeating the same thing twenty times over; for they all dealt with the same system, and tried to bring out the same type of thought in more and more determinate forms.

The earliest literature of India is the Vedas. These consist mostly of hymns in praise of nature gods, such as fire, wind, etc. Excepting in some of the hymns of the later parts of the work (probably about 1000 B.C.), there is not much philosophy in them in our sense of the term. It is here that we first find intensely interesting philosophical questions of a more or less cosmological character expressed in terms of poetry and imagination. In the later Vedic works called the Brāhmaṇas and the Āraṇyakas written mostly in prose, which followed the Vedic hymns, there are two tendencies, viz. one that sought to establish the magical forms of ritualistic worship, and the other which indulged in speculative thinking through crude generalizations. This latter tendency was indeed much feebler than the former, and it might appear that the ritualistic tendency had actually swallowed up what little of philosophy the later parts of the Vedic hymns were trying to express, but there are unmistakable marks that this tendency existed and worked. Next to this come certain treatises written in prose and verse called the Upaniṣads, which contain various sorts of philosophical thoughts mostly monistic or singularistic but also some pluralistic and dualistic ones. These are not reasoned statements, but utterances of truths intuitively perceived or felt as unquestionably real and indubitable, and carrying great force, vigour, and persuasiveness with them. It is very probable that many of the earliest parts of this literature are as old as 500 B.C. to 700 B.C. Buddhist philosophy began with the Buddha from some time about 500 B.C. There is reason to believe that Buddhist philosophy continued to develop in India in one or other of its vigorous forms till some time about the tenth or eleventh century A.D. The earliest beginnings of the other Indian systems of thought are also to be sought chiefly between the age of the Buddha to about 200 B.C. Jaina philosophy was probably prior to the Buddha. But except in its earlier days, when it came in conflict with the doctrines of the Buddha, it does not seem to me that the Jaina thought came much in contact with other systems of Hindu thought. Excepting in some forms of Vaiṣṇava thought in later times, Jaina thought is seldom alluded to by the Hindu writers or later Buddhists, though some Jains like Haribhadra and Guṇaratna tried to refute the Hindu and Buddhist systems. The non-aggressive nature of their religion and ideal may to a certain extent explain it, but there may be other reasons too which it is difficult for us to guess. It is interesting to note that, though there have been some dissensions amongst the Jains about dogmas and creeds, Jaina philosophy has not split into many schools of thought more or less differing from one another as Buddhist thought did.

The first volume of this work will contain Buddhist and Jaina philosophy and the six systems of Hindu thought. These six systems of orthodox Hindu thought are the Sāṃkhya, the Yoga, the Nyāya, the Vaiśeṣika, the Mīmāṃsā (generally known as Pūrva Mīmāṃsā), and the Vedānta (known also as Uttara Mīmāṃsā). Of these what is differently known as Sāṃkhya and Yoga are but different schools of one system. The Vaiśeṣika and the Nyāya in later times became so mixed up that, though in early times the similarity of the former with Mīmāṃsā was greater than that with Nyāya, they came to be regarded as fundamentally almost the same systems. Nyāya and Vaiśeṣika have therefore been treated together. In addition to these systems some theistic systems began to grow prominent from the ninth century A.D. They also probably had their early beginnings at the time of the Upaniṣads. But at that time their interest was probably concentrated on problems of morality and religion. It is not improbable that these were associated with certain metaphysical theories also, but no works treating them in a systematic way are now available. One of their most important early works is the *Bhagavadgītā*. This book is rightly regarded as one of the greatest masterpieces of Hindu thought. It is written in verse, and deals with moral, religious, and metaphysical problems, in a loose form. It is its lack of system and method which gives it its peculiar charm more akin to the poetry of the Upaniṣads than to the dialectical and systematic Hindu thought. From the ninth century onwards attempts were made to supplement these loose theistic ideas which were floating about and forming integral parts of religious creeds, by metaphysical theories. Theism is often dualistic and pluralistic, and so are all these systems, which are known as different schools of Vaiṣṇava philosophy. Most of the Vaiṣṇava thinkers wished to show that their systems were taught in the Upaniṣads, and thus wrote commentaries thereon to prove their interpretations, and also wrote commentaries on the *Brahmasūtra*, the classical exposition of the philosophy of the Upaniṣads. In addition to the works of these Vaiṣṇava thinkers there sprang up another class of theistic works which were of a more eclectic nature. These also had their beginnings in periods as old as the Upaniṣads. They are known as the Śaiva and Tantra thought, and are dealt with in the second volume of this work.

We thus see that the earliest beginnings of most systems of Hindu thought can be traced to some time between 600 B.C. to 100 or 200 B.C. It is extremely difficult to say anything about the relative priority of the systems with any degree of certainty. Some conjectural attempts have been made in this work with regard to some of the systems, but how far they are correct, it will be for our readers to judge. Moreover during the earliest manifestation of a system some crude outlines only are traceable. As time went on the systems of thought began to develop side by side. Most of them were taught from the time in which they were first conceived to about the seventeenth century A.D. in an unbroken chain of teachers and pupils. Even now each system of Hindu thought has its own adherents, though few people now care to write any new works upon them. In the history of the growth of any system of Hindu thought we find that as time went on, and as new problems were suggested, each system tried to answer them consistently with its own doctrines. The order in which we have taken the philosophical systems could not be strictly a chronological one. Thus though it is possible that the earliest speculations of some form of Sāṃkhya, Yoga, and Mīmāṃsā were prior to Buddhism yet they have been treated after Buddhism and Jainism, because the elaborate works of these systems which we now possess are later than Buddhism. In my opinion the Vaiśeṣika system is also probably pre-Buddhistic, but it has been treated later, partly on account of its association with Nyāya, and partly on account of the fact that all its commentaries are of a much later date. It seems to me almost certain that enormous quantities of old philosophical literature have been lost, which if found could have been of use to us in showing the stages of the early growth of the systems and their mutual relations. But as they are not available we have to be satisfied with what remains. The original sources from which I have drawn my materials have all been indicated in the brief accounts of the literature of each system which I have put in before beginning the study of any particular system of thought.

In my interpretations I have always tried to follow the original sources as accurately as I could. This has sometimes led to old and unfamiliar modes of expression, but this course seemed to me to be preferable to the adoption of European modes of thought for the expression of Indian ideas. But even in spite of this striking similarities to many of the modern philosophical doctrines and ideas will doubtless be noticed. This only proves that the human mind follows more or less the same modes of rational thought. I have never tried to compare any phase of Indian thought with European, for this is beyond the scope of my present attempt, but if I may be allowed to express my own conviction, I might say that many of the philosophical doctrines of European philosophy are essentially the same as those found in Indian philosophy. The main difference is often the difference of the point of view from which the same problems appeared in such a variety of forms in the two countries. My own view with regard to the net value of Indian philosophical development will be expressed in the concluding chapter of the second volume of the present work.

CHAPTER II

THE VEDAS, BRĀHMANAS AND THEIR PHILOSOPHY

The Vedas and their antiquity.

THE sacred books of India, the Vedas, are generally believed to be the earliest literary record of the Indo-European race. It is indeed difficult to say when the earliest portions of these compositions came into existence. Many shrewd guesses have been offered, but none of them can be proved to be incontestably true. Max Müller supposed the date to be 1200 B.C., Haug 2400 B.C. and Bāl Gaṅgādhar Tilak 4000 B.C. The ancient Hindus seldom kept any historical record of their literary, religious or political achievements. The Vedas were handed down from mouth to mouth from a period of unknown antiquity; and the Hindus generally believed that they were never composed by men. It was therefore generally supposed that either they were taught by God to the sages, or that they were of themselves revealed to the sages who were the "seers" (*mantradraṣṭā*) of the hymns. Thus we find that when some time had elapsed after the composition of the Vedas, people had come to look upon them not only as very old, but so old that they had, theoretically at least, no beginning in time, though they were believed to have been revealed at some unknown remote period at the beginning of each creation.

The place of the Vedas in the Hindu mind.

When the Vedas were composed, there was probably no system of writing prevalent in India. But such was the scrupulous zeal of the Brahmins, who got the whole Vedic literature by heart by hearing it from their preceptors, that it has been transmitted most faithfully to us through the course of the last 3000 years or more with little or no interpolations at all. The religious history of India had suffered considerable changes in the latter periods, since the time of the Vedic civilization, but such was the reverence paid to the Vedas that they had ever remained as the highest religious authority for all sections of the Hindus at all times. Even at this day all the obligatory duties of the Hindus at birth, marriage, death, etc., are performed according to the old

Vedic ritual. The prayers that a Brahmin now says three times a day are the same selections of Vedic verses as were used as prayer verses two or three thousand years ago. A little insight into the life of an ordinary Hindu of the present day will show that the system of image-worship is one that has been grafted upon his life, the regular obligatory duties of which are ordered according to the old Vedic rites. Thus an orthodox Brahmin can dispense with image-worship if he likes, but not so with his daily Vedic prayers or other obligatory ceremonies. Even at this day there are persons who bestow immense sums of money for the performance and teaching of Vedic sacrifices and rituals. Most of the Sanskrit literatures that flourished after the Vedas base upon them their own validity, and appeal to them as authority. Systems of Hindu philosophy not only own their allegiance to the Vedas, but the adherents of each one of them would often quarrel with others and maintain its superiority by trying to prove that it and it alone was the faithful follower of the Vedas and represented correctly their views. The laws which regulate the social, legal, domestic and religious customs and rites of the Hindus even to the present day are said to be but mere systematized memories of old Vedic teachings, and are held to be obligatory on their authority. Even under British administration, in the inheritance of property, adoption, and in such other legal transactions, Hindu Law is followed, and this claims to draw its authority from the Vedas. To enter into details is unnecessary. But suffice it to say that the Vedas, far from being regarded as a dead literature of the past, are still looked upon as the origin and source of almost all literatures except purely secular poetry and drama. Thus in short we may say that in spite of the many changes that time has wrought, the orthodox Hindu life may still be regarded in the main as an adumbration of the Vedic life, which had never ceased to shed its light all through the past.

Classification of the Vedic literature.

A beginner who is introduced for the first time to the study of later Sanskrit literature is likely to appear somewhat confused when he meets with authoritative texts of diverse purport and subjects having the same generic name "Veda" or "Śruti" (from *śru* to hear); for Veda in its wider sense is not the name of any particular book, but of the literature of a particular epoch extending over a long period, say two thousand years or so. As this literature represents the total achievements of the Indian people in different directions for such a long period, it must of necessity be of a diversified character. If we roughly classify this huge literature from the points of view of age, language, and subject matter, we can point out four different types, namely the Saṃhitā or collection of verses (*sam* together, *hita* put), Brāhmaṇas, Āraṇyakas ("forest treatises") and the Upanisads. All these literatures, both prose and verse, were looked upon as so holy that in early times it was thought almost a sacrilege to write them; they were therefore learnt by heart by the Brahmins from the mouth of their preceptors and were hence called *śruti* (literally anything heard)[1].

The Saṃhitās.

There are four collections or Saṃhitās, namely Ṛg-Veda, Sāma-Veda, Yajur-Veda and Atharva-Veda. Of these the Ṛg-Veda is probably the earliest. The Sāma-Veda has practically no independent value, for it consists of stanzas taken (excepting only 75) entirely from the Ṛg-Veda, which were meant to be sung to certain fixed melodies, and may thus be called the book of chants. The Yajur-Veda however contains in addition to the verses taken from the Rg-Veda many original prose formulas. The arrangement of the verses of the Sāma-Veda is solely with reference to their place and use in the Soma sacrifice; the contents of the Yajur-Veda are arranged in the order in which the verses were actually employed in the various religious sacrifices. It is therefore called the Veda of Yajus—sacrificial prayers. These may be contrasted with the arrangement in the Ṛg-Veda in this, that there the verses are generally arranged in accordance with the gods who are adored in them. Thus, for example, first we get all the poems addressed to Agni or the Fire-god, then all those to the god Indra and so on. The fourth collection, the Atharva-Veda, probably attained its present form considerably later than the Ṛg-Veda. In spirit, however, as Professor Macdonell says, "it is not only entirely different from the *Rigveda* but represents a much more primitive stage of thought. While the *Rigveda* deals almost exclusively with the higher gods as conceived by a com-

[1] Pāṇini, III. iii. 94.

paratively advanced and refined sacerdotal class, the *Atharva-Veda* is, in the main a book of spells and incantations appealing to the demon world, and teems with notions about witchcraft current among the lower grades of the population, and derived from an immemorial antiquity. These two, thus complementary to each other in contents are obviously the most important of the four Vedas[1]."

The Brāhmaṇas[2].

After the Saṃhitās there grew up the theological treatises called the Brāhmaṇas, which were of a distinctly different literary type. They are written in prose, and explain the sacred significance of the different rituals to those who are not already familiar with them. "They reflect," says Professor Macdonell, "the spirit of an age in which all intellectual activity is concentrated on the sacrifice, describing its ceremonies, discussing its value, speculating on its origin and significance." These works are full of dogmatic assertions, fanciful symbolism and speculations of an unbounded imagination in the field of sacrificial details. The sacrificial ceremonials were probably never so elaborate at the time when the early hymns were composed. But when the collections of hymns were being handed down from generation to generation the ceremonials became more and more complicated. Thus there came about the necessity of the distribution of the different sacrificial functions among several distinct classes of priests. We may assume that this was a period when the caste system was becoming established, and when the only thing which could engage wise and religious minds was sacrifice and its elaborate rituals. Free speculative thinking was thus subordinated to the service of the sacrifice, and the result was the production of the most fanciful sacramental and symbolic

[1] A. A. Macdonell's *History of Sanskrit Literature*, p. 31.

[2] Weber (*Hist. Ind. Lit.*, p. 11, note) says that the word Brāhmaṇa signifies "that which relates to prayer *brahman*." Max Müller (*S. B. E.* I. p. lxvi) says that Brāhmaṇa meant "originally the sayings of Brahmans, whether in the general sense of priests, or in the more special sense of Brahman-priests." Eggeling (*S. B E.* XII. Introd. p. xxii) says that the Brāhmaṇas were so called "probably either because they were intended for the instruction and guidance of priests (brahman) generally; or because they were, for the most part, the authoritative utterances of such as were thoroughly versed in Vedic and sacrificial lore and competent to act as Brahmans or superintending priests." But in view of the fact that the Brāhmaṇas were also supposed to be as much revealed as the Vedas, the present writer thinks that Weber's view is the correct one.

system, unparalleled anywhere but among the Gnostics. It is now generally believed that the close of the Brāhmaṇa period was not later than 500 B.C.

The Āraṇyakas.

As a further development of the Brāhmaṇas however we get the Āraṇyakas or forest treatises. These works were probably composed for old men who had retired into the forest and were thus unable to perform elaborate sacrifices requiring a multitude of accessories and articles which could not be procured in forests. In these, meditations on certain symbols were supposed to be of great merit, and they gradually began to supplant the sacrifices as being of a superior order. It is here that we find that amongst a certain section of intelligent people the ritualistic ideas began to give way, and philosophic speculations about the nature of truth became gradually substituted in their place. To take an illustration from the beginning of the Bṛhadāraṇyaka we find that instead of the actual performance of the horse sacrifice (*aśvamedha*) there are directions for meditating upon the dawn (*Uṣas*) as the head of the horse, the sun as the eye of the horse, the air as its life, and so on. This is indeed a distinct advancement of the claims of speculation or meditation over the actual performance of the complicated ceremonials of sacrifice. The growth of the subjective speculation, as being capable of bringing the highest good, gradually resulted in the supersession of Vedic ritualism and the establishment of the claims of philosophic meditation and self-knowledge as the highest goal of life. Thus we find that the Āraṇyaka age was a period during which free thinking tried gradually to shake off the shackles of ritualism which had fettered it for a long time. It was thus that the Āraṇyakas could pave the way for the Upaniṣads, revive the germs of philosophic speculation in the Vedas, and develop them in a manner which made the Upaniṣads the source of all philosophy that arose in the world of Hindu thought.

The Ṛg-Veda, its civilization.

The hymns of the Ṛg-Veda are neither the productions of a single hand nor do they probably belong to any single age. They were composed probably at different periods by different sages, and it is not improbable that some of them were composed before the Aryan people entered the plains of India. They were handed down from mouth to mouth and gradually swelled through the new additions that were made by the poets of succeeding generations. It was when the collection had increased to a very considerable extent that it was probably arranged in the present form, or in some other previous forms to which the present arrangement owes its origin. They therefore reflect the civilization of the Aryan people at different periods of antiquity before and after they had come to India. This unique monument of a long vanished age is of great aesthetic value, and contains much that is genuine poetry. It enables us to get an estimate of the primitive society which produced it—the oldest book of the Aryan race. The principal means of sustenance were cattle-keeping and the cultivation of the soil with plough and harrow, mattock and hoe, and watering the ground when necessary with artificial canals. "The chief food consists," as Kaegi says, "together with bread, of various preparations of milk, cakes of flour and butter, many sorts of vegetables and fruits; meat cooked on the spits or in pots, is little used, and was probably eaten only at the great feasts and family gatherings. Drinking plays throughout a much more important part than eating[1]." The wood-worker built war-chariots and wagons, as also more delicate carved works and artistic cups. Metal-workers, smiths and potters continued their trade. The women understood the plaiting of mats, weaving and sewing; they manufactured the wool of the sheep into clothing for men and covering for animals. The group of individuals forming a tribe was the highest political unit; each of the different families forming a tribe was under the sway of the father or the head of the family. Kingship was probably hereditary and in some cases electoral. Kingship was nowhere absolute, but limited by the will of the people. Most developed ideas of justice, right and law, were present in the country. Thus Kaegi says, "the hymns strongly prove how deeply the prominent minds in the people were persuaded that the eternal ordinances of the rulers of the world were as inviolable in mental and moral matters as in the realm of nature, and that every wrong act, even the unconscious, was punished and the sin expiated[2]." Thus it is only right and proper to think that the Aryans had attained a pretty high degree

[1] *The Rigveda*, by Kaegi, 1886 edition, p. 13. [2] *Ibid.* p. 18.

of civilization, but nowhere was the sincere spirit of the Aryans more manifested than in religion, which was the most essential and dominant feature of almost all the hymns, except a few secular ones. Thus Kaegi says, "The whole significance of the Rigveda in reference to the general history of religion, as has repeatedly been pointed out in modern times, rests upon this, that it presents to us the development of religious conceptions from the earliest beginnings to the deepest apprehension of the godhead and its relation to man[1]."

The Vedic Gods.

The hymns of the Ṛg-Veda were almost all composed in praise of the gods. The social and other materials are of secondary importance, as these references had only to be mentioned incidentally in giving vent to their feelings of devotion to the god. The gods here are however personalities presiding over the diverse powers of nature or forming their very essence. They have therefore no definite, systematic and separate characters like the Greek gods or the gods of the later Indian mythical works, the Purāṇas. The powers of nature such as the storm, the rain, the thunder, are closely associated with one another, and the gods associated with them are also similar in character. The same epithets are attributed to different gods and it is only in a few specific qualities that they differ from one another. In the later mythological compositions of the Purāṇas the gods lost their character as hypostatic powers of nature, and thus became actual personalities and characters having their tales of joy and sorrow like the mortal here below. The Vedic gods may be contrasted with them in this, that they are of an impersonal nature, as the characters they display are mostly but expressions of the powers of nature. To take an example, the fire or Agni is described, as Kaegi has it, as one that "lies concealed in the softer wood, as in a chamber, until, called forth by the rubbing in the early morning hour, he suddenly springs forth in gleaming brightness. The sacrificer takes and lays him on the wood. When the priests pour melted butter upon him, he leaps up crackling and neighing like a horse—he whom men love to see increasing like their own prosperity. They wonder at him, when, decking himself with

[1] *The Rigveda*, by Kaegi, p. 26.

changing colors like a suitor, equally beautiful on all sides, he presents to all sides his front.

> All-searching is his beam, the gleaming of his light,
> His, the all-beautiful, of beauteous face and glance,
> The changing shimmer like that floats upon the stream,
> So Agni's rays gleam over bright and never cease[1]."
>
> R. V. I. 143. 3.

They would describe the wind (Vāta) and adore him and say

> "In what place was he born, and from whence comes he?
> The vital breath of gods, the world's great offspring,
> The God where'er he will moves at his pleasure:
> His rushing sound we hear—what his appearance, no one[2]."
>
> R. V. X. 168. 3, 4.

It was the forces of nature and her manifestations, on earth here, the atmosphere around and above us, or in the Heaven beyond the vault of the sky that excited the devotion and imagination of the Vedic poets. Thus with the exception of a few abstract gods of whom we shall presently speak and some dual divinities, the gods may be roughly classified as the terrestrial, atmospheric, and celestial.

Polytheism, Henotheism and Monotheism.

The plurality of the Vedic gods may lead a superficial enquirer to think the faith of the Vedic people polytheistic. But an intelligent reader will find here neither polytheism nor monotheism but a simple primitive stage of belief to which both of these may be said to owe their origin. The gods here do not preserve their proper places as in a polytheistic faith, but each one of them shrinks into insignificance or shines as supreme according as it is the object of adoration or not. The Vedic poets were the children of nature. Every natural phenomenon excited their wonder, admiration or veneration. The poet is struck with wonder that "the rough red cow gives soft white milk." The appearance or the setting of the sun sends a thrill into the minds of the Vedic sage and with wonder-gazing eyes he exclaims:

> "Undropped beneath, not fastened firm, how comes it
> That downward turned he falls not downward?
> The guide of his ascending path,—who saw it[1]?" R. V. IV. 13. 5.

The sages wonder how "the sparkling waters of all rivers flow into one ocean without ever filling it." The minds of the Vedic

[1] *The Rigveda*, by Kaegi, p. 35. [2] *Ibid.* p. 38.

people as we find in the hymns were highly impressionable and fresh. At this stage the time was not ripe enough for them to accord a consistent and well-defined existence to the multitude of gods nor to universalize them in a monotheistic creed. They hypostatized unconsciously any force of nature that overawed them or filled them with gratefulness and joy by its beneficent or aesthetic character, and adored it. The deity which moved the devotion or admiration of their mind was the most supreme for the time. This peculiar trait of the Vedic hymns Max Müller has called Henotheism or Kathenotheism: "a belief in single gods, each in turn standing out as the highest. And since the gods are thought of as specially ruling in their own spheres, the singers, in their special concerns and desires, call most of all on that god to whom they ascribe the most power in the matter,—to whose department if I may say so, their wish belongs. This god alone is present to the mind of the suppliant; with him for the time being is associated everything that can be said of a divine being;—he is the highest, the only god, before whom all others disappear, there being in this, however, no offence or depreciation of any other god[1]." "Against this theory it has been urged," as Macdonell rightly says in his *Vedic Mythology*[2], "that Vedic deities are not represented 'as independent of all the rest,' since no religion brings its gods into more frequent and varied juxtaposition and combination, and that even the mightiest gods of the Veda are made dependent on others. Thus Varuṇa and Sūrya are subordinate to Indra (I. 101), Varuṇa and the Aśvins submit to the power of Viṣṇu (I. 156)....Even when a god is spoken of as unique or chief (*eka*), as is natural enough in laudations, such statements lose their temporarily monotheistic force, through the modifications or corrections supplied by the context or even by the same verse[3]." "Henotheism is therefore an appearance," says Macdonell, "rather than a reality, an appearance produced by the indefiniteness due to undeveloped anthropomorphism, by the lack of any Vedic god occupying the position of a Zeus as the constant head of the pantheon, by the natural tendency of the priest or singer in extolling a particular god to exaggerate his greatness and to ignore other gods, and by the

[1] *The Rigveda*, by Kaegi, p. 27.

[2] See *Ibid*. p. 33. See also Arrowsmith's note on it for other references to Henotheism.

[3] Macdonell's *Vedic Mythology*, pp. 16, 17.

growing belief in the unity of the gods (cf. the refrain of 3, 35) each of whom might be regarded as a type of the divine[1]." But whether we call it Henotheism or the mere temporary exaggeration of the powers of the deity in question, it is evident that this stage can neither be properly called polytheistic nor monotheistic, but one which had a tendency towards them both, although it was not sufficiently developed to be identified with either of them. The tendency towards extreme exaggeration could be called a monotheistic bias in germ, whereas the correlation of different deities as independent of one another and yet existing side by side was a tendency towards polytheism.

Growth of a Monotheistic tendency; Prajāpati, Viśvakarma.

This tendency towards extolling a god as the greatest and highest gradually brought forth the conception of a supreme Lord of all beings (Prajāpati), not by a process of conscious generalization but as a necessary stage of development of the mind, able to imagine a deity as the repository of the highest moral and physical power, though its direct manifestation cannot be perceived. Thus the epithet Prajāpati or the Lord of beings, which was originally an epithet for other deities, came to be recognized as a separate deity, the highest and the greatest. Thus it is said in R. V. x. 121[2]:

In the beginning rose Hiraṇyagarbha,
Born as the only lord of all existence.
This earth he settled firm and heaven established:
What god shall we adore with our oblations?
Who gives us breath, who gives us strength, whose bidding
All creatures must obey, the bright gods even;
Whose shade is death, whose shadow life immortal:
What god shall we adore with our oblations?
Who by his might alone became the monarch
Of all that breathes, of all that wakes or slumbers,
Of all, both man and beast, the lord eternal:
What god shall we adore with our oblations?
Whose might and majesty these snowy mountains,
The ocean and the distant stream exhibit;
Whose arms extended are these spreading regions:
What god shall we adore with our oblations?
Who made the heavens bright, the earth enduring,
Who fixed the firmament, the heaven of heavens;
Who measured out the air's extended spaces:
What god shall we adore with our oblations?

[1] Macdonell's *Vedic Mythology*, p. 17. [2] *The Rigveda*, by Kaegi, pp. 88, 89.

Similar attributes are also ascribed to the deity Viśvakarma (All-creator)[1]. He is said to be father and procreator of all beings, though himself uncreated. He generated the primitive waters. It is to him that the sage says,

> Who is our father, our creator, maker,
> Who every place doth know and every creature,
> By whom alone to gods their names were given,
> To him all other creatures go to ask him[2]. R. V. x. 82. 3.

Brahma.

The conception of Brahman which has been the highest glory for the Vedānta philosophy of later days had hardly emerged in the Ṛg-Veda from the associations of the sacrificial mind. The meanings that Sāyaṇa the celebrated commentator of the Vedas gives of the word as collected by Haug are: (*a*) food, food offering, (*b*) the chant of the sāma-singer, (*c*) magical formula or text, (*d*) duly completed ceremonies, (*e*) the chant and sacrificial gift together, (*f*) the recitation of the hotṛ priest, (*g*) great. Roth says that it also means "the devotion which manifests itself as longing and satisfaction of the soul and reaches forth to the gods." But it is only in the Śatapatha Brāhmaṇa that the conception of Brahman has acquired a great significance as the supreme principle which is the moving force behind the gods. Thus the Śatapatha says, "Verily in the beginning this (universe) was the Brahman (neut.). It created the gods; and, having created the gods, it made them ascend these worlds: Agni this (terrestrial) world, Vāyu the air, and Sūrya the sky....Then the Brahman itself went up to the sphere beyond. Having gone up to the sphere beyond, it considered, 'How can I descend again into these worlds?' It then descended again by means of these two, Form and Name. Whatever has a name, that is name; and that again which has no name and which one knows by its form, 'this is (of a certain) form,' that is form : as far as there are Form and Name so far, indeed, extends this (universe). These indeed are the two great forces of Brahman; and, verily, he who knows these two great forces of Brahman becomes himself a great force[3]. In another place Brahman is said to be the ultimate thing in the Universe and is identified with Prajāpati, Puruṣa and Prāṇa

[1] See *The Rigveda*, by Kaegi, p. 89, and also Muir's *Sanskrit Texts*, vol. IV. pp. 5–11.
[2] Kaegi's translation.
[3] See Eggeling's translation of Śatapatha Brāhmaṇa *S. B. E.* vol. XLIV. pp. 27, 28.

(the vital air[1]). In another place Brahman is described as being the Svayambhū (self-born) performing austerities, who offered his own self in the creatures and the creatures in his own self, and thus compassed supremacy, sovereignty and lordship over all creatures[2]. The conception of the supreme man (Puruṣa) in the Ṛg-Veda also supposes that the supreme man pervades the world with only a fourth part of Himself, whereas the remaining three parts transcend to a region beyond. He is at once the present, past and future[3].

Sacrifice; the First Rudiments of the Law of Karma.

It will however be wrong to suppose that these monotheistic tendencies were gradually supplanting the polytheistic sacrifices. On the other hand, the complications of ritualism were gradually growing in their elaborate details. The direct result of this growth contributed however to relegate the gods to a relatively unimportant position, and to raise the dignity of the magical characteristics of the sacrifice as an institution which could give the desired fruits of themselves. The offerings at a sacrifice were not dictated by a devotion with which we are familiar under Christian or Vaiṣṇava influence. The sacrifice taken as a whole is conceived as Haug notes "to be a kind of machinery in which every piece must tally with the other," the slightest discrepancy in the performance of even a minute ritualistic detail, say in the pouring of the melted butter on the fire, or the proper placing of utensils employed in the sacrifice, or even the misplacing of a mere straw contrary to the injunctions was sufficient to spoil the whole sacrifice with whatsoever earnestness it might be performed. Even if a word was mispronounced the most dreadful results might follow. Thus when Tvaṣṭṛ performed a sacrifice for the production of a demon who would be able to kill his enemy Indra, owing to the mistaken accent of a single word the object was reversed and the demon produced was killed by Indra. But if the sacrifice could be duly performed down to the minutest detail, there was no power which could arrest or delay the fruition of the object. Thus the objects of a sacrifice were fulfilled not by the grace of the gods, but as a natural result of the sacrifice. The performance of the rituals invariably produced certain mystic or magical results by virtue of which the object desired

[1] See *S. B. E.* XLIII. pp. 59, 60, 400 and XLIV. p. 409.

[2] See *Ibid.* XLIV. p. 418.

[3] R. V. X. 90, Puruṣa Sūkta.

by the sacrificer was fulfilled in due course like the fulfilment of a natural law in the physical world. The sacrifice was believed to have existed from eternity like the Vedas. The creation of the world itself was even regarded as the fruit of a sacrifice performed by the supreme Being. It exists as Haug says "as an invisible thing at all times and is like the latent power of electricity in an electrifying machine, requiring only the operation of a suitable apparatus in order to be elicited." The sacrifice is not offered to a god with a view to propitiate him or to obtain from him welfare on earth or bliss in Heaven; these rewards are directly produced by the sacrifice itself through the correct performance of complicated and interconnected ceremonies which constitute the sacrifice. Though in each sacrifice certain gods were invoked and received the offerings, the gods themselves were but instruments in bringing about the sacrifice or in completing the course of mystical ceremonies composing it. Sacrifice is thus regarded as possessing a mystical potency superior even to the gods, who it is sometimes stated attained to their divine rank by means of sacrifice. Sacrifice was regarded as almost the only kind of duty, and it was also called *karma* or *kriyā* (action) and the unalterable law was, that these mystical ceremonies for good or for bad, moral or immoral (for there were many kinds of sacrifices which were performed for injuring one's enemies or gaining worldly prosperity or supremacy at the cost of others) were destined to produce their effects. It is well to note here that the first recognition of a cosmic order or law prevailing in nature under the guardianship of the highest gods is to be found in the use of the word Ṛta (literally the course of things). This word was also used, as Macdonell observes, to denote the "'order' in the moral world as truth and 'right' and in the religious world as sacrifice or 'rite'[1]" and its unalterable law of producing effects. It is interesting to note in this connection that it is here that we find the first germs of the law of karma, which exercises such a dominating control over Indian thought up to the present day. Thus we find the simple faith and devotion of the Vedic hymns on one hand being supplanted by the growth of a complex system of sacrificial rites, and on the other bending their course towards a monotheistic or philosophic knowledge of the ultimate reality of the universe.

[1] Macdonell's *Vedic Mythology*, p. 11.

Cosmogony—Mythological and philosophical.

The cosmogony of the Ṛg-Veda may be looked at from two aspects, the mythological and the philosophical. The mythological aspect has in general two currents, as Professor Macdonell says, "The one regards the universe as the result of mechanical production, the work of carpenter's and joiner's skill; the other represents it as the result of natural generation[1]." Thus in the Ṛg-Veda we find that the poet in one place says, "what was the wood and what was the tree out of which they built heaven and earth[2]?" The answer given to this question in Taittirīya-Brāhmaṇa is "Brahman the wood and Brahman the tree from which the heaven and earth were made[3]." Heaven and Earth are sometimes described as having been supported with posts[4]. They are also sometimes spoken of as universal parents, and parentage is sometimes attributed to Aditi and Dakṣa.

Under this philosophical aspect the semi-pantheistic Man-hymn[5] attracts our notice. The supreme man as we have already noticed above is there said to be the whole universe, whatever has been and shall be; he is the lord of immortality who has become diffused everywhere among things animate and inanimate, and all beings came out of him; from his navel came the atmosphere; from his head arose the sky; from his feet came the earth; from his ear the four quarters. Again there are other hymns in which the Sun is called the soul (*ātman*) of all that is movable and all that is immovable[6]. There are also statements to the effect that the Being is one, though it is called by many names by the sages[7]. The supreme being is sometimes extolled as the supreme Lord of the world called the golden egg (Hiraṇyagarbha[8]). In some passages it is said "Brahmaṇaspati blew forth these births like a blacksmith. In the earliest age of the gods, the existent sprang from the non-existent. In the first age of the gods, the existent sprang from the non-existent: thereafter the regions sprang, thereafter, from Uttānapada[9]." The most remarkable and sublime hymn in which the first germs of philosophic speculation

[1] Macdonell's *Vedic Mythology*, p. 11.

[2] R. V. x. 81. 4.

[3] Taitt. Br. II. 8. 9. 6.

[4] Macdonell's *Vedic Mythology*, p. 11; also R. V. II. 15 and IV. 56.

[5] R. V. x. 90.

[6] R. V. I. 115.

[7] R. V. I. 164. 46.

[8] R. V. x. 121.

[9] Muir's translation of R. V. x. 72; Muir's *Sanskrit Texts*, vol. v. p. 48.

with regard to the wonderful mystery of the origin of the world are found is the 129th hymn of R. V. X.

1. Then there was neither being nor not-being.
The atmosphere was not, nor sky above it.
What covered all? and where? by what protected?
Was there the fathomless abyss of waters?

2. Then neither death nor deathless existed;
Of day and night there was yet no distinction.
Alone that one breathed calmly, self-supported,
Other than It was none, nor aught above It.

3. Darkness there was at first in darkness hidden;
The universe was undistinguished water.
That which in void and emptiness lay hidden
Alone by power of fervor was developed.

4. Then for the first time there arose desire,
Which was the primal germ of mind, within it.
And sages, searching in their heart, discovered
In Nothing the connecting bond of Being.

. . . .

6. Who is it knows? Who here can tell us surely
From what and how this universe has risen?
And whether not till after it the gods lived?
Who then can know from what it has arisen?

7. The source from which this universe has risen,
And whether it was made, or uncreated,
He only knows, who from the highest heaven
Rules, the all-seeing lord—or does not He know[1]?

The earliest commentary on this is probably a passage in the Śatapatha Brāhmaṇa (X. 5. 3. 1) which says that "in the beginning this (universe) was as it were neither non-existent nor existent; in the beginning this (universe) was as it were, existed and did not exist: there was then only that Mind. Wherefore it has been declared by the Rishi (Ṛg-Veda X. 129. 1), 'There was then neither the non-existent nor the existent' for Mind was, as it were, neither existent nor non-existent. This Mind when created, wished to become manifest,—more defined, more substantial: it sought after a self (a body); it practised austerity: it acquired consistency[2]." In the Atharva-Veda also we find it stated that all forms of the universe were comprehended within the god Skambha[3].

Thus we find that even in the period of the Vedas there sprang forth such a philosophic yearning, at least among some who could

[1] *The Rigveda*, by Kaegi, p. 90. R. V. X. 129.
[2] See Eggeling's translation of *Ś. B.*, *S. B. E.* vol. XLIII. pp. 374, 375.
[3] *A. V.* X. 7. 10.

question whether this universe was at all a creation or not, which could think of the origin of the world as being enveloped in the mystery of a primal non-differentiation of being and non-being; and which could think that it was the primal One which by its inherent fervour gave rise to the desire of a creation as the first manifestation of the germ of mind, from which the universe sprang forth through a series of mysterious gradual processes. In the Brāhmaṇas, however, we find that the cosmogonic view generally requires the agency of a creator, who is not however always the starting point, and we find that the theory of evolution is combined with the theory of creation, so that Prajāpati is sometimes spoken of as the creator while at other times the creator is said to have floated in the primeval water as a cosmic golden egg.

Eschatology; the Doctrine of Ātman.

There seems to be a belief in the Vedas that the soul could be separated from the body in states of swoon, and that it could exist after death, though we do not find there any trace of the doctrine of transmigration in a developed form. In the Śatapatha Brāhmaṇa it is said that those who do not perform rites with correct knowledge are born again after death and suffer death again. In a hymn of the Ṛg-Veda (X. 58) the soul (*manas*) of a man apparently unconscious is invited to come back to him from the trees, herbs, the sky, the sun, etc. In many of the hymns there is also the belief in the existence of another world, where the highest material joys are attained as a result of the performance of the sacrifices and also in a hell of darkness underneath where the evil-doers are punished. In the Śatapatha Brāhmaṇa we find that the dead pass between two fires which burn the evil-doers, but let the good go by[1]; it is also said there that everyone is born again after death, is weighed in a balance, and receives reward or punishment according as his works are good or bad. It is easy to see that scattered ideas like these with regard to the destiny of the soul of man according to the sacrifice that he performs or other good or bad deeds form the first rudiments of the later doctrine of metempsychosis. The idea that man enjoys or suffers, either in another world or by being born in this world according to his good or bad deeds, is the first beginning of the moral idea, though in the Brahmanic days the good deeds were

[1] See *S. B.* I. 9. 3, and also Macdonell's *Vedic Mythology*, pp. 166, 167.

more often of the nature of sacrificial duties than ordinary good works. These ideas of the possibilities of a necessary connection of the enjoyments and sorrows of a man with his good and bad works when combined with the notion of an inviolable law or order, which we have already seen was gradually growing with the conception of ṛta, and the unalterable law which produces the effects of sacrificial works, led to the Law of Karma and the doctrine of transmigration. The words which denote soul in the Ṛg-Veda are *manas*, *ātman* and *asu*. The word *ātman* however which became famous in later Indian thought is generally used to mean vital breath. Manas is regarded as the seat of thought and emotion, and it seems to be regarded, as Macdonell says, as dwelling in the heart[1]. It is however difficult to understand how ātman as vital breath, or as a separable part of man going out of the dead man came to be regarded as the ultimate essence or reality in man and the universe. There is however at least one passage in the Ṛg-Veda where the poet penetrating deeper and deeper passes from the vital breath (*asu*) to the blood, and thence to ātman as the inmost self of the world; "Who has seen how the first-born, being the Bone-possessing (the shaped world), was born from the Boneless (the shapeless)? where was the vital breath, the blood, the Self (*ātman*) of the world? Who went to ask him that knows it[2]?" In Taittirīya Āraṇyaka I. 23, however, it is said that Prajāpati after having created his self (as the world) with his own self entered into it. In Taittirīya Brāhmaṇa the ātman is called omnipresent, and it is said that he who knows him is no more stained by evil deeds. Thus we find that in the pre-Upaniṣad Vedic literature ātman probably was first used to denote "vital breath" in man, then the self of the world, and then the self in man. It is from this last stage that we find the traces of a growing tendency to looking at the self of man as the omnipresent supreme principle of the universe, the knowledge of which makes a man sinless and pure.

Conclusion.

Looking at the advancement of thought in the Ṛg-Veda we find first that a fabric of thought was gradually growing which not only looked upon the universe as a correlation of parts or a

[1] Macdonell's *Vedic Mythology*, p. 166 and R. V. VIII. 89.

[2] R. V. I. 164. 4 and Deussen's article on Ātman in *Encyclopaedia of Religion and Ethics*.

construction made of them, but sought to explain it as having emanated from one great being who is sometimes described as one with the universe and surpassing it, and at other times as being separate from it; the agnostic spirit which is the mother of philosophic thought is seen at times to be so bold as to express doubts even on the most fundamental questions of creation—"Who knows whether this world was ever created or not?" Secondly, the growth of sacrifices has helped to establish the unalterable nature of the law by which the (sacrificial) actions produced their effects of themselves. It also lessened the importance of deities as being the supreme masters of the world and our fate, and the tendency of henotheism gradually diminished their multiple character and advanced the monotheistic tendency in some quarters. Thirdly, the soul of man is described as being separable from his body and subject to suffering and enjoyment in another world according to his good or bad deeds; the doctrine that the soul of man could go to plants, etc., or that it could again be re-born on earth, is also hinted at in certain passages, and this may be regarded as sowing the first seeds of the later doctrine of transmigration. The self (*ātman*) is spoken of in one place as the essence of the world, and when we trace the idea in the Brāhmaṇas and the Āraṇyakas we see that ātman has begun to mean the supreme essence in man as well as in the universe, and has thus approached the great Ātman doctrine of the Upaniṣads.

CHAPTER III

THE EARLIER UPANIṢADS[1]. (700 B.C.—600 B.C.)

The place of the Upaniṣads in Vedic literature.

THOUGH it is generally held that the Upaniṣads are usually attached as appendices to the Āraṇyakas which are again attached to the Brāhmaṇas, yet it cannot be said that their distinction as separate treatises is always observed. Thus we find in some cases that subjects which we should expect to be discussed in a Brāhmaṇa are introduced into the Āraṇyakas and the Āraṇyaka materials are sometimes fused into the great bulk of Upaniṣad teaching. This shows that these three literatures gradually grew up in one

[1] There are about 112 Upaniṣads which have been published by the "Nirṇaya-Sāgara" Press, Bombay, 1917. These are 1 Īśā, 2 Kena, 3 Kaṭha, 4 Praśna, 5 Muṇḍaka, 6 Māṇḍūkya, 7 Taittirīya, 8 Aitareya, 9 Chāndogya, 10 Bṛhadāraṇyaka, 11 Śvetāśvatara, 12 Kauṣītaki, 13 Maitreyī, 14 Kaivalya, 15 Jābāla, 16 Brahmabindu, 17 Haṃsa, 18 Āruṇika, 19 Garbha, 20 Nārāyaṇa, 21 Nārāyaṇa, 22 Paramahaṃsa, 23 Brahma, 24 Amṛtanāda, 25 Atharvaśiras, 26 Atharvaśikhā, 27 Maitrāyaṇī, 28 Bṛhajjābāla, 29 Nṛsiṃhapūrvatāpinī, 30 Nṛsiṃhottaratāpinī, 31 Kālāgnirudra, 32 Subāla, 33 Kṣurikā, 34 Yantrikā, 35 Sarvasāra, 36 Nirālamba, 37 Śukarahasya, 38 Vajrasūcikā, 39 Tejobindu, 40 Nādabindu, 41 Dhyānabindu, 42 Brahmavidyā, 43 Yogatattva, 44 Ātmabodha, 45 Nāradaparivrājaka, 46 Triśikhibrāhmaṇa, 47 Sītā, 48 Yogacūḍāmaṇi, 49 Nirvāṇa, 50 Maṇḍalabrāhmaṇa, 51 Dakṣiṇāmūrtti, 52 Śarabha, 53 Skanda, 54 Tripādvibhūtimahānārāyaṇa, 55 Advayatāraka, 56 Rāmarahasya, 57 Rāmapūrvatāpinī, 58 Rāmottaratāpinī, 59 Vāsudeva, 60 Mudgala, 61 Sāṇḍilya, 62 Paiṅgala, 63 Bhikṣuka, 64 Mahā, 65 Śārīraka, 66 Yogaśikhā, 67 Turīyātīta, 68 Saṃnyāsa, 69 Paramahaṃsaparivrājaka, 70 Akṣamālā, 71 Avyakta, 72 Ekākṣara, 73 Annapūrnā, 74 Sūrya, 75 Akṣi, 76 Adhyātma, 77 Kuṇḍika, 78 Sāvitrī, 79 Ātman, 80 Pāśupatabrahma, 81 Parabrahma, 82 Avadhūta, 83 Tripurātāpinī, 84 Devī, 85 Tripurā, 86 Kaṭharudra, 87 Bhāvanā, 88 Rudrahṛdaya, 89 Yogakuṇḍalī, 90 Bhasmajābāla, 91 Rudrākṣajābāla, 92 Gaṇapati, 93 Jābāladarśana, 94 Tārasāra, 95 Mahāvākya, 96 Pañcabrahma, 97 Prāṇāgnihotra, 98 Gopālapūrvatāpinī, 99 Gopālottaratāpinī, 100 Kṛṣṇa, 101 Yājñavalkya, 102 Varāha, 103 Śāṭhyāyanīya, 104 Hayagrīva, 105 Dattātreya, 106 Garuḍa, 107 Kalisantaraṇa, 108 Jābāli, 109 Saubhāgyalakṣmī, 110 Sarasvatīrahasya, 111 Bahvṛca, 112 Muktika.

The collection of Upaniṣads translated by Dara shiko, Aurangzeb's brother, contained 50 Upaniṣads. The Muktika Upaniṣad gives a list of 108 Upaniṣads. With the exception of the first 13 Upaniṣads most of them are of more or less later date. The Upaniṣads dealt with in this chapter are the earlier ones. Amongst the later ones there are some which repeat the purport of these, there are others which deal with the Śaiva, Śākta, the Yoga and the Vaiṣṇava doctrines. These will be referred to in connection with the consideration of those systems in Volume II. The later Upaniṣads which only repeat the purport of those dealt with in this chapter do not require further mention. Some of the later Upaniṣads were composed even as late as the fourteenth or the fifteenth century.

process of development and they were probably regarded as parts of one literature, in spite of the differences in their subject-matter. Deussen supposes that the principle of this division was to be found in this, that the Brāhmaṇas were intended for the householders, the Āraṇyakas for those who in their old age withdrew into the solitude of the forests and the Upaniṣads for those who renounced the world to attain ultimate salvation by meditation. Whatever might be said about these literary classifications the ancient philosophers of India looked upon the Upaniṣads as being of an entirely different type from the rest of the Vedic literature as dictating the path of knowledge (*jñāna-mārga*) as opposed to the path of works (*karma-mārga*) which forms the content of the latter. It is not out of place here to mention that the orthodox Hindu view holds that whatever may be written in the Veda is to be interpreted as commandments to perform certain actions (*vidhi*) or prohibitions against committing certain others (*niṣedha*). Even the stories or episodes are to be so interpreted that the real objects of their insertion might appear as only to praise the performance of the commandments and to blame the commission of the prohibitions. No person has any right to argue why any particular Vedic commandment is to be followed, for no reason can ever discover that, and it is only because reason fails to find out why a certain Vedic act leads to a certain effect that the Vedas have been revealed as commandments and prohibitions to show the true path of happiness. The Vedic teaching belongs therefore to that of the Karma-mārga or the performance of Vedic duties of sacrifice, etc. The Upaniṣads however do not require the performance of any action, but only reveal the ultimate truth and reality, a knowledge of which at once emancipates a man. Readers of Hindu philosophy are aware that there is a very strong controversy on this point between the adherents of the Vedānta (*Upaniṣads*) and those of the Veda. For the latter seek in analogy to the other parts of the Vedic literature to establish the principle that the Upaniṣads should not be regarded as an exception, but that they should also be so interpreted that they might also be held out as commending the performance of duties; but the former dissociate the Upaniṣads from the rest of the Vedic literature and assert that they do not make the slightest reference to any Vedic duties, but only delineate the ultimate reality which reveals the highest knowledge in the minds of the deserving.

Śaṅkara the most eminent exponent of the Upaniṣads holds that they are meant for such superior men who are already above worldly or heavenly prosperities, and for whom the Vedic duties have ceased to have any attraction. Wheresoever there may be such a deserving person, be he a student, a householder or an ascetic, for him the Upaniṣads have been revealed for his ultimate emancipation and the true knowledge. Those who perform the Vedic duties belong to a stage inferior to those who no longer care for the fruits of the Vedic duties but are eager for final emancipation, and it is the latter who alone are fit to hear the Upaniṣads[1].

The names of the Upaniṣads; Non-Brahmanic influence.

The Upaniṣads are also known by another name Vedānta, as they are believed to be the last portions of the Vedas (*veda-anta*, end); it is by this name that the philosophy of the Upaniṣads, the Vedānta philosophy, is so familiar to us. A modern student knows that in language the Upaniṣads approach the classical Sanskrit; the ideas preached also show that they are the culmination of the intellectual achievement of a great epoch. As they thus formed the concluding parts of the Vedas they retained their Vedic names which they took from the name of the different schools or branches (*śākhā*) among which the Vedas were studied[2]. Thus the Upaniṣads attached to the Brāhmaṇas of the Aitareya and Kauṣītaki schools are called respectively Aitareya and Kauṣītaki Upaniṣads. Those of the Tāṇḍins and Talavakāras of the Sāma-veda are called the Chāndogya and Talavakāra (or Kena) Upaniṣads. Those of the Taittirīya school of the Yajurveda

[1] This is what is called the difference of fitness (*adhikāribheda*). Those who perform the sacrifices are not fit to hear the Upaniṣads and those who are fit to hear the Upaniṣads have no longer any necessity to perform the sacrificial duties.

[2] When the Saṃhitā texts had become substantially fixed, they were committed to memory in different parts of the country and transmitted from teacher to pupil along with directions for the practical performance of sacrificial duties. The latter formed the matter of prose compositions, the Brāhmaṇas. These however were gradually liable to diverse kinds of modifications according to the special tendencies and needs of the people among which they were recited. Thus after a time there occurred a great divergence in the readings of the texts of the Brāhmaṇas even of the same Veda among different people. These different schools were known by the name of particular Śākhās (e.g. Aitareya, Kauṣītaki) with which the Brāhmaṇas were associated or named. According to the divergence of the Brāhmaṇas of the different Śākhās there occurred the divergences of content and the length of the Upaniṣads associated with them.

form the Taittirīya and Mahānārayaṇa, of the Kaṭha school the Kāṭhaka, of the Maitrāyaṇī school the Maitrāyaṇī. The Bṛhadāraṇyaka Upaniṣad forms part of the Śatapatha Brāhmaṇa of the Vājasaneyi schools. The Īśā Upaniṣad also belongs to the latter school. But the school to which the Śvetāśvatara belongs cannot be traced, and has probably been lost. The presumption with regard to these Upaniṣads is that they represent the enlightened views of the particular schools among which they flourished, and under whose names they passed. A large number of Upaniṣads of a comparatively later age were attached to the Atharva-Veda, most of which were named not according to the Vedic schools but according to the subject-matter with which they dealt[1].

It may not be out of place here to mention that from the frequent episodes in the Upaniṣads in which the Brahmins are described as having gone to the Kṣattriyas for the highest knowledge of philosophy, as well as from the disparateness of the Upaniṣad teachings from that of the general doctrines of the Brāhmaṇas and from the allusions to the existence of philosophical speculations amongst the people in Pāli works, it may be inferred that among the Kṣattriyas in general there existed earnest philosophic enquiries which must be regarded as having exerted an important influence in the formation of the Upaniṣad doctrines. There is thus some probability in the supposition that though the Upaniṣads are found directly incorporated with the Brāhmaṇas it was not the production of the growth of Brahmanic dogmas alone, but that non-Brahmanic thought as well must have either set the Upaniṣad doctrines afoot, or have rendered fruitful assistance to their formulation and cultivation, though they achieved their culmination in the hands of the Brahmins.

Brāhmaṇas and the Early Upaniṣads.

The passage of the Indian mind from the Brāhmanic to the Upaniṣad thought is probably the most remarkable event in the history of philosophic thought. We know that in the later Vedic hymns some monotheistic conceptions of great excellence were developed, but these differ in their nature from the absolutism of the Upaniṣads as much as the Ptolemaic and the Copernican

[1] Garbha Upaniṣad, Ātman Upaniṣad, Praśna Upaniṣad, etc. There were however some exceptions such as the Māṇḍūkya, Jābāla, Paiṅgala, Śaunaka, etc.

systems in astronomy. The direct translation of Viśvakarman or Hiraṇyagarbha into the ātman and the Brahman of the Upaniṣads seems to me to be very improbable, though I am quite willing to admit that these conceptions were swallowed up by the ātman doctrine when it had developed to a proper extent. Throughout the earlier Upaniṣads no mention is to be found of Viśvakarman, Hiraṇyagarbha or Brahmaṇaspati and no reference of such a nature is to be found as can justify us in connecting the Upaniṣad ideas with those conceptions[1]. The word puruṣa no doubt occurs frequently in the Upaniṣads, but the sense and the association that come along with it are widely different from that of the puruṣa of the Puruṣasūkta of the Ṛg-Veda.

When the Ṛg-Veda describes Viśvakarman it describes him as a creator from outside, a controller of mundane events, to whom they pray for worldly benefits. "What was the position, which and whence was the principle, from which the all-seeing Viśvakarman produced the earth, and disclosed the sky by his might? The one god, who has on every side eyes, on every side a face, on every side arms, on every side feet, when producing the sky and earth, shapes them with his arms and with his wings....Do thou, Viśvakarman, grant to thy friends those thy abodes which are the highest, and the lowest, and the middle...may a generous son remain here to us[2]"; again in R.V. X. 82 we find "Viśvakarman is wise, energetic, the creator, the disposer, and the highest object of intuition....He who is our father, our creator, disposer, who knows all spheres and creatures, who alone assigns to the gods their names, to him the other creatures resort for instruction[3]." Again about Hiraṇyagarbha we find in R.V. I. 121, "Hiraṇyagarbha arose in the beginning; born, he was the one lord of things existing. He established the earth and this sky; to what god shall we offer our oblation?... May he not injure us, he who is the generator of the earth, who ruling by fixed ordinances, produced the heavens, who produced the great and brilliant waters!—to what god, etc.? Prajāpati, no other than thou is lord over all these created things: may we obtain that, through desire of which we have invoked thee; may we become masters of riches[4]." Speaking of the puruṣa the Ṛg-Veda

[1] The name Viśvakarma appears in Śvet. IV. 17. Hiraṇyagarbha appears in Śvet. III. 4 and IV. 12, but only as the first created being. The phrase Sarvāhammānī Hiraṇyagarbha which Deussen refers to occurs only in the later Nṛsiṃh. 9. The word Brahmaṇaspati does not occur at all in the Upaniṣads.

[2] Muir's *Sanskrit Texts*, vol. IV. pp. 6, 7. [3] *Ibid.* p. 7. [4] *Ibid.* pp. 16, 17.

says "Purusha has a thousand heads...a thousand eyes, and a thousand feet. On every side enveloping the earth he transcended [it] by a space of ten fingers....He formed those aerial creatures, and the animals, both wild and tame[1]," etc. Even that famous hymn (R.V. X. 129) which begins with "There was then neither being nor non-being, there was no air nor sky above" ends with saying "From whence this creation came into being, whether it was created or not—he who is in the highest sky, its ruler, probably knows or does not know."

In the Upaniṣads however, the position is entirely changed, and the centre of interest there is not in a creator from outside but in the self: the natural development of the monotheistic position of the Vedas could have grown into some form of developed theism, but not into the doctrine that the self was the only reality and that everything else was far below it. There is no relation here of the worshipper and the worshipped and no prayers are offered to it, but the whole quest is of the highest truth, and the true self of man is discovered as the greatest reality. This change of philosophical position seems to me to be a matter of great interest. This change of the mind from the objective to the subjective does not carry with it in the Upaniṣads any elaborate philosophical discussions, or subtle analysis of mind. It comes there as a matter of direct perception, and the conviction with which the truth has been grasped cannot fail to impress the readers. That out of the apparently meaningless speculations of the Brāhmaṇas this doctrine could have developed, might indeed appear to be too improbable to be believed.

On the strength of the stories of Bālāki Gārgya and Ajātaśatru (Bṛh. II. 1), Śvetaketu and Pravāhaṇa Jaibali (Chā. V. 3 and Bṛh. VI. 2) and Āruṇi and Aśvapati Kaikeya (Chā. V. 11) Garbe thinks "that it can be proven that the Brahman's profoundest wisdom, the doctrine of All-one, which has exercised an unmistakable influence on the intellectual life even of our time, did not have its origin in the circle of Brahmans at all[2]" and that "it took its rise in the ranks of the warrior caste[3]." This if true would of course lead the development of the Upaniṣads away from the influence of the Veda, Brāhmaṇas and the Āraṇyakas. But do the facts prove this? Let us briefly examine the evidences that Garbe him-

[1] Muir's *Sanskrit Texts*, vol. V. pp. 368, 371.

[2] Garbe's article, "*Hindu Monism*," p. 68. [3] *Ibid.* p. 78.

self has produced. In the story of Bālāki Gārgya and Ajātaśatru (Bṛh. II. 1) referred to by him, Bālāki Gārgya is a boastful man who wants to teach the Kṣattriya Ajātaśatru the true Brahman, but fails and then wants it to be taught by him. To this Ajātaśatru replies (following Garbe's own translation) "it is contrary to the natural order that a Brahman receive instruction from a warrior and expect the latter to declare the Brahman to him[1]." Does this not imply that in the natural order of things a Brahmin always taught the knowledge of Brahman to the Kṣattriyas, and that it was unusual to find a Brahmin asking a Kṣattriya about the true knowledge of Brahman? At the beginning of the conversation, Ajātaśatru had promised to pay Bālāki one thousand coins if he could tell him about Brahman, since all people used to run to Janaka to speak about Brahman[2]. The second story of Śvetaketu and Pravāhaṇa Jaibali seems to be fairly conclusive with regard to the fact that the transmigration doctrines, the way of the gods (*devayāna*) and the way of the fathers (*pitṛyāna*) had originated among the Kṣattriyas, but it is without any relevancy with regard to the origin of the superior knowledge of Brahman as the true self.

The third story of Āruṇi and Aśvapati Kaikeya (Chā. V. 11) is hardly more convincing, for here five Brahmins wishing to know what the Brahman and the self were, went to Uddālaka Āruṇi; but as he did not know sufficiently about it he accompanied them to the Kṣattriya king Aśvapati Kaikeya who was studying the subject. But Aśvapati ends the conversation by giving them certain instructions about the fire doctrine (*vaiśvānara agni*) and the import of its sacrifices. He does not say anything about the true self as Brahman. We ought also to consider that there are only the few exceptional cases where Kṣattriya kings were instructing the Brahmins. But in all other cases the Brahmins were discussing and instructing the ātman knowledge. I am thus led to think that Garbe owing to his bitterness of feeling against the Brahmins as expressed in the earlier part of the essay had been too hasty in his judgment. The opinion of Garbe seems to have been shared to some extent by Winternitz also, and the references given by him to the Upaniṣad passages are also the same as we

[1] Garbe's article, "*Hindu Monism*," p. 74.

[2] Bṛh. II., compare also Bṛh. IV. 3, how Yājñavalkya speaks to Janaka about the *brahmavidyā*.

just examined[1]. The truth seems to me to be this, that the Kṣattriyas and even some women took interest in the religio-philosophical quest manifested in the Upaniṣads. The enquirers were so eager that either in receiving the instruction of Brahman or in imparting it to others, they had no considerations of sex and birth[2]; and there seems to be no definite evidence for thinking that the Upaniṣad philosophy originated among the Kṣattriyas or that the germs of its growth could not be traced in the Brāhmaṇas and the Āraṇyakas which were the productions of the Brahmins.

The change of the Brāhmaṇa into the Āraṇyaka thought is signified by a transference of values from the actual sacrifices to their symbolic representations and meditations which were regarded as being productive of various earthly benefits. Thus we find in the Bṛhadāraṇyaka (I. I) that instead of a horse sacrifice the visible universe is to be conceived as a horse and meditated upon as such. The dawn is the head of the horse, the sun is the eye, wind is its life, fire is its mouth and the year is its soul, and so on. What is the horse that grazes in the field and to what good can its sacrifice lead? This moving universe is the horse which is most significant to the mind, and the meditation of it as such is the most suitable substitute of the sacrifice of the horse, the mere animal. Thought-activity as meditation, is here taking the place of an external worship in the form of sacrifices. The material substances and the most elaborate and accurate sacrificial rituals lost their value and bare meditations took their place. Side by side with the ritualistic sacrifices of the generality of the Brahmins, was springing up a system where thinking and symbolic meditations were taking the place of gross matter and action involved in sacrifices. These symbols were not only chosen from the external world as the sun, the wind, etc., from the body of man, his various vital functions and the senses, but even arbitrary alphabets were taken up and it was believed that the meditation of these as the highest and the greatest was productive of great beneficial results. Sacrifice in itself was losing value in the eyes of these men and diverse mystical significances and imports were beginning to be considered as their real truth[3].

[1] Winternitz's *Geschichte der indischen Litteratur*, I. pp. 197 ff.

[2] The story of Maitreyī and Yājñavalkya (Bṛh. II. 4) and that of Satyakāma son of Jabālā and his teacher (Chā. IV. 4).

[3] Chā. V. II.

The Uktha (verse) of Ṛg-Veda was identified in the Aitareya Āraṇyaka under several allegorical forms with the Prāṇa[1], the Udgītha of the Sāmaveda was identified with Om, Prāṇa, sun and eye; in Chāndogya II. the Sāman was identified with Om, rain, water, seasons, Prāṇa, etc., in Chāndogya III. 16–17 man was identified with sacrifice; his hunger, thirst, sorrow, with initiation; laughing, eating, etc., with the utterance of the Mantras; and asceticism, gift, sincerity, restraint from injury, truth, with sacrificial fees (*dakṣiṇā*). The gifted mind of these cultured Vedic Indians was anxious to come to some unity, but logical precision of thought had not developed, and as a result of that we find in the Āraṇyakas the most grotesque and fanciful unifications of things which to our eyes have little or no connection. Any kind of instrumentality in producing an effect was often considered as pure identity. Thus in Ait. Āraṇ. II. I. 3 we find "Then comes the origin of food. The seed of Prajāpati are the gods. The seed of the gods is rain. The seed of rain is herbs. The seed of herbs is food. The seed of food is seed. The seed of seed is creatures. The seed of creatures is the heart. The seed of the heart is the mind. The seed of the mind is speech. The seed of speech is action. The act done is this man the abode of Brahman[2]."

The word Brahman according to Sāyaṇa meant mantras (magical verses), the ceremonies, the hotṛ priest, the great. Hillebrandt points out that it is spoken of in R.V. as being new, "as not having hitherto existed," and as "coming into being from the fathers." It originates from the seat of the Ṛta, springs forth at the sound of the sacrifice, begins really to exist when the soma juice is pressed and the hymns are recited at the savana rite, endures with the help of the gods even in battle, and soma is its guardian (R.V. VIII. 37. I, VIII. 69. 9, VI. 23. 5, I. 47. 2, VII. 22. 9, VI. 52. 3, etc.). On the strength of these Hillebrandt justifies the conjecture of Haug that it signifies a mysterious power which can be called forth by various ceremonies, and his definition of it, as the magical force which is derived from the orderly cooperation of the hymns, the chants and the sacrificial gifts[3]. I am disposed to think that this meaning is closely connected with the meaning as we find it in many passages in the Āraṇyakas and the Upaniṣads. The meaning in many of these seems to be midway between

[1] Ait. Āraṇ. II. I–3.
[2] Keith's *Translation of Aitareya Āraṇyaka.*
[3] Hillebrandt's article on Brahman, *E. R. E.*

"magical force" and "great," transition between which is rather easy. Even when the sacrifices began to be replaced by meditations, the old belief in the power of the sacrifices still remained, and as a result of that we find that in many passages of the Upaniṣads people are thinking of meditating upon this great force "Brahman" as being identified with diverse symbols, natural objects, parts and functions of the body.

When the main interest of sacrifice was transferred from its actual performance in the external world to certain forms of meditation, we find that the understanding of particular allegories of sacrifice having a relation to particular kinds of bodily functions was regarded as Brahman, without a knowledge of which nothing could be obtained. The fact that these allegorical interpretations of the Pañcāgnividyā are so much referred to in the Upaniṣads as a secret doctrine, shows that some people came to think that the real efficacy of sacrifices depended upon such meditations. When the sages rose to the culminating conception, that he is really ignorant who thinks the gods to be different from him, they thought that as each man was nourished by many beasts, so the gods were nourished by each man, and as it is unpleasant for a man if any of his beasts are taken away, so it is unpleasant for the gods that men should know this great truth[1].

In the Kena we find it indicated that all the powers of the gods such as that of Agni (fire) to burn, Vāyu (wind) to blow, depended upon Brahman, and that it is through Brahman that all the gods and all the senses of man could work. The whole process of Upaniṣad thought shows that the magic power of sacrifices as associated with Ṛta (unalterable law) was being abstracted from the sacrifices and conceived as the supreme power. There are many stories in the Upaniṣads of the search after the nature of this great power the Brahman, which was at first only imperfectly realized. They identified it with the dominating power of the natural objects of wonder, the sun, the moon, etc. with bodily and mental functions and with various symbolical representations, and deluded themselves for a time with the idea that these were satisfactory. But as these were gradually found inadequate, they came to the final solution, and the doctrine of the inner self of man as being the highest truth the Brahman originated.

[1] Bṛh. I. 4. 10.

The meaning of the word Upaniṣad.

The word Upaniṣad is derived from the root *sad* with the prefix *ni* (to sit), and Max Müller says that the word originally meant the act of sitting down near a teacher and of submissively listening to him. In his introduction to the Upaniṣads he says, "The history and the genius of the Sanskrit language leave little doubt that Upaniṣad meant originally session, particularly a session consisting of pupils, assembled at a respectful distance round their teacher[1]." Deussen points out that the word means "secret" or "secret instruction," and this is borne out by many of the passages of the Upaniṣads themselves. Max Müller also agrees that the word was used in this sense in the Upaniṣads[2]. There we find that great injunctions of secrecy are to be observed for the communication of the doctrines, and it is said that it should only be given to a student or pupil who by his supreme moral restraint and noble desires proves himself deserving to hear them. Śaṅkara however, the great Indian exponent of the Upaniṣads, derives the word from the root *sad* to destroy and supposes that it is so called because it destroys inborn ignorance and leads to salvation by revealing the right knowledge. But if we compare the many texts in which the word Upaniṣad occurs in the Upaniṣads themselves it seems that Deussen's meaning is fully justified[3].

The composition and growth of diverse Upaniṣads.

The oldest Upaniṣads are written in prose. Next to these we have some in verses very similar to those that are to be found in classical Sanskrit. As is easy to see, the older the Upaniṣad the more archaic is it in its language. The earliest Upaniṣads have an almost mysterious forcefulness in their expressions at least to Indian ears. They are simple, pithy and penetrate to the heart. We can read and read them over again without getting tired. The lines are always as fresh as ever. As such they have a charm apart from the value of the ideas they intend to convey. The word Upaniṣad was used, as we have seen, in the sense of "secret doctrine or instruction"; the Upaniṣad teachings were also intended to be conveyed in strictest secrecy to earnest enquirers of high morals and superior self-restraint for the purpose of achieving

[1] Max Müller's *Translation of the Upanishads*, *S. B. E.* vol. I. p. lxxxi.

[2] *S. B. E.* vol. I. p. lxxxiii.

[3] Deussen's *Philosophy of the Upanishads*, pp. 10–15.

emancipation. It was thus that the Upaniṣad style of expression, when it once came into use, came to possess the greatest charm and attraction for earnest religious people; and as a result of that we find that even when other forms of prose and verse had been adapted for the Sanskrit language, the Upaniṣad form of composition had not stopped. Thus though the earliest Upaniṣads were compiled by 500 B.C., they continued to be written even so late as the spread of Mahommedan influence in India. The earliest and most important are probably those that have been commented upon by Śaṅkara namely Bṛhadāraṇyaka, Chāndogya, Aitareya, Taittirīya, Íśā, Kena, Kaṭha, Praśna, Muṇḍaka and Māṇḍūkya[1]. It is important to note in this connection that the separate Upaniṣads differ much from one another with regard to their content and methods of exposition. Thus while some of them are busy laying great stress upon the monistic doctrine of the self as the only reality, there are others which lay stress upon the practice of Yoga, asceticism, the cult of Śiva, of Viṣṇu and the philosophy or anatomy of the body, and may thus be respectively called the Yoga, Śaiva, Viṣṇu and Śārīra Upaniṣads. These in all make up the number to one hundred and eight.

Revival of Upaniṣad studies in modern times.

How the Upaniṣads came to be introduced into Europe is an interesting story. Dārā Shiko the eldest son of the Emperor Shāh Jahān heard of the Upaniṣads during his stay in Kashmir in 1640. He invited several Pandits from Benares to Delhi, who undertook the work of translating them into Persian. In 1775 Anquetil Duperron, the discoverer of the Zend-Avesta, received a manuscript of it presented to him by his friend Le Gentil, the French resident in Faizabad at the court of Shujā-uddaulah. Anquetil translated it into Latin which was published in 1801–1802. This translation though largely unintelligible was read by Schopenhauer with great enthusiasm. It had, as Schopenhauer himself admits, profoundly influenced his philosophy. Thus he

[1] Deussen supposes that Kauṣītaki is also one of the earliest. Max Müller and Schroeder think that Maitrāyaṇī also belongs to the earliest group, whereas Deussen counts it as a comparatively later production. Winternitz divides the Upaniṣads into four periods. In the first period he includes Bṛhadāraṇyaka, Chāndogya, Taittirīya, Aitareya, Kauṣītaki and Kena. In the second he includes Kāṭhaka, Íśā, Śvetāśvatara, Muṇḍaka, Mahānārāyaṇa, and in the third period he includes Praśna, Maitrāyaṇī and Māṇḍūkya. The rest of the Upaniṣads he includes in the fourth period.

writes in the preface to his *Welt als Wille und Vorstellung*[1], "And if, indeed, in addition to this he is a partaker of the benefit conferred by the Vedas, the access to which, opened to us through the Upanishads, is in my eyes the greatest advantage which this still young century enjoys over previous ones, because I believe that the influence of the Sanskrit literature will penetrate not less deeply than did the revival of Greek literature in the fifteenth century: if, I say, the reader has also already received and assimilated the sacred, primitive Indian wisdom, then is he best of all prepared to hear what I have to say to him....I might express the opinion that each one of the individual and disconnected aphorisms which make up the Upanishads may be deduced as a consequence from the thought I am going to impart, though the converse, that my thought is to be found in the Upanishads is by no means the case." Again, "How does every line display its firm, definite, and throughout harmonious meaning! From every sentence deep, original, and sublime thoughts arise, and the whole is pervaded by a high and holy and earnest spirit....In the whole world there is no study, except that of the originals, so beneficial and so elevating as that of the Oupanikhat. It has been the solace of my life, it will be the solace of my death![2]" Through Schopenhauer the study of the Upaniṣads attracted much attention in Germany and with the growth of a general interest in the study of Sanskrit, they found their way into other parts of Europe as well.

The study of the Upaniṣads has however gained a great impetus by the earnest attempts of our Ram Mohan Roy who not only translated them into Bengali, Hindi and English and published them at his own expense, but founded the Brahma Samaj in Bengal, the main religious doctrines of which were derived directly from the Upaniṣads.

[1] Translation by Haldane and Kemp, vol. I. pp. xii and xiii.

[2] Max Müller says in his introduction to the Upanishads (*S. B. E.* I. p. lxii; see also pp. lx, lxi) "that Schopenhauer should have spoken of the Upanishads as 'products of the highest wisdom'...that he should have placed the pantheism there taught high above the pantheism of Bruno, Malebranche, Spinoza and Scotus Erigena, as brought to light again at Oxford in 1681, may perhaps secure a more considerate reception for those relics of ancient wisdom than anything that I could say in their favour."

The Upaniṣads and their interpretations.

Before entering into the philosophy of the Upaniṣads it may be worth while to say a few words as to the reason why diverse and even contradictory explanations as to the real import of the Upaniṣads had been offered by the great Indian scholars of past times. The Upaniṣads, as we have seen, formed the concluding portion of the revealed Vedic literature, and were thus called the Vedānta. It was almost universally believed by the Hindus that the highest truths could only be found in the revelation of the Vedas. Reason was regarded generally as occupying a comparatively subservient place, and its proper use was to be found in its judicious employment in getting out the real meaning of the apparently conflicting ideas of the Vedas. The highest knowledge of ultimate truth and reality was thus regarded as having been once for all declared in the Upaniṣads. Reason had only to unravel it in the light of experience. It is important that readers of Hindu philosophy should bear in mind the contrast that it presents to the ruling idea of the modern world that new truths are discovered by reason and experience every day, and even in those cases where the old truths remain, they change their hue and character every day, and that in matters of ultimate truths no finality can ever be achieved; we are to be content only with as much as comes before the purview of our reason and experience at the time. It was therefore thought to be extremely audacious that any person howsoever learned and brilliant he might be should have any right to say anything regarding the highest truths simply on the authority of his own opinion or the reasons that he might offer. In order to make himself heard it was necessary for him to show from the texts of the Upaniṣads that they supported him, and that their purport was also the same. Thus it was that most schools of Hindu philosophy found it one of their principal duties to interpret the Upaniṣads in order to show that they alone represented the true Vedānta doctrines. Any one who should feel himself persuaded by the interpretations of any particular school might say that in following that school he was following the Vedānta.

The difficulty of assuring oneself that any interpretation is absolutely the right one is enhanced by the fact that germs of diverse kinds of thoughts are found scattered over the Upaniṣads which are not worked out in a systematic manner. Thus each interpreter in his turn made the texts favourable to his own doctrines prominent and brought them to the forefront, and tried to repress others or explain them away. But comparing the various systems of Upaniṣad interpretation we find that the interpretation offered by Śaṅkara very largely represents the view of the general body of the earlier Upaniṣad doctrines, though there are some which distinctly foreshadow the doctrines of other systems, but in a crude and germinal form. It is thus that Vedānta is generally associated with the interpretation of Śaṅkara and Śaṅkara's system of thought is called the Vedānta system, though there are many other systems which put forth their claim as representing the true Vedānta doctrines.

Under these circumstances it is necessary that a modern interpreter of the Upaniṣads should turn a deaf ear to the absolute claims of these exponents, and look upon the Upaniṣads not as a systematic treatise but as a repository of diverse currents of thought—the melting pot in which all later philosophic ideas were still in a state of fusion, though the monistic doctrine of Śaṅkara, or rather an approach thereto, may be regarded as the purport of by far the largest majority of the texts. It will be better that a modern interpreter should not agree to the claims of the ancients that all the Upaniṣads represent a connected system, but take the texts independently and separately and determine their meanings, though keeping an attentive eye on the context in which they appear. It is in this way alone that we can detect the germs of the thoughts of other Indian systems in the Upaniṣads, and thus find in them the earliest records of those tendencies of thoughts.

The quest after Brahman: the struggle and the failures.

The fundamental idea which runs through the early Upaniṣads is that underlying the exterior world of change there is an unchangeable reality which is identical with that which underlies the essence in man[1]. If we look at Greek philosophy in Parmenides or Plato or at modern philosophy in Kant, we find the same tendency towards glorifying one unspeakable entity as the reality or the essence. I have said above that the Upaniṣads are

[1] Bṛh. IV. 4. 5, 22.

no systematic treatises of a single hand, but are rather collations or compilations of floating monologues, dialogues or anecdotes. There are no doubt here and there simple discussions but there is no pedantry or gymnastics of logic. Even the most casual reader cannot but be struck with the earnestness and enthusiasm of the sages. They run from place to place with great eagerness in search of a teacher competent to instruct them about the nature of Brahman. Where is Brahman? What is his nature?

We have noticed that during the closing period of the Saṃhitā there were people who had risen to the conception of a single creator and controller of the universe, variously called Prajāpati, Viśvakarman, Puruṣa, Brahmaṇaspati and Brahman. But this divine controller was yet only a deity. The search as to the nature of this deity began in the Upaniṣads. Many visible objects of nature such as the sun or the wind on one hand and the various psychological functions in man were tried, but none could render satisfaction to the great ideal that had been aroused. The sages in the Upaniṣads had already started with the idea that there was a supreme controller or essence presiding over man and the universe. But what was its nature? Could it be identified with any of the deities of Nature, was it a new deity or was it no deity at all? The Upaniṣads present to us the history of this quest and the results that were achieved.

When we look merely to this quest we find that we have not yet gone out of the Āraṇyaka ideas and of symbolic (*pratīka*) forms of worship. *Prāṇa* (vital breath) was regarded as the most essential function for the life of man, and many anecdotes are related to show that it is superior to the other organs, such as the eye or ear, and that on it all other functions depend. This recognition of the superiority of prāṇa brings us to the meditations on prāṇa as Brahman as leading to the most beneficial results. So also we find that owing to the presence of the exalting characters of omnipresence and eternality *ākāśa* (space) is meditated upon as Brahman. So also manas and Āditya (sun) are meditated upon as Brahman. Again side by side with the visible material representation of Brahman as the pervading Vāyu, or the sun and the immaterial representation as ākāśa, manas or prāṇa, we find also the various kinds of meditations as substitutes for actual sacrifice. Thus it is that there was an earnest quest after the discovery of Brahman. We find a stratum of thought which shows that the sages were still blinded by the old ritualistic associations, and though meditation had taken the place of sacrifice yet this was hardly adequate for the highest attainment of Brahman.

Next to the failure of the meditations we have to notice the history of the search after Brahman in which the sages sought to identify Brahman with the presiding deity of the sun, moon, lightning, ether, wind, fire, water, etc., and failed; for none of these could satisfy the ideal they cherished of Brahman. It is indeed needless here to multiply these examples, for they are tiresome not only in this summary treatment but in the original as well. They are of value only in this that they indicate how toilsome was the process by which the old ritualistic associations could be got rid of; what struggles and failures the sages had to undergo before they reached a knowledge of the true nature of Brahman.

Unknowability of Brahman and the Negative Method.

It is indeed true that the magical element involved in the discharge of sacrificial duties lingered for a while in the symbolic worship of Brahman in which He was conceived almost as a deity. The minds of the Vedic poets so long accustomed to worship deities of visible manifestation could not easily dispense with the idea of seeking after a positive and definite content of Brahman. They tried some of the sublime powers of nature and also many symbols, but these could not render ultimate satisfaction. They did not know what the Brahman was like, for they had only a dim and dreamy vision of it in the deep craving of their souls which could not be translated into permanent terms. But this was enough to lead them on to the goal, for they could not be satisfied with anything short of the highest.

They found that by whatever means they tried to give a positive and definite content of the ultimate reality, the Brahman, they failed. Positive definitions were impossible. They could not point out what the Brahman was like in order to give an utterance to that which was unutterable, they could only say that it was not like aught that we find in experience. Yājñavalkya said "He the ātman is not this, nor this (*neti neti*). He is inconceivable, for he cannot be conceived, unchangeable, for he is not changed, untouched, for nothing touches him; he cannot suffer by a stroke of the sword, he cannot suffer any injury[1]." He is *asat*, non-being, for the being which Brahman is, is not to be understood as such being as is known to us by experience; yet he is being, for he alone is supremely real, for the universe subsists by him. We ourselves are but he, and yet we know not what he is. Whatever we can experience, whatever we can express, is limited, but he is the unlimited, the basis of all. "That which is inaudible, intangible, invisible, indestructible, which cannot be tasted, nor smelt, eternal, without beginning or end, greater than the great (*mahat*), the fixed. He who knows it is released from the jaws of death[2]." Space, time and causality do not appertain to him, for he at once forms their essence and transcends them. He is the infinite and the vast, yet the smallest of the small, at once here as there, there as here; no characterisation of him is possible, otherwise than by the denial to him of all empirical attributes, relations and definitions. He is independent of all limitations of space, time, and cause which rules all that is objectively presented, and therefore the empirical universe. When Bāhva was questioned by Vaṣkali, he expounded the nature of Brahman to him by maintaining silence—"Teach me," said Vaṣkali, "most reverent sir, the nature of Brahman." Bāhva however remained silent. But when the question was put forth a second or third time he answered, "I teach you indeed but you do not understand; the Ātman is silence[3]." The way to indicate it is thus by *neti neti*, it is not this, it is not this. We cannot describe it by any positive content which is always limited by conceptual thought.

The Ātman doctrine.

The sum and substance of the Upaniṣad teaching is involved in the equation Ātman = Brahman. We have already seen that the word Ātman was used in the Rg-Veda to denote on the one hand the ultimate essence of the universe, and on the other the vital breath in man. Later on in the Upaniṣads we see that the word Brahman is generally used in the former sense, while the word Ātman is reserved to denote the inmost essence in man, and the

[1] Bṛh. IV. 5. 15. Deussen, Max Müller and Röer have all misinterpreted this passage; *asito* has been interpreted as an adjective or participle, though no evidence has ever been adduced; it is evidently the ablative of *asi*, a sword.

[2] Katha III. 15.

[3] Śaṅkara on *Brahmasūtra*, III. 2. 17, and also Deussen, *Philosophy of the Upanishads*, p. 156.

Upaniṣads are emphatic in their declaration that the two are one and the same. But what is the inmost essence of man? The self of man involves an ambiguity, as it is used in a variety of senses. Thus so far as man consists of the essence of food (i.e. the physical parts of man) he is called *annamaya*. But behind the sheath of this body there is the other self consisting of the vital breath which is called the self as vital breath (*prāṇamaya ātman*). Behind this again there is the other self "consisting of will" called the *manomaya ātman*. This again contains within it the self "consisting of consciousness" called the *vijñānamaya ātman*. But behind it we come to the final essence the self as pure bliss (the *ānandamaya ātman*). The texts say: "Truly he is the rapture; for whoever gets this rapture becomes blissful. For who could live, who could breathe if this space (*ākāśa*) was not bliss? For it is he who behaves as bliss. For whoever in that Invisible, Self-surpassing, Unspeakable, Supportless finds fearless support, he really becomes fearless. But whoever finds even a slight difference, between himself and this Ātman there is fear for him[1]."

Again in another place we find that Prajāpati said: "The self (*ātman*) which is free from sin, free from old age, from death and grief, from hunger and thirst, whose desires are true, whose cogitations are true, that is to be searched for, that is to be enquired; he gets all his desires and all worlds who knows that self[2]." The gods and the demons on hearing of this sent Indra and Virocana respectively as their representatives to enquire of this self from Prajāpati. He agreed to teach them, and asked them to look into a vessel of water and tell him how much of self they could find. They answered: "We see, this our whole self, even to the hair, and to the nails." And he said, "Well, that is the self, that is the deathless and the fearless, that is the Brahman." They went away pleased, but Prajāpati thought, "There they go away, without having discovered, without having realized the self." Virocana came away with the conviction that the body was the self; but Indra did not return back to the gods, he was afraid and pestered with doubts and came back to Prajāpati and said, "just as the self becomes decorated when the body is decorated, well-dressed when the body is well-dressed, well-cleaned when the body is well-cleaned, even so that image self will be blind when the body is blind, injured in one eye when the body is injured in one eye, and mutilated when the body is mutilated, and it perishes

[1] Taitt. II. 7.

[2] Chā. VIII. 7. 1.

when the body perishes, therefore I can see no good in this theory." Prajāpati then gave him a higher instruction about the self, and said, "He who goes about enjoying dreams, he is the self, this is the deathless, the fearless, this is Brahman." Indra departed but was again disturbed with doubts, and was afraid and came back and said "that though the dream self does not become blind when the body is blind, or injured in one eye when the body is so injured and is not affected by its defects, and is not killed by its destruction, but yet it is as if it was overwhelmed, as if it suffered and as if it wept—in this I see no good." Prajāpati gave a still higher instruction: "When a man, fast asleep, in total contentment, does not know any dreams, this is the self, this is the deathless, the fearless, this is Brahman." Indra departed but was again filled with doubts on the way, and returned again and said "the self in deep sleep does not know himself, that I am this, nor does he know any other existing objects. He is destroyed and lost. I see no good in this." And now Prajāpati after having given a course of successively higher instructions as self as the body, as the self in dreams and as the self in deep dreamless sleep, and having found that the enquirer in each case could find out that this was not the ultimate truth about the self that he was seeking, ultimately gave him the ultimate and final instruction about the full truth about the self, and said "this body is the support of the deathless and the bodiless self. The self as embodied is affected by pleasure and pain, the self when associated with the body cannot get rid of pleasure and pain, but pleasure and pain do not touch the bodiless self[1]."

As the anecdote shows, they sought such a constant and unchangeable essence in man as was beyond the limits of any change. This inmost essence has sometimes been described as pure subject-object-less consciousness, the reality, and the bliss. He is the seer of all seeing, the hearer of all hearing and the knower of all knowledge. He sees but is not seen, hears but is not heard, knows but is not known. He is the light of all lights. He is like a lump of salt, with no inner or outer, which consists through and through entirely of savour; as in truth this Ātman has no inner or outer, but consists through and through entirely of knowledge. Bliss is not an attribute of it but it is bliss itself. The state of Brahman is thus likened unto the state of dreamless sleep. And he who has reached this bliss is beyond any fear. It is dearer to us than

[1] Chā. VIII. 7–12.

son, brother, wife, or husband, wealth or prosperity. It is for it and by it that things appear dear to us. It is the dearest *par excellence*, our inmost Ātman. All limitation is fraught with pain; it is the infinite alone that is the highest bliss. When a man receives this rapture, then is he full of bliss; for who could breathe, who live, if that bliss had not filled this void (*ākāśa*)? It is he who behaves as bliss. For when a man finds his peace, his fearless support in that invisible, supportless, inexpressible, unspeakable one, then has he attained peace.

Place of Brahman in the Upaniṣads.

There is the ātman not in man alone but in all objects of the universe, the sun, the moon, the world; and Brahman is this ātman. There is nothing outside the ātman, and therefore there is no plurality at all. As from a lump of clay all that is made of clay is known, as from an ingot of black iron all that is made of black iron is known, so when this ātman the Brahman is known everything else is known. The essence in man and the essence of the universe are one and the same, and it is Brahman.

Now a question may arise as to what may be called the nature of the phenomenal world of colour, sound, taste, and smell. But we must also remember that the Upaniṣads do not represent so much a conceptional system of philosophy as visions of the seers who are possessed by the spirit of this Brahman. They do not notice even the contradiction between the Brahman as unity and nature in its diversity. When the empirical aspect of diversity attracts their notice, they affirm it and yet declare that it is all Brahman. From Brahman it has come forth and to it will it return. He has himself created it out of himself and then entered into it as its inner controller (*antaryāmin*). Here is thus a glaring dualistic trait of the world of matter and Brahman as its controller, though in other places we find it asserted most emphatically that these are but names and forms, and when Brahman is known everything else is known. No attempts at reconciliation are made for the sake of the consistency of conceptual utterance, as Śaṅkara the great professor of Vedānta does by explaining away the dualistic texts. The universe is said to be a reality, but the real in it is Brahman alone. It is on account of Brahman that the fire burns and the wind blows. He is the active principle in the entire universe, and yet the most passive and unmoved. The world is his body, yet he is the soul within. "He creates all, wills all, smells all, tastes all, he has pervaded all, silent and unaffected[1]". He is below, above, in the back, in front, in the south and in the north, he is all this[2]. "These rivers in the east and in the west originating from the ocean, return back into it and become the ocean themselves, though they do not know that they are so. So also all these people coming into being from the Being do not know that they have come from the Being....That which is the subtlest that is the self, that is all this, the truth, that self thou art O Śvetaketu[3]." "Brahman," as Deussen points out, "was regarded as the cause antecedent in time, and the universe as the effect proceeding from it; the inner dependence of the universe on Brahman and its essential identity with him was represented as a creation of the universe by and out of Brahman." Thus it is said in Muṇḍ. I. I. 7:

As a spider ejects and retracts (the threads),
As the plants shoot forth on the earth,
As the hairs on the head and body of the living man,
So from the imperishable all that is here.
As the sparks from the well-kindled fire,
In nature akin to it, spring forth in their thousands,
So, my dear sir, from the imperishable
Living beings of many kinds go forth,
And again return into him[4].

Yet this world principle is the dearest to us and the highest teaching of the Upaniṣads is "That art thou."

Again the growth of the doctrine that Brahman is the "inner controller" in all the parts and forces of nature and of mankind as the ātman thereof, and that all the effects of the universe are the result of his commands which no one can outstep, gave rise to a theistic current of thought in which Brahman is held as standing aloof as God and controlling the world. It is by his ordaining, it is said, that the sun and moon are held together, and the sky and earth stand held together[5]. God and soul are distinguished again in the famous verse of Śvetāśvatara[6]:

Two bright-feathered bosom friends
Flit around one and the same tree;
One of them tastes the sweet berries,
The other without eating merely gazes down.

[1] Chā. III. 14. 4. [2] *Ibid.* VII. 25. 1; also Muṇḍaka II. 2. 11. [3] Chā. VI. 10.
[4] Deussen's translation in *Philosophy of the Upanishads*, p. 164. [5] Bṛh. III. 8. I.
[6] Śvetāśvatara IV. 6, and Muṇḍaka III. I. I, also Deussen's translation in *Philosophy of the Upanishads*, p. 177.

But in spite of this apparent theistic tendency and the occasional use of the word *Īśa* or *Īśāna*, there seems to be no doubt that theism in its true sense was never prominent, and this acknowledgement of a supreme Lord was also an offshoot of the exalted position of the ātman as the supreme principle. Thus we read in Kauṣītaki Upaniṣad 3. 9, "He is not great by good deeds nor low by evil deeds, but it is he makes one do good deeds whom he wants to raise, and makes him commit bad deeds whom he wants to lower down. He is the protector of the universe, he is the master of the world and the lord of all; he is my soul (*ātman*)." Thus the lord in spite of his greatness is still my soul. There are again other passages which regard Brahman as being at once immanent and transcendent. Thus it is said that there is that eternally existing tree whose roots grow upward and whose branches grow downward. All the universes are supported in it and no one can transcend it. This is that, "...from its fear the fire burns, the sun shines, and from its fear Indra, Vāyu and Death the fifth (with the other two) run on[1]."

If we overlook the different shades in the development of the conception of Brahman in the Upaniṣads and look to the main currents, we find that the strongest current of thought which has found expression in the majority of the texts is this that the Ātman or the Brahman is the only reality and that besides this everything else is unreal. The other current of thought which is to be found in many of the texts is the pantheistic creed that identifies the universe with the Ātman or Brahman. The third current is that of theism which looks upon Brahman as the Lord controlling the world. It is because these ideas were still in the melting pot, in which none of them were systematically worked out, that the later exponents of Vedānta, Śaṅkara, Rāmānuja, and others quarrelled over the meanings of texts in order to develop a consistent systematic philosophy out of them. Thus it is that the doctrine of Māyā which is slightly hinted at once in Bṛhadāraṇyaka and thrice in Śvetāśvatara, becomes the foundation of Śaṅkara's philosophy of the Vedānta in which Brahman alone is real and all else beside him is unreal[2].

[1] Kaṭha II. 6. 1 and 3.

[2] Bṛh. II. 5. 19, Śvet. I. 10, IV. 9, 10.

The World.

We have already seen that the universe has come out of Brahman, has its essence in Brahman, and will also return back to it. But in spite of its existence as Brahman its character as represented to experience could not be denied. Śaṅkara held that the Upaniṣads referred to the external world and accorded a reality to it consciously with the purpose of treating it as merely relatively real, which will eventually appear as unreal as soon as the ultimate truth, the Brahman, is known. This however remains to be modified to this extent that the sages had not probably any conscious purpose of according a relative reality to the phenomenal world, but in spite of regarding Brahman as the highest reality they could not ignore the claims of the exterior world, and had to accord a reality to it. The inconsistency of this reality of the phenomenal world with the ultimate and only reality of Brahman was attempted to be reconciled by holding that this world is not beside him but it has come out of him, it is maintained in him and it will return back to him.

The world is sometimes spoken of in its twofold aspect, the organic and the inorganic. All organic things, whether plants, animals or men, have souls[1]. Brahman desiring to be many created fire (*tejas*), water (*ap*) and earth (*kṣiti*). Then the self-existent Brahman entered into these three, and it is by their combination that all other bodies are formed[2]. So all other things are produced as a result of an alloying or compounding of the parts of these three together. In this theory of the threefold division of the primitive elements lies the earliest germ of the later distinction (especially in the Sāṃkhya school) of pure infinitesimal substances (*tanmātra*) and gross elements, and the theory that each gross substance is composed of the atoms of the primary elements. And in Praśna IV. 8 we find the gross elements distinguished from their subtler natures, e.g. earth (*pṛthivī*), and the subtler state of earth (*pṛthivīmātra*). In the Taittirīya, II. I, however, ether (*ākāśa*) is also described as proceeding from Brahman, and the other elements, air, fire, water, and earth, are described as each proceeding directly from the one which directly preceded it.

[1] Chā. VI. II. [2] *ibid.* VI. 2, 3, 4.

The World-Soul.

The conception of a world-soul related to the universe as the soul of man to his body is found for the first time in R.V. x. 121. 1, where he is said to have sprung forth as the firstborn of creation from the primeval waters. This being has twice been referred to in the Śvetāśvatara, in III. 4 and IV. 12. It is indeed very strange that this being is not referred to in any of the earlier Upaniṣads. In the two passages in which he has been spoken of, his mythical character is apparent. He is regarded as one of the earlier products in the process of cosmic creation, but his importance from the point of view of the development of the theory of Brahman or Ātman is almost nothing. The fact that neither the Puruṣa, nor the Viśvakarma, nor the Hiraṇyagarbha played an important part in the earlier development of the Upaniṣads leads me to think that the Upaniṣad doctrines were not directly developed from the monotheistic tendencies of the later Ṛg-Veda speculations. The passages in Śvetāśvatara clearly show how from the supreme eminence that he had in R.V. x. 121, Hiraṇyagarbha had been brought to the level of one of the created beings. Deussen in explaining the philosophical significance of the Hiraṇyagarbha doctrine of the Upaniṣads says that the "entire objective universe is possible only in so far as it is sustained by a knowing subject. This subject as a sustainer of the objective universe is manifested in all individual objects but is by no means identical with them. For the individual objects pass away but the objective universe continues to exist without them; there exists therefore the eternal knowing subject also (*hiraṇyagarbha*) by whom it is sustained. Space and time are derived from this subject. It is itself accordingly not in space and does not belong to time, and therefore from an empirical point of view it is in general non-existent; it has no empirical but only a metaphysical reality[1]." This however seems to me to be wholly irrelevant, since the Hiraṇyagarbha doctrine cannot be supposed to have any philosophical importance in the Upaniṣads.

The Theory of Causation.

There was practically no systematic theory of causation in the Upaniṣads. Śaṅkara, the later exponent of Vedānta philosophy, always tried to show that the Upaniṣads looked upon the cause

[1] Deussen's *Philosophy of the Upanishads*, p. 201.

as mere ground of change which though unchanged in itself in reality had only an appearance of suffering change. This he did on the strength of a series of examples in the Chāndogya Upaniṣad (VI. I) in which the material cause, e.g. the clay, is spoken of as the only reality in all its transformations as the pot, the jug or the plate. It is said that though there are so many diversities of appearance that one is called the plate, the other the pot, and the other the jug, yet these are only empty distinctions of name and form, for the only thing real in them is the earth which in its essence remains ever the same whether you call it the pot, plate, or jug. So it is that the ultimate cause, the unchangeable Brahman, remains ever constant, though it may appear to suffer change as the manifold world outside. This world is thus only an unsubstantial appearance, a mirage imposed upon Brahman, the real *par excellence*.

It seems however that though such a view may be regarded as having been expounded in the Upaniṣads in an imperfect manner, there is also side by side the other view which looks upon the effect as the product of a real change wrought in the cause itself through the action and combination of the elements of diversity in it. Thus when the different objects of nature have been spoken of in one place as the product of the combination of the three elements fire, water and earth, the effect signifies a real change produced by their compounding. This is in germ (as we shall see hereafter) the Pariṇāma theory of causation advocated by the Sāṃkhya school[1].

Doctrine of Transmigration.

When the Vedic people witnessed the burning of a dead body they supposed that the eye of the man went to the sun, his breath to the wind, his speech to the fire, his limbs to the different parts of the universe. They also believed as we have already seen in the recompense of good and bad actions in worlds other than our own, and though we hear of such things as the passage of the human soul into trees, etc., the tendency towards transmigration had but little developed at the time.

In the Upaniṣads however we find a clear development in the direction of transmigration in two distinct stages. In the one the Vedic idea of a recompense in the other world is combined with

[1] Chā. VI. 2-4.

the doctrine of transmigration, whereas in the other the doctrine of transmigration comes to the forefront in supersession of the idea of a recompense in the other world. Thus it is said that those who performed charitable deeds or such public works as the digging of wells, etc., follow after death the way of the fathers (*pitṛyāna*), in which the soul after death enters first into smoke, then into night, the dark half of the month, etc., and at last reaches the moon; after a residence there as long as the remnant of his good deeds remains he descends again through ether, wind, smoke, mist, cloud, rain, herbage, food and seed, and through the assimilation of food by man he enters the womb of the mother and is born again. Here we see that the soul had not only a recompense in the world of the moon, but was re-born again in this world[1].

The other way is the way of gods (*devayāna*), meant for those who cultivate faith and asceticism (*tapas*). These souls at death enter successively into flame, day, bright half of the month, bright half of the year, sun, moon, lightning, and then finally into Brahman never to return. Deussen says that "the meaning of the whole is that the soul on the way of the gods reaches regions of ever-increasing light, in which is concentrated all that is bright and radiant as stations on the way to Brahman the 'light of lights'" (*jyotiṣāṃ jyotiḥ*)[2].

The other line of thought is a direct reference to the doctrine of transmigration unmixed with the idea of reaping the fruits of his deeds (*karma*) by passing through the other worlds and without reference to the doctrine of the ways of the fathers and gods, the *Yānas*. Thus Yājñavalkya says, "when the soul becomes weak (apparent weakness owing to the weakness of the body with which it is associated) and falls into a swoon as it were, these senses go towards it. It (Soul) takes these light particles within itself and centres itself only in the heart. Thus when the person in the eye turns back, then the soul cannot know colour; (the senses) become one (with him); (people about him) say he does not see; (the senses) become one (with him), he does not smell, (the senses) become one (with him), he does not taste, (the senses) become one (with him), he does not speak, (the senses) become one (with him), he does not hear, (the senses) become one (with him), he does not think, (the senses) become one with him, he does not touch, (the senses) become one with him, he does not know, they say. The

[1] Chā. V. 10.

[2] Deussen's *Philosophy of the Upanishads*, p. 335.

tip of his heart shines and by that shining this soul goes out. When he goes out either through the eye, the head, or by any other part of the body, the vital function (*prāṇa*) follows and all the senses follow the vital function (*prāṇa*) in coming out. He is then with determinate consciousness and as such he comes out. Knowledge, the deeds as well as previous experience (*prajñā*) accompany him. Just as a caterpillar going to the end of a blade of grass, by undertaking a separate movement collects itself, so this self after destroying this body, removing ignorance, by a separate movement collects itself. Just as a goldsmith taking a small bit of gold, gives to it a newer and fairer form, so the soul after destroying this body and removing ignorance fashions a newer and fairer form as of the Pitṛs, the Gandharvas, the gods, of Prajāpati or Brahma or of any other being....As he acts and behaves so he becomes, good by good deeds, bad by bad deeds, virtuous by virtuous deeds and vicious by vice. The man is full of desires. As he desires so he wills, as he wills so he works, as the work is done so it happens. There is also a verse, being attached to that he wants to gain by karma that to which he was attached. Having reaped the full fruit (lit. gone to the end) of the karma that he does here, he returns back to this world for doing karma[1]. So it is the case with those who have desires. He who has no desires, who had no desires, who has freed himself from all desires, is satisfied in his desires and in himself, his senses do not go out. He being Brahma attains Brahmahood. Thus the verse says, when all the desires that are in his heart are got rid of, the mortal becomes immortal and attains Brahma here" (Bṛh. IV. iv. 1–7).

A close consideration of the above passage shows that the self itself destroyed the body and built up a newer and fairer frame by its own activity when it reached the end of the present life. At the time of death, the self collected within itself all senses and faculties and after death all its previous knowledge, work and experience accompanied him. The falling off of the body at the time of death is only for the building of a newer body either in this world or in the other worlds. The self which thus takes rebirth is regarded as an aggregation of diverse categories. Thus it is said that "he is of the essence of understanding,

[1] It is possible that there is a vague and obscure reference here to the doctrine that the fruits of our deeds are reaped in other worlds.

of the vital function, of the visual sense, of the auditory sense, of the essence of the five elements (which would make up the physical body in accordance with its needs) or the essence of desires, of the essence of restraint of desires, of the essence of anger, of the essence of turning off from all anger, of the essence of dharma, of the essence of adharma, of the essence of all that is this (manifest) and that is that (unmanifest or latent)" (Bṛh. IV. iv. 5). The self that undergoes rebirth is thus a unity not only of moral and psychological tendencies, but also of all the elements which compose the physical world. The whole process of his changes follows from this nature of his; for whatever he desires, he wills and whatever he wills he acts, and in accordance with his acts the fruit happens. The whole logic of the genesis of karma and its fruits is held up within him, for he is a unity of the moral and psychological tendencies on the one hand and elements of the physical world on the other.

The self that undergoes rebirth being a combination of diverse psychological and moral tendencies and the physical elements holds within itself the principle of all its transformations. The root of all this is the desire of the self and the consequent fruition of it through will and act. When the self continues to desire and act, it reaps the fruit and comes again to this world for performing acts. This world is generally regarded as the field for performing karma, whereas other worlds are regarded as places where the fruits of karma are reaped by those born as celestial beings. But there is no emphasis in the Upaniṣads on this point. The Pitṛyāna theory is not indeed given up, but it seems only to form a part in the larger scheme of rebirth in other worlds and sometimes in this world too. All the course of these rebirths is effected by the self itself by its own desires, and if it ceases to desire, it suffers no rebirth and becomes immortal. The most distinctive feature of this doctrine is this, that it refers to desires as the cause of rebirth and not karma. Karma only comes as the connecting link between desires and rebirth—for it is said that whatever a man desires he wills, and whatever he wills he acts.

Thus it is said in another place "he who knowingly desires is born by his desires in those places (accordingly), but for him whose desires have been fulfilled and who has realized himself, all his desires vanish here" (Muṇḍ III. 2. 2). This destruction of desires is effected by the right knowledge of the self. "He who knows his self as 'I am the person' for what wish and for what desire will he trouble the body,...even being here if we know it, well if we do not, what a great destruction" (Bṛh. IV. iv. 12 and 14). "In former times the wise men did not desire sons, thinking what shall we do with sons since this our self is the universe" (Bṛh. IV. iv. 22). None of the complexities of the karma doctrine which we find later on in more recent developments of Hindu thought can be found in the Upaniṣads. The whole scheme is worked out on the principle of desire (*kāma*) and karma only serves as the link between it and the actual effects desired and willed by the person.

It is interesting to note in this connection that consistently with the idea that desires (*kāma*) led to rebirth, we find that in some Upaniṣads the discharge of the semen in the womb of a woman as a result of desires is considered as the first birth of man, and the birth of the son as the second birth and the birth elsewhere after death is regarded as the third birth. Thus it is said, "It is in man that there comes first the embryo, which is but the semen which is produced as the essence of all parts of his body and which holds itself within itself, and when it is put in a woman, that is his first birth. That embryo then becomes part of the woman's self like any part of her body; it therefore does not hurt her; she protects and develops the embryo within herself. As she protects (the embryo) so she also should be protected. It is the woman who bears the embryo (before birth) but when after birth the father takes care of the son always, he is taking care only of himself, for it is through sons alone that the continuity of the existence of people can be maintained. This is his second birth. He makes this self of his a representative for performing all the virtuous deeds. The other self of his after realizing himself and attaining age goes away and when going away he is born again that is his third birth" (Aitareya, II. 1–4)[1]. No special emphasis is given in the Upaniṣads to the sex-desire or the desire for a son; for, being called kāma, whatever was the desire for a son was the same as the desire for money and the desire for money was the same as any other worldly desire (Bṛh. IV. iv. 22), and hence sex-desires stand on the same plane as any other desire.

[1] See also Kauṣītaki, II. 15.

Emancipation.

The doctrine which next attracts our attention in this connection is that of emancipation (*mukti*). Already we know that the doctrine of Devayāna held that those who were faithful and performed asceticism (*tapas*) went by the way of the gods through successive stages never to return to the world and suffer rebirth. This could be contrasted with the way of the fathers (*pitṛyāna*) where the dead were for a time recompensed in another world and then had to suffer rebirth. Thus we find that those who are faithful and perform *śraddhā* had a distinctly different type of goal from those who performed ordinary virtues, such as those of a general altruistic nature. This distinction attains its fullest development in the doctrine of emancipation. Emancipation or Mukti means in the Upaniṣads the state of infiniteness that a man attains when he knows his own self and thus becomes Brahman. The ceaseless course of transmigration is only for those who are ignorant. The wise man however who has divested himself of all passions and knows himself to be Brahman, at once becomes Brahman and no bondage of any kind can ever affect him.

> He who beholds that loftiest and deepest,
> For him the fetters of the heart break asunder,
> For him all doubts are solved,
> And his works become nothingness[1].

The knowledge of the self reveals the fact that all our passions and antipathies, all our limitations of experience, all that is ignoble and small in us, all that is transient and finite in us is false. We "do not know" but are "pure knowledge" ourselves. We are not limited by anything, for we are the infinite; we do not suffer death, for we are immortal. Emancipation thus is not a new acquisition, product, an effect, or result of any action, but it always exists as the Truth of our nature. We are always emancipated and always free. We do not seem to be so and seem to suffer rebirth and thousands of other troubles only because we do not know the true nature of our self. Thus it is that the true knowledge of self does not lead to emancipation but is emancipation itself. All sufferings and limitations are true only so long as we do not know our self. Emancipation is the natural and only goal of man simply because it represents the true nature and essence of man. It is the realization of our own nature that

[1] Deussen's *Philosophy of the Upanishads*, p. 352.

is called emancipation. Since we are all already and always in our own true nature and as such emancipated, the only thing necessary for us is to know that we are so. Self-knowledge is therefore the only desideratum which can wipe off all false knowledge, all illusions of death and rebirth. The story is told in the Kaṭha Upaniṣad that Yama, the lord of death, promised Naciketas, the son of Gautama, to grant him three boons at his choice. Naciketas, knowing that his father Gautama was offended with him, said, "O death let Gautama be pleased in mind and forget his anger against me." This being granted Naciketas asked the second boon that the fire by which heaven is gained should be made known to him. This also being granted Naciketas said, "There is this enquiry, some say the soul exists after the death of man; others say it does not exist. This I should like to know instructed by thee. This is my third boon." Yama said, "It was inquired of old, even by the gods; for it is not easy to understand it. Subtle is its nature, choose another boon. Do not compel me to this." Naciketas said, "Even by the gods was it inquired before, and even thou O Death sayest that it is not easy to understand it, but there is no other speaker to be found like thee. There is no other boon like this." Yama said, "Choose sons and grandsons who may live a hundred years, choose herds of cattle; choose elephants and gold and horses; choose the wide expanded earth, and live thyself as many years as thou wishest. Or if thou knowest a boon like this choose it together with wealth and far-extending life. Be a king on the wide earth. I will make thee the enjoyer of all desires. All those desires that are difficult to gain in the world of mortals, all those ask thou at thy pleasure; those fair nymphs with their chariots, with their musical instruments; the like of them are not to be gained by men. I will give them to thee, but do not ask the question regarding death." Naciketas replied, "All those enjoyments are of to-morrow and they only weaken the senses. All life is short, with thee the dance and song. Man cannot be satisfied with wealth, we could obtain wealth, as long as we did not reach you we live only as long as thou pleasest. The boon which I choose I have said." Yama said, "One thing is good, another is pleasant. Blessed is he who takes the good, but he who chooses the pleasant loses the object of man. But thou considering the objects of desire, hast abandoned them. These two, ignorance (whose object is what is pleasant) and knowledge (whose object is what is good), are known to be far asunder, and to lead to different goals. Believing that this world exists and not the other, the careless youth is subject to my sway. That knowledge which thou hast asked is not to be obtained by argument. I know worldly happiness is transient for that firm one is not to be obtained by what is not firm. The wise by concentrating on the soul, knowing him whom it is hard to behold, leaves both grief and joy. Thee O Naciketas, I believe to be like a house whose door is open to Brahman. Brahman is deathless, whoever knows him obtains whatever he wishes. The wise man is not born; he does not die; he is not produced from anywhere. Unborn, eternal, the soul is not slain, though the body is slain; subtler than what is subtle, greater than what is great, sitting it goes far, lying it goes everywhere. Thinking the soul as unbodily among bodies, firm among fleeting things, the wise man casts off all grief. The soul cannot be gained by eloquence, by understanding, or by learning. It can be obtained by him alone whom it chooses. To him it reveals its own nature[1]." So long as the Self identifies itself with its desires, he wills and acts according to them and reaps the fruits in the present and in future lives. But when he comes to know the highest truth about himself, that he is the highest essence and principle of the universe, the immortal and the infinite, he ceases to have desires, and receding from all desires realizes the ultimate truth of himself in his own infinitude. Man is as it were the epitome of the universe and he holds within himself the fine constituents of the gross body (*annamaya koṣa*), the vital functions (*prāṇamaya koṣa*) of life, the will and desire (*manomaya*) and the thoughts and ideas (*vijñānamaya*), and so long as he keeps himself in these spheres and passes through a series of experiences in the present life and in other lives to come, these experiences are willed by him and in that sense created by him. He suffers pleasures and pains, disease and death. But if he retires from these into his true unchangeable being, he is in a state where he is one with his experience and there is no change and no movement. What this state is cannot be explained by the use of concepts. One could only indicate it by pointing out that it is not any of those concepts found in ordinary knowledge; it is not

[1] Kaṭha II. The translation is not continuous. There are some parts in the extract which may be differently interpreted.

whatever one knows as this and this (*neti neti*). In this infinite and true self there is no difference, no diversity, no *meum* and *tuum*. It is like an ocean in which all our phenomenal existence will dissolve like salt in water. "Just as a lump of salt when put in water will disappear in it and it cannot be taken out separately but in whatever portion of water we taste we find the salt, so, Maitreyī, does this great reality infinite and limitless consisting only of pure intelligence manifesting itself in all these (phenomenal existences) vanish in them and there is then no phenomenal knowledge" (Bṛh. II. 4. 12). The true self manifests itself in all the processes of our phenomenal existences, but ultimately when it retires back to itself, it can no longer be found in them. It is a state of absolute infinitude of pure intelligence, pure being, and pure blessedness.

CHAPTER IV

GENERAL OBSERVATIONS ON THE SYSTEMS OF INDIAN PHILOSOPHY

In what Sense is a History of Indian Philosophy possible?

It is hardly possible to attempt a history of Indian philosophy in the manner in which the histories of European philosophy have been written. In Europe from the earliest times, thinkers came one after another and offered their independent speculations on philosophy. The work of a modern historian consists in chronologically arranging these views and in commenting upon the influence of one school upon another or upon the general change from time to time in the tides and currents of philosophy. Here in India, however, the principal systems of philosophy had their beginning in times of which we have but scanty record, and it is hardly possible to say correctly at what time they began, or to compute the influence that led to the foundation of so many divergent systems at so early a period, for in all probability these were formulated just after the earliest Upaniṣads had been composed or arranged.

The systematic treatises were written in short and pregnant half-sentences (*sūtras*) which did not elaborate the subject in detail, but served only to hold before the reader the lost threads of memory of elaborate disquisitions with which he was already thoroughly acquainted. It seems, therefore, that these pithy half-sentences were like lecture hints, intended for those who had had direct elaborate oral instructions on the subject. It is indeed difficult to guess from the sūtras the extent of their significance, or how far the discussions which they gave rise to in later days were originally intended by them. The sūtras of the Vedānta system, known as the Śārīraka-sūtras or Brahma-sūtras of Bādarāyaṇa for example were of so ambiguous a nature that they gave rise to more than half a dozen divergent interpretations, each one of which claimed to be the only faithful one. Such was the high esteem and respect in which these writers of the sūtras were held by later writers that whenever they had any new speculations to offer, these were reconciled with the doctrines of one or other of the existing systems, and put down as faithful interpretations of the system in the form of commentaries. Such was the hold of these systems upon scholars that all the orthodox teachers since the foundation of the systems of philosophy belonged to one or other of these schools. Their pupils were thus naturally brought up in accordance with the views of their teachers. All the independence of their thinking was limited and enchained by the faith of the school to which they were attached. Instead of producing a succession of free-lance thinkers having their own systems to propound and establish, India had brought forth schools of pupils who carried the traditionary views of particular systems from generation to generation, who explained and expounded them, and defended them against the attacks of other rival schools which they constantly attacked in order to establish the superiority of the system to which they adhered. To take an example, the Nyāya system of philosophy consisting of a number of half-sentences or sūtras is attributed to Gautama, also called Akṣapāda. The earliest commentary on these sūtras, called the *Vātsyāyana bhāṣya*, was written by Vātsyāyana. This work was sharply criticized by the Buddhist Diṅnāga, and to answer these criticisms Udyotakara wrote a commentary on this commentary called the *Bhāṣyavāttika*[1]. As time went on the original force of this work was lost, and it failed to maintain the old dignity of the school. At this Vācaspati Miśra wrote a commentary called *Vārttika-tātparyaṭīkā* on this second commentary, where he tried to refute all objections against the Nyāya system made by other rival schools and particularly by the Buddhists. This commentary, called *Nyāya-tātparyaṭīkā*, had another commentary called *Nyāya-tātparyaṭīkā-pariśuddhi* written by the great Udayana. This commentary had another commentary called *Nyāya-nibandha-prakāśa* written by Varddhamāna the son of the illustrious Gaṅgeśa. This again had another commentary called *Varddhamānendu* upon it by Padmanābha Miśra, and this again had another named *Nyāya-tātparyamaṇḍana* by Śaṅkara Miśra. The names of Vātsyāyana, Vācaspati, and Udayana are indeed very great, but even they contented themselves by writing commentaries on commentaries, and did not try to formulate any

[1] I have preferred to spell Diṅnāga after Vācaspati's *Tātparyaṭīkā* (p. 1) and not Dignāga as it is generally spelt.

original system. Even Śaṅkara, probably the greatest man of India after Buddha, spent his life in writing commentaries on the *Brahma-sūtras*, the Upaniṣads, and the *Bhagavadgītā*.

As a system passed on it had to meet unexpected opponents and troublesome criticisms for which it was not in the least prepared. Its adherents had therefore to use all their ingenuity and subtlety in support of their own positions, and to discover the defects of the rival schools that attacked them. A system as it was originally formulated in the sūtras had probably but few problems to solve, but as it fought its way in the teeth of opposition of other schools, it had to offer consistent opinions on other problems in which the original views were more or less involved but to which no attention had been given before.

The contributions of the successive commentators served to make each system more and more complete in all its parts, and stronger and stronger to enable it to hold its own successfully against the opposition and attacks of the rival schools. A system in the sūtras is weak and shapeless as a newborn babe, but if we take it along with its developments down to the beginning of the seventeenth century it appears as a fully developed man strong and harmonious in all its limbs. It is therefore not possible to write any history of successive philosophies of India, but it is necessary that each system should be studied and interpreted in all the growth it has acquired through the successive ages of history from its conflicts with the rival systems as one whole[1]. In the history of Indian philosophy we have no place for systems which had their importance only so long as they lived and were then forgotten or remembered only as targets of criticism. Each system grew and developed by the untiring energy of its adherents through all the successive ages of history, and a history of this growth is a history of its conflicts. No study of any Indian system is therefore adequate unless it is taken throughout all the growth it attained by the work of its champions, the commentators whose selfless toil for it had kept it living through the ages of history.

[1] In the case of some systems it is indeed possible to suggest one or two earlier phases of the system, but this principle cannot be carried all through, for the supplementary information and arguments given by the later commentators often appear as harmonious elaborations of the earlier writings and are very seldom in conflict with them.

Growth of the Philosophic Literature.

It is difficult to say how the systems were originally formulated, and what were the influences that led to it. We know that a spirit of philosophic enquiry had already begun in the days of the earliest Upaniṣads. The spirit of that enquiry was that the final essence or truth was the ātman, that a search after it was our highest duty, and that until we are ultimately merged in it we can only feel this truth and remain uncontented with everything else and say that it is not the truth we want, it is not the truth we want (*neti neti*). Philosophical enquires were however continuing in circles other than those of the Upaniṣads. Thus the Buddha who closely followed the early Upaniṣad period, spoke of and enumerated sixty-two kinds of heresies[1], and these can hardly be traced in the Upaniṣads. The Jaina activities were also probably going on contemporaneously but in the Upaniṣads no reference to these can be found. We may thus reasonably suppose that there were different forms of philosophic enquiry in spheres other than those of the Upaniṣad sages, of which we have but scanty records. It seems probable that the Hindu systems of thought originated among the sages who though attached chiefly to the Upaniṣad circles used to take note of the discussions and views of the antagonistic and heretical philosophic circles. In the assemblies of these sages and their pupils, the views of the heretical circles were probably discussed and refuted. So it continued probably for some time when some illustrious member of the assembly such as Gautama or Kaṇāda collected the purport of these discussions on various topics and problems, filled up many of the missing links, classified and arranged these in the form of a system of philosophy and recorded it in sūtras. These sūtras were intended probably for people who had attended the elaborate oral discussions and thus could easily follow the meaning of the suggestive phrases contained in the aphorisms. The sūtras thus contain sometimes allusions to the views of the rival schools and indicate the way in which they could be refuted. The commentators were possessed of the general drift of the different discussions alluded to and conveyed from generation to generation through an unbroken chain of succession of teachers and pupils. They were however free to supplement these traditionary explanations with their own

[1] *Brahmajāla-sutta*, *Dīgha*, I. p. 12 ff.

views or to modify and even suppress such of the traditionary views with which they did not agree or which they found it difficult to maintain. Brilliant oppositions from the opposing schools often made it necessary for them to offer solutions to new problems unthought of before, but put forward by some illustrious adherent of a rival school. In order to reconcile these new solutions with the other parts of the system, the commentators never hesitated to offer such slight modifications of the doctrines as could harmonize them into a complete whole. These elaborations or modifications generally developed the traditionary system, but did not effect any serious change in the system as expounded by the older teachers, for the new exponents always bound themselves to the explanations of the older teachers and never contradicted them. They would only interpret them to suit their own ideas, or say new things only in those cases where the older teachers had remained silent. It is not therefore possible to describe the growth of any system by treating the contributions of the individual commentators separately. This would only mean unnecessary repetition. Except when there is a specially new development, the system is to be interpreted on the basis of the joint work of the commentators treating their contributions as forming one whole.

The fact that each system had to contend with other rival systems in order to hold its own has left its permanent mark upon all the philosophic literatures of India which are always written in the form of disputes, where the writer is supposed to be always faced with objections from rival schools to whatever he has got to say. At each step he supposes certain objections put forth against him which he answers, and points out the defects of the objector or shows that the objection itself is ill founded. It is thus through interminable byways of objections, counter-objections and their answers that the writer can wend his way to his destination. Most often the objections of the rival schools are referred to in so brief a manner that those only who know the views can catch them. To add to these difficulties the Sanskrit style of most of the commentaries is so condensed and different from literary Sanskrit, and aims so much at precision and brevity, leading to the use of technical words current in the diverse systems, that a study of these becomes often impossible without the aid of an expert preceptor; it is difficult therefore for all who are not widely read in all the different systems to follow any advanced work of any particular system, as the deliberations of that particular system are expressed in such close interconnection with the views of other systems that these can hardly be understood without them. Each system of India has grown (at least in particular epochs) in relation to and in opposition to the growth of other systems of thought, and to be a thorough student of Indian philosophy one should study all the systems in their mutual opposition and relation from the earliest times to a period at which they ceased to grow and came to a stop—a purpose for which a work like the present one may only be regarded as forming a preliminary introduction.

Besides the sūtras and their commentaries there are also independent treatises on the systems in verse called *kārikās*, which try to summarize the important topics of any system in a succinct manner; the *Sāṃkhya kārikā* may be mentioned as a work of this kind. In addition to these there were also long dissertations, commentaries, or general observations on any system written in verses called the vārttikas; the *Ślokavārttika*, of Kumārila or the *Vārttika* of Sureśvara may be mentioned as examples. All these of course had their commentaries to explain them. In addition to these there were also advanced treatises on the systems in prose in which the writers either nominally followed some selected sūtras or proceeded independently of them. Of the former class the *Nyāyamañjarī* of Jayanta may be mentioned as an example and of the latter the *Praśastapāda bhāṣya*, the *Advaitasiddhi* of Madhusūdana Sarasvatī or the *Vedānta-paribhāṣā* of Dharmarājādhvarīndra. The more remarkable of these treatises were of a masterly nature in which the writers represented the systems they adhered to in a highly forcible and logical manner by dint of their own great mental powers and genius. These also had their commentaries to explain and elaborate them. The period of the growth of the philosophic literatures of India begins from about 500 B.C. (about the time of the Buddha) and practically ends in the later half of the seventeenth century, though even now some minor publications are seen to come out.

The Indian Systems of Philosophy.

The Hindus classify the systems of philosophy into two classes, namely, the *nāstika* and the *āstika*. The nāstika (*na asti* "it is not") views are those which neither regard the Vedas as infallible nor try to establish their own validity on their authority. These are principally three in number, the Buddhist, Jaina and the Cārvāka. The āstika-mata or orthodox schools are six in number, Sāṃkhya, Yoga, Vedānta, Mīmāṃsā, Nyāya and Vaiśeṣika, generally known as the six systems (*ṣaḍdarśana*[1]).

The Sāṃkhya is ascribed to a mythical Kapila, but the earliest works on the subject are probably now lost. The Yoga system is attributed to Patañjali and the original sūtras are called the *Pātañjala Yoga sūtras*. The general metaphysical position of these two systems with regard to soul, nature, cosmology and the final goal is almost the same, and the difference lies in this that the Yoga system acknowledges a god (*Īśvara*) as distinct from Ātman and lays much importance on certain mystical practices (commonly known as Yoga practices) for the achievement of liberation, whereas the Sāṃkhya denies the existence of Īśvara and thinks that sincere philosophic thought and culture are sufficient to produce the true conviction of the truth and thereby bring about liberation. It is probable that the system of Sāṃkhya associated with Kapila and the Yoga system associated with Patañjali are but two divergent modifications of an original Sāṃkhya school, of which we now get only references here and there. These systems therefore though generally counted as two should more properly be looked upon as two different schools of the same Sāṃkhya system—one may be called the Kāpila Sāṃkhya and the other Pātañjala Sāṃkhya.

The Pūrva Mīmāṃsā (from the root *man* to think—rational conclusions) cannot properly be spoken of as a system of philosophy. It is a systematized code of principles in accordance with which the Vedic texts are to be interpreted for purposes of sacrifices.

[1] The word "*darśana*" in the sense of true philosophic knowledge has its earliest use in the *Vaiśeṣika sūtras* of Kaṇāda (IX. ii. 13) which I consider as pre-Buddhistic. The Buddhist piṭakas (400 B.C.) called the heretical opinions "*diṭṭhi*" (Sanskrit—dṛṣṭi from the same root *dṛś* from which darśana is formed). Haribhadra (fifth century A.D.) uses the word Darśana in the sense of systems of philosophy (*sarvadarśanavācyo' rthaḥ—Ṣaḍdarśanasamuccaya* I.). Ratnakīrtti (end of the tenth century A.D.) uses the word also in the same sense ("*Yadi nāma darśane darśane nānāprakāram sattvalakṣaṇam uktamasti.*" *Kṣaṇabhaṅgasiddhi* in *Six Buddhist Nyāya tracts*, p. 20). Mādhava (1331 A.D.) calls his Compendium of all systems of philosophy, *Sarvadarśanasaṃgraha*. The word "*mata*" (opinion or view) was also freely used in quoting the views of other systems. But there is no word to denote 'philosophers' in the technical sense. The Buddhists used to call those who held heretical views "*tairthika*." The words "siddha," "*jñānin*," etc. do not denote philosophers in the modern sense, they are used rather in the sense of "seers" or "perfects."

The Vedic texts were used as mantras (incantations) for sacrifices, and people often disputed as to the relation of words in a sentence or their mutual relative importance with reference to the general drift of the sentence. There were also differences of view with regard to the meaning of a sentence, the use to which it may be applied as a mantra, its relative importance or the exact nature of its connection with other similar sentences in a complex Vedic context. The Mīmāṃsā formulated some principles according to which one could arrive at rational and uniform solutions for all these difficulties. Preliminary to these its main objects, it indulges in speculations with regard to the external world, soul, perception, inference, the validity of the Vedas, or the like, for in order that a man might perform sacrifices with mantras, a definite order of the universe and its relation to man or the position and nature of the mantras of the Veda must be demonstrated and established. Though its interest in such abstract speculations is but secondary yet it briefly discusses these in order to prepare a rational ground for its doctrine of the mantras and their practical utility for man. It is only so far as there are these preliminary discussions in the Mīmāṃsā that it may be called a system of philosophy. Its principles and maxims for the interpretation of the import of words and sentences have a legal value even to this day. The sūtras of Mīmāṃsā are attributed to Jaimini, and Śabara wrote a bhāṣya upon it. The two great names in the history of Mīmāṃsā literature after Jaimini and Śabara are Kumārila Bhaṭṭa and his pupil Prabhākara, who criticized the opinions of his master so much, that the master used to call him guru (master) in sarcasm, and to this day his opinions pass as *guru-mata*, whereas the views of Kumārila Bhaṭṭa pass as *bhaṭṭa-mata*[1]. It may not be out of place to mention here that Hindu Law (*smṛti*) accepts without any reservation the maxims and principles settled and formulated by the Mīmāṃsā.

[1] There is a story that Kumārila could not understand the meaning of a Sanskrit sentence "*Atra tunoktam tatrāpinoktam* iti paunaruktam" (hence spoken twice). *Tunoktam* phonetically admits of two combinations, *tu noktam* (but not said) and *tunā uktam* (said by the particle *tu*) and *tatrāpi noktam* as *tatra api na uktam* (not said also there) and *tatra apinā uktam* (said there by the particle *api*). Under the first interpretation the sentence would mean, "Not spoken here, not spoken there, it is thus spoken twice." This puzzled Kumārila, when Prabhākara taking the second meaning pointed out to him that the meaning was "here it is indicated by *tu* and there by *api*, and so it is indicated twice." Kumārila was so pleased that he called his pupil "Guru" (master) at this.

The *Vedānta sūtras*, also called Uttara Mīmāṃsā, written by Bādarāyaṇa, otherwise known as the *Brahma-sūtras*, form the original authoritative work of Vedānta. The word Vedānta means "end of the Veda," i.e. the Upaniṣads, and the *Vedānta sūtras* are so called as they are but a summarized statement of the general views of the Upaniṣads. This work is divided into four books or adhyāyas and each adhyāya is divided into four pādas or chapters. The first four sūtras of the work commonly known as *Catuḥsūtrī* are (1) How to ask about Brahman, (2) From whom proceed birth and decay, (3) This is because from him the Vedas have come forth, (4) This is shown by the harmonious testimony of the Upaniṣads. The whole of the first chapter of the second book is devoted to justifying the position of the Vedānta against the attacks of the rival schools. The second chapter of the second book is busy in dealing blows at rival systems. All the other parts of the book are devoted to settling the disputed interpretations of a number of individual Upaniṣad texts. The really philosophical portion of the work is thus limited to the first four sūtras and the first and second chapters of the second book. The other portions are like commentaries to the Upaniṣads, which however contain many theological views of the system. The first commentary of the *Brahma-sūtra* was probably written by Baudhāyana, which however is not available now. The earliest commentary that is now found is that of the great Śaṅkara. His interpretations of the *Brahma-sūtras* together with all the commentaries and other works that follow his views are popularly known as Vedānta philosophy, though this philosophy ought more properly to be called Viśuddhādvaitavāda school of Vedānta philosophy (i.e. the Vedānta philosophy of the school of absolute monism). Variant forms of dualistic philosophy as represented by the Vaiṣṇavas, Śaivas, Rāmāyatas, etc., also claim to express the original purport of the Brahma sūtras. We thus find that apostles of dualistic creeds such as Rāmānuja, Vallabha, Madhva, Śrīkaṇṭha, Baladeva, etc., have written independent commentaries on the *Brahma-sūtra* to show that the philosophy as elaborated by themselves is the view of the Upaniṣads and as summarized in the *Brahma-sūtras*. These differed largely and often vehemently attacked Śaṅkara's interpretations of the same sūtras. These systems as expounded by them also pass by the name of Vedānta as these are also claimed to be the real interpretations intended by the Vedānta (Upaniṣads) and the *Vedānta sūtras*. Of these the system of Rāmānuja has great philosophical importance.

The *Nyāya sūtras* attributed to Gautama, called also Akṣapāda, and the *Vaiśeṣika sūtras* attributed to Kaṇāda, called also Ulūka, represent the same system for all practical purposes. They are in later times considered to differ only in a few points of minor importance. So far as the sūtras are concerned the *Nyāya sūtras* lay particular stress on the cultivation of logic as an art, while the *Vaiśeṣika sūtras* deal mostly with metaphysics and physics. In addition to these six systems, the Tantras had also philosophies of their own, which however may generally be looked upon largely as modifications of the Sāṃkhya and Vedānta systems, though their own contributions are also noteworthy.

Some fundamental Points of Agreement.

1. *The Karma Theory.*

It is, however, remarkable that with the exception of the Cārvāka materialists all the other systems agree on some fundamental points of importance. The systems of philosophy in India were not stirred up merely by the speculative demands of the human mind which has a natural inclination for indulging in abstract thought, but by a deep craving after the realization of the religious purpose of life. It is surprising to note that the postulates, aims and conditions for such a realization were found to be identical in all the conflicting systems. Whatever may be their differences of opinion in other matters, so far as the general postulates for the realization of the transcendent state, the *summum bonum* of life, were concerned, all the systems were practically in thorough agreement. It may be worth while to note some of them at this stage.

First, the theory of Karma and rebirth. All the Indian systems agree in believing that whatever action is done by an individual leaves behind it some sort of potency which has the power to ordain for him joy or sorrow in the future according as it is good or bad. When the fruits of the actions are such that they cannot be enjoyed in the present life or in a human life, the individual has to take another birth as a man or any other being in order to suffer them.

The Vedic belief that the mantras uttered in the correct accent at the sacrifices with the proper observance of all ritualistic details, exactly according to the directions without the slightest error even in the smallest trifle, had something like a magical virtue automatically to produce the desired object immediately or after a lapse of time, was probably the earliest form of the Karma doctrine. It postulates a semi-conscious belief that certain mystical actions can produce at a distant time certain effects without the ordinary process of the instrumentality of visible agents of ordinary cause and effect. When the sacrifice is performed, the action leaves such an unseen magical virtue, called the *adṛṣṭa* (the unseen) or the *apūrva* (new), that by it the desired object will be achieved in a mysterious manner, for the *modus operandi* of the *apūrva* is unknown. There is also the notion prevalent in the Saṃhitās, as we have already noticed, that he who commits wicked deeds suffers in another world, whereas he who performs good deeds enjoys the highest material pleasures. These were probably associated with the conception of *ṛta*, the inviolable order of things. Thus these are probably the elements which built up the Karma theory which we find pretty well established but not emphasized in the Upaniṣads, where it is said that according to good or bad actions men will have good or bad births.

To notice other relevant points in connection with the Karma doctrine as established in the āstika systems we find that it was believed that the unseen (*adṛṣṭa*) potency of the action generally required some time before it could be fit for giving the doer the merited punishment or enjoyment. These would often accumulate and prepare the items of suffering and enjoyment for the doer in his next life. Only the fruits of those actions which are extremely wicked or particularly good could be reaped in this life. The nature of the next birth of a man is determined by the nature of pleasurable or painful experiences that have been made ready for him by his maturing actions of this life. If the experiences determined for him by his action are such that they are possible to be realized in the life of a goat, the man will die and be born as a goat. As there is no ultimate beginning in time of this world process, so there is no time at which any person first began his actions or experiences. Man has had an infinite number of past lives of the most varied nature, and the instincts of each kind of life exist dormant in the life of every individual, and thus whenever he has any particular birth as this or that animal or man, the special instincts of that life (technically called *vāsanā*) come forth. In accordance with these vāsanās the person passes through the painful or pleasurable experiences as determined for him by his action. The length of life is also determined by the number and duration of experiences as preordained by the fructifying actions of his past life. When once certain actions become fit for giving certain experiences, these cannot be avoided, but those actions which have not matured are uprooted once for all if the person attains true knowledge as advocated by philosophy. But even such an emancipated (*mukta*) person has to pass through the pleasurable or painful experiences ordained for him by the actions just ripened for giving their fruits. There are four kinds of actions, white or virtuous (*śukla*), black or wicked (*kṛṣṇa*), white-black or partly virtuous and partly vicious (*śukla-kṛṣṇa*) as most of our actions are, neither black nor white (*aśuklākṛṣṇa*), i.e. those acts of self-renunciation or meditation which are not associated with any desires for the fruit. It is only when a person can so restrain himself as to perform only the last kind of action that he ceases to accumulate any new karma for giving fresh fruits. He has thus only to enjoy the fruits of his previous karmas which have ripened for giving fruits. If in the meantime he attains true knowledge, all his past accumulated actions become destroyed, and as his acts are only of the aśuklākṛṣṇa type no fresh karma for ripening is accumulated, and thus he becomes divested of all karma after enjoying the fruits of the ripened karmas alone.

The Jains think that through the actions of body, speech and mind a kind of subtle matter technically called karma is produced. The passions of a man act like a viscous substance that attracts this karma matter, which thus pours into the soul and sticks to it. The karma matter thus accumulated round the soul during the infinite number of past lives is technically called *kārmaśarīra*, which encircles the soul as it passes on from birth to birth. This karma matter sticking to the soul gradually ripens and exhausts itself in ordaining the sufferance of pains or the enjoyment of pleasures for the individual. While some karma matter is being expended in this way, other karma matters are accumulating by his activities, and thus keep him in a continuous process of suffering and enjoyment. The karma matter thus accumulated in the soul produces a kind of coloration called *leśyā*, such as white, black, etc., which marks the character of the soul. The idea of the śukla and kṛṣṇa karmas of the Yoga system was probably suggested by the Jaina view. But when a man is free from passions, and acts in strict compliance with the rules of conduct, his actions produce karma which lasts but for a moment and is then annihilated. Every karma that the sage has previously earned has its predestined limits within which it must take effect and be purged away. But when by contemplation and the strict adherence to the five great vows, no new karma is generated, and when all the karmas are exhausted the worldly existence of the person rapidly draws towards its end. Thus in the last stage of contemplation, all karma being annihilated, and all activities having ceased, the soul leaves the body and goes up to the top of the universe, where the liberated souls stay for ever.

Buddhism also contributes some new traits to the karma theory which however being intimately connected with their metaphysics will be treated later on.

2. *The Doctrine of Mukti.*

Not only do the Indian systems agree as to the cause of the inequalities in the share of sufferings and enjoyments in the case of different persons, and the manner in which the cycle of births and rebirths has been kept going from beginningless time, on the basis of the mysterious connection of one's actions with the happenings of the world, but they also agree in believing that this beginningless chain of karma and its fruits, of births and rebirths, this running on from beginningless time has somewhere its end. This end was not to be attained at some distant time or in some distant kingdom, but was to be sought within us. Karma leads us to this endless cycle, and if we could divest ourselves of all such emotions, ideas or desires as lead us to action we should find within us the actionless self which neither suffers nor enjoys, neither works nor undergoes rebirth. When the Indians, wearied by the endless bustle and turmoil of worldly events, sought for and believed that somewhere a peaceful goal could be found, they generally hit upon the self of man. The belief that the soul could be realized in some stage as being permanently divested of all action, feelings or ideas, led logically to the conclusion that the connection of the soul with these worldly elements was extraneous, artificial or even illusory. In its true nature the soul is untouched by the impurities of our ordinary life, and it is through ignorance and passion as inherited from the cycle of karma from beginningless time that we connect it with these. The realization of this transcendent state is the goal and final achievement of this endless cycle of births and rebirths through karma. The Buddhists did not admit the existence of soul, but recognized that the final realization of the process of karma is to be found in the ultimate dissolution called Nirvāṇa, the nature of which we shall discuss later on.

3. *The Doctrine of Soul.*

All the Indian systems except Buddhism admit the existence of a permanent entity variously called ātman, puruṣa or jīva. As to the exact nature of this soul there are indeed divergences of view. Thus while the Nyāya calls it absolutely qualityless and characterless, indeterminate unconscious entity, Sāṃkhya describes it as being of the nature of pure consciousness, the Vedānta says that it is that fundamental point of unity implied in pure consciousness (*cit*), pure bliss (*ānanda*), and pure being (*sat*). But all agree in holding that it is pure and unsullied in its nature and that all impurities of action or passion do not form a real part of it. The *summum bonum* of life is attained when all impurities are removed and the pure nature of the self is thoroughly and permanently apprehended and all other extraneous connections with it are absolutely dissociated.

The Pessimistic Attitude towards the World and the Optimistic Faith in the end.

Though the belief that the world is full of sorrow has not been equally prominently emphasized in all systems, yet it may be considered as being shared by all of them. It finds its strongest utterance in Sāṃkhya, Yoga, and Buddhism. This interminable chain of pleasurable and painful experiences was looked upon as nearing no peaceful end but embroiling and entangling us in the meshes of karma, rebirth, and sorrow. What appear as pleasures are but a mere appearance for the attempt to keep them steady is painful, there is pain when we lose the pleasures or when we are anxious to have them. When the pleasures are so much associated with pains they are but pains themselves. We are but duped when we seek pleasures, for they are sure to lead us to pain. All our experiences are essentially sorrowful and ultimately sorrow-begetting. Sorrow is the ultimate truth of this process of the world. That which to an ordinary person seems pleasurable appears to a wise person or to a yogin who has a clearer vision as painful. The greater the knowledge the higher is the sensitiveness to sorrow and dissatisfaction with world experiences. The yogin is like the pupil of the eye to which even the smallest grain of disturbance is unbearable. This sorrow of worldly experiences cannot be removed by bringing in remedies for each sorrow as it comes, for the moment it is remedied another sorrow comes in. It cannot also be avoided by mere inaction or suicide, for we are continually being forced to action by our nature, and suicide will but lead to another life of sorrow and rebirth. The only way to get rid of it is by the culmination of moral greatness and true knowledge which uproot sorrow once for all. It is our ignorance that the self is intimately connected with the experiences of life or its pleasures, that leads us to action and arouses passion in us for the enjoyment of pleasures and other emotions and activities. Through the highest moral elevation a man may attain absolute dispassion towards world-experiences and retire in body, mind, and speech from all worldly concerns. When the mind is so purified, the self shines in its true light, and its true nature is rightly conceived. When this is once done the self can never again be associated with passion or ignorance. It becomes at this stage ultimately dissociated from *citta* which contains within it the root of all emotions, ideas, and actions. Thus emancipated the self for ever conquers all sorrow. It is important, however, to note in this connection that emancipation is not based on a general aversion to intercourse with the world or on such feelings as a disappointed person may have, but on the appreciation of the state of mukti as the supremely blessed one. The details of the pessimistic creed of each system have developed from the logical necessity peculiar to each system. There was never the slightest tendency to shirk the duties of this life, but to rise above them through right performance and right understanding. It is only when a man rises to the highest pinnacle of moral glory that he is fit for aspiring to that realization of selfhood in comparison with which all worldly things or even the joys of Heaven would not only shrink into insignificance, but appear in their true character as sorrowful and loathsome. It is when his mind has thus turned from all ordinary joys that he can strive towards his ideal of salvation. In fact it seems to me that a sincere religious craving after some ideal blessedness and quiet of self-realization is indeed the fundamental fact from which not only her philosophy but many of the complex phenomena of the civilization of India can be logically deduced. The sorrow around us has no fear for us if we remember that we are naturally sorrowless and blessed in ourselves. The pessimistic view loses all terror as it closes in absolute optimistic confidence in one's own self and the ultimate destiny and goal of emancipation.

Unity in Indian Sādhana (philosophical, religious and ethical endeavours).

As might be expected the Indian systems are all agreed upon the general principles of ethical conduct which must be followed for the attainment of salvation. That all passions are to be controlled, no injury to life in any form should be done, and that all desire for pleasures should be checked, are principles which are almost universally acknowledged. When a man attains a very high degree of moral greatness he has to strengthen and prepare his mind for further purifying and steadying it for the attainment of his ideal; and most of the Indian systems are unanimous with regard to the means to be employed for the purpose. There are indeed divergences in certain details or technical names, but the means to be adopted for purification are almost everywhere essentially the same as those advocated by the Yoga system. It is only in later times that devotion (*bhakti*) is seen to occupy a more prominent place specially in Vaiṣṇava schools of thought. Thus it was that though there were many differences among the various systems, yet their goal of life, their attitude towards the world and the means for the attainment of the goal (*sādhana*) being fundamentally the same, there was a unique unity in the practical sādhana of almost all the Indian systems. The religious craving has been universal in India and this uniformity of sādhana has therefore secured for India a unity in all her aspirations and strivings.

CHAPTER V

BUDDHIST PHILOSOPHY

MANY scholars are of opinion that the Sāṃkhya and the Yoga represent the earliest systematic speculations of India. It is also suggested that Buddhism drew much of its inspiration from them. It may be that there is some truth in such a view, but the systematic Sāṃkhya and Yoga treatises as we have them had decidedly been written after Buddhism. Moreover it is well-known to every student of Hindu philosophy that a conflict with the Buddhists has largely stimulated philosophic enquiry in most of the systems of Hindu thought. A knowledge of Buddhism is therefore indispensable for a right understanding of the different systems in their mutual relation and opposition to Buddhism. It seems desirable therefore that I should begin with Buddhism first.

The State of Philosophy in India before the Buddha.

It is indeed difficult to give a short sketch of the different philosophical speculations that were prevalent in India before Buddhism. The doctrines of the Upaniṣads are well known, and these have already been briefly described. But these were not the only ones. Even in the Upaniṣads we find references to diverse atheistical creeds[1]. We find there that the origin of the world and its processes were sometimes discussed, and some thought that "time" was the ultimate cause of all, others that all these had sprung forth by their own nature (*svabhāva*), others that everything had come forth in accordance with an inexorable destiny or a fortuitous concourse of accidental happenings, or through matter combinations in general. References to diverse kinds of heresies are found in Buddhist literature also, but no detailed accounts of these views are known. Of the Upaniṣad type of materialists the two schools of Cārvākas (Dhūrtta and Suśikṣita) are referred to in later literature, though the time in which these flourished cannot rightly be discovered[2]. But it seems

[1] Śvetāśvatara, I. 2, *kālaḥ svabhābo niyatiryadṛcchā bhūtāni yoniḥ puruṣa iti cintyam.*

[2] Lokāyata (literally, that which is found among people in general) seems to have been the name by which all cārvāka doctrines were generally known. See Guṇaratna on the Lokāyatas.

probable however that the allusion to the materialists contained in the Upaniṣads refers to these or to similar schools. The Cārvākas did not believe in the authority of the Vedas or any other holy scripture. According to them there was no soul. Life and consciousness were the products of the combination of matter, just as red colour was the result of mixing up white with yellow or as the power of intoxication was generated in molasses (*madaśakti*). There is no after-life, and no reward of actions, as there is neither virtue nor vice. Life is only for enjoyment. So long as it lasts it is needless to think of anything else, as everything will end with death, for when at death the body is burnt to ashes there cannot be any rebirth. They do not believe in the validity of inference. Nothing is trustworthy but what can be directly perceived, for it is impossible to determine that the distribution of the middle term (*hetu*) has not depended upon some extraneous condition, the absence of which might destroy the validity of any particular piece of inference. If in any case any inference comes to be true, it is only an accidental fact and there is no certitude about it. They were called Cārvāka because they would only eat but would not accept any other religious or moral responsibility. The word comes from *carv* to eat. The Dhūrtta Cārvākas held that there was nothing but the four elements of earth, water, air and fire, and that the body was but the result of atomic combination. There was no self or soul, no virtue or vice. The Suśikṣita Cārvākas held that there was a soul apart from the body but that it also was destroyed with the destruction of the body. The original work of the Cārvākas was written in sūtras probably by Bṛhaspati. Jayanta and Guṇaratna quote two sūtras from it. Short accounts of this school may be found in Jayanta's *Nyāyamañjarī*, Mādhava's *Sarvadarśanasaṃgraha* and Guṇaratna's *Tarkarahasyadīpikā*. *Mahābhārata* gives an account of a man called Cārvāka meeting Yudhiṣṭhira.

Side by side with the doctrine of the Cārvāka materialists we are reminded of the Ājīvakas of which Makkhali Gosāla, probably a renegade disciple of the Jain saint Mahāvīra and a contemporary of Buddha and Mahāvīra, was the leader. This was a thoroughgoing determinism denying the free will of man and his moral responsibility for any so-called good or evil. The essence of Makkhali's system is this, that "there is no cause, either proximate or remote, for the depravity of beings or for their purity. They become so without any cause. Nothing depends either on one's own efforts or on the efforts of others, in short nothing depends on any human effort, for there is no such thing as power or energy, or human exertion. The varying conditions at any time are due to fate, to their environment and their own nature[1]."

Another sophistical school led by Ajita Kesakambali taught that there was no fruit or result of good or evil deeds; there is no other world, nor was this one real; nor had parents nor any former lives any efficacy with respect to this life. Nothing that we can do prevents any of us alike from being wholly brought to an end at death[2].

There were thus at least three currents of thought: firstly the sacrificial Karma by the force of the magical rites of which any person could attain anything he desired; secondly the Upaniṣad teaching that the Brahman, the self, is the ultimate reality and being, and all else but name and form which pass away but do not abide. That which permanently abides without change is the real and true, and this is self. Thirdly the nihilistic conceptions that there is no law, no abiding reality, that everything comes into being by a fortuitous concourse of circumstances or by some unknown fate. In each of these schools, philosophy had probably come to a deadlock. There were the Yoga practices prevalent in the country and these were accepted partly on the strength of traditional custom among certain sections, and partly by virtue of the great spiritual, intellectual and physical power which they gave to those who performed them. But these had no rational basis behind them on which they could lean for support. These were probably then just tending towards being affiliated to the nebulous Sāṃkhya doctrines which had grown up among certain sections. It was at this juncture that we find Buddha erecting a new superstructure of thought on altogether original lines which thenceforth opened up a new avenue of philosophy for all posterity to come. If the Being of the Upaniṣads, the superlatively motionless, was the only real, how could it offer scope for further new speculations, as it had already discarded all other matters of interest? If everything was due to a reasonless fortuitous concourse of circumstances, reason could not proceed further in the direction to create any philosophy of the unreason. The magical

[1] *Sāmaññaphala-sutta*, *Dīgha*, II. 20. Hoernlé's article on the Ājīvakas, E. R. E.

[2] *Sāmaññaphala-sutta*, II. 23.

force of the hocus-pocus of sorcery or sacrifice had but little that was inviting for philosophy to proceed on. If we thus take into account the state of Indian philosophic culture before Buddha, we shall be better able to understand the value of the Buddhistic contribution to philosophy.

Buddha: his Life.

Gautama the Buddha was born in or about the year 560 B.C. in the Lumbini Grove near the ancient town of Kapilavastu in the now dense terai region of Nepal. His father was Suddhodana, a prince of the Sākya clan, and his mother Queen Mahāmāyā. According to the legends it was foretold of him that he would enter upon the ascetic life when he should see "A decrepit old man, a diseased man, a dead man, and a monk." His father tried his best to keep him away from these by marrying him and surrounding him with luxuries. But on successive occasions, issuing from the palace, he was confronted by those four things, which filled him with amazement and distress, and realizing the impermanence of all earthly things determined to forsake his home and try if he could to discover some means to immortality to remove the sufferings of men. He made his "Great Renunciation" when he was twenty-nine years old. He travelled on foot to Rājagṛha (Rajgir) and thence to Uruvelā, where in company with other five ascetics he entered upon a course of extreme self-discipline, carrying his austerities to such a length that his body became utterly emaciated and he fell down senseless and was believed to be dead. After six years of this great struggle he was convinced that the truth was not to be won by the way of extreme asceticism, and resuming an ordinary course of life at last attained absolute and supreme enlightenment. Thereafter the Buddha spent a life prolonged over forty-five years in travelling from place to place and preaching the doctrine to all who would listen. At the age of over eighty years Buddha realized that the time drew near for him to die. He then entered into Dhyāna and passing through its successive stages attained nirvāṇa[1]. The vast developments which the system of this great teacher underwent in the succeeding centuries in India and in other countries have not been thoroughly studied, and it will probably take yet many years more before even the materials for

[1] *Mahāparinibbānasuttanta*, *Dīgha*, XVI. 6, 8, 9.

such a study can be collected. But from what we now possess it is proved incontestably that it is one of the most wonderful and subtle productions of human wisdom. It is impossible to overestimate the debt that the philosophy, culture and civilization of India owe to it in all her developments for many succeeding centuries.

Early Buddhist Literature.

The Buddhist Pāli Scriptures contain three different collections: the Sutta (relating to the doctrines), the Vinaya (relating to the discipline of the monks) and the Abhidhamma (relating generally to the same subjects as the suttas but dealing with them in a scholastic and technical manner). Scholars of Buddhistic religious history of modern times have failed as yet to fix any definite dates for the collection or composition of the different parts of the aforesaid canonical literature of the Buddhists. The suttas were however composed before the Abhidhamma and it is very probable that almost the whole of the canonical works were completed before 241 B.C., the date of the third council during the reign of King Asoka. The suttas mainly deal with the doctrine (Dhamma) of the Buddhistic faith whereas the Vinaya deals only with the regulations concerning the discipline of the monks. The subject of the Abhidhamma is mostly the same as that of the suttas, namely, the interpretation of the Dhamma. Buddhaghoṣa in his introduction to *Atthasālinī*, the commentary on the *Dhammasaṅgaṇi*, says that the Abhidhamma is so called (*abhi* and *dhamma*) because it describes the same Dhammas as are related in the suttas in a more intensified (*dhammātireka*) and specialized (*dhammavisesatthena*) manner. The Abhidhammas do not give any new doctrines that are not in the suttas, but they deal somewhat elaborately with those that are already found in the suttas. Buddhaghoṣa in distinguishing the special features of the suttas from the Abhidhammas says that the acquirement of the former leads one to attain meditation (*samādhi*) whereas the latter leads one to attain wisdom (*paññāsampadam*). The force of this statement probably lies in this, that the dialogues of the suttas leave a chastening effect on the mind, the like of which is not to be found in the Abhidhammas, which busy themselves in enumerating the Buddhistic doctrines and defining them in a technical manner, which is more fitted to produce a reasoned insight into the doctrines than directly to generate a craving for following the path of meditation for the extinction of sorrow. The Abhidhamma known as the *Kathāvatthu* differs from the other Abhidhammas in this, that it attempts to reduce the views of the heterodox schools to absurdity. The discussions proceed in the form of questions and answers, and the answers of the opponents are often shown to be based on contradictory assumptions.

The suttas contain five groups of collections called the Nikāyas. These are (1) *Dīgha Nikāya*, called so on account of the length of the suttas contained in it; (2) *Majjhima Nikāya* (middling Nikāya), called so on account of the middling extent of the suttas contained in it; (3) *Saṃyutta Nikāya* (Nikāyas relating to special meetings), called saṃyutta on account of their being delivered owing to the meetings (*saṃyoga*) of special persons which were the occasions for them; (4) *Aṅguttara Nikāya*, so called because in each succeeding book of this work the topics of discussion increase by one[1]; (5) *Khuddaka Nikāya* containing *Khuddaka pāṭha*, *Dhammapada*, *Udāna*, *Itivuttaka*, *Sutta Nipāta*, *Vimānavatthu*, *Petavatthu*, *Theragathā*, *Therīgāthā*, *Jātaka*, *Niddesa*, *Paṭisambhidāmagga*, *Apadāna*, *Buddhavaṃsa*, *Caryāpiṭaka*.

The Abhidhammas are *Paṭṭhāna*, *Dhammasaṅgaṇi*, *Dhātukathā*, *Puggalapaññatti*, *Vibhaṅga*, *Yamaka* and *Kathāvatthu*. There exists also a large commentary literature on diverse parts of the above works known as atthakathā. The work known as *Milinda Pañha* (questions of King Milinda), of uncertain date, is of considerable philosophical value.

The doctrines and views incorporated in the above literature is generally now known as Sthaviravāda or Theravāda. On the origin of the name Theravāda (the doctrine of the elders) *Dīpavaṃsa* says that since the Theras (elders) met (at the first council) and collected the doctrines it was known as the Thera Vāda[2]. It does not appear that Buddhism as it appears in this Pāli literature developed much since the time of Buddhaghoṣa (400 A.D.), the writer of *Visuddhimagga* (a compendium of theravāda doctrines) and the commentator of *Dīghanikāya*, *Dhammasaṅgaṇi*, etc.

Hindu philosophy in later times seems to have been influenced by the later offshoots of the different schools of Buddhism, but it does not appear that Pāli Buddhism had any share in it. I

[1] See Buddhaghoṣa's *Atthasālinī*, p. 25.

[2] Oldenberg's *Dīpavaṃsa*, p. 31.

have not been able to discover any old Hindu writer who could be considered as being acquainted with Pāli.

The Doctrine of Causal Connection of early Buddhism[1].

The word Dhamma in the Buddhist scriptures is used generally in four senses: (1) Scriptural texts, (2) quality (*guṇa*), (3) cause (*hetu*) and (4) unsubstantial and soulless (*nissatta nijjīva*[2]). Of these it is the last meaning which is particularly important from the point of view of Buddhist philosophy. The early Buddhist philosophy did not accept any fixed entity as determining all reality; the only things with it were the unsubstantial phenomena and these were called dhammas. The question arises that if there is no substance or reality how are we to account for the phenomena? But the phenomena are happening and passing away and the main point of interest with the Buddha was to find out "What being what else is," "What happening what else happens" and "What not being what else is not." The phenomena are happening in a series and we see that there being certain phenomena there become some others; by the happening of some events others also are produced. This is called (*paṭicca-samuppāda*) dependent origination. But it is difficult to understand what is the exact nature of this dependence. The question as *Saṃyutta Nikāya* (II. 5) has it with which the Buddha started before attaining Buddhahood was this: in what miserable condition are the people! they are born, they decay, they die, pass away and are born again; and they do not know the path of escape from this decay, death and misery.

How to know the way to escape from this misery of decay and death. Then it occurred to him what being there, are decay and death, depending on what do they come? As he thought deeply into the root of the matter, it occurred to him that decay and death can only occur when there is birth (*jāti*), so they depend

[1] There are some differences of opinion as to whether one could take the doctrine of the twelve links of causes as we find it in the *Saṃyutta Nikāya* as the earliest Buddhist view, as Saṃyutta does not represent the oldest part of the suttas. But as this doctrine of the twelve causes became regarded as a fundamental Buddhist doctrine and as it gives us a start in philosophy I have not thought it fit to enter into conjectural discussions as to the earliest form. Dr E. J. Thomas drew my attention to this fact.

[2] *Atthasāḷinī*, p. 38. There are also other senses in which the word is used, as *dhamma-desanā* where it means religious teaching. The *Laṅkāvatāra* described Dharmma as *guṇadravyapūrvakā dharmmā*, i.e. Dharmmas are those which are associated as attributes and substances.

on birth. What being there, is there birth, on what does birth
depend? Then it occurred to him that birth could only be if
there were previous existence (*bhava*)[1]. But on what does this
existence depend, or what being there is there *bhava*. Then it
occurred to him that there could not be existence unless there
were holding fast (*upādāna*)[2]. But on what did upādāna depend?
It occurred to him that it was desire (*taṇhā*) on which upādāna
depended. There can be upādāna if there is desire (*taṇhā*)[3]. But
what being there, can there be desire? To this question it
occurred to him that there must be feeling (*vedanā*) in order that
there may be desire. But on what does vedanā depend, or rather
what must be there, that there may be feeling (*vedanā*)? To this
it occurred to him that there must be a sense-contact (*phassa*)
in order that there may be feeling[4]. If there should be no sense-
contact there would be no feeling. But on what does sense-
contact depend? It occurred to him that as there are six sense-
contacts, there are the six fields of contact (*āyatana*)[5]. But on
what do the six āyatanas depend? It occurred to him that
there must be the mind and body (*nāmarūpa*) in order that there
may be the six fields of contact[5]; but on what does nāmarūpa
depend? It occurred to him that without consciousness (*viññāna*)
there could be no nāmarūpa[6]. But what being there would there

1 This word bhava is interpreted by Candrakīrtti in his *Mādhyamīka vṛtti*, p. 565
(La Vallée Poussin's edition) as the deed which brought about rebirth (*punarbhava-
janakaṃ karma samutthāpayati kāyena vācā manasā ca*).

2 *Atthasālinī*, p. 385, upādānanti daḷhagahaṇaṃ. Candrakīrtti in explaining upādāna
says that whatever thing a man desires he holds fast to the materials necessary for
attaining it (*yatra vastuni satṛṣṇastasya vastuno 'rjanāya viḍhapanāya upādānamupā-
datte tatra tatra prārthayate*). *Mādhyamīka vṛtti*, p. 565.

3 Candrakīrtti describes tṛṣṇā as *āsvādanābhinandanādhyavasānasthānādātmapri-
yarūpairviyogo mā bhūt, nityamaparityāgo bhavediti, yeyam prārthanā*—the desire
that there may not ever be any separation from those pleasures, etc., which are dear to
us. *Ibid.* 565.

4 We read also of phassāyatana and phassakāya. *M. N.* II. 261, III. 280, etc. Candrakīrtti says that *saḍbhirāyatanadvāraiḥ kṛtyaprakṛiyāḥ pravarttante prajñāyante,
tannāmarūpapratyayaṃ ṣaḍāyatanamucyate. saḍbhyaścāyatanebhyaḥ ṣaṭsparśakāyāḥ
pravarttante. M. V.* 565.

5 Āyatana means the six senses together with their objects. Āyatana literally is
"Field of operation." Saḷāyatana means six senses as six fields of operation. Candrakīrtti has *āyatanadvāraiḥ.*

6 I have followed the translation of Aung in rendering nāmarūpa as mind and body,
Compendium, p. 271. This seems to me to be fairly correct. The four skandhas are called
nāma in each birth. These together with rūpa (matter) give us nāmarūpa (mind
and body) which being developed render the activities through the six sense-gates
possible so that there may be knowledge. Cf. *M. V.* 564. Govindānanda, the commentator

be viññāna. Here it occurred to him that in order that there might be viññāna there must be the conformations (*saṅkhāra*)[1]. But what being there are there the saṅkhāras? Here it occurred to him that the saṅkhāras can only be if there is ignorance (*avijjā*). If avijjā could be stopped then the saṅkhāras will be stopped, and if the saṅkhāras could be stopped viññāna could be stopped and so on[2].

It is indeed difficult to be definite as to what the Buddha actually wished to mean by this cycle of dependence of existence sometimes called Bhavacakra (wheel of existence). Decay and death (*jarāmaraṇa*) could not have happened if there was no birth[3]. This seems to be clear. But at this point the difficulty begins. We must remember that the theory of rebirth was

on Śaṅkara's bhāṣya on the *Brahma-sūtras* (II. ii. 19), gives a different interpretation of Nāmarūpa which may probably refer to the Vijñānavāda view though we have no means at hand to verify it. He says—To think the momentary as the permanent is Avidyā; from there come the saṃskāras of attachment, antipathy or anger, and infatuation; from there the first vijñāna or thought of the foetus is produced; from that ālayavijñāna, and the four elements (which are objects of name and are hence called nāma) are produced, and from those are produced the white and black, semen and blood called rūpa. Both Vācaspati and Amalānanda agree with Govindānanda in holding that nāma signifies the semen and the ovum while rūpa means the visible physical body built out of them. Vijñāña entered the womb and on account of it nāmarūpa were produced through the association of previous karma. See *Vedāntakalpataru*, pp. 274, 275. On the doctrine of the entrance of vijñāña into the womb compare *D. N.* II. 63.

[1] It is difficult to say what is the exact sense of the word here. The Buddha was one of the first few earliest thinkers to introduce proper philosophical terms and phraseology with a distinct philosophical method and he had often to use the same word in more or less different senses. Some of the philosophical terms at least are therefore rather elastic when compared with the terms of precise and definite meaning which we find in later Sanskrit thought. Thus in *S. N.* III. p. 87, "*Saṅkhataṃ abhisaṅkharonti,*" saṅkhāra means that which synthesises the complexes. In the *Compendium* it is translated as will, action. Mr Aung thinks that it means the same as karma; it is here used in a different sense from what we find in the word saṅkhāra khandha (viz. mental states). We get a list of 51 mental states forming saṅkhāra khandha in *Dhamma Saṅgaṇi*, p. 18, and another different set of 40 mental states in *Dharmasaṃgraha*, p. 6. In addition to these forty *cittasamprayuktasaṃskāra*, it also counts thirteen *cittaviprayuktasaṃskāra*. Candrakīrtti interprets it as meaning attachment, antipathy and infatuation, p. 563. Govindānanda, the commentator on Śaṅkara's *Brahma-sūtra* (II. ii. 19), also interprets the word in connection with the doctrine of *Pratītyasamutpāda* as attachment, antipathy and infatuation.

[2] *Saṃyutta Nikāya*, II. 7–8.

[3] Jarā and maraṇa bring in śoka (grief), paridevanā (lamentation), duḥkha (suffering), daurmanasya (feeling of wretchedness and miserableness) and upāyāsa (feeling of extreme destitution) at the prospect of one's death or the death of other dear ones. All these make up suffering and are the results of jāti (birth). *M. V.* (B. T. S. p. 208). Śaṅkara in his bhāṣya counted all the terms from jarā, separately. The whole series is to be taken as representing the entirety of duḥkhaskandha.

enunciated in the Upaniṣads. The Bṛhadāraṇyaka says that just as an insect going to the end of a leaf of grass by a new effort collects itself in another so does the soul coming to the end of this life collect itself in another. This life thus presupposes another existence. So far as I remember there has seldom been before or after Buddha any serious attempt to prove or disprove the doctrine of rebirth[1]. All schools of philosophy except the Cārvākas believed in it and so little is known to us of the Cārvāka sūtras that it is difficult to say what they did to refute this doctrine. The Buddha also accepts it as a fact and does not criticize it. This life therefore comes only as one which had an infinite number of lives before, and which except in the case of a few emancipated ones would have an infinite number of them in the future. It was strongly believed by all people, and the Buddha also, when he came to think to what our present birth might be due, had to fall back upon another existence (*bhava*). If bhava means karma which brings rebirth as Candrakīrtti takes it to mean, then it would mean that the present birth could only take place on account of the works of a previous existence which determined it. Here also we are reminded of the Upaniṣad note "as a man does so will he be born" (*Yat karma kurute tadabhisampadyate*, Bṛh. IV. iv. 5). Candrakīrtti's interpretation of "bhava" as Karma (*punarbhavajanakam karma*) seems to me to suit better than "existence." The word was probably used rather loosely for *kammabhava*. The word bhava is not found in the earlier Upaniṣads and was used in the Pāli scriptures for the first time as a philosophical term. But on what does this bhava depend? There could not have been a previous existence if people had not betaken themselves to things or works they desired. This betaking oneself to actions or things in accordance with desire is called upādāna. In the Upaniṣads we read, "whatever one betakes himself to, so does he work" (*Yatkraturbhavati tatkarmma kurute*, Bṛh. IV. iv. 5). As this betaking to the thing depends upon desire (*tṛṣṇā*), it is said that in order that there may be upādāna there must be taṇhā. In the Upaniṣads also we read "Whatever one desires so does he betake himself to" (*sa yathākāmo bhavati tatkraturbhavati*). Neither the word upādāna nor tṛṣṇā (the Sanskrit word corresponding

[1] The attempts to prove the doctrine of rebirth in the Hindu philosophical works such as the Nyāya, etc., are slight and inadequate.

to taṇhā) is found in the earlier Upaniṣads, but the ideas contained in them are similar to the words "*kratu*" and "*kāma*." Desire (*taṇhā*) is then said to depend on feeling or sense-contact. Sense-contact presupposes the six senses as fields of operation[1]. These six senses or operating fields would again presuppose the whole psychosis of the man (the body and the mind together) called nāmarūpa. We are familiar with this word in the Upaniṣads but there it is used in the sense of determinate forms and names as distinguished from the indeterminate indefinable reality[2]. Buddhaghoṣa in the *Visuddhimagga* says that by "Name" are meant the three groups beginning with sensation (i.e. sensation, perception and the predisposition); by "Form" the four elements and form derivative from the four elements[3]. He further says that name by itself can produce physical changes, such as eating, drinking, making movements or the like. So form also cannot produce any of those changes by itself. But like the cripple and the blind they mutually help one another and effectuate the changes[4]. But there exists no heap or collection of material for the production of Name and Form; "but just as when a lute is played upon, there is no previous store of sound; and when the sound comes into existence it does not come from any such store; and when it ceases, it does not go to any of the cardinal or intermediate points of the compass;...in exactly the same way all the elements of being both those with form and those without, come into existence after having previously been non-existent and having come into existence pass away[5]." Nāmarūpa taken in this sense will not mean the whole of mind and body, but only the sense functions and the body which are found to operate in the six doors of sense (*saḷāyatana*). If we take nāmarūpa in this sense, we can see that it may be said to depend upon the viññāna (consciousness). Consciousness has been compared in the *Milinda Pañha* with a watchman at the middle of

[1] The word āyatana is found in many places in the earlier Upaniṣads in the sense of "field or place," Chā. I. 5, Bṛh. III. 9. 10, but ṣaḍāyatana does not occur.

[2] Candrakīrtti interprets nāma as *Vedanādayo'rūpiṇaścatvāraḥ skandhāstatra tatra bhave nāmayantīti nāma. saha rūpaskandhena ca nāma rūpam ceti nāmarūpamucyate.* The four skandhas in each specific birth act as name. These together with rūpa make nāmarūpa. *M. V.* 564.

[3] Warren's *Buddhism in Translations*, p. 184.

[4] *Ibid.* p. 185, *Visuddhimagga*, Ch. XVII.

[5] *Ibid.* pp. 185–186, *Visuddhimagga*, Ch. XVII.

the cross-roads beholding all that come from any direction[1]. Buddhaghoṣa in the *Atthasālinī* also says that consciousness means that which thinks its object. If we are to define its characteristics we must say that it knows (*vijānana*), goes in advance (*pubbaṅgama*), connects (*sandhāna*), and stands on nāmarūpa (*nāmarūpa-padaṭṭhānam*). When the consciousness gets a door, at a place the objects of sense are discerned (*ārammana-vibhāvanaṭṭhāne*) and it goes first as the precursor. When a visual object is seen by the eye it is known only by the consciousness, and when the dhammas are made the objects of (mind) mano, it is known only by the consciousness[2]. Buddhaghoṣa also refers here to the passage in the *Milinda Pañha* we have just referred to. He further goes on to say that when states of consciousness rise one after another, they leave no gap between the previous state and the later and consciousness therefore appears as connected. When there are the aggregates of the five khandhas it is lost; but there are the four aggregates as nāmarūpa, it stands on nāma and therefore it is said that it stands on nāmarūpa. He further asks, Is this consciousness the same as the previous consciousness or different from it? He answers that it is the same. Just so, the sun shows itself with all its colours, etc., but he is not different from those in truth; and it is said that just when the sun rises, its collected heat and yellow colour also rise then, but it does not mean that the sun is different from these. So the citta or consciousness takes the phenomena of contact, etc., and cognizes them. So though it is the same as they are yet in a sense it is different from them[3].

To go back to the chain of twelve causes, we find that jāti (birth) is the cause of decay and death, *jarāmaraṇa*, etc. Jāti is the appearance of the body or the totality of the five skandhas[4]. Coming to bhava which determines jāti, I cannot think of any better rational explanation of bhava, than that I have already

[1] Warren's *Buddhism in Translations*, p. 182. *Milinda Pañha* (62⁸).

[2] *Atthasālinī*, p. 112.

[3] *Ibid.* p. 113, *Yathā hi rūpādīni upādāya paññattā suriyādayo na atthato rūpādīhi aññe honti ten' eva yasmin samaye suriyo udeti tasmin samaye tassa tejā-saṅkhātam rūpaṃ pīti evaṃ vuccamāne pi na rūpādihi añño suriyo nāma atthi. Tathā cittam phassādayo dhamme upādāya paññapiyati. Atthato pan' ettha tehi aññam eva. Tena yasmin samaye cittam uppannaṃ hoti ekaṃsen eva tasmin samaye phassādihi atthato aññad eva hotī ti.*

[4] "*Jātirdehajanma pañcaskandhasamudāyaḥ*," Govindānanda's *Ratnaprabhā* on Śaṅkara's bhāṣya, II. ii. 19.

suggested, namely, the works (*karma*) which produce the birth[1]. Upādāna is an advanced tṛṣṇā leading to positive clinging[2]. It is produced by tṛṣṇā (desire) which again is the result of vedanā (pleasure and pain). But this vedanā is of course vedanā with ignorance (*avidyā*), for an Arhat may have also vedanā but as he has no avidyā, the vedanā cannot produce tṛṣṇā in turn. On its development it immediately passes into upādāna. Vedanā means pleasurable, painful or indifferent feeling. On the one side it leads to tṛṣṇā (desire) and on the other it is produced by sense-contact (*sparśa*). Prof. De la Vallée Poussin says that Śrīlābha distinguishes three processes in the production of vedanā. Thus first there is the contact between the sense and the object; then there is the knowledge of the object, and then there is the vedanā. Depending on *Majjhima Nikāya*, iii. 242, Poussin gives the other opinion that just as in the case of two sticks heat takes place simultaneously with rubbing, so here also vedanā takes place simultaneously with sparśa for they are "produits par un même complexe de causes (*sāmagrī*)[3]."

Sparśa is produced by ṣaḍāyatana, ṣaḍāyatana by nāmarūpa, and nāmarūpa by vijñāna, and is said to descend in the womb of the mother and produce the five skandhas as nāmarūpa, out of which the six senses are specialized.

Vijñāna in this connection probably means the principle or germ of consciousness in the womb of the mother upholding the five elements of the new body there. It is the product of the past karmas (*saṅkhāra*) of the dying man and of his past consciousness too.

We sometimes find that the Buddhists believed that the last thoughts of the dying man determined the nature of his next

[1] Govindānanda in his *Ratnaprabhā* on Śaṅkara's bhāṣya, II. ii. 19, explains "bhava" as that from which anything becomes, as merit and demerit (*dharmādi*). See also *Vibhaṅga*, p. 137 and Warren's *Buddhism in Translations*, p. 201. Mr Aung says in *Abhidhammatthasaṅgaha*, p. 189, that bhavo includes kammabhavo (the active side of an existence) and upapattibhavo (the passive side). And the commentators say that bhava is a contraction of "*kammabhava*" or Karma—becoming i.e. karmic activity.

[2] Prof. De la Vallée Poussin in his *Théorie des Douze Causes*, p. 26, says that *Śālistambhasūtra* explains the word "upādāna" as "tṛṣṇāvaipulya" or hyper-tṛṣṇā and Candrakīrtti also gives the same meaning, *M. V.* (B. T. S. p. 210). Govindānanda explains "upādāna" as pravṛtti (movement) generated by tṛṣṇā (desire), i.e. the active tendency in pursuance of desire. But if upādāna means "support" it would denote all the five skandhas. Thus *Madhyamaka vṛtti* says *upādānam pañcaskandhalakṣaṇam... pañcopādānaskandhākhyam upādānam. M. V.* XXVII. 6.

[3] Poussin's *Théorie des Douze Causes*, p. 23.

birth[1]. The manner in which the vijñāna produced in the womb is determined by the past vijñāna of the previous existence is according to some authorities of the nature of a reflected image, like the transmission of learning from the teacher to the disciple, like the lighting of a lamp from another lamp or like the impress of a stamp on wax. As all the skandhas are changing in life, so death also is but a similar change; there is no great break, but the same uniform sort of destruction and coming into being. New skandhas are produced as simultaneously as the two scale pans of a balance rise up and fall, in the same manner as a lamp is lighted or an image is reflected. At the death of the man the vijñāna resulting from his previous karmas and vijñānas enters into the womb of that mother (animal, man or the gods) in which the next skandhas are to be matured. This vijñāna thus forms the principle of the new life. It is in this vijñāna that name (*nāma*) and form (*rūpa*) become associated.

The vijñāna is indeed a direct product of the saṃskāras and the sort of birth in which vijñāna should bring down (*nāmayati*) the new existence (*upapatti*) is determined by the saṃskāras[2], for in reality the happening of death (*maraṇabhava*) and the instillation of the vijñāna as the beginning of the new life (*upapatti-bhava*) cannot be simultaneous, but the latter succeeds just at the next moment, and it is to signify this close succession that they are said to be simultaneous. If the vijñāna had not entered the womb then no nāmarūpa could have appeared[3].

This chain of twelve causes extends over three lives. Thus avidyā and saṃskāra of the past life produce the vijñāna, nāma-

[1] The deities of the gardens, the woods, the trees and the plants, finding the master of the house, Citta, ill said "make your resolution, 'May I be a cakravarttī king in a next existence,'" *Saṃyutta*, IV. 303.

[2] "*sa cedānandavijñānaṃ mātuḥkukṣim nāvakrāmeta, na tat kalalam kalalatvāya sannivartteta*," *M. V.* 552. Compare *Caraka*, *Śārīra*, III. 5–8, where he speaks of a "upapāduka sattva" which connects the soul with body and by the absence of which the character is changed, the senses become affected and life ceases, when it is in a pure condition one can remember even the previous births; character, purity, antipathy, memory, fear, energy, all mental qualities are produced out of it. Just as a chariot is made by the combination of many elements, so is the foetus.

[3] *Madhyamaka vṛtti* (B.T.S. 202–203). Poussin quotes from *Dīgha*, II. 63, "si le vijñāna ne descendait pas dans le sein maternel la namarupa s'y constituerait-il?" Govindānanda on Śaṅkara's commentary on the *Brahma-sūtras* (II. ii. 19) says that the first consciousness (vijñāna) of the foetus is produced by the saṃskāras of the previous birth, and from that the four elements (which he calls nāma) and from that the white and red, semen and ovum, and the first stage of the foetus (*kalala-budbudāvasthā*) is produced.

rūpa, ṣaḍāyatana, sparśa, vedanā, tṛṣṇā, upādāna and the bhava (leading to another life) of the present actual life. This bhava produces the jāti and jarāmaraṇa of the next life[1].

It is interesting to note that these twelve links in the chain extending in three sections over three lives are all but the manifestations of sorrow to the bringing in of which they naturally determine one another. Thus *Abhidhammatthasaṅgaha* says "each of these twelve terms is a factor. For the composite term 'sorrow,' etc. is only meant to show incidental consequences of birth. Again when 'ignorance' and 'the actions of the mind' have been taken into account, craving (*tṛṣṇā*), grasping (*upādāna*) and (*karma*) becoming (*bhava*) are implicitly accounted for also. In the same manner when craving, grasping and (*karma*) becoming have been taken into account, ignorance and the actions of the mind are (implicitly) accounted for, also; and when birth, decay, and death are taken into account, even the fivefold fruit, to wit (rebirth), consciousness, and the rest are accounted for. And thus:

Five causes in the Past and Now a fivefold 'fruit.'

Five causes Now and yet to come a fivefold 'fruit' make up the Twenty Modes, the Three Connections (1. saṅkhāra and viññāna, 2. vedanā and taṇhā, 3. bhava and jāti) and the four groups (one causal group in the Past, one resultant group in the Present, one causal group in the Present and one resultant group in the Future, each group consisting of five modes)[2]."

These twelve interdependent links (*dvādaśāṅga*) represent the paṭiccasamuppāda (*pratītyasamutpāda*) doctrines (dependent origination)[3] which are themselves but sorrow and lead to cycles of sorrow. The term paṭiccasamuppāda or pratītyasamutpāda has been differently interpreted in later Buddhist literature[4].

[1] This explanation probably cannot be found in the early Pāli texts; but Buddhaghoṣa mentions it in *Sumaṅgalavilāsinī* on *Mahānidāna suttanta*. We find it also in *Abhidhammatthasaṅgaha*, VIII. 3. Ignorance and the actions of the mind belong to the past; "birth," "decay and death" to the future; the intermediate eight to the present. It is styled as trikāṇḍaka (having three branches) in *Abhidharmakośa*, III. 20–24. Two in the past branch, two in the future and eight in the middle "*sa pratītyasamutpādo dvādaśāṅgastrikāṇḍakaḥ pūrvāparāntayordve dve madhyeṣṭau.*"

[2] Aung and Mrs Rhys Davids' translation of *Abhidhammatthasaṅgaha*, pp. 189–190.

[3] The twelve links are not always constant. Thus in the list given in the *Dialogues of the Buddha*, II. 23 f., avijjā and saṅkhāra have been omitted and the start has been made with consciousness, and it has been said that "Cognition turns back from name and form; it goes not beyond."

[4] *M. V.* p. 5 f.

Samutpāda means appearance or arising (*prādurbhāva*) and pratītya means after getting (*prati+i+ya*); combining the two we find, arising after getting (something). The elements, depending on which there is some kind of arising, are called hetu (cause) and paccaya (ground). These two words however are often used in the same sense and are interchangeable. But paccaya is also used in a specific sense. Thus when it is said that avijjā is the paccaya of saṅkhāra it is meant that avijjā is the ground (*ṭhiti*) of the origin of the saṅkhāras, is the ground of their movement, of the instrument through which they stand (*nimittaṭṭhiti*), of their āyuhana (conglomeration), of their interconnection, of their intelligibility, of their conjoint arising, of their function as cause and of their function as the ground with reference to those which are determined by them. Avijjā in all these nine ways is the ground of saṅkhāra both in the past and also in the future, though avijjā itself is determined in its turn by other grounds[1]. When we take the hetu aspect of the causal chain, we cannot think of anything else but succession, but when we take the paccaya aspect we can have a better vision into the nature of the cause as ground. Thus when avijjā is said to be the ground of the saṅkhāras in the nine ways mentioned above, it seems reasonable to think that the saṅkhāras were in some sense regarded as special manifestations of avijjā[2]. But as this point was not further developed in the early Buddhist texts it would be unwise to proceed further with it.

The Khandhas.

The word khandha (Skr. skandha) means the trunk of a tree and is generally used to mean group or aggregate[3]. We have seen that Buddha said that there was no ātman (soul). He said that when people held that they found the much spoken of soul, they really only found the five khandhas together or any one of them. The khandhas are aggregates of bodily and psychical states which are immediate with us and are divided into five

[1] See *Paṭisambhidāmagga*, vol. I. p. 50; see also *Majjhima Nikāya*, I. 67, *saṅkhārā...avijjānidānā avijjāsamudayā avijjājātikā avijjāpabhavā*.

[2] In the Yoga derivation of asmitā (egoism), rāga (attachment), dveṣa (antipathy) and abhiniveśa (self love) from avidyā we find also that all the five are regarded as the five special stages of the growth of avidyā (*pañcaparvā avidyā*).

[3] The word skandha is used in Chāndogya, II. 23 (*trayo dharmaskandhāḥ yajñaḥ adhyayanam dānam*) in the sense of branches and in almost the same sense in Maitrī, VII. 11.

classes: (1) rūpa (four elements, the body, the senses), sense data, etc., (2) vedanā (feeling—pleasurable, painful and indifferent), (3) saññā (conceptual knowledge), (4) saṅkhāra (synthetic mental states and the synthetic functioning of compound sense-affections, compound feelings and compound concepts), (5) viññāna (consciousness)[1].

All these states rise depending one upon the other (*paṭicca-samuppanna*) and when a man says that he perceives the self he only deludes himself, for he only perceives one or more of these. The word rūpa in rūpakhandha stands for matter and material qualities, the senses, and the sense data[2]. But "rūpa" is also used in the sense of pure organic affections or states of mind as we find in the *Khandha Yamaka*, I. p. 16, and also in *Saṃyutta Nikāya*, III. 86. Rūpaskandha according to *Dharmasaṃgraha* means the aggregate of five senses, the five sensations, and the implicatory communications associated in sense perceptions (*vijñapti*).

The elaborate discussion of *Dhammasaṅgaṇi* begins by defining rūpa as "*cattāro ca mahābhūtā catunnañca mahābhūtānam upādāya rūpam*" (the four mahābhūtas or elements and that proceeding from the grasping of that is called rūpa)[3]. Buddhaghoṣa explains it by saying that rūpa means the four mahābhūtas and those which arise depending (*nissāya*) on them as a modification of them. In the rūpa the six senses including their affections are also included. In explaining why the four elements are called mahābhūtas, Buddhaghoṣa says: "Just as a magician (*māyākāra*) makes the water which is not hard appear as hard, makes the stone which is not gold appear as gold; just as he himself though not a ghost nor a bird makes himself appear as a ghost or a bird, so these elements though not themselves blue make themselves appear as blue (*nīlam upādā rūpam*), not yellow, red, or white make themselves appear as yellow, red or white (*odātam upādārūpam*), so on account of their similarity to the appearances created by the magician they are called mahābhūta[4]."

In the *Saṃyutta Nikāya* we find that the Buddha says, "O Bhikkhus it is called rūpam because it manifests (*rūpyati*); how

[1] *Saṃyutta Nikāya*, III. 86, etc.

[2] *Abhidhammatthasaṅgaha*, J. P. T. S. 1884, p. 27 ff.

[3] *Dhammasaṅgaṇi*, pp. 124–179.

[4] *Atthasālinī*, p. 299.

does it manifest? It manifests as cold, and as heat, as hunger and as thirst, it manifests as the touch of gnats, mosquitos, wind, the sun and the snake; it manifests, therefore it is called rūpa[1]."

If we take the somewhat conflicting passages referred to above for our consideration and try to combine them so as to understand what is meant by rūpa, I think we find that that which manifested itself to the senses and organs was called rūpa. No distinction seems to have been made between the sense-data as colours, smells, etc., as existing in the physical world and their appearance as sensations. They were only numerically different and the appearance of the sensations was dependent upon the sense-data and the senses but the sense-data and the sensations were "rūpa." Under certain conditions the sense-data were followed by the sensations. Buddhism did not probably start with the same kind of division of matter and mind as we now do. And it may not be out of place to mention that such an opposition and duality were found neither in the Upaniṣads nor in the Sāṃkhya system which is regarded by some as pre-Buddhistic. The four elements manifested themselves in certain forms and were therefore called rūpa; the forms of affection that appeared were also called rūpa; many other mental states or features which appeared with them were also called rūpa[2]. The āyatanas or the senses were also called rūpa[3]. The mahābhūtas or four elements were themselves but changing manifestations, and they together with all that appeared in association with them were called rūpa and formed the rūpa khandha (the classes of sense-materials, sense-data, senses and sensations).

In *Saṃyutta Nikāya* (III. 101) it is said that "the four mahābhūtas were the hetu and the paccaya for the communication of the rūpakkhandha (*rūpakkhandhassa paññāpanāya*). Contact (sense-contact, phassa) is the cause of the communication of feelings (*vedanā*); sense-contact was also the hetu and paccaya for the communication of the saññākkhandha; sense-contact is also the hetu and paccaya for the communication of the saṅkhārakkhandha. But nāmarūpa is the hetu and the paccaya for the communication of the viññānakkhandha." Thus not only feelings arise on account of the sense-contact but saññā and saṅkhāra also arise therefrom. Saññā is that where specific knowing or

[1] *Saṃyutta Nikāya*, III. 86.

[2] *Khandhayamaka.*

[3] *Dhammasaṅgaṇi*, p. 124 ff.

conceiving takes place. This is the stage where the specific distinctive knowledge as the yellow or the red takes place.

Mrs Rhys Davids writing on saññā says: "In editing the second book of the Abhidhamma piṭaka I found a classification distinguishing between saññā as cognitive assimilation on occasion of sense, and saññā as cognitive assimilation of ideas by way of naming. The former is called perception of resistance, or opposition (*patigha-saññā*). This, writes Buddhaghoṣa, is perception on occasion of sight, hearing, etc., when consciousness is aware of the impact of impressions; of external things as different, we might say. The latter is called perception of the equivalent word or name (*adhivachānā-saññā*) and is exercised by the *sensus communis* (mano), when e.g. 'one is seated...and asks another who is thoughtful: "What are you thinking of?" one perceives through his speech.' Thus there are two stages of saññā-consciousness, 1. contemplating sense-impressions, 2. ability to know what they are by naming[1]."

About saṅkhāra we read in *Saṃyutta Nikāya* (III. 87) that it is called saṅkhāra because it synthesises (*abhisaṅkharonti*), it is that which conglomerated rūpa as rūpa, conglomerated saññā as saññā, saṅkhāra as saṅkhāra and consciousness (*viññāna*) as consciousness. It is called saṅkhāra because it synthesises the conglomerated (*saṅkhatam abhisaṅkharonti*). It is thus a synthetic function which synthesises the passive rūpa, saññā, saṅkhāra and viññāna elements. The fact that we hear of 52 saṅkhāra states and also that the saṅkhāra exercises its synthetic activity on the conglomerated elements in it, goes to show that probably the word saṅkhāra is used in two senses, as mental states and as synthetic activity.

Viññāna or consciousness meant according to Buddhaghoṣa, as we have already seen in the previous section, both the stage at which the intellectual process started and also the final resulting consciousness.

Buddhaghoṣa in explaining the process of Buddhist psychology says that "consciousness (*citta*) first comes into touch (*phassa*) with its object (*ārammaṇa*) and thereafter feeling, conception (*saññā*) and volition (*cetanā*) come in. This contact is like the pillars of a palace, and the rest are but the superstructure built upon it (*dabbasambhārasadisā*). But it should not be thought that contact

[1] *Buddhist Psychology*, pp. 49, 50.

is the beginning of the psychological processes, for in one whole consciousness (*ekacittasmiṃ*) it cannot be said that this comes first and that comes after, so we can take contact in association with feeling (*vedanā*), conceiving (*saññā*) or volition (*cetanā*); it is itself an immaterial state but yet since it comprehends objects it is called contact." "There is no impinging on one side of the object (as in physical contact), nevertheless contact causes consciousness and object to be in collision, as visible object and visual organs, sound and hearing; thus impact is its *function*; or it has impact as its *essential property* in the sense of attainment, owing to the impact of the physical basis with the mental object. For it is said in the Commentary:—"contact in the four planes of existence is never without the characteristic of touch with the object; but the function of impact takes place in the five doors. For to sense, or five-door contact, is given the name 'having the characteristic of touch' as well as 'having the function of impact.' But to contact in the mind-door there is only the characteristic of touch, but not the function of impact. And then this Sutta is quoted 'As if, sire, two rams were to fight, one ram to represent the eye, the second the visible object, and their collision contact. And as if, sire, two cymbals were to strike against each other, or two hands were to clap against each other; one hand would represent the eye, the second the visible object and their collision contact. Thus contact has the characteristic of touch and the function of impact[1]'. Contact is the manifestation of the union of the three (the object, the consciousness and the sense) and its effect is feeling (*vedanā*); though it is generated by the objects it is felt in the consciousness and its chief feature is experiencing (*anubhava*) the taste of the object. As regards enjoying the taste of an object, the remaining associated states enjoy it only partially. Of contact there is (the function of) the mere touching, of perception the mere noting or perceiving, of volition the mere coordinating, of consciousness the mere cognizing. But feeling alone, through governance, proficiency, mastery, enjoys the taste of an object. For feeling is like the king, the remaining states are like the cook. As the cook, when he has prepared food of diverse tastes, puts it in a basket, seals it, takes it to the king, breaks the seal, opens the basket, takes the best of all the soup and curries, puts them in a dish, swallows (a portion) to find out

[1] *Atthasālinī*, p. 108; translation, pp. 143–144.

whether they are faulty or not and afterwards offers the food of various excellent tastes to the king, and the king, being lord, expert, and master, eats whatever he likes, even so the mere tasting of the food by the cook is like the partial enjoyment of the object by the remaining states, and as the cook tastes a portion of the food, so the remaining states enjoy a portion of the object, and as the king, being lord, expert and master, eats the meal according to his pleasure so feeling being lord expert, and master, enjoys the taste of the object and therefore it is said that enjoyment or experience is its function[1]."

The special feature of saññā is said to be the recognizing (*paccabhiññā*) by means of a sign (*abhiññānena*). According to another explanation, a recognition takes place by the inclusion of the totality (of aspects)—*sabbasaṅgahikavasena*. The work of volition (*cetanā*) is said to be coordination or binding together (*abhisandahana*). "Volition is exceedingly energetic and makes a double effort, a double exertion. Hence the Ancients said 'Volition is like the nature of a landowner, a cultivator who taking fifty-five strong men, went down to the fields to reap. He was exceedingly energetic and exceedingly strenuous; he doubled his strength and said "Take your sickles" and so forth, pointed out the portion to be reaped, offered them drink, food, scent, flowers, etc., and took an equal share of the work.' The simile should be thus applied: volition is like the cultivator, the fifty-five moral states which arise as factors of consciousness are like the fifty-five strong men; like the time of doubling strength, doubling effort by the cultivator is the doubled strength, doubled effort of volition as regards activity in moral and immoral acts[2]." It seems that probably the active side operating in saṅkhāra was separately designated as cetanā (volition).

"When one says 'I,' what he does is that he refers either to all the khandhas combined or any one of them and deludes himself that that was 'I.' Just as one could not say that the fragrance of the lotus belonged to the petals, the colour or the pollen, so one could not say that the rūpa was 'I' or that the vedanā was 'I' or any of the other khandhas was 'I.' There is nowhere to be found in the khandhas 'I am[3]'."

[1] *Atthasālinī*, pp. 109–110; translation, pp. 145–146.
[2] *Ibid.* p. 111; translation, pp. 147–148.
[3] *Saṃyutta Nikāya*, III. 130.

Avijjā and Āsava.

As to the question how the avijjā (ignorance) first started there can be no answer, for we could never say that either ignorance or desire for existence ever has any beginning[1]. Its fruition is seen in the cycle of existence and the sorrow that comes in its train, and it comes and goes with them all. Thus as we can never say that it has any beginning, it determines the elements which bring about cycles of existence and is itself determined by certain others. This mutual determination can only take place in and through the changing series of dependent phenomena, for there is nothing which can be said to have any absolute priority in time or stability. It is said that it is through the coming into being of the āsavas or depravities that the avijjā came into being, and that through the destruction of the depravities (*āsava*) the avijjā was destroyed[2]. These āsavas are classified in the *Dhammasaṅgaṇi* as kāmāsava, bhavāsava, diṭṭhāsava and avijjāsava. Kāmāsava means desire, attachment, pleasure, and thirst after the qualities associated with the senses; bhavāsava means desire, attachment and will for existence or birth; diṭṭhāsava means the holding of heretical views, such as, the world is eternal or non-eternal, or that the world will come to an end or will not come to an end, or that the body and the soul are one or are different; avijjāsava means the ignorance of sorrow, its cause, its extinction and its means of extinction. *Dhammasaṅgaṇi* adds four more supplementary ones, viz. ignorance about the nature of anterior mental khandhas, posterior mental khandhas, anterior and posterior together, and their mutual dependence[3]. Kāmāsava and bhavāsava can as Buddhaghoṣa says be counted as one, for they are both but depravities due to attachment[4].

[1] Warren's *Buddhism in Translations* (*Visuddhimagga*, chap. XVII.), p. 175.

[2] *M. N.* I. p. 54. Childers translates "āsava" as "depravities" and Mrs Rhys Davids as "intoxicants." The word "āsava" in Skr. means "old wine." It is derived from "su" to produce by Buddhaghoṣa and the meaning that he gives to it is "*cira pārivāsikaṭṭhena*" (on account of its being stored up for a long time like wine). They work through the eye and the mind and continue to produce all beings up to Indra. As those wines which are kept long are called "āsavas" so these are also called āsavas for remaining a long time. The other alternative that Buddhaghoṣa gives is that they are called āsava on account of their producing saṃsāradukkha (sorrows of the world), *Atthasālinī*, p. 48. Contrast it with Jaina āsrava (flowing in of karma matter). Finding it difficult to translate it in one word after Buddhaghosa, I have translated it as "depravities," after Childers.

[3] See *Dhammasaṅgaṇi*, p. 195.

[4] Buddhaghoṣa's *Atthasālinī*, p. 371.

The diṭṭhāsavas by clouding the mind with false metaphysical views stand in the way of one's adopting the true Buddhistic doctrines. The kāmāsavas stand in the way of one's entering into the way of Nirvāṇa (*anāgāmimagga*) and the bhavāsavas and avijjāsavas stand in the way of one's attaining arhattva or final emancipation. When the *Majjhima Nikāya* says that from the rise of the āsavas avijjā rises, it evidently counts avijjā there as in some sense separate from the other āsavas, such as those of attachment and desire of existence which veil the true knowledge about sorrow.

The afflictions (*kilesas*) do not differ much from the āsavas for they are but the specific passions in forms ordinarily familiar to us, such as covetousness (*lobha*), anger or hatred (*dosa*), infatuation (*moha*), arrogance, pride or vanity (*māna*), heresy (*diṭṭhi*), doubt or uncertainty (*vicikicchā*), idleness (*thīna*), boastfulness (*udhacca*), shamelessness (*ahirika*) and hardness of heart (*anottapa*); these kilesas proceed directly as a result of the āsavas. In spite of these varieties they are often counted as three (lobha, dosa, moha) and these together are called kilesa. They are associated with the vedanākkhandha, saññākkhandha, saṅkhārakkhandha and viññānakkhandha. From these arise the three kinds of actions, of speech, of body, and of mind[1].

Sīla and Samādhi.

We are intertwined all through outside and inside by the tangles of desire (*taṇhā jaṭā*), and the only way by which these may be loosened is by the practice of right discipline (*sīla*), concentration (*samādhi*) and wisdom (*paññā*). Sīla briefly means the desisting from committing all sinful deeds (*sabbapāpassa akaraṇam*). With sīla therefore the first start has to be made, for by it one ceases to do all actions prompted by bad desires and thereby removes the inrush of dangers and disturbances. This serves to remove the kilesas, and therefore the proper performance of the sīla would lead one to the first two successive stages of sainthood, viz. the sotāpannabhāva (the stage in which one is put in the right current) and the sakadāgāmibhāva (the stage when one has only one more birth to undergo). Samādhi is a more advanced effort, for by it all the old roots of the old kilesas are destroyed and the taṇhā or desire is removed and

[1] *Dhammasaṅgaṇi*, p. 180.

by it one is led to the more advanced states of a saint. It directly brings in paññā (true wisdom) and by paññā the saint achieves final emancipation and becomes what is called an arhat[1]. Wisdom (*paññā*) is right knowledge about the four āriya saccas, viz. sorrow, its cause, its destruction and its cause of destruction.

Sīla means those particular volitions and mental states, etc. by which a man who desists from committing sinful actions maintains himself on the right path. Sīla thus means 1. right volition (*cetanā*), 2. the associated mental states (*cetasika*), 3. mental control (*saṃvara*) and 4. the actual non-transgression (in body and speech) of the course of conduct already in the mind by the preceding three sīlas called avītikkama. Saṃvara is spoken of as being of five kinds. 1. Pāṭimokkhasaṃvara (the control which saves him who abides by it), 2. Satisaṃvara (the control of mindfulness), 3. Ñānasaṃvara (the control of knowledge), 4. Khantisaṃvara (the control of patience), 5. Viriyasaṃvara (the control of active self-restraint). Pāṭimokkhasaṃvara means all self-control in general. Satisaṃvara means the mindfulness by which one can bring in the right and good associations when using one's cognitive senses. Even when looking at any tempting object he will by virtue of his mindfulness (*sati*) control himself from being tempted by avoiding to think of its tempting side and by thinking on such aspects of it as may lead in the right direction. Khantisaṃvara is that by which one can remain unperturbed in heat and cold. By the proper adherence to sīla all our bodily, mental and vocal activities (*kamma*) are duly systematized, organized, stabilized (*samādhānam, upadhāraṇaṃ, patiṭṭhā*)[2].

The sage who adopts the full course should also follow a number of healthy monastic rules with reference to dress, sitting, dining, etc., which are called the dhūtaṅgas or pure disciplinary parts[3]. The practice of sīla and the dhūtaṅgas help the sage to adopt the course of samādhi. Samādhi as we have seen means the concentration of the mind bent on right endeavours (*kusalacittekaggatā samādhiḥ*) together with its states upon one particular object (*ekārammaṇa*) so that they may completely cease to shift and change (*sammā ca avikkhipamānā*)[4].

[1] *Visuddhimagga Nidānādikathā.*
[2] *Visuddhimagga-sīlaniddeso*, pp. 7 and 8.
[3] *Visuddhimagga*, II.
[4] *Visuddhimagga*, pp. 84–85.

The man who has practised sīla must train his mind first in particular ways, so that it may be possible for him to acquire the chief concentration of meditation called jhāna (fixed and steady meditation). These preliminary endeavours of the mind for the acquirement of jhānasamādhi eventually lead to it and are called upacāra samādhi (preliminary samādhi) as distinguished from the jhānasamādhi called the appanāsamādhi (achieved samādhi)[1]. Thus as a preparatory measure, firstly he has to train his mind continually to view with disgust the appetitive desires for eating and drinking (*āhāre paṭikkūlasaññā*) by emphasizing in the mind the various troubles that are associated in seeking food and drink and their ultimate loathsome transformations as various nauseating bodily elements. When a man continually habituates himself to emphasize the disgusting associations of food and drink, he ceases to have any attachment to them and simply takes them as an unavoidable evil, only awaiting the day when the final dissolution of all sorrows will come[2]. Secondly he has to habituate his mind to the idea that all the parts of our body are made up of the four elements, kṣiti (earth), ap (water), tejas (fire) and wind (air), like the carcase of a cow at the butcher's shop. This is technically called catudhātuvavatthānabhāvanā (the meditation of the body as being made up of the four elements)[3]. Thirdly he has to habituate his mind to think again and again (*anussati*) about the virtues or greatness of the Buddha, the saṅgha (the monks following the Buddha), the gods and the law (*dhamma*) of the Buddha, about the good effects of sīla, and the making of gifts (*cāgānussati*), about the nature of death (*maraṇānussati*) and about the deep nature and qualities of the final extinction of all phenomena (*upasamānussati*)[4].

[1] As it is not possible for me to enter into details, I follow what appears to me to be the main line of division showing the interconnection of jhāna (Skr. *dhyāna*) with its accessory stages called parikammas (*Visuddhimagga*, pp. 85 f.).

[2] *Visuddhimagga*, pp. 341–347; mark the intense pessimistic attitude, "*Imañ ca pana āhāre paṭikulasaññāṃ anuyuttassa bhikkhuṇo rasataṇhāya cittaṃ paṭilīyati, paṭikuṭṭati, paṭivaṭṭati; so, kantāranittharaṇatthiko viya puttamaṃsaṃ vigatamado āhāraṃ āhāreti yāvad eva dukkhassa nittharaṇatthāya*," p. 347. The mind of him who inspires himself with this supreme disgust to all food, becomes free from all desires for palatable tastes, and turns its back to them and flies off from them. As a means of getting rid of all sorrow he takes his food without any attachment as one would eat the flesh of his own son to sustain himself in crossing a forest.

[3] *Visuddhimagga*, pp. 347–370.

[4] *Visuddhimagga*, pp. 197–294.

Advancing further from the preliminary meditations or preparations called the upacāra samādhi we come to those other sources of concentration and meditation called the appanāsamādhi which directly lead to the achievement of the highest samādhi. The processes of purification and strengthening of the mind continue in this stage also, but these represent the last attempts which lead the mind to its final goal Nibbāna. In the first part of this stage the sage has to go to the cremation grounds and notice the diverse horrifying changes of the human carcases and think how nauseating, loathsome, unsightly and impure they are, and from this he will turn his mind to the living human bodies and convince himself that they being in essence the same as the dead carcases are as loathsome as they[1]. This is called asubhakammaṭṭhāna or the endeavour to perceive the impurity of our bodies. He should think of the anatomical parts and constituents of the body as well as their processes, and this will help him to enter into the first jhāna by leading his mind away from his body. This is called the kāyagatāsati or the continual mindfulness about the nature of the body[2]. As an aid to concentration the sage should sit in a quiet place and fix his mind on the inhaling (*passāsa*) and the exhaling (*āssāsa*) of his breath, so that instead of breathing in a more or less unconscious manner he may be aware whether he is breathing quickly or slowly; he ought to mark it definitely by counting numbers, so that by fixing his mind on the numbers counted he may fix his mind on the whole process of inhalation and exhalation in all stages of its course. This is called the ānapānasati or the mindfulness of inhalation and exhalation[3].

Next to this we come to Brahmavihāra, the fourfold meditation of mettā (universal friendship), karuṇā (universal pity), muditā (happiness in the prosperity and happiness of all) and upekkhā (indifference to any kind of preferment of oneself, his friend, enemy or a third party). In order to habituate oneself to the meditation on universal friendship, one should start with thinking how he should himself like to root out all misery and become happy, how he should himself like to avoid death and live cheerfully, and then pass over to the idea that other beings would also have the same desires. He should thus habituate himself to think that his friends, his enemies, and all those with whom he is not

[1] *Visuddhimagga*, VI. [2] *Ibid.* pp. 239–266. [3] *Ibid.* pp. 266–292.

connected might all live and become happy. He should fix himself to such an extent in this meditation that he would not find any difference between the happiness or safety of himself and of others. He should never become angry with any person. Should he at any time feel himself offended on account of the injuries inflicted on him by his enemies, he should think of the futility of doubling his sadness by becoming sorry or vexed on that account. He should think that if he should allow himself to be affected by anger, he would spoil all his sīla which he was so carefully practising. If anyone has done a vile action by inflicting injury, should he himself also do the same by being angry at it? If he were finding fault with others for being angry, could he himself indulge in anger? Moreover he should think that all the dhammas are momentary (*khaṇikattā*); that there no longer existed the khandhas which had inflicted the injury, and moreover the infliction of any injury being only a joint product, the man who was injured was himself an indispensable element in the production of the infliction as much as the man who inflicted the injury, and there could not thus be any special reason for making him responsible and of being angry with him. If even after thinking in this way the anger does not subside, he should think that by indulging in anger he could only bring mischief on himself through his bad deeds, and he should further think that the other man by being angry was only producing mischief to himself but not to him. By thinking in these ways the sage would be able to free his mind from anger against his enemies and establish himself in an attitude of universal friendship[1]. This is called the mettā-bhāvanā. In the meditation of universal pity (*karuṇā*) also one should sympathize with the sorrows of his friends and foes alike. The sage being more keen-sighted will feel pity for those who are apparently leading a happy life, but are neither acquiring merits nor endeavouring to proceed on the way to Nibbāna, for they are to suffer innumerable lives of sorrow[2].

We next come to the jhānas with the help of material things as objects of concentration called the Kasiṇam. These objects of concentration may either be earth, water, fire, wind, blue colour, yellow colour, red colour, white colour, light or limited space (*paricchinnākāsa*). Thus the sage may take a brown ball of earth and concentrate his mind upon it as an earth ball, sometimes

[1] *Visuddhimagga*, pp. 295–314. [2] *Ibid.* pp. 314–315.

with eyes open and sometimes with eyes shut. When he finds that even in shutting his eyes he can visualize the object in his mind, he may leave off the object and retire to another place to concentrate upon the image of the earth ball in his mind.

In the first stages of the first meditation (*pathamam jhānam*) the mind is concentrated on the object in the way of understanding it with its form and name and of comprehending it with its diverse relations. This state of concentration is called vitakka (discursive meditation). The next stage of the first meditation is that in which the mind does not move in the object in relational terms but becomes fixed and settled in it and penetrates into it without any quivering. This state is called vicāra (steadily moving). The first stage vitakka has been compared in Buddhaghoṣa's *Visuddhimagga* to the flying of a kite with its wings flapping, whereas the second stage is compared to its flying in a sweep without the least quiver of its wings. These two stages are associated with a buoyant exaltation (*pīti*) and a steady inward bliss called sukha[1] instilling the mind. The formation of this first jhāna roots out five ties of avijjā, kāmacchando (dallying with desires), vyāpādo (hatred), thīnamiddham (sloth and torpor), uddhaccakukkuccam (pride and restlessness), and vicikicchā (doubt). The five elements of which this jhāna is constituted are vitakka, vicāra, pīti, sukham and ekaggatā (one pointedness).

When the sage masters the first jhāna he finds it defective and wants to enter into the second meditation (*dutiyaṃ jhānam*), where there is neither any vitakka nor vicāra of the first jhāna, but the mind is in one unruffled state (*ekodibhāvam*). It is a much steadier state and does not possess the movement which characterized the vitakka and the vicāra stages of the first jhāna and is therefore a very placid state (*vitakka-vicārakkhobha-viraheṇa ativiya acalatā suppasannatā ca*). It is however associated with pīti, sukha and ekaggatā as the first jhāna was.

When the second jhāna is mastered the sage becomes disinclined towards the enjoyment of the pīti of that stage and becomes indifferent to them (*upekkhako*). A sage in this stage sees the objects but is neither pleased nor displeased. At this stage all the āsavas of the sage become loosened (*khīṇāsava*). The enjoyment of sukha however still remains in the stage and the

[1] Where there is pīti there is sukha, but where there is sukha there may not necessarily be pīti. *Visuddhimagga*, p. 145.

mind if not properly and carefully watched would like sometimes to turn back to the enjoyment of pīti again. The two characteristics of this jhāna are sukha and ekaggatā. It should however be noted that though there is the feeling of highest sukha here, the mind is not only not attached to it but is indifferent to it (*atimadhurasukhe sukhapāramippatte pi tatiyajjhāne upekkhako, na tattha sukhābhisangena ākaḍḍhiyati*)[1]. The earth ball (*paṭhavī*) is however still the object of the jhāna.

In the fourth or the last jhāna both the sukha (happiness) and the dukkha (misery) vanish away and all the roots of attachment and antipathies are destroyed. This state is characterized by supreme and absolute indifference (*upekkhā*) which was slowly growing in all the various stages of the jhānas. The characteristics of this jhāna are therefore upekkhā and ekaggatā. With the mastery of this jhāna comes final perfection and total extinction of the citta called cetovimutti, and the sage becomes thereby an arhat[2]. There is no further production of the khandhas, no rebirth, and there is the absolute cessation of all sorrows and sufferings—Nibbāna.

Kamma.

In the Kaṭha (II. 6) Yama says that "a fool who is blinded with the infatuation of riches does not believe in a future life; he thinks that only this life exists and not any other, and thus he comes again and again within my grasp." In the Dīgha Nikāya also we read how Pāyāsi was trying to give his reasons in support of his belief that "Neither is there any other world, nor are there beings, reborn otherwise than from parents, nor is there fruit or result of deeds well done or ill done[3]." Some of his arguments were that neither the vicious nor the virtuous return to tell us that they suffered or enjoyed happiness in the other world, that if the virtuous had a better life in store, and if they believed in it, they would certainly commit suicide in order to get it at the earliest opportunity, that in spite of taking the best precautions we do not find at the time of the death of any person that his soul goes out, or that his body weighs less on account of the departure of his soul, and so on. Kassapa refutes his arguments with apt illustrations. But in spite of a few agnostics of

[1] *Visuddhimagga*, p. 163.
[2] *Majjhima Nikāya*, I. p. 296, and *Visuddhimagga*, pp. 167–168.
[3] *Dialogues of the Buddha*, II. p. 349; *D. N.* II. pp. 317 ff.

Pāyāsi's type, we have every reason to believe that the doctrine of rebirth in other worlds and in this was often spoken of in the Upaniṣads and taken as an accepted fact by the Buddha. In the *Milinda Pañha*, we find Nāgasena saying "it is through a difference in their karma that men are not all alike, but some long lived, some short lived, some healthy and some sickly, some handsome and some ugly, some powerful and some weak, some rich and some poor, some of high degree and some of low degree, some wise and some foolish[1]." We have seen in the third chapter that the same sort of views was enunciated by the Upaniṣad sages.

But karma could produce its effect in this life or any other life only when there were covetousness, antipathy and infatuation. But "when a man's deeds are performed without covetousness, arise without covetousness and are occasioned without covetousness, then inasmuch as covetousness is gone these deeds are abandoned, uprooted, pulled out of the ground like a palmyra tree and become non-existent and not liable to spring up again in the future[2]." Karma by itself without craving (*taṇhā*) is incapable of bearing good or bad fruits. Thus we read in the *Mahāsatipaṭṭhāna sutta*, "even this craving, potent for rebirth, that is accompanied by lust and self-indulgence, seeking satisfaction now here, now there, to wit, the craving for the life of sense, the craving for becoming (renewed life) and the craving for not becoming (for no new rebirth)[3]." "Craving for things visible, craving for things audible, craving for things that may be smelt, tasted, touched, for things in memory recalled. These are the things in this world that are dear, that are pleasant. There does craving take its rise, there does it dwell[4]." Pre-occupation and deliberation of sensual gratification giving rise to craving is the reason why sorrow comes. And this is the first ārya satya (noble truth).

The cessation of sorrow can only happen with "the utter cessation of and disenchantment about that very craving, giving it up, renouncing it and emancipation from it[5]."

When the desire or craving (*taṇhā*) has once ceased the sage becomes an arhat, and the deeds that he may do after that will bear no fruit. An arhat cannot have any good or bad

[1] Warren's *Buddhism in Translations*, p. 215. [2] *Ibid.* pp. 216–217.
[3] *Dialogues of the Buddha*, II. p. 340. [4] *Ibid.* p. 341. [5] *Ibid.* p. 341.

fruits of whatever he does. For it is through desire that karma finds its scope of giving fruit. With the cessation of desire all ignorance, antipathy and grasping cease and consequently there is nothing which can determine rebirth. An arhat may suffer the effects of the deeds done by him in some previous birth just as Moggallāna did, but in spite of the remnants of his past karma an arhat was an emancipated man on account of the cessation of his desire[1].

Kammas are said to be of three kinds, of body, speech and mind (*kāyika, vācika* and *mānasika*). The root of this kamma is however volition (*cetanā*) and the states associated with it[2]. If a man wishing to kill animals goes out into the forest in search of them, but cannot get any of them there even after a long search, his misconduct is not a bodily one, for he could not actually commit the deed with his body. So if he gives an order for committing a similar misdeed, and if it is not actually carried out with the body, it would be a misdeed by speech (*vācika*) and not by the body. But the merest bad thought or ill will alone whether carried into effect or not would be a kamma of the mind (*mānasika*)[3]. But the mental kamma must be present as the root of all bodily and vocal kammas, for if this is absent, as in the case of an arhat, there cannot be any kammas at all for him.

Kammas are divided from the point of view of effects into four classes, viz. (1) those which are bad and produce impurity, (2) those which are good and productive of purity, (3) those which are partly good and partly bad and thus productive of both purity and impurity, (4) those which are neither good nor bad and productive neither of purity nor of impurity, but which contribute to the destruction of kammas[4].

Final extinction of sorrow (*nibbāna*) takes place as the natural result of the destruction of desires. Scholars of Buddhism have tried to discover the meaning of this ultimate happening, and various interpretations have been offered. Professor De la Vallée Poussin has pointed out that in the Pāli texts Nibbāna has sometimes been represented as a happy state, as pure annihilation, as an inconceivable existence or as a changeless state[5].

[1] See *Kathāvatthu* and Warren's *Buddhism in Translations*, pp. 221 ff.

[2] *Atthasālinī*, p. 88. [3] See *Atthasālinī*, p. 90. [4] See *Atthasālinī*, p. 89.

[5] Prof. De la Vallée Poussin's article in the *E. R. E.* on Nirvāṇa. See also *Cullavagga*, IX. i. 4; Mrs Rhys Davids's *Psalms of the early Buddhists*, I. and II., Introduction, p. xxxvii; *Dīgha*, II. 15; *Udāna*, VIII.; *Saṃyutta*, III. 109.

Mr Schrader, in discussing Nibbāna in *Pali Text Society Journal*, 1905, says that the Buddha held that those who sought to become identified after death with the soul of the world as infinite space (*ākāsa*) or consciousness (*viññāna*) attained to a state in which they had a corresponding feeling of infiniteness without having really lost their individuality. This latter interpretation of Nibbāna seems to me to be very new and quite against the spirit of the Buddhistic texts. It seems to me to be a hopeless task to explain Nibbāna in terms of worldly experience, and there is no way in which we can better indicate it than by saying that it is a cessation of all sorrow; the stage at which all worldly experiences have ceased can hardly be described either as positive or negative. Whether we exist in some form eternally or do not exist is not a proper Buddhistic question, for it is a heresy to think of a Tathāgata as existing eternally (*śāśvata*) or not-existing (*aśāśvata*) or whether he is existing as well as not existing or whether he is neither existing nor non-existing. Any one who seeks to discuss whether Nibbāna is either a positive and eternal state or a mere state of non-existence or annihilation, takes a view which has been discarded in Buddhism as heretical. It is true that we in modern times are not satisfied with it, for we want to know what it all means. But it is not possible to give any answer since Buddhism regarded all these questions as illegitimate.

Later Buddhistic writers like Nāgārjuna and Candrakīrtti took advantage of this attitude of early Buddhism and interpreted it as meaning the non-essential character of all existence. Nothing existed, and therefore any question regarding the existence or non-existence of anything would be meaningless. There is no difference between the wordly stage (*saṃsāra*) and Nibbāna, for as all appearances are non-essential, they never existed during the saṃsāra so that they could not be annihilated in Nibbāna.

Upaniṣads and Buddhism.

The Upaniṣads had discovered that the true self was ānanda (bliss)[1]. We could suppose that early Buddhism tacitly presupposes some such idea. It was probably thought that if there was the self (*attā*) it must be bliss. The Upaniṣads had asserted that the self (*ātman*) was indestructible and eternal[2]. If we are allowed

[1] Tait. II. 5.

[2] Bṛh. IV. 5. 14. Kaṭha. V. 13.

to make explicit what was implicit in early Buddhism we could conceive it as holding that if there was the self it must be bliss, because it was eternal. This causal connection has not indeed been anywhere definitely pronounced in the Upaniṣads, but he who carefully reads the Upaniṣads cannot but think that the reason why the Upaniṣads speak of the self as bliss is that it is eternal. But the converse statement that what was not eternal was sorrow does not appear to be emphasized clearly in the Upaniṣads. The important postulate of the Buddha is that that which is changing is sorrow, and whatever is sorrow is not self[1]. The point at which Buddhism parted from the Upaniṣads lies in the experiences of the self. The Upaniṣads doubtless considered that there were many experiences which we often identify with self, but which are impermanent. But the belief is found in the Upaniṣads that there was associated with these a permanent part as well, and that it was this permanent essence which was the true and unchangeable self, the blissful. They considered that this permanent self as pure bliss could not be defined as this, but could only be indicated as not this, not this (*neti neti*)[2]. But the early Pāli scriptures hold that we could nowhere find out such a permanent essence, any constant self, in our changing experiences. All were but changing phenomena and therefore sorrow and therefore non-self, and what was non-self was not mine, neither I belonged to it, nor did it belong to me as my self[3].

The true self was with the Upaniṣads a matter of transcendental experience as it were, for they said that it could not be described in terms of anything, but could only be pointed out as "there," behind all the changing mental categories. The Buddha looked into the mind and saw that it did not exist. But how was it that the existence of this self was so widely spoken of as demonstrated in experience? To this the reply of the Buddha was that what people perceived there when they said that they perceived the self was but the mental experiences either individually or together. The ignorant ordinary man did not know the noble truths and was not trained in the way of wise men, and considered himself to be endowed with form (*rūpa*) or found the forms in his self or the self in the forms. He

[1] *Saṃyutta Nikāya*, III. pp. 44–45 ff.

[2] See Bṛh. IV. iv. Chāndogya, VIII. 7–12.

[3] *Saṃyutta Nikāya*, III. 45.

experienced the thought (of the moment) as it were the self or experienced himself as being endowed with thought, or the thought in the self or the self in the thought. It is these kinds of experiences that he considered as the perception of the self[1].

The Upaniṣads did not try to establish any school of discipline or systematic thought. They revealed throughout the dawn of an experience of an immutable Reality as the self of man, as the only abiding truth behind all changes. But Buddhism holds that this immutable self of man is a delusion and a false knowledge. The first postulate of the system is that impermanence is sorrow. Ignorance about sorrow, ignorance about the way it originates, ignorance about the nature of the extinction of sorrow, and ignorance about the means of bringing about this extinction represent the fourfold ignorance (*avijjā*)[2]. The avidyā, which is equivalent to the Pāli word avijjā, occurs in the Upaniṣads also, but there it means ignorance about the ātman doctrine, and it is sometimes contrasted with vidyā or true knowledge about the self (*ātman*)[3]. With the Upaniṣads the highest truth was the permanent self, the bliss, but with the Buddha there was nothing permanent; and all was change; and all change and impermanence was sorrow[4]. This is, then, the cardinal truth of Buddhism, and ignorance concerning it in the above fourfold ways represented the fourfold ignorance which stood in the way of the right comprehension of the fourfold cardinal truths (*āriya sacca*)—sorrow, cause of the origination of sorrow, extinction of sorrow, and the means thereto.

There is no Brahman or supreme permanent reality and no self, and this ignorance does not belong to any ego or self as we may ordinarily be led to suppose.

Thus it is said in the *Visuddhimagga* "inasmuch however as ignorance is empty of stability from being subject to a coming into existence and a disappearing from existence...and is empty of a self-determining Ego from being subject to dependence,—...or in other words inasmuch as ignorance is not an Ego, and similarly with reference to Karma and the rest—therefore is it to be understood of the wheel of existence that it is empty with a twelvefold emptiness[5]."

[1] *Saṃyutta Nikāya*, III. 46. [2] *Majjhima Nikāya*, I. p. 54.

[3] Chā. I. I. 10. Bṛh. IV. 3. 20. There are some passages where vidyā and avidyā have been used in a different and rather obscure sense, Íśā 9–11.

[4] *Aṅg. Nikāya*, III. 85.

[5] Warren's *Buddhism in Translations* (*Visuddhimagga*, chap. XVII.), p. 175.

The Schools of Theravāda Buddhism.

There is reason to believe that the oral instructions of the Buddha were not collected until a few centuries after his death. Serious quarrels arose amongst his disciples or rather amongst the successive generations of the disciples of his disciples about his doctrines and other monastic rules which he had enjoined upon his followers. Thus we find that when the council of Vesāli decided against the Vṛjin monks, called also the Vajjiputtakas, they in their turn held another great meeting (Mahāsaṅgha) and came to their own decisions about certain monastic rules and thus came to be called as the Mahāsaṅghikas[1]. According to Vasumitra as translated by Vassilief, the Mahāsaṅghikas seceded in 400 B.C. and during the next one hundred years they gave rise first to the three schools Ekavyavahārikas, Lokottaravādins, and Kukkulikas and after that the Bahuśrutīyas. In the course of the next one hundred years, other schools rose out of it namely the Prajñaptivādins, Caittikas, Aparaśailas and Uttaraśailas. The Theravāda or the Sthaviravāda school which had convened the council of Vesāli developed during the second and first century B.C. into a number of schools, viz. the Haimavatas, Dharmaguptikas, Mahīśāsakas, Kāśyapīyas, Saṅkrāntikas (more well known as Sautrāntikas) and the Vātsiputtrīyas which latter was again split up into the Dharmottarīyas, Bhadrayānīyas, Sammitīyas and Channāgarikas. The main branch of the Theravāda school was from the second century downwards known as the Hetuvādins or Sarvāstivādins[2]. The *Mahābodhivaṃsa* identifies the Theravāda school with the Vibhajjavādins. The commentator of the *Kathāvatthu* who probably lived according to Mrs Rhys Davids sometime in the fifth century A.D. mentions a few other schools of Buddhists. But of all these Buddhist schools we know very little. Vasumitra (100 A.D.) gives us some very meagre accounts of

[1] The *Mahāvaṃsa* differs from *Dīpavaṃsa* in holding that the Vajjiputtakas did not develop into the Mahāsaṅghikas, but it was the Mahāsaṅghikas who first seceded while the Vajjiputtakas seceded independently of them. The *Mahābodhivaṃsa*, which according to Professor Geiger was composed 975 A.D.—1000 A.D., follows the Mahāvaṃsa in holding the Mahāsaṅghikas to be the first seceders and Vajjiputtakas to have seceded independently.

Vasumitra confuses the council of Vesāli with the third council of Pāṭaliputra. See introduction to translation of *Kathāvatthu* by Mrs Rhys Davids.

[2] For other accounts of the schism see Mr Aung and Mrs Rhys Davids's translation of *Kathāvatthu*, pp. xxxvi–xlv.

certain schools, of the Mahāsaṅghikas, Lokottaravādins, Ekavyavahārikas, Kukkulikas, Prajñaptivādins and Sarvāstivādins, but these accounts deal more with subsidiary matters of little philosophical importance. Some of the points of interest are (1) that the Mahāsaṅghikas were said to believe that the body was filled with mind (*citta*) which was represented as sitting, (2) that the Prajñaptivādins held that there was no agent in man, that there was no untimely death, for it was caused by the previous deeds of man, (3) that the Sarvāstivādins believed that everything existed. From the discussions found in the *Kathāvatthu* also we may know the views of some of the schools on some points which are not always devoid of philosophical interest. But there is nothing to be found by which we can properly know the philosophy of these schools. It is quite possible however that these so-called schools of Buddhism were not so many different systems but only differed from one another on some points of dogma or practice which were considered as being of sufficient interest to them, but which to us now appear to be quite trifling. But as we do not know any of their literatures, it is better not to make any unwarrantable surmises. These schools are however not very important for a history of later Indian Philosophy, for none of them are even referred to in any of the systems of Hindu thought. The only schools of Buddhism with which other schools of philosophical thought came in direct contact, are the Sarvāstivādins including the Sautrāntikas and the Vaibhāṣikas, the Yogācāra or the Vijñānavādins and the Mādhyamikas or the Śūnyavādins. We do not know which of the diverse smaller schools were taken up into these four great schools, the Sautrāntika, Vaibhāṣika, Yogācāra and the Mādhyamika schools. But as these schools were most important in relation to the development of the different systems in Hindu thought, it is best that we should set ourselves to gather what we can about these systems of Buddhistic thought.

When the Hindu writers refer to the Buddhist doctrine in general terms such as "the Buddhists say" without calling them the Vijñānavādins or the Yogācāras and the Śūnyavādins, they often refer to the Sarvāstivādins by which they mean both the Sautrāntikas and the Vaibhāṣikas, ignoring the difference that exists between these two schools. It is well to mention that there is hardly any evidence to prove that the Hindu writers were acquainted with the Theravāda doctrines as expressed in the Pāli works. The Vaibhāṣikas and the Sautrāntikas have been more or less associated with each other. Thus the *Abhidharmakośaśāstra* of Vasubandhu who was a Vaibhāṣika was commented upon by Yaśomitra who was a Sautrāntika. The difference between the Vaibhāṣikas and the Sautrāntikas that attracted the notice of the Hindu writers was this, that the former believed that external objects were directly perceived, whereas the latter believed that the existence of the external objects could only be inferred from our diversified knowledge[1]. Guṇaratna (fourteenth century A.D.) in his commentary *Tarkarahasyadīpikā* on *Ṣaḍdarśanasamuccaya* says that the Vaibhāṣika was but another name of the Āryasammitīya school. According to Guṇaratna the Vaibhāṣikas held that things existed for four moments, the moment of production, the moment of existence, the moment of decay and the moment of annihilation. It has been pointed out in Vasubandhu's *Abhidharmakośa* that the Vaibhāṣikas believed these to be four kinds of forces which by coming in combination with the permanent essence of an entity produced its impermanent manifestations in life (see Prof. Stcherbatsky's translation of Yaśomitra on *Abhidharmakośa kārikā*, V. 25). The self called pudgala also possessed those characteristics. Knowledge was formless and was produced along with its object by the very same conditions (*arthasahabhāśī ekasamāgryadhīnaḥ*). The Sautrāntikas according to Guṇaratna held that there was no soul but only the five skandhas. These skandhas transmigrated. The past, the future, annihilation, dependence on cause, ākāśa and pudgala are but names (*saṃjñāmātram*), mere assertions (*pratijñāmātram*), mere limitations (*samvṛtamātram*) and mere phenomena (*vyavahāramātram*). By pudgala they meant that which other people called eternal and all pervasive soul. External objects are never directly perceived but are only inferred as existing for explaining the diversity of knowledge. Definite cognitions are valid; all compounded things are momentary (*kṣaṇikāḥ sarvasaṃskārāḥ*).

[1] Mādhavācārya's *Sarvadarśanasaṃgraha*, chapter II. *Śāstradīpikā*, the discussions on Pratyakṣa, Amalānanda's commentary (on *Bhāmatī*) *Vedāntakalpataru*, p. 286, "*vaibhāṣikasya bāhyo'rthaḥ pratyakṣaḥ, sautrāntikasya jñānagatākāravaicitryeṇ anumeyaḥ.*" The nature of the inference of the Sautrāntikas is shown thus by Amalānanda (1247–1260 A.D.) "*ye yasmin satyapi kādācitkāḥ te tadatiriktāpekṣāḥ*" (those (i.e. cognitions) which in spite of certain unvaried conditions are of unaccounted diversity must depend on other things in addition to these, i.e. the external objects) *Vedāntakalpataru*, p. 289.

The atoms of colour, taste, smell and touch, and cognition are being destroyed every moment. The meanings of words always imply the negations of all other things, excepting that which is intended to be signified by that word (*anyāpohaḥ śabdārthaḥ*). Salvation (*mokṣa*) comes as the result of the destruction of the process of knowledge through continual meditation that there is no soul[1].

One of the main differences between the Vibhajjavādins, Sautrāntikas and the Vaibhāṣikas or the Sarvāstivādins appears to refer to the notion of time which is a subject of great interest with Buddhist philosophy. Thus *Abhidharmakośa* (v. 24...) describes the Sarvāstivādins as those who maintain the universal existence of everything past, present and future. The Vibhajjavādins are those "who maintain that the present elements and those among the past that have not yet produced their fruition, are existent, but they deny the existence of the future ones and of those among the past that have already produced fruition." There were four branches of this school represented by Dharmatrāta, Ghoṣa, Vasumitra and Buddhadeva. Dharmatrāta maintained that when an element enters different times, its existence changes but not its essence, just as when milk is changed into curd or a golden vessel is broken, the form of the existence changes though the essence remains the same. Ghoṣa held that "when an element appears at different times, the past one retains its past aspects without being severed from its future and present aspects, the present likewise retains its present aspect without completely losing its past and future aspects," just as a man in passionate love with a woman does not lose his capacity to love other women though he is not actually in love with them. Vasumitra held that an entity is called present, past and future according as it produces its efficiency, ceases to produce after having once produced it or has not yet begun to produce it. Buddhadeva maintained the view that just as the same woman may be called mother, daughter, wife, so the same entity may be called present, past or future in accordance with its relation to the preceding or the succeeding moment.

All these schools are in some sense Sarvāstivādins, for they maintain universal existence. But the Vaibhāṣika finds them all defective excepting the view of Vasumitra. For Dharmatrāta's

[1] Guṇaratna's *Tarkarahasyadīpikā*, pp. 46–47.

view is only a veiled Sāṃkhya doctrine; that of Ghoṣa is a confusion of the notion of time, since it presupposes the co-existence of all the aspects of an entity at the same time, and that of Buddhadeva is also an impossible situation, since it would suppose that all the three times were found together and included in one of them. The Vaibhāṣika finds himself in agreement with Vasumitra's view and holds that the difference in time depends upon the difference of the function of an entity; at the time when an entity does not actually produce its function it is future; when it produces it, it becomes present; when after having produced it, it stops, it becomes past; there is a real existence of the past and the future as much as of the present. He thinks that if the past did not exist and assert some efficiency it could not have been the object of my knowledge, and deeds done in past times could not have produced its effects in the present time. The Sautrāntika however thought that the Vaibhāṣika's doctrine would imply the heretical doctrine of eternal existence, for according to them the stuff remained the same and the time-difference appeared in it. The true view according to him was, that there was no difference between the efficiency of an entity, the entity and the time of its appearance. Entities appeared from non-existence, existed for a moment and again ceased to exist. He objected to the Vaibhāṣika view that the past is to be regarded as existent because it exerts efficiency in bringing about the present on the ground that in that case there should be no difference between the past and the present, since both exerted efficiency. If a distinction is made between past, present and future efficiency by a second grade of efficiencies, then we should have to continue it and thus have a vicious infinite. We can know non-existent entities as much as we can know existent ones, and hence our knowledge of the past does not imply that the past is exerting any efficiency. If a distinction is made between an efficiency and an entity, then the reason why efficiency started at any particular time and ceased at another would be inexplicable. Once you admit that there is no difference between efficiency and the entity, you at once find that there is no time at all and the efficiency, the entity and the moment are all one and the same. When we remember a thing of the past we do not know it as existing in the past, but in the same way in which we knew it when it was present. We are never attracted to past passions as the Vaibhāṣika suggests, but past passions leave residues which become the causes of new passions of the present moment[1].

Again we can have a glimpse of the respective positions of the Vātsīputtrīyas and the Sarvāstivādins as represented by Vasubandhu if we attend to the discussion on the subject of the existence of soul in *Abhidharmakośa*. The argument of Vasubandhu against the existence of soul is this, that though it is true that the sense organs may be regarded as a determining cause of perception, no such cause can be found which may render the inference of the existence of soul necessary. If soul actually exists, it must have an essence of its own and must be something different from the elements or entities of a personal life. Moreover, such an eternal, uncaused and unchanging being would be without any practical efficiency (*arthakriyākāritva*) which alone determines or proves existence. The soul can thus be said to have a mere nominal existence as a mere object of current usage. There is no soul, but there are only the elements of a personal life. But the Vātsīputtrīya school held that just as fire could not be said to be either the same as the burning wood or as different from it, and yet it is separate from it, so the soul is an individual (*pudgala*) which has a separate existence, though we could not say that it was altogether different from the elements of a personal life or the same as these. It exists as being conditioned by the elements of personal life, but it cannot further be defined. But its existence cannot be denied, for wherever there is an activity, there must be an agent (e.g. Devadatta walks). To be conscious is likewise an action, hence the agent who is conscious must also exist. To this Vasubandhu replies that Devadatta (the name of a person) does not represent an unity. "It is only an unbroken continuity of momentary forces (flashing into existence), which simple people believe to be a unity and to which they give the name Devadatta. Their belief that Devadatta moves is conditioned, and is based on an analogy with their own experience, but their own continuity of life consists in constantly moving from one place to another. This movement, though regarded as

[1] I am indebted for the above account to the unpublished translation from Tibetan of a small portion of *Abhidharmakośa* by my esteemed friend Prof. Th. Stcherbatsky of Petrograd. I am grateful to him that he allowed me to utilize it.

belonging to a permanent entity, is but a series of new productions in different places, just as the expressions 'fire moves,' 'sound spreads' have the meaning of continuities (of new productions in new places). They likewise use the words 'Devadatta cognises' in order to express the fact that a cognition (takes place in the present moment) which has a cause (in the former moments, these former moments coming in close succession being called Devadatta)."

The problem of memory also does not bring any difficulty, for the stream of consciousness being one throughout, it produces its recollections when connected with a previous knowledge of the remembered object under certain conditions of attention, etc., and absence of distractive factors, such as bodily pains or violent emotions. No agent is required in the phenomena of memory. The cause of recollection is a suitable state of mind and nothing else. When the Buddha told his birth stories saying that he was such and such in such and such a life, he only meant that his past and his present belonged to one and the same lineage of momentary existences. Just as when we say "this same fire which had been consuming that has reached this object," we know that the fire is not identical at any two moments, but yet we overlook the difference and say that it is the same fire. Again, what we call an individual can only be known by descriptions such as "this venerable man, having this name, of such a caste, of such a family, of such an age, eating such food, finding pleasure or displeasure in such things, of such an age, the man who after a life of such length, will pass away having reached an age." Only so much description can be understood, but we have never a direct acquaintance with the individual; all that is perceived are the momentary elements of sensations, images, feelings, etc., and these happening at the former moments exert a pressure on the later ones. The individual is thus only a fiction, a mere nominal existence, a mere thing of description and not of acquaintance; it cannot be grasped either by the senses or by the action of pure intellect. This becomes evident when we judge it by analogies from other fields. Thus whenever we use any common noun, e.g. milk, we sometimes falsely think that there is such an entity as milk, but what really exists is only certain momentary colours, tastes, etc., fictitiously unified as milk; and "just as milk and water are conventional names (for a set of independent elements) for some colour, smell (taste and touch) taken together, so is the designation 'individual' but a common name for the different elements of which it is composed."

The reason why the Buddha declined to decide the question whether the "living being is identical with the body or not" is just because there did not exist any living being as "individual," as is generally supposed. He did not declare that the living being did not exist, because in that case the questioner would have thought that the continuity of the elements of a life was also denied. In truth the "living being" is only a conventional name for a set of constantly changing elements[1].

The only book of the Sammitīyas known to us and that by name only is the *Sammitīyaśāstra* translated into Chinese between 350 A.D. to 431 A.D.; the original Sanskrit works are however probably lost[2].

The Vaibhāṣikas are identified with the Sarvāstivādins who according to *Dīpavaṃsa* v. 47, as pointed out by Takakusu, branched off from the Mahīśāsakas, who in their turn had separated from the Theravāda school.

From the *Kathāvatthu* we know (1) that the Sabbatthivādins believed that everything existed, (2) that the dawn of right attainment was not a momentary flash of insight but by a gradual process, (3) that consciousness or even samādhi was nothing but

[1] This account is based on the translation of *Aṣṭamakośasthānanibaddhaḥ pudgalaviniścayaḥ*, a special appendix to the eighth chapter of *Abhidharmakośa*, by Prof. Th. Stcherbatsky, *Bulletin de l'Académie des Sciences de Russie*, 1919.

[2] Professor De la Vallée Poussin has collected some of the points of this doctrine in an article on the Sammitīyas in the *E. R. E.* He there says that in the *Abhidharmakośavyākhyā* the Sammitīyas have been identified with the Vātsīputtrīyas and that many of its texts were admitted by the Vaibhāṣikas of a later age. Some of their views are as follows: (1) An arhat in possession of nirvāṇa can fall away; (2) there is an intermediate state between death and rebirth called *antarābhava*; (3) merit accrues not only by gift (*tyagānvaya*) but also by the fact of the actual use and advantage reaped by the man to whom the thing was given (*paribhogānvaya puṇya*); (4) not only abstention from evil deeds but a declaration of intention to that end produces merit by itself alone; (5) they believe in a pudgala (soul) as distinct from the skandhas from which it can be said to be either different or non-different. "The pudgala cannot be said to be transitory (*anitya*) like the skandhas since it transmigrates laying down the burden (*skandhas*) shouldering a new burden; it cannot be said to be permanent, since it is made of transitory constituents." This pudgala doctrine of the Sammitīyas as sketched by Professor De la Vallée Poussin is not in full agreement with the pudgala doctrine of the Sammitīyas as sketched by Guṇaratna which we have noticed above.

a flux and (4) that an arhat (saint) may fall away[1]. The Sabbatthivādins or Sarvāstivādins have a vast Abhidharma literature still existing in Chinese translations which is different from the Abhidharma of the Theravāda school which we have already mentioned[2]. These are 1. *Jñānaprasthāna Śāstra* of Kātyāyanīputtra which passed by the name of *Mahā Vibhāṣā* from which the Sabbatthivādins who followed it are called Vaibhāṣikas[3]. This work is said to have been given a literary form by Aśvaghoṣa. 2. *Dharmaskandha* by Śāriputtra. 3. *Dhātukāya* by Pūrṇa. 4. *Prajñaptiśāstra* by Maudgalyāyana. 5. *Vijñānakāya* by Devakṣema. 6. *Saṅgītiparyyāya* by Sāriputtra and *Prakaraṇapāda* by Vasumitra. Vasubandhu (420 A.D.—500 A.D.) wrote a work on the Vaibhāṣika[4] system in verses (*kārikā*) known as the *Abhidharmakośa*, to which he appended a commentary of his own which passes by the name *Abhidharma Kośabhāṣya* in which he pointed out some of the defects of the Vaibhāṣika school from the Sautrāntika point of view[5]. This work was commented upon by Vasumitra and Guṇamati and later on by Yaśomitra who was himself a Sautrāntika and called his work *Abhidharmakośa vyākhyā*; Saṅghabhadra a contemporary of Vasubandhu wrote *Samayapradīpa* and *Nyāyānusāra* (Chinese translations of which are available) on strict Vaibhāṣika lines. We hear also of other Vaibhāṣika writers such as Dharmatrāta, Ghoṣaka, Vasumitra and Bhadanta, the writer of *Saṃyuktābhidharmaśāstra* and *Mahāvibhāṣā*. Diṅnāga (480 A.D.), the celebrated logician, a Vaibhāṣika or a Sautrāntika and reputed to be a pupil of Vasubandhu, wrote his famous work *Pramāṇasamuccaya* in which he established Buddhist logic and refuted many of the views of Vātsyāyana the celebrated commentator of the *Nyāya sūtras*; but we regret

[1] See Mrs Rhys Davids's translation *Kathāvatthu*, p. xix, and Sections I. 6, 7; II. 9 and XI. 6.

[2] *Mahāvyutpatti* gives two names for Sarvāstivāda, viz. Mūlasarvāstivāda and Āryyasarvāstivāda. Itsing (671–695 A.D.) speaks of Āryyamūlasarvāstivāda and Mūlasarvāstivāda. In his time he found it prevailing in Magadha, Guzrat, Sind, S. India, E. India. Takakusu says (*P. T. S.* 1904–1905) that Paramārtha, in his life of Vasubandhu, says that it was propagated from Kashmere to Middle India by Vasubhadra, who studied it there.

[3] Takakusu says (*P. T. S.* 1904–1905) that Kātyāyanīputtra's work was probably a compilation from other Vibhāṣās which existed before the Chinese translations and Vibhāṣā texts dated 383 A.D.

[4] See Takakusu's article *J. R. A. S.* 1905.

[5] The Sautrāntikas did not regard the Abhidharmas of the Vaibhāṣikas as authentic and laid stress on the suttanta doctrines as given in the Suttapiṭaka.

to say that none of the above works are available in Sanskrit, nor have they been retranslated from Chinese or Tibetan into any of the modern European or Indian languages.

The Japanese scholar Mr Yamakami Sogen, late lecturer at Calcutta University, describes the doctrine of the Sabbatthivādins from the Chinese versions of the *Abhidharmakośa*, *Mahāvibhāṣāśāstra*, etc., rather elaborately[1]. The following is a short sketch, which is borrowed mainly from the accounts given by Mr Sogen.

The Sabbatthivādins admitted the five skandhas, twelve āyatanas, eighteen dhātus, the three asaṃskṛta dharmas of pratisaṃkhyānirodha apratisaṃkhyānirodha and ākāśa, and the saṃskṛta dharmas (things composite and interdependent) of rūpa (matter), citta (mind), caitta (mental) and cittaviprayukta (non-mental)[2]. All effects are produced by the coming together (saṃskṛta) of a number of causes. The five skandhas, and the rūpa, citta, etc., are thus called saṃskṛta dharmas (composite things or collocations—*sambhūyakāri*). The rūpa dharmas are eleven in number, one citta dharma, 46 caitta dharmas and 14 cittaviprayukta saṃskāra dharmas (non-mental composite things); adding to these the three asaṃskṛta dharmas we have the seventy-five dharmas. Rūpa is that which has the capacity to obstruct the sense organs. Matter is regarded as the collective organism or collocation, consisting of the fourfold substratum of colour, smell, taste and contact. The unit possessing this fourfold substratum is known as paramāṇu, which is the minutest form of rūpa. It cannot be pierced through or picked up or thrown away. It is indivisible, unanalysable, invisible, inaudible, untastable and intangible. But yet it is not permanent, but is like a momentary flash into being. The simple atoms are called *dravyaparamāṇu* and the compound ones *saṃghātaparamāṇu*. In the words of Prof. Stcherbatsky "the universal elements of matter are manifested in their actions or functions. They are consequently more energies than substances." The organs of sense are also regarded as modifications of atomic matter. Seven such paramāṇus combine together to form an aṇu, and it is in this combined form only that they become perceptible. The combination takes place in the form of a cluster having one atom at the centre and

[1] *Systems of Buddhistic Thought*, published by the Calcutta University.

[2] Śaṅkara in his meagre sketch of the doctrine of the Sarvāstivādins in his bhāṣya on the *Brahma-sūtras* II. 2 notices some of the categories mentioned by Sogen.

others around it. The point which must be remembered in connection with the conception of matter is this, that the qualities of all the mahābhūtas are inherent in the paramāṇus. The special characteristics of roughness (which naturally belongs to earth), viscousness (which naturally belongs to water), heat (belonging to fire), movableness (belonging to wind), combine together to form each of the elements; the difference between the different elements consists only in this, that in each of them its own special characteristics were predominant and active, and other characteristics though present remained only in a potential form. The mutual resistance of material things is due to the quality of earth or the solidness inherent in them; the mutual attraction of things is due to moisture or the quality of water, and so forth. The four elements are to be observed from three aspects, namely, (1) as things, (2) from the point of view of their natures (such as activity, moisture, etc.), and (3) function (such as *dhṛti* or attraction, *saṃgraha* or cohesion, *pakti* or chemical heat, and *vyūhana* or clustering and collecting). These combine together naturally by other conditions or causes. The main point of distinction between the Vaibhāṣika Sarvāstivādins and other forms of Buddhism is this, that here the five skandhas and matter are regarded as permanent and eternal; they are said to be momentary only in the sense that they are changing their phases constantly, owing to their constant change of combination. Avidyā is not regarded here as a link in the chain of the causal series of pratītyasamutpāda; nor is it ignorance of any particular individual, but is rather identical with "moha" or delusion and represents the ultimate state of immaterial dharmas. Avidyā, which through saṃskāra, etc., produces nāmarūpa in the case of a particular individual, is not his avidyā in the present existence but the avidyā of his past existence bearing fruit in the present life.

"The cause never perishes but only changes its name, when it becomes an effect, having changed its state." For example, clay becomes jar, having changed its state; and in this case the name clay is lost and the name jar arises[1]. The Sarvāstivādins allowed simultaneousness between cause and effect only in the case of composite things (*saṃprayukta hetu*) and in the case of

[1] Sogen's quotation from Kumārajīva's Chinese version of Āryyadeva's commentary on the *Mādhyamika śāstra* (chapter XX. Kārikā 9).

the interaction of mental and material things. The substratum of "vijñāna" or "consciousness" is regarded as permanent and the aggregate of the five senses (*indriyas*) is called the perceiver. It must be remembered that the indriyas being material had a permanent substratum, and their aggregate had therefore also a substratum formed of them.

The sense of sight grasps the four main colours of blue, yellow, red, white, and their combinations, as also the visual forms of appearance (*saṃsthāna*) of long, short, round, square, high, low, straight, and crooked. The sense of touch (*kāyendriya*) has for its object the four elements and the qualities of smoothness, roughness, lightness, heaviness, cold, hunger and thirst. These qualities represent the feelings generated in sentient beings by the objects of touch, hunger, thirst, etc., and are also counted under it, as they are the organic effects produced by a touch which excites the physical frame at a time when the energy of wind becomes active in our body and predominates over other energies; so also the feeling of thirst is caused by a touch which excites the physical frame when the energy of the element of fire becomes active and predominates over the other energies. The indriyas (senses) can after grasping the external objects arouse thought (*vijñāna*); each of the five senses is an agent without which none of the five vijñānas would become capable of perceiving an external object. The essence of the senses is entirely material. Each sense has two subdivisions, namely, the principal sense and the auxiliary sense. The substratum of the principal senses consists of a combination of paramāṇus, which are extremely pure and minute, while the substratum of the latter is the flesh, made of grosser materials. The five senses differ from one another with respect to the manner and form of their respective atomic combinations. In all sense-acts, whenever an act is performed and an idea is impressed, a latent energy is impressed on our person which is designated as avijñapti rūpa. It is called rūpa because it is a result or effect of rūpa-contact; it is called avijñapti because it is latent and unconscious; this latent energy is bound sooner or later to express itself in karma effects and is the only bridge which connects the cause and the effect of karma done by body or speech. Karma in this school is considered as twofold, namely, that as thought (*cetana karma*) and that as activity (*caitasika karma*). This last, again, is of two kinds, viz.

that due to body-motion (*kāyika karma*) and speech (*vācika karma*). Both these may again be latent (*avijñapti*) and patent (*vijñapti*), giving us the kāyika-vijñapti karma, kāyikāvijñapti karma, vācika-vijñapti karma and vācikāvijñapti karma. Avijñapti rūpa and avijñapti karma are what we should call in modern phraseology sub-conscious ideas, feelings and activity. Corresponding to each conscious sensation, feeling, thought or activity there is another similar sub-conscious state which expresses itself in future thoughts and actions; as these are not directly known but are similar to those which are known, they are called avijñapti.

The mind, says Vasubandhu, is called cittam, because it wills (*cetati*), manas because it thinks (*manvate*) and vijñāna because it discriminates (*nirdiśati*). The discrimination may be of three kinds: (1) svabhāva nirdeśa (natural perceptual discrimination), (2) prayoga nirdeśa (actual discrimination as present, past and future), and (3) anusmṛti nirdeśa (reminiscent discrimination referring only to the past). The senses only possess the *svabhāva nirdeśa*, the other two belong exclusively to manovijñāna. Each of the vijñānas as associated with its specific sense discriminates its particular object and perceives its general characteristics; the six vijñānas combine to form what is known as the Vijñānaskandha, which is presided over by mind (*mano*). There are forty-six caitta saṃskṛta dharmas. Of the three asaṃskṛta dharmas ākāśa (ether) is in essence the freedom from obstruction, establishing it as a permanent omnipresent immaterial substance (*nīrūpākhya*, non-rūpa). The second asaṃskṛta dharma, apratisaṃkhyā nirodha, means the non-perception of dharmas caused by the absence of pratyayas or conditions. Thus when I fix my attention on one thing, other things are not seen then, not because they are non-existent but because the conditions which would have made them visible were absent. The third asaṃskṛta dharma, pratisaṃkhyā nirodha, is the final deliverance from bondage. Its essential characteristic is everlastingness. These are called asaṃskṛta because being of the nature of negation they are non-collocative and hence have no production or dissolution. The eightfold noble path which leads to this state consists of right views, right aspirations, right speech, right conduct, right livelihood, right effort, right mindfulness, right rapture[1].

[1] Mr Sogen mentions the name of another Buddhist Hīnayāna thinker (about 250 A.D.), Harivarman, who founded a school known as Satyasiddhi school, which

Mahāyānism.

It is difficult to say precisely at what time Mahāyānism took its rise. But there is reason to think that as the Mahāsaṅghikas separated themselves from the Theravādins probably some time in 400 B.C. and split themselves up into eight different schools, those elements of thoughts and ideas which in later days came to be labelled as Mahāyāna were gradually on the way to taking their first inception. We hear in about 100 A.D. of a number of works which are regarded as various Mahāyāna sūtras, some of which are probably as old as at least 100 B.C. (if not earlier) and others as late as 300 or 400 A.D.[1]. These Mahāyānasūtras, also called the Vaipulyasūtras, are generally all in the form of instructions given by the Buddha. Nothing is known about their authors or compilers, but they are all written in some form of Sanskrit and were probably written by those who seceded from the Theravāda school.

The word Hīnayāna refers to the schools of Theravāda, and as such it is contrasted with Mahāyāna. The words are generally translated as small vehicle (*hīna*= small, *yāna* =vehicle) and great vehicle (*mahā* = great, *yāna* = vehicle). But this translation by no means expresses what is meant by Mahāyāna and Hīnayāna[2]. Asaṅga (480 A.D.) in his *Mahāyānasūtrālaṃkāra* gives

propounded the same sort of doctrines as those preached by Nāgārjuna. None of his works are available in Sanskrit and I have never come across any allusion to his name by Sanskrit writers.

[1] Quotations and references to many of these sūtras are found in Candrakīrtti's commentary on the *Mādhyamika kārikās* of Nāgārjuna; some of these are the following: *Aṣṭasāhasrikāprajñāpāramitā* (translated into Chinese 164 A.D.–167 A.D.), *Śatasāhasrikāprajñāpāramitā*, *Gaganagañja*, *Samādhisūtra*, *Tathāgataguhyasūtra*, *Dṛḍhādhyāśayasañcodanāsūtra*, *Dhyāyitamuṣṭisūtra*, *Pitāputrasamāgamasūtra*, *Mahāyānasūtra*, *Māradamanasūtra*, *Ratnakūṭasūtra*, *Ratnacūḍāparipṛcchāsūtra*, *Ratnameghasūtra*, *Ratnarāśisūtra*, *Ratnākarasūtra*, *Rāṣṭrapālaparipṛcchāsūtra*, *Laṅkāvatārasūtra*, *Lalitavistarasūtra*, *Vajracchedikāsūtra*, *Vimalakīrttinirdeśasūtra*, *Śālistambhasūtra*, *Samādhirajasūtra*, *Sukhāvatīvyūha*, *Suvarṇaprabhāsasūtra*, *Saddharmapuṇḍarīka* (translated into Chinese A.D. 255), *Amitāyurdhyānasūtra*, *Hastikākhyasūtra*, etc.

[2] The word Yāna is generally translated as vehicle, but a consideration of numerous contexts in which the word occurs seems to suggest that it means career or course or way, rather than vehicle (*Lalitavistara*, pp. 25, 38; *Prajñāpāramitā*, pp. 24, 319; *Samādhirājasūtra*, p. 1; *Karuṇāpuṇḍarīka*, p. 67; *Laṅkāvatārasūtra*, pp. 68, 108, 132). The word Yāna is as old as the Upaniṣads where we read of Devayāna and Pitṛyāna. There is no reason why this word should be taken in a different sense. We hear in *Laṅkāvatāra* of Śrāvakayāna (career of the Śrāvakas or the Theravādin Buddhists), Pratyekabuddhayāna (the career of saints before the coming of the Buddha), Buddha yāna (career of the Buddhas), Ekayāna (one career), Devayāna (career of the gods),

us the reason why one school was called Hīnayāna whereas the other, which he professed, was called Mahāyāna. He says that, considered from the point of view of the ultimate goal of religion, the instructions, attempts, realization, and time, the Hīnayāna occupies a lower and smaller place than the other called Mahā (great) Yāna, and hence it is branded as Hīna (small, or low). This brings us to one of the fundamental points of distinction between Hīnayāna and Mahāyāna. The ultimate good of an adherent of the Hīnayāna is to attain his own nirvāṇa or salvation, whereas the ultimate goal of those who professed the Mahāyāna creed was not to seek their own salvation but to seek the salvation of all beings. So the Hīnayāna goal was lower, and in consequence of that the instructions that its followers received, the attempts they undertook, and the results they achieved were narrower than that of the Mahāyāna adherents. A Hīnayāna man had only a short business in attaining his own salvation, and this could be done in three lives, whereas a Mahāyāna adherent was prepared to work for infinite time in helping all beings to attain salvation. So the Hīnayāna adherents required only a short period of work and may from that point of view also be called *hīna*, or lower.

This point, though important from the point of view of the difference in the creed of the two schools, is not so from the point of view of philosophy. But there is another trait of the Mahāyānists which distinguishes them from the Hīnayānists from the philosophical point of view. The Mahāyānists believed that all things were of a non-essential and indefinable character and void at bottom, whereas the Hīnayānists only believed in the impermanence of all things, but did not proceed further than that.

It is sometimes erroneously thought that Nāgārjuna first preached the doctrine of Śūnyavāda (essencelessness or voidness of all appearance), but in reality almost all the Mahāyāna sūtras either definitely preach this doctrine or allude to it. Thus if we take some of those sūtras which were in all probability earlier than Nāgārjuna, we find that the doctrine which Nāgārjuna expounded

Brahmayāna (career of becoming a Brahmā), Tathāgatayāna (career of a Tathāgata). In one place *Laṅkāvatāra* says that ordinarily distinction is made between the three careers and one career and no career, but these distinctions are only for the ignorant (*Laṅkāvatāra*, p. 68).

with all the rigour of his powerful dialectic was quietly accepted as an indisputable truth. Thus we find Subhūti saying to the Buddha that vedanā (feeling), saṃjñā (concepts) and the saṃskāras (conformations) are all māyā (illusion)[1]. All the skandhas, dhātus (elements) and āyatanas are void and absolute cessation. The highest knowledge of everything as pure void is not different from the skandhas, dhātus and āyatanas, and this absolute cessation of dharmas is regarded as the highest knowledge (*prajñāpāramitā*)[2]. Everything being void there is in reality no process and no cessation. The truth is neither eternal (*śāśvata*) nor non-eternal (*aśāśvata*) but pure void. It should be the object of a saint's endeavour to put himself in the "thatness" (*tathatā*) and consider all things as void. The saint (*bodhisattva*) has to establish himself in all the virtues (*pāramitā*), benevolence (*dānapāramitā*), the virtue of character (*śīlapāramitā*), the virtue of forbearance (*kṣāntipāramitā*), the virtue of tenacity and strength (*vīryyapāramitā*) and the virtue of meditation (*dhyānapāramitā*). The saint (*bodhisattva*) is firmly determined that he will help an infinite number of souls to attain nirvāṇa. In reality, however, there are no beings, there is no bondage, no salvation; and the saint knows it but too well, yet he is not afraid of this high truth, but proceeds on his career of attaining for all illusory beings illusory emancipation from illusory bondage. The saint is actuated with that feeling and proceeds in his work on the strength of his pāramitās, though in reality there is no one who is to attain salvation in reality and no one who is to help him to attain it[3]. The true prajñāpāramitā is the absolute cessation of all appearance (*yaḥ anupalambhaḥ sarvadharmāṇām sa prajñāpāramitā ityucyate*)[4].

The Mahāyāna doctrine has developed on two lines, viz. that of Śūnyavāda or the Mādhyamika doctrine and Vijñānavāda. The difference between Śūnyavāda and Vijñānavāda (the theory that there is only the appearance of phenomena of consciousness) is not fundamental, but is rather one of method. Both of them agree in holding that there is no truth in anything, everything is only passing appearance akin to dream or magic. But while the Śūnyavādins were more busy in showing this indefinableness of all phenomena, the Vijñānavādins, tacitly accepting

[1] *Aṣṭasāhasrikāprajñāpāramitā*, p. 16.
[2] *Ibid.* p. 177.
[3] *Ibid.* p. 21.
[4] *Ibid.* p. 177.

the truth preached by the Śūnyavādins, interested themselves in explaining the phenomena of consciousness by their theory of beginningless illusory root-ideas or instincts of the mind (*vāsanā*).

Aśvaghoṣa (100 A.D.) seems to have been the greatest teacher of a new type of idealism (*vijñānavāda*) known as the Tathatā philosophy. Trusting in Suzuki's identification of a quotation in Aśvaghoṣa's *Śraddhotpādaśāstra* as being made from *Laṅkāvatārasūtra*, we should think of the *Laṅkāvatārasūtra* as being one of the early works of the Vijñānavādins[1]. The greatest later writer of the Vijñānavāda school was Asaṅga (400 A.D.), to whom are attributed the *Saptadaśabhūmi sūtra*, *Mahāyāna sūtra*, *Upadeśa*, *Mahāyānasamparigraha śāstra*, *Yogācārabhūmi śāstra* and *Mahāyānasūtrālaṃkāra*. None of these works excepting the last one is available to readers who have no access to the Chinese and Tibetan manuscripts, as the Sanskrit originals are in all probability lost. The Vijñānavāda school is known to Hindu writers by another name also, viz. Yogācāra, and it does not seem an improbable supposition that Asaṅga's *Yogācārabhūmi śāstra* was responsible for the new name. Vasubandhu, a younger brother of Asaṅga, was, as Paramārtha (499–569) tells us, at first a liberal Sarvāstivādin, but was converted to Vijñānavāda, late in his life, by Asaṅga. Thus Vasubandhu, who wrote in his early life the great standard work of the Sarvāstivādins, *Abhidharmakośa*, devoted himself in his later life to Vijñānavāda[2]. He is said to have commented upon a number of Mahāyāna sūtras, such as *Avataṃsaka*, *Nirvāṇa*, *Saddharmapuṇḍarīka*, *Prajñāpāramitā*, *Vimalakīrtti* and *Śrīmālāsiṃhanāda*, and compiled some Mahāyāna sūtras, such as *Vijñānamātrasiddhi*, *Ratnatraya*, etc. The school of Vijñānavāda continued for at least a century or two after Vasubandhu, but we are not in possession of any work of great fame of this school after him.

We have already noticed that the Śūnyavāda formed the fundamental principle of all schools of Mahāyāna. The most powerful exponent of this doctrine was Nāgārjuna (100 A.D.), a brief account of whose system will be given in its proper place. Nāgārjuna's kārikās (verses) were commented upon by Āryyadeva, a disciple of his, Kumārajīva (383 A.D.), Buddhapālita and Candrakīrtti (550 A.D.). Āryyadeva in addition to this commentary wrote at

[1] Dr S. C. Vidyābhūshana thinks that *Laṅkāvatāra* belongs to about 300 A.D.

[2] Takakusu's "A study of the Paramārtha's life of Vasubandhu," *J. R. A. S.* 1905.

least three other books, viz. *Catuḥśataka, Hastabālaprakaraṇavṛtti* and *Cittaviśuddhiprakaraṇa*[1]. In the small work called *Hastabālaprakaraṇavṛtti* Āryyadeva says that whatever depends for its existence on anything else may be proved to be illusory; all our notions of external objects depend on space perceptions and notions of part and whole and should therefore be regarded as mere appearance. Knowing therefore that all that is dependent on others for establishing itself is illusory, no wise man should feel attachment or antipathy towards these mere phenomenal appearances. In his *Cittaviśuddhiprakaraṇa* he says that just as a crystal appears to be coloured, catching the reflection of a coloured object, even so the mind though in itself colourless appears to show diverse colours by coloration of imagination (*vikalpa*). In reality the mind (*citta*) without a touch of imagination (*kalpanā*) in it is the pure reality.

It does not seem however that the Śūnyavādins could produce any great writers after Candrakīrtti. References to Śūnyavāda show that it was a living philosophy amongst the Hindu writers until the time of the great Mīmaṃsā authority Kumārila who flourished in the eighth century; but in later times the Śūnyavādins were no longer occupying the position of strong and active disputants.

The Tathatā Philosophy of Aśvaghoṣa (80 A.D.)[2].

Aśvaghoṣa was the son of a Brahmin named Saiṃhaguhya who spent his early days in travelling over the different parts of India and defeating the Buddhists in open debates. He was probably converted to Buddhism by Pārśva who was an important person in the third Buddhist Council promoted, according to some authorities, by the King of Kashmere and according to other authorities by Puṇyayaśas[3].

[1] Āryyadeva's *Hastabālaprakaraṇavṛtti* has been reclaimed by Dr F. W. Thomas. Fragmentary portions of his *Cittaviśuddhiprakaraṇa* were published by Mahāmahopādhyāya Haraprasāda śāstrī in the Bengal Asiatic Society's journal, 1898.

[2] The above section is based on the *Awakening of Faith*, an English translation by Suzuki of the Chinese version of *Śraddhotpādaśāstra* by Aśvaghoṣa, the Sanskrit original of which appears to have been lost. Suzuki has brought forward a mass of evidence to show that Aśvaghoṣa was a contemporary of Kaniṣka.

[3] Tāranātha says that he was converted by Āryadeva, a disciple of Nāgārjuna, *Geschichte des Buddhismus*, German translation by Schiefner, pp. 84–85. See Suzuki's *Awakening of Faith*, pp. 24–32. Aśvaghoṣa wrote the *Buddhacaritakāvya*, of great poetical excellence, and the *Mahālaṃkāraśāstra*. He was also a musician and had

He held that in the soul two aspects may be distinguished —the aspect as thatness (*bhūtatathatā*) and the aspect as the cycle of birth and death (*saṃsāra*). The soul as bhūtatathatā means the oneness of the totality of all things (*dharmadhātu*). Its essential nature is uncreate and external. All things simply on account of the beginningless traces of the incipient and unconscious memory of our past experiences of many previous lives (*smṛti*) appear under the forms of individuation[1]. If we could overcome this smrti "the signs of individuation would disappear and there would be no trace of a world of objects." "All things in their fundamental nature are not nameable or explicable. They cannot be adequately expressed in any form of language. They possess absolute sameness (*samatā*). They are subject neither to transformation nor to destruction. They are nothing but one soul" —thatness (*bhūtatathatā*). This "thatness" has no attribute and it can only be somehow pointed out in speech as "thatness." As soon as you understand that when the totality of existence is spoken of or thought of, there is neither that which speaks nor that which is spoken of, there is neither that which thinks nor that which is thought of, "this is the stage of thatness." This bhūtatathatā is neither that which is existence, nor that which is non-existence, nor that which is at once existence and non-existence, nor that which is not at once existence and non-existence; it is neither that which is plurality, nor that which is at once unity and plurality, nor that which is not at once unity and plurality. It is a negative concept in the sense that it is beyond all that is conditional and yet it is a positive concept in the sense that it holds all within it. It cannot be comprehended by any kind of particularization or distinction. It is only by transcending the range of our intellectual categories of the comprehension of the limited range of finite phenomena that we can get a glimpse of it. It cannot be comprehended by the particularizing consciousness of all beings, and we thus may call it negation, "śūnyatā," in this sense. The truth is that which

invented a musical instrument called Rāstavara that he might by that means convert the people of the city. "Its melody was classical, mournful, and melodious, inducing the audience to ponder on the misery, emptiness, and non-ātmanness of life." Suzuki, p. 35.

[1] I have ventured to translate "*smṛti*" in the sense of vāsanā in preference to Suzuki's "confused subjectivity" because smṛti in the sense of vāsanā is not unfamiliar to the readers of such Buddhist works as *Laṅkāvatāra*. The word "subjectivity" seems to be too European a term to be used as a word to represent the Buddhist sense.

subjectively does not exist by itself, that the negation (*śūnyatā*) is also void (*śūnya*) in its nature, that neither that which is negated nor that which negates is an independent entity. It is the pure soul that manifests itself as eternal, permanent, immutable, and completely holds all things within it. On that account it may be called affirmation. But yet there is no trace of affirmation in it, because it is not the product of the creative instinctive memory (*smṛti*) of conceptual thought and the only way of grasping the truth—the thatness, is by transcending all conceptual creations.

"The soul as birth and death (*saṃsāra*) comes forth from the Tathāgata womb (*tathāgatagarbha*), the ultimate reality. But the immortal and the mortal coincide with each other. Though they are not identical they are not duality either. Thus when the absolute soul assumes a relative aspect by its self-affirmation it is called the all-conserving mind (*ālayavijñāna*). It embraces two principles, (1) enlightenment, (2) non-enlightenment. Enlightenment is the perfection of the mind when it is free from the corruptions of the creative instinctive incipient memory (*smṛti*). It penetrates all and is the unity of all (*dharmadhātu*). That is to say, it is the universal dharmakāya of all Tathāgatas constituting the ultimate foundation of existence.

"When it is said that all consciousness starts from this fundamental truth, it should not be thought that consciousness had any real origin, for it was merely phenomenal existence—a mere imaginary creation of the perceivers under the influence of the delusive smṛti. The multitude of people (*bahujana*) are said to be lacking in enlightenment, because ignorance (*avidyā*) prevails there from all eternity, because there is a constant succession of smṛti (past confused memory working as instinct) from which they have never been emancipated. But when they are divested of this smṛti they can then recognize that no states of mentation, viz. their appearance, presence, change and disappearance, have any reality. They are neither in a temporal nor in a spatial relation with the one soul, for they are not self-existent.

"This high enlightenment shows itself imperfectly in our corrupted phenomenal experience as prajñā (wisdom) and karma (incomprehensible activity of life). By pure wisdom we understand that when one, by virtue of the perfuming power of dharma, disciplines himself truthfully (i.e. according to the dharma) and accomplishes meritorious deeds, the mind (i.e. the *ālayavijñāna*) which implicates itself with birth and death will be broken down and the modes of the evolving consciousness will be annulled, and the pure and the genuine wisdom of the Dharmakāya will manifest itself. Though all modes of consciousness and mentation are mere products of ignorance, ignorance in its ultimate nature is identical and non-identical with enlightenment; and therefore ignorance is in one sense destructible, though in another sense it is indestructible. This may be illustrated by the simile of the water and the waves which are stirred up in the ocean. Here the water can be said to be both identical and non-identical with the waves. The waves are stirred up by the wind, but the water remains the same. When the wind ceases the motion of the waves subsides, but the water remains the same. Likewise when the mind of all creatures, which in its own nature is pure and clean, is stirred up by the wind of ignorance (*avidyā*), the waves of mentality (*vijñāna*) make their appearance. These three (i.e. the mind, ignorance, and mentality) however have no existence, and they are neither unity nor plurality. When the ignorance is annihilated, the awakened mentality is tranquillized, whilst the essence of the wisdom remains unmolested." The truth or the enlightenment "is absolutely unobtainable by any modes of relativity or by any outward signs of enlightenment. All events in the phenomenal world are reflected in enlightenment, so that they neither pass out of it, nor enter into it, and they neither disappear nor are destroyed." It is for ever cut off from the hindrances both affectional (*kleśāvaraṇa*) and intellectual (*jñeyāvaraṇa*), as well as from the mind (i.e. *ālayavijñāna*) which implicates itself with birth and death, since it is in its true nature clean, pure, eternal, calm, and immutable. The truth again is such that it transforms and unfolds itself wherever conditions are favourable in the form of a tathāgata or in some other forms, in order that all beings may be induced thereby to bring their virtue to maturity.

"Non-elightenment has no existence of its own aside from its relation with enlightenment *a priori*." But enlightenment *a priori* is spoken of only in contrast to non-enlightenment, and as non-enlightenment is a non-entity, true enlightenment in turn loses its significance too. They are distinguished only in mutual relation as enlightenment or non-enlightenment. The manifestations of non-enlightenment are made in three ways: (1) as a disturbance of the mind (*ālayavijñāna*), by the avidyākarma (ignorant action), producing misery (*duḥkha*); (2) by the appearance of an ego or of a perceiver; and (3) by the creation of an external world which does not exist in itself, independent of the perceiver. Conditioned by the unreal external world six kinds of phenomena arise in succession. The first phenomenon is intelligence (sensation); being affected by the external world the mind becomes conscious of the difference between the agreeable and the disagreeable. The second phenomenon is succession. Following upon intelligence, memory retains the sensations, agreeable as well as disagreeable, in a continuous succession of subjective states. The third phenomenon is clinging. Through the retention and succession of sensations, agreeable as well as disagreeable, there arises the desire of clinging. The fourth phenomenon is an attachment to names or ideas (*saṃjñā*), etc. By clinging the mind hypostatizes all names whereby to give definitions to all things. The fifth phenomenon is the performance of deeds (*karma*). On account of attachment to names, etc., there arise all the variations of deeds, productive of individuality. "The sixth phenomenon is the suffering due to the fetter of deeds. Through deeds suffering arises in which the mind finds itself entangled and curtailed of its freedom." All these phenomena have thus sprung forth through avidyā.

The relation between this truth and avidyā is in one sense a mere identity and may be illustrated by the simile of all kinds of pottery which though different are all made of the same clay[1]. Likewise the undefiled (*anāsrava*) and ignorance (*avidyā*) and their various transient forms all come from one and the same entity. Therefore Buddha teaches that all beings are from all eternity abiding in Nirvāṇa.

It is by the touch of ignorance (*avidyā*) that this truth assumes all the phenomenal forms of existence.

In the all-conserving mind (*ālayavijñāna*) ignorance manifests itself; and from non-enlightenment starts that which sees, that which represents, that which apprehends an objective world, and that which constantly particularizes. This is called ego (*manas*). Five different names are given to the ego (according to its different modes of operation). The first name is activity-consciousness (*karmavijñāna*) in the sense that through the agency of ignorance an unenlightened mind begins to be disturbed (or

[1] Compare Chāndogya, VI. I. 4.

awakened). The second name is evolving-consciousness (*pravṛtti-vijñāna*) in the sense that when the mind is disturbed, there evolves that which sees an external world. The third name is representation-consciousness in the sense that the ego (*manas*) represents (or reflects) an external world. As a clean mirror reflects the images of all description, it is even so with the representation-consciousness. When it is confronted, for instance, with the objects of the five senses, it represents them instantaneously and without effort. The fourth is particularization-consciousness, in the sense that it discriminates between different things defiled as well as pure. The fifth name is succession-consciousness, in the sense that continuously directed by the awakening consciousness of attention (*manaskāra*) it (*manas*) retains all experiences and never loses or suffers the destruction of any karma, good as well as evil, which had been sown in the past, and whose retribution, painful or agreeable, it never fails to mature, be it in the present or in the future, and also in the sense that it unconsciously recollects things gone by and in imagination anticipates things to come. Therefore the three domains (*kāmaloka*, domain of feeling—*rūpaloka*, domain of bodily existence—*arūpaloka*, domain of incorporeality) are nothing but the self manifestation of the mind (i.e. *ālayavijñāna* which is practically identical with *bhūtatathatā*). Since all things, owing the principle of their existence to the mind (*ālayavijñāna*), are produced by smṛti, all the modes of particularization are the self-particularizations of the mind. The mind in itself (or the soul) being however free from all attributes is not differentiated. Therefore we come to the conclusion that all things and conditions in the phenomenal world, hypostatized and established only through ignorance (*avidyā*) and memory (*smṛti*), have no more reality than the images in a mirror. They arise simply from the ideality of a particularizing mind. When the mind is disturbed, the multiplicity of things is produced; but when the mind is quieted, the multiplicity of things disappears. By ego-consciousness (*manovijñāna*) we mean the ignorant mind which by its succession-consciousness clings to the conception of I and Not-I and misapprehends the nature of the six objects of sense. The ego-consciousness is also called separation-consciousness, because it is nourished by the perfuming influence of the prejudices (*āsrava*), intellectual as well as affectional. Thus believing in the external world produced by memory, the mind becomes oblivious of the principle of sameness (*samatā*) that underlies all things which are one and perfectly calm and tranquil and show no sign of becoming.

Non-enlightenment is the *raison d'être* of saṃsāra. When this is annihilated the conditions—the external world—are also annihilated and with them the state of an interrelated mind is also annihilated. But this annihilation does not mean the annihilation of the mind but of its modes only. It becomes calm like an unruffled sea when all winds which were disturbing it and producing the waves have been annihilated.

In describing the relation of the interaction of avidyā (ignorance), karmavijñāna (activity-consciousness—the subjective mind), viṣaya (external world—represented by the senses) and the tathatā (suchness), Aśvaghoṣa says that there is an interperfuming of these elements. Thus Aśvaghoṣa says, "By perfuming we mean that while our worldly clothes (viz. those which we wear) have no odour of their own, neither offensive nor agreeable, they can yet acquire one or the other odour according to the nature of the substance with which they are perfumed. Suchness (*tathatā*) is likewise a pure dharma free from all defilements caused by the perfuming power of ignorance. On the other hand ignorance has nothing to do with purity. Nevertheless we speak of its being able to do the work of purity because it in its turn is perfumed by suchness. Determined by suchness ignorance becomes the *raison d'être* of all forms of defilement. And this ignorance perfumes suchness and produces smṛti. This smṛti in its turn perfumes ignorance. On account of this (reciprocal) perfuming, the truth is misunderstood. On account of its being misunderstood an external world of subjectivity appears. Further, on account of the perfuming power of memory, various modes of individuation are produced. And by clinging to them various deeds are done, and we suffer as the result miseries mentally as well as bodily." Again "suchness perfumes ignorance, and in consequence of this perfuming the individual in subjectivity is caused to loathe the misery of birth and death and to seek after the blessing of Nirvāṇa. This longing and loathing on the part of the subjective mind in turn perfumes suchness. On account of this perfuming influence we are enabled to believe that we are in possession within ourselves of suchness whose essential nature is pure and immaculate; and we also recognize that all phenomena in the world are nothing but the illusory manifestations of the mind (*ālayavijñāna*) and have no reality of their own. Since we thus rightly understand the truth, we can practise the means of liberation, can perform those actions which are in accordance with the dharma. We should neither particularize, nor cling to objects of desire. By virtue of this discipline and habituation during the lapse of innumerable āsaṅkhyeyakalpas[1] we get ignorance annihilated. As ignorance is thus annihilated, the mind (*ālayavijñāna*) is no longer disturbed, so as to be subject to individuation. As the mind is no longer disturbed, the particularization of the surrounding world is annihilated. When in this wise the principle and the condition of defilement, their products, and the mental disturbances are all annihilated, it is said that we attain Nirvāṇa and that various spontaneous displays of activity are accomplished." The Nirvāṇa of the tathatā philosophy is not nothingness, but tathatā (suchness or thatness) in its purity unassociated with any kind of disturbance which produces all the diversity of experience.

To the question that if all beings are uniformly in possession of suchness and are therefore equally perfumed by it, how is it that there are some who do not believe in it, while others do, Aśvaghoṣa's reply is that though all beings are uniformly in possession of suchness, the intensity of ignorance and the principle of individuation, that work from all eternity, vary in such manifold grades as to outnumber the sands of the Ganges, and hence the difference. There is an inherent perfuming principle in one's own being which, embraced and protected by the love (*maitrī*) and compassion (*karuṇā*) of all Buddhas and Bodhisattvas, is caused to loathe the misery of birth and death, to believe in nirvāṇa, to cultivate the root of merit (*kuśalamūla*), to habituate oneself to it and to bring it to maturity. In consequence of this, one is enabled to see all Buddhas and Bodhisattvas and, receiving instructions from them, is benefited, gladdened and induced to practise good deeds, etc., till one can attain to Buddhahood and enter into Nirvāṇa. This implies that all beings have such perfuming power in them that they may be affected by the good wishes of the Buddhas and Bodhisattvas for leading them to the path of virtue, and thus it is that sometimes hearing the Bodhisattvas and sometimes seeing them, "all beings thereby acquire (spiritual) benefits (*hitatā*)" and "entering into the samādhi of purity, they

[1] Technical name for a very vast period of time.

destroy hindrances wherever they are met with and obtain all-penetrating insight that enables them to become conscious of the absolute oneness (*samatā*) of the universe (*sarvaloka*) and to see innumerable Buddhas and Bodhisattvas."

There is a difference between the perfuming which is not in unison with suchness, as in the case of śrāvakas (theravādin monks), pratyekabuddhas and the novice bodhisattvas, who only continue their religious discipline but do not attain to the state of non-particularization in unison with the essence of suchness. But those bodhisattvas whose perfuming is already in unison with suchness attain to the state of non-particularization and allow themselves to be influenced only by the power of the dharma. The incessant perfuming of the defiled dharma (ignorance from all eternity) works on, but when one attains to Buddhahood one at once puts an end to it. The perfuming of the pure dharma (i.e. suchness) however works on to eternity without any interruption. For this suchness or thatness is the effulgence of great wisdom, the universal illumination of the dharmadhātu (universe), the true and adequate knowledge, the mind pure and clean in its own nature, the eternal, the blessed, the self-regulating and the pure, the tranquil, the inimitable and the free, and this is called the tathāgatagarbha or the dharmakāya. It may be objected that since thatness or suchness has been described as being without characteristics, it is now a contradiction to speak of it as embracing all merits, but it is held, that in spite of its embracing all merits, it is free in its nature from all forms of distinction, because all objects in the world are of one and the same taste; and being of one reality they have nothing to do with the modes of particularization or of dualistic character. "Though all things in their (metaphysical) origin come from the soul alone and in truth are free from particularization, yet on account of non-enlightenment there originates a subjective mind (*ālayavijñāna*) that becomes conscious of an external world." This is called ignorance or avidyā. Nevertheless the pure essence of the mind is perfectly pure and there is no awakening of ignorance in it. Hence we assign to suchness this quality, the effulgence of great wisdom. It is called universal illumination, because there is nothing for it to illumine. This perfuming of suchness therefore continues for ever, though the stage of the perfuming of avidyā comes to an end with the Buddhas when they attain to nirvāṇa. All Buddhas while at the stage of discipline feel a deep compassion (*mahākaruṇā*) for all beings, practise all virtues (*pāramitās*) and many other meritorious deeds, treat others as their own selves, and wish to work out a universal salvation of mankind in ages to come, through limitless numbers of *kalpas*, recognize truthfully and adequately the principle of equality (*samatā*) among people; and do not cling to the individual existence of a sentient being. This is what is meant by the activity of tathatā. The main idea of this tathatā philosophy seems to be this, that this transcendent "thatness" is at once the quintessence of all thought and activity; as avidyā veils it or perfumes it, the world-appearance springs forth, but as the pure thatness also perfumes the avidyā there is a striving for the good as well. As the stage of avidyā is passed its luminous character shines forth, for it is the ultimate truth which only illusorily appeared as the many of the world.

This doctrine seems to be more in agreement with the view of an absolute unchangeable reality as the ultimate truth than that of the nihilistic idealism of *Laṅkāvatāra*. Considering the fact that Aśvaghoṣa was a learned Brahmin scholar in his early life, it is easy to guess that there was much Upaniṣad influence in this interpretation of Buddhism, which compares so favourably with the Vedānta as interpreted by Śaṅkara. The *Laṅkāvatāra* admitted a reality only as a make-believe to attract the Tairthikas (heretics) who had a prejudice in favour of an unchangeable self (*ātman*). But Aśvaghoṣa plainly admitted an unspeakable reality as the ultimate truth. Nāgārjuna's Mādhyamika doctrines which eclipsed the profound philosophy of Aśvaghoṣa seem to be more faithful to the traditional Buddhist creed and to the Vijñānavāda creed of Buddhism as explained in the *Laṅkāvatāra*[1].

The Mādhyamika or the Śūnyavāda school.—Nihilism.

Candrakīrtti, the commentator of Nāgārjuna's verses known as "*Mādhyamika kārikā*," in explaining the doctrine of dependent origination (*pratītyasamutpāda*) as described by Nāgārjuna starts with two interpretations of the word. According to one the word pratītyasamutpāda means the origination (*utpāda*) of the non-existent (*abhāva*) depending on (*pratītya*) reasons and causes

[1] As I have no access to the Chinese translation of Aśvaghoṣa's *Śraddhotpāda Śāstra*, I had to depend entirely on Suzuki's expressions as they appear in his translation.

(hetupratyaya). According to the other interpretation pratītya means each and every destructible individual and pratītyasamutpāda means the origination of each and every destructible individual. But he disapproves of both these meanings. The second meaning does not suit the context in which the Pāli Scriptures generally speak of pratītyasamutpāda (e.g. *cakṣuḥ pratītya rūpāni ca utpadyante cakṣurvijñānam*) for it does not mean the origination of each and every destructible individual, but the originating of specific individual phenomena (e.g. perception of form by the operation in connection with the eye) depending upon certain specific conditions.

The first meaning also is equally unsuitable. Thus for example if we take the case of any origination, e.g. that of the visual percept, we see that there cannot be any contact between visual knowledge and physical sense, the eye, and so it would not be intelligible that the former should depend upon the latter. If we interpret the maxim of pratītyasamutpāda as this happening that happens, that would not explain any specific origination. All origination is false, for a thing can neither originate by itself nor by others, nor by a co-operation of both nor without any reason. For if a thing exists already it cannot originate again by itself. To suppose that it is originated by others would also mean that the origination was of a thing already existing. If again without any further qualification it is said that depending on one the other comes into being, then depending on anything any other thing could come into being—from light we could have darkness! Since a thing could not originate from itself or by others, it could not also be originated by a combination of both of them together. A thing also could not originate without any cause, for then all things could come into being at all times. It is therefore to be acknowledged that wherever the Buddha spoke of this so-called dependent origination (*pratītyasamutpāda*) it was referred to as illusory manifestations appearing to intellects and senses stricken with ignorance. This dependent origination is not thus a real law, but only an appearance due to ignorance (*avidyā*). The only thing which is not lost (*amoṣadharma*) is nirvāṇa; but all other forms of knowledge and phenomena (*saṃskāras*) are false and are lost with their appearances (*sarvasaṃskārāśca mṛṣāmoṣadharmāṇaḥ*).

It is sometimes objected to this doctrine that if all appearances are false, then they do not exist at all. There are then no good or bad works and no cycle of existence, and if such is the case, then it may be argued that no philosophical discussion should be attempted. But the reply to such an objection is that the nihilistic doctrine is engaged in destroying the misplaced confidence of the people that things are true. Those who are really wise do not find anything either false or true, for to them clearly they do not exist at all and they do not trouble themselves with the question of their truth or falsehood. For him who knows thus there are neither works nor cycles of births (*saṃsāra*) and also he does not trouble himself about the existence or non-existence of any of the appearances. Thus it is said in the Ratnakūṭasūtra that howsoever carefully one may search one cannot discover consciousness (*citta*); what cannot be perceived cannot be said to exist, and what does not exist is neither past, nor future, nor present, and as such it cannot be said to have any nature at all; and that which has no nature is subject neither to origination nor to extinction. He who through his false knowledge (*viparyyāsa*) does not comprehend the falsehood of all appearances, but thinks them to be real, works and suffers the cycles of rebirth (*saṃsāra*). Like all illusions, though false these appearances can produce all the harm of rebirth and sorrow.

It may again be objected that if there is nothing true according to the nihilists (*śūnyavādins*), then their statement that there is no origination or extinction is also not true. Candrakīrtti in replying to this says that with śūnyavādins the truth is absolute silence. When the Śūnyavādin sages argue, they only accept for the moment what other people regard as reasons, and deal with them in their own manner to help them to come to a right comprehension of all appearances. It is of no use to say, in spite of all arguments tending to show the falsehood of all appearances, that they are testified by our experience, for the whole thing that we call "our experience" is but false illusion inasmuch as these phenomena have no true essence.

When the doctrine of pratītyasamutpāda is described as "this being that is," what is really meant is that things can only be indicated as mere appearances one after another, for they have no essence or true nature. Nihilism (*śūnyavāda*) also means just this. The true meaning of pratītyasamutpāda or śūnyavāda is this, that there is no truth, no essence in all phenomena that appear[1]. As the phenomena have no essence they are neither produced nor destroyed; they really neither come nor go. They are merely the appearance of māyā or illusion. The void (*śūnya*) does not mean pure negation, for that is relative to some kind of position. It simply means that none of the appearances have any intrinsic nature of their own (*niḥsvabhāvatvaṃ*).

The Madhyamaka or Śūnya system does not hold that anything has any essence or nature (*svabhāva*) of its own; even heat cannot be said to be the essence of fire; for both the heat and the fire are the result of the combination of many conditions, and what depends on many conditions cannot be said to be the nature or essence of the thing. That alone may be said to be the true essence or nature of anything which does not depend on anything else, and since no such essence or nature can be pointed out which stands independently by itself we cannot say that it exists. If a thing has no essence or existence of its own, we cannot affirm the essence of other things to it (*parabhāva*). If we cannot affirm anything of anything as positive, we cannot consequently assert anything of anything as negative. If anyone first believes in things positive and afterwards discovers that they are not so, he no doubt thus takes his stand on a negation (*abhāva*), but in reality since we cannot speak of anything positive, we cannot speak of anything negative either[2].

It is again objected that we nevertheless perceive a process going on. To this the Madhyamaka reply is that a process of change could not be affirmed of things that are permanent. But we can hardly speak of a process with reference to momentary things; for those which are momentary are destroyed the next moment after they appear, and so there is nothing which can continue to justify a process. That which appears as being neither comes from anywhere nor goes anywhere, and that which appears as destroyed also does not come from anywhere nor go anywhere, and so a process (*saṃsāra*) cannot be affirmed of them. It cannot be that when the second moment arose, the first moment had suffered a change in the process, for it was not the same as the second, as there is no so-called cause-effect connection. In fact there being no relation between the two, the temporal determination as prior and later is wrong. The supposition that there is a self which suffers changes is also not valid, for howsoever we

[1] See *Mādhyamikavṛtti* (B.T.S.), p. 50. [2] *Ibid.* pp. 93–100.

may search we find the five skandhas but no self. Moreover if the soul is a unity it cannot undergo any process or progression, for that would presuppose that the soul abandons one character and takes up another at the same identical moment which is inconceivable[1].

But then again the question arises that if there is no process, and no cycle of worldly existence of thousands of afflictions, what is then the nirvāṇa which is described as the final extinction of all afflictions (*kleśa*)? To this the Madhyamaka reply is that it does not agree to such a definition of nirvāṇa. Nirvāṇa on the Madhyamaka theory is the absence of the essence of all phenomena, that which cannot be conceived either as anything which has ceased or as anything which is produced (*aniruddham anutpannam*). In nirvāṇa all phenomena are lost; we say that the phenomena cease to exist in nirvāṇa, but like the illusory snake in the rope they never existed[2]. Nirvāṇa cannot be any positive thing or any sort of state of being (*bhāva*), for all positive states or things are joint products of combined causes (*saṃskṛta*) and are liable to decay and destruction. Neither can it be a negative existence, for since we cannot speak of any positive existence, we cannot speak of a negative existence either. The appearances or the phenomena are communicated as being in a state of change and process coming one after another, but beyond that no essence, existence, or truth can be affirmed of them. Phenomena sometimes appear to be produced and sometimes to be destroyed, but they cannot be determined as existent or non-existent. Nirvāṇa is merely the cessation of the seeming phenomenal flow (*prapañcapravṛtti*). It cannot therefore be designated either as positive or as negative for these conceptions belong to phenomena (*na cāpravṛttimātram bhāvābhāveti parikalpitum pāryyate evam na bhāvābhāvanirvāṇam*, M.V. 197). In this state there is nothing which is known, and even the knowledge that the phenomena have ceased to appear is not found. Even the Buddha himself is a phenomenon, a mirage or a dream, and so are all his teachings[3].

It is easy to see that in this system there cannot exist any bondage or emancipation; all phenomena are like shadows, like the mirage, the dream, the māyā, and the magic without any real nature (*niḥsvabhāva*). It is mere false knowledge to suppose that

[1] See *Mādhyamikavṛtti* (B.T.S.), pp. 101–102.
[2] *Ibid.* p. 194.
[3] *Ibid.* pp. 162 and 201.

one is trying to win a real nirvāṇa[1]. It is this false egoism that is to be considered as avidyā. When considered deeply it is found that there is not even the slightest trace of any positive existence. Thus it is seen that if there were no ignorance (*avidyā*), there would have been no conformations (*saṃskāras*), and if there were no conformations there would have been no consciousness, and so on; but it cannot be said of the ignorance "I am generating the saṃskāras," and it can be said of the saṃskāras "we are being produced by the avidyā." But there being avidyā, there come the saṃskāras and so on with other categories too. This character of the pratītyasamutpāda is known as the coming of the consequent depending on an antecedent reason (*hetūpanibandha*).

It can be viewed from another aspect, namely that of dependence on conglomeration or combination (*pratyayopanibandha*). It is by the combination (*samavāya*) of the four elements, space (*ākāśa*) and consciousness (*vijñāna*) that a man is made. It is due to earth (*pṛthivī*) that the body becomes solid, it is due to water that there is fat in the body, it is due to fire that there is digestion, it is due to wind that there is respiration; it is due to ākāśa that there is porosity, and it is due to vijñāna that there is mind-consciousness. It is by their mutual combination that we find a man as he is. But none of these elements think that they have done any of the functions that are considered to be allotted to them. None of these are real substances or beings or souls. It is by ignorance that these are thought of as existents and attachment is generated for them. Through ignorance thus come the saṃskāras, consisting of attachment, antipathy and thoughtlessness (*rāga*, *dveṣa*, *moha*); from these proceed the vijñāna and the four skandhas. These with the four elements bring about name and form (*nāmarūpa*), from these proceed the senses (*ṣaḍāyatana*), from the coming together of those three comes contact (*sparśa*); from that feelings, from that comes desire (*tṛṣṇā*) and so on. These flow on like the stream of a river, but there is no essence or truth behind them all or as the ground of them all[2]. The phenomena therefore cannot be said to be either existent or non-existent, and no truth can be affirmed of either eternalism (*śāśvatavāda*) or nihilism (*ucchedavāda*), and it is for this reason

[1] See *Mādhyamikavṛtti* (B.T.S.), pp. 101–108.

[2] *Ibid.* pp. 209–211, quoted from *Śālistambhasūtra.* Vācaspatimiśra also quotes this passage in his *Bhāmatī* on Śaṅkara's *Brahma-sūtra.*

that this doctrine is called the middle doctrine (*madhyamaka*)[1]. Existence and non-existence have only a relative truth (*saṃvṛtisatya*) in them, as in all phenomena, but there is no true reality (*paramārthasatya*) in them or anything else. Morality plays as high a part in this nihilistic system as it does in any other Indian system. I quote below some stanzas from Nāgārjuna's *Suhṛllekha* as translated by Wenzel (P.T.S. 1886) from the Tibetan translation.

6. Knowing that riches are unstable and void (*asāra*) give according to the moral precepts, to Bhikshus, Brahmins, the poor and friends for there is no better friend than giving.

7. Exhibit morality (*śīla*) faultless and sublime, unmixed and spotless, for morality is the supporting ground of all eminence, as the earth is of the moving and immovable.

8. Exercise the imponderable, transcendental virtues of charity, morality, patience, energy, meditation, and likewise wisdom, in order that, having reached the farther shore of the sea of existence, you may become a Jina prince.

9. View as enemies, avarice (*mātsaryya*), deceit (*śāṭhya*), duplicity (*māyā*), lust, indolence (*kausīdya*), pride (*māna*), greed (*rāga*), hatred (*dveṣa*) and pride (*mada*) concerning family, figure, glory, youth, or power.

15. Since nothing is so difficult of attainment as patience, open no door for anger; the Buddha has pronounced that he who renounces anger shall attain the degree of an anāgāmin (a saint who never suffers rebirth).

21. Do not look after another's wife; but if you see her, regard her, according to age, like your mother, daughter or sister.

24. Of him who has conquered the unstable, ever moving objects of the six senses and him who has overcome the mass of his enemies in battle, the wise praise the first as the greater hero.

29. Thou who knowest the world, be equanimous against the eight worldly conditions, gain and loss, happiness and suffering, fame and dishonour, blame and praise, for they are not objects for your thoughts.

37. But one (a woman) that is gentle as a sister, winning as a friend, careful of your well being as a mother, obedient as a servant her (you must) honour as the guardian god(dess) of the family.

40. Always perfectly meditate on (turn your thoughts to) kindness, pity, joy and indifference; then if you do not obtain a higher degree you (certainly) will obtain the happiness of Brahman's world (*brahmavihāra*).

41. By the four dhyānas completely abandoning desire (*kāma*), reflection (*vicāra*), joy (*prīti*), and happiness and pain (*sukha*, *duḥkha*) you will obtain as fruit the lot of a Brahman.

49. If you say "I am not the form, you thereby will understand I am not endowed with form, I do not dwell in form, the form does not dwell in me; and in like manner you will understand the voidness of the other four aggregates."

50. The aggregates do not arise from desire, nor from time, nor from

[1] See *Mādhyamikavṛtti* (B.T.S.), p. 160.

nature (*prakṛti*), not from themselves (*svabhāvāt*), nor from the Lord (*īśvara*), nor yet are they without cause; know that they arise from ignorance (*avidyā*) and desire (*tṛṣṇā*).

51. Know that attachment to religious ceremonies (*śīlabrataparāmarśa*), wrong views (*mithyādṛṣṭi*) and doubt (*vicikitsā*) are the three fetters.

53. Steadily instruct yourself (more and more) in the highest morality, the highest wisdom and the highest thought, for the hundred and fifty one rules (of the *prātimokṣa*) are combined perfectly in these three.

58. Because thus (as demonstrated) all this is unstable (*anitya*) without substance (*anātma*) without help (*aśaraṇa*) without protector (*anātha*) and without abode (*asthāna*) thou O Lord of men must become discontented with this worthless (*asāra*) kadali-tree of the orb.

104. If a fire were to seize your head or your dress you would extinguish and subdue it, even then endeavour to annihilate desire, for there is no other higher necessity than this.

105. By morality, knowledge and contemplation, attain the spotless dignity of the quieting and the subduing nirvāṇa not subject to age, death or decay, devoid of earth, water, fire, wind, sun and moon.

107. Where there is no wisdom (*prajñā*) there is also no contemplation (*dhyāna*), where there is no contemplation there is also no wisdom; but know that for him who possesses these two the sea of existence is like a grove.

Uncompromising Idealism or the School of Vijñānavāda Buddhism.

The school of Buddhist philosophy known as the Vijñānavāda or Yogācāra has often been referred to by such prominent teachers of Hindu thought as Kumārila and Śaṅkara. It agrees to a great extent with the Śūnyavādins whom we have already described. All the dharmas (qualities and substances) are but imaginary constructions of ignorant minds. There is no movement in the so-called external world as we suppose, for it does not exist. We construct it ourselves and then are ourselves deluded that it exists by itself (*nirmmitapratimohi*)[1]. There are two functions involved in our consciousness, viz. that which holds the perceptions (*khyāti vijñāna*), and that which orders them by imaginary constructions (*vastuprativikalpavijñāna*). The two functions however mutually determine each other and cannot be separately distinguished (*abhinnalakṣaṇe anyonyahetuke*). These functions are set to work on account of the beginningless instinctive tendencies inherent in them in relation to the world of appearance (*anādikāla-prapañca-vāsanāhetukañca*)[2].

All sense knowledge can be stopped only when the diverse

[1] *Laṅkāvatārasūtra*, pp. 21–22. [2] *Ibid.* p. 44.

unmanifested instincts of imagination are stopped (*abhūta-parikalpa-vāsanā-vaicitra-nirodha*)[1]. All our phenomenal knowledge is without any essence or truth (*nihsvabhāva*) and is but a creation of māyā, a mirage or a dream. There is nothing which may be called external, but all is the imaginary creation of the mind (*svacitta*), which has been accustomed to create imaginary appearances from beginningless time. This mind by whose movement these creations take place as subject and object has no appearance in itself and is thus without any origination, existence and extinction (*utpādasthitibhaṅgavarjjam*) and is called the ālaya-vijñāna. The reason why this ālayavijñāna itself is said to be without origination, existence, and extinction is probably this, that it is always a hypothetical state which merely explains all the phenomenal states that appear, and therefore it has no existence in the sense in which the term is used and we could not affirm any special essence of it.

We do not realize that all visible phenomena are of nothing external but of our own mind (*svacitta*), and there is also the beginningless tendency for believing and creating a phenomenal world of appearance. There is also the nature of knowledge (which takes things as the perceiver and the perceived) and there is also the instinct in the mind to experience diverse forms. On account of these four reasons there are produced in the ālayavijñāna (mind) the ripples of our sense experiences (*pravṛttivijñāna*) as in a lake, and these are manifested as sense experiences. All the five skandhas called *pañcavijñānakāya* thus appear in a proper synthetic form. None of the phenomenal knowledge that appears is either identical or different from the ālayavijñāna just as the waves cannot be said to be either identical or different from the ocean. As the ocean dances on in waves so the citta or the ālayavijñāna is also dancing as it were in its diverse operations (*vṛtti*). As citta it collects all movements (*karma*) within it, as manas it synthesizes (*vidhīyate*) and as vijñāna it constructs the fivefold perceptions (*vijñānen vijānāti dṛśyam kalpate pañcabhiḥ*)[2].

It is only due to māyā (illusion) that the phenomena appear in their twofold aspect as subject and object. This must always be regarded as an appearance (*samvṛtisatyatā*) whereas in the real aspect we could never say whether they existed (*bhāva*) or did not exist[3].

[1] *Laṅkāvatārasūtra*, p. 44. [2] *Ibid.* pp. 50–55.

[3] Asaṅga's *Mahāyānasūtrālaṃkāra*, pp. 58–59.

All phenomena both being and non-being are illusory (*sadasantaḥ māyopamāḥ*). When we look deeply into them we find that there is an absolute negation of all appearances, including even all negations, for they are also appearances. This would make the ultimate truth positive. But this is not so, for it is that in which the positive and negative are one and the same (*bhāvābhāvasamānatā*)[1]. Such a state which is complete in itself and has no name and no substance had been described in the Laṅkāvatārasūtra as thatness (*tathatā*)[2]. This state is also described in another place in the *Laṅkāvatāra* as voidness (*śūnyatā*) which is one and has no origination and no essence[3]. In another place it is also designated as tathāgatagarbha[4].

It may be supposed that this doctrine of an unqualified ultimate truth comes near to the Vedantic ātman or Brahman like the tathatā doctrine of Aśvaghoṣa; and we find in Laṅkāvatāra that Rāvaṇa asks the Buddha "How can you say that your doctrine of tathāgatagarbha was not the same as the ātman doctrine of the other schools of philosophers, for those heretics also consider the ātman as eternal, agent, unqualified, all-pervading and unchanged?" To this the Buddha is found to reply thus—"Our doctrine is not the same as the doctrine of those heretics; it is in consideration of the fact that the instruction of a philosophy which considered that there was no soul or substance in anything (*nairātmya*) would frighten the disciples, that I say that all things are in reality the tathāgatagarbha. This should not be regarded as ātman. Just as a lump of clay is made into various shapes, so it is the non-essential nature of all phenomena and their freedom from all characteristics (*sarvavikalpalakṣaṇavinivṛttam*) that is variously described as the garbha or the nairātmya (essencelessness). This explanation of tathāgatagarbha as the ultimate truth and reality is given in order to attract to our creed those heretics who are superstitiously inclined to believe in the ātman doctrine[5]."

So far as the appearance of the phenomena was concerned the idealistic Buddhists (*vijñānavādins*) agreed to the doctrine of pratītyasamutpāda with certain modifications. There was with them an external pratītyasamutpāda just as it appeared in the

1 Asaṅga's *Mahāyānasūtrālaṃkāra*, p. 65.

2 *Laṅkāvatārasūtra*, p. 70.

3 *Ibid.* p. 78.

4 *Ibid.* p. 80.

5 *Ibid.* pp. 80–81.

objective aspect and an internal pratītyasamutpāda. The external pratītyasamutpāda (dependent origination) is represented in the way in which material things (e.g. a jug) came into being by the co-operation of diverse elements—the lump of clay, the potter, the wheel, etc. The internal (*ādhyātmika*) pratītyasamutpāda was represented by avidyā, tṛṣṇā, karma, the skandhas, and the āyatanas produced out of them[1].

Our understanding is composed of two categories called the *pravicayabuddhi* and the *vikalpalakṣaṇagrahābhiniveśapratiṣṭhāpikābuddhi.* The pravicayabuddhi is that which always seeks to take things in either of the following four ways, that they are either this or the other (*ekatvānyatva*); either both or not both (*ubhayānubhaya*), either are or are not (*astināsti*), either eternal or non-eternal (*nityānitya*). But in reality none of these can be affirmed of the phenomena. The second category consists of that habit of the mind by virtue of which it constructs diversities and arranges them (created in their turn by its own constructive activity —*parikalpa*) in a logical order of diverse relations of subject and predicate, causal and other relations. He who knows the nature of these two categories of the mind knows that there is no external world of matter and that they are all experienced only in the mind. There is no water, but it is the sense construction of smoothness (*sneha*) that constructs the water as an external substance; it is the sense construction of activity or energy that constructs the external substance of fire; it is the sense construction of movement that constructs the external substance of air. In this way through the false habit of taking the unreal as the real (*mithyāsatyābhiniveśa*) five skandhas appear. If these were to appear all together, we could not speak of any kind of causal relations, and if they appeared in succession there could be no connection between them, as there is nothing to bind them together. In reality there is nothing which is produced or destroyed, it is only our constructive imagination that builds up things as perceived with all their relations, and ourselves as perceivers. It is simply a convention (*vyavahāra*) to speak of things as known[2]. Whatever we designate by speech is mere speech-construction (*vāgvikalpa*) and unreal. In speech one could not speak of anything without relating things in some kind of causal

[1] *Laṅkāvatārasūtra*, p. 85.

[2] *Laṅkāvatārasūtra*, p. 87, compare the term "vyavahārika" as used of the phenomenal and the conventional world in almost the same sense by Śaṅkara.

relation, but none of these characters may be said to be true; the real truth (*paramārtha*) can never be referred to by such speech-construction.

The nothingness (*śūnyatā*) of things may be viewed from seven aspects—(1) that they are always interdependent, and hence have no special characteristics by themselves, and as they cannot be determined in themselves they cannot be determined in terms of others, for, their own nature being undetermined, a reference to an "other" is also undetermined, and hence they are all indefinable (*lakṣaṇaśūnyatā*); (2) that they have no positive essence (*bhāvasvabhāvaśūnyatā*), since they spring up from a natural non-existence (*svabhāvābhāvotpatti*); (3) that they are of an unknown type of non-existence (*apracaritaśūnyatā*), since all the skandhas vanish in the nirvāṇa; (4) that they appear phenomenally as connected though non-existent (*pracaritaśūnyatā*), for their skandhas have no reality in themselves nor are they related to others, but yet they appear to be somehow causally connected; (5) that none of the things can be described as having any definite nature, they are all undemonstrable by language (*nirabhilapyaśūnyatā*); (6) that there cannot be any knowledge about them except that which is brought about by the long-standing defects of desires which pollute all our vision; (7) that things are also non-existent in the sense that we affirm them to be in a particular place and time in which they are not (*itaretaraśūnyatā*).

There is thus only non-existence, which again is neither eternal nor destructible, and the world is but a dream and a māyā; the two kinds of negation (*nirodha*) are ākāśa (space) and nirvāṇa; things which are neither existent nor non-existent are only imagined to be existent by fools.

This view apparently comes into conflict with the doctrine of this school, that the reality is called the tathāgatagarbha (the womb of all that is merged in thatness) and all the phenomenal appearances of the clusters (*skandhas*), elements (*dhātus*), and fields of sense operation (*āyatanas*) only serve to veil it with impurities, and this would bring it nearer to the assumption of a universal soul as the reality. But the *Laṅkāvatāra* attempts to explain away this conflict by suggesting that the reference to the tathāgatagarbha as the reality is only a sort of false bait to attract those who are afraid of listening to the nairātmya (non-soul) doctrine[1].

[1] *Laṅkāvatārasūtra*, p. 80.

The Bodhisattvas may attain their highest by the fourfold knowledge of (1) *svacittadṛśyabhāvanā*, (2) *utpādasthitibhaṅga-vivarjjanatā*, (3) *bāhyabhāvābhāvopalakṣaṇatā* and (4) *svapratyāryyajñānādhigamābhinnalakṣaṇatā*. The first means that all things are but creations of the imagination of one's mind. The second means that as things have no essence there is no origination, existence or destruction. The third means that one should know the distinctive sense in which all external things are said either to be existent or non-existent, for their existence is merely like the mirage which is produced by the beginningless desire (*vāsanā*) of creating and perceiving the manifold. This brings us to the fourth one, which means the right comprehension of the nature of all things.

The four dhyānas spoken of in the *Laṅkāvatāra* seem to be different from those which have been described in connection with the Theravāda Buddhism. These dhyānas are called (1) *bālopacārika*, (2) *arthapravicaya*, (3) *tathatālambana* and (4) *tathāgata*. The first one is said to be that practised by the śrāvakas and the pratyekabuddhas. It consists in concentrating upon the doctrine that there is no soul (*pudgalanairātmya*), and that everything is transitory, miserable and impure. When considering all things in this way from beginning to end the sage advances on till all conceptual knowing ceases (*āsaṃjñānirodhāt*); we have what is called the vālopacārika dhyāna (the meditation for beginners).

The second is the advanced state where not only there is full consciousness that there is no self, but there is also the comprehension that neither these nor the doctrines of other heretics may be said to exist, and that there is none of the dharmas that appears. This is called the *arthapravicayadhyāna*, for the sage concentrates here on the subject of thoroughly seeking out (*pravicaya*) the nature of all things (*artha*).

The third dhyāna, that in which the mind realizes that the thought that there is no self nor that there are the appearances, is itself the result of imagination and thus lapses into the thatness (*tathatā*). This dhyāna is called *tathatālambana*, because it has for its object tathatā or thatness.

The last or the fourth dhyāna is that in which the lapse of the mind into the state of thatness is such that the nothingness and incomprehensibility of all phenomena is perfectly realized;

and nirvāṇa is that in which all root desires (*vāsanā*) manifesting themselves in knowledge are destroyed and the mind with knowledge and perceptions, making false creations, ceases to work. This cannot be called death, for it will not have any rebirth and it cannot be called destruction, for only compounded things (*saṃskṛta*) suffer destruction, so that it is different from either death or destruction. This nirvāṇa is different from that of the śrāvakas and the pratyekabuddhas for they are satisfied to call that state nirvāṇa, in which by the knowledge of the general characteristics of all things (transitoriness and misery) they are not attached to things and cease to make erroneous judgments[1].

Thus we see that there is no cause (in the sense of ground) of all these phenomena as other heretics maintain. When it is said that the world is māyā or illusion, what is meant to be emphasized is this, that there is no cause, no ground. The phenomena that seem to originate, stay, and be destroyed are mere constructions of tainted imagination, and the tathatā or thatness is nothing but the turning away of this constructive activity or nature of the imagination (*vikalpa*) tainted with the associations of beginningless root desires (*vāsanā*)[2]. The tathatā has no separate reality from illusion, but it is illusion itself when the course of the construction of illusion has ceased. It is therefore also spoken of as that which is cut off or detached from the mind (*cittavimukta*), for here there is no construction of imagination (*sarvakalpanāvirahitam*)[3].

Sautrāntika Theory of Perception.

Dharmottara (847 A.D.), a commentator of Dharmakīrtti's[4] (about 635 A.D.) *Nyāyabindu*, a Sautrāntika logical and epistemological work, describes right knowledge (*samyagjñāna*) as an invariable antecedent to the accomplishment of all that a man

[1] *Laṅkāvatārasūtra*, p. 100. [2] *Ibid.* p. 109.

[3] This account of the Vijñānavāda school is collected mainly from *Laṅkāvatārasūtra*, as no other authentic work of the Vijñānavāda school is available. Hindu accounts and criticisms of this school may be had in such books as Kumarila's *Śloka vārttika* or Śaṅkara's bhāṣya, II. ii, etc. Asaṅga's *Mahāyānasūtrālaṃkāra* deals more with the duties concerning the career of a saint (*Bodhisattva*) than with the metaphysics of the system.

[4] Dharmakīrtti calls himself an adherent of Vijñānavāda in his *Santānāntarasiddhi*, a treatise on solipsism, but his *Nyāyabindu* seems rightly to have been considered by the author of *Nyāyabinduṭīkāṭippanī* (p. 19) as being written from the Sautrāntika point of view.

desires to have (*samyagjñānapūrvikā sarvapuruṣārthasiddhi*)[1]. When on proceeding, in accordance with the presentation of any knowledge, we get a thing as presented by it we call it right knowledge. Right knowledge is thus the knowledge by which one can practically acquire the thing he wants to acquire (*arthādhigati*). The process of knowledge, therefore, starts with the perceptual presentation and ends with the attainment of the thing represented by it and the fulfilment of the practical need by it (*arthādhigamāt samāptaḥ pramāṇavyāpāraḥ*). Thus there are three moments in the perceptual acquirement of knowledge: (1) the presentation, (2) our prompting in accordance with it, and (3) the final realization of the object in accordance with our endeavour following the direction of knowledge. Inference is also to be called right knowledge, as it also serves our practical need by representing the presence of objects in certain connections and helping us to realize them. In perception this presentation is direct, while in inference this is brought about indirectly through the liṅga (reason). Knowledge is sought by men for the realization of their ends, and the subject of knowledge is discussed in philosophical works only because knowledge is sought by men. Any knowledge, therefore, which will not lead us to the realization of the object represented by it could not be called right knowledge. All illusory perceptions, therefore, such as the perception of a white conch-shell as yellow or dream perceptions, are not right knowledge, since they do not lead to the realization of such objects as are presented by them. It is true no doubt that since all objects are momentary, the object which was perceived at the moment of perception was not the same as that which was realized at a later moment. But the series of existents which started with the first perception of a blue object finds itself realized by the realization of other existents of the same series (*nīlādau ya eva santānaḥ paricchinno nīlajñānena sa eva tena prāpitaḥ tena nīlajñānam pramāṇam*)[2].

When it is said that right knowledge is an invariable antecedent of the realization of any desirable thing or the retarding of any undesirable thing, it must be noted that it is not meant

[1] Brief extracts from the opinions of two other commentators of *Nyāyabindu*, Vinītadeva and Śāntabhadra (seventh century), are found in *Nyāyabinduṭīkāṭippanī*, a commentary of *Nyāyabinduṭīkā* of Dharmmottara, but their texts are not available to us.

[2] *Nyāyabinduṭīkāṭippanī*, p. 11.

that right knowledge is directly the cause of it; for, with the rise of any right perception, there is a memory of past experiences, desire is aroused, through desire an endeavour in accordance with it is launched, and as a result of that there is realization of the object of desire. Thus, looked at from this point of view, right knowledge is not directly the cause of the realization of the object. Right knowledge of course directly indicates the presentation, the object of desire, but so far as the object is a mere presentation it is not a subject of enquiry. It becomes a subject of enquiry only in connection with our achieving the object presented by perception.

Perception (*pratyakṣa*) has been defined by Dharmakīrtti as a presentation, which is generated by the objects alone, unassociated by any names or relations (*kalpanā*) and which is not erroneous (*kalpanāpoḍhamabhrāntam*)[1]. This definition does not indeed represent the actual nature (*svarūpa*) of perception, but only shows the condition which must be fulfilled in order that anything may be valid perception. What is meant by saying that a perception is not erroneous is simply this, that it will be such that if one engages himself in an endeavour in accordance with it, he will not be baffled in the object which was presented to him by his perception (*tasmādgrāhye arthe vasturūpe yadaviparyastam tadabhrāntamiha veditavyam*). It is said that a right perception could not be associated with names (*kalpanā* or *abhilāpa*). This qualification is added only with a view of leaving out all that is not directly generated by the object. A name is given to a thing only when it is associated in the mind, through memory, as being the same as perceived before. This cannot, therefore, be regarded as being produced by the object of perception. The senses present the objects by coming in contact with them, and the objects also must of necessity allow themselves to be presented as they are when they are in contact with the proper senses. But the work of recognition or giving names is not what is directly produced by the objects themselves, for this involves the unification of previous experiences, and this is certainly not what is presented

[1] The definition first given in the *Pramāṇasamuccaya* (not available in Sanskrit) of Diṅnāga (500 A.D.) was "*Kalpanāpoḍham.*" According to Dharmakīrtti it is the indeterminate knowledge (*nirvikalpa jñāna*) consisting only of the copy of the object presented to the senses that constitutes the valid element presented to perception. The determinate knowledge (*savikalpa jñāna*), as formed by the conceptual activity of the mind identifying the object with what has been experienced before, cannot be regarded as truly representing what is really presented to the senses.

to the sense (*pūrvadṛṣṭāparadṛṣṭañcārthamekīkurvadvijñānam-asannihitaviṣayam pūrvadṛṣṭasyāsannihitatvāt*). In all illusory perceptions it is the sense which is affected either by extraneous or by inherent physiological causes. If the senses are not perverted they are bound to present the object correctly. Perception thus means the correct presentation through the senses of an object in its own uniqueness as containing only those features which are its and its alone (*svalakṣaṇam*). The validity of knowledge consists in the sameness that it has with the objects presented by it (*arthena saha yatsārūpyam sādṛśyamasya jñānasya tatpramāṇamiha*). But the objection here is that if our percept is only similar to the external object then this similarity is a thing which is different from the presentation, and thus perception becomes invalid. But the similarity is not different from the percept which appears as being similar to the object. It is by virtue of their sameness that we refer to the object by the percept (*taditi sārūpyam tasya vaśāt*) and our perception of the object becomes possible. It is because we have an awareness of blueness that we speak of having perceived a blue object. The relation, however, between the notion of similarity of the perception with the blue object and the indefinite awareness of blue in perception is not one of causation but of a determinant and a determinate (*vyavasthāpya-vyavasthāpakabhāvena*). Thus it is the same cognition which in one form stands as signifying the similarity with the object of perception and is in another indefinite form the awareness as the percept (*tata ekasya vastunaḥ kiñcidrūpam pramāṇam kiñcitpramānaphalam na virudhyate*). It is on account of this similarity with the object that a cognition can be a determinant of the definite awareness (*vyavasthāpanaheturhi sārūpyam*), so that by the determinate we know the determinant and thus by the similarity of the sense-datum with the object (*pramāṇa*) we come to think that our awareness has this particular form as "blue" (*pramāṇaphala*). If this sameness between the knowledge and its object was not felt we could not have spoken of the object from the awareness (*sārūpyamanubhūtam vyavasthāpanahetuḥ*). The object generates an awareness similar to itself, and it is this correspondence that can lead us to the realization of the object so presented by right knowledge[1].

[1] See also pp. 340 and 409. It is unfortunate that, excepting the *Nyāyabindu*, *Nyāyabinduṭīkā*, *Nyāyabinduṭīkāṭippanī* (St Petersburg, 1909), no other works dealing with this interesting doctrine of perception are available to us. *Nyāyabindu* is probably

Sautrāntika theory of Inference[1].

According to the Sautrāntika doctrine of Buddhism as described by Dharmakīrtti and Dharmmottara which is probably the only account of systematic Buddhist logic that is now available to us in Sanskrit, inference (*anumāna*) is divided into two classes, called svārthānumāna (inferential knowledge attained by a person arguing in his own mind or judgments), and parārthānumāna (inference through the help of articulated propositions for convincing others in a debate). The validity of inference depended, like the validity of perception, on copying the actually existing facts of the external world. Inference copied external realities as much as perception did; just as the validity of the immediate perception of blue depends upon its similarity to the external blue thing perceived, so the validity of the inference of a blue thing also, so far as it is knowledge, depends upon its resemblance to the external fact thus inferred (*sārūpyavaśāddhi tannīlapratītirūpam sidhyati*).

The reason by which an inference is made should be such that it may be present only in those cases where the thing to be inferred exists, and absent in every case where it does not exist. It is only when the reason is tested by both these joint conditions that an unfailing connection (*pratibandha*) between the reason and the thing to be inferred can be established. It is not enough that the reason should be present in all cases where the thing to be inferred exists and absent where it does not exist, but it is necessary that it should be present only in the above case. This law (*niyama*) is essential for establishing the unfailing condition necessary for inference[2]. This unfailing natural connection (*svabhāvapratibandha*) is found in two types

one of the earliest works in which we hear of the doctrine of *arthakriyākāritva* (practical fulfilment of our desire as a criterion of right knowledge). Later on it was regarded as a criterion of existence, as Ratnakīrtti's works and the profuse references by Hindu writers to the Buddhistic doctrines prove. The word *arthakriyā* is found in Candrakīrtti's commentary on Nāgārjuna and also in such early works as *Lalitavistara* (pointed out to me by Dr E. J. Thomas of the Cambridge University Library) but the word has no philosophical significance there.

[1] As the *Pramāṇasamuccaya* of Diṅnāga is not available in Sanskrit, we can hardly know anything of developed Buddhist logic except what can be got from the *Nyāyabinduṭīkā* of Dharmmottara.

[2] *tasmāt niyamavatorevānvayavyatirekayoḥ prayogaḥ karttavyaḥ yena pratibandho gamyeta sādhanyasa sādhyena. Nyāyabinduṭīkā*, p. 24.

of cases. The first is that where the nature of the reason is contained in the thing to be inferred as a part of its nature, i.e. where the reason stands for a species of which the thing to be inferred is a genus; thus a stupid person living in a place full of tall pines may come to think that pines are called trees because they are tall and it may be useful to point out to him that even a small pine plant is a tree because it is pine; the quality of pineness forms a part of the essence of treeness, for the former being a species is contained in the latter as a genus; the nature of the species being identical with the nature of the genus, one could infer the latter from the former but not *vice versa*; this is called the unfailing natural connection of identity of nature (*tādātmya*). The second is that where the cause is inferred from the effect which stands as the reason of the former. Thus from the smoke the fire which has produced it may be inferred. The ground of these inferences is that reason is naturally indissolubly connected with the thing to be inferred, and unless this is the case, no inference is warrantable.

This natural indissoluble connection (*svabhāvapratibandha*), be it of the nature of identity of essence of the species in the genus or inseparable connection of the effect with the cause, is the ground of all inference[1]. The svabhāvapratibandha determines the inseparability of connection (*avinābhāvaniyama*) and the inference is made not through a series of premisses but directly by the liṅga (reason) which has the inseparable connection[2].

The second type of inference known as parārthānumāna agrees with svārthānumāna in all essential characteristics; the main difference between the two is this, that in the case of parārthānumāna, the inferential process has to be put verbally in premisses.

Pandit Ratnākaraśānti, probably of the ninth or the tenth century A.D., wrote a paper named *Antarvyāptisamarthana* in which

[1] *na hi yo yatra svabhāvena na pratibaddhaḥ sa tam apratibaddhaviṣayamavaśyameva na vyabhicaratīti nāsti tayoravyabhicāraniyamah. Nyāyabinduṭīkā*, p. 29.

[2] The inseparable connection determining inference is only possible when the liṅga satisfies the three following conditions, viz. (1) pakṣasattva (existence of the liṅga in the pakṣa—the thing about which something is inferred); (2) sapakṣasattva (existence of the liṅga in those cases where the sādhya or probandum existed), and (3) vipakṣāsattva (its non-existence in all those places where the sādhya did not exist). The Buddhists admitted three propositions in a syllogism, e.g. The hill has fire, because it has smoke, like a kitchen but unlike a lake.

he tried to show that the concomitance is not between those cases which possess the liṅga or reason with the cases which possess the sādhya (probandum) but between that which has the characteristics of the liṅga with that which has the characteristics of the sādhya (probandum); or in other words the concomitance is not between the places containing the smoke such as kitchen, etc., and the places containing fire but between that which has the characteristic of the liṅga, viz. the smoke, and that which has the characteristic of the sādhya, viz. the fire. This view of the nature of concomitance is known as inner concomitance (*antarvyāpti*), whereas the former, viz. the concomitance between the thing possessing liṅga and that possessing sādhya, is known as outer concomitance (*bahirvyāpti*) and generally accepted by the Nyāya school of thought. This antarvyāpti doctrine of concomitance is indeed a later Buddhist doctrine.

It may not be out of place here to remark that evidences of some form of Buddhist logic probably go back at least as early as the *Kathāvatthu* (200 B.C.). Thus Aung on the evidence of the *Yamaka* points out that Buddhist logic at the time of Aśoka "was conversant with the distribution of terms" and the process of conversion. He further points out that the logical premisses such as the udāharaṇa (*Yo yo aggimā so so dhūmavā*—whatever is fiery is smoky), the upanayana (*ayam pabbato dhūmavā*—this hill is smoky) and the niggama (*tasmādayam aggimā*—therefore that is fiery) were also known. (Aung further sums up the method of the arguments which are found in the *Kathāvatthu* as follows:

"Adherent. Is *A B*? (*ṭhāpanā*).
Opponent. Yes.
Adherent. Is *C D*? (*pāpanā*).
Opponent. No.
Adherent. But if *A* be *B* then (you should have said) *C* is *D*. That *B* can be affirmed of *A* but *D* of *C* is false. Hence your first answer is refuted.")

The antecedent of the hypothetical major premiss is termed ṭhāpanā, because the opponent's position, *A* is *B*, is conditionally established for the purpose of refutation.

The consequent of the hypothetical major premiss is termed pāpanā because it is got from the antecedent. And the conclusion is termed ropaṇa because the regulation is placed on the opponent. Next:

"If *D* be derived of *C*.
Then *B* should have been derived of *A*.
But you affirmed *B* of *A*.
(therefore) That *B* can be affirmed of *A* but not of *D* or *C* is wrong."

This is the paṭiloma, inverse or indirect method, as contrasted with the former or direct method, anuloma. In both methods the consequent is derived. But if we reverse the hypothetical major in the latter method we get

If *A* is *B* *C* is *D*.
But *A* is *B*.
Therefore *C* is *D*.

By this indirect method the opponent's second answer is re-established[1]."

The Doctrine of Momentariness.

Ratnakīrtti (950 A.D.) sought to prove the momentariness of all existence (*sattva*), first, by the concomitance discovered by the method of agreement in presence (*anvayavyāpti*), and then by the method of difference by proving that the production of effects could not be justified on the assumption of things being permanent and hence accepting the doctrine of momentariness as the only alternative. Existence is defined as the capacity of producing anything (*arthakriyākāritva*). The form of the first type of argument by anvayavyāpti may be given thus: "Whatever exists is momentary, by virtue of its existence, as for example the jug; all things about the momentariness of which we are discussing are existents and are therefore momentary." It cannot be said that the jug which has been chosen as an example of an existent is not momentary; for the jug is producing certain effects at the present moment; and it cannot be held that these are all identical in the past and the future or that it is producing no effect at all in the past and future, for the first is impossible, for those which are done now could not be done again in the future; the second is impossible, for if it has any capacity to

[1] See introduction to the translation of *Kathāvatthu* (*Points of Controversy*) by Mrs Rhys Davids.

produce effects it must not cease doing so, as in that case one might as well expect that there should not be any effect even at the present moment. Whatever has the capacity of producing anything at any time must of necessity do it. So if it does produce at one moment and does not produce at another, this contradiction will prove the supposition that the things were different at the different moments. If it is held that the nature of production varies at different moments, then also the thing at those two moments must be different, for a thing could not have in it two contradictory capacities.

Since the jug does not produce at the present moment the work of the past and the future moments, it cannot evidently do so, and hence is not identical with the jug in the past and in the future, for the fact that the jug has the capacity and has not the capacity as well, proves that it is not the same jug at the two moments (*śaktāśaktasvabhāvatayā pratikṣaṇam bhedaḥ*). The capacity of producing effects (*arthakṛiyāśakti*), which is but the other name of existence, is universally concomitant with momentariness (*kṣaṇikatvavyāpta*).

The Nyāya school of philosophy objects to this view and says that the capacity of anything cannot be known until the effect produced is known, and if capacity to produce effects be regarded as existence or being, then the being or existence of the effect cannot be known, until that has produced another effect and that another *ad infinitum*. Since there can be no being that has not capacity of producing effects, and as this capacity can demonstrate itself only in an infinite chain, it will be impossible to know any being or to affirm the capacity of producing effects as the definition of existence. Moreover if all things were momentary there would be no permanent perceiver to observe the change, and there being nothing fixed there could hardly be any means even of taking to any kind of inference. To this Ratnakīrtti replies that capacity (*sāmarthya*) cannot be denied, for it is demonstrated even in making the denial. The observation of any concomitance in agreement in presence, or agreement in absence, does not require any permanent observer, for under certain conditions of agreement there is the knowledge of the concomitance of agreement in presence, and in other conditions there is the knowledge of the concomitance in absence. This knowledge of concomitance at the succeeding moment holds within itself the experience of the conditions of the preceding moment, and this alone is what we find and not any permanent observer.

The Buddhist definition of being or existence (*sattva*) is indeed capacity, and we arrived at this when it was observed that in all proved cases capacity was all that could be defined of being;—seed was but the capacity of producing shoots, and even if this capacity should require further capacity to produce effects, the fact which has been perceived still remains, viz. that the existence of seeds is nothing but the capacity of producing the shoots and thus there is no vicious infinite[1]. Though things are momentary, yet we could have concomitance between things only so long as their apparent forms are not different (*atadrūpa-parāvṛttayoreva sādhyasādhanayoḥ pratyakṣeṇa vyāptigrahaṇāt*). The vyāpti or concomitance of any two things (e.g. the fire and the smoke) is based on extreme similarity and not on identity.

Another objection raised against the doctrine of momentariness is this, that a cause (e.g. seed) must wait for a number of other collocations of earth, water, etc., before it can produce the effect (e.g. the shoots) and hence the doctrine must fail. To this Ratnakīrtti replies that the seed doos not exist before and produce the effect when joined by other collocations, but such is the special effectiveness of a particular seed-moment, that it produces both the collocations or conditions as well as the effect, the shoot. How a special seed-moment became endowed with such special effectiveness is to be sought in other causal moments which preceded it, and on which it was dependent. Ratnakīrtti wishes to draw attention to the fact that as one perceptual moment reveals a number of objects, so one causal moment may produce a number of effects. Thus he says that the inference that whatever has being is momentary is valid and free from any fallacy.

It is not important to enlarge upon the second part of Ratnakīrtti's arguments in which he tries to show that the production of effects could not be explained if we did not suppose

[1] The distinction between vicious and harmless infinites was known to the Indians at least as early as the sixth or the seventh century. Jayanta quotes a passage which differentiates the two clearly (*Nyāyamañjarī*, p. 22):

"*mūlakṣatikarīmāhuranavasthāṃ hi dūṣaṇam.*
mūlasiddhau tvarucyāpi nānavasthā nivāryate."

The infinite regress that has to be gone through in order to arrive at the root matter awaiting to be solved destroys the root and is hence vicious, whereas if the root is saved there is no harm in a regress though one may not be willing to have it.

all things to be momentary, for this is more an attempt to refute the doctrines of Nyāya than an elaboration of the Buddhist principles.

The doctrine of momentariness ought to be a direct corollary of the Buddhist metaphysics. But it is curious that though all dharmas were regarded as changing, the fact that they were all strictly momentary (*kṣaṇika*—i.e. existing only for one moment) was not emphasized in early Pāli literature. Aśvaghoṣa in his *Śraddhotpādaśāstra* speaks of all skandhas as kṣaṇika (Suzuki's translation, p. 105). Buddhaghoṣa also speaks of the meditation of the khandhas as khaṇika in his *Visuddhimagga.* But from the seventh century A.D. till the tenth century this doctrine together with the doctrine of arthakriyākāritva received great attention at the hands of the Sautrāntikas and the Vaibhāṣikas. All the Nyāya and Vedānta literature of this period is full of refutations and criticisms of these doctrines. The only Buddhist account available of the doctrine of momentariness is from the pen of Ratnakīrtti. Some of the general features of his argument in favour of the view have been given above. Elaborate accounts of it may be found in any of the important Nyāya works of this period such as *Nyāyamañjari*, *Tātparyyaṭīkā* of Vācaspati Miśra, etc.

Buddhism did not at any time believe anything to be permanent. With the development of this doctrine they gave great emphasis to this point. Things came to view at one moment and the next moment they were destroyed. Whatever is existent is momentary. It is said that our notion of permanence is derived from the notion of permanence of ourselves, but Buddhism denied the existence of any such permanent selves. What appears as self is but the bundle of ideas, emotions, and active tendencies manifesting at any particular moment. The next moment these dissolve, and new bundles determined by the preceding ones appear and so on. The present thought is thus the only thinker. Apart from the emotions, ideas, and active tendencies, we cannot discover any separate self or soul. It is the combined product of these ideas, emotions, etc., that yield the illusory appearance of self at any moment. The consciousness of self is the resultant product as it were of the combination of ideas, emotions, etc., at any particular moment. As these ideas, emotions, etc., change every moment there is no such thing as a permanent self.

The fact that I remember that I have been existing for

a long time past does not prove that a permanent self has been existing for such a long period. When I say this is that book, I perceive the book with my eye at the present moment, but that "this book" is the same as "that book" (i.e. the book arising in memory), cannot be perceived by the senses. It is evident that the "that book" of memory refers to a book seen in the past, whereas "this book" refers to the book which is before my eyes. The feeling of identity which is adduced to prove permanence is thus due to a confusion between an object of memory referring to a past and different object with the object as perceived at the present moment by the senses[1]. This is true not only of all recognition of identity and permanence of external objects but also of the perception of the identity of self, for the perception of self-identity results from the confusion of certain ideas or emotions arising in memory with similar ideas of the present moment. But since memory points to an object of past perception, and the perception to another object of the present moment, identity cannot be proved by a confusion of the two. Every moment all objects of the world are suffering dissolution and destruction, but yet things appear to persist, and destruction cannot often be noticed. Our hair and nails grow and are cut, but yet we think that we have the same hair and nail that we had before, in place of old hairs new ones similar to them have sprung forth, and they leave the impression as if the old ones were persisting. So it is that though things are destroyed every moment, others similar to these often rise into being and are destroyed the next moment and so on, and these similar things succeeding in a series produce the impression that it is one and the same thing which has been persisting through all the passing moments[2]. Just as the flame of a candle is changing every moment and yet it seems to us as if we have been perceiving the same flame all the while, so all our bodies, our ideas, emotions, etc., all external objects around us are being destroyed every moment, and new ones are being generated at every succeeding moment, but so long as the objects of the succeeding moments are similar to those of the preceding moments, it appears to us that things have remained the same and no destruction has taken place.

[1] See pratyabhijñānirāsa of the Buddhists, *Nyāyamañjarī*, V.S. Series, pp. 449, etc.

[2] See *Tarkarahasyadīpikā* of Guṇaratna, p. 30, and also *Nyāyamañjarī*, V.S. edition, p. 450.

The Doctrine of Momentariness and the Doctrine of Causal Efficiency (Arthakriyākāritva).

It appears that a thing or a phenomenon may be defined from the Buddhist point of view as being the combination of diverse characteristics[1]. What we call a thing is but a conglomeration of diverse characteristics which are found to affect, determine or influence other conglomerations appearing as sentient or as inanimate bodies. So long as the characteristics forming the elements of any conglomeration remain perfectly the same, the conglomeration may be said to be the same. As soon as any of these characteristics is supplanted by any other new characteristic, the conglomeration is to be called a new one[2]. Existence or being of things means the work that any conglomeration does or the influence that it exerts on other conglomerations. This in Sanskrit is called *arthakriyākāritva* which literally translated means—the power of performing actions and purposes of some kind[3]. The criterion of existence or being is the performance of certain specific actions, or rather existence means that a certain effect has been produced in some way (causal efficiency). That which has produced such an effect is then called existent or *sat*. Any change in the effect thus produced means a corresponding change of existence. Now, that selfsame definite specific effect

[1] Compare *Milindapañha*, II. I. I—The Chariot Simile.

[2] Compare *Tarkarahasyadīpikā* of Guṇaratna, A. S.'s edition, pp. 24, 28 and *Nyāyamañjarī*, V.S. edition, pp. 445, etc., and also the paper on *Kṣaṇabhaṅga-siddhi* by Ratnakīrtti in *Six Buddhist Nyāya tracts*.

[3] This meaning of the word "arthakriyākāritva" is different from the meaning of the word as we found in the section "sautrāntika theory of perception." But we find the development of this meaning both in Ratnakīrtti as well as in Nyāya writers who referred to this doctrine. With Vinītadeva (seventh century A.D.) the word "*arthakriyā-siddhi*" meant the fulfilment of any need such as the cooking of rice by fire (*artha-śabdena prayojanamucyate puruṣasya prayojanaṃ dārupākādi tasya siddhiḥ niṣpattiḥ*—the word *artha* means need; the need of man such as cooking by logs, etc.; *siddhi* of that, means accomplishment). With Dharmottara who flourished about a century and a half later *arthasiddhi* means action (*anuṣṭhiti*) with reference to undesirable and desirable objects (*heyopādeyārthaviṣayā*). But with Ratnakīrtti (950 A.D.) the word *arthakriyākāritva* has an entirely different sense. It means with him efficiency of producing any action or event, and as such it is regarded as the characteristic definition of existence (*sattva*). Thus he says in his *Kṣaṇabhaṅgasiddhi*, pp. 20, 21, that though in different philosophies there are different definitions of existence or being, he will open his argument with the universally accepted definition of existence as *arthakriyā-kāritva* (efficiency of causing any action or event). Whenever Hindu writers after Ratnakīrtti refer to the Buddhist doctrine of *arthakriyākāritva* they usually refer to this doctrine in Ratnakīrtti's sense.

which is produced now was never produced before, and cannot be repeated in the future, for that identical effect which is once produced cannot be produced again. So the effects produced in us by objects at different moments of time may be similar but cannot be identical. Each moment is associated with a new effect and each new effect thus produced means in each case the coming into being of a correspondingly new existence of things. If things were permanent there would be no reason why they should be performing different effects at different points of time. Any difference in the effect produced, whether due to the thing itself or its combination with other accessories, justifies us in asserting that the thing has changed and a new one has come in its place. The existence of a jug for example is known by the power it has of forcing itself upon our minds; if it had no such power then we could not have said that it existed. We can have no notion of the meaning of existence other than the impression produced on us; this impression is nothing else but the power exerted by things on us, for there is no reason why one should hold that beyond such powers as are associated with the production of impressions or effects there should be some other permanent entity to which the power adhered, and which existed even when the power was not exerted. We perceive the power of producing effects and define each unit of such power as amounting to a unit of existence. And as there would be different units of power at different moments, there should also be as many new existences, i.e. existents must be regarded as momentary, existing at each moment that exerts a new power. This definition of existence naturally brings in the doctrine of momentariness shown by Ratnakīrtti.

Some Ontological Problems on which the Different Indian Systems Diverged.

We cannot close our examination of Buddhist philosophy without briefly referring to its views on some ontological problems which were favourite subjects of discussion in almost all philosophical circles of India. These are in brief: (1) the relation of cause and effect, (2) the relation of the whole (*avayavī*) and the part (*avayava*), (3) the relation of generality (*sāmānya*) to the specific individuals, (4) the relation of attributes or qualities and the substance and the problem of the relation of inherence, (5) the relation of power (*śakti*) to the power-possessor (*śaktimān*). Thus on the relation of cause and effect, Śaṅkara held that cause alone was permanent, real, and all effects as such were but impermanent illusions due to ignorance, Sāṃkhya held that there was no difference between cause and effect, except that the former was only the earlier stage which when transformed through certain changes became the effect. The history of any causal activity is the history of the transformation of the cause into the effects. Buddhism holds everything to be momentary, so neither cause nor effect can abide. One is called the effect because its momentary existence has been determined by the destruction of its momentary antecedent called the cause. There is no permanent reality which undergoes the change, but one change is determined by another and this determination is nothing more than "that happening, this happened." On the relation of parts to whole, Buddhism does not believe in the existence of wholes. According to it, it is the parts which illusorily appear as the whole, the individual atoms rise into being and die the next moment and thus there is no such thing as "whole[1]." The Buddhists hold again that there are no universals, for it is the individuals alone which come and go. There are my five fingers as individuals but there is no such thing as fingerness (*aṅgulitva*) as the abstract universal of the fingers. On the relation of attributes and substance we know that the Sautrāntika Buddhists did not believe in the exist ence of any substance apart from its attributes; what we call a substance is but a unit capable of producing a unit of sensation. In the external world there are as many individual simple units (atoms) as there are points of sensations. Corresponding to each unit of sensation there is a separate simple unit in the objective world. Our perception of a thing is thus the perception of the assemblage of these sensations. In the objective world also there are no substances but atoms or reals, each representing a unit of sensation, force or attribute, rising into being and dying the next moment. Buddhism thus denies the existence of any such relation as that of inherence (*samavāya*) in which relation the attributes are said to exist in the substance, for since there are no separate substances there is no necessity for admitting the relation of inherence. Following the same logic Buddhism also does not

[1] See *Avayavinirākaraṇa, Six Buddhist Nyāya tracts, Bibliotheca Indica*, Calcutta, 1910.

believe in the existence of a power-possessor separate from the power.

Brief survey of the evolution of Buddhist Thought.

In the earliest period of Buddhism more attention was paid to the four noble truths than to systematic metaphysics. What was sorrow, what was the cause of sorrow, what was the cessation of sorrow and what could lead to it? The doctrine of *paṭiccasamuppāda* was offered only to explain how sorrow came in and not with a view to the solving of a metaphysical problem. The discussion of ultimate metaphysical problems, such as whether the world was eternal or non-eternal, or whether a Tathāgata existed after death or not, were considered as heresies in early Buddhism. Great emphasis was laid on sīla, samādhi and paññā and the doctrine that there was no soul. The Abhidhammas hardly give us any new philosophy which was not contained in the Suttas. They only elaborated the materials of the suttas with enumerations and definitions. With the evolution of Mahāyāna scriptures from some time about 200 B.C. the doctrine of the non-essentialness and voidness of all *dhammas* began to be preached. This doctrine, which was taken up and elaborated by Nāgārjuna, Āryyadeva, Kumārajīva and Candrakīrtti, is more or less a corollary from the older doctrine of Buddhism. If one could not say whether the world was eternal or non-eternal, or whether a Tathāgata existed or did not exist after death, and if there was no permanent soul and all the dhammas were changing, the only legitimate way of thinking about all things appeared to be to think of them as mere void and non-essential appearances. These appearances appear as being mutually related but apart from their appearance they have no other essence, no being or reality. The Tathatā doctrine which was preached by Aśvaghoṣa oscillated between the position of this absolute non-essentialness of all dhammas and the Brahminic idea that something existed as the background of all these non-essential dhammas. This he called tathatā, but he could not consistently say that any such permanent entity could exist. The Vijñānavāda doctrine which also took its rise at this time appears to me to be a mixture of the Śūnyavāda doctrine and the Tathatā doctrine; but when carefully examined it seems to be nothing but Śūnyavāda, with an attempt at explaining all the observed phenomena. If everything was non-essential how did it originate? Vijñānavāda proposes to give an answer, and says that these phenomena are all but ideas of the mind generated by the beginningless vāsanā (desire) of the mind. The difficulty which is felt with regard to the Tathatā doctrine that there muct be some reality which is generating all these ideas appearing as phenomena, is the same as that in the Vijñānavāda doctrine. The Vijñānavādins could not admit the existence of such a reality, but yet their doctrines led them to it. They could not properly solve the difficulty, and admitted that their doctrine was some sort of a compromise with the Brahminical doctrines of heresy, but they said that this was a compromise to make the doctrine intelligible to the heretics; in truth however the reality assumed in the doctrine was also non-essential. The Vijñānavāda literature that is available to us is very scanty and from that we are not in a position to judge what answers Vijñānavāda could give on the point. These three doctrines developed almost about the same time and the difficulty of conceiving śūnya (void), tathatā, (thatness) and the ālayavijñāna of Vijñānavāda is more or less the same.

The Tathatā doctrine of Aśvaghoṣa practically ceased with him. But the Śūnyavāda and the Vijñānavāda doctrines which originated probably about 200 B.C. continued to develop probably till the eighth century A.D. Vigorous disputes with Śūnyavāda doctrines are rarely made in any independent work of Hindu philosophy, after Kumārila and Śaṅkara. From the third or the fourth century A.D. some Buddhists took to the study of systematic logic and began to criticize the doctrine of the Hindu logicians. Diṅnāga the Buddhist logician (500 A.D.) probably started these hostile criticisms by trying to refute the doctrines of the great Hindu logician Vātsyāyana, in his Pramāṇa-samuccaya. In association with this logical activity we find the activity of two other schools of Buddhism, viz. the Sarvāstivādins (known also as Vaibhāṣikas) and the Sautrāntikas. Both the Vaibhāṣikas and the Sautrāntikas accepted the existence of the external world, and they were generally in conflict with the Hindu schools of thought Nyāya-Vaiśeṣika and Sāṃkhya which also admitted the existence of the external world. Vasubandhu (420–500 A.D.) was one of the most illustrious names of this school. We have from this time forth a number of great Buddhist thinkers such as Yaśomitra (commentator of Vasubandhu's work),

Dharmmakīrtti (writer of Nyāyabindu 635 A.D.), Vinītadeva and Śāntabhadra (commentators of Nyāyabindu), Dharmmottara (commentator of Nyāyabindu 847 A.D.), Ratnakīrtti (950 A.D.), Paṇḍita Aśoka, and Ratnākara Śānti, some of whose contributious have been published in the *Six Buddhist Nyāya Tracts*, published in Calcutta in the *Bibliotheca Indica* series. These Buddhist writers were mainly interested in discussions regarding the nature of perception, inference, the doctrine of momentariness, and the doctrine of causal efficiency (*arthakriyākāritva*) as demonstrating the nature of existence. On the negative side they were interested in denying the ontological theories of Nyāya and Sāṃkhya with regard to the nature of class-concepts, negation, relation of whole and part, connotation of terms, etc. These problems hardly attracted any notice in the non-Sautrāntika and non-Vaibhāṣika schools of Buddhism of earlier times. They of course agreed with the earlier Buddhists in denying the existence of a permanent soul, but this they did with the help of their doctrine of causal efficiency. The points of disagreement between Hindu thought up to Śaṅkara (800 A.D.) and Buddhist thought till the time of Śaṅkara consisted mainly in the denial by the Buddhists of a permanent soul and the permanent external world. For Hindu thought was more or less realistic, and even the Vedānta of Śaṅkara admitted the existence of the permanent external world in some sense. With Śaṅkara the forms of the external world were no doubt illusory, but they all had a permanent background in the Brahman, which was the only reality behind all mental and the physical phenomena. The Sautrāntikas admitted the existence of the external world and so their quarrel with Nyāya and Sāṃkhya was with regard to their doctrine of momentariness; their denial of soul and their views on the different ontological problems were in accordance with their doctrine of momentariness. After the twelfth century we do not hear much of any new disputes with the Buddhists. From this time the disputes were mainly between the different systems of Hindu philosophers, viz. Nyāya, the Vedānta of the school of Śaṅkara and the Theistic Vedānta of Rāmānuja, Madhva, etc

CHAPTER VI

THE JAINA PHILOSOPHY

The Origin of Jainism.

NOTWITHSTANDING the radical differences in their philosophical notions Jainism and Buddhism, which were originally both orders of monks outside the pale of Brahmanism, present some resemblance in outward appearance, and some European scholars who became acquainted with Jainism through inadequate samples of Jaina literature easily persuaded themselves that it was an offshoot of Buddhism, and even Indians unacquainted with Jaina literature are often found to commit the same mistake. But it has now been proved beyond doubt that this idea is wrong and Jainism is at least as old as Buddhism. The oldest Buddhist works frequently mention the Jains as a rival sect, under their old name Nigantha and their leader Nātaputta Varddhamāna Mahāvīra, the last prophet of the Jains. The canonical books of the Jains mention as contemporaries of Mahāvīra the same kings as reigned during Buddha's career.

Thus Mahāvīra was a contemporary of Buddha, but unlike Buddha he was neither the author of the religion nor the founder of the sect, but a monk who having espoused the Jaina creed afterwards became the seer and the last prophet (Tīrthaṅkara) of Jainism[1]. His predecessor Pārśva, the last Tīrthaṅkara but one, is said to have died 250 years before Mahāvīra, while Pārśva's predecessor Ariṣṭanemi is said to have died 84,000 years before Mahāvīra's Nirvāṇa. The story in *Uttarādhyayanasūtra* that a disciple of Pārśva met a disciple of Mahāvīra and brought about the union of the old Jainism and that propounded by Mahāvīra seems to suggest that this Pārśva was probably a historical person.

According to the belief of the orthodox Jains, the Jaina religion is eternal, and it has been revealed again and again in every one of the endless succeeding periods of the world by innumerable Tīrthaṅkaras. In the present period the first Tīrthaṅkara was Ṛṣabha and the last, the 24th, was Vardhamāna Mahāvīra. All

[1] See Jacobi's article on Jainism, *E. R. E.*

Tīrthaṅkaras have reached mokṣa at their death, and they neither care for nor have any influence on worldly affairs; but yet they are regarded as "Gods" by the Jains and are worshipped[1]

Two Sects of Jainism[2].

There are two main sects of Jains, Śvetāmbaras (wearers of white cloths) and Digambaras (the naked). They are generally agreed on all the fundamental principles of Jainism. The tenets peculiar to the Digambaras are firstly that perfect saints such as the Tīrthaṅkaras live without food, secondly that the embryo of Mahāvīra was not removed from the womb of Devanandā to that of Triśalā as the Śvetāmbaras contend, thirdly that a monk who owns any property and wears clothes cannot reach Mokṣa, fourthly that no woman can reach Mokṣa[3]. The Digambaras deny the canonical works of the Śvetāmbaras and assert that these had been lost immediately after Mahāvīra. The origin of the Digambaras is attributed to Śivabhūti (A.D. 83) by the Śvetāmbaras as due to a schism in the old Śvetāmbara church, of which there had already been previous to that seven other schisms. The Digambaras in their turn deny this, and say that they themselves alone have preserved the original practices, and that under Bhadrabāhu, the eighth sage after Mahāvīra, the last Tīrthaṅkara, there rose the sect of Ardhaphālakas with laxer principles, from which developed the present sect of Śvetāmbaras (A.D. 80). The Digambaras having separated in early times from the Śvetāmbaras developed peculiar religious ceremonies of their own, and have a different ecclesiastical and literary history, though there is practically no difference about the main creed. It may not be out of place here to mention that the Sanskrit works of the Digambaras go back to a greater antiquity than those of the Śvetāmbaras, if we except the canonical books of the latter. It may be noted in this connection that there developed in later times about 84 different schools of Jainism differing from one another only in minute details of conduct. These were called *gacchas*, and the most important of these is the Kharatara Gaccha, which had split into many minor gacchas. Both sects of Jains have

---

[1] See "*Digumbara Jain Iconography* (I. A, xxxii [1903] p. 459" of J. Burgess, and Bühler's "Specimens of Jina sculptures from Mathurā," in *Epigraphica Indica*, II. pp. 311 etc. See also Jacobi's article on Jainism, *E. R. E.*

[2] See Jacobi's article on Jainism, *E. R. E.*

[3] See Guṇaratna's commentary on Jainism in *Ṣaḍḍarśanasamuccaya*.

preserved a list of the succession of their teachers from Mahāvīra (*sthavirāvali*, *paṭṭāvali*, *gurvāvali*) and also many legends about them such as those in the *Kalpasūtra*, the *Pariśiṣṭa-parvan* of Hemacandra, etc.

The Canonical and other Literature of the Jains.

According to the Jains there were originally two kinds of sacred books, the fourteen Pūrvas and the eleven Aṅgas. The Pūrvas continued to be transmitted for some time but were gradually lost. The works known as the eleven Aṅgas are now the oldest parts of the existing Jain canon. The names of these are *Ācāra*, *Sūtrakṛta*, *Sthāna*, *Samavāya Bhagavatī*, *Jñatadharmakathās*, *Upāsakadaśās*, *Antakṛtadaśās Anuttaraupapātikadaśās*, *Praśnavyākaraṇa*, *Vipāka*. In addition to these there are the twelve *Upāṅgas*[1], the ten *Prakīrṇas*[2], six *Chedasūtras*[3], *Nāndī* and *Anuyogadvāra* and four *Mūlasūtras* (*Uttarādhyayana*, *Āvaśyaka*, *Daśavaikālika*, and *Piṇḍaniryukti*). The Digambaras however assert that these original works have all been lost, and that the present works which pass by the old names are spurious. The original language of these according to the Jains was Ardhamāgadhī, but these suffered attempts at modernization and it is best to call the language of the sacred texts Jaina Prākrit and that of the later works Jaina Mahārāṣṭrī. A large literature of glosses and commentaries has grown up round the sacred texts. And besides these, the Jains possess separate works, which contain systematic expositions of their faith in Prākrit and Sanskrit. Many commentaries have also been written upon these independent treatises. One of the oldest of these treatises is Umāsvāti's *Tattvārthādhigamasūtra* (1–85 A.D.). Some of the most important later Jaina works on which this chapter is based are *Viśeṣāvaśyakabhāṣya*, Jaina *Tarkavārttika*, with the commentary of Śāntyācāryya, *Dravyasaṃgraha* of Nemicandra (1150 A.D.), *Syādvādamañjarī* of Malliṣena (1292 A.D.), *Nyāyāvatāra* of Siddhasena Divākara (533 A.D.), *Parīkṣāmukhasūtralaghuvṛtti* of Anantavīryya (1039 A.D.), *Prameyakamalamārtaṇḍa* of Prabhā-

[1] *Aupapātika*, *Rājapraśnīya*, *Jīvābhigama*, *Prajñāpanā*, *Jambudvīpaprajñapti*, *Candraprajñapti*, *Sūryaprajñapti*, *Nirayāvali*, *Kalpāvataṃsikā*, *Puṣpikā*, *Puṣpacūlikā*, *Vṛṣṇidaśās*.

[2] *Catuḥśaraṇa*, *Saṃstāra*, *Āturapratyākhyāna*, *Bhaktāparijñā*, *Taṇḍulavaiyālī*, *Caṇḍāvīja*, *Devendrastava*, *Gaṇivīja*, *Mahāpratyākhyāna*, *Vīrastava*.

[3] *Niśītha*, *Mahāniśītha*, *Vyavahāra*, *Daśaśrutaskandha*, *Bṛhatkalpa*, *Pañcakalpa*.

candra (825 A.D.), *Yogaśāstra* of Hemacandra (1088–1172 A.D.), and *Pramāṇanayatattvālokālaṃkāra* of Deva Sūri (1086–1169 A.D.). I am indebted for these dates to Vidyābhūṣaṇa's *Indian Logic*.

It may here be mentioned that the Jains also possess a secular literature of their own in poetry and prose, both Sanskrit and Prākrit. There are also many moral tales (e.g. *Samarāicca-kahā*, *Upamitabhavaprapañca-kathā* in Prākrit, and the *Yaśastilaka* of Somadeva and Dhanapāla's *Tilakamañjarī*); Jaina Sanskrit poems both in the Purāṇa and Kāvya style and hymns in Prākrit and Sanskrit are also very numerous. There are also many Jaina dramas. The Jaina authors have also contributed many works, original treatises as well as commentaries, to the scientific literature of India in its various branches: grammar, biography, metrics, poetics, philosophy, etc. The contributions of the Jains to logic deserve special notice[1].

Some General Characteristics of the Jains.

The Jains exist only in India and their number is a little less than a million and a half. The Digambaras are found chiefly in Southern India but also in the North, in the North-western provinces, Eastern Rājputāna and the Punjab. The head-quarters of the Śvetāmbaras are in Gujarat and Western Rājputāna, but they are to be found also all over Northern and Central India.

The outfit of a monk, as Jacobi describes it, is restricted to bare necessaries, and these he must beg—clothes, a blanket, an alms-bowl, a stick, a broom to sweep the ground, a piece of cloth to cover his mouth when speaking lest insects should enter it[2]. The outfit of nuns is the same except that they have additional clothes. The Digambaras have a similar outfit, but keep no clothes, use brooms of peacock's feathers or hairs of the tail of a cow (*cāmara*)[3]. The monks shave the head or remove the hair by plucking it out. The latter method of getting rid of the hair is to be preferred, and is regarded sometimes as an essential rite. The duties of monks are very hard. They should sleep only three hours and spend the rest of the time in repenting of and expiating sins, meditating, studying, begging alms (in the afternoon), and careful inspection of their clothes and other things for the removal of insects. The laymen should try to approach the ideal of conduct of the monks

[1] See Jacobi's article on Jainism, *E. R. E.*

[2] See Jacobi, *loc. cit.*

[3] See *Ṣaḍdarśanasamuccaya*, chapter IV.

by taking upon themselves particular vows, and the monks are required to deliver sermons and explain the sacred texts in the upāśrayas (separate buildings for monks like the Buddhist vihāras). The principle of extreme carefulness not to destroy any living being has been in monastic life carried out to its very last consequences, and has shaped the conduct of the laity in a great measure. No layman will intentionally kill any living being, not even an insect, however troublesome. He will remove it carefully without hurting it. The principle of not hurting any living being thus bars them from many professions such as agriculture, etc., and has thrust them into commerce[1].

Life of Mahāvīra.

Mahāvīra, the last prophet of the Jains, was a Kṣattriya of the Jñāta clan and a native of Vaiśāli (modern Besarh, 27 miles north of Patna). He was the second son of Siddhārtha and Triśalā. The Śvetāmbaras maintain that the embryo of the Tīrthaṅkara which first entered the womb of the Brahmin lady Devanandā was then transferred to the womb of Triśalā. This story the Digambaras do not believe as we have already seen. His parents were the worshippers of Pārśva and gave him the name Varddhamāna (Vīra or Mahāvīra). He married Yaśodā and had a daughter by her. In his thirtieth year his parents died and with the permission of his brother Nandivardhana he became a monk. After twelve years of self-mortification and meditation he attained omniscience (*kevala*, cf. *bodhi* of the Buddhists). He lived to preach for forty-two years more, and attained mokṣa (emancipation) some years before Buddha in about 480 B.C.[2].

The Fundamental Ideas of Jaina Ontology.

A thing (such as clay) is seen to assume various shapes and to undergo diverse changes (such as the form of a jug, or pan, etc.), and we have seen that the Chāndogya Upaniṣad held that since in all changes the clay-matter remained permanent, that alone was true, whereas the changes of form and state were but appearances, the nature of which cannot be rationally

[1] See Jacobi's article on Jainism, *E. R. E.*

[2] See Hoernlé's translation of *Uvāsagadasāo*, Jacobi, *loc. cit.*, and Hoernlé's articl on the Ājīvakas, *E. R. E.* The Śvetāmbaras, however, say that this date was 527 B.C. and the Digambaras place it eighteen years later.

demonstrated or explained. The unchangeable substance (e.g. the clay-matter) alone is true, and the changing forms are mere illusions of the senses, mere objects of name (*nāma-rūpa*)[1]. What we call tangibility, visibility, or other sense-qualities, have no real existence, for they are always changing, and are like mere phantoms of which no conception can be made by the light of reason.

The Buddhists hold that changing qualities can alone be perceived and that there is no unchanging substance behind them. What we perceive as clay is but some specific quality, what we perceive as jug is also some quality. Apart from these qualities we do not perceive any qualitiless substance, which the Upaniṣads regard as permanent and unchangeable. The permanent and unchangeable substance is thus a mere fiction of ignorance, as there are only the passing collocations of qualities. Qualities do not imply that there are substances to which they adhere, for the so-called pure substance does not exist, as it can neither be perceived by the senses nor inferred. There are only the momentary passing qualities. We should regard each change of quality as a new existence.

The Jains we know were the contemporaries of Buddha and possibly of some of the Upaniṣads too, and they had also a solution to offer. They held that it was not true that substance alone was true and qualities were mere false and illusory appearances. Further it was not true as the Buddhists said that there was no permanent substance but merely the change of passing qualities, for both these represent two extreme views and are contrary to experience. Both of them, however, contain some elements of truth but not the whole truth as given in experience. Experience shows that in all changes there are three elements: (1) that some collocations of qualities appear to remain unchanged; (2) that some new qualities are generated; (3) that some old qualities are destroyed. It is true that qualities of things are changing every minute, but all qualities are not changing. Thus when a jug is made, it means that the clay-lump has been destroyed, a jug has been generated and the clay is permanent, i.e. all production means that some old qualities have been lost, some new ones brought in, and there is some part in it which is permanent The clay has become lost in some form, has generated itself in another, and remained permanent in still

[1] See Chāndogya, VI. I.

another form. It is by virtue of these unchanged qualities that a thing is said to be permanent though undergoing change. Thus when a lump of gold is turned into a rod or a ring, all the specific qualities which come under the connotation of the word "gold" are seen to continue, though the forms are successively changed, and with each such change some of its qualities are lost and some new ones are acquired. Such being the case, the truth comes to this, that there is always a permanent entity as represented by the permanence of such qualities as lead us to call it a substance in spite of all its diverse changes. The nature of being (*sat*) then is neither the absolutely unchangeable, nor the momentary changing qualities or existences, but involves them both. Being then, as is testified by experience, is that which involves a permanent unit, which is incessantly every moment losing some qualities and gaining new ones. The notion of being involves a permanent (*dhruva*) accession of some new qualities (*utpāda*) and loss of some old qualities (*vyaya*)[1]. The solution of Jainism is thus a reconciliation of the two extremes of Vedāntism and Buddhism on grounds of common-sense experience.

The Doctrine of Relative Pluralism (anekāntavāda).

This conception of being as the union of the permanent and change brings us naturally to the doctrine of Anekāntavāda or what we may call relative pluralism as against the extreme absolutism of the Upaniṣads and the pluralism of the Buddhists. The Jains regarded all things as *anekānta* (*na-ekānta*), or in other words they held that nothing could be affirmed absolutely, as all affirmations were true only under certain conditions and limitations. Thus speaking of a gold jug, we see that its existence as a substance (*dravya*) is of the nature of a collocation of atoms and not as any other substance such as space (*ākāśa*), i.e. a gold jug is a *dravya* only in one sense of the term and not in every sense; so it is a *dravya* in the sense that it is a collocation of atoms and not a *dravya* in the sense of space or time (*kāla*). It is thus both a dravya and not a dravya at one and the same time. Again it is atomic in the sense that it is a composite of earth-atoms and not atomic in the sense that it is

[1] See *Tattvārthādhigamasūtra*, and Guṇaratna's treatment of Jainism in *Ṣaḍdarśanasamuccaya*.

not a composite of water-atoms. Again it is a composite of earth-atoms only in the sense that gold is a metallic modification of earth, and not any other modification of earth as clay or stone. Its being constituted of metal-atoms is again true in the sense that it is made up of gold-atoms and not of iron-atoms. It is made up again of gold-atoms in the sense of melted and unsullied gold and not as gold in the natural condition. It is again made up of such unsullied and melted gold as has been hammered and shaped by the goldsmith Devadatta and not by Yajñadatta. Its being made up of atoms conditioned as above is again only true in the sense that the collocation has been shaped as a jug and not as a pot and so on. Thus proceeding in a similar manner the Jains say that all affirmations are true of a thing only in a certain limited sense. All things (*vastu*) thus possess an infinite number of qualities (*anantadharmātmakaṃ vastu*), each of which can only be affirmed in a particular sense. Such an ordinary thing as a jug will be found to be the object of an infinite number of affirmations and the possessor of an infinite number of qualities from infinite points of view, which are all true in certain restricted senses and not absolutely[1]. Thus in the positive relation riches cannot be affirmed of poverty but in the negative relation such an affirmation is possible as when we say "the poor man has no riches." The poor man possesses riches not in a positive but in a negative way. Thus in some relation or other anything may be affirmed of any other thing, and again in other relations the very same thing cannot be affirmed of it. The different standpoints from which things (though possessed of infinite determinations) can be spoken of as possessing this or that quality or as appearing in relation to this or that, are technically called *naya*[2].

The Doctrine of Nayas.

In framing judgments about things there are two ways open to us, firstly we may notice the manifold qualities and characteristics of anything but view them as unified in the thing; thus when we say "this is a book" we do not look at its characteristic qualities as being different from it, but rather the qualities or characteristics are perceived as having no separate existence from

[1] See Guṇaratna on Jainamata in *Ṣaḍdarśanasamuccaya*, pp. 211, etc., and also *Tattvārthādhigamasūtra*.

[2] See *Tattvārthādhigamasūtra*, and *Viśeṣāvaśyaka bhāṣya*, pp. 895–923.

the thing. Secondly we may notice the qualities separately and regard the thing as a mere non-existent fiction (cf. the Buddhist view); thus I may speak of the different qualities of the book separately and hold that the qualities of things are alone perceptible and the book apart from these cannot be found. These two points of view are respectively called *dravyanaya* and *paryāyanaya*[1]. The dravyanaya again shows itself in three forms, and paryāyanaya in four forms, of which the first form only is important for our purposes, the other three being important rather from the point of view of grammar and language had better be omitted here. The three nayas under dravyanaya are called naigama-naya, saṃgraha-naya and vyavahāra-naya.

When we speak of a thing from a purely common sense point of view, we do not make our ideas clear or precise. Thus I may hold a book in my hand and when asked whether my hands are empty, I may say, no, I have something in my hand, or I may say, I have a book in my hand. It is evident that in the first answer I looked at the book from the widest and most general point of view as a "thing," whereas in the second I looked at it in its special existence as a book. Again I may be reading a page of a book, and I may say I am reading a book, but in reality I was reading only one of the pages of the book. I may be scribbling on loose sheets, and may say this is my book on Jaina philosophy, whereas in reality there were no books but merely some loose sheets. This looking at things from the loose common sense view, in which we do not consider them from the point of view of their most general characteristic as "being" or as any of their special characteristics, but simply as they appear at first sight, is technically called the naigama standpoint. This empirical view probably proceeds on the assumption that a thing possesses the most general as well as the most special qualities, and hence we may lay stress on any one of these at any time and ignore the other ones. This is the point of view from which according to the Jains the Nyāya and Vaiśeṣika schools interpret experience.

Saṃgraha-naya is the looking at things merely from the most general point of view. Thus we may speak of all individual things from their most general and fundamental aspect as "being." This according to the Jains is the Vedānta way of looking at things.

[1] *Syādvādamañjarī*, pp. 171–173.

The vyavahāra-naya standpoint holds that the real essence of things is to be regarded from the point of view of actual practical experience of the thing, which unifies within it some general as well as some special traits, which has been existing from past times and remain in the future, but yet suffer trifling changes all the while, changes which are serviceable to us in a thousand ways. Thus a "book" has no doubt some general traits, shared by all books, but it has some special traits as well. Its atoms are continually suffering some displacement and rearrangement, but yet it has been existing as a book for some time past and will exist foı some time in the future as well. All these characteristics, go to make up the essence of the "book" of our everyday experience, and none of these can be separated and held up as being the concept of a "book." This according to the Jains is the Sāṃkhya way of looking at things.

The first view of paryāya-naya called *ṛjusūtra* is the Buddhist view which does not believe in the existence of the thing in the past or in the future, but holds that a thing is a mere conglomeration of characteristics which may be said to produce effects at any given moment. At each new moment there are new collocations of new qualities and it is these which may be regarded as the true essence of our notion of things[1].

The nayas as we have already said are but points of view, or aspects of looking at things, and as such are infinite in number. The above four represent only a broad classification of these. The Jains hold that the Nyāya-Vaiśeṣika, the Vēdanta, the Sāṃkhya, and the Buddhist, have each tried to interpret and systematize experience from one of the above four points of view, and each regards the interpretation from his point of view as being absolutely true to the exclusion of all other points of view. This is their error (*nayābhāsa*), for each standpoint represents only one of the many points of view from which a thing can be looked at. The affirmations from any point of view are thus true in a limited sense and under limited conditions. Infinite numbers of affirmations may be made of things from infinite points of view. Affirmations or judgments according to any naya or standpoint cannot therefore be absolute, for even contrary affirmations of the very selfsame

[1] The other standpoints of paryāya-naya, which represent grammatical and linguistic points of view, are *śabda-naya*, *samabhirūḍha-naya*, and *evambhūta-naya*. See *Viśeṣāvaśyaka bhāṣya*, pp. 895–923.

things may be held to be true from other points of view. The truth of each affirmation is thus only conditional, and inconceivable from the absolute point of view. To guarantee correctness therefore each affirmation should be preceded by the phrase *syāt* (may be). This will indicate that the affirmation is only relative, made somehow, from some point of view and under some reservations and not in any sense absolute. There is no judgment which is absolutely true, and no judgment which is absolutely false. All judgments are true in some sense and false in another. This brings us to the famous Jaina doctrine of Syādvāda[1].

The Doctrine of Syādvāda.

The doctrine of Syādvāda holds that since the most contrary characteristics of infinite variety may be associated with a thing, affirmation made from whatever standpoint (*naya*) cannot be regarded as absolute. All affirmations are true (in some *syādasti* or "may be it is" sense); all affirmations are false in some sense; all affirmations are indefinite or inconceivable in some sense (*syādavaktavya*); all affirmations are true as well as false in some sense (*syādasti syānnāsti*); all affirmations are true as well as indefinite (*syādasti cāvaktavyaśca*); all affirmations are false as well as indefinite; all affirmations are true and false and indefinite in some sense (*syādasti syānnāsti syādavaktavyaśca*). Thus we may say "the jug is" or the jug has being, but it is more correct to say explicitly that "may be (*syāt*) that the jug is," otherwise if "being" here is taken absolutely of any and every kind of being, it might also mean that there is a lump of clay or a pillar, or a cloth or any other thing. The existence here is limited and defined by the form of the jug. "The jug is" does not mean absolute existence but a limited kind of existence as determined by the form of the jug, "The jug is" thus means that a limited kind of existence, namely the jug-existence is affirmed and not existence in general in the absolute or unlimited sense, for then the sentence "the jug is" might as well mean "the clay is," "the tree is," "the cloth is," etc. Again the existence of the jug is determined by the negation of all other things in the world; each quality or characteristic (such as red colour) of the jug is apprehended and defined by the negation of all the infinite varieties (such as black, blue, golden), etc., of its class, and it is by the combined negation of all

[1] See *Viśeṣāvaśyaka bhāṣya*, pp. 895, etc., and *Syādvādamañjarī*, pp. 170, etc.

the infinite number of characteristics or qualities other than those constituting the jug that a jug may be apprehended or defined. What we call the being of the jug is thus the non-being of all the rest except itself. Thus though looked at from one point of view the judgment "the jug is" may mean affirmation of being, looked at from another point of view it means an affirmation of non-being (of all other objects). Thus of the judgment "the jug is" one may say, may be it is an affirmation of being (*syādasti*), may be it is a negation of being (*syānnāsti*); or I may proceed in quite another way and say that "the jug is" means "this jug is here," which naturally indicates that "this jug is not there" and thus the judgment "the jug is" (i.e. is here) also means that "the jug is not there," and so we see that the affirmation of the being of the jug is true only of this place and false of another, and this justifies us in saying that "may be that in some sense the jug is," and "may be in some sense that the jug is not." Combining these two aspects we may say that in some sense "may be that the jug is," and in some sense "may be that the jug is not." We understood here that if we put emphasis on the side of the characteristics constituting being, we may say "the jug is," but if we put emphasis on the other side, we may as well say "the jug is not." Both the affirmations hold good of the jug according as the emphasis is put on either side. But if without emphasis on either side we try to comprehend the two opposite and contradictory judgments regarding the jug, we see that the nature of the jug or of the existence of the jug is indefinite, unspeakable and inconceivable—*avaktavya*, for how can we affirm both being and non-being of the same thing, and yet such is the nature of things that we cannot but do it. Thus all affirmations are true, are not true, are both true and untrue, and are thus unspeakable, inconceivable, and indefinite. Combining these four again we derive another three, (1) that in some sense it may be that the jug is, and (2) is yet unspeakable, or (3) that the jug is not and is unspeakable, or finally that the jug is, is not, and is unspeakable. Thus the Jains hold that no affirmation, or judgment, is absolute in its nature, each is true in its own limited sense only, and for each one of them any of the above seven alternatives (technically called *saptabhaṅgī*) holds good[1]. The Jains say that other Indian systems each from its own point of view asserts itself to be the absolute and the only

[1] See *Syādvādamañjarī*, with Hemacandra's commentary, pp. 166, etc.

point of view. They do not perceive that the nature of reality is such that the truth of any assertion is merely conditional, and holds good only in certain conditions, circumstances, or senses (*upādhi*). It is thus impossible to make any affirmation which is universally and absolutely valid. For a contrary or contradictory affirmation will always be found to hold good of any judgment in some sense or other. As all reality is partly permanent and partly exposed to change of the form of losing and gaining old and new qualities, and is thus relatively permanent and changeful, so all our affirmations regarding truth are also only relatively valid and invalid. Being, non-being and indefinite, the three categories of logic, are all equally available in some sense or other in all their permutations for any and every kind of judgment. There is no universal and absolute position or negation, and all judgments are valid only conditionally. The relation of the naya doctrine with the syādvāda doctrine is therefore this, that for any judgment according to any and every naya there are as many alternatives as are indicated by syādvāda. The validity of such a judgment is therefore only conditional. If this is borne in mind when making any judgment according to any naya, the naya is rightly used. If, however, the judgments are made absolutely according to any particular naya without any reference to other nayas as required by the syādvāda doctrine the nayas are wrongly used as in the case of other systems, and then such judgments are false and should therefore be called false nayas (*nayābhāsa*)[1].

Knowledge, its value for us.

The Buddhist Dharmottara in his commentary on *Nyāyabindu* says that people who are anxious to fulfil some purpose or end in which they are interested, value the knowledge which helps them to attain that purpose. It is because knowledge is thus found to be useful and sought by men that philosophy takes upon it the task of examining the nature of true knowledge (*samyagjñāna* or *pramāṇa*). The main test of true knowledge is that it helps us to attain our purpose. The Jains also are in general agreement with the above view of knowledge of the Buddhists[2]. They also

[1] The earliest mention of the doctrine of syādvāda and saptabhaṅgī probably occurs in Bhadrabāhu's (433–357 B.C.) commentary *Sūtrakṛtāṅganiryukti*.

[2] See *Pramāṇa-naya-tattvālokālaṃkāra* (Benares), p. 26; also *Parīkṣā-mukha-sūtra-vṛtti* (Asiatic Society), ch. I.

say that knowledge is not to be valued for its own sake. The validity (*prāmāṇya*) of anything consists in this, that it directly helps us to get what is good for us and to avoid what is bad for us. Knowledge alone has this capacity, for by it we can adapt ourselves to our environments and try to acquire what is good for us and avoid what is bad[1]. The conditions that lead to the production of such knowledge (such as the presence of full light and proximity to the eye in the case of seeing an object by visual perception) have but little relevancy in this connection. For we are not concerned with how a cognition is produced, as it can be of no help to us in serving our purposes. It is enough for us to know that external objects under certain conditions assume such a special fitness (*yogyatā*) that we can have knowledge of them. We have no guarantee that they generate knowledge in us, for we are only aware that under certain conditions we know a thing, whereas under other conditions we do not know it[2]. The enquiry as to the nature of the special fitness of things which makes knowledge of them possible does not concern us. Those conditions which confer such a special fitness on things as to render them perceivable have but little to do with us; for our purposes which consist only in the acquirement of good and avoidance of evil, can only be served by knowledge and not by those conditions of external objects.

Knowledge reveals our own self as a knowing subject as well as the objects that are known by us. We have no reason to suppose (like the Buddhists) that all knowledge by perception of external objects is in the first instance indefinite and indeterminate, and that all our determinate notions of form, colour, size and other characteristics of the thing are not directly given in our perceptual experience, but are derived only by imagination (*utprekṣā*), and that therefore true perceptual knowledge only certifies the validity of the indefinite and indeterminate crude sense data (*nirvikalpa jñāna*). Experience shows that true knowledge on the one hand reveals us as subjects or knowers, and on the other hand gives a correct sketch of the external objects in all the diversity of their characteristics. It is for this reason that knowledge is our immediate and most prominent means of serving our purposes.

[1] *Pramāṇa-naya-tattvālokālaṃkāra*, p. 26.

[2] See *Parīkṣā-mukha-sūtra*, II. 9, and its vṛtti, and also the concluding vṛtti of ch. II.

Of course knowledge cannot directly and immediately bring to us the good we want, but since it faithfully communicates to us the nature of the objects around us, it renders our actions for the attainment of good and the avoidance of evil, possible; for if knowledge did not possess these functions, this would have been impossible. The validity of knowledge thus consists in this, that it is the most direct, immediate, and indispensable means for serving our purposes. So long as any knowledge is uncontradicted it should be held as true. False knowledge is that which represents things in relations in which they do not exist. When a rope in a badly lighted place gives rise to the illusion of a snake, the illusion consists in taking the rope to be a snake, i.e. perceiving a snake where it does not exist. Snakes exist and ropes also exist, there is no untruth in that[1]. The error thus consists in this, that the snake is perceived where the rope exists. The perception of a snake under relations and environments in which it was not then existing is what is meant by error here. What was at first perceived as a snake was later on contradicted and thus found false. Falsehood therefore consists in the misrepresentation of objective facts in experience. True knowledge therefore is that which gives such a correct and faithful representation of its object as is never afterwards found to be contradicted. Thus knowledge when imparted directly in association with the organs in sense-perception is very clear, vivid, and distinct, and is called perceptional (*pratyakṣa*); when attained otherwise the knowledge is not so clear and vivid and is then called non-perceptional (*parokṣa*[2]).

Theory of Perception.

The main difference of the Jains from the Buddhists in the theory of perception lies, as we have already seen, in this, that the Jains think that perception (*pratyakṣa*) reveals to us the external objects just as they are with most of their diverse characteristics of colour, form, etc., and also in this, that knowledge arises in the soul

[1] Illusion consists in attributing such spatial, temporal or other kinds of relations to the objects of our judgment as do not actually exist, but the objects themselves actually exist in other relations. When I mistake the rope for the snake, the snake actually exists though its relationing with the "this" as "this is a snake" does not exist, for the snake is not the rope. This illusion is thus called *satkhyāti* or misrelationing of existents (*sat*).

[2] See *Jaina-tarka-vārttika* of Siddhasena, ch. I., and vṛtti by Śantyācārya, Pramāṇanayatattvālokālaṃkāra, ch. I., *Parīkṣā-mukha-sūtra-vṛtti*, ch. I.

from within it as if by removing a veil which had been covering it before. Objects are also not mere forms of knowledge (as the Vijñānavādin Buddhist thinks) but are actually existing. Knowledge of external objects by perception is gained through the senses. The exterior physical sense such as the eye must be distinguished from the invisible faculty or power of vision of the soul, which alone deserves the name of sense. We have five such cognitive senses. But the Jains think that since by our experience we are only aware of five kinds of sense knowledge corresponding to the five senses, it is better to say that it is the "self" which gains of itself those different kinds of sense-knowledge in association with those exterior senses as if by removal of a covering, on account of the existence of which the knowledge could not reveal itself before. The process of external perception does not thus involve the exercise of any separate and distinct sense, though the rise of the sense-knowledge in the soul takes place in association with the particular sense-organ such as eye, etc. The soul is in touch with all parts of the body, and visual knowledge is that knowledge which is generated in the soul through that part of it which is associated with, or is in touch with the eye. To take an example, I look before me and see a rose. Before looking at it the knowledge of rose was in me, but only in a covered condition, and hence could not get itself manifested. The act of looking at the rose means that such a fitness has come into the rose and into myself that the rose is made visible, and the veil over my knowledge of rose is removed. When visual knowledge arises, this happens in association with the eye; I say that I see through the visual sense, whereas in reality experience shows that I have only a knowledge of the visual type (associated with eye). As experience does not reveal the separate senses, it is unwarrantable to assert that they have an existence apart from the self. Proceeding in a similar way the Jains discard the separate existence of manas (mind-organ) also, for manas also is not given in experience, and the hypothesis of its existence is unnecessary, as self alone can serve its purpose[1]. Perception of an object means

[1] *Tanna indriyam bhautikam kim tu ātmā ca indriyam...anupahatacakṣurādideśeṣu eva āṭmanaḥ karmakṣayopaśamastenāsthagitagavākṣatulyāni cakṣurādīni upakaraṇāni. Jaina-Vāttika-Vṛtti*, II. p. 98. In many places, however, the five senses, such as eye, ear, etc., are mentioned as senses, and living beings are often classified according to the number of senses they possess. (See *Pramāṇamīmāṃsā*. See also *Tattvārthādhigamasūtra*, ch. II. etc.) But this is with reference to the sense organs. The denial

that the veil of ignorance upon the "self" regarding the object has been removed. Inwardly this removal is determined by the karma of the individual, outwardly it is determined by the presence of the object of perception, light, the capacity of the sense organs, and such other conditions. Contrary to the Buddhists and many other Indian systems, the Jains denied the existence of any nirvikalpa (indeterminate) stage preceding the final savikalpa (determinate) stage of perception. There was a direct revelation of objects from within and no indeterminate sense-materials were necessary for the development of determinate perceptions. We must contrast this with the Buddhists who regarded that the first stage consisting of the presentation of indeterminate sense materials was the only valid part of perception. The determinate stage with them is the result of the application of mental categories, such as imagination, memory, etc., and hence does not truly represent the presentative part[1].

Non-Perceptual Knowledge.

Non-perceptual knowledge (*parokṣa*) differs from pratyakṣa in this, that it does not give us so vivid a picture of objects as the latter. Since the Jains do not admit that the senses had any function in determining the cognitions of the soul, the only distinction they could draw between perception and other forms of knowledge was that the knowledge of the former kind (perception) gave us clearer features and characteristics of objects than the latter. Parokṣa thus includes inference, recognition, implication, memory, etc.; and this knowledge is decidedly less vivid than perception.

Regarding inference, the Jains hold that it is unnecessary to have five propositions, such as: (1) "the hill is fiery," (2) "because of smoke," (3) "wherever there is smoke there is fire, such as the kitchen," (4) "this hill is smoky," (5) "therefore it is fiery," called respectively *pratijñā*, *hetu*, *dṛṣṭānta*, *upanaya* and *nigamana*, except for the purpose of explicitness. It is only the first two propositions which actually enter into the inferential process (*Prameyakamalamārtaṇḍa*, pp. 108, 109). When we make an

of separate senses is with reference to admitting them as entities or capacities having a distinct and separate category of existence from the soul. The sense organs are like windows for the soul to look out. They cannot thus modify the sense-knowledge which rises in the soul by inward determination; for it is already existent in it; the perceptual process only means that the veil which was observing it is removed.

[1] *Prameyakamalamārtaṇḍa*, pp. 8–11.

inference we do not proceed through the five propositions as above. They who know that the reason is inseparably connected with the probandum either as coexistence (*sahabhāva*) or as invariable antecedence (*kramabhāva*) will from the mere statement of the existence of the reason (e.g. smoke) in the hill jump to the conclusion that the hill has got fire. A syllogism consisting of five propositions is rather for explaining the matter to a child than for representing the actual state of the mind in making an inference[1].

As regards proof by testimony the Jains do not admit the authority of the Vedas, but believe that the Jaina scriptures give us right knowledge, for these are the utterances of persons who have lived a worldly life but afterwards by right actions and right knowledge have conquered all passions and removed all ignorance[2].

Knowledge as Revelation.

The Buddhists had affirmed that the proof of the existence of anything depended upon the effect that it could produce on us. That which could produce any effect on us was existent, and that

[1] As regards concomitance (*vyāpti*) some of the Jaina logicians like the Buddhists prefer *antarvyāpti* (between smoke and fire) to bahirvyāpti (the place containing smoke with the place containing fire). They also divide inference into two classes, *svārthānumāna* for one's own self and *parārthānumāna* for convincing others. It may not be out of place to note that the earliest Jaina view as maintained by Bhadrabāhu in his Daśavaikālikaniryukti was in favour of ten propositions for making an inference; (1) *Pratijñā* (e.g. non-injury to life is the greatest virtue), (2) *Pratijñāvibhakti* (non-injury to life is the greatest virtue according to Jaina scriptures), (3) *Hetu* (because those who adhere to non-injury are loved by gods and it is meritorious to do them honour), (4) *Hetu vibhakti* (those who do so are the only persons who can live in the highest places of virtue), (5) *Vipakṣa* (but even by doing injury one may prosper and even by reviling Jaina scriptures one may attain merit as is the case with Brahmins), (6) *Vipakṣa pratiṣedha* (it is not so, it is impossible that those who despise Jaina scriptures should be loved by gods or should deserve honour), (7) *Dṛṣṭānta* (the Arhats take food from householders as they do not like to cook themselves for fear of killing insects), (8) *Āśaṅkā* (but the sins of the householders should touch the arhats, for they cook for them), (9) *Āśaṅkāpratiṣedha* (this cannot be, for the arhats go to certain houses unexpectedly, so it could not be said that the cooking was undertaken for them), (10) *Naigamana* (non-injury is therefore the greatest virtue) (Vidyābhūṣaṇa's *Indian Logic*). These are persuasive statements which are often actually adopted in a discussion, but from a formal point of view many of these are irrelevant. When Vātsyāyana in his *Nyāyasūtrabhāṣya*, I. I. 32, says that Gautama introduced the doctrine of five propositions as against the doctrine of ten propositions as held by other logicians, he probably had this Jaina view in his mind.

[2] See *Jainatarkavārttika*, and *Parīkṣāmukhasūtravṛtti*, and *Ṣaḍdarśanasamuccaya* with Guṇaratna on Jainism.

which could not non-existent. In fact production of effect was with them the only definition of existence (being). Theoretically each unit of effect being different from any other unit of effect, they supposed that there was a succession of different units of effect or, what is the same thing, acknowledged a succession of new substances every moment. All things were thus momentary. The Jains urged that the reason why the production of effect may be regarded as the only proof of being is that we can assert only that thing the existence of which is indicated by a corresponding experience. When we have a unit of experience we suppose the existence of the object as its ground. This being so, the theoretical analysis of the Buddhists that each unit of effect produced in us is not exactly the same at each new point of time, and that therefore all things are momentary, is fallacious; for experience shows that not all of an object is found to be changing every moment; some part of it (e.g. gold in a gold ornament) is found to remain permanent while other parts (e.g. its form as earrings or bangles) are seen to undergo change. How in the face of such an experience can we assert that the whole thing vanishes every moment and that new things are being renewed at each succeeding moment? Hence leaving aside mere abstract and unfounded speculations, if we look to experience we find that the conception of being or existence involves a notion of permanence associated with change—*paryāya* (acquirement of new qualities and the loss of old ones). The Jains hold that the defects of other systems lie in this, that they interpret experience only from one particular standpoint (*naya*) whereas they alone carefully weigh experience from all points of view and acquiesce in the truths indicated by it, not absolutely but under proper reservations and limitations. The Jains hold that in formulating the doctrine of *arthakriyākāritva* the Buddhists at first showed signs of starting on their enquiry on the evidence of experience, but soon they became one-sided in their analysis and indulged in unwarrantable abstract speculations which went directly against experience. Thus if we go by experience we can neither reject the self nor the external world as some Buddhists did. Knowledge which reveals to us the clear-cut features of the external world certifies at the same time that such knowledge is part and parcel of myself as the subject. Knowledge is thus felt to be an expression of my own self. We do not perceive in experience that knowledge in us is generated by the external world, but there is in us the rise of knowledge and of certain objects made known to us by it. The rise of knowledge is thus only parallel to certain objective collocations of things which somehow have the special fitness that they and they alone are perceived at that particular moment. Looked at from this point of view all our experiences are centred in ourselves, for determined somehow, our experiences come to us as modifications of our own self. Knowledge being a character of the self, it shows itself as manifestations of the self independent of the senses. No distinction should be made between a conscious and an unconscious element in knowledge as Sāṃkhya does. Nor should knowledge be regarded as a copy of the objects which it reveals, as the Sautrāntikas think, for then by copying the materiality of the object, knowledge would itself become material. Knowledge should thus be regarded as a formless quality of the self revealing all objects by itself. But the Mīmāṃsā view that the validity (*prāmāṇya*) of all knowledge is proved by knowledge itself (*svataḥprāmāṇya*) is wrong. Both logically and psychologically the validity of knowledge depends upon outward correspondence (*saṃvāda*) with facts. But in those cases where by previous knowledge of correspondence a right belief has been produced there may be a psychological ascertainment of validity without reference to objective facts (*prāmāṇyamutpattau parata eva jñaptau svakārye ca svataḥ parataśca abhyāsānabhyāsāpekṣayā*)[1]. The objective world exists as it is certified by experience. But that it generates knowledge in us is an unwarrantable hypothesis, for knowledge appears as a revelation of our own self. This brings us to a consideration of Jaina metaphysics.

The Jīvas.

The Jains say that experience shows that all things may be divided into the living (*jīva*) and the non-living (*ajīva*). The principle of life is entirely distinct from the body, and it is most erroneous to think that life is either the product or the property of the body[2]. It is on account of this life-principle that the body appears to be living. This principle is the soul. The soul is directly perceived (by introspection) just as the external things are. It is not a mere symbolical object indicated by a phrase or

[1] *Prameyakamalamārtaṇḍa*, pp. 38–43.

[2] See *Jaina Vārttika*, p. 60.

a description. This is directly against the view of the great Mīmāṃsā authority Prabhākara[1]. The soul in its pure state is possessed of infinite perception (*ananta-darśana*), infinite knowledge (*ananta-jñāna*), infinite bliss (*ananta-sukha*) and infinite power (*ananta-vīrya*)[2]. It is all perfect. Ordinarily however, with the exception of a few released pure souls (*mukta-jīva*), all the other jīvas (*saṃsārin*) have all their purity and power covered with a thin veil of karma matter which has been accumulating in them from beginningless time. These souls are infinite in number. They are substances and are eternal. They in reality occupy innumerable space-points in our mundane world (*lokākāśa*), have a limited size (*madhyama-parimāṇa*) and are neither all-pervasive (*vibhu*) nor atomic (*aṇu*); it is on account of this that *jīva* is called *Jivāstikāya.* The word *astikāya* means anything that occupies space or has some pervasiveness; but these souls expand and contract themselves according to the dimensions of the body which they occupy at any time (bigger in the elephant and smaller in the ant life). It is well to remember that according to the Jains the soul occupies the whole of the body in which it lives, so that from the tip of the hair to the nail of the foot, wherever there may be any cause of sensation, it can at once feel it. The manner in which the soul occupies the body is often explained as being similar to the manner in which a lamp illumines the whole room though remaining in one corner of the room. The Jains divide the jīvas according to the number of sense-organs they possess. The lowest class consists of plants, which possess only the sense-organ of touch. The next higher class is that of worms, which possess two sense-organs of touch and taste. Next come the ants, etc., which possess touch, taste, and smell. The next higher one that of bees, etc., possessing vision in addition to touch, taste, and smell. The vertebrates possess all the five sense-organs. The higher animals among these, namely men, denizens of hell, and the gods possess in addition to these an inner sense-organ namely *manas* by virtue of which they are

[1] See *Prameyakamalamārtaṇḍa*, p. 33.

[2] The Jains distinguish between *darśana* and *jñāna*. Darśana is the knowledge of things without their details, e.g. I see a cloth. Jñāna means the knowledge of details, e.g. I not only see the cloth, but know to whom it belongs, of what quality it is, where it was prepared, etc. In all cognition we have first darśana and then jñāna. The pure souls possess infinite general perception of all things as well as infinite knowledge of all things in all their details.

called rational (*saṃjñin*) while the lower animals have no reason and are called *asaṃjñin.*

Proceeding towards the lowest animal we find that the Jains regard all the four elements (earth, water, air, fire) as being animated by souls. Thus particles of earth, etc., are the bodies of souls, called earth-lives, etc. These we may call elementary lives; they live and die and are born again in another elementary body. These elementary lives are either gross or subtle; in the latter case they are invisible. The last class of one-organ lives are plants. Of some plants each is the body of one soul only; but of other plants, each is an aggregation of embodied souls, which have all the functions of life such as respiration and nutrition in common. Plants in which only one soul is embodied are always gross; they exist in the habitable part of the world only. But those plants of which each is a colony of plant lives may also be subtle and invisible, and in that case they are distributed all over the world. The whole universe is full of minute beings called *nigodas*; they are groups of infinite number of souls forming very small clusters, having respiration and nutrition in common and experiencing extreme pains. The whole space of the world is closely packed with them like a box filled with powder. The nigodas furnish the supply of souls in place of those that have reached Mokṣa. But an infinitesimally small fraction of one single nigoda has sufficed to replace the vacancy caused in the world by the Nirvāṇa of all the souls that have been liberated from beginningless past down to the present. Thus it is evident the saṃsāra will never be empty of living beings. Those of the *nigodas* who long for development come out and contiune their course of progress through successive stages[1].

Karma Theory.

It is on account of their merits or demerits that the jīvas are born as gods, men, animals, or denizens of hell. We have already noticed in Chapter III that the cause of the embodiment of soul is the presence in it of karma matter. The natural perfections of the pure soul are sullied by the different kinds of karma matter. Those which obscure right knowledge of details (*jñāna*) are called *jñānāvaraṇīya*, those which obscure right perception (*darśana*) as in sleep are called *darśanāvaraṇīya*, those which

[1] See Jacobi's article on Jainism, *E. R. E.*, and *Lokaprakāśa*, VI. pp. 31 ff.

obscure the bliss-nature of the soul and thus produce pleasure and pain are *vedanīya*, and those which obscure the right attitude of the soul towards faith and right conduct *mohanīya*[1]. In addition to these four kinds of karma there are other four kinds of karma which determine (1) the length of life in any birth, (2) the peculiar body with its general and special qualities and faculties, (3) the nationality, caste, family, social standing, etc., (4) the inborn energy of the soul by the obstruction of which it prevents the doing of a good action when there is a desire to do it. These are respectively called (1) *āyuṣka karma*, (2) *nāma karma*, (3) *gotra karma*, (4) *antarāya karma*. By our actions of mind, speech and body, we are continually producing certain subtle karma matter which in the first instance is called *bhāva karma*, which transforms itself into *dravya karma* and pours itself into the soul and sticks there by coming into contact with the passions (*kaṣāya*) of the soul. These act like viscous substances in retaining the inpouring karma matter. This matter acts in eight different ways and it is accordingly divided into eight classes, as we have already noticed. This karma is the cause of bondage and sorrow. According as good or bad karma matter sticks to the soul it gets itself coloured respectively as golden, lotus-pink, white and black, blue and grey and they are called the *leśyās*. The feelings generated by the accumulation of the karma-matter are called *bhāva-leśyā* and the actual coloration of the soul by it is called *dravya-leśyā*. According as any karma matter has been generated by good, bad, or indifferent actions, it gives us pleasure, pain, or feeling of indifference. Even the knowledge that we are constantly getting by perception, inference, etc., is but the result of the effect of karmas in accordance with which the particular kind of veil which was obscuring any particular kind of knowledge is removed at any time and we have a knowledge of a corresponding nature. By our own karmas the veils over our knowledge, feeling, etc., are so removed that we have just that kind of knowledge and feeling that we deserved to have. All knowledge, feeling, etc., are thus in one sense generated from within, the external objects which are ordinarily said to be generating them all being but mere coexistent external conditions.

[1] The Jains acknowledge five kinds of knowledge: (1) *matijñāna* (ordinary cognition), (2) *śruti* (testimony), (3) *avadhi* (supernatural cognition), (4) *manaḥparyāya* (thought-reading), (5) *kevala-jñāna* (omniscience).

After the effect of a particular karma matter (*karma-vargaṇā*) is once produced, it is discharged and purged from off the soul. This process of purging off the karmas is called *nirjarā*. If no new karma matter should accumulate then, the gradual purging off of the karmas might make the soul free of karma matter, but as it is, while some karma matter is being purged off, other karma matter is continually pouring in, and thus the purging and binding processes continuing simultaneously force the soul to continue its mundane cycle of existence, transmigration, and rebirth. After the death of each individual his soul, together with its karmic body (*kārmaṇaśarīra*), goes in a few moments to the place of its new birth and there assumes a new body, expanding or contracting in accordance with the dimensions of the latter.

In the ordinary course karma takes effect and produces its proper results, and at such a stage the soul is said to be in the *audayika* state. By proper efforts karma may however be prevented from taking effect, though it still continues to exist, and this is said to be the *aupaśamika* state of the soul. When karma is not only prevented from operating but is annihilated, the soul is said to be in the *kṣāyika* state, and it is from this state that Mokṣa is attained. There is, however, a fourth state of ordinary good men with whom some karma is annihilated, some neutralized, and some active (*kṣāyopaśamika*)[1].

Karma, Āsrava and Nirjarā.

It is on account of karma that the souls have to suffer all the experiences of this world process, including births and rebirths in diverse spheres of life as gods, men or animals, or insects. The karmas are certain sorts of infra-atomic particles of matter (*karma-vargaṇā*). The influx of these karma particles into the soul is called āsrava in Jainism. These karmas are produced by body, mind, and speech. The āsravas represent the channels or modes through which the karmas enter the soul, just like the channels through which water enters into a pond. But the Jains distinguish between the channels and the karmas which actually

[1] The stages through which a developing soul passes are technically called *guṇasthānas* which are fourteen in number. The first three stages represent the growth of faith in Jainism, the next five stages are those in which all the passions are controlled, in the next four stages the ascetic practises yoga and destroys all his karmas, at the thirteenth stage he is divested of all karmas but he still practises yoga and at the fourteenth stage he attains liberation (see Dravyasaṃgrahavṛtti, 13th verse).

enter through those channels. Thus they distinguish two kinds of āsravas, bhāvāsrava and karmāsrava. Bhāvāsrava means the thought activities of the soul through which or on account of which the karma particles enter the soul[1]. Thus Nemicandra says that bhāvāsrava is that kind of change in the soul (which is the contrary to what can destroy the karmāsrava), by which the karmas enter the soul[2]. Karmāsrava, however, means the actual entrance of the karma matter into the soul. These bhāvāsravas are in general of five kinds, namely delusion (*mithyātva*), want of control (*avirati*), inadvertence (*pramāda*), the activities of body, mind and speech (*yoga*) and the passions (*kaṣāyas*). Delusion again is of five kinds, namely *ekānta* (a false belief unknowingly accepted and uncritically followed), *viparīta* (uncertainty as to the exact nature of truth), *vinaya* (retention of a belief knowing it to be false, due to old habit), *saṃśaya* (doubt as to right or wrong) and *ajñāna* (want of any belief due to the want of application of reasoning powers). Avirati is again of five kinds, injury (*hiṃsā*), falsehood (*anṛta*), stealing (*cauryya*), incontinence (*abrahma*), and desire to have things which one does not already possess (*parigrahākāṅkṣā*). Pramāda or inadvertence is again of five kinds, namely bad conversation (*vikathā*), passions (*kaṣāya*), bad use of the five senses (*indriya*), sleep (*nidrā*), attachment (*rāga*)[3].

Coming to dravyāsrava we find that it means that actual influx of karma which affects the soul in eight different manners in accordance with which these karmas are classed into eight different kinds, namely jñānāvaraṇīya, darśanāvaraṇīya, vedanīya, mohanīya, āyu, nāma, gotra and antarāya. These actual influxes take place only as a result of the bhāvāsrava or the reprehensible thought activities, or changes (*pariṇāma*) of the soul. The states of thought which condition the coming in of the karmas is called bhāvabandha and the actual bondage of the soul by the actual impure connections of the karmas is technically called dravyabandha. It is on account of bhāvabandha that the actual connection between the karmas and the soul can take place[4]. The actual connections of the karmas with the soul are like the sticking

[1] *Dravyasaṃgraha*, Śl. 29.

[2] Nemicandra's commentary on *Dravyasaṃgraha*, Śl. 29, edited by S. C. Ghoshal, Arrah, 1917.

[3] See Nemicandra's commentary on Śl. 30.

[4] Nemicandra on 31, and *Vardhamānapurāṇa* XVI. 44, quoted by Ghoshal.

of dust on the body of a person who is besmeared all over with oil. Thus Guṇaratna says: "The influx of karma means the contact of the particles of karma matter, in accordance with the particular kind of karma, with the soul, just like the sticking of dust on the body of a person besmeared with oil. In all parts of the soul there being infinite number of karma atoms it becomes so completely covered with them that in some sense when looked at from that point of view the soul is sometimes regarded as a material body during its saṃsāra stage[1]." From one point of view the bondage of karma is only of *puṇya* and *pāpa* (good and bad karmas)[2]. From another this bondage is of four kinds, according to the nature of karma (*prakṛti*), duration of bondage (*sthiti*), intensity (*anubhāga*) and extension (*pradeśa*). The nature of karma refers to the eight classes of karma already mentioned, namely the jñānāvaraṇīya karma which obscures the infinite knowledge of the soul of all things in detail, darśanāvaraṇīya karma which obscures the infinite general knowledge of the soul, vedanīya karma which produces the feelings of pleasure and pain in the soul, mohanīya karma, which so infatuates souls that they fail to distinguish what is right from what is wrong, āyu karma, which determines the tenure of any particular life, nāma karma which gives them personalities, gotra karma which brings about a particular kind of social surrounding for the soul and antarāya karma which tends to oppose the performance of right actions by the soul. The duration of the stay of any karma in the soul is called sthiti. Again a karma may be intense, middling or mild, and this indicates the third principle of division, anubhāga. Pradeśa refers to the different parts of the soul to which the karma particles attach themselves. The duration of stay of any karma and its varying intensity are due to the nature of the kaṣāyas or passions of the soul, whereas the different classification of karmas as jñānāvaraṇīya, etc., are due to the nature of specific contact of the soul with karma matter[3].

Corresponding to the two modes of inrush of karmas (bhāvāsrava and dravyāsrava) are two kinds of control opposing this inrush, by actual thought modification of a contrary nature and by the actual stoppage of the inrush of karma particles, and these are respectively called bhāvasaṃvara and dravyasaṃvara[4].

[1] See Guṇaratna, p. 181. [2] *Ibid.* [3] Nemicandra, 33.
[4] *Varddhamānapurāṇa*, XVI. 67–68, and *Dravyasaṃgrahavṛtti*, Śl. 35.

The bhāvasaṃvaras are (1) the vows of non-injury, truthfulness, abstinence from stealing, sex-control, and non-acceptance of objects of desire, (2) samitis consisting of the use of trodden tracks in order to avoid injury to insects (*īryā*), gentle and holy talk (*bhāṣā*), receiving proper alms (*eṣaṇā*), etc., (3) *guptis* or restraints of body, speech and mind, (4) *dharmas* consisting of habits of forgiveness, humility, straightforwardness, truth, cleanliness, restraint, penance, abandonment, indifference to any kind of gain or loss, and supreme sex-control[1], (5) *anuprekṣā* consisting of meditation about the transient character of the world, about our helplessness without the truth, about the cycles of world-existence, about our own responsibilities for our good and bad actions, about the difference between the soul and the non-soul, about the uncleanliness of our body and all that is associated with it, about the influx of karma and its stoppage and the destruction of those karmas which have already entered the soul, about soul, matter and the substance of the universe, about the difficulty of attaining true knowledge, faith, and conduct, and about the essential principles of the world[2], (6) the *parīṣahajaya* consisting of the conquering of all kinds of physical troubles of heat, cold, etc., and of feelings of discomforts of various kinds, (7) *cāritra* or right conduct.

Next to this we come to nirjarā or the purging off of the karmas or rather their destruction. This nirjarā also is of two kinds, bhāvanirjarā and dravyanirjarā. Bhāvanirjarā means that change in the soul by virtue of which the karma particles are destroyed. Dravyanirjarā means the actual destruction of these karma particles either by the reaping of their effects or by penances before their time of fruition, called savipāka and avipāka nirjarās respectively. When all the karmas are destroyed mokṣa or liberation is effected.

Pudgala.

The *ajīva* (non-living) is divided into *pudgalāstikāya*, *dharma stikāya*, *adharmāstikāya*, *ākāśāstikāya*, *kāla*, *puṇya*, *pāpa*. The word *pudgala* means matter[3], and it is called *astikāya* in the sense that it occupies space. Pudgala is made up of atoms

1 *Tattvārthādhigamasūtra*.

2 *Ibid.*

3 This is entirely different from the Buddhist sense. With the Buddhists *pudgala* means an individual or a person.

which are without size and eternal. Matter may exist in two states, gross (such as things we see around us), and subtle (such as the karma matter which sullies the soul). All material things are ultimately produced by the combination of atoms. The smallest indivisible particle of matter is called an atom (*aṇu*). The atoms are all eternal and they all have touch, taste, smell, and colour. The formation of different substances is due to the different geometrical, spherical or cubical modes of the combination of the atoms, to the diverse modes of their inner arrangement and to the existence of different degrees of inter-atomic space (*ghanapratarabhedena*). Some combinations take place by simple mutual contact at two points (*yugmapradeśa*) whereas in others the atoms are only held together by the points of attractive force (*ojaḥpradeśa*) (*Prajñāpanopāṅgasūtra*, pp. 10–12). Two atoms form a compound (*skandha*), when the one is viscous and the other dry or both are of different degrees of viscosity or dryness. It must be noted that while the Buddhists thought that there was no actual contact between the atoms the Jains regarded the contact as essential and as testified by experience. These compounds combine with other compounds and thus produce the gross things of the world. They are, however, liable to constant change (*pariṇāma*) by which they lose some of their old qualities (*guṇas*) and acquire new ones. There are four elements, earth, water, air, and fire, and the atoms of all these are alike in character. The perception of grossness however is not an error which is imposed upon the perception of the atoms by our mind (as the Buddhists think) nor is it due to the perception of atoms scattered spatially lengthwise and breadthwise (as the Sāṃkhya-Yoga supposes), but it is due to the accession of a similar property of grossness, blueness or hardness in the combined atoms, so that such knowledge is generated in us as is given in the perception of a gross, blue, or a hard thing. When a thing appears as blue, what happens is this, that the atoms there have all acquired the property of blueness and on the removal of the darśanavaraṇīya and jñānavaraṇīya veil, there arises in the soul the perception and knowledge of that blue thing. This sameness (*samāna-rūpatā*) of the accession of a quality in an aggregate of atoms by virtue of which it appears as one object (e.g. a cow) is technically called *tiryaksāmānya*. This sāmānya or generality is thus neither an imposition of the mind nor an abstract entity (as maintained by the Naiyāyikas) but represents only the accession of similar qualities by a similar development of qualities of atoms forming an aggregate. So long as this similarity of qualities continues we perceive the thing to be the same and to continue for some length of time. When we think of a thing to be permanent, we do so by referring to this sameness in the developing tendencies of an aggregate of atoms resulting in the relative permanence of similar qualities in them. According to the Jains things are not momentary and in spite of the loss of some old qualities and the accession of other ones, the thing as a whole may remain more or less the same for some time. This sameness of qualities in time is technically called *ūrdhvasāmānya*[1]. If the atoms are looked at from the point of view of the change and accession of new qualities, they may be regarded as liable to destruction, but if they are looked at from the point of view of substance (*dravya*) they are eternal.

Dharma, Adharma, Ākāśa.

The conception of dharma and adharma in Jainism is absolutely different from what they mean in other systems of Indian philosophy. Dharma is devoid of taste, touch, smell, sound and colour; it is conterminous with the mundane universe (*lokākāśa*) and pervades every part of it. The term *astikāya* is therefore applied to it. It is the principle of motion, the accompanying circumstance or cause which makes motion possible, like water to a moving fish. The water is a passive condition or circumstance of the movement of a fish, i.e. it is indifferent or passive (*udāsīna*) and not an active or solicitous (*preraka*) cause. The water cannot compel a fish at rest to move; but if the fish wants to move, water is then the necessary help to its motion. Dharma cannot make the soul or matter move; but if they are to move, they cannot do so without the presence of dharma. Hence at the extremity of the mundane world (*loka*) in the region of the liberated souls, there being no dharma, the liberated souls attain perfect rest. They cannot move there because there is not the necessary motion-element, dharma[2]. Adharma is also regarded as a similar pervasive entity which

[1] See *Prameyakamalamārtaṇḍa*, pp. 136–143; *Jainatarkavārttika*, p. 106.
[2] *Dravyasaṃgrahavṛtti*, 17–20.

helps jīvas and pudgalas to keep themselves at rest. No substance could move if there were no dharma, or could remain at rest if there were no adharma. The necessity of admitting these two categories seems probably to have been felt by the Jains on account of their notion that the inner activity of the jīva or the atoms required for its exterior realization the help of some other extraneous entity, without which this could not have been transformed into actual exterior motion. Moreover since the jīvas were regarded as having activity inherent in them they would be found to be moving even at the time of liberation (mokṣa), which was undesirable; thus it was conceived that actual motion required for its fulfilment the help of an extraneous entity which was absent in the region of the liberated souls.

The category of ākāśa is that subtle entity which pervades the mundane universe (*loka*) and the transcendent region of liberated souls (*aloka*) which allows the subsistence of all other substances such as dharma, adharma, jīva, pudgala. It is not a mere negation and absence of veil or obstruction, or mere emptiness, but a positive entity which helps other things to interpenetrate it. On account of its pervasive character it is called *ākāśāstikāya*[1].

Kāla and Samaya.

Time (*kāla*) in reality consists of those innumerable particles which never mix with one another, but which help the happening of the modification or accession of new qualities and the change of qualities of the atoms. Kāla does not bring about the changes of qualities, in things, but just as ākāśa helps interpenetration and dharma motion, so also kāla helps the action of the transformation of new qualities in things. Time perceived as moments, hours, days, etc., is called *samaya.* This is the appearance of the unchangeable kāla in so many forms. Kāla thus not only aids the modifications of other things, but also allows its own modifications as moments, hours, etc. It is thus a dravya (substance), and the moments, hours, etc., are its paryāyas. The unit of samaya is the time required by an atom to traverse a unit of space by a slow movement.

[1] *Dravyasaṃgrahavṛtti*, 19.

Jaina Cosmography.

According to the Jains, the world is eternal, without beginning or end. Loka is that place in which happiness and misery are experienced as results of virtue and vice. It is composed of three parts, *ūrdhva* (where the gods reside), *madhya* (this world of ours), and *adho* (where the denizens of hell reside). The mundane universe (*lokākāśa*) is pervaded with dharma which makes all movement possible. Beyond the lokākāśa there is no dharma and therefore no movement, but only space (*ākāśa*). Surrounding this lokākāśa are three layers of air. The perfected soul rising straight over the ūrdhvaloka goes to the top of this lokākāśa and (there being no dharma) remains motionless there.

Jaina Yoga.

Yoga according to Jainism is the cause of mokṣa (salvation). This yoga consists of jñāna (knowledge of reality as it is), śraddhā (faith in the teachings of the Jinas), and cāritra (cessation from doing all that is evil). This cāritra consists of *ahiṃsā* (not taking any life even by mistake or unmindfulness), *sūnṛta* (speaking in such a way as is true, good and pleasing), *asteya* (not taking anything which has not been given), *brahmacaryya* (abandoning lust for all kinds of objects, in mind, speech and body), and *aparigraha* (abandoning attachment for all things)[1]. These strict rules of conduct only apply to ascetics who are bent on attaining perfection. The standard proposed for the ordinary householders is fairly workable. Thus it is said by Hemacandra, that ordinary householders should earn money honestly, should follow the customs of good people, should marry a good girl from a good family, should follow the customs of the country and so forth. These are just what we should expect from any good and

[1] Certain external rules of conduct are also called cāritra. These are: *Īryyā* (to go by the path already trodden by others and illuminated by the sun's rays, so that proper precaution may be taken while walking to prevent oneself from treading on insects, etc., which may be lying on the way), *bhāṣā* (to speak well and pleasantly to all beings), *iṣaṇa* (to beg alms in the proper monastic manner), *dānasamiti* (to inspect carefully the seats avoiding all transgressions when taking or giving anything), *utsargasamiti* (to take care that bodily refuse may not be thrown in such a way as to injure any being), *manogupti* (to remove all false thoughts, to remain satisfied within oneself, and hold all people to be the same in mind), *vāggupti* (absolute silence), and *kāyagupti* (absolute steadiness and fixity of the body). Five other kinds of cāritra are counted in *Dravyasaṃgrahavṛtti* 35.

honest householder of the present day. Great stress is laid upon the virtues of ahiṃsā, sūnṛta, asteya and brahmacaryya, but the root of all these is ahiṃsā. The virtues of sūnṛta, asteya and brahmacaryya are made to follow directly as secondary corrollaries of ahiṃsā. Ahiṃsā may thus be generalized as the fundamental ethical virtue of Jainism; judgment on all actions may be passed in accordance with the standard of ahiṃsā; sūnṛta, asteya and brahmacaryya are regarded as virtues as their transgression leads to hiṃsā (injury to beings). A milder form of the practice of these virtues is expected from ordinary householders and this is called anubrata (small vows). But those who are struggling for the attainment of emancipation must practise these virtues according to the highest and strictest standard, and this is called mahābrata (great vows). Thus for example brahmacaryya for a householder according to the anubrata standard would be mere cessation from adultery, whereas according to mahābrata it would be absolute abstention from sex-thoughts, sex-words and sex-acts. Ahiṃsā according to a householder, according to anubrata, would require abstinence from killing any animals, but according to mahāvrata it would entail all the rigour and carefulness to prevent oneself from being the cause of any kind of injury to any living being in any way.

Many other minor duties are imposed upon householders, all of which are based upon the cardinal virtue of ahiṃsā. These are (1) *digvirati* (to carry out activities within a restricted area and thereby desist from injuring living beings in different places), (2) *bhogopabhogamāna* (to desist from drinking liquors, taking flesh, butter, honey, figs, certain other kinds of plants, fruits, and vegetables, to observe certain other kinds of restrictions regarding time and place of taking meals), (3) *anarthadaṇḍa* consisting of (*a*) *apadhyāna* (cessation from inflicting any bodily injuries, killing of one's enemies, etc.), (*b*) *pāpopadeśa* (desisting from advising people to take to agriculture which leads to the killing of so many insects), (*c*) *hiṃsopakāridāna* (desisting from giving implements of agriculture to people which will lead to the injury of insects), (*d*) *pramādācaraṇa* (to desist from attending musical parties, theatres, or reading sex-literature, gambling, etc.), (4) *śikṣāpadabrata* consisting of (*a*) *sāmayikabrata* (to try to treat all beings equally), (*b*) *deśāvakāśikabrata* (gradually to practise the *digviratibrata* more and more extensively), (*c*) *poṣadhabrata* (certain other kinds of restriction), (*d*) *atithisaṃvibhāgabrata* (to make gifts to guests). All transgressions of these virtues, called *aticāra*, should be carefully avoided.

All perception, wisdom, and morals belong to the soul, and to know the soul as possessing these is the right knowledge of the soul. All sorrows proceeding out of want of self-knowledge can be removed only by true self-knowledge. The soul in itself is pure intelligence, and it becomes endowed with the body only on account of its karma. When by meditation, all the karmas are burnt (*dhyānāgnidagdhakarma*) the self becomes purified. The soul is itself the saṃsāra (the cycle of rebirths) when it is overpowered by the four kaṣāyas (passions) and the senses. The four kaṣāyas are *krodha* (anger), *māna* (vanity and pride), *māyā* (insincerity and the tendency to dupe others), and *lobha* (greed). These kaṣāyas cannot be removed except by a control of the senses; and self-control alone leads to the purity of the mind (*manaḥśuddhi*). Without the control of the mind no one can proceed in the path of yoga. All our acts become controlled when the mind is controlled, so those who seek emancipation should make every effort to control the mind. No kind of asceticism (*tapas*) can be of any good until the mind is purified. All attachment and antipathy (*rāgadveṣa*) can be removed only by the purification of the mind. It is by attachment and antipathy that man loses his independence. It is thus necessary for the yogin (sage) that he should be free from them and become independent in the real sense of the term. When a man learns to look upon all beings with equality (*samatva*) he can effect such a conquest over rāga and dveṣa as one could never do even by the strictest asceticism through millions of years. In order to effect this samatva towards all, we should take to the following kinds of meditation (*bhāvanā*):

We should think of the transitoriness (*anityatā*) of all things, that what a thing was in the morning, it is not at mid-day, what it was at mid-day it is not at night; for all things are transitory and changing. Our body, all our objects of pleasure, wealth and youth all are fleeting like dreams, or cotton particles in a whirlwind.

All, even the gods, are subject to death. All our relatives will by their works fall a prey to death. This world is thus full of misery and there is nothing which can support us in it. Thus in whatever way we look for anything, on which we can depend, we find that it fails us. This is called aśaraṇabhāvanā (the meditation of helplessness).

Some are born in this world, some suffer, some reap the fruits of the karma done in another life. We are all different from one another by our surroundings, karma, by our separate bodies and by all other gifts which each of us severally enjoy. To meditate on these aspects is called ekatvabhāvanā and anyatvabhāvanā.

To think that the body is made up of defiled things, the flesh, blood, and bones, and is therefore impure is called aśucibhāvanā (meditation of the impurity of the body).

To think that if the mind is purified by the thoughts of universal friendship and compassion and the passions are removed, then only will good (*śubha*) accrue to me, but if on the contrary I commit sinful deeds and transgress the virtues, then all evil will befall me, is called āsravabhāvanā (meditation of the befalling of evil). By the control of the āsrava (inrush of karma) comes the saṃvara (cessation of the influx of karma) and the destruction of the karmas already accumulated leads to nirjarā (decay and destruction of karma matter).

Again one should think that the practice of the ten dharmas (virtues) of self control (*saṃyama*), truthfulness (*sūnṛtà*), purity (*śauca*), chastity (*brahma*), absolute want of greed (*akiñcanatā*), asceticism (*tapas*), forbearance, patience (*kṣānti*), mildness (*mārdava*), sincerity (*ṛjutā*), and freedom or emancipation from all sins (*mukti*) can alone help us in the achievement of the highest goal. These are the only supports to which we can look. It is these which uphold the world-order. This is called dharmasvākhyātatābhāvanā.

Again one should think of the Jaina cosmology and also of the nature of the influence of karma in producing all the diverse conditions of men. These two are called *lokabhāvanā* and *bodhibhāvanā*.

When by the continual practice of the above thoughts man becomes unattached to all things and adopts equality to all beings, and becomes disinclined to all worldly enjoyments, then with a mind full of peace he gets rid of all passions, and then he should take to the performance of dhyāna or meditation by deep concentration. The samatva or perfect equality of the mind and dhyāna are interdependent, so that without dhyanā there is no samatva and without samatva there is no dhyāna. In order to make the mind steady by dhyāna one should think of *maitrī* (universal friendship), *pramoda* (the habit of emphasizing the good sides of men), *karuṇā* (universal compassion) and *mādhyastha* (indifference to the wickedness of people, i.e. the habit of not taking any note of sinners). The Jaina dhyāna consists in concentrating the mind on the syllables of the Jaina prayer phrases. The dhyāna however as we have seen is only practised as an aid to making the mind steady and perfectly equal and undisturbed towards all things. Emancipation comes only as the result of the final extinction of the karma materials. Jaina yoga is thus a complete course of moral discipline which leads to the purification of the mind and is hence different from the traditional Hindu yoga of Patañjali or even of the Buddhists[1].

Jaina Atheism[2].

The Naiyāyikas assert that as the world is of the nature of an effect, it must have been created by an intelligent agent and this agent is Īśvara (God). To this the Jain replies, "What does the Naiyāyika mean when he says that the world is of the nature of an effect"? Does he mean by "effect," (1) that which is made up of parts (*sāvayava*), or, (2) the coinherence of the causes of a non-existent thing, or, (3) that which is regarded by anyone as having been made, or, (4) that which is liable to change (*vikāritvam*). Again, what is meant by being "made up of parts"? If it means existence in parts, then the class-concepts (*sāmānya*) existing in the parts should also be regarded as effects, and hence destructible, but these the Naiyāyikas regard as being partless and eternal. If it means "that which has parts," then even "space" (*ākāśa*) has to be regarded as "effect," but the Naiyāyika regards it as eternal.

Again "effect" cannot mean "coinherence of the causes of a thing which were previously non-existent," for in that case one could not speak of the world as an effect, for the atoms of the elements of earth, etc., are regarded as eternal.

Again if "effect" means "that which is regarded by anyone as

[1] *Yogaśāstra*, by Hemacandra, edited by Windisch, in *Zeitschrift der Deutschen Morg. Gesellschaft*, Leipsig, 1874, and *Dravyasaṃgraha*, edited by Ghoshal, 1917.

[2] See Guṇaratna's *Tarkarahasyadīpikā*.

having been made," then it would apply even to space, for when a man digs the ground he thinks that he has made new space in the hollow which he dug.

If it means "that which is liable to change," then one could suppose that God was also liable to change and he would require another creator to create him and he another, and so on *ad infinitum*. Moreover, if God creates he cannot but be liable to change with reference to his creative activity.

Moreover, we know that those things which happen at some time and do not happen at other times are regarded as "effects." But the world as a whole exists always. If it is argued that things contained within it such as trees, plants, etc., are "effects," then that would apply even to this hypothetical God, for, his will and thought must be diversely operating at diverse times and these are contained in him. He also becomes a created being by virtue of that. And even atoms would be "effects," for they also undergo changes of colour by heat.

Let us grant for the sake of argument that the world as a whole is an "effect." And every effect has a cause, and so the world as a whole has a cause. But this does not mean that the cause is an intelligent one, as God is supposed to be. If it is argued that he is regarded as intelligent on the analogy of human causation then he might also be regarded as imperfect as human beings. If it is held that the world as a whole is not exactly an effect of the type of effects produced by human beings but is similar to those, this will lead to no inference. Because water-vapour is similar to smoke, nobody will be justified in inferring fire from water-vapour, as he would do from smoke. If it is said that this is so different an effect that from it the inference is possible, though nobody has ever been seen to produce such an effect, well then, one could also infer on seeing old houses ruined in course of time that these ruins were produced by intelligent agents. For these are also effects of which we do not know of any intelligent agent, for both are effects, and the invisibility of the agent is present in both cases. If it is said that the world is such that we have a sense that it has been made by some one, then the question will be, whether you infer the agency of God from this sense or infer the sense of its having been made from the fact of its being made by God, and you have a vicious circle (*anyonyāśraya*).

Again, even if we should grant that the world was created by an agent, then such an agent should have a body, for we have never seen any intelligent creator without a body. If it is held that we should consider the general condition of agency only, namely, that the agent is intelligent, the objection will be that this is impossible, for agency is always associated with some kind of body. If you take the instances of other kinds of effects such as the shoots of corn growing in the fields, it will be found that these had no intelligent agents behind them to create them. If it is said that these are also made by God, then you have an argument in a circle (*cakraka*), for this was the very matter which you sought to prove.

Let it be granted for the sake of argument that God exists. Does his mere abstract existence produce the world? Well, in that case, the abstract existence of a potter may also create the world, for the abstract existence is the same in both cases. Does he produce the world by knowledge and will? Well, that is impossible, for there cannot be any knowledge and will without a body. Does he produce the world by physical movement or any other kind of movement? In any case that is impossible, for there cannot be any movement without a body. If you suppose that he is omniscient, you may do so, but that does not prove that he can be all-creator.

Let us again grant for the sake of argument that a bodiless God can create the world by his will and activity. Did he take to creation through a personal whim? In that case there would be no natural laws and order in the world. Did he take to it in accordance with the moral and immoral actions of men? Then he is guided by a moral order and is not independent. Is it through mercy that he took to creation? Well then, we suppose there should have been only happiness in the world and nothing else. If it is said that it is by the past actions of men that they suffer pains and enjoy pleasure, and if men are led to do vicious actions by past deeds which work like blind destiny, then such a blind destiny (*adṛṣṭa*) might take the place of God. If He took to creation as mere play, then he must be a child who did things without a purpose. If it was due to his desire of punishing certain people and favouring others, then he must harbour favouritism on behalf of some and hatred against others. If the creation took place simply through his own nature, then, what is the good of admitting him at all? You may rather say that the world came into being out of its own nature.

It is preposterous to suppose that one God without the help of any instruments or other accessories of any kind, could create this world. This is against all experience.

Admitting for the sake of argument that such a God exists, you could never justify the adjectives with which you wish to qualify him. Thus you say that he is eternal. But since he has no body, he must be of the nature of intelligence and will. But this nature must have changed in diverse forms for the production of diverse kinds of worldly things, which are of so varied a nature. If there were no change in his knowledge and will, then there could not have been diverse kinds of creation and destruction. Destruction and creation cannot be the result of one unchangeable will and knowledge. Moreover it is the character of knowledge to change, if the word is used in the sense in which knowledge is applied to human beings, and surely we are not aware of any other kind of knowledge. You say that God is omniscient, but it is difficult to suppose how he can have any knowledge at all, for as he has no organs he cannot have any perception, and since he cannot have any perception he cannot have any inference either. If it is said that without the supposition of a God the variety of the world would be inexplicable, this also is not true, for this implication would only be justified if there were no other hypothesis left. But there are other suppositions also. Even without an omniscient God you could explain all things merely by the doctrine of moral order or the law of karma. If there were one God, there could be a society of Gods too. You say that if there were many Gods, then there would be quarrels and differences of opinion. This is like the story of a miser who for fear of incurring expenses left all his sons and wife and retired into the forest. When even ants and bees can co-operate together and act harmoniously, the supposition that if there were many Gods they would have fallen out, would indicate that in spite of all the virtues that you ascribe to God you think his nature to be quite unreliable, if not vicious. Thus in whichever way one tries to justify the existence of God he finds that it is absolutely a hopeless task. The best way then is to dispense with the supposition altogether[1].

[1] See *Ṣaḍdarśanasamuccaya*, Guṇaratna on Jainism, pp. 115–124.

Mokṣa (emancipation).

The motive which leads a man to strive for release (*mokṣa*) is the avoidance of pain and the attainment of happiness, for the state of mukti is the state of the soul in pure happiness. It is also a state of pure and infinite knowledge (*anantajñāna*) and infinite perception (*anantadarśana*). In the saṃsāra state on account of the karma veils this purity is sullied, and the veils are only worn out imperfectly and thus reveal this and that object at this and that time as ordinary knowledge (*mati*), testimony (*śruta*), supernatural cognition, as in trance or hypnotism (*avadhi*), and direct knowledge of the thoughts of others or thought reading (*manaḥparyāya*). In the state of release however there is omniscience (*kevala-jñāna*) and all things are simultaneously known to the perfect (*kevalin*) as they are. In the saṃsāra stage the soul always acquires new qualities, and thus suffers a continual change though remaining the same in substance. But in the emancipated stage the changes that a soul suffers are all exactly the same, and thus it is that at this stage the soul appears to be the same in substance as well as in its qualities of infinite knowledge, etc., the change meaning in this state only the repetition of the same qualities.

It may not be out of place to mention here that though the karmas of man are constantly determining him in various ways yet there is in him infinite capacity or power for right action (*anantavīrya*), so that karma can never subdue this freedom and infinite capacity, though this may be suppressed from time to time by the influence of karma. It is thus that by an exercise of this power man can overcome all karma and become finally liberated. If man had not this anantavīrya in him he might have been eternally under the sway of the accumulated karma which secured his bondage (*bandha*). But since man is the repository of this indomitable power the karmas can only throw obstacles and produce sufferings, but can never prevent him from attaining his highest good.

CHAPTER VII

THE KAPILA AND THE PĀTAÑJALA SĀṂKHYA (YOGA)[1].

A Review.

THE examination of the two ancient Nāstika schools of Buddhism and Jainism of two different types ought to convince us that serious philosophical speculations were indulged in, in circles other than those of the Upaniṣad sages. That certain practices known as Yoga were generally prevalent amongst the wise seems very probable, for these are not only alluded to in some of the Upaniṣads but were accepted by the two nāstika schools of Buddhism and Jainism. Whether we look at them from the point of view of ethics or metaphysics, the two Nāstika schools appear to have arisen out of a reaction against the sacrificial disciplines of the Brāhmaṇas. Both these systems originated with the Kṣattriyas and were marked by a strong aversion against the taking of animal life, and against the doctrine of offering animals at the sacrifices.

The doctrine of the sacrifices supposed that a suitable combination of rites, rituals, and articles of sacrifice had the magical power of producing the desired effect—a shower of rain, the birth of a son, the routing of a huge army, etc. The sacrifices were enjoined generally not so much for any moral elevation, as for the achievement of objects of practical welfare. The Vedas were the eternal revelations which were competent so to dictate a detailed procedure, that we could by following it proceed on a certain course of action and refrain from other injurious courses in such a manner that we might obtain the objects we desired by the accurate performance of any sacrifice. If we are to define truth in accordance with the philosophy of such a ritualistic culture we might say that, that alone is true, in accordance with which we may realize our objects in the world about us; the truth of Vedic injunctions is shown by the practical attainment of our

[1] This chapter is based on my *Study of Patanjali*, published by the Calcutta University, and my *Yoga philosophy in relation to other Indian Systems of thought*, awaiting publication with the same authority. The system has been treated in detail in those two works.

objects. Truth cannot be determined *a priori* but depends upon the test of experience[1].

It is interesting to notice that Buddhism and Jainism though probably born out of a reactionary movement against this artificial creed, yet could not but be influenced by some of its fundamental principles which, whether distinctly formulated or not, were at least tacitly implied in all sacrificial performances. Thus we see that Buddhism regarded all production and destruction as being due to the assemblage of conditions, and defined truth as that which could produce any effect. But to such a logical extreme did the Buddhists carry these doctrines that they ended in formulating the doctrine of absolute momentariness[2]. Turning to the Jains we find that they also regarded the value of knowledge as consisting in the help that it offers in securing what is good for us and avoiding what is evil; truth gives us such an account of things that on proceeding according to its directions we may verify it by actual experience. Proceeding on a correct estimate of things we may easily avail ourselves of what is good and avoid what is bad. The Jains also believed that changes were produced by the assemblage of conditions, but they did not carry this doctrine to its logical extreme. There was change in the world as well as permanence. The Buddhists had gone so far that they had even denied the existence of any permanent soul. The Jains said that no ultimate, one-sided and absolute view of things could be taken, and held that not only the happening of events was conditional, but even all our judgments, are true only in a limited sense. This is indeed true for common sense, which we acknowledge as superior to mere *a priori* abstractions, which lead to absolute and one-sided conclusions. By the assemblage of conditions, old qualities in things disappeared, new qualities came in, and a part remained permanent. But this common-sense view, though in agreement with our ordinary experience, could not satisfy our inner *a priori* demands for finding out ultimate truth, which was true not relatively but absolutely. When asked whether anything was true, Jainism

[1] The philosophy of the Vedas as formulated by the Mīmāṃsā of Kumārila and Prabhākara holds the opposite view. Truth according to them is determined *a priori* while error is determined by experience.

[2] Historically the doctrine of momentariness is probably prior to the doctrine of *arthakriyākāritva*. But the later Buddhists sought to prove that momentariness was the logical result of the doctrine of *arthakriyākāritva*.

would answer, "yes, this is true from this point of view, but untrue from that point of view, while that is also true from such a point of view and untrue from another." But such an answer cannot satisfy the mind which seeks to reach a definite pronouncement, an absolute judgment.

The main departure of the systems of Jainism and Buddhism from the sacrificial creed consisted in this, that they tried to formulate a theory of the universe, the reality and the position of sentient beings and more particularly of man. The sacrificial creed was busy with individual rituals and sacrifices, and cared for principles or maxims only so far as they were of use for the actual performances of sacrifices. Again action with the new systems did not mean sacrifice but any general action that we always perform. Actions were here considered bad or good according as they brought about our moral elevation or not. The followers of the sacrificial creed refrained from untruth not so much from a sense of personal degradation, but because the Vedas had dictated that untruth should not be spoken, and the Vedas must be obeyed. The sacrificial creed wanted more and more happiness here or in the other world. The systems of Buddhist and Jain philosophy turned their backs upon ordinary happiness and wanted an ultimate and unchangeable state where all pains and sorrows were for ever dissolved (Buddhism) or where infinite happiness, ever unshaken, was realized. A course of right conduct to be followed merely for the moral elevation of the person had no place in the sacrificial creed, for with it a course of right conduct could be followed only if it was so dictated in the Vedas. Karma and the fruit of karma (*karmaphala*) only meant the karma of sacrifice and its fruits—temporary happiness, such as was produced as the fruit of sacrifices; knowledge with them meant only the knowledge of sacrifice and of the dictates of the Vedas. In the systems however, karma, karmaphala, happiness, knowledge, all these were taken in their widest and most universal sense. Happiness or absolute extinction of sorrow was still the goal, but this was no narrow sacrificial happiness but infinite and unchangeable happiness or destruction of sorrow; karma was still the way, but not sacrificial karma, for it meant all moral and immoral actions performed by us; knowledge here meant the knowledge of truth or reality and not the knowledge of sacrifice.

Such an advance had however already begun in the Upaniṣads which had anticipated the new systems in all these directions. The pioneers of these new systems probably drew their suggestions both from the sacrificial creed and from the Upaniṣads, and built their systems independently by their own rational thinking. But if the suggestions of the Upaniṣads were thus utilized by heretics who denied the authority of the Vedas, it was natural to expect that we should find in the Hindu camp such germs of rational thinking as might indicate an attempt to harmonize the suggestions of the Upaniṣads and of the sacrificial creed in such a manner as might lead to the construction of a consistent and well-worked system of thought. Our expectations are indeed fulfilled in the Sāṃkhya philosophy, germs of which may be discovered in the Upaniṣads.

The Germs of Sāṃkhya in the Upaniṣads.

It is indeed true that in the Upaniṣads there is a large number of texts that describe the ultimate reality as the Brahman, the infinite, knowledge, bliss, and speak of all else as mere changing forms and names. The word Brahman originally meant in the earliest Vedic literature, *mantra*, duly performed sacrifice, and also the power of sacrifice which could bring about the desired result[1]. In many passages of the Upaniṣads this Brahman appears as the universal and supreme principle from which all others derived their powers. Such a Brahman is sought for in many passages for personal gain or welfare. But through a gradual process of development the conception of Brahman reached a superior level in which the reality and truth of the world are tacitly ignored, and the One, the infinite, knowledge, the real is regarded as the only Truth. This type of thought gradually developed into the monistic Vedānta as explained by Śaṅkara. But there was another line of thought which was developing alongside of it, which regarded the world as having a reality and as being made up of water, fire, and earth. There are also passages in Śvetāśvatara and particularly in Maitrāyaṇī from which it appears that the Sāṃkhya line of thought had considerably developed, and many of its technical terms were already in use[2]. But the date of Maitrāyaṇī has not yet been definitely settled, and the details

[1] See Hillebrandt's article, "Brahman" (*E. R. E.*).

[2] Kaṭha III. 10, V. 7. Śveta. V. 7, 8, 12, IV. 5, I. 3. This has been dealt with in detail in my *Yoga Philosophy in relation to other Indian Systems of Thought*, in the first chapter.

found there are also not such that we can form a distinct notion of the Sāṃkhya thought as it developed in the Upaniṣads. It is not improbable that at this stage of development it also gave some suggestions to Buddhism or Jainism, but the Sāṃkhya-Yoga philosophy as we now get it is a system in which are found all the results of Buddhism and Jainism in such a manner that it unites the doctrine of permanence of the Upaniṣads with the doctrine of momentariness of the Buddhists and the doctrine of relativism of the Jains.

Sāṃkhya and Yoga Literature.

The main exposition of the system of Sāṃkhya and Yoga in this section has been based on the *Sāṃkhya kārikā*, the *Sāṃkhya sūtras*, and the *Yoga sūtras* of Patañjali with their commentaries and sub-commentaries. The *Sāṃkhya kārikā* (about 200 A.D.) was written by Īśvarakṛṣṇa. The account of Sāṃkhya given by Caraka (78 A.D.) represents probably an earlier school and this has been treated separately. Vācaspati Miśra (ninth century A.D.) wrote a commentary on it known as *Tattvakaumudī*. But before him Gauḍapāda and Rājā wrote commentaries on the *Sāṃkhya kārikā*[1]. Nārāyaṇatīrtha wrote his *Candrikā* on Gauḍapāda's commentary. The *Sāṃkhya sūtras* which have been commented on by Vijñāna Bhikṣu (called *Pravacanabhāṣya*) of the sixteenth century seems to be a work of some unknown author after the ninth century. Aniruddha of the latter half of the fifteenth century was the first man to write a commentary on the *Sāṃkhya sūtras*. Vijñāna Bhikṣu wrote also another elementary work on Sāṃkhya known as *Sāṃkhyasāra*. Another short work of late origin is *Tattvasamāsa* (probably fourteenth century). Two other works on Sāṃkhya, viz. Sīmānanda's *Sāṃkhyatattvavivecana* and Bhāvāgaṇeśa's *Sāṃkhyatattvayāthārthyadīpana* (both later than Vijñānabhikṣu) of real philosophical value have also been freely consulted. Patañjali's *Yoga sūtra* (not earlier than 147 B.C.) was commented on by Vyāsa (400 A.D.) and Vyāsa's bhāṣya commented on by Vācaspati Miśra is called *Tattvavaiśāradī*, by Vijñāna Bhikṣu *Yogavārttika*, by Bhoja in the tenth century *Bhojavṛtti*, and by Nāgeśa (seventeenth century) *Chāyāvyākhyā*.

[1] I suppose that Rājā's commentary on the *Kārikā* was the same as *Rājavārttika* quoted by Vācaspati. Rājā's commentary on the *Kārikā* has been referred to by Jayanta in his *Nyāyamañjarī*, p. 109. This book is probably now lost.

Amongst the modern works to which I owe an obligation I may mention the two treatises *Mechanical, physical and chemical theories of the Ancient Hindus* and the *Positive Sciences of the Ancient Hindus* by Dr B. N. Seal and my two works on Yoga *Study of Patanjali* published by the Calcutta University, and *Yoga Philosophy in relation to other Indian Systems of Thought* which is shortly to be published, and my *Natural Philosophy of the Ancient Hindus*, awaiting publication with the Calcutta University.

Guṇaratna mentions two other authoritative Sāṃkhya works, viz. *Māṭharabhāṣya* and *Ātreyatantra.* Of these the second is probably the same as Caraka s treatment of Sāṃkhya, for we know that the sage Atri is the speaker in Caraka's work and for that it was called *Ātreyasaṃhitā* or *Ātreyatantra.* Nothing is known of the *Māṭharabhāṣya*[1].

An Early School of Sāṃkhya.

It is important for the history of Sāṃkhya philosophy that Caraka's treatment of it, which so far as I know has never been dealt with in any of the modern studies of Sāṃkhya, should be brought before the notice of the students of this philosophy. According to Caraka there are six elements (*dhātus*), viz. the five elements such as ākāśa, vāyu etc. and cetanā, called also puruṣa. From other points of view, the categories may be said to be twenty-four only, viz. the ten senses (five cognitive and five conative), manas, the five objects of senses and the eightfold prakṛti (prakṛti, mahat, ahaṃkāra and the five elements)[2]. The manas works through the senses. It is atomic and its existence is proved by the fact that in spite of the existence of the senses there cannot be any knowledge unless manas is in touch with them. There are two movements of manas as indeterminate sensing (*ūha*) and conceiving (*vicāra*) before definite understanding (*buddhi*) arises. Each of the five senses is the product of the combination of five elements but the auditory sense is made with a preponderance of ākāśa, the sense of touch with a preponderance

[1] Readers unacquainted with Sāṃkhya-Yoga may omit the following three sections at the time of first reading.

[2] Puruṣa is here excluded from the list. Cakrapāṇi, the commentator, says that the prakṛti and puruṣa both being unmanifested, the two together have been counted as one. *Prakṛtivyatiriktañcodāsīnaṃ puruṣamavyaktatvasādharmyāt avyaktāyām prakṛtāveva prakṣipya avyaktaśabdenaiva gṛhṇāti.* Harinātha Viśārada's edition of *Caraka*, *Śārīra*, p. 4.

of air, the visual sense with a preponderance of light, the taste with a preponderance of water and the sense of smell with a preponderance of earth. Caraka does not mention the tanmātras at all[1]. The conglomeration of the sense-objects (*indriyārtha*) or gross matter, the ten senses, manas, the five subtle bhūtas and prakṛti, mahat and ahaṃkāra taking place through rajas make up what we call man. When the sattva is at its height this conglomeration ceases. All karma, the fruit of karma, cognition, pleasure, pain, ignorance, life and death belongs to this conglomeration. But there is also the puruṣa, for had it not been so there would be no birth, death, bondage, or salvation. If the ātman were not regarded as cause, all illuminations of cognition would be without any reason. If a permanent self were not recognized, then for the work of one others would be responsible. This puruṣa, called also *paramātman*, is beginningless and it has no cause beyond itself. The self is in itself without consciousness. Consciousness can only come to it through its connection with the sense organs and manas. By ignorance, will, antipathy, and work, this conglomeration of puruṣa and the other elements takes place. Knowledge, feeling, or action, cannot be produced without this combination. All positive effects are due to conglomerations of causes and not by a single cause, but all destruction comes naturally and without cause. That which is eternal is never the product of anything. Caraka identifies the avyakta part of prakṛti with puruṣa as forming one category. The vikāra or evolutionary products of prakṛti are called kṣetra, whereas the avyakta part of prakṛti is regarded as the kṣetrajña (*avyaktamasya kṣetrasya kṣetrajñamṛṣayo viduh*). This avyakta and cetanā are one and the same entity. From this unmanifested prakṛti or cetanā is derived the buddhi, and from the buddhi is derived the ego (*ahaṃkāra*) and from the ahaṃkāra the five elements and the senses are produced, and when this production is complete, we say that creation has taken place. At the time of pralaya (periodical cosmic dissolution) all the evolutes return back to prakṛti, and thus become unmanifest with it, whereas at the time of a new creation from the puruṣa the unmanifest (*avyakta*), all the manifested forms—the evolutes of buddhi, ahaṃkāra, etc.—

[1] But some sort of subtle matter, different from gross matter, is referred to as forming part of *prakṛti* which is regarded as having eight elements in it (*prakṛtiścāṣṭadhātuki*), viz. avyakta, mahat, ahaṃkāra, and five other elements. In addition to these elements forming part of the prakṛti we hear of indriyārthā, the five sense objects which have evolved out of the prakṛti.

appear[1]. This cycle of births or rebirths or of dissolution and new creation acts through the influence of rajas and tamas, and so those who can get rid of these two will never again suffer this revolution in a cycle. The manas can only become active in association with the self, which is the real agent. This self of itself takes rebirth in all kinds of lives according to its own wish, undetermined by anyone else. It works according to its own free will and reaps the fruits of its karma. Though all the souls are pervasive, yet they can only perceive in particular bodies where they are associated with their own specific senses. All pleasures and pains are felt by the conglomeration (*rāśi*), and not by the ātman presiding over it. From the enjoyment and suffering of pleasure and pain comes desire (*tṛṣṇā*) consisting of wish and antipathy, and from desire again comes pleasure and pain. Mokṣa means complete cessation of pleasure and pain, arising through the association of the self with the manas, the sense, and sense-objects. If the manas is settled steadily in the self, it is the state of yoga when there is neither pleasure nor pain. When true knowledge dawns that "all are produced by causes, are transitory, rise of themselves, but are not produced by the self and are sorrow, and do not belong to me the self," the self transcends all. This is the last renunciation when all affections and knowledge become finally extinct. There remains no indication of any positive existence of the self at this time, and the self can no longer be perceived[2]. It is the state of Brahman. Those who know Brahman call this state the Brahman, which is eternal and absolutely devoid of any characteristic. This state is spoken of by the Sāṃkhyas as their goal, and also that of the Yogins. When rajas and tamas are rooted out and the karma of the past whose fruits have to be enjoyed are exhausted, and there is no new karma and new birth,

1 This passage has been differently explained in a commentary previous to Cakrapāṇi as meaning that at the time of death these resolve back into the prakṛti—the puruṣa—and at the time of rebirth they become manifest again. See Cakrapāṇi on Śārīra, I. 46.

2 Though this state is called brahmabhūta, it is not in any sense like the Brahman of Vedānta which is of the nature of pure being, pure intelligence and pure bliss. This indescribable state is more like absolute annihilation without any sign of existence (*alakṣaṇam*), resembling Nāgārjuna's Nirvāṇa. Thus Caraka writes:—*tasmiṃścarama-sannyāse samūlāḥsarvavedanāḥ asaṃjñājñānavijñānā nivṛttiṃ yāntyaśeṣataḥ. ataḥ-paraṃ brahmabhūto bhūtātmā nopalabhyate niḥsṛtaḥ sarvabhāvebhyaḥ cihnaṃ yasya na vidyate. gatirbrahmavidāṃ brahma taccākṣaramalakṣaṇam. Caraka, Śārīra* I. 98–100.

the state of mokṣa comes about. Various kinds of moral endeavours in the shape of association with good people, abandoning of desires, determined attempts at discovering the truth with fixed attention, are spoken of as indispensable means. Truth (tattva) thus discovered should be recalled again and again[1] and this will ultimately effect the disunion of the body with the self. As the self is avyakta (unmanifested) and has no specific nature or character, this state can only be described as absolute cessation (*mokṣe nivṛttirniḥśeṣā*).

The main features of the Sāṃkhya doctrine as given by Caraka are thus: 1. Puruṣa is the state of avyakta. 2. By a conglomera- of this avyakta with its later products a conglomeration is formed which generates the so-called living being. 3. The tanmātras are not mentioned. 4. Rajas and tamas represent the bad states of the mind and sattva the good ones. 5. The ultimate state of emancipation is either absolute annihilation or characterless absolute existence and it is spoken of as the Brahman state; there is no consciousness in this state, for consciousness is due to the conglomeration of the self with its evolutes, buddhi, ahaṃkāra etc. 6. The senses are formed of matter (*bhautika*).

This account of Sāṃkhya agrees with the system of Sāṃkhya propounded by Pañcaśikha (who is said to be the direct pupil of Āsuri the pupil of Kapila, the founder of the system) in the Mahābhārata XII. 219. Pañcaśikha of course does not describe the system as elaborately as Caraka does. But even from what little he says it may be supposed that the system of Sāṃkhya he sketches is the same as that of Caraka[2]. Pañcaśikha speaks of the ultimate truth as being avyakta (a term applied in all Sāṃkhya literature to prakṛti) in the state of puruṣa (*puruṣāvasthamavyaktam*). If man is the product of a mere combination of the different elements, then one may assume that all ceases with death. Caraka in answer to such an objection introduces a discussion, in which he tries to establish the existence of a self as the postulate of all our duties and sense of moral responsibility. The same discussion occurs in Pañcaśikha also, and the proofs

[1] Four causes are spoken of here as being causes of memory: (1) Thinking of the cause leads to the remembering of the effect, (2) by similarity, (3) by opposite things, and (4) by acute attempt to remember.

[2] Some European scholars have experienced great difficulty in accepting Pañcaśikha's doctrine as a genuine Sāṃkhya doctrine. This may probably be due to the fact that the Sāṃkhya doctrines sketched in *Caraka* did not attract their notice.

for the existence of the self are also the same. Like Caraka again Pañcaśikha also says that all consciousness is due to the conditions of the conglomeration of our physical body mind,—and the element of "cetas." They are mutually independent, and by such independence carry on the process of life and work. None of the phenomena produced by such a conglomeration are self. All our suffering comes in because we think these to be the self. Mokṣa is realized when we can practise absolute renunciation of these phenomena. The guṇas described by Pañcaśikha are the different kinds of good and bad qualities of the mind as Caraka has it. The state of the conglomeration is spoken of as the kṣetra, as Caraka says, and there is no annihilation or eternality; and the last state is described as being like that when all rivers lose themselves in the ocean and it is called aliṅga (without any characteristic)—a term reserved for prakṛti in later Sāṃkhya. This state is attainable by the doctrine of ultimate renunciation which is also called the doctrine of complete destruction (*samyagbadha*).

Guṇaratna (fourteenth century A.D.), a commentator of *Ṣaḍdarśanasamuccaya*, mentions two schools of Sāṃkhya, the Maulikya (original) and the Uttara or (later)[1]. Of these the doctrine of the Maulikya Sāṃkhya is said to be that which believed that there was a separate pradhāna for each ātman (*maulikyasāṃkhyā hyātmānamātmānam prati pṛthak pradhānam vadanti*). This seems to be a reference to the Sāṃkhya doctrine I have just sketched. I am therefore disposed to think that this represents the earliest systematic doctrine of Sāṃkhya.

In *Mahābhārata* XII. 318 three schools of Sāṃkhya are mentioned, viz. those who admitted twenty-four categories (the school I have sketched above), those who admitted twenty-five (the well-known orthodox Sāṃkhya system) and those who admitted twenty-six categories. This last school admitted a supreme being in addition to puruṣa and this was the twenty-sixth principle. This agrees with the orthodox Yoga system and the form of Sāṃkhya advocated in the *Mahābhārata*. The schools of Sāṃkhya of twenty-four and twenty-five categories are here denounced as unsatisfactory. Doctrines similar to the school of Sāṃkhya we have sketched above are referred to in some of the

[1] Guṇaratna's *Tarkarahasyadīpikā*, p. 99.

other chapters of the *Mahābhārata* (XII. 203, 204). The self apart from the body is described as the moon of the new moon day; it is said that as Rāhu (the shadow on the sun during an eclipse) cannot be seen apart from the sun, so the self cannot be seen apart from the body. The selfs (*śarīriṇaḥ*) are spoken of as manifesting from prakṛti.

We do not know anything about Āsuri the direct disciple of Kapila[1]. But it seems probable that the system of Sāṃkhya we have sketched here which appears in fundamentally the same form in the *Mahābhārata* and has been attributed there to Pañcaśikha is probably the earliest form of Sāṃkhya available to us in a systematic form. Not only does Guṇaratna's reference to the school of Maulikya Sāṃkhya justify it, but the fact that Caraka (78 A.D.) does not refer to the Sāṃkhya as described by Īśvarakṛṣṇa and referred to in other parts of *Mahābhārata* is a definite proof that Īśvarakṛṣṇa's Sāṃkhya is a later modification, which was either non-existent in Caraka's time or was not regarded as an authoritative old Sāṃkhya view.

Wassilief says quoting Tibetan sources that Vindhyavāsin altered the Sāṃkhya according to his own views[2]. Takakusu thinks that Vindhyavāsin was a title of Īśvarakṛṣṇa[3] and Garbe holds that the date of Īśvarakṛṣṇa was about 100 A.D. It seems to be a very plausible view that Īśvarakṛṣṇa was indebted for his kārikās to another work, which was probably written in a style different from what he employs. The seventh verse of his *Kārikā* seems to be in purport the same as a passage which is found quoted in the

[1] A verse attributed to Āsuri is quoted by Guṇaratna (*Tarkarahasyadīpikā*, p. 104). The purport of this verse is that when buddhi is transformed in a particular manner, it (puruṣa) has experience. It is like the reflection of the moon in transparent water.

[2] Vassilief's *Buddhismus*, p. 240.

[3] Takakusu's "A study of Paramārtha's life of Vasubandhu," *J. R. A. S.*, 1905. This identification by Takakusu, however, appears to be extremely doubtful, for Guṇaratna mentions Īśvarakṛṣṇa and Vindhyavāsin as two different authorities (*Tarkarahasyadīpikā*, pp. 102 and 104). The verse quoted from Vindhyavāsin (p. 104) in anuṣṭubh metre cannot be traced as belonging to Īśvarakṛṣṇa. It appears that Īśvarakṛṣṇa wrote two books; one is the *Sāṃkhya kārikā* and another an independent work on Sāṃkhya, a line from which, quoted by Guṇaratna, stands as follows:

"*Pratiniyatādhyavasāyaḥ śrotrādisamuttha adhyakṣam*" (p. 108).

If Vācaspati's interpretation of the classification of anumāna in his *Tattvakaumudī* be considered to be a correct explanation of *Sāṃkhya kārikā* then Īśvarakṛṣṇa must be a different person from Vindhyavāsin whose views on anumāna as referred to in *Ślokavārttika*, p. 393, are altogether different. But Vācaspati's own statement in the *Tātparyyaṭīkā* (pp. 109 and 131) shows that his treatment there was not faithful.

Mahābhāṣya of Patañjali the grammarian (147 B.C.)[1]. The subject of the two passages are the enumeration of reasons which frustrate visual perception. This however is not a doctrine concerned with the strictly technical part of Sāṃkhya, and it is just possible that the book from which Patañjali quoted the passage, and which was probably paraphrased in the Āryā metre by Īśvarakṛṣṇa was not a Sāṃkhya book at all. But though the subject of the verse is not one of the strictly technical parts of Sāṃkhya, yet since such an enumeration is not seen in any other system of Indian philosophy, and as it has some special bearing as a safeguard against certain objections against the Sāṃkhya doctrine of prakṛti, the natural and plausible supposition is that it was the verse of a Sāṃkhya book which was paraphrased by Īśvarakṛṣṇa.

The earliest descriptions of a Sāṃkhya which agrees with Īśvarakṛṣṇa's Sāṃkhya (but with an addition of Iśvara) are to be found in Patañjali's *Yoga sūtras* and in the *Mahābhārata*; but we are pretty certain that the Sāṃkhya of *Caraka* we have sketched here was known to Patañjali, for in *Yoga sūtra* I. 19 a reference is made to a view of Sāṃkhya similar to this.

From the point of view of history of philosophy the Sāṃkhya of Caraka and Pañcaśikha is very important; for it shows a transitional stage of thought between the Upaniṣad ideas and the orthodox Sāṃkhya doctrine as represented by Īśvarakṛṣṇa. On the one hand its doctrine that the senses are material, and that effects are produced only as a result of collocations, and that the puruṣa is unconscious, brings it in close relation with Nyāya, and on the other its connections with Buddhism seem to be nearer than the orthodox Sāṃkhya.

We hear of a *Ṣaṣṭitantraśāstra* as being one of the oldest Sāṃkhya works. This is described in the *Ahirbudhnya Saṃhitā* as containing two books of thirty-two and twenty-eight chapters[2]. A quotation from *Rājavārttika* (a work about which there is no definite information) in Vācaspati Miśra's commentary on the *Sāṃkhya kārika*(72) says that it was called the *Ṣaṣṭitantra* because it dealt with the existence of prakṛti, its oneness, its difference from puruṣas, its purposefulness for puruṣas, the multiplicity of puruṣas, connection and separation from puruṣas, the evolution of

[1] Patañjali's Mahābhāṣya, IV. I. 3. *Atisannikarṣādativiprakarṣāt mūrttyantaravyavadhānāt tamasāvṛtatvāt indriyadaurvalyādatipramādāt*, etc. (Benares edition.)

[2] *Ahirbudhnya Saṃhitā*, pp. 108, 110.

the categories, the inactivity of the puruṣas and the five *viparyyayas*, nine *tuṣṭis*, the defects of organs of twenty-eight kinds, and the eight siddhis[1].

But the content of the *Ṣaṣṭitantra* as given in *Ahirbudhnya Saṃhitā* is different from it, and it appears from it that the Sāṃkhya of the *Ṣaṣṭitantra* referred to in the *Ahirbudhnya Saṃhitā* was of a theistic character resembling the doctrine of the Pañcarātra Vaiṣṇavas and the *Ahirbudhnya Saṃhitā* says that Kapila's theory of Sāṃkhya was a Vaiṣṇava one. Vijñāna Bhikṣu, the greatest expounder of Sāṃkhya, says in many places of his work *Vijñānāmṛta Bhāṣya* that Sāṃkhya was originally theistic, and that the atheistic Sāṃkhya is only a *prauḍhivāda* (an exaggerated attempt to show that no supposition of Īśvara is necessary to explain the world process) though the *Mahābhārata* points out that the difference between Sāṃkhya and Yoga is this, that the former is atheistic, while the latter is theistic. The discrepancy between the two accounts of *Ṣaṣṭitantra* suggests that the original *Ṣaṣṭitantra* as referred to in the *Ahirbudhnya Saṃhitā* was subsequently revised and considerably changed. This supposition is corroborated by the fact that Guṇaratna does not mention among the important Sāṃkhya works *Ṣaṣṭitantra* but *Ṣaṣṭitantroddhāra*

[1] The doctrine of the *viparyyaya*, *tuṣṭi*, defects of organs, and the *siddhi* are mentioned in the *Kārikā* of Īśvarakṛṣṇa, but I have omitted them in my account of Sāṃkhya as these have little philosophical importance. The viparyyaya (false knowledge) are five, viz. avidyā (ignorance), asmitā (egoism), rāga (attachment), dveṣa (antipathy), abhiniveśa (self-love), which are also called *tamo*, *moha*, *mahāmoha*, *tamisrā*, and *andhatāmisra*. These are of nine kinds of tuṣṭi, such as the idea that no exertion is necessary, since prakṛti will herself bring our salvation (*ambhas*), that it is not necessary to meditate, for it is enough if we renounce the householder's life (*salila*), that there is no hurry, salvation will come in time (*megha*), that salvation will be worked out by fate (*bhāgya*), and the contentment leading to renunciation proceeding from five kinds of causes, e.g. the troubles of earning (*para*), the troubles of protecting the earned money (*supara*), the natural waste of things earned by enjoyment (*parāpara*), increase of desires leading to greater disappointments (*anuttamāmbhas*), all gain leads to the injury of others (*uttamāmbhas*). This renunciation proceeds from external considerations with those who consider prakṛti and its evolutes as the self. The siddhis or ways of success are eight in number, viz. (1) reading of scriptures (*tāra*), (2) enquiry into their meaning (*sutāra*), (3) proper reasoning (*tāratāra*), (4) corroborating one's own ideas with the ideas of the teachers and other workers of the same field (*ramyaka*), (5) clearance of the mind by long-continued practice (*sadāmudita*). The three other siddhis called pramoda, mudita, and modamāna lead directly to the separation of the prakṛti from the puruṣa. The twenty-eight sense defects are the eleven defects of the eleven senses and seventeen kinds of defects of the understanding corresponding to the absence of siddhis and the presence of tuṣṭis. The viparyyayas, tuṣṭis and the defects of the organs are hindrances in the way of the achievement of the Sāṃkhya goal.

(revised edition of *Ṣaṣṭitantra*)[1]. Probably the earlier Ṣaṣṭitantra was lost even before Vācaspati's time.

If we believe the Ṣaṣṭitantra referred to in the *Ahirbudhnya Saṃhitā* to be in all essential parts the same work which was composed by Kapila and based faithfully on his teachings, then it has to be assumed that Kapila's Sāṃkhya was theistic[2]. It seems probable that his disciple Āsuri tried to popularise it. But it seems that a great change occurred when Pañcaśikha the disciple of Āsuri came to deal with it. For we know that his doctrine differed from the traditional one in many important respects. It is said in *Sāṃkhya kārikā* (70) that the literature was divided by him into many parts (*tena bahudhākṛtam tantram*). The exact meaning of this reference is difficult to guess. It might mean that the original *Ṣaṣṭitantra* was rewritten by him in various treatises. It is a well-known fact that most of the schools of Vaiṣṇavas accepted the form of cosmology which is the same in most essential parts as the Sāṃkhya cosmology. This justifies the assumption that Kapila's doctrine was probably theistic. But there are a few other points of difference between the Kapila and the Pātañjala Sāṃkhya (Yoga). The only supposition that may be ventured is that Pañcaśikha probably modified Kapila's work in an atheistic way and passed it as Kapila's work. If this supposition is held reasonable, then we have three strata of Sāṃkhya, first a theistic one, the details of which are lost, but which is kept in a modified form by the Pātañjala school of Sāṃkhya, second an atheistic one as represented by Pañcaśikha, and a third atheistic modification as the orthodox Sāṃkhya system. An important change in the Sāṃkhya doctrine seems to have been introduced by Vijñāna Bhikṣu (sixteenth century A.D.) by his treatment of guṇas as types of reals. I have myself accepted this interpretation of Sāṃkhya as the most rational and philosophical one, and have therefore followed it in giving a connected system of the accepted Kapila and the Pātañjala school of Sāṃkhya. But it must be pointed out that originally the notion of guṇas was applied to different types of good and bad mental states, and then they were supposed in some mysterious way by mutual increase and decrease to form the objective world on the one hand and the

[1] *Tarkarahasyadīpikā*, p. 109.

[2] *evaṃ ṣaḍviṃśakaṃ prāhuḥ śarīramih mānavāḥ sāṃkhyam saṃkhyātmakatvācca kapilādibhirucyate. Matsyapurāṇa*, IV. 28.

totality of human psychosis on the other. A systematic explanation of the guṇas was attempted in two different lines by Vijñāna Bhikṣu and the Vaiṣṇava writer Veṅkaṭa[1]. As the Yoga philosophy compiled by Patañjali and commented on by Vyāsa, Vācaspati and Vijñāna Bhikṣu, agree with the Sāṃkhya doctrine as explained by Vācaspati and Vijñāna Bhikṣu in most points I have preferred to call them the Kapila and the Pātañjala schools of Sāṃkhya and have treated them together—a principle which was followed by Haribhadra in his *Ṣaḍdarśanasamuccaya.*

The other important Sāṃkhya teachers mentioned by Gauḍapāda are Sanaka, Sananda, Sanātana and Voḍhu. Nothing is known about their historicity or doctrines.

Sāṃkhya kārikā, Sāṃkhya sūtra, Vācaspati Miśra and Vijñāna Bhikṣu.

A word of explanation is necessary as regards my interpretation of the Sāṃkhya-Yoga system. The *Sāṃkhya kārikā* is the oldest Sāṃkhya text on which we have commentaries by later writers. The *Sāṃkhya sūtra* was not referred to by any writer until it was commented upon by Aniruddha (fifteenth century A.D.). Even Guṇaratna of the fourteenth century A.D. who made allusions to a number of Sāṃkhya works, did not make any reference to the *Sāṃkhya sūtra,* and no other writer who is known to have flourished before Guṇaratna seems to have made any reference to the *Sāṃkhya sūtra.* The natural conclusion therefore is that these sūtras were probably written some time after the fourteenth century. But there is no positive evidence to prove that it was so late a work as the fifteenth century. It is said at the end of the *Sāṃkhya kārikā* of Īśvarakṛṣṇa that the kārikās give an exposition of the Sāṃkhya doctrine excluding the refutations of the doctrines of other people and excluding the parables attached to the original Sāṃkhya works—the *Ṣaṣṭitantraśāstra.* The *Sāṃkhya sūtras* contain refutations of other doctrines and also a number of parables. It is not improbable that these were collected from some earlier Sāṃkhya work which is now lost to us. It may be that it was done from some later edition of the *Ṣaṣṭitantraśāstra* (*Saṣṭitantroddhāra* as mentioned by

[1] Veṅkaṭa's philosophy will be dealt with in the second volume of the present work.

Guṇaratna), but this is a mere conjecture. There is no reason to suppose that the Sāṃkhya doctrine found in the sūtras differs in any important way from the Sāṃkhya doctrine as found in the *Sāṃkhya kārikā*. The only point of importance is this, that the *Sāṃkhya sūtras* hold that when the Upaniṣads spoke of one absolute pure intelligence they meant to speak of unity as involved in the class of intelligent puruṣas as distinct from the class of the guṇas. As all puruṣas were of the nature of pure intelligence, they were spoken of in the Upaniṣads as one, for they all form the category or class of pure intelligence, and hence may in some sense be regarded as one. This compromise cannot be found in the *Sāṃkhya kārikā*. This is, however, a case of omission and not of difference. Vijñāna Bhikṣu, the commentator of the *Sāṃkhya sūtra*, was more inclined to theistic Sāṃkhya or Yoga than to atheistic Sāṃkhya. This is proved by his own remarks in his *Sāṃkhyapravacanabhāṣya*, *Yogavārttika*, and *Vijñānāmṛtabhāsya* (an independent commentary on the Brahmasūtras of Bādarāyaṇa on theistic Sāṃkhya lines). Vijñāna Bhikṣu's own view could not properly be called a thorough Yoga view, for he agreed more with the views of the Sāṃkhya doctrine of the Purāṇas, where both the diverse puruṣas and the prakṛti are said to be merged in the end in Īśvara, by whose will the creative process again began in the prakṛti at the end of each pralaya. He could not avoid the distinctively atheistic arguments of the *Sāṃkhya sūtras*, but he remarked that these were used only with a view to showing that the Sāṃkhya system gave such a rational explanation that even without the intervention of an Īśvara it could explain all facts. Vijñāna Bhikṣu in his interpretation of Sāṃkhya differed on many points from those of Vācaspati, and it is difficult to say who is right. Vijñāna Bhikṣu has this advantage that he has boldly tried to give interpretations on some difficult points on which Vācaspati remained silent. I refer principally to the nature of the conception of the guṇas, which I believe is the most important thing in Sāṃkhya. Vijñāna Bhikṣu described the guṇas as reals or super-subtle substances, but Vācaspati and Gauḍapāda (the other commentator of the *Sāṃkhya kārikā*) remained silent on the point. There is nothing, however, in their interpretations which would militate against the interpretation of Vijñāna Bhikṣu, but yet while they were silent as to any definite explanations regarding the nature of the guṇas, Bhikṣu definitely came forward with a very satisfactory and rational interpretation of their nature.

Since no definite explanation of the guṇas is found in any other work before Bhikṣu, it is quite probable that this matter may not have been definitely worked out before. Neither Caraka nor the *Mahābhārata* explains the nature of the guṇas. But Bhikṣu's interpretation suits exceedingly well all that is known of the manifestations and the workings of the guṇas in all early documents. I have therefore accepted the interpretation of Bhikṣu in giving my account of the nature of the guṇas. The *Kārikā* speaks of the guṇas as being of the nature of pleasure, pain, and dullness (*sattva, rajas* and *tamas*). It also describes sattva as being light and illuminating, rajas as of the nature of energy and causing motion, and tamas as heavy and obstructing. Vācaspati merely paraphrases this statement of the *Kārikā* but does not enter into any further explanations. Bhikṣu's interpretation fits in well with all that is known of the guṇas, though it is quite possible that this view might not have been known before, and when the original Sāṃkhya doctrine was formulated there was a real vagueness as to the conception of the guṇas.

There are some other points in which Bhikṣu's interpretation differs from that of Vācaspati. The most important of these may be mentioned here. The first is the nature of the connection of the buddhi states with the puruṣa. Vācaspati holds that there is no contact (*saṃyoga*) of any buddhi state with the puruṣa but that a reflection of the puruṣa is caught in the state of buddhi by virtue of which the buddhi state becomes intelligized and transformed into consciousness. But this view is open to the objection that it does not explain how the puruṣa can be said to be the experiencer of the conscious states of the buddhi, for its reflection in the buddhi is merely an image, and there cannot be an experience (*bhoga*) on the basis of that image alone without any actual connection of the puruṣa with the buddhi. The answer of Vācaspati Miśra is that there is no contact of the two in space and time, but that their proximity (*sannidhi*) means only a specific kind of fitness (*yogyatā*) by virtue of which the puruṣa, though it remains aloof, is yet felt to be united and identified in the buddhi, and as a result of that the states of the buddhi appear as ascribed to a person. Vijñāna Bhikṣu differs from Vācaspati and says that if such a special kind of fitness be admitted, then there is no reason why puruṣa should be deprived of such a fitness at the time of emancipation, and thus there would be no emancipation at all, for the fitness being in the puruṣa, he could not be divested of it, and he would continue to enjoy the experiences represented in the buddhi for ever. Vijñāna Bhikṣu thus holds that there is a real contact of the puruṣa with the buddhi state in any cognitive state. Such a contact of the puruṣa and the buddhi does not necessarily mean that the former will be liable to change on account of it, for contact and change are not synonymous. Change means the rise of new qualities. It is the buddhi which suffers changes, and when these changes are reflected in the puruṣa, there is the notion of a person or experiencer in the puruṣa, and when the puruṣa is reflected back in the buddhi the buddhi state appears as a conscious state. The second, is the difference between Vācaspati and Bhikṣu as regards the nature of the perceptual process. Bhikṣu thinks that the senses can directly perceive the determinate qualities of things without any intervention of manas, whereas Vācaspati ascribes to manas the power of arranging the sense-data in a definite order and of making the indeterminate sense-data determinate. With him the first stage of cognition is the stage when indeterminate sense materials are first presented, at the next stage there is assimilation, differentiation, and association by which the indeterminate materials are ordered and classified by the activity of manas called saṃkalpa which coordinates the indeterminate sense materials into determinate perceptual and conceptual forms as class notions with particular characteristics. Bhikṣu who supposes that the determinate character of things is directly perceived by the senses has necessarily to assign a subordinate position to manas as being only the faculty of desire, doubt, and imagination.

It may not be out of place to mention here that there are one or two passages in Vācaspati's commentary on the *Sāṃkhya kārikā* which seem to suggest that he considered the ego (*ahaṃkāra*) as producing the subjective series of the senses and the objective series of the external world by a sort of desire or will, but he did not work out this doctrine, and it is therefore not necessary to enlarge upon it. There is also a difference of view with regard to the evolution of the tanmātras from the mahat; for contrary to the view of *Vyāsabhāṣya* and Vijñāna Bhikṣu etc. Vācaspati holds that from the mahat there was ahaṃkāra and from ahaṃkāra the tanmātras[1]. Vijñāna Bhikṣu however holds that both the separation of ahaṃkāra and the evolution of the tanmātras take place in the mahat, and as this appeared to me to be more reasonable, I have followed this interpretation. There are some other minor points of difference about the Yoga doctrines between Vācaspati and Bhikṣu which are not of much philosophical importance.

Yoga and Patañjali.

The word yoga occurs in the Ṛg-Veda in various senses such as yoking or harnessing, achieving the unachieved, connection, and the like. The sense of yoking is not so frequent as the other senses; but it is nevertheless true that the word was used in this sense in Ṛg-Veda and in such later Vedic works as the Śatapatha Brāhmaṇa and the Bṛhadāraṇyaka Upaniṣad[2]. The word has another derivative "yugya" in later Sanskrit literature[3].

With the growth of religious and philosophical ideas in the Ṛg-Veda, we find that the religious austerities were generally very much valued. Tapas (asceticism) and brahmacarya (the holy vow of celibacy and life-long study) were regarded as greatest virtues and considered as being productive of the highest power[4].

As these ideas of asceticism and self-control grew the force of the flying passions was felt to be as uncontrollable as that of a spirited steed, and thus the word yoga which was originally applied to the control of steeds began to be applied to the control of the senses[5].

In Pāṇini's time the word yoga had attained its technical meaning, and he distinguished this root "*yuj samādhau*" (*yuj* in the sense of concentration) from "*yujir yoge*" (root *yujir* in the sense of connecting). *Yuj* in the first sense is seldom used as a verb. It is more or less an imaginary root for the etymological derivation of the word yoga[6].

[1] See my *Study of Patanjali*, p. 60 ff.

[2] Compare R.V. I. 34. 9/VII. 67. 8/III. 27. 11/X. 30. 11/X. 114. 9/IV. 24. 4/I. 5. 3/I. 30. 7; Śatapatha Brāhmaṇa 14. 7. 1. 11.

[3] It is probably an old word of the Aryan stock; compare German Joch, A.S. geoc, Latin jugum.

[4] See Chāndogya III. 17. 4; Bṛh. I. 2. 6; Bṛh. III. 8. 10; Taitt. I. 9. 1/III. 2. 1/III. 3. 1; Taitt. Brāh. II. 2. 3. 3; R.V. X. 129; Śatap. Brāh. XI. 5. 8. 1.

[5] Kaṭha III. 4, *indriyāṇi hayānāhuḥ viṣayāteṣugocarān.* The senses are the horses and whatever they grasp are their objects. Maitr. 2. 6. *Karmendriyāṇyasya hayāḥ* the conative senses are its horses.

[6] *Yugyaḥ* is used from the root of *yujir yoge* and not from *yuja samādhau.* A consideration of Pāṇini's rule "*Tadasya brahmacaryam,*" V. i. 94 shows that not only

In the *Bhagavadgītā*, we find that the word yoga has been used not only in conformity with the root "*yuj-samādhau*" but also with "*yujir yoge*." This has been the source of some confusion to the readers of the *Bhagavadgītā*. "Yogin" in the sense of a person who has lost himself in meditation is there regarded with extreme veneration. One of the main features of the use of this word lies in this that the *Bhagavadgītā* tried to mark out a middle path between the austere discipline of meditative abstraction on the one hand and the course of duties of sacrificial action of a Vedic worshipper in the life of a new type of Yogin (evidently from *yujir yoge*) on the other, who should combine in himself the best parts of the two paths, devote himself to his duties, and yet abstract himself from all selfish motives associated with desires.

Kauṭilya in his *Arthaśāstra* when enumerating the philosophic sciences of study names Sāṃkhya, Yoga, and Lokāyata. The oldest Buddhist sūtras (e.g. the *Satipaṭṭhāna sutta*) are fully familiar with the stages of Yoga concentration. We may thus infer that self-concentration and Yoga had developed as a technical method of mystic absorption some time before the Buddha.

As regards the connection of Yoga with Sāṃkhya, as we find it in the *Yoga sūtras* of Patañjali, it is indeed difficult to come to any definite conclusion. The science of breath had attracted notice in many of the earlier Upaniṣads, though there had not probably developed any systematic form of prāṇāyāma (a system of breath control) of the Yoga system. It is only when we come to Maitrāyaṇī that we find that the Yoga method had attained a systematic development. The other two Upaniṣads in which the Yoga ideas can be traced are the Śvetāśvatara and the Kaṭha. It is indeed curious to notice that these three Upaniṣads of Kṛṣṇa Yajurveda, where we find reference to Yoga methods, are the only ones where we find clear references also to the Sāṃkhya tenets, though the Sāṃkhya and Yoga ideas do not appear there as related to each other or associated as parts of the same system. But there is a remarkable passage in the Maitrāyaṇī in the conversation between Śākyāyana and Bṛhad ratha where we find that the Sāṃkhya metaphysics was offered

different kinds of asceticism and rigour which passed by the name of brahmacarya were prevalent in the country at the time (Pāṇini as Goldstücker has proved is pre-buddhistic), but associated with these had grown up a definite system of mental discipline which passed by the name of Yoga.

in some quarters to explain the validity of the Yoga processes, and it seems therefore that the association and grafting of the Sāṃkhya metaphysics on the Yoga system as its basis, was the work of the followers of this school of ideas which was subsequently systematized by Patañjali. Thus Śākyāyana says: "Here some say it is the guṇa which through the differences of nature goes into bondage to the will, and that deliverance takes place when the fault of the will has been removed, because he sees by the mind; and all that we call desire, imagination, doubt, belief, unbelief, certainty, uncertainty, shame, thought, fear, all that is but mind. Carried along by the waves of the qualities darkened in his imagination, unstable, fickle, crippled, full of desires, vacillating he enters into belief, believing I am he, this is mine, and he binds his self by his self as a bird with a net. Therefore, a man being possessed of will, imagination and belief is a slave, but he who is the opposite is free. For this reason let a man stand free from will, imagination and belief—this is the sign of liberty, this is the path that leads to Brahman, this is the opening of the door, and through it he will go to the other shore of darkness. All desires are there fulfilled. And for this, they quote a verse: 'When the five instruments of knowledge stand still together with the mind, and when the intellect does not move, that is called the highest state[1].'"

An examination of such Yoga Upaniṣads as Śāṇḍilya, Yogatattva, Dhyānabindu, Haṃsa, Amṛtanāda, Varāha, Maṇḍala Brāhmaṇa, Nādabindu, and Yogakuṇḍalī, shows that the Yoga practices had undergone diverse changes in diverse schools, but none of these show any predilection for the Sāṃkhya. Thus the Yoga practices grew in accordance with the doctrines of the

[1] Vātsyāyana, however, in his bhāṣya on *Nyāya sūtra*, I. i. 29, distinguishes Sāṃkhya from Yoga in the following way: The Sāṃkhya holds that nothing can come into being nor be destroyed, there cannot be any change in the pure intelligence (*niratiśayāḥ cetanāḥ*). All changes are due to changes in the body, the senses, the manas and the objects. Yoga holds that all creation is due to the karma of the puruṣa. Doṣas (passions) and the pravṛtti (action) are the cause of karma. The intelligences or souls (cetana) are associated with qualities. Non-being can come into being and what is produced may be destroyed. The last view is indeed quite different from the Yoga of *Vyāsabhāṣya*. It is closer to Nyāya in its doctrines. If Vātsyāyana's statement is correct, it would appear that the doctrine of there being a moral purpose in creation was borrowed by Sāṃkhya from Yoga. Udyotakara's remarks on the same sūtra do not indicate a difference but an agreement between Sāṃkhya and Yoga on the doctrine of the *indriyas* being "*abhautika.*" Curiously enough Vātsyāyana quotes a passage from *Vyāsabhāṣya*, III. 13, in his bhāṣya, I. ii. 6, and criticizes it as self-contradictory (*viruddha*).

Śaivas and Śāktas and assumed a peculiar form as the Mantrayoga; they grew in another direction as the Haṭhayoga which was supposed to produce mystic and magical feats through constant practices of elaborate nervous exercises, which were also associated with healing and other supernatural powers. The Yogatattva Upaniṣad says that there are four kinds of yoga, the Mantra Yoga, Laya Yoga, Haṭhayoga and Rājayoga[1]. In some cases we find that there was a great attempt even to associate Vedāntism with these mystic practices. The influence of these practices in the development of Tantra and other modes of worship was also very great, but we have to leave out these from our present consideration as they have little philosophic importance and as they are not connected with our present endeavour.

Of the Pātañjala school of Sāṃkhya, which forms the subject of the Yoga with which we are now dealing, Patañjali was probably the most notable person for he not only collected the different forms of Yoga practices, and gleaned the diverse ideas which were or could be associated with the Yoga, but grafted them all on the Sāṃkhya metaphysics, and gave them the form in which they have been handed down to us. Vācaspati and Vijñāna Bhikṣu, the two great commentators on the *Vyāsabhāṣya*, agree with us in holding that Patañjali was not the founder of the Yoga, but an editor. Analytic study of the sūtras also brings the conviction that the sūtras do not show any original attempt, but a masterly and systematic compilation which was also supplemented by fitting contributions. The systematic manner also in which the first three chapters are written by way of definition and classification shows that the materials were already in existence and that Patañjali only systematized them. There was no missionizing zeal, no attempt to overthrow the doctrines of other systems, except as far as they might come in, by way of explaining the system. Patañjali is not even anxious to establish the system, but he is only engaged in systematizing the facts as he had them. Most of the criticisms against the Buddhists occur in the last chapter. The doctrines of the Yoga are described in the first three chapters, and this part is separated from the last chapter where the views of the Buddhists are

[1] The Yoga writer Jaigīṣavya wrote "*Dhāranāśāstra*" which dealt with Yoga more in the fashion of Tantra than that given by Patañjali. He mentions different places in the body (e.g. heart, throat, tip of the nose, palate, forehead, centre of the brain) which are centres of memory where concentration is to be made. See Vācaspati's *Tātparyaṭīkā* or Vātsyāyana's bhāṣya on *Nyāya sūtra*, III. ii. 43.

criticized; the putting of an "*iti*" (the word to denote the conclusion of any work) at the end of the third chapter is evidently to denote the conclusion of his Yoga compilation. There is of course another "*iti*" at the end of the fourth chapter to denote the conclusion of the whole work. The most legitimate hypothesis seems to be that the last chapter is a subsequent addition by a hand other than that of Patañjali who was anxious to supply some new links of argument which were felt to be necessary for the strengthening of the Yoga position from an internal point of view, as well as for securing the strength of the Yoga from the supposed attacks of Buddhist metaphysics. There is also a marked change (due either to its supplementary character or to the manipulation of a foreign hand) in the style of the last chapter as compared with the style of the other three.

The sūtras, 30–34, of the last chapter seem to repeat what has already been said in the second chapter and some of the topics introduced are such that they could well have been dealt with in a more relevant manner in connection with similar discussions in the preceding chapters. The extent of this chapter is also disproportionately small, as it contains only 34 sūtras, whereas the average number of sūtras in other chapters is between 51 to 55.

We have now to meet the vexed question of the probable date of this famous Yoga author Patañjali. Weber had tried to connect him with Kāpya Patamchala of Śatapatha Brāhmaṇa[1]; in Kātyāyana's *Vārttika* we get the name Patañjali which is explained by later commentators as *patantaḥ añjalayaḥ yasmai* (for whom the hands are folded as a mark of reverence), but it is indeed difficult to come to any conclusion merely from the similarity of names. There is however another theory which identifies the writer of the great commentary on Pāṇini called the *Mahābhāṣya* with the Patañjali of the *Yoga sūtra*. This theory has been accepted by many western scholars probably on the strength of some Indian commentators who identified the two Patañjalis. Of these one is the writer of the *Patañjalicarita* (Rāmabhadra Dīkṣita) who could not have flourished earlier than the eighteenth century. The other is that cited in Śivarāma's commentary on *Vāsavadattā* which Aufrecht assigns to the eighteenth century. The other two are king Bhoja of Dhār and Cakrapāṇidatta,

[1] Weber's *History of Indian Literature*, p. 223 n.

the commentator of *Caraka*, who belonged to the eleventh century A.D. Thus Cakrapāṇi says that he adores the Ahipati (mythical serpent chief) who removed the defects of mind, speech and body by his *Pātañjala mahābhāṣya* and the revision of *Caraka*. Bhoja says: "Victory be to the luminous words of that illustrious sovereign Raṇaraṅgamalla who by composing his grammar, by writing his commentary on the Pātañjala and by producing a treatise on medicine called *Rājamṛgāṅka* has like the lord of the holder of serpents removed defilement from speech, mind and body." The adoration hymn of Vyāsa (which is considered to be an interpolation even by orthodox scholars) is also based upon the same tradition. It is not impossible therefore that the later Indian commentators might have made some confusion between the three Patañjalis, the grammarian, the Yoga editor, and the medical writer to whom is ascribed the book known as *Pātañjalatantra*, and who has been quoted by Śivadāsa in his commentary on *Cakradatta* in connection with the heating of metals.

Professor J. H. Woods of Harvard University is therefore in a way justified in his unwillingness to identify the grammarian and the Yoga editor on the slender evidence of these commentators. It is indeed curious to notice that the great commentators of the grammar school such as Bhartṛhari, Kaiyyaṭa, Vāmana, Jayāditya, Nāgeśa, etc. are silent on this point. This is indeed a point against the identification of the two Patañjalis by some Yoga and medical commentators of a later age. And if other proofs are available which go against such an identification, we could not think the grammarian and the Yoga writer to be the same person.

Let us now see if Patañjali's grammatical work contains anything which may lead us to think that he was not the same person as the writer on Yoga. Professor Woods supposes that the philosophic concept of substance (*dravya*) of the two Patañjalis differs and therefore they cannot be identified. He holds that dravya is described in *Vyāsabhāṣya* in one place as being the unity of species and qualities (*sāmānyaviśeṣātmaka*), whereas the *Mahābhāṣya* holds that a dravya denotes a genus and also specific qualities according as the emphasis or stress is laid on either side. I fail to see how these ideas are totally antagonistic. Moreover, we know that these two views were held by

Vyāḍi and Vājapyāyana (Vyāḍi holding that words denoted qualities or dravya and Vājapyāyana holding that words denoted species[1]). Even Pāṇini had these two different ideas in "*jātyākhyāyāmekasmin bahuvacanamanyatarasyām*," and "*sarūpānamekaśeṣamekavibhaktau*," and Patañjali the writer of the *Mahābhāṣya* only combined these two views. This does not show that he opposes the view of *Vyāsabhāṣya*, though we must remember that even if he did, that would not prove anything with regard to the writer of the sūtras. Moreover, when we read that dravya is spoken of in the *Mahābhāṣya* as that object which is the specific kind of the conglomeration of its parts, just as a cow is of its tail, hoofs, horns, etc.—"*yat sāsnālāṅgulakakudakhuraviṣāṇyartharūpaṁ*," we are reminded of its similarity with "*ayutasiddhāvayavabhedānugataḥ samūhaḥ dravyam*" (a conglomeration of interrelated parts is called dravya) in the *Vyāsabhāṣya*. So far as I have examined the *Mahābhāṣya* I have not been able to discover anything there which can warrant us in holding that the two Patañjalis cannot be identified. There are no doubt many apparent divergences of view, but even in these it is only the traditional views of the old grammarians that are exposed and reconciled, and it would be very unwarrantable for us to judge anything about the personal views of the grammarian from them. I am also convinced that the writer of the *Mahābhāṣya* knew most of the important points of the Sāṃkhya-Yoga metaphysics; as a few examples I may refer to the guṇa theory (1. 2. 64, 4. 1. 3), the Sāṃkhya dictum of ex nihilo nihil fit (1. 1. 56), the ideas of time (2. 2. 5, 3. 2. 123), the idea of the return of similars into similars (1. 1. 50), the idea of change *vikāra* as production of new qualities *guṇāntarādhāna* (5. 1. 2, 5. 1. 3) and the distinction of indriya and Buddhi (3. 3. 133). We may add to it that the *Mahābhāṣya* agrees with the Yoga view as regards the Sphoṭavāda, which is not held in common by any other school of Indian philosophy. There is also this external similarity, that unlike any other work they both begin their works in a similar manner (*atha yogānuśāsanam* and *atha śābdānuśāsanam*)—"now begins the compilation of the instructions on Yoga" (*Yoga sūtra*)—and "now begins the compilation of the instructions of words" (*Mahābhāṣya*).

It may further be noticed in this connection that the arguments

[1] Patañjali's *Mahābhāṣya*, 1. 2. 64.

which Professor Woods has adduced to assign the date of the *Yoga sūtra* between 300 and 500 A.D. are not at all conclusive, as they stand on a weak basis; for firstly if the two Patañjalis cannot be identified, it does not follow that the editor of the Yoga should necessarily be made later; secondly, the supposed Buddhist[1] reference is found in the fourth chapter which, as I have shown above, is a later interpolation; thirdly, even if they were written by Patañjali it cannot be inferred that because Vācaspati describes the opposite school as being of the Vijñānavādi type, we are to infer that the sūtras refer to Vasubandhu or even to Nāgārjuna, for such ideas as have been refuted in the sūtras had been developing long before the time of Nāgārjuna.

Thus we see that though the tradition of later commentators may not be accepted as a sufficient ground to identify the two Patañjalis, we cannot discover anything from a comparative critical study of the *Yoga sūtras* and the text of the *Mahābhāṣya*, which can lead us to say that the writer of the *Yoga sūtras* flourished at a later date than the other Patañjali.

Postponing our views about the time of Patañjali the Yoga editor, I regret I have to increase the confusion by introducing the other work *Kitāb Pātanjal*, of which Alberuni speaks, for our consideration. Alberuni considers this work as a very famous one and he translates it along with another book called *Sānka* (Sāṃkhya) ascribed to Kapila. This book was written in the form of dialogue between master and pupil, and it is certain that this book was not the present *Yoga sūtra* of Patañjali, though it had the same aim as the latter, namely the search for liberation and for the union of the soul with the object of its meditation. The book was called by Alberuni *Kitāb Pātanjal*, which is to be translated as the book of Pātañjala, because in another place, speaking of its author, he puts in a Persian phrase which when translated stands as "the author of the book of Pātanjal." It had also an elaborate commentary from which Alberuni quotes many extracts, though he does not tell us the author's name. It treats of God, soul, bondage, karma, salvation, etc., as we find in the *Yoga sūtra*, but the manner in which these are described (so

[1] It is important to notice that the most important Buddhist reference *nacaikacittatantram vastu tadapramāṇakam tadā kim syāt* (IV. 16) was probably a line of the *Vyāsabhāṣya*, as Bhoja, who had consulted many commentaries as he says in the preface, does not count it as a sūtra.

far as can be judged from the copious extracts supplied by Alberuni) shows that these ideas had undergone some change from what we find in the *Yoga sūtra*. Following the idea of God in Alberuni we find that he retains his character as a timeless emancipated being, but he speaks, hands over the Vedas and shows the way to Yoga and inspires men in such a way that they could obtain by cogitation what he bestowed on them. The name of God proves his existence, for there cannot exist anything of which the name existed, but not the thing. The soul perceives him and thought comprehends his qualities. Meditation is identical with worshipping him exclusively, and by practising it uninterruptedly the individual comes into supreme absorption with him and beatitude is obtained[1].

The idea of soul is the same as we find in the *Yoga sūtra*. The idea of metempsychosis is also the same. He speaks of the eight siddhis (miraculous powers) at the first stage of meditation on the unity of God. Then follow the other four stages of meditation corresponding to the four stages we have as in the *Yoga sūtra*. He gives four kinds of ways for the achievement of salvation, of which the first is the *abhyāsa* (habit) of Patañjali, and the object of this abhyāsa is unity with God[2]. The second stands for vairāgya; the third is the worship of God with a view to seek his favour in the attainment of salvation (cf. *Yoga sūtra*, I. 23 and I. 29). The fourth is a new introduction, namely that of rasāyana or alchemy. As regards liberation the view is almost the same as in the *Yoga sūtra*, II. 25 and IV. 34, but the liberated state is spoken of in one place as absorption in God or being one with him. The Brahman is conceived as an *ūrddhvamūla avākśākha aśvattha* (a tree with roots upwards and branches below), after the Upaniṣad fashion, the upper root is pure Brahman, the trunk is Veda, the branches are the different doctrines and schools, its leaves are the different modes of interpretation. Its nourishment comes from the three forces; the

[1] Cf. *Yoga sūtra* I. 23–29 and II. 1, 45. The *Yoga sūtras* speak of Īśvara (God) as an eternally emancipated puruṣa, omniscient, and the teacher of all past teachers. By meditating on him many of the obstacles such as illness, etc., which stand in the way of Yoga practice are removed. He is regarded as one of the alternative objects of concentration. The commentator Vyāsa notes that he is the best object, for being drawn towards the Yogin by his concentration He so wills that he can easily attain concentration and through it salvation. No argument is given in the *Yoga sūtras* of the existence of God.

[2] Cf. Yoga II. 1.

object of the worshipper is to leave the tree and go back to the roots.

The difference of this system from that of the *Yoga sūtra* is: (1) the conception of God has risen here to such an importance that he has become the only object of meditation, and absorption in him is the goal; (2) the importance of the yama[1] and the niyama has been reduced to the minimum; (3) the value of the Yoga discipline as a separate means of salvation apart from any connection with God as we find in the *Yoga sūtra* has been lost sight of; (4) liberation and Yoga are defined as absorption in God; (5) the introduction of Brahman; (6) the very significance of Yoga as control of mental states (*cittavṛttinirodha*) is lost sight of, and (7) rasāyana (alchemy) is introduced as one of the means of salvation.

From this we can fairly assume that this was a new modification of the Yoga doctrine on the basis of Patañjali's *Yoga sūtra* in the direction of Vedānta and Tantra, and as such it probably stands as the transition link through which the Yoga doctrine of the sūtras entered into a new channel in such a way that it could be easily assimilated from there by later developments of Vedānta, Tantra and Śaiva doctrines[2]. As the author mentions rasāyana as a means of salvation, it is very probable that he flourished after Nāgārjuna and was probably the same person who wrote *Pātañjala tantra*, who has been quoted by Śivadāsa in connection with alchemical matters and spoken of by Nāgeśa as "*Carake* Patañjaliḥ." We can also assume with some degree of probability that it is with reference to this man that Cakrapāṇi and Bhoja made the confusion of identifying him with the writer of the *Mahābhāṣya*. It is also very probable that Cakrapāṇi by his line "*pātañjalamahābhāṣyacarakapratisaṃskṛtaiḥ*" refers to this work which was called "Pātañjala." The commentator of this work gives some description of the lokas, dvīpas and the sāgaras, which runs counter to the descriptions given in the *Vyāsabhāṣya*, III. 26, and from this we can infer that it was probably written at a time when the *Vyāsabhāṣya* was not written or had not attained any great sanctity or authority. Alberuni

[1] Alberuni, in his account of the book of Sāṃkhya, gives a list of commandments which practically is the same as yama and niyama, but it is said that through them one cannot attain salvation.

[2] Cf. the account of *Pāśupatadarśana* in *Sarvadarśanasaṃgraha*.

also described the book as being very famous at the time, and Bhoja and Cakrapāṇi also probably confused him with Patañjali the grammarian; from this we can fairly assume that this book of Patañjali was probably written by some other Patañjali within the first 300 or 400 years of the Christian era; and it may not be improbable that when *Vyāsabhāṣya* quotes in III. 44 as "*iti* Patañjaliḥ," he refers to this Patañjali.

The conception of Yoga as we meet it in the Maitrāyaṇa Upaniṣad consisted of six aṅgas or accessories, namely prāṇāyāma, pratyāhāra, dhyāna, dhāraṇā, tarka and samādhi[1]. Comparing this list with that of the list in the *Yoga sūtras* we find that two new elements have been added, and tarka has been replaced by āsana. Now from the account of the sixty-two heresies given in the *Brahmajāla sutta* we know that there were people who either from meditation of three degrees or through logic and reasoning had come to believe that both the external world as a whole and individual souls were eternal. From the association of this last mentioned logical school with the Samādhi or Dhyāna school as belonging to one class of thinkers called śāśvatavāda, and from the inclusion of tarka as an aṅga in samādhi, we can fairly assume that the last of the aṅgas given in Maitrāyaṇī Upaniṣad represents the oldest list of the Yoga doctrine, when the Sāṃkhya and the Yoga were in a process of being grafted on each other, and when the Saṃkhya method of discussion did not stand as a method independent of the Yoga. The substitution of āsana for tarka in the list of Patañjali shows that the Yoga had developed a method separate from the Saṃkhya. The introduction of ahiṃsā (non-injury), satya (truthfulness), asteya (want of stealing), brahmacaryya (sex-control), aparigraha (want of greed) as yama and śauca (purity), santoṣa (contentment) as niyama, as a system of morality without which Yoga is deemed impossible (for the first time in the sūtras), probably marks the period when the disputes between the Hindus and the Buddhists had not become so keen. The introduction of maitrī, karuṇā, muditā, upekṣā is also equally significant, as we do not find them mentioned in such a prominent form in any other literature of the Hindus dealing with the subject of emancipation. Beginning from the *Ācārāṅgasūtra*, *Uttarādhyayanasūtra*,

[1] *prāṇāyāmaḥ pratyāhāraḥ dhyānam dhāraṇā tarkaḥ samādhiḥ ṣaḍaṅga ityucyate yogaḥ* (Maitr. 6. 8).

the *Sūtrakṛtāṅgasūtra*, etc., and passing through Umāsvāti's *Tattvārthādhigamasūtra* to Hemacandra's *Yogaśāstra* we find that the Jains had been founding their Yoga discipline mainly on the basis of a system of morality indicated by the yamas, and the opinion expressed in Alberuni's *Pātanjal* that these cannot give salvation marks the divergence of the Hindus in later days from the Jains. Another important characteristic of Yoga is its thoroughly pessimistic tone. Its treatment of sorrow in connection with the statement of the scope and ideal of Yoga is the same as that of the four sacred truths of the Buddhists, namely suffering, origin of suffering, the removal of suffering; and of the path to the removal of suffering[1]. Again, the metaphysics of the saṃsāra (rebirth) cycle in connection with sorrow, origination, decease, rebirth, etc. is described with a remarkable degree of similarity with the cycle of causes as described in early Buddhism. Avidyā is placed at the head of the group; yet this avidyā should not be confused with the Vedānta avidyā of Śaṅkara, as it is an avidyā of the Buddhist type; it is not a cosmic power of illusion nor anything like a mysterious original sin, but it is within the range of earthly tangible reality. Yoga avidyā is the ignorance of the four sacred truths, as we have in the sūtra "*anityāśuciduḥkhānātmasu nityaśuciduḥkhātmakhyātiravidyā*" (II. 5).

The ground of our existing is our will to live (*abhiniveśa*). "This is our besetting sin that we will to be, that we will to be ourselves, that we fondly will our being to blend with other kinds of existence and extend. The negation of the will to be, cuts off being for us at least[2]." This is true as much of Buddhism as of the Yoga abhiniveśa, which is a term coined and used in the Yoga for the first time to suit the Buddhist idea, and which has never been accepted, so far as I know, in any other Hindu literature in this sense. My sole aim in pointing out these things in this section is to show that the *Yoga sūtras* proper (first three chapters) were composed at a time when the later forms of Buddhism had not developed, and when the quarrels between the Hindus and the Buddhists and Jains had not reached such

[1] *Yoga sūtra*, II. 15, 16, 17. *Yathācikitsāśāstraṃ caturvyūhaṃ rogo rogahetuḥ ārogyaṃ bhaiṣajyamiti evamidamapi śāstram caturvyūhameva; tadyathā saṃsāraḥ, saṃsārahetuḥ mokṣaḥ mokṣopāyaḥ; duḥkhabahulaḥ saṃsāro heyaḥ, pradhānapuruṣayoḥ saṃyogo heyahetuḥ, saṃyogasyātyantikī nivṛttirhānaṃ hanopāyaḥ samyagdarśanam*, *Vyāsabhāṣya*, II. 15

[2] Oldenberg's *Buddhism*[1].

a stage that they would not like to borrow from one another. As this can only be held true of earlier Buddhism I am disposed to think that the date of the first three chapters of the *Yoga sūtras* must be placed about the second century B.C. Since there is no evidence which can stand in the way of identifying the grammarian Patañjali with the Yoga writer, I believe we may take them as being identical[1].

The Saṃkhya and the Yoga Doctrine of Soul or Puruṣa.

The Sāṃkhya philosophy as we have it now admits two principles, souls and *prakṛti*, the root principle of matter. Souls are many, like the Jaina souls, but they are without parts and qualities. They do not contract or expand according as they occupy a smaller or a larger body, but are always all-pervasive, and are not contained in the bodies in which they are manifested. But the relation between body or rather the mind associated with it and soul is such that whatever mental phenomena happen in the mind are interpreted as the experience of its soul. The souls are many, and had it not been so (the Sāṃkhya argues) with the birth of one all would have been born and with the death of one all would have died[2].

The exact nature of soul is however very difficult of comprehension, and yet it is exactly this which one must thoroughly grasp in order to understand the Sāṃkhya philosophy. Unlike the Jaina soul possessing *anantajñāna*, *anantadarśana*, *anantasukha*, and *anantavīryya*, the Sāṃkhya soul is described as being devoid of any and every characteristic; but its nature is absolute pure consciousness (*cit*). The Sāṃkhya view differs from the Vedānta, firstly in this that it does not consider the soul to be of the nature of pure intelligence and bliss (*ānanda*)[3]. Bliss with Sāṃkhya is but another name for pleasure and as such it belongs to prakṛti and does not constitute the nature of soul; secondly, according to Vedānta the individual souls (*jīva*) are

[1] See S. N. Das Gupta, *Yoga Philosophy in relation to other Indian systems of thought*, ch. II. The most important point in favour of this identification seems to be that both the Patañjalis as against the other Indian systems admitted the doctrine of *sphoṭa* which was denied even by Sāṃkhya. On the doctrine of Sphoṭa see my *Study of Patanjali*, Appendix I.

[2] *Kārikā*, 18.

[3] See Citsukha's *Tattvapradīpikā*, IV.

but illusory manifestations of one soul or pure consciousness the Brahman, but according to Sāṃkhya they are all real and many.

The most interesting feature of Sāṃkhya as of Vedānta is the analysis of knowledge. Sāṃkhya holds that our knowledge of things are mere ideational pictures or images. External things are indeed material, but the sense data and images of the mind, the coming and going of which is called knowledge, are also in some sense matter-stuff, since they are limited in their nature like the external things. The sense-data and images come and go, they are often the prototypes, or photographs of external things, and as such ought to be considered as in some sense material, but the matter of which these are composed is the subtlest. These images of the mind could not have appeared as conscious, if there were no separate principles of consciousness in connection with which the whole conscious plane could be interpreted as the experience of a person[1]. We know that the Upaniṣads consider the soul or ātman as pure and infinite consciousness, distinct from the forms of knowledge, the ideas, and the images. In our ordinary ways of mental analysis we do not detect that beneath the forms of knowledge there is some other principle which has no change, no form, but which is like a light which illumines the mute, pictorial forms which the mind assumes. The self is nothing but this light. We all speak of our "self" but we have no mental picture of the self as we have of other things, yet in all our knowledge we seem to know our self. The Jains had said that the soul was veiled by karma matter, and every act of knowledge meant only the partial removal of the veil. Sāṃkhya says that the self cannot be found as an image of knowledge, but that is because it is a distinct, transcendent principle, whose real nature as such is behind or beyond the subtle matter of knowledge. Our cognitions, so far as they are mere forms or images, are merely compositions or complexes of subtle mind-substance, and thus are like a sheet of painted canvas immersed in darkness; as the canvas gets prints from outside and moves, the pictures appear one by one before the light and are illuminated. So it is with our knowledge. The special characteristic of self is that it is like a light, without which all knowledge would be blind. Form and motion are the characteristics of matter, and

[1] *Tattakaumudī*, 5; *Yogavārttika*, IV. 22; *Vijñānāmṛtabhāṣya*, p. 74; *Yogavārttika* and *Tattvavaiśāradī*, I. 4, II. 6, 18, 20; *Vyāsabhāṣya*, I. 6, 7.

so far as knowledge is mere limited form and movement it is the same as matter; but there is some other principle which enlivens these knowledge-forms, by virtue of which they become conscious. This principle of consciousness (*cit*) cannot indeed be separately perceived *per se*, but the presence of this principle in all our forms of knowledge is distinctly indicated by inference. This principle of consciousness has no motion, no form, no quality, no impurity[1]. The movement of the knowledge-stuff takes place in relation to it, so that it is illuminated as consciousness by it, and produces the appearance of itself as undergoing all changes of knowledge and experiences of pleasure and pain. Each item of knowledge so far as it is an image or a picture of some sort is but a subtle knowledge-stuff which has been illumined by the principle of consciousness, but so far as each item of knowledge carries with it the awakening or the enlivening of consciousness, it is the manifestation of the principle of consciousness. Knowledge-revelation is not the unveiling or revelation of a particular part of the self, as the Jains supposed, but it is a revelation of the self only so far as knowledge is pure awakening, pure enlivening, pure consciousness. So far as the content of knowledge or the image is concerned, it is not the revelation of self but is the blind knowledge-stuff.

The Buddhists had analysed knowledge into its diverse constituent parts, and had held that the coming together of these brought about the conscious states. This coming together was to them the point of the illusory notion of self, since this unity or coming together was not a permanent thing but a momentary collocation. With Sāṃkhya however the self, the pure *cit*, is neither illusory nor an abstraction; it is concrete but transcendent. Coming into touch with it gives unity to all the movements of the knowledge-composites of subtle stuff, which would otherwise have remained aimless and unintelligent. It is by coming into connection with this principle of intelligence that they are interpreted as the systematic and coherent experience of a person, and may thus be said to be intelligized. Intelligizing means the expression and interpretation of the events or the happenings of

[1] It is important to note that Sāṃkhya has two terms to denote the two aspects involved in knowledge, viz. the relating element of awareness as such (*cit*), and the content (*buddhi*) which is the form of the mind-stuff representing the sense-data and the image. Cognition takes place by the reflection of the former in the latter.

knowledge in connection with a person, so as to make them a system of experience. This principle of intelligence is called puruṣa. There is a separate puruṣa in Sāṃkhya for each individual, and it is of the nature of pure intelligence. The Vedānta ātman however is different from the Sāṃkhya puruṣa in this that it is one and is of the nature of pure intelligence, pure being, and pure bliss. It alone is the reality and by illusory māyā it appears as many.

Thought and Matter.

A question naturally arises, that if the knowledge forms are made up of some sort of stuff as the objective forms of matter are, why then should the puruṣa illuminate it and not external material objects. The answer that Sāṃkhya gives is that the knowledge-complexes are certainly different from external objects in this, that they are far subtler and have a preponderance of a special quality of plasticity and translucence (*sattva*), which resembles the light of puruṣa, and is thus fit for reflecting and absorbing the light of the puruṣa. The two principal characteristics of external gross matter are mass and energy. But it has also the other characteristic of allowing itself to be photographed by our mind; this thought-photograph of matter has again the special privilege of being so translucent as to be able to catch the reflection of the *cit*—the super-translucent transcendent principle of intelligence. The fundamental characteristic of external gross matter is its mass; energy is common to both gross matter and the subtle thought-stuff. But mass is at its lowest minimum in thought-stuff, whereas the capacity of translucence, or what may be otherwise designated as the intelligence-stuff, is at its highest in thought-stuff. But if the gross matter had none of the characteristics of translucence that thought possesses, it could not have made itself an object of thought; for thought transforms itself into the shape, colour, and other characteristics of the thing which has been made its object. Thought could not have copied the matter, if the matter did not possess some of the essential substances of which the copy was made up. But this plastic entity (*sattva*) which is so predominant in thought is at its lowest limit of subordination in matter. Similarly mass is not noticed in thought, but some such notions as are associated with mass may be discernible in thought; thus the images of thought are limited, separate, have movement, and have more or less clear cut forms. The images do not extend in space, but they can represent space. The translucent and plastic element of thought (*sattva*) in association with movement (*rajas*) would have resulted in a simultaneous revelation of all objects; it is on account of mass or tendency of obstruction (*tamas*) that knowledge proceeds from image to image and discloses things in a successive manner. The buddhi (thought-stuff) holds within it all knowledge immersed as it were in utter darkness, and actual knowledge comes before our view as though by the removal of the darkness or veil, by the reflection of the light of the puruṣa. This characteristic of knowledge, that all its stores are hidden as if lost at any moment, and only one picture or idea comes at a time to the arena of revelation, demonstrates that in knowledge there is a factor of obstruction which manifests itself in its full actuality in gross matter as mass. Thus both thought and gross matter are made up of three elements, a plasticity of intelligence-stuff (*sattva*), energy-stuff (*rajas*), and mass-stuff (*tamas*), or the factor of obstruction. Of these the last two are predominant in gross matter and the first two in thought.

Feelings, the Ultimate Substances[1].

Another question that arises in this connection is the position of feeling in such an analysis of thought and matter. Sāṃkhya holds that the three characteristic constituents that we have analyzed just now are feeling substances. Feeling is the most interesting side of our consciousness. It is in our feelings that we think of our thoughts as being parts of ourselves. If we should analyze any percept into the crude and undeveloped sensations of which it is composed at the first moment of its appearance, it comes more as a shock than as an image, and we find that it is felt more as a feeling mass than as an image. Even in our ordinary life the elements which precede an act of knowledge are probably mere feelings. As we go lower down the scale of evolution the automatic actions and relations of matter are concomitant with crude manifestations of feeling which never rise to the level of knowledge. The lower the scale of evolution the less is the keenness of feeling, till at last there comes a stage where matter-complexes do not give rise to feeling

[1] *Kārikā*, 12, with Gauḍpāda and Nārāyaṇatīrtha.

reactions but to mere physical reactions. Feelings thus mark the earliest track of consciousness, whether we look at it from the point of view of evolution or of the genesis of consciousness in ordinary life. What we call matter-complexes become at a certain stage feeling-complexes and what we call feeling-complexes at a certain stage of descent sink into mere matter-complexes with matter reaction. The feelings are therefore the things-in-themselves, the ultimate substances of which consciousness and gross matter are made up. Ordinarily a difficulty might be felt in taking feelings to be the ultimate substances of which gross matter and thought are made up; for we are more accustomed to take feelings as being merely subjective, but if we remember the Sāṃkhya analysis, we find that it holds that thought and matter are but two different modifications of certain subtle substances which are in essence but three types of feeling entities. The three principal characteristics of thought and matter that we have noticed in the preceding section are but the manifestations of three types of feeling substances. There is the class of feelings that we call the sorrowful, there is another class of feelings that we call pleasurable, and there is still another class which is neither sorrowful nor pleasurable, but is one of ignorance, depression (*viṣāda*) or dullness. Thus corresponding to these three types of manifestations as pleasure, pain, and dullness, and materially as shining (*prakāśa*), energy (*pravṛtti*), obstruction (*niyama*), there are three types of feeling-substances which must be regarded as the ultimate things which make up all the diverse kinds of gross matter and thought by their varying modifications.

The Guṇas[1].

These three types of ultimate subtle entities are technically called *guṇa* in Sāṃkhya philosophy. Guṇa in Sanskrit has three meanings, namely (1) quality, (2) rope, (3) not primary. These entities, however, are substances and not mere qualities. But it may be mentioned in this connection that in Sāṃkhya philosophy there is no separate existence of qualities; it holds that each and every unit of quality is but a unit of substance. What we call quality is but a particular manifestation or appearance of a subtle entity. Things do not possess quality, but quality

[1] *Yogavārttika*, II. 18; Bhāvāgaṇeśa's *Tattvayāthārthyadīpana*, pp. 1–3; *Vijñānāmṛtabhāṣya*, p. 100; *Tattvakaumudī*, 13; also Gauḍapāda and Nārāyaṇatīrtha, 13.

signifies merely the manner in which a substance reacts; any object we see seems to possess many qualities, but the Sāṃkhya holds that corresponding to each and every new unit of quality, however fine and subtle it may be, there is a corresponding subtle entity, the reaction of which is interpreted by us as a quality. This is true not only of qualities of external objects but also of mental qualities as well. These ultimate entities were thus called guṇas probably to suggest that they are the entities which by their various modifications manifest themselves as guṇas or qualities. These subtle entities may also be called guṇas in the sense of ropes because they are like ropes by which the soul is chained down as if it were to thought and matter. These may also be called guṇas as things of secondary importance, because though permanent and indestructible, they continually suffer modifications and changes by their mutual groupings and re-groupings, and thus not primarily and unalterably constant like the souls (*puruṣa*). Moreover the object of the world process being the enjoyment and salvation of the puruṣas, the matter-principle could not naturally be regarded as being of primary importance. But in whatever senses we may be inclined to justify the name guṇa as applied to these subtle entities, it should be borne in mind that they are substantive entities or subtle substances and not abstract qualities. These guṇas are infinite in number, but in accordance with their three main characteristics as described above they have been arranged in three classes or types called *sattva* (intelligence-stuff), *rajas* (energy-stuff) and *tamas* (mass-stuff). An infinite number of subtle substances which agree in certain characteristics of self-shining or plasticity are called the *sattva-guṇas* and those which behave as units of activity are called the *rajo-guṇas* and those which behave as factors of obstruction, mass or materiality are called *tamo-guṇas*. These subtle guṇa substances are united in different proportions (e.g. a larger number of sattva substances with a lesser number of rajas or tamas, or a larger number of tamas substances with a smaller number of rajas and sattva substances and so on in varying proportions), and as a result of this, different substances with different qualities come into being. Though attached to one another when united in different proportions, they mutually act and react upon one another, and thus by their combined resultant produce new characters, qualities and substances. There is however one and only one stage in which the guṇas are not compounded in varying proportions. In this state each of the guṇa substances is opposed by each of the other guṇa substances, and thus by their equal mutual opposition create an equilibrium, in which none of the characters of the guṇas manifest themselves. This is a state which is so absolutely devoid of all characteristics that it is absolutely incoherent, indeterminate, and indefinite. It is a qualitiless simple homogeneity. It is a state of being which is as it were non-being. This state of the mutual equilibrium of the guṇas is called prakṛti[1]. This is a state which cannot be said either to exist or to non-exist for it serves no purpose, but it is hypothetically the mother of all things. This is however the earliest stage, by the breaking of which, later on, all modifications take place.

Prakṛti and its Evolution.

Sāṃkhya believes that before this world came into being there was such a state of dissolution—a state in which the guṇa compounds had disintegrated into a state of disunion and had by their mutual opposition produced an equilibrium the prakṛti. Then later on disturbance arose in the prakṛti, and as a result of that a process of unequal aggregation of the guṇas in varying proportions took place, which brought forth the creation of the manifold. Prakṛti, the state of perfect homogeneity and incoherence of the guṇas, thus gradually evolved and became more and more determinate, differentiated, heterogeneous, and coherent. The guṇas are always uniting, separating, and uniting again[2]. Varying qualities of essence, energy, and mass in varied groupings act on one another and through their mutual interaction and interdependence evolve from the indefinite or qualitatively indeterminate the definite or qualitatively determinate. And though co-operating to produce the world of effects, these diverse moments with diverse tendencies never coalesce. Thus in the phenomenal product whatever energy there is is due to the element of rajas and rajas alone; all matter, resistance, stability, is due to tamas, and all conscious manifestation to sattva. The particular guṇa which happens to be predominant in any phenomenon becomes manifest in that phenomenon and others become latent, though their presence is inferred by their

[1] *Yogavārttika*, II. 19, and *Pravacanabhāṣya*, I. 61.

[2] *Kaumudī*, 13–16; *Tattvavaiśāradī*, II. 20, IV. 13, 14; also *Yogavārttika*, IV. 13, 14.

effect. Thus, for example, in a body at rest mass is patent, energy latent and potentiality of conscious manifestation sublatent. In a moving body, the rajas is predominant (kinetic) and the mass is partially overcome. All these transformations of the groupings of the guṇas in different proportions presuppose the state of prakṛti as the starting point. It is at this stage that the tendencies to conscious manifestation, as well as the powers of doing work, are exactly counterbalanced by the resistance of inertia or mass, and the process of cosmic evolution is at rest. When this equilibrium is once destroyed, it is supposed that out of a natural affinity of all the sattva reals for themselves, of rajas reals for other reals of their type, of tamas reals for others of their type, there arises an unequal aggregation of sattva, rajas, or tamas at different moments. When one guṇa is preponderant in any particular collocation, the others are co-operant. This evolutionary series beginning from the first disturbance of the prakṛti to the final transformation as the world-order, is subject to "a definite law which it cannot overstep." In the words of Dr B. N. Seal[1], "the process of evolution consists in the development of the differentiated (*vaiṣamya*) within the undifferentiated (*sāmyāvasthā*) of the determinate (*viśeṣa*) within the indeterminate (*aviśeṣa*) of the coherent (*yutasiddha*) within the incoherent (*ayutasiddha*). The order of succession is neither from parts to whole nor from whole to the parts, but ever from a relatively less differentiated, less determinate, less coherent whole to a relatively more differentiated, more determinate, more coherent whole." The meaning of such an evolution is this, that all the changes and modifications in the shape of the evolving collocations of guṇa reals take place within the body of the prakṛti. Prakṛti consisting of the infinite reals is infinite, and that it has been disturbed does not mean that the whole of it has been disturbed and upset, or that the totality of the guṇas in the prakṛti has been unhinged from a state of equilibrium. It means rather that a very vast number of guṇas constituting the worlds of thought and matter has been upset. These guṇas once thrown out of balance begin to group themselves together first in one form, then in another, then in another, and so on. But such a change in the formation of aggregates should not be thought to take place in such a way that the later aggregates appear in supersession of the former ones, so that when the former comes into being the latter ceases to exist.

[1] Dr B. N. Seal's *Positive Sciences of the Ancient Hindus*, 1915, p. 7.

For the truth is that one stage is produced after another; this second stage is the result of a new aggregation of some of the reals of the first stage. This deficiency of the reals of the first stage which had gone forth to form the new aggregate as the second stage is made good by a refilling from the prakṛti. So also, as the third stage of aggregation takes place from out of the reals of the second stage, the deficiency of the reals of the second stage is made good by a refilling from the first stage and that of the first stage from the prakṛti. Thus by a succession of refillings the process of evolution proceeds, till we come to its last limit, where there is no real evolution of new substance, but mere chemical and physical changes of qualities in things which had already evolved. Evolution (*tattvāntarapariṇāma*) in Sāṃkhya means the development of categories of existence and not mere changes of qualities of substances (physical, chemical, biological or mental). Thus each of the stages of evolution remains as a permanent category of being, and offers scope to the more and more differentiated and coherent groupings of the succeeding stages. Thus it is said that the evolutionary process is regarded as a differentiation of new stages as integrated in previous stages (*saṃsṛṣṭa-viveka*).

Pralaya and the disturbance of the Prakṛti Equilibrium.

But how or rather why prakṛti should be disturbed is the most knotty point in Sāṃkhya. It is postulated that the prakṛti or the sum-total of the guṇas is so connected with the puruṣas, and there is such an inherent teleology or blind purpose in the lifeless prakṛti, that all its evolution and transformations take place for the sake of the diverse puruṣas, to serve the enjoyment of pleasures and sufferance of pain through experiences, and finally leading them to absolute freedom or mukti. A return of this manifold world into the quiescent state (*pralaya*) of prakṛti takes place when the karmas of all puruṣas collectively require that there should be such a temporary cessation of all experience. At such a moment the guṇa compounds are gradually broken, and there is a backward movement (*pratisañcara*) till everything is reduced to the guṇas in their elementary disintegrated state when their mutual opposition brings about their equilibrium. This equilibrium however is not a mere passive state, but one of utmost tension; there is intense activity, but the activity here does not lead to the generation of new things and qualities (*visadṛśa-pariṇāma*); this course of new production being suspended, the activity here repeats the same state (*sadṛśa-pariṇāma*) of equilibrium, so that there is no change or new production. The state of pralaya thus is not a suspension of the teleology or purpose of the guṇas, or an absolute break of the course of guṇa evolution; for the state of pralaya, since it has been generated to fulfil the demands of the accumulated karmas of puruṣas, and since there is still the activity of the guṇas in keeping themselves in a state of suspended production, is also a stage of the saṃsāra cycle. The state of mukti (liberation) is of course quite different, for in that stage the movement of the guṇas ceases for ever with reference to the liberated soul. But still the question remains, what breaks the state of equilibrium? The Sāṃkhya answer is that it is due to the transcendental (non-mechanical) influence of the puruṣa[1]. This influence of the puruṣa again, if it means anything, means that there is inherent in the guṇas a teleology that all their movements or modifications should take place in such a way that these may serve the purposes of the puruṣas. Thus when the karmas of the puruṣas had demanded that there should be a suspension of all experience, for a period there was a pralaya. At the end of it, it is the same inherent purpose of the prakṛti that wakes it up for the formation of a suitable world for the experiences of the puruṣas by which its quiescent state is disturbed. This is but another way of looking at the inherent teleology of the prakṛti, which demands that a state of pralaya should cease and a state of world-framing activity should begin. Since there is a purpose in the guṇas which brought them to a state of equilibrium, the state of equilibrium also presupposes that it also may be broken up again when the purpose so demands. Thus the inherent purpose of the prakṛti brought about the state of pralaya and then broke it up for the creative work again, and it is this natural change in the prakṛti that may be regarded from another point of view as the transcendental influence of the puruṣas.

Mahat and Ahaṃkāra.

The first evolute of the prakṛti is generated by a preponderance of the sattva (intelligence-stuff). This is indeed the earliest state from which all the rest of the world has sprung forth; and it is a state in which the stuff of sattva predominates. It thus holds

[1] The Yoga answer is of course different. It believes that the disturbance of the equilibrium of the prakṛti for new creation takes place by the will of Īśvara (God).

within it the minds (*buddhi*) of all puruṣas which were lost in the prakṛti during the pralaya. The very first work of the evolution of prakṛti to serve the puruṣas is thus manifested by the separating out of the old buddhis or minds (of the puruṣas) which hold within themselves the old specific ignorance (*avidyā*) inherent in them with reference to each puruṣa with which any particular buddhi is associated from beginningless time before the pralaya. This state of evolution consisting of all the collected minds (buddhi) of all the puruṣas is therefore called *buddhitattva.* It is a state which holds or comprehends within it the buddhis of all individuals. The individual buddhis of individual puruṣas are on one hand integrated with the buddhitattva and on the other associated with their specific puruṣas. When some buddhis once begin to be separated from the prakṛti, other buddhi evolutions take place. In other words, we are to understand that once the transformation of buddhis is effected for the service of the puruṣas, all the other direct transformations that take place from the prakṛti take the same line, i.e. a preponderance of sattva being once created by the bringing out of some buddhis, other transformations of prakṛti that follow them have also the sattva preponderance, which thus have exactly the same composition as the first buddhis. Thus the first transformation from prakṛti becomes buddhi-transformation. This stage of buddhis may thus be regarded as the most universal stage, which comprehends within it all the buddhis of individuals and potentially all the matter of which the gross world is formed. Looked at from this point of view it has the widest and most universal existence comprising all creation, and is thus called *mahat* (the great one). It is called *liṅga* (sign), as the other later existences or evolutes give us the ground of inferring its existence, and as such must be distinguished from the prakṛti which is called *aliṅga*, i.e. of which no liṅga or characteristic may be affirmed.

This mahat-tattva being once produced, further modifications begin to take place in three lines by three different kinds of undulations representing the sattva preponderance, rajas preponderance and tamas preponderance. This state when the mahat is disturbed by the three parallel tendencies of a preponderance of tamas, rajas and sattva is called *ahaṃkāra*, and the above three tendencies are respectively called *tāmasika ahaṃkāra* or *bhūtādi*, *rājasika* or *taijasa ahaṃkāra*, and *vaikārika ahaṃkāra*. The rājasika ahaṃkāra cannot mark a new preponderance by itself; it only helps (*sahakāri*) the transformations of the sattva preponderance and the tamas preponderance. The development of the former preponderance, as is easy to see, is only the assumption of a more and more determinate character of the buddhi, for we remember that buddhi itself has been the resulting transformation of a sattva preponderance. Further development with the help of rajas on the line of sattva development could only take place when the buddhi as mind determined itself in specific ways. The first development of the buddhi on this line is called *sāttvika* or *vaikārika ahaṃkāra.* This ahaṃkāra represents the development in buddhi to produce a consciousness-stuff as I or rather "mine," and must thus be distinguished from the first stage as buddhi, the function of which is a mere understanding and general datum as thisness.

The ego or ahaṃkāra (*abhimāna-dravya*) is the specific expression of the general consciousness which takes experience as mine. The function of the ego is therefore called *abhimāna* (self-assertion). From this again come the five cognitive senses of vision, touch, smell, taste, and hearing, the five conative senses of speech, handling, foot-movement, the ejective sense and the generative sense; the *prāṇas* (bio-motor force) which help both conation and cognition are but aspects of buddhi-movement as life. The individual ahaṃkāras and senses are related to the individual buddhis by the developing sattva determinations from which they had come into being. Each buddhi with its own group of ahaṃkāra (ego) and sense-evolutes thus forms a microcosm separate from similar other buddhis with their associated groups. So far therefore as knowledge is subject to sense-influence and the ego, it is different for each individual, but so far as a general mind (*kāraṇa buddhi*) apart from sense knowledge is concerned, there is a community of all buddhis in the buddhitattva. Even there however each buddhi is separated from other buddhis by its own peculiarly associated ignorance (*avidyā*). The buddhi and its sattva evolutes of ahaṃkāra and the senses are so related that though they are different from buddhi in their functions, they are all comprehended in the buddhi, and mark only its gradual differentiations and modes. We must again remember in this connection the doctrine of refilling, for as buddhi exhausts its part in giving rise to ahaṃkāra, the deficiency of buddhi is made good by prakṛti; again as ahaṃkāra partially exhausts itself in generating sense-faculties, the deficiency is made good by a refilling from the buddhi. Thus the change and wastage of each of the stadia are always made good and kept constant by a constant refilling from each higher state and finally from prakṛti.

The Tanmātras and the Paramāṇus[1].

The other tendency, namely that of tamas, has to be helped by the liberated rajas of ahaṃkāra, in order to make itself preponderant, and this state in which the tamas succeeds in overcoming the sattva side which was so preponderant in the buddhi, is called *bhūtādi*. From this bhūtādi with the help of rajas are generated the *tanmātras*, the immediately preceding causes of the gross elements. The bhūtādi thus represents only the intermediate stage through which the differentiations and regroupings of tamas reals in the mahat proceed for the generation of the tanmātras. There has been some controversy between Sāṃkhya and Yoga as to whether the tanmātras are generated from the mahat or from ahaṃkāra. The situation becomes intelligible if we remember that evolution here does not mean coming out or emanation, but increasing differentiation in integration within the evolving whole. Thus the regroupings of tamas reals marks the differentiation which takes place within the mahat but through its stage as bhūtādi. Bhūtādi is absolutely homogeneous and inert, devoid of all physical and chemical characters except quantum or mass. The second stadium tanmātra represents subtle matter, vibratory, impingent, radiant, instinct with potential energy. These "potentials" arise from the unequal aggregation of the original mass-units in different proportions and collocations with an unequal distribution of the original energy (*rajas*). The tanmātras possess something more than quantum of mass and energy; they possess physical characters, some of them penetrability, others powers of impact or pressure, others radiant heat, others again capability of viscous and cohesive attraction[2].

In intimate relation with those physical characters they also possess the potentials of the energies represented by sound, touch, colour, taste, and smell; but, being subtle matter, they are devoid

[1] I have accepted in this section and in the next many of the translations of Sanskrit terms and expressions of Dr Seal and am largely indebted to him for his illuminating exposition of this subject as given in Ray's *Hindu Chemistry*. The credit of explaining Sāṃkhya physics in the light of the text belongs entirely to him.

[2] Dr Seal's *Positive Sciences of the Ancient Hindus*.

of the peculiar forms which these "potentials" assume in particles of gross matter like the atoms and their aggregates. In other words, the potentials lodged in subtle matter must undergo peculiar transformations by new groupings or collocations before they can act as sensory stimuli as gross matter, though in the minutest particles thereof the sensory stimuli may be infra-sensible (*atīndriya* but not *anudbhūta*)[1].

Of the tanmātras the *śabda* or *ākāśa tanmātra* (the sound-potential) is first generated directly from the bhūtādi. Next comes the *sparśa* or the *vāyu tanmātra* (touch-potential) which is generated by the union of a unit of tamas from bhūtādi with the ākāśa tanmātra. The *rūpa tanmātra* (colour-potential) is generated similarly by the accretion of a unit of tamas from bhūtādi; the *rasa tanmātra* (taste-potential) or the *ap tanmātra* is also similarly formed. This ap tanmātra again by its union with a unit of tamas from bhūtādi produces the *gandha tanmātra* (smell-potential) or the *kṣiti tanmātra*[2]. The difference of tanmātras or infra-atomic units and atoms (*paramāṇu*) is this, that the tanmātras have only the potential power of affecting our senses, which must be grouped and regrouped in a particular form to constitute a new existence as atoms before they can have the power of affecting our senses. It is important in this connection to point out that the classification of all gross objects as kṣiti, ap, tejas, marut and vyoman is not based upon a chemical analysis, but from the points of view of the five senses through which knowledge of them could be brought home to us. Each of our senses can only apprehend a particular quality and thus five different ultimate substances are said to exist corresponding to the five qualities which may be grasped by the five senses. In accordance with the existence of these five elements, the existence of the five potential states or tanmātras was also conceived to exist as the ground of the five gross forms.

The five classes of atoms are generated from the tanmātras as follows: the sound-potential, with accretion of rudiment matter from *bhūtādi* generates the ākāśa-atom. The touch-potentials combine with the vibratory particles (sound-potential) to generate the

[1] Dr Seal's *Positive Sciences of the Ancient Hindus.*

[2] There were various ways in which the genesis of tanmātras and atoms were explained in literatures other than Sāṃkhya; for some account of it see Dr Seal's *Positive Sciences of the Ancient Hindus.*

vāyu-atom. The light-and-heat potentials combine with touch-potentials and sound-potentials to produce the tejas-atom. The taste-potentials combine with light-and-heat potentials, touch-potentials and sound-potentials to generate the ap-atom and the smell-potentials combine with the preceding potentials to generate the earth-atom. The ākāśa-atom possesses penetrability, the vāyu-atom impact or mechanical pressure, the tejas-atom radiant heat and light, the ap-atom viscous attraction and the earth-atom cohesive attraction. The ākāśa we have seen forms the transition link from the bhūtādi to the tanmātra and from the tanmātra to the atomic production; it therefore deserves a special notice at this stage. Sāṃkhya distinguishes between a kāraṇa-ākāśa and kāryākāśa. The kāraṇa-ākāśa (non-atomic and all-pervasive) is the formless tamas—the mass in prakṛti or bhūtādi; it is indeed all-pervasive, and is not a mere negation, a mere un-occupiedness (*āvaraṇābhāva*) or vacuum[1]. When energy is first associated with this tamas element it gives rise to the sound-potential; the atomic ākāśa is the result of the integration of the original mass-units from bhūtādi with this sound-potential (*śabda tanmātra*). Such an ākāśa-atom is called the kāryākāśa; it is formed everywhere and held up in the original kāraṇa ākāśa as the medium for the development of vāyu atoms. Being atomic it occupies limited space.

The ahaṃkāra and the five tanmātras are technically called *aviśeṣa* or indeterminate, for further determinations or differentiations of them for the formation of newer categories of existence are possible. The eleven senses and the five atoms are called *viśeṣa*, i.e. determinate, for they cannot further be so determined as to form a new category of existence. It is thus that the course of evolution which started in the prakṛti reaches its furthest limit in the production of the senses on the one side and the atoms on the other. Changes no doubt take place in bodies having atomic constitution, but these changes are changes of quality due to spatial changes in the position of the atoms or to the introduction of new atoms and their re-arrangement. But these are not such that a newer category of existence could be formed by them which was substantially different from the combined atoms.

[1] Dr B. N. Seal in describing this ākāśa says "Ākāśa corresponds in some respects to the ether of the physicists and in others to what may be called proto-atom (protyle)." Ray's *History of Hindu Chemistry*, p. 88.

The changes that take place in the atomic constitution of things certainly deserve to be noticed. But before we go on to this, it will be better to enquire about the principle of causation according to which the Sāṃkhya-Yoga evolution should be comprehended or interpreted.

Principle of Causation and Conservation of Energy[1].

The question is raised, how can the prakṛti supply the deficiences made in its evolutes by the formation of other evolutes from them? When from mahat some tanmātras have evolved, or when from the tanmātras some atoms have evolved, how can the deficiency in mahat and the tanmātras be made good by the prakṛti?

Or again, what is the principle that guides the transformations that take place in the atomic stage when one gross body, say milk, changes into curd, and so on? Sāṃkhya says that "as the total energy remains the same while the world is constantly evolving, cause and effect are only more or less evolved forms of the same ultimate Energy. The sum of effects exists in the sum of causes in a potential form. The grouping or collocation alone changes, and this brings on the manifestation of the latent powers of the guṇas, but without creation of anything new. What is called the (material) cause is only the power which is efficient in the production or rather the vehicle of the power. This power is the unmanifested (or potential) form of the Energy set free (*udbhūta-vṛtti*) in the effect. But the concomitant conditions are necessary to call forth the so-called material cause into activity[2]." The appearance of an effect (such as the manifestation of the figure of the statue in the marble block by the causal efficiency of the sculptor's art) is only its passage from potentiality to actuality and the concomitant conditions (*sahakāri-śakti*) or efficient cause (*nimitta-kāraṇa*, such as the sculptor's art) is a sort of mechanical help or instrumental help to this passage or the transition[3]. The refilling from prakṛti thus means nothing more than this, that by the inherent teleology of the prakṛti, the reals there are so collocated as to be transformed into mahat as those of the mahat have been collocated to form the bhūtādi or the tanmātras.

[1] *Vyāsabhāṣya* and *Yogavārttika*, IV. 3; *Tattvavaiśāradī*, IV. 3.

[2] Ray, *History of Hindu Chemistry*, p. 72.

[3] *Ibid.* p. 73.

Yoga however explains this more vividly on the basis of transformation of the liberated potential energy. The sum of material causes potentially contains the energy manifested in the sum of effects. When the effectuating condition is added to the sum of material conditions in a given collocation, all that happens is that a stimulus is imparted which removes the arrest, disturbs the relatively stable equilibrium, and brings on a liberation of energy together with a fresh collocation (*guṇasanniveśaviśeṣa*). As the owner of an adjacent field in transferring water from one field to another of the same or lower level has only to remove the obstructing mud barriers, whereupon the water flows of itself to the other field, so when the efficient or instrumental causes (such as the sculptor's art) remove the barrier inherent in any collocation against its transformation into any other collocation, the energy from that collocation flows out in a corresponding manner and determines the collocation. Thus for example the energy which collocated the milk-atoms to form milk was in a state of arrest in the milk state. If by heat or other causes this barrier is removed, the energy naturally changes direction in a corresponding manner and collocates the atoms accordingly for the formation of curd. So also as soon as the barriers are removed from the prakṛti, guided by the constant will of Īśvara, the reals in equilibrium in the state of prakṛti leave their state of arrest and evolve themselves into mahat, etc.

Change as the formation of new collocations.

It is easy to see from what we have already said that any collocation of atoms forming a thing could not change its form, unless the barrier inherent or caused by the formation of the present collocation could be removed by some other extraneous instrumental cause. All gross things are formed by the collocation of the five atoms of kṣiti, ap, tejas, marut, and vyoman. The difference between one thing and another is simply this, that its collocation of atoms or the arrangement or grouping of atoms is different from that in another. The formation of a collocation has an inherent barrier against any change, which keeps that collocation in a state of equilibrium, and it is easy to see that these barriers exist in infinite directions in which all the other infinite objects of the world exist. From whichever side the barrier is removed, the energy flows in that direction and helps the formation of a corresponding object. Provided the suitable barriers could be removed, anything could be changed into any other thing. And it is believed that the Yogins can acquire the powers by which they can remove any barriers, and thus make anything out of any other thing. But generally in the normal course of events the line of evolution follows "a definite law which cannot be overstepped" (*pariṇāmakramaniyama*) or in other words there are some natural barriers which cannot be removed, and thus the evolutionary course has to take a path to the exclusion of those lines where the barriers could not be removed. Thus saffron grows in countries like Kashmere and not in Bengal, this is limitation of countries (*deśāpabandha*); certain kinds of paddy grow in the rainy season only, this is limitation of season or time (*kālāpabandha*); deer cannot beget men, this is limitation by form (*ākārāpabandha*); curd can come out of milk, this is the limitation of causes (*nimittāpabandha*). The evolutionary course can thus follow only that path which is not barricaded by any of these limitations or natural obstructions[1].

Change is taking place everywhere, from the smallest and least to the highest. Atoms and reals are continually vibrating and changing places in any and every object. At each moment the whole universe is undergoing change, and the collocation of atoms at any moment is different from what it was at the previous moment. When these changes are perceivable, they are perceived as *dharmapariṇāma* or changes of *dharma* or quality; but perceived or unperceived the changes are continually going on. This change of appearance may be viewed from another aspect by virtue of which we may call it present or past, and old or new, and these are respectively called the *lakṣaṇapariṇāma* and *avasthāpariṇāma*. At every moment every object of the world is undergoing evolution or change, change as past, present and future, as new, old or unborn. When any change is in a potential state we call it future, when manifested present, when it becomes sub-latent again it is said to be past. Thus it is that the potential, manifest, and sub-latent changes of a thing are called future, present and past[2].

[1] *Vyāsabhāṣya*, *Tattvavaiśāradī* and *Yogavārttika*, III. 14.

[2] It is well to note in this connection that Sāṃkhya-yoga does not admit the existence of time as an independent entity like the Nyāya-Vaiśesika Time represents the order of moments in which the mind grasps the phenomenal changes. It is hence a construction of the mind (*buddhi-nirmāṇa*). The time required by an atom to move

Causation as Satkāryavāda (the theory that the effect potentially exists before it is generated by the movement of the cause).

The above consideration brings us to an important aspect of the Sāṃkhya view of causation as *satkāryavāda*. Sāṃkhya holds that there can be no production of a thing previously non-existent; causation means the appearance or manifestation of a quality due to certain changes of collocations in the causes which were already held in them in a potential form. Production of effect only means an internal change of the arrangement of atoms in the cause, and this exists in it in a potential form, and just a little loosening of the barrier which was standing in the way of the happening of such a change of arrangement will produce the desired new collocation—the effect. This doctrine is called *satkāryavāda*, i.e. that the kārya or effect is *sat* or existent even before the causal operation to produce the effect was launched. The oil exists in the sesamum, the statue in the stone, the curd in the milk. The causal operation (*kārakavyāpāra*) only renders that manifest (*āvirbhūta*) which was formerly in an unmanifested condition (*tirohita*)[1].

The Buddhists also believed in change, as much as Sāṃkhya did, but with them there was no background to the change; every change was thus absolutely a new one, and when it was past, the next moment the change was lost absolutely. There were only the passing dharmas or manifestations of forms and qualities, but there was no permanent underlying dharma or substance. Sāṃkhya also holds in the continual change of dharmas, but it also holds that these dharmas represent only the conditions of the permanent reals. The conditions and collocations of the reals change constantly, but the reals themselves are unchangeable. The effect according to the Buddhists was non-existent, it came into being for a moment and was lost. On account of this theory of causation and also on account of their doctrine of śūnya, they were called *vaināśikas* (nihilists) by the Vedāntins. This doctrine is therefore contrasted to Sāṃkhya doctrine as *asatkāryavāda*.

its own measure of space is called a moment (*kṣaṇa*) or one unit of time. Vijñāna Bhikṣu regards one unit movement of the guṇas or reals as a moment. When by true wisdom the guṇas are perceived as they are both the illusory notions of time and space vanish. *Vyāsabhāṣya*, *Tattvavaiśāradī*, and *Yogavārttika*, III. 52 and III. 13.

[1] *Tattvakaumudī*, 9.

The Jain view holds that both these views are relatively true and that from one point of view satkāryavāda is true and from another asatkāryavāda. The Sāṃkhya view that the cause is continually transforming itself into its effects is technically called *pariṇāma-vāda* as against the Vedānta view called the *vivarttavāda*: that cause remains ever the same, and what we call effects are but illusory impositions of mere unreal appearance of name and form —mere Māyā[1].

Sāṃkhya Atheism and Yoga Theism.

Granted that the interchange of the positions of the infinite number of reals produce all the world and its transformations; whence comes this fixed order of the universe, the fixed order of cause and effect, the fixed order of the so-called barriers which prevent the transformation of any cause into any effect or the first disturbance of the equilibrium of the prakṛti? Sāṃkhya denies the existence of Īśvara (God) or any other exterior influence, and holds that there is an inherent tendency in these reals which guides all their movements. This tendency or teleology demands that the movements of the reals should be in such a manner that they may render some service to the souls either in the direction of enjoyment or salvation. It is by the natural course of such a tendency that prakṛti is disturbed, and the guṇas develop on two lines—on the mental plane, *citta* or mind comprising the sense faculties, and on the objective plane as material objects; and it is in fulfilment of the demands of this tendency that on the one hand take place subjective experiences as the changes of the buddhi and on the other the infinite modes of the changes of objective things. It is this tendency to be of service to the puruṣas (*puruṣārthatā*) that guides all the movements of the reals, restrains all disorder, renders the world a fit object of experience, and finally rouses them to turn back from the world and seek to attain liberation from the association of prakṛti and its gratuitous service, which causes us all this trouble of saṃsāra.

Yoga here asks, how the blind tendency of the non-intelligent

[1] Both the Vedānta and the Sāṃkhya theories of causation are sometimes loosely called *satkāryyavāda*. But correctly speaking as some discerning commentators have pointed out, the Vedānta theory of causation should be called satkāraṇavāda for according to it the *kāraṇa* (cause) alone exists (*sat*) and all *kāryyas* (effects) are illusory appearances of the kāraṇa; but according to Sāṃkhya the kāryya exists in a potential state in the kāraṇa and is hence always existing and real.

prakṛti can bring forth this order and harmony of the universe, how can it determine what course of evolution will be of the best service to the puruṣas, how can it remove its own barriers and lend itself to the evolutionary process from the state of prakṛti equilibrium? How too can this blind tendency so regulate the evolutionary order that all men must suffer pains according to their bad karmas, and happiness according to their good ones? There must be some intelligent Being who should help the course of evolution in such a way that this system of order and harmony may be attained. This Being is Īśvara. Īśvara is a puruṣa who had never been subject to ignorance, afflictions, or passions. His body is of pure sattva quality which can never be touched by ignorance. He is all knowledge and all powerful. He has a permanent wish that those barriers in the course of the evolution of the reals by which the evolution of the guṇas may best serve the double interest of the puruṣa's experience (*bhoga*) and liberation (*apavarga*) should be removed. It is according to this permanent will of Īśvara that the proper barriers are removed and the guṇas follow naturally an intelligent course of evolution for the service of the best interests of the puruṣas. Īśvara has not created the prakṛti; he only disturbs the equilibrium of the prakṛti in its quiescent state, and later on helps it to follow an intelligent order by which the fruits of karma are properly distributed and the order of the world is brought about. This acknowledgement of Īśvara in Yoga and its denial by Sāṃkhya marks the main theoretic difference between the two according to which the Yoga and Sāṃkhya are distinguished as Seśvara Sāṃkhya (Sāṃkhya with Īśvara) and Nirīśvara Sāṃkhya (Atheistic Sāṃkhya)[1].

Buddhi and Puruṣa.

The question again arises that though puruṣa is pure intelligence, the guṇas are non-intelligent subtle substances, how can the latter come into touch with the former? Moreover, the puruṣa is pure inactive intelligence without any touch of impurity and what service or need can such a puruṣa have of the guṇas? This difficulty is anticipated by Sāṃkhya, which has already made room for its answer by assuming that one class of the guṇas called sattva is such that it resembles the purity and the intelligence of the puruṣa to a very high degree, so much so

[1] *Tattvavaiśāradī*, IV. 3; *Yogavārttika*, I. 24; and *Pravacanabhāṣya*, V. 1–12.

that it can reflect the intelligence of the puruṣa, and thus render its non-intelligent transformations to appear as if they were intelligent. Thus all our thoughts and other emotional or volitional operations are really the non-intelligent transformations of the buddhi or citta having a large sattva preponderance; but by virtue of the reflection of the puruṣa in the buddhi, these appear as if they are intelligent. The self (puruṣa) according to Sāṃkhya-Yoga is not directly demonstrated by self-consciousness. Its existence is a matter of inference on teleological grounds and grounds of moral responsibility. The self cannot be directly noticed as being separate from the buddhi modifications. Through beginningless ignorance there is a confusion and the changing states of buddhi are regarded as conscious. These buddhi changes are further so associated with the reflection of the puruṣa in the buddhi that they are interpreted as the experiences of the puruṣa. This association of the buddhi with the reflection of the puruṣa in the buddhi has such a special fitness (*yogyatā*) that it is interpreted as the experience of the puruṣa. This explanation of Vācaspati of the situation is objected to by Vijñāna Bhikṣu. Vijñāna Bhikṣu says that the association of the buddhi with the image of the puruṣa cannot give us the notion of a real person who undergoes the experiences. It is to be supposed therefore that when the buddhi is intelligized by the reflection of the puruṣa, it is then superimposed upon the puruṣa, and we have the notion of an abiding person who experiences[1]. Whatever may be the explanation, it seems that the union of the buddhi with the puruṣa is somewhat mystical. As a result of this reflection of *cit* on buddhi and the superimposition of the buddhi the puruṣa cannot realize that the transformations of the buddhi are not its own. Buddhi resembles puruṣa in transparency, and the puruṣa fails to differentiate itself from the modifications of the buddhi, and as a result of this non-distinction the puruṣa becomes bound down to the buddhi, always failing to recognize the truth that the buddhi and its transformations are wholly alien to it. This non-distinction of puruṣa from buddhi which is itself a mode of buddhi is what is meant by *avidyā* (non-knowledge) in Sāṃkhya, and is the root of all experience and all misery[2].

[1] *Tattvavaiśāradī* and *Yogavārttika*, I. 4.

[2] This indicates the nature of the analysis of illusion with Sāṃkhya. It is the non-apprehension of the distinction of two things (e.g. the snake and the rope) that

Yoga holds a slightly different view and supposes that the puruṣa not only fails to distinguish the difference between itself and the buddhi but positively takes the transformations of buddhi as its own. It is no non-perception of the difference but positively false knowledge, that we take the puruṣa to be that which it is not (*anyathākhyāti*). It takes the changing, impure, sorrowful, and objective prakṛti or buddhi to be the changeless, pure, happiness-begetting subject. It wrongly thinks buddhi to be the self and regards it as pure, permanent and capable of giving us happiness. This is the avidyā of Yoga. A buddhi associated with a puruṣa is dominated by such an avidyā, and when birth after birth the same buddhi is associated with the same puruṣa, it cannot easily get rid of this avidyā. If in the meantime pralaya takes place, the buddhi is submerged in the prakṛti, and the avidyā also sleeps with it. When at the beginning of the next creation the individual buddhis associated with the puruṣas emerge, the old avidyās also become manifest by virtue of it and the buddhis associate themselves with the puruṣas to which they were attached before the pralaya. Thus proceeds the course of saṃsāra. When the avidyā of a person is rooted out by the rise of true knowledge, the buddhi fails to attach itself to the purūṣa and is forever dissociated from it, and this is the state of mukti.

The Cognitive Process and some characteristics of Citta.

It has been said that buddhi and the internal objects have evolved in order to giving scope to the experience of the puruṣa. What is the process of this experience? Sāṃkhya (as explained by Vācaspati) holds that through the senses the buddhi comes into touch with external objects. At the first moment of this touch there is an indeterminate consciousness in which the particulars of the thing cannot be noticed. This is called *nirvikalpa pratyakṣa* (indeterminate perception). At the next moment by the function of the *saṃkalpa* (synthesis) and *vikalpa* (abstraction or imagination) of manas (mind-organ) the thing is perceived in all its determinate character; the manas differentiates, integrates, and associates the sense-data received through the senses, and

is the cause of illusion; it is therefore called the *akhyāti* (non-apprehension) theory of illusion which must be distinguished from the *anyathākhyāti* (misapprehension) theory of illusion of Yoga which consists in positively misapprehending one (e.g. the rope) for the other (e.g. snake). *Yogavārttika*, I. 8.

thus generates the determinate perception, which when intelligized by the puruṣa and associated with it becomes interpreted as the experience of the person. The action of the senses, ahaṃkāra, and buddhi, may take place sometimes successively and at other times as in cases of sudden fear simultaneously. Vijñāna Bhikṣu differs from this view of Vācaspati, and denies the synthetic activity of the mind-organ (manas), and says that the buddhi directly comes into touch with the objects through the senses. At the first moment of touch the perception is indeterminate, but at the second moment it becomes clear and determinate[1]. It is evident that on this view the importance of manas is reduced to a minimum and it is regarded as being only the faculty of desire, doubt and imagination.

Buddhi, including ahaṃkāra and the senses, often called *citta* in Yoga, is always incessantly suffering changes like the flame of a lamp; it is made up of a large preponderance of the pure sattva substances, and is constantly moulding itself from one content to another. These images by the dual reflection of buddhi and puruṣa are constantly becoming conscious, and are being interpreted as the experiences of a person. The existence of the puruṣa is to be postulated for explaining the illumination of consciousness and for explaining experience and moral endeavour. The buddhi is spread all over the body, as it were, for it is by its functions that the life of the body is kept up; for the Sāṃkhya does not admit any separate prāṇa vāyu (vital breath) to keep the body living. What are called *vāyus* (bio-motor force) in Vedānta are but the different modes of operation of this category of buddhi, which acts all through the body and by its diverse movements performs the life-functions and sense-functions of the body.

[1] As the contact of the buddhi with the external objects takes place through the senses, the sense-data of colours, etc., are modified by the senses if they are defective. The spatial qualities of things are however perceived by the senses directly, but the time-order is a scheme of the citta or the buddhi. Generally speaking Yoga holds that the external objects are faithfully copied by the buddhi in which they are reflected, like trees in a lake:

"*tasmiṃśca darpaṇe sphāre samastā vastudṛṣṭayaḥ*
imāstāḥ pratibimbanti sarasīva taṭadrumāḥ." *Yogavārttika*, I. 4.

The buddhi assumes the form of the object which is reflected on it by the senses, or rather the mind flows out through the senses to the external objects and assumes their forms: "*indriyāṇyeva praṇālikā cittasañcaraṇamārgaḥ taiḥ saṃyujya tadgolakadvārā bāhyavastuṣūparaktasya cittasyendriyasāhityenaivārthākāraḥ pariṇāmo bhavati.*" *Yogavārttika*, I. vi. 7. Contrast *Tattvakaumudī*, 27 and 30.

Apart from the perceptions and the life-functions, buddhi, or rather citta as Yoga describes it, contains within it the root impressions (*saṃskāras*) and the tastes and instincts or tendencies of all past lives (*vāsanā*)[1]. These saṃskāras are revived under suitable associations. Every man had had infinite numbers of births in their past lives as man and as some animal. In all these lives the same citta was always following him. The citta has thus collected within itself the instincts and tendencies of all those different animal lives. It is knotted with these vāsanās like a net. If a man passes into a dog life by rebirth, the vāsanās of a dog life, which the man must have had in some of his previous infinite number of births, are revived, and the man's tendencies become like those of a dog. He forgets the experiences of his previous life and becomes attached to enjoyment in the manner of a dog. It is by the revival of the vāsanā suitable to each particular birth that there cannot be any collision such as might have occurred if the instincts and tendencies of a previous dog-life were active when any one was born as man.

The saṃskāras represent the root impressions by which any habit of life that man has lived through, or any pleasure in which he took delight for some time, or any passions which were

[1] The word saṃskāra is used by Pāṇini who probably preceded Buddha in three different senses: (1) improving a thing as distinguished from generating a new quality (*Sata utkarṣādhānaṃ saṃskāraḥ*, Kāśikā on Paṇini, VI. ii. 16), (2) conglomeration or aggregation, and (3) adornment (Pāṇini, VI. i. 137, 138). In the Piṭakas the word saṅkhāra is used in various senses such as constructing, preparing, perfecting, embellishing, aggregation, matter, karma, the skandhas (collected by Childers). In fact saṅkhāra stands for almost anything of which impermanence could be predicated. But in spite of so many diversities of meaning I venture to suggest that the meaning of aggregation (*samavāya* of Pāṇini) is prominent. The word *saṃskaroti* is used in Kauṣītaki, II. 6, Chāndogya, IV. xvi. 2, 3, 4, viii. 8, 5, and Bṛhadāraṇyaka, VI. iii. 1, in the sense of improving. I have not yet come across any literary use of the second meaning in Sanskrit. The meaning of saṃskāra in Hindu philosophy is altogether different. It means the impressions (which exist sub-consciously in the mind) of the objects experienced. All our experiences whether cognitive, emotional or conative exist in sub-conscious states and may under suitable conditions be reproduced as memory (smṛti). The word vāsanā (*Yoga sūtra*, IV. 24) seems to be a later word. The earlier Upaniṣads do not mention it and so far as I know it is not mentioned in the Pāḷi piṭakas. *Abhidhānappadīpikā* of Moggallāna mentions it, and it occurs in the Muktika Upaniṣad. It comes from the root "*vas*" to stay. It is often loosely used in the sense of saṃskāra, and in *Vyāsabhāṣya* they are identified in IV. 9. But vāsanā generally refers to the tendencies of past lives most of which lie dormant in the mind. Only those appear which can find scope in this life. But saṃskāras are the sub-conscious states which are being constantly generated by experience. Vāsanās are innate saṃskāras not acquired in this life. See *Vyāsabhāṣya*, *Tattvāvaiśāradī* and *Yogavārttika*, II. 13.

engrossing to him, tend to be revived, for though these might not now be experienced, yet the fact that they were experienced before has so moulded and given shape to the citta that the citta will try to reproduce them by its own nature even without any such effort on our part. To safeguard against the revival of any undesirable idea or tendency it is therefore necessary that its roots as already left in the citta in the form of saṃskāras should be eradicated completely by the formation of the habit of a contrary tendency, which if made sufficiently strong will by its own saṃskāra naturally stop the revival of the previous undesirable saṃskāras.

Apart from these the citta possesses volitional activity (*ceṣṭā*) by which the conative senses are brought into relation to their objects. There is also the reserved potent power (*śakti*) of citta, by which it can restrain itself and change its courses or continue to persist in any one direction. These characteristics are involved in the very essence of citta, and form the groundwork of the Yoga method of practice, which consists in steadying a particular state of mind to the exclusion of others.

Merit or demerit (*puṇya, pāpa*) also is imbedded in the citta as its tendencies, regulating the mode of its movements, and giving pleasures and pains in accordance with it.

Sorrow and its Dissolution[1].

Sāṃkhya and the Yoga, like the Buddhists, hold that all experience is sorrowful. Tamas, we know, represents the pain substance. As tamas must be present in some degree in all combinations, all intellectual operations are fraught with some degree of painful feeling. Moreover even in states of temporary pleasure, we had sorrow at the previous moment when we had solicited it, and we have sorrow even when we enjoy it, for we have the fear that we may lose it. The sum total of sorrows is thus much greater than the pleasures, and the pleasures only strengthen the keenness of the sorrow. The wiser the man the greater is his capacity of realizing that the world and our experiences are all full of sorrow. For unless a man is convinced of this great truth that all is sorrow, and that temporary pleasures, whether generated by ordinary worldly experience or by enjoying heavenly experiences through the performance of Vedic sacrifices, are quite unable to

[1] *Tattvavaiśāradī* and *Yogavārttika*, II. 15, and *Tattvakaumudī*, I.

eradicate the roots of sorrow, he will not be anxious for mukti or the final uprooting of pains. A man must feel that all pleasures lead to sorrow, and that the ordinary ways of removing sorrows by seeking enjoyment cannot remove them ultimately; he must turn his back on the pleasures of the world and on the pleasures of paradise. The performances of sacrifices according to the Vedic rites may indeed give happiness, but as these involve the sacrifice of animals they must involve some sins and hence also some pains. Thus the performance of these cannot be regarded as desirable. It is when a man ceases from seeking pleasures that he thinks how best he can eradicate the roots of sorrow. Philosophy shows how extensive is sorrow, why sorrow comes, what is the way to uproot it, and what is the state when it is uprooted. The man who has resolved to uproot sorrow turns to philosophy to find out the means of doing it.

The way of eradicating the root of sorrow is thus the practical enquiry of the Sāṃkhya philosophy[1]. All experiences are sorrow. Therefore some means must be discovered by which all experiences may be shut out for ever. Death cannot bring it, for after death we shall have rebirth. So long as citta (mind) and puruṣa are associated with each other, the sufferings will continue. Citta must be dissociated from puruṣa. Citta or buddhi, Sāṃkhya says, is associated with puruṣa because of the non-distinction of itself from buddhi[2]. It is necessary therefore that in buddhi we should be able to generate the true conception of the nature of puruṣa; when this true conception of puruṣa arises in the buddhi it feels itself to be different, and distinct, from and quite unrelated to puruṣa, and thus ignorance is destroyed. As a result of that, buddhi turns its back on puruṣa and can no longer bind it to its experiences, which are all irrevocably connected with sorrow, and thus the puruṣa remains in its true form. This according to Sāṃkhya philosophy is alone adequate to bring about the liberation of the puruṣa. Prakṛti which was leading us through cycles of experiences from birth to birth, fulfils its final purpose when this true knowledge arises differentiating

[1] Yoga puts it in a slightly modified form. Its object is the cessation of the rebirth-process which is so much associated with sorrow (*duḥkhabahulaḥ saṃsāraḥ heyaḥ*).

[2] The word *citta* is a Yoga term. It is so called because it is the repository of all sub-conscious states. Sāṃkhya generally uses the word buddhi. Both the words mean the same substance, the mind, but they emphasize its two different functions. Buddhi means intellection.

puruṣa from prakṛti. This final purpose being attained the prakṛti can never again bind the puruṣa with reference to whom this right knowledge was generated; for other puruṣas however the bondage remains as before, and they continue their experiences from one birth to another in an endless cycle.

Yoga, however, thinks that mere philosophy is not sufficient. In order to bring about liberation it is not enough that a true knowledge differentiating puruṣa and buddhi should arise, but it is necessary that all the old habits of experience of buddhi, all its saṃskāras should be once for all destroyed never to be revived again. At this stage the buddhi is transformed into its purest state, reflecting steadily the true nature of the puruṣa. This is the *kevala* (oneness) state of existence after which (all saṃskāras, all avidyā being altogether uprooted) the citta is impotent any longer to hold on to the puruṣa, and like a stone hurled from a mountain top, gravitates back into the prakṛti[1]. To destroy the old saṃskāras, knowledge alone not being sufficient, a graduated course of practice is necessary. This graduated practice should be so arranged that by generating the practice of living higher and better modes of life, and steadying the mind on its subtler states, the habits of ordinary life may be removed. As the yogin advances he has to give up what he had adopted as good and try for that which is still better. Continuing thus he reaches the state when the buddhi is in its ultimate perfection and purity. At this stage the buddhi assumes the form of the puruṣa, and final liberation takes place.

Karmas in Yoga are divided into four classes: (1) *śukla* or white (*puṇya*, those that produce happiness), (2) *kṛṣṇa* or black (*pāpa*, those that produce sorrow), (3) *śukla-kṛṣṇa* (*puṇya-pāpa*, most of our ordinary actions are partly virtuous and partly vicious as they involve, if not anything else, at least the death of many insects), (4) *aśuklākṛṣṇa* (those inner acts of self-abnegation, and meditation which are devoid of any fruits as pleasures or pains). All external actions involve some sins, for it is difficult to work in the world and avoid taking the lives of insects[2]. All karmas

[1] Both Sāṃkhya and Yoga speak of this emancipated state as *Kaivalya* (alone-ness), the former because all sorrows have been absolutely uprooted, never to grow up again and the latter because at this state puruṣa remains for ever alone without any association with buddhi, see *Sāṃkhya kārikā*, 68 and *Yoga sūtras*, IV. 34.

[2] *Vyāsabhāṣya* and *Tattvavaiśāradī*, IV. 7.

proceed from the five-fold afflictions (*kleśas*), namely *avidyā*, *asmitā*, *rāga*, *dveṣa* and *abhiniveśa*.

We have already noticed what was meant by avidyā. It consists generally in ascribing intelligence to buddhi, in thinking it as permanent and leading to happiness. This false knowledge while remaining in this form further manifests itself in the other four forms of asmitā, etc. Asmitā means the thinking of worldly objects and our experiences as really belonging to us—the sense of "mine" or "I" to things that really are the qualities or transformations of the guṇas. Rāga means the consequent attachment to pleasures and things. Dveṣa means aversion or antipathy to unpleasant things. Abhiniveśa is the desire for life or love of life—the will to be. We proceed to work because we think our experiences to be our own, our body to be our own, our family to be our own, our possessions to be our own; because we are attached to these; because we feel great antipathy against any mischief that might befall them, and also because we love our life and always try to preserve it against any mischief. These all proceed, as is easy to see, from their root avidyā, which consists in the false identification of buddhi with puruṣa. These five, avidyā, asmitā, rāga, dveṣa and abhiniveśa, permeate our buddhi, and lead us to perform karma and to suffer. These together with the performed karmas which lie inherent in the buddhi as a particular mode of it transmigrate with the buddhi from birth to birth, and it is hard to get rid of them[1]. The karma in the aspect in which it lies in the buddhi as a mode or modification of it is called *karmāśaya* (the bed of karma for the puruṣa to lie in). We perform a karma actuated by the vicious tendencies (*kleśa*) of the buddhi. The karma when thus performed leaves its stain or modification on the buddhi, and it is so ordained according to the teleology of the prakṛti and the removal of obstacles in the course of its evolution in accordance with it by the permanent will of Īśvara that each vicious action brings sufferance and a virtuous one pleasure.

The karmas performed in the present life will generally accumulate, and when the time for giving their fruits comes, such a life is ordained for the person, such a body is made ready for him according to the evolution of prakṛti as shall make it possible for him to suffer or enjoy the fruits thereof. The karma of the

[1] *Vyāsabhāṣya* and *Tattvavaiśāradī*, II. 3–9.

present life thus determines the particular kind of future birth (as this or that animal or man), the period of life (*āyuṣ*) and the painful or pleasurable experiences (*bhoga*) destined for that life. Exceedingly good actions and extremely bad actions often produce their effects in this life. It may also happen that a man has done certain bad actions, for the realization of the fruits of which he requires a dog-life and good actions for the fruits of which he requires a man-life. In such cases the good action may remain in abeyance and the man may suffer the pains of a dog-life first and then be born again as a man to enjoy the fruits of his good actions. But if we can remove ignorance and the other afflictions, all his previous unfulfilled karmas are for ever lost and cannot again be revived. He has of course to suffer the fruits of those karmas which have already ripened. This is the *jīvanmukti* stage, when the sage has attained true knowledge and is yet suffering mundane life in order to experience the karmas that have already ripened (*tiṣṭhati saṃskāravaśāt cakrabhramivaddhṛtaśarīraḥ*).

Citta.

The word Yoga which was formerly used in Vedic literature in the sense of the restraint of the senses is used by Patañjali in his *Yoga sūtra* in the sense of the partial or full restraint or steadying of the states of citta. Some sort of concentration may be brought about by violent passions, as when fighting against a mortal enemy, or even by an ignorant attachment or instinct. The citta which has the concentration of the former type is called *kṣipta* (wild) and of the latter type *pramūḍha* (ignorant). There is another kind of citta, as with all ordinary people, in which concentration is only possible for a time, the mind remaining steady on one thing for a short time leaves that off and clings to another thing and so on. This is called the *vikṣipta* (unsteady) stage of mind (*cittabhūmi*). As distinguished from these there is an advanced stage of citta in which it can concentrate steadily on an object for a long time. This is the *ekāgra* (one-pointed) stage. There is a still further advanced stage in which the citta processes are absolutely stopped. This happens immediately before mukti, and is called the *nirodha* (cessation) state of citta. The purpose of Yoga is to achieve the conditions of the last two stages of citta.

The cittas have five processes (*vṛtti*), (1) *pramāṇa*[1] (valid

[1] Sāṃkhya holds that both validity and invalidity of any cognition depend upon the cognitive state itself and not on correspondence with external facts or objects (*svataḥ prāmāṇyaṃ svataḥ aprāmāṇyaṃ*). The contribution of Sāṃkhya to the doc-

cognitive states such as are generated by perception, inference and scriptural testimony), (2) *viparyaya* (false knowledge, illusion, etc.), (3) *vikalpa* (abstraction, construction and different kinds of imagination), (4) *nidrā* (sleep, is a vacant state of mind, in which tamas tends to predominate), (5) *smṛti* (memory).

These states of mind (*vṛtti*) comprise our inner experience. When they lead us towards saṃsāra into the course of passions and their satisfactions, they are said to be *kliṣṭa* (afflicted or leading to affliction); when they lead us towards liberation, they are called *akliṣṭa* (unafflicted). To whichever side we go, towards saṃsāra or towards mukti, we have to make use of our states of mind; the states which are bad often alternate with good states, and whichever state should tend towards our final good (liberation) must be regarded as good.

This draws attention to that important characteristic of citta, that it sometimes tends towards good (i.e. liberation) and sometimes towards bad (saṃsāra). It is like a river, as the *Vyāsabhāṣya* says, which flows both ways, towards sin and towards the good. The teleology of prakṛti requires that it should produce in man the saṃsāra as well as the liberation tendency.

Thus in accordance with it in the midst of many bad thoughts and bad habits there come good moral will and good thoughts, and in the midst of good thoughts and habits come also bad thoughts and vicious tendencies. The will to be good is therefore never lost in man, as it is an innate tendency in him which is as strong as his desire to enjoy pleasures. This point is rather remarkable, for it gives us the key of Yoga ethics and shows that our desire of liberation is not actuated by any hedonistic attraction for happiness or even removal of pain, but by an innate tendency of the mind to follow the path of liberation[1]. Removal of pains

trine of inference is not definitely known. What little Vācaspati says on the subject has been borrowed from Vātsyāyana such as the *pūrvavat*, *śeṣavat* and *sāmānyatodṛṣṭa* types of inference, and these may better be consulted in our chapter on Nyāya or in the *Tātparyaṭīkā* of Vācaspati. Sāṃkhya inference was probably from particular to particular on the ground of seven kinds of relations according to which they had seven kinds of inference "*mātrānimittasaṃyogivirodhisahacāribhiḥ. Svasvāmibadhyaghātādyaiḥ sāṃkhyānāṃ saptadhānumā*" (*Tātparyaṭīkā*, p. 109). Sāṃkhya definition of inference as given by Udyotakara (I. I. V) is "*sambandhādekasmāt pratyakṣāccheṣasiddhiranumānam.*"

[1] Sāṃkhya however makes the absolute and complete destruction of three kinds of sorrows, *ādhyātmika* (generated internally by the illness of the body or the unsatisfied passions of the mind), *ādhibhautika* (generated externally by the injuries inflicted by other men, beasts, etc.) and *ādhidaivika* (generated by the injuries inflicted by demons and ghosts) the object of all our endeavours (*puruṣārtha*).

is of course the concomitant effect of following such a course, but still the motive to follow this path is a natural and irresistible tendency of the mind. Man has power (*śakti*) stored up in his citta, and he has to use it in such a way that this tendency may gradually grow stronger and stronger and ultimately uproot the other. He must succeed in this, since prakṛti wants liberation for her final realization[1].

Yoga Purificatory Practices (Parikarma).

The purpose of Yoga meditation is to steady the mind on the gradually advancing stages of thoughts towards liberation, so that vicious tendencies may gradually be more and more weakened and at last disappear altogether. But before the mind can be fit for this lofty meditation, it is necessary that it should be purged of ordinary impurities. Thus the intending yogin should practise absolute non-injury to all living beings (*ahiṃsā*), absolute and strict truthfulness (*satya*), non-stealing (*asteya*), absolute sexual restraint (*brahmacarya*) and the acceptance of nothing but that which is absolutely necessary (*aparigraha*). These are collectively called *yama*. Again side by side with these abstinences one must also practise external cleanliness by ablutions and inner cleanliness of the mind, contentment of mind, the habit of bearing all privations of heat and cold, or keeping the body unmoved and remaining silent in speech (*tapas*), the study of philosophy (*svādhyāya*) and meditation on Īśvara (*Īśvara-praṇidhāna*). These are collectively called *niyamas*. To these are also to be added certain other moral disciplines such as *pratipakṣa-bhāvanā*, *maitrī*, *karuṇā*, *muditā* and *upekṣā*. Pratipakṣa-bhāvanā means that whenever a bad thought (e.g. selfish motive) may come one should practise the opposite good thought (self-sacrifice); so that the bad thoughts may not find any scope. Most of our vices are originated by our unfriendly relations with our fellow-beings. To remove these the practice of mere abstinence may not be sufficient, and therefore one should habituate the mind to keep itself in positive good relations with our fellow-beings. The practice of maitrī means to think of all beings as friends. If we continually habituate ourselves to think this, we can never be displeased with them. So too one should practise karuṇā or kindly feeling for sufferers, muditā

[1] See my "*Yoga Psychology*," *Quest*, October, 1921.

or a feeling of happiness for the good of all beings, and upekṣā or a feeling of equanimity and indifference for the vices of others. The last one indicates that the yogin should not take any note of the vices of vicious men.

When the mind becomes disinclined to all worldly pleasures (*vairāgya*) and to all such as are promised in heaven by the performances of Vedic sacrifices, and the mind purged of its dross and made fit for the practice of Yoga meditation, the yogin may attain liberation by a constant practice (*abhyāsa*) attended with faith, confidence (*śraddhā*), strength of purpose and execution (*vīrya*) and wisdom (*prajñā*) attained at each advance.

The Yoga Meditation.

When the mind has become pure the chances of its being ruffled by external disturbances are greatly reduced. At such a stage the yogin takes a firm posture (*āsana*) and fixes his mind on any object he chooses. It is, however, preferable that he should fix it on Īśvara, for in that case Īśvara being pleased removes many of the obstacles in his path, and it becomes easier for him to attain success. But of course he makes his own choice, and can choose anything he likes for the unifying concentration (*samādhi*) of his mind. There are four states of this unifying concentration namely *vitarka, vicāra, ānanda* and *asmitā*. Of these vitarka and vicāra have each two varieties, *savitarka, nirvitarka, savicāra, nirvicāra*[1]. When the mind concentrates on objects, remembering their names and qualities, it is called the savitarka stage; when on the five tanmātras with a remembrance of their qualities it is called savicāra, and when it is one with the tanmātras without any notion of their qualities it is called nirvicāra. Higher than these are the ānanda and the asmitā states. In the ānanda state the mind concentrates on the buddhi with its functions of the senses causing pleasure. In the asmitā stage buddhi concentrates on pure substance as divested of all modifications. In all these stages there are objects on which the mind consciously concentrates, these are therefore called the *samprajñāta* (with knowledge of objects) types of samādhi. Next to this comes the last stage of samādhi called the *asamprajñāta* or nirodha samādhi, in which the mind is without any object. By remaining

[1] Vācaspati, however, thinks that ānanda and asmitā have also two other varieties, which is denied by Bhikṣu.

long in this stage the old potencies (saṃskāras) or impressions due to the continued experience of worldly events tending towards the objective world or towards any process of experiencing inner thinking are destroyed by the production of a strong habit of the nirodha state. At this stage dawns the true knowledge, when the buddhi becomes as pure as the puruṣa, and after that the citta not being able to bind the puruṣa any longer returns back to prakṛti.

In order to practise this concentration one has to see that there may be no disturbance, and the yogin should select a quiet place on a hill or in a forest. One of the main obstacles is, however, to be found in our constant respiratory action. This has to be stopped by the practice of *prāṇāyāma*. Prāṇāyāma consists in taking in breath, keeping it for a while and then giving it up. With practice one may retain breath steadily for hours, days, months and even years. When there is no need of taking in breath or giving it out, and it can be retained steady for a long time, one of the main obstacles is removed.

The process of practising concentration is begun by sitting in a steady posture, holding the breath by prāṇāyāma, excluding all other thoughts, and fixing the mind on any object (*dhāraṇā*). At first it is difficult to fix steadily on any object, and the same thought has to be repeated constantly in the mind, this is called *dhyāna*. After sufficient practice in dhyāna the mind attains the power of making itself steady; at this stage it becomes one with its object and there is no change or repetition. There is no consciousness of subject, object or thinking, but the mind becomes steady and one with the object of thought. This is called *samādhi*[1]. We have already described the six stages of samādhi. As the yogin acquires strength in one stage of samādhi, he passes on to a still higher stage and so on. As he progresses onwards he attains miraculous powers (*vibhūti*) and his faith and hope in the practice increase. Miraculous powers bring with them many temptations, but the yogin is firm of purpose and even though the position of Indra is offered to him he does not relax. His wisdom (*prajñā*) also increases at each step. Prajñā knowledge is as clear as perception, but while perception is limited to

[1] It should be noted that the word *samādhi* cannot properly be translated either by "concentration" or by "meditation." It means that peculiar kind of concentration in the Yoga sense by which the mind becomes one with its object and there is no movement of the mind into its passing states.

certain gross things and certain gross qualities[1] prajñā has no such limitations, penetrating into the subtlest things, the tanmātras, the guṇas, and perceiving clearly and vividly all their subtle conditions and qualities[2]. As the potencies (*saṃskāra*) of the prajñā wisdom grow in strength the potencies of ordinary knowledge are rooted out, and the yogin continues to remain always in his prajñā wisdom. It is a peculiarity of this prajñā that it leads a man towards liberation and cannot bind him to saṃsāra. The final prajñās which lead to liberation are of seven kinds, namely, (1) I have known the world, the object of suffering and misery, I have nothing more to know of it. (2) The grounds and roots of saṃsāra have been thoroughly uprooted, nothing more of it remains to be uprooted. (3) Removal has become a fact of direct cognition by inhibitive trance. (4) The means of knowledge in the shape of a discrimination of puruṣa from prakṛti has been understood. The other three are not psychological but are rather metaphysical processes associated with the situation. They are as follows: (5) The double purpose of buddhi experience and emancipation (*bhoga* and *apavarga*) has been realized. (6) The strong gravitating tendency of the disintegrated guṇas drives them into prakṛti like heavy stones dropped from high hill tops. (7) The buddhi disintegrated into its constituents the guṇas become merged in the prakṛti and remain there for ever. The puruṣa having passed beyond the bondage of the guṇas shines forth in its pure intelligence. There is no bliss or happiness in this Sāṃkhya-Yoga mukti, for all feeling belongs to prakṛti. It is thus a state of pure intelligence. What the Sāṃkhya tries to achieve through knowledge, Yoga achieves through the perfected discipline of the will and psychological control of the mental states.

[1] The limitations which baffle perception are counted in the *Kārikā* as follows: Extreme remoteness (e.g. a lark high up in the sky), extreme proximity (e.g. collyrium inside the eye), loss of sense-organ (e.g. a blind man), want of attention, extreme smallness of the object (e.g. atoms), obstruction by other intervening objects (e.g. by walls), presence of superior lights (the star cannot be seen in daylight), being mixed up with other things of its own kind (e.g. water thrown into a lake).

[2] Though all things are but the modifications of guṇas yet the real nature of the guṇas is never revealed by the sense-knowledge. What appears to the senses are but illusory characteristics like those of magic (māyā):

> "*Guṇānāṃ paramaṃ rūpam na dṛṣṭipathamṛcchati*
> *Yattu dṛṣṭipatham prāptam tanmāyeva sutucchakam.*"
>
> *Vyāsabhāṣya*, IV. 13.

The real nature of the guṇas is thus revealed only by *prajñā*.

CHAPTER VIII

THE NYĀYA-VAIŚEṢIKA PHILOSOPHY

Criticism of Buddhism and Sāṃkhya from the Nyāya standpoint.

THE Buddhists had upset all common sense convictions of substance and attribute, cause and effect, and permanence of things, on the ground that all collocations are momentary; each group of collocations exhausts itself in giving rise to another group and that to another and so on. But if a collocation representing milk generates the collocation of curd it is said to be due to a joint action of the elements forming the cause-collocation and the *modus operandi* is unintelligible; the elements composing the cause-collocation cannot separately generate the elements composing the effect-collocation, for on such a supposition it becomes hard to maintain the doctrine of momentariness as the individual and separate exercise of influence on the part of the cause-elements and their coordination and manifestation as effect cannot but take more than one moment. The supposition that the whole of the effect-collocation is the result of the joint action of the elements of cause-collocation is against our universal uncontradicted experience that specific elements constituting the cause (e.g. the whiteness of milk) are the cause of other corresponding elements of the effect (e.g. the whiteness of the curd); and we could not say that the hardness, blackness, and other properties of the atoms of iron in a lump state should not be regarded as the cause of similar qualities in the iron ball, for this is against the testimony of experience. Moreover there would be no difference between material (*upādāna*, e.g. clay of the jug), instrumental and concomitant causes (*nimitta* and *sahakāri*, such as the potter, and the wheel, the stick etc. in forming the jug), for the causes jointly produce the effect, and there was no room for distinguishing the material and the instrumental causes, as such.

Again at the very moment in which a cause-collocation is brought into being, it cannot exert its influence to produce its effect-collocation. Thus after coming into being it would take the cause-collocation at least another moment to exercise its influence to produce the effect. How can the thing which is destroyed the moment after it is born produce any effect? The truth is that causal elements remain and when they are properly collocated the effect is produced. Ordinary experience also shows that we perceive things as existing from a past time. The past time is perceived by us as past, the present as present and the future as future and things are perceived as existing from a past time onwards.

The Sāṃkhya assumption that effects are but the actualized states of the potential cause, and that the causal entity holds within it all the future series of effects, and that thus the effect is already existent even before the causal movement for the production of the effect, is also baseless. Sāṃkhya says that the oil was already existent in the sesamum and not in the stone, and that it is thus that oil can be got from sesamum and not from the stone. The action of the instrumental cause with them consists only in actualizing or manifesting what was already existent in a potential form in the cause. This is all nonsense. A lump of clay is called the cause and the jug the effect; of what good is it to say that the jug exists in the clay since with clay we can never carry water? A jug is made out of clay, but clay is not a jug. What is meant by saying that the jug was unmanifested or was in a potential state before, and that it has now become manifest or actual? What does potential state mean? The potential state of the jug is not the same as its actual state; thus the actual state of the jug must be admitted as non-existent before. If it is meant that the jug is made up of the same parts (the atoms) of which the clay is made up, of course we admit it, but this does not mean that the jug was existent in the atoms of the lump of clay. The potency inherent in the clay by virtue of which it can expose itself to the influence of other agents, such as the potter, for being transformed into a jug is not the same as the effect, the jug. Had it been so, then we should rather have said that the jug came out of the jug. The assumption of Sāṃkhya that the substance and attribute have the same reality is also against all experience, for we all perceive that movement and attribute belong to substance and not to attribute. Again Sāṃkhya holds a preposterous doctrine that buddhi is different from intelligence. It is absolutely unmeaning to call buddhi non-intelligent. Again what is the good of all this fictitious fuss that the qualities of buddhi are reflected on puruṣa and then again on buddhi. Evidently in all our experience we find that the soul (*ātman*) knows, feels and wills, and it is difficult to understand why Sāṃkhya does not accept this patent fact and declare that knowledge, feeling, and willing, all belonged to buddhi. Then again in order to explain experience it brought forth a theory of double reflection. Again Sāṃkhya prakṛti is non-intelligent, and where is the guarantee that she (prakṛti) will not bind the wise again and will emancipate him once for all? Why did the puruṣa become bound down? Prakṛti is being utilized for enjoyment by the infinite number of puruṣas, and she is no delicate girl (as Sāṃkhya supposes) who will leave the presence of the puruṣa ashamed as soon as her real nature is discovered. Again pleasure (*sukha*), sorrow (*duḥkha*) and a blinding feeling through ignorance (*moha*) are but the feeling-experiences of the soul, and with what impudence could Sāṃkhya think of these as material substances? Again their cosmology of a mahat, ahaṃkāra, the tanmātras, is all a series of assumptions never testified by experience nor by reason. They are all a series of hopeless and foolish blunders. The phenomena of experience thus call for a new careful reconstruction in the light of reason and experience such as cannot be found in other systems. (See *Nyāyamañjarī*, pp. 452–466 and 490–496.)

Nyāya and Vaiśeṣika sūtras.

It is very probable that the earliest beginnings of Nyāya are to be found in the disputations and debates amongst scholars trying to find out the right meanings of the Vedic texts for use in sacrifices and also in those disputations which took place between the adherents of different schools of thought trying to defeat one another. I suppose that such disputations occurred in the days of the Upaniṣads, and the art of disputation was regarded even then as a subject of study, and it probably passed then by the name of *vākovākya*. Mr Bodas has pointed out that Āpastamba who according to Bühler lived before the third century B.C. used the word Nyāya in the sense of Mīmāṃsā[1]. The word Nyāya derived

[1] *Āpastamba*, trans. by Bühler, Introduction, p. XXVII., and Bodas's article on the *Historical Survey of Indian Logic* in the Bombay Branch of J.R.A.S., vol. XIX.

from the root *nī* is sometimes explained as that by which sentences and words could be interpreted as having one particular meaning and not another, and on the strength of this even Vedic accents of words (which indicate the meaning of compound words by pointing out the particular kind of compound in which the words entered into combination) were called Nyāya[1]. Prof. Jacobi on the strength of Kauṭilya's enumeration of the *vidyā* (sciences) as Ānvīkṣikī (the science of testing the perceptual and scriptural knowledge by further scrutiny), *trayī* (the three Vedas), *vārttā* (the sciences of agriculture, cattle keeping etc.), and *daṇḍanīti* (polity), and the enumeration of the philosophies as Sāṃkhya, Yoga, Lokāyata and Ānvīkṣikī, supposes that the *Nyāya sūtra* was not in existence in Kauṭilya's time 300 B.C.)[2]. Kauṭilya's reference to Nyāya as Ānvīkṣikī only suggests that the word Nyāya was not a familiar name for Ānvīkṣikī in Kauṭilya's time. He seems to misunderstand Vātsyāyana in thinking that Vātsyāyana distinguishes Nyāya from the Ānvīkṣikī in holding that while the latter only means the science of logic the former means logic as well as metaphysics. What appears from Vātsyāyana's statement in *Nyāya sūtra* I. i. I is this that he points out that the science which was known in his time as Nyāya was the same as was referred to as Ānvīkṣikī by Kauṭilya. He distinctly identifies Nyāyavidyā with Ānvīkṣikī, but justifies the separate enumeration of certain logical categories such as *saṃśaya* (doubt) etc., though these were already contained within the first two terms *pramāṇa* (means of cognition) and *prameya* (objects of cognition), by holding that unless these its special and separate branches (*pṛthakprasthāna*) were treated, Nyāyavidyā would simply become metaphysics (*adhyātmavidyā*) like the Upaniṣads. The old meaning of Nyāya as the means of determining the right meaning or the right thing is also agreed upon by Vātsyāyana and is sanctioned by Vācaspati in his *Nyāyavārttikatātparyaṭīkā* I. i. I). He compares the meaning of the word Nyāya (*pramāṇairarthaparīkṣaṇam*—to scrutinize an object by means of logical proof) with the etymological meaning of the word ānvīkṣikī (to scrutinize anything after it has been known by perception and scriptures). Vātsyāyana of course points out that so far as this logical side of Nyāya is concerned it has the widest scope for

[1] Kālidāsa's *Kumārasambhava* "*Udghāto praṇavo yāsām nyāyaistribhirudīraṇam,*" also Mallinātha's gloss on it.

[2] Prof. Jacobi's "*The early history of Indian Philosophy,*" *Indian Antiquary*, 1918.

itself as it includes all beings, all their actions, and all the sciences[1]. He quotes Kauṭilya to show that in this capacity Nyāya is like light illumining all sciences and is the means of all works. In its capacity as dealing with the truths of metaphysics it may show the way to salvation. I do not dispute Prof. Jacobi's main point that the metaphysical portion of the work was a later addition, for this seems to me to be a very probable view. In fact Vātsyāyana himself designates the logical portion as a pṛthakprasthāna (separate branch). But I do not find that any statement of Vātsyāyana or Kauṭilya can justify us in concluding that this addition was made after Kauṭilya. Vātsyāyana has no doubt put more stress on the importance of the logical side of the work, but the reason of that seems to be quite obvious, for the importance of metaphysics or *adhyātmavidyā* was acknowledged by all. But the importance of the mere logical side would not appeal to most people. None of the dharmaśāstras (religious scriptures) or the Vedas would lend any support to it, and Vātsyāyana had to seek the support of Kauṭilya in the matter as the last resource. The fact that Kauṭilya was not satisfied by counting Ānvīkṣikī as one of the four vidyās but also named it as one of the philosophies side by side with Sāṃkhya seems to lead to the presumption that probably even in Kauṭilya's time Nyāya was composed of two branches, one as adhyātmavidyā and another as a science of logic or rather of debate. This combination is on the face of it loose and external, and it is not improbable that the metaphysical portion was added to increase the popularity of the logical part, which by itself might not attract sufficient attention. Mahāmahopādhyāya Haraprasāda Śāstrī in an article in the *Journal of the Bengal Asiatic Society* 1905 says that as Vācaspati made two attempts to collect the *Nyāya sūtras*, one as *Nyāyasūci* and the other as *Nyāyasūtroddhāra*, it seems that even in Vācaspati's time he was not certain as to the authenticity of many of the *Nyāya sūtras*. He further points out that there are unmistakable signs that many of the sūtras were interpolated, and relates the Buddhist tradition from China and Japan that Mirok mingled Nyāya and Yoga. He also

[1] *Yena prayuktaḥ pravarttate tat prayojanam* (that by which one is led to act is called *prayojanam*); *yamartham abhīpsan jihāsan vā karma ārabhate tenānena sarve prāṇinaḥ sarvāṇi karmāṇi sarvāśca vidyāḥ vyāptāḥ tadāśrayāśca nyāyaḥ pravarttate* (all those which one tries to have or to fly from are called prayojana, therefore all beings, all their actions, and all sciences, are included within prayojana, and all these depend on Nyāya). *Vātsyāyana bhāṣya*, I. i. 1.

thinks that the sūtras underwent two additions, one at the hands of some Buddhists and another at the hands of some Hindu who put in Hindu arguments against the Buddhist ones. These suggestions of this learned scholar seem to be very probable, but we have no clue by which we can ascertain the time when such additions were made. The fact that there are unmistakable proofs of the interpolation of many of the sūtras makes the fixing of the date of the original part of the *Nyāya sūtras* still more difficult, for the Buddhist references can hardly be of any help, and Prof. Jacobi's attempt to fix the date of the *Nyāya sūtras* on the basis of references to Śūnyavāda naturally loses its value, except on the supposition that all references to Śūnyavāda must be later than Nāgārjuna, which is not correct, since the *Mahāyāna sūtras* written before Nāgārjuna also held the Śūnyavāda doctrine.

The late Dr S. C. Vidyābhūṣaṇa in *J.R.A.S.* 1918 thinks that the earlier part of Nyāya was written by Gautama about 550 B.C. whereas the *Nyāya sūtras* of Akṣapāda were written about 150 A.D. and says that the use of the word Nyāya in the sense of logic in *Mahābhārata* I. I. 67, I. 70. 42–51, must be regarded as interpolations. He, however, does not give any reasons in support of his assumption. It appears from his treatment of the subject that the fixing of the date of Akṣapāda was made to fit in somehow with his idea that Akṣapāda wrote his *Nyāya sūtras* under the influence of Aristotle—a supposition which does not require serious refutation, at least so far as Dr Vidyābhūṣaṇa has proved it. Thus after all this discussion we have not advanced a step towards the ascertainment of the date of the original part of the Nyāya. Goldstücker says that both Patañjali (140 B.C.) and Kātyāyana (fourth century B.C.) knew the *Nyāya sūtras*[1]. We know that Kauṭilya knew the Nyāya in some form as Ānvīkṣikī in 300 B.C., and on the strength of this we may venture to say that the Nyāya existed in some form as early as the fourth century B.C. But there are other reasons which lead me to think that at least some of the present sūtras were written some time in the second century A.D. Bodas points out that Bādarāyaṇa's sūtras make allusions to the Vaiśeṣika doctrines and not to Nyāya. On this ground he thinks that *Vaiśeṣika sūtras* were written before Bādarāyaṇa's *Brahma-sūtras*, whereas the *Nyāya sūtras* were written later. Candrakānta Tarkālaṃkāra also contends in his

[1] Goldstücker's *Pāṇini*, p. 157.

edition of Vaiśeṣika that the *Vaiśeṣika sūtras* were earlier than the Nyāya. It seems to me to be perfectly certain that the *Vaiśeṣika sūtras* were written before Caraka (80 A.D.); for he not only quotes one of the *Vaiśeṣika sūtras*, but the whole foundation of his medical physics is based on the Vaiśeṣika physics[1]. The *Laṅkāvatāra sūtra* (which as it was quoted by Aśvaghoṣa is earlier than 80 A.D.) also makes allusions to the atomic doctrine. There are other weightier grounds, as we shall see later on, for supposing that the *Vaiśeṣika sūtras* are probably pre-Buddhistic[2].

It is certain that even the logical part of the present *Nyāya sūtras* was preceded by previous speculations on the subject by thinkers of other schools. Thus in commenting on I. i. 32 in which the sūtra states that a syllogism consists of five premisses (*avayava*) Vātsyāyana says that this sūtra was written to refute the views of those who held that there should be ten premisses[3]. The *Vaiśeṣika sūtras* also give us some of the earliest types of inference, which do not show any acquaintance with the technic of the Nyāya doctrine of inference[4].

Does Vaiśeṣika represent an Old School of Mīmāṃsā?

The Vaiśeṣika is so much associated with Nyāya by tradition that it seems at first sight quite unlikely that it could be supposed to represent an old school of Mīmāṃsā, older than that represented in the *Mīmāṃsā sūtras*. But a closer inspection of the *Vaiśeṣika sūtras* seems to confirm such a supposition in a very remarkable way. We have seen in the previous section that Caraka quotes a *Vaiśeṣika sūtra*. An examination of Caraka's *Sūtrasthāna* (I. 35–38) leaves us convinced that the writer of the verses had some compendium of Vaiśeṣika such as that of the *Bhāṣāparicchedа* before him. *Caraka sūtra* or *kārikā* (I. i. 36) says that the guṇas are those which have been enumerated such as heaviness, etc., cognition, and those which begin with the guṇa "*para*" (universality) and end with "*prayatna*" (effort) together with the sense-qualities (*sārthā*). It seems that this is a reference to some well-known enumeration. But this enumeration is not to be found in the *Vaiśeṣika sūtra* (I. i. 6) which leaves out the six guṇas,

[1] *Caraka, Śārīra*, 39.

[2] See the next section.

[3] Vātsyāyana's Bhāṣya on the *Nyāya sūtras*, I. i. 32. This is undoubtedly a reference the Jaina view as found in *Daśavaikālikaniryukti* as noted before.

[4] *Nyāya sūtra* I. i. 5, and *Vaiśeṣika sūtras* IX. ii. 1–2, 4–5, and III. i. 8–17.

heaviness (*gurutva*), liquidity (*dravatva*), oiliness (*sneha*), elasticity (*saṃskāra*), merit (*dharma*) and demerit (*adharma*); in one part of the sūtra the enumeration begins with "para" (universality) and ends in "prayatna," but buddhi (cognition) comes within the enumeration beginning from para and ending in prayatna, whereas in Caraka buddhi does not form part of the list and is separately enumerated. This leads me to suppose that Caraka's sūtra was written at a time when the six guṇas left out in the Vaiśeṣika enumeration had come to be counted as guṇas, and compendiums had been made in which these were enumerated. *Bhāṣāpariccheda* (a later Vaiśeṣika compendium), is a compilation from some very old kārikās which are referred to by Viśvanātha as being collected from "*atisaṃkṣiptacirantanoktibhiḥ*"—(from very ancient aphorisms[1]); Caraka's definition of sāmānya and viśeṣa shows that they had not then been counted as separate categories as in later Nyāya-Vaiśeṣika doctrines; but though slightly different it is quite in keeping with the sort of definition one finds in the *Vaiśeṣika sūtra* that sāmānya (generality) and viśeṣa are relative to each other[2]. Caraka's sūtras were therefore probably written at a time when the Vaiśeṣika doctrines were undergoing changes, and well-known compendiums were beginning to be written on them.

The *Vaiśeṣika sūtras* seem to be ignorant of the Buddhist doctrines. In their discussions on the existence of soul, there is no reference to any view as to non-existence of soul, but the argument turned on the point as to whether the self is to be an object of inference or revealed to us by our notion of "I." There is also no other reference to any other systems except to some Mīmāṃsā doctrines and occasionally to Sāṃkhya. There is no reason to suppose that the Mīmāṃsā doctrines referred to allude to the *Mīmāṃsā sūtras* of Jaimini. The manner in which the nature of inference has been treated shows that the Nyāya phraseology of "*pūrvavat*" and "*śeṣavat*" was not known. *Vaiśeṣika sūtras* in more than one place refer to time as the ultimate cause[3]. We know that the Śvetāśvatara Upaniṣad refers to those who regard time as the cause of all things, but in none of the

[1] Professor Vanamālī Vedāntatīrtha's article in *J. A. S. B.*, 1908.

[2] Caraka (I. I. 33) says that sāmānya is that which produces unity and viśeṣa is that which separates. V. S. II. ii. 7. Sāmānya and viśeṣa depend upon our mode of thinking (as united or as separate).

[3] *Vaiśeṣika sūtra* (II. ii. 9 and V. ii. 26).

systems that we have can we trace any upholding of this ancient view[1]. These considerations as well as the general style of the work and the methods of discussion lead me to think that these sūtras are probably the oldest that we have and in all probability are pre-Buddhistic.

The *Vaiśeṣika sūtra* begins with the statement that its object is to explain virtue, "dharma." This is we know the manifest duty of Mīmāṃsā and we know that unlike any other system Jaimini begins his *Mīmāṃsā sūtras* by defining "dharma." This at first seems irrelevant to the main purpose of Vaiśeṣika, viz., the description of the nature of padārtha[2]. He then defines dharma as that which gives prosperity and ultimate good (*niḥśreyasa*) and says that the Veda must be regarded as valid, since it can dictate this. He ends his book with the remarks that those injunctions (of Vedic deeds) which are performed for ordinary human motives bestow prosperity even though their efficacy is not known to us through our ordinary experience, and in this matter the Veda must be regarded as the authority which dictates those acts[3]. The fact that the Vaiśeṣika begins with a promise to describe dharma and after describing the nature of substances, qualities and actions and also the *adṛṣṭa* (unknown virtue) due to dharma (merit accruing from the performance of Vedic deeds) by which many of our unexplained experiences may be explained, ends his book by saying that those Vedic works which are not seen to produce any direct effect, will produce prosperity through adṛṣṭa, shows that Kaṇāda's method of explaining dharma has been by showing that physical phenomena involving substances, qualities, and actions can only be explained up to a certain extent while a good number cannot be explained at all except on the assumption of adṛṣṭa (unseen virtue) produced by dharma. The

[1] Śvetāśvatara I. i. 2.

[2] I remember a verse quoted in an old commentary of the *Kalāpa Vyākaraṇa*, in which it is said that the description of the six categories by Kaṇāda in his *Vaiśeṣika sūtras*, after having proposed to describe the nature of dharma, is as irrelevant as to proceed towards the sea while intending to go to the mountain Himavat (Himālaya). "*Dharmaṃ vyākhyātukāmasya ṣaṭpadārthopavarṇanaṃ Himavadgantukāmasya sāgaragamanopamam.*"

[3] The sūtra "*Tadvacanād āmnāyasya prāmāṇyam* (I. i. 3 and X. ii. 9) has been explained by *Upaskāra* as meaning "The Veda being the word of Īśvara (God) must be regarded as valid," but since there is no mention of "Īśvara" anywhere in the text this is simply reading the later Nyāya ideas into the Vaiśeṣika. Sūtra X. ii. 8 is only a repetition of VI. ii. I.

description of the categories of substance is not irrelevant, but is the means of proving that our ordinary experience of these cannot explain many facts which are only to be explained on the supposition of adṛṣṭa proceeding out of the performance of Vedic deeds. In V. i. 15 the movement of needles towards magnets, in V. ii. 7 the circulation of water in plant bodies, V. ii. 13 and IV. ii. 7 the upward motion of fire, the side motion of air, the combining movement of atoms (by which all combinations have taken place), and the original movement of the mind are said to be due to adṛṣṭa. In V. ii. 17 the movement of the soul after death, its taking hold of other bodies, the assimilation of food and drink and other kinds of contact (the movement and development of the foetus as enumerated in *Upaskāra*) are said to be due to adṛṣṭa. Salvation (mokṣa) is said to be produced by the annihilation of adṛṣṭa leading to the annihilation of all contacts and non-production of rebirths. Vaiśeṣika marks the distinction between the dṛṣṭa (experienced) and the adṛṣṭa. All the categories that he describes are founded on dṛṣṭa (experience) and those unexplained by known experience are due to adṛṣṭa. These are the acts on which depend all life-process of animals and plants, the continuation of atoms or the construction of the worlds, natural motion of fire and air, death and rebirth (VI. ii. 15) and even the physical phenomena by which our fortunes are affected in some way or other (V. ii. 2), in fact all with which we are vitally interested in philosophy. Kaṇāda's philosophy gives only some facts of experience regarding substances, qualities and actions, leaving all the graver issues of metaphysics to adṛṣṭa. But what leads to adṛṣṭa? In answer to this, Kaṇāda does not speak of good or bad or virtuous or sinful deeds, but of Vedic works, such as holy ablutions (*snāna*), fasting, holy student life (*brahmacarya*), remaining at the house of the teacher (*gurukulavāsa*), retired forest life (*vānaprastha*), sacrifice (*yajña*), gifts (*dāna*), certain kinds of sacrificial sprinkling and rules of performing sacrificial works according to the prescribed time of the stars, the prescribed hymns (mantras) (VI. ii. 2).

He described what is pure and what is impure food, pure food being that which is sacrificially purified (VI. ii. 5) the contrary being impure; and he says that the taking of pure food leads to prosperity through adṛṣṭa. He also described how feelings of attachment to things are also generated by adṛṣṭa. Throughout almost the whole of VI. i Kaṇāda is busy in showing the special conditions of making gifts and receiving them. A reference to our chapter on Mīmāṃsā will show that the later Mīmāṃsā writers agreed with the Nyāya-Vaiśeṣika doctrines in most of their views regarding substance, qualities, etc. Some of the main points in which Mīmāṃsā differs from Nyāya-Vaiśeṣika are (1) self-validity of the Vedas, (2) the eternality of the Vedas, (3) disbelief in any creator or god, (4) eternality of sound (śabda), (5) (according to Kumārila) direct perception of self in the notion of the ego. Of these the first and the second points do not form any subject of discussion in the Vaiśeṣika. But as no Īśvara is mentioned, and as all adṛṣṭa depends upon the authority of the Vedas, we may assume that Vaiśeṣika had no dispute with Mīmāṃsā. The fact that there is no reference to any dissension is probably due to the fact that really none had taken place at the time of the *Vaiśeṣika sūtras*. It is probable that Kaṇāda believed that the Vedas were written by some persons superior to us (II. i. 18, VI. i. 1–2). But the fact that there is no reference to any conflict with Mīmāṃsā suggests that the doctrine that the Vedas were never written by anyone was formulated at a later period, whereas in the days of the *Vaiśeṣika sūtras*, the view was probably what is represented in the *Vaiśeṣika sūtras*. As there is no reference to Īśvara and as adṛṣṭa proceeding out of the performance of actions in accordance with Vedic injunctions is made the cause of all atomic movements, we can very well assume that Vaiśeṣika was as atheistic or non-theistic as the later Mīmāṃsā philosophers. As regards the eternality of sound, which in later days was one of the main points of quarrel between the Nyāya-Vaiśeṣika and the Mīmāṃsā, we find that in II. ii. 25–32, Kaṇāda gives reasons in favour of the non-eternality of sound, but after that from II. ii. 33 till the end of the chapter he closes the argument in favour of the eternality of sound, which is the distinctive Mīmāṃsā view as we know from the later Mīmāṃsā writers[1]. Next comes the question of the proof of the existence of self. The traditional Nyāya view is

[1] The last two concluding sūtras II. ii. 36 and 37 are in my opinion wrongly interpreted by Śaṅkara Miśra in his *Upaskāra* (II. ii. 36 by adding an "*api*" to the sūtra and thereby changing the issue, and II. ii. 37 by misreading the phonetic combination "saṃkhyābhāva" as saṃkhyā and bhāva instead of samkhyā and abhāva, which in my opinion is the right combination here) in favour of the non-eternality of sound as we find in the later Nyāya-Vaiśeṣika view.

that the self is supposed to exist because it must be inferred as the seat of the qualities of pleasure, pain, cognition, etc. Traditionally this is regarded as the Vaiśeṣika view as well. But in Vaiśeṣika III. ii. 4 the existence of soul is first inferred by reason of its activity and the existence of pleasure, pain, etc., in III. ii. 6–7 this inference is challenged by saying that we do not perceive that the activity, etc. belongs to the soul and not to the body and so no certainty can be arrived at by inference, and in III. ii. 8 it is suggested that therefore the existence of soul is to be accepted on the authority of the scriptures (*āgama*). To this the final Vaiśeṣika conclusion is given that we can directly perceive the self in our feeling as "I" (*aham*), and we have therefore not to depend on the scriptures for the proof of the existence of the self, and thus the inference of the existence of the self is only an additional proof of what we already find in perception as "I" (*aham*) (III. ii. 10–18, also IX. i. 11).

These considerations lead me to think that the Vaiśeṣika represented a school of Mīmāṃsā thought which supplemented a metaphysics to strengthen the grounds of the Vedas.

Philosophy in the Vaiśeṣika sūtras.

The *Vaiśeṣika sūtras* begin with the ostensible purpose of explaining virtue (*dharma*) (I. i. 1) and dharma according to it is that by which prosperity (*abhyudaya*) and salvation (*niḥśreyasa*) are attained. Then it goes on to say that the validity of the Vedas depends on the fact that it leads us to prosperity and salvation. Then it turns back to the second sūtra and says that salvation comes as the result of real knowledge, produced by special excellence of dharma, of the characteristic features of the categories of substance (*dravya*), quality (*guṇa*), class concept (*sāmānya*), particularity (*viśeṣa*), and inherence (*samavāya*)[1]. The dravyas are earth, water, fire, air, ether, time, space, soul, and mind. The guṇas are colour, taste, odour, touch, number, measure, separations, contact, disjoining, quality of belonging to high genus or to species[2]. Action (*karma*) means upward move-

[1] *Upaskāra* notes that viśeṣa here refers to the ultimate differences of things and not to species. A special doctrine of this system is this, that each of the indivisible atoms of even the same element has specific features of difference.

[2] Here the well known qualities of heaviness (*gurutva*), liquidity (*dravatva*), oiliness (*sneha*), elasticity (*saṃskāra*), merit (*dharma*), and demerit (*adharma*) have been altogether omitted. These are all counted in later Vaiśeṣika commentaries and com-

ment, downward movement, contraction, expansion and horizontal movement. The three common qualities of dravya, guṇa and karma are that they are existent, non-eternal, substantive, effect, cause, and possess generality and particularity. Dravya produces other dravyas and the guṇas other guṇas. But karma is not necessarily produced by karma. Dravya does not destroy either its cause or its effect, but the guṇas are destroyed both by the cause and by the effect. Karma is destroyed by karma. Dravya possesses karma and guṇa and is regarded as the material (*samavāyi*) cause. Guṇas inhere in dravya, cannot possess further guṇas, and are not by themselves the cause of contact or disjoining. Karma is devoid of guṇa, cannot remain at one time in more than one object, inheres in dravya alone, and is an independent cause of contact or disjoining. Dravya is the material cause (samavāyi) of (derivative) dravyas, guṇa, and karma; guṇa is also the non-material cause (*asamāvāyi*) of dravya, guṇa and karma. Karma is the general cause of contact, disjoining, and inertia in motion (*vega*). Karma is not the cause of dravya. For dravya may be produced even without karma[1]. Dravya is the general effect of dravya. Karma is dissimilar to guṇa in this that it does not produce karma. The numbers two, three, etc., separateness, contact and disjoining are effected by more than one dravya. Each karma not being connected with more than one thing is not produced by more than one thing[2]. A dravya is the result of many contacts (of the atoms). One colour may be the result of many colours. Upward movement is the result of heaviness, effort and contact. Contact and disjoining are also the result of karma. In denying the causality of karma it is meant that karma is not the cause of dravya and karma[3].

In the second chapter of the first book Kaṇāda first says that if there is no cause, there is no effect, but there may be the cause even though there may not be the effect. He next says that genus (*sāmānya*) and species (*viśeṣa*) are relative to the under-

pendiums. It must be noted that "*guṇa*" in Vaiśeṣika means qualities and not subtle reals or substances as in Sāṃkhya-Yoga. Guṇa in Vaiśeṣika would be akin to what Yoga would call *dharma*.

1 It is only when the kārya ceases that dravya is produced. See *Upaskāra* I. i. 22.

2 If karma is related to more than one thing, then with the movement of one we should have felt that two or more things were moving.

3 It must be noted that "karma" in this sense is quite different from the more extensive use of karma as meritorious or vicious action which is the cause of rebirth.

standing; being (*bhāva*) indicates continuity only and is hence only a genus. The universals of substance, quality and action may be both genus and species, but viśeṣa as constituting the ultimate differences (of atoms) exists (independent of any percipient). In connection with this he says that the ultimate genus is being (*sattā*) in virtue of which things appear as existent; all other genera may only relatively be regarded as relative genera or species. Being must be regarded as a separate category, since it is different from dravya, guṇa and karma, and yet exists in them, and has no genus or species. It gives us the notion that something is and must be regarded as a category existing as one identical entity in all dravya, guṇa, and karma, for in its universal nature as being it has no special characteristics in the different objects in which it inheres. The specific universals of thingness (*dravyatva*), qualitiness (*guṇatva*) or actionness (*karmatva*) are also categories which are separate from universal being (*bhāva* or *sattā*) for they also have no separate genus or species and yet may be distinguished from one another, but bhāva or being was the same in all.

In the first chapter of the second book Kaṇāda deals with substances. Earth possesses colour, taste, smell, and touch; water, colour, taste, touch, liquidity, and smoothness (*snigdha*); fire, colour and touch; air, touch; but none of these qualities can be found in ether (*ākāśa*). Liquidity is a special quality of water because butter, lac, wax, lead, iron, silver, gold, become liquids only when they are heated, while water is naturally liquid itself[1]. Though air cannot be seen, yet its existence can be inferred by touch, just as the existence of the genus of cows may be inferred from the characteristics of horns, tails, etc. Since this thing inferred from touch possesses motion and quality, and does not itself inhere in any other substance, it is a substance (dravya) and is eternal[2]. The inference of air is of the type of inference of imperceptible things from certain known characteristics called *sāmānyato dṛṣṭa*. The name of air "*vāyu*" is derived from the scriptures. The existence of others different from us has (*asmadviśiṣṭānāṃ*) to be admitted for accounting for the

[1] It should be noted that mercury is not mentioned. This is important for mercury was known at a time later than Caraka.

[2] Substance is that which possesses quality and action. It should be noted that the word "*adravyatvena*" in II. i. 13 has been interpreted by me as "*adravyavattvena.*"

giving of names to things (*saṃjñākarma*). Because we find that the giving of names is already in usage (and not invented by us)[1]. On account of the fact that movements rest only in one thing, the phenomenon that a thing can enter into any unoccupied space, would not lead us to infer the existence of ākāśa (ether). Ākāśa has to be admitted as the hypothetical substance in which the quality of sound inheres, because, since sound (a quality) is not the characteristic of things which can be touched, there must be some substance of which it is a quality. And this substance is ākāśa. It is a substance and eternal like air. As being is one so ākāśa is one[2].

In the second chapter of the second book Kaṇāda tries to prove that smell is a special characteristic of earth, heat of fire, and coldness of water. Time is defined as that which gives the notion of youth in the young, simultaneity, and quickness. It is one like being. Time is the cause of all non-eternal things, because the notion of time is absent in eternal things. Space supplies the notion that this is so far away from this or so much nearer to this. Like being it is one. One space appears to have diverse inter-space relations in connection with the motion of the sun. As a preliminary to discussing the problem whether sound is eternal or not, he discusses the notion of doubt, which arises when a thing is seen in a general way, but the particular features coming under it are not seen, either when these are only remembered, or when some such attribute is seen which resembles some other attribute seen before, or when a thing is seen in one way but appears in another, or when what is seen is not definitely grasped, whether rightly seen or not. He then discusses the question whether sound is eternal or non-eternal and gives his reasons to show that it is non-eternal, but concludes the discussion with a number of other reasons proving that it is eternal.

The first chapter of the third book is entirely devoted to the inference of the existence of soul from the fact that there must be some substance in which knowledge produced by the contact of the senses and their object inheres.

The knowledge of sense-objects (*indriyārtha*) is the reason by

[1] I have differed from *Upaskāra* in interpreting "*saṃjñākarma*" in II. i. 18, 19 as a genitive compound while *Upaskāra* makes it a *dvandva* compound. Upaskāra's interpretation seems to be far-fetched. He wants to twist it into an argument for the existence of God.

[2] This interpretation is according to Śaṅkara Miśra's *Upaskāra*.

which we can infer the existence of something different from the senses and the objects which appear in connection with them. The types of inferences referred to are (1) inference of non-existence of some things from the existence of some things, (2) of the existence of some things from the non-existence of some things, (3) of the existence of some things from the existence of others. In all these cases inference is possible only when the two are known to be connected with each other (*prasiddhipūrvakatvāt apadeśasya*)[1]. When such a connection does not exist or is doubtful, we have *anapadeśa* (fallacious middle) and *sandigdha* (doubtful middle); thus, it is a horse because it has a horn, or it is a cow because it has a horn are examples of fallacious reason. The inference of soul from the cognition produced by the contact of soul, senses and objects is not fallacious in the above way. The inference of the existence of the soul in others may be made in a similar way in which the existence of one's own soul is inferred[2], i.e. by virtue of the existence of movement and cessation of movement. In the second chapter it is said that the fact that there is cognition only when there is contact between the self, the senses and the objects proves that there is manas (mind), and this manas is a substance and eternal, and this can be proved because there is no simultaneity of production of efforts and various kinds of cognition; it may also be inferred that this manas is one (with each person).

The soul may be inferred from inhalation, exhalation, twinkling of the eye, life, the movement of the mind, the sense-affections pleasure, pain, will, antipathy, and effort. That it is a substance and eternal can be proved after the manner of vāyu. An objector is supposed to say that since when I see a man I do not see his soul, the inference of the soul is of the type of *sāmānyatodṛṣṭa* inference, i.e., from the perceived signs of pleasure, pain, cognition to infer an unknown entity to which they belong, but that this was the self could not be affirmed. So the existence of soul has to be admitted on the strength of the scriptures. But the Vaiśeṣika reply is that since there is nothing else but self to which the expression "I" may be applied, there is no need of falling back on the scriptures for the existence of the soul. But

[1] In connection with this there is a short reference to the methods of fallacy in which Gautama's terminology does not appear. There is no generalised statement, but specific types of inference are only pointed out as the basis.

[2] The forms of inference used show that Kaṇāda was probably not aware of Gautama's terminology.

then it is said that if the self is directly perceived in such experiences as "I am Yajñadatta" or "I am Devadatta," what is the good of turning to inference? The reply to this is that inference lending its aid to the same existence only strengthens the conviction. When we say that Devadatta goes or Yajñadatta goes, there comes the doubt whether by Devadatta or Yajñadatta the body alone is meant; but the doubt is removed when we think that the notion of "I" refers to the self and not to anything else. As there is no difference regarding the production of pleasure, pain, and cognition, the soul is one in all. But yet it is many by special limitations as individuals and this is also proved on the strength of the scriptures[1].

In the first chapter of the fourth book it is said that that which is existent, but yet has no cause, should be considered eternal (*nitya*). It can be inferred by its effect, for the effect can only take place because of the cause. When we speak of anything as non-eternal, it is only a negation of the eternal, so that also proves that there is something eternal. The non-eternal is ignorance (*avidyā*)[2]. Colour is visible in a thing which is great (*mahat*) and compounded. Air (*vāyu*) is not perceived to have colour, though it is great and made up of parts, because it has not the actuality of colour (*rūpasaṃskāra*—i.e. in air there is only colour in its unmanifested form) in it Colour is thus visible only when there is colour with special qualifications and conditions[3]. In this way the cognition of taste, smell, and touch is also explained. Number, measure, separateness, contact, and disjoining, the quality of belonging to a higher or lower class, action, all these as they abide in things possessing colour are visible to the eye. The number etc. of those which have no colour are not perceived by the eye. But the notion of being and also of genus of quality (guṇatva)

[1] I have differed here from the meaning given in *Upaskāra*. I think the three sūtras "*Sukhaduḥkhajñānaniṣpattyaviśeṣādekātmyam*," "*vyavasthāto nānā*," and "*śastrasāmarthyāt ca*" originally meant that the self was one, though for the sake of many limitations, and also because of the need of the performance of acts enjoined by the scriptures, they are regarded as many.

[2] I have differed here also in my meaning from the *Upaskāra*, which regards this sūtra "*avidyā*" to mean that we do not know of any reasons which lead to the non-eternality of the atoms.

[3] This is what is meant in the later distinctions of *udbhūtarūpavattva* and *anudbhūtarūpavattva*. The word *saṃskāra* in Vaiśeṣika has many senses. It means inertia, elasticity, collection (*samavāya*), production (*udbhava*) and not being overcome (*anabhibhava*). For the last three senses see *Upaskāra* IV. i. 7.

are perceived by all the senses (just as colour, taste, smell, touch, and sound are perceived by one sense, cognition, pleasure, pain, etc. by the manas and number etc. by the visual and the tactile sense)[1].

In the second chapter of the fourth book it is said that the earth, etc. exist in three forms, body, sense, and objects. There cannot be any compounding of the five elements or even of the three, but the atoms of different elements may combine when one of them acts as the central radicle (*upaṣṭambhaka*). Bodies are of two kinds, those produced from ovaries and those which are otherwise produced by the combination of the atoms in accordance with special kinds of dharma. All combinations of atoms are due to special kinds of dharmas. Such super-mundane bodies are to be admitted for explaining the fact that things must have been given names by beings having such super-mundane bodies, and also on account of the authority of the Vedas.

In the first chapter of the fifth book action (*karma*) is discussed. Taking the example of threshing the corn, it is said that the movement of the hand is due to its contact with the soul in a state of effort, and the movement of the flail is due to its contact with the hand. But in the case of the uprising of the flail in the threshing pot due to impact the movement is not due to contact with the hands, and so the uplifting of the hand in touch with the flail is not due to its contact with the soul; for it is due to the impact of the flail. On account of heaviness (*gurutva*) the flail will fall when not held by the hand. Things may have an upward or side motion by specially directed motions (*nodanaviśeṣa*) which are generated by special kinds of efforts. Even without effort the body may move during sleep. The movement of needles towards magnets is due to an unknown cause (*adṛṣṭakāraṇaka*). The arrow first acquires motion by specially directed movement, and then on account of its inertia (*vegasaṃskāra*) keeps on moving and when that ceases it falls down through heaviness.

The second chapter abounds with extremely crude explana-

[1] This portion has been taken from the *Upaskāra* of Śaṅkara Miśra on the *Vaiśeṣika sūtras* of Kaṇāda. It must be noted here that the notion of number according to Vaiśeṣika is due to mental relativity or oscillation (*apekṣābuddhijanya*). But this mental relativity can only start when the thing having number is either seen or touched; and it is in this sense that notion of number is said to depend on the visual or the tactual sense.

tions of certain physical phenomena which have no philosophical importance. All the special phenomena of nature are explained as being due to unknown cause (*adṛṣṭakāritam*) and no explanation is given as to the nature of this unknown (*adṛṣṭa*). It is however said that with the absence of *adṛṣṭa* there is no contact of body with soul, and thus there is no rebirth, and therefore mokṣa (salvation); pleasure and pain are due to contact of the self, manas, senses and objects. Yoga is that in which the mind is in contact with the self alone, by which the former becomes steady and there is no pain in the body. Time, space, ākāśa are regarded as inactive.

The whole of the sixth book is devoted to showing that gifts are made to proper persons not through sympathy but on account of the injunction of the scriptures, the enumeration of certain Vedic performances, which brings in adṛṣṭa, purification and impurities of things, how passions are often generated by adṛṣṭa, how dharma and adharma lead to birth and death and how mokṣa takes place as a result of the work of the soul.

In the seventh book it is said that the qualities in eternal things are eternal and in non-eternal things non-eternal. The change of qualities produced by heat in earth has its beginning in the cause (the atoms). Atomic size is invisible while great size is visible. Visibility is due to a thing's being made up of many causes[1], but the atom is therefore different from those that have great size. The same thing may be called great and small relatively at the same time. In accordance with aṇutva (atomic) and mahattva (great) there are also the notions of small and big. The eternal size of *parimaṇḍala* (round) belongs to the atoms. Ākāśa and ātman are called *mahān* or *paramamahān* (the supremely great or all-pervasive); since manas is not of the great measure it is of atomic size. Space and time are also considered as being of the measure "supremely great" (paramamahat). Atomic size (parimaṇḍala) belonging to the atoms and the mind (manas) and the supremely great size belonging to space, time, soul and ether (ākāśa) are regarded as eternal.

In the second chapter of the seventh book it is said that unity and separateness are to be admitted as entities distinct from other qualities. There is no number in movement and quality; the appearance of number in them is false. Cause and effect are

[1] I have differed from the *Upaskāra* in the interpretation of this sūtra.

neither one, nor have they distinctive separateness (*ekapṛthaktva*). The notion of unity is the cause of the notion of duality, etc. Contact may be due to the action of one or two things, or the effect of another contact and so is disjoining. There is neither contact nor disjoining in cause and effect since they do not exist independently (*yutasiddhyabhāvāt*). In the eighth book it is said that soul and manas are not perceptible, and that in the apprehension of qualities, action, generality, and particularity perception is due to their contact with the thing. Earth is the cause of perception of smell, and water, fire, and air are the cause of taste, colour and touch[1]. In the ninth book negation is described; non-existence (*asat*) is defined as that to which neither action nor quality can be attributed. Even existent things may become non-existent and that which is existent in one way may be non-existent in another; but there is another kind of non-existence which is different from the above kinds of existence and non-existence[2]. All negation can be directly perceived through the help of the memory which keeps before the mind the thing to which the negation applies. Allusion is also made in this connection to the special perceptual powers of the yogins (sages attaining mystical powers through Yoga practices).

In the second chapter the nature of hetu (reason) or the middle term is described. It is said that anything connected with any other thing, as effect, cause, as in contact, or as contrary or as inseparably connected, will serve as liṅga (reason). The main point is the notion "this is associated with this," or "these two are related as cause and effect," and since this may also be produced through premisses, there may be a formal syllogism from propositions fulfilling the above condition. Verbal cognition comes without inference. False knowledge (*avidyā*) is due to the defect of the senses or non-observation and malobservation due to wrong expectant impressions. The opposite of this is true knowledge (*vidyā*). In the tenth it is said that pleasure and pain are not cognitions, since they are not related to doubt and certainty.

1 *Upaskāra* here explains that it is intended that the senses are produced by those specific elements, but this cannot be found in the sūtras.

2 In the previous three kinds of non-existence, *prāgabhāva* (negation before production), *dhvaṃsābhāva* (negation after destruction), and *anyonyābhāva* (mutual negation of each other in each other), have been described. The fourth one is *sāmānyābhāva* (general negation).

A dravya may be caused by the inhering of the effect in it, for because of its contact with another thing the effect is produced. Karma (motion) is also a cause since it inheres in the cause. Contact is also a cause since it inheres in the cause. A contact which inheres in the cause of the cause and thereby helps the production of the effect is also a cause. The special quality of the heat of fire is also a cause.

Works according to the injunctions of the scriptures since they have no visible effect are the cause of prosperity, and because the Vedas direct them, they have validity.

Philosophy in the Nyāya sūtras[1].

The *Nyāya sūtras* begin with an enumeration of the sixteen subjects, viz. means of right knowledge (*pramāṇa*), object of right knowledge (*prameya*), doubt (*saṃśaya*), purpose (*prayojana*), illustrative instances (*dṛṣṭānta*), accepted conclusions (*siddhānta*), premisses (*avayava*), argumentation (*tarka*), ascertainment (*nirṇaya*), debates (*vāda*), disputations (*jalpa*), destructive criticisms (*vitaṇḍā*), fallacy (*hetvābhāsa*), quibble (*chala*), refutations (*jāti*), points of opponent's defeat (*nigrahasthāna*), and hold that by a thorough knowledge of these the highest good (*niḥśreyasa*), is attained. In the second sūtra it is said that salvation (*apavarga*) is attained by the successive disappearance of false knowledge (*mithyājñāna*), defects (*doṣa*), endeavours (*pravṛtti*), birth (*janma*), and ultimately of sorrow. Then the means of proof are said to be of four kinds, perception (*pratyakṣa*), inference (*anumāna*), analogy (*upamāna*), and testimony (*śabda*). Perception is defined as uncontradicted determinate knowledge unassociated with names proceeding out of sense contact with objects. Inference is of three kinds, from cause to effect (*pūrvavat*), effect to cause (*śeṣavat*), and inference from common characteristics (*sāmānyato dṛṣṭa*). Upamāna is the knowing of anything by similarity with any well-known thing.

Śabda is defined as the testimony of reliable authority (āpta)[2].

[1] This is a brief summary of the doctrines found in *Nyāya sūtras*, supplemented here and there with the views of Vātsyāyana, the commentator. This follows the order of the sūtras, and tries to present their ideas with as little additions from those of later day Nyāya as possible. The general treatment of Nyāya-Vaiśeṣika expounds the two systems in the light of later writers and commentators.

[2] It is curious to notice that Vātsyāyana says that an ārya, a ṛṣi or a mlechha (foreigner), may be an āpta (reliable authority).

Such a testimony may tell us about things which may be experienced and which are beyond experience. Objects of knowledge are said to be self (*ātman*), body, senses, sense-objects, understanding (*buddhi*), mind (*manas*), endeavour (*pravṛtti*), rebirths, enjoyment of pleasure and suffering of pain, sorrow and salvation. Desire, antipathy, effort (*prayatna*), pleasure, pain, and knowledge indicate the existence of the self. Body is that which upholds movement, the senses and the rise of pleasure and pain as arising out of the contact of sense with sense-objects[1]; the five senses are derived from the five elements, such as pṛthivī, ap, tejas, vāyu and ākāśa; smell, taste, colour, touch, and sound are the qualities of the above five elements, and these are also the objects of the senses. The fact that many cognitions cannot occur at any one moment indicates the existence of mind (*manas*). Endeavour means what is done by speech, understanding, and body. Doṣas (attachment, antipathy, etc.) are those which lead men to virtue and vice. Pain is that which causes suffering[2]. Ultimate cessation from pain is called *apavarga*[3]. Doubt arises when through confusion of similar qualities or conflicting opinions etc., one wants to settle one of the two alternatives. That for attaining which, or for giving up which one sets himself to work is called *prayojana*.

Illustrative example (*dṛṣṭānta*) is that on which both the common man and the expert (*parīkṣaka*) hold the same opinion. Established texts or conclusions (*siddhānta*) are of four kinds, viz. (1) those which are accepted by all schools of thought called the *sarvatantrasiddhānta*; (2) those which are held by one school or similar schools but opposed by others called the *pratitantrasiddhānta*; (3) those which being accepted other conclusions will also naturally follow called *adhikaraṇasiddhānta*; (4) those of the opponent's views which are uncritically granted by a debater, who proceeds then to refute the consequences that follow and thereby show his own special skill and bring the opponent's intellect to disrepute (*abhyupagamasiddhānta*)[4]. The premisses are five:

[1] Here I have followed Vātsyāyana's meaning.

[2] Vātsyāyana comments here that when one finds all things full of misery, he wishes to avoid misery, and finding birth to be associated with pain becomes unattached and thus is emancipated.

[3] Vātsyāyana wants to emphasize that there is no bliss in salvation, but only cessation from pain.

[4] I have followed Vātsyāyana's interpretation here.

(1) *pratijñā* (the first enunciation of the thing to be proved); (2) *hetu* (the reason which establishes the conclusion on the strength of the similarity of the case in hand with known examples or negative instances); (3) *udāharaṇa* (positive or negative illustrative instances); (4) *upanaya* (corroboration by the instance); (5) *nigamana* (to reach the conclusion which has been proved). Then come the definitions of tarka, nirṇaya, vāda, jalpa, vitaṇḍā, the fallacies (hetvābhāsa), chala, jāti, and nigrahasthāna, which have been enumerated in the first sūtra.

The second book deals with the refutations of objections against the means of right knowledge (pramāṇa). In refutation of certain objections against the possibility of the happening of doubt, which held that doubt could not happen, since there was always a difference between the two things regarding which doubt arose, it is held that doubt arises when the special differentiating characteristics between the two things are not noted. Certain objectors, probably the Buddhists, are supposed to object to the validity of the pramāṇa in general and particularly of perceptions on the ground that if they were generated before the sense-object contact, they could not be due to the latter, and if they are produced after the sense-object contact, they could not establish the nature of the objects, and if the two happened together then there would be no notion of succession in our cognitions. To this the Nyāya reply is that if there were no means of right knowledge, then there would be no means of knowledge by means of which the objector would refute all means of right knowledge; if the objector presumes to have any means of valid knowledge then he cannot say that there are no means of valid knowledge at all. Just as from the diverse kinds of sounds of different musical instruments, one can infer the previous existence of those different kinds of musical instruments, so from our knowledge of objects we can infer the previous existence of those objects of knowledge[1].

The same things (e.g. the senses, etc.) which are regarded as instruments of right knowledge with reference to the right cognition of other things may themselves be the objects of right

[1] *Yathāpaścātsiddhena śabdena pūrvasiddham ātodyamanumīyate sādhyam ca ātodyam sādhanam ca śabdaḥ antarhite hyātodye svanataḥ anumānam bhavatīti, vīṇā vādyate veṇuḥ pūryyate iti svanaviśeṣeṇa ātodyaviśeṣam pratipadyate tathā pūrvasiddham upalabdhiviṣayam paścātsiddhena upalabdhihetunā pratipadyate. Vātsyāyana bhāṣya*, II. i. 15.

knowledge. There are no hard and fast limits that those which are instruments of knowledge should always be treated as mere instruments, for they themselves may be objects of right knowledge. The means of right knowledge (pramāṇa) do not require other sets of means for revealing them, for they like the light of a lamp in revealing the objects of right knowledge reveal themselves as well.

Coming to the question of the correctness of the definition of perception, it is held that the definition includes the contact of the soul with the mind[1]. Then it is said that though we perceive only parts of things, yet since there is a whole, the perception of the part will naturally refer to the whole. Since we can pull and draw things wholes exist, and the whole is not merely the parts collected together, for were it so one could say that we perceived the ultimate parts or the atoms[2]. Some objectors hold that since there may be a plurality of causes it is wrong to infer particular causes from particular effects. To this the Nyāya answer is that there is always such a difference in the specific nature of each effect that if properly observed each particular effect will lead us to a correct inference of its own particular cause[3]. In refuting those who object to the existence of time on the ground of relativity, it is said that if the present time did not exist, then no perception of it would have been possible. The past and future also exist, for otherwise we should not have perceived things as being done in the past or as going to be done in the future. The validity of analogy (*upamāna*) as a means of knowledge and the validity of the Vedas is then proved. The four pramāṇas of perception, inference, analogy, and scripture

[1] Here the sūtras, II. i. 20–28, are probably later interpolations to answer criticisms, not against the Nyāya doctrine of perception, but against the wording of the definition of perception as given in the *Nyāya sūtra*, II. i. 4.

[2] This is a refutation of the doctrines of the Buddhists, who rejected the existence of wholes (avayavī). On this subject a later Buddhist monograph by Paṇḍita Aśoka (9th century A.D.), *Avayavinirākaraṇa* in *Six Buddhist Nyāya Tracts*, may be referred to.

[3] *Pūrvodakaviśiṣṭam khalu varṣodakan śīghrataram srotasā bahutaraphenaphalaparṇakāsṭhādivahanañcopalabhamānaḥ pūrṇatvena, nadyā upari vṛṣto deva ityanuminoti nodakabṛddhimātreṇa. Vātsyāyana bhāṣya*, II. I. 38. The inference that there has been rain up the river is not made merely from seeing the rise of water, but from the rainwater augmenting the previous water of the river and carrying with its current large quantities of foam, fruits, leaves, wood, etc. These characteristics, associated with the rise of water, mark it as a special kind of rise of water, which can only be due to the happening of rain up the river.

are quite sufficient and it is needless to accept arthāpatti (implication), aitihya (tradition), sambhava (when a thing is understood in terms of higher measure the lower measure contained in it is also understood—if we know that there is a bushel of corn anywhere we understand that the same contains eight gallons of corn as well) and abhāva (non-existence) as separate pramāṇas for the tradition is included in verbal testimony and arthāpatti, sambhava and abhāva are included within inference.

The validity of these as pramāṇas is recognized, but they are said to be included in the four pramāṇas mentioned before. The theory of the eternity of sound is then refuted and the non-eternity proved in great detail. The meaning of words is said to refer to class-notions (*jāti*), individuals (*vyakti*), and the specific position of the limbs (*ākṛti*), by which the class notion is manifested. Class (*jāti*) is defined as that which produces the notion of sameness (*samānaprasavātmikā jātiḥ*).

The third book begins with the proofs for the existence of the self or ātman. It is said that each of the senses is associated with its own specific object, but there must exist some other entity in us which gathered together the different sense-cognitions and produced the perception of the total object as distinguished from the separate sense-perceptions. If there were no self then there would be no sin in injuring the bodies of men; again if there were no permanent self, no one would be able to recognize things as having seen them before; the two images produced by the eyes in visual perception could not also have been united together as one visual perception of the things[1]; moreover if there were no permanent cognizer then by the sight of a sour fruit one could not be reminded of its sour taste. If consciousness belonged to the senses only, then there would be no recognition, for the experience of one could not be recognized by another. If it is said that the unity of sensations could as well be effected by manas (mind), then the manas would serve the same purpose as self and it would only be a quarrel over a name, for this entity the knower would require some instrument by which it would co-ordinate the sensations and cognize; unless manas is admitted as a separate instrument of the soul, then though the sense perceptions could be explained as being the work of the

[1] According to Vātsyāyana, in the two eyes we have two different senses. Udyotakara, however, thinks that there is one visual sense which works in both eyes.

senses, yet imagining, thinking, etc., could not be explained. Another argument for the admission of soul is this, that infants show signs of pleasure and pain in quite early stages of infancy and this could not be due to anything but similar experiences in previous lives. Moreover every creature is born with some desires, and no one is seen to be born without desires. All attachments and desires are due to previous experiences, and therefore it is argued that desires in infants are due to their experience in previous existences.

The body is made up of the kṣiti element. The visual sense is material and so also are all other senses[1]. Incidentally the view held by some that the skin is the only organ of sensation is also refuted. The earth possesses four qualities, water three, fire two, air one, and ether one, but the sense of smell, taste, eye, and touch which are made respectively by the four elements of earth, etc., can only grasp the distinctive features of the elements of which they are made. Thus though the organ of smell is made by earth which contains four qualities, it can only grasp the distinctive quality of earth, viz. smell.

Against the Sāṃkhya distinction of *buddhi* (cognition) and *cit* (pure intelligence) it is said that there is no difference between the *buddhi* and *cit*. We do not find in our consciousness two elements of a phenomenal and a non-phenomenal consciousness, but only one, by whichever name it may be called. The Sāṃkhya epistemology that the antaḥkaraṇa assumes diverse forms in cognitive acts is also denied, and these are explained on the supposition of contacts of manas with the senses, ātman and external objects. The Buddhist objection against the Sāṃkhya explanation that the antaḥkaraṇas catch reflection from the external world just as a crystal does from the coloured objects that may lie near it, that there were really momentary productions of crystals and no permanent crystal catching different reflections at different times is refuted by Nyāya; for it says that it cannot be said that all creations are momentary, but it can only be agreed to in those cases where momentariness was actually experienced. In the case of the transformation of milk into curd there is no coming in of new qualities and disappearance of old ones, but

[1] It is well to remember that Sāṃkhya did not believe that the senses were constituted of the gross elements. But the Sāṃkhya-Yoga view represented in *Ātreya-saṃhitā* (*Caraka*) regarded the senses as bhautika or constituted of the gross elements.

the old milk is destroyed and the curd originates anew. The contact of manas with soul (*ātman*) takes place within the body and not in that part of ātman which is outside the body; knowledge belongs to the self and not to the senses or the object for even when they are destroyed knowledge remains. New cognitions destroy the old ones. No two recollections can be simultaneous. Desire and antipathy also belong to the soul. None of these can belong either to the body or to the mind (manas). Manas cannot be conscious for it is dependent upon self. Again if it was conscious then the actions done by it would have to be borne by the self and one cannot reap the fruits of the actions of another. The causes of recollection on the part of self are given as follows: (1) attention, (2) context, (3) repetition, (4) sign, (5) association, (6) likeness, (7) association of the possessor and the possessed or master and servant, or things which are generally seen to follow each other, (8) separation (as of husband and wife), (9) simpler employment, (10) opposition, (11) excess, (12) that from which anything can be got, (13) cover and covered, (14) pleasure and pain causing memory of that which caused them, (15) fear, (16) entreaty, (17) action such as that of the chariot reminding the charioteer, (18) affection, (19) merit and demerit[1]. It is said that knowledge does not belong to body, and then the question of the production of the body as due to adṛṣṭa is described. Salvation (*apavarga*) is effected by the manas being permanenly separated from the soul (ātman) through the destruction of karma.

In the fourth book in course of the examination of doṣa (defects), it is said that moha (ignorance), is at the root of all other defects such as rāga (attachment) and dveṣa (antipathy). As against the Buddhist view that a thing could be produced by destruction, it is said that destruction is only a stage in the process of origination. Īśvara is regarded as the cause of the production of effects of deeds performed by men's efforts, for man is not always found to attain success according to his efforts. A reference is made to the doctrine of those who say that all things have come into being by no-cause (*animitta*), for then no-cause would be the cause, which is impossible.

The doctrine of some that all things are eternal is next refuted on the ground that we always see things produced and destroyed.

[1] *Nyāya sūtra* III. ii. 44.

The doctrine of the nihilistic Buddhists (śūnyavādin Bauddhas) that all things are what they are by virtue of their relations to other things, and that of other Buddhists who hold that there are merely the qualities and parts but no substances or wholes, are then refuted. The fruits of karmas are regarded as being like the fruits of trees which take some time before they can ripen. Even though there may be pleasures here and there, birth means sorrow for men, for even the man who enjoys pleasure is tormented by many sorrows, and sometimes one mistakes pains for pleasures. As there is no sorrow in the man who is in deep dreamless sleep, so there is no affliction (*kleśa*) in the man who attains apavarga (salvation)[1]. When once this state is attained all efforts (*pravṛtti*) cease for ever, for though efforts were beginningless with us they were all due to attachment, antipathy, etc. Then there are short discussions regarding the way in which egoism (*ahaṃkāra*) ceases with the knowledge of the true causes of defects (*doṣa*); about the nature of whole and parts and about the nature of atoms (*aṇus*) which cannot further be divided. A discussion is then introduced against the doctrine of the Vijñānavādins that nothing can be regarded as having any reality when separated from thoughts. Incidentally Yoga is mentioned as leading to right knowledge.

The whole of the fifth book which seems to be a later addition is devoted to the enumeration of different kinds of refutations (*nigrahasthāna*) and futilities (*jāti*).

Caraka, Nyāya sūtras and Vaiśeṣika sūtras.

When we compare the *Nyāya sūtras* with the *Vaiśeṣika sūtras* we find that in the former two or three different streams of purposes have met, whereas the latter is much more homogeneous. The large amount of materials relating to debates treated as a practical art for defeating an opponent would lead one to suppose that it was probably originally compiled from some other existing treatises which were used by Hindus and Buddhists alike for rendering themselves fit to hold their own in debates with their opponents[2]. This assumption is justified when

[1] Vātsyāyana notes that this is the salvation of him who has known Brahman, IV. i. 63.

[2] A reference to the *Suvarṇaprabhāsa sūtra* shows that the Buddhist missionaries used to get certain preparations for improving their voice in order to be able to argue with force, and they took to the worship of Sarasvatī (goddess of learning), who they supposed would help them in bringing readily before their mind all the information and ideas of which they stood so much in need at the time of debates.

we compare the futilities (jāti) quibbles (chala), etc., relating to disputations as found in the *Nyāya sūtra* with those that are found in the medical work of Caraka (78 A.D.), III. viii. There are no other works in early Sanskrit literature, excepting the *Nyāya sūtra* and *Caraka-saṃhitā* which have treated of these matters. Caraka's description of some of the categories (e.g. dṛṣṭānta, prayojana, pratijñā and vitaṇḍā) follows very closely the definitions given of those in the *Nyāya sūtras*. There are others such as the definitions of jalpa, chala, nigrahasthāna, etc., where the definitions of two authorities differ more. There are some other logical categories mentioned in Caraka (e.g. *pratiṣṭhāpanā*, *jijñāsā*, *vyavasāya*, *vākyadoṣa*, *vākyapraśaṃsā*, *upalambha*, *parihāra*, *abhyanujñā*, etc.) which are not found in the *Nyāya sūtra*[1]. Again, the various types of futilities (jāti) and points of opponent's refutation (*nigrahasthāna*) mentioned in the *Nyāya sūtra* are not found in *Caraka*. There are some terms which are found in slightly variant forms in the two works, e.g. *aupamya* in *Caraka*, *upamāna* in *Nyāya sūtra*, *arthāpatti* in *Nyāya sūtra* and *arthaprāpti* in *Caraka*. Caraka does not seem to know anything about the Nyāya work on this subject, and it is plain that the treatment of these terms of disputations in the *Caraka* is much simpler and less technical than what we find in the *Nyāya sūtras*. If we leave out the varieties of jāti and nigrahasthāna of the fifth book, there is on the whole a great agreement between the treatment of Caraka and that of the *Nyāya sūtras*. It seems therefore in a high degree probable that both Caraka and the *Nyāya sūtras* were indebted for their treatment of these terms of disputation to some other earlier work. Of these, Caraka's compilation was earlier, whereas the compilation of the *Nyāya sūtras* represents a later work when a hotter atmosphere of disputations had necessitated the use of more technical terms which are embodied in this work, but which were not contained in the earlier work. It does not seem therefore that this part of the work could have been earlier than the second century A.D. Another stream flowing through the *Nyāya sūtras* is that of a polemic against the doctrines which could be attributed to the Sautrāntika Buddhists, the Vijñānavāda Buddhists, the nihilists, the Sāṃkhya, the Cārvāka, and some other unknown schools of thought to which we find no

[1] Like Vaiśeṣika, Caraka does not know the threefold division of inference (*anumāna*) as *pūrvavat*, *śeṣavat* and *sāmānyatodṛṣṭa*.

further allusion elsewhere. The *Vaiśeṣika sūtras* as we have already seen had argued only against the Mīmāṃsā, and ultimately agreed with them on most points. The dispute with Mīmāṃsā in the *Nyāya sūtras* is the same as in the Vaiśeṣika over the question of the doctrine of the eternality of sound. The question of the self-validity of knowledge (*svataḥ prāmāṇyavāda*) and the akhyāti doctrine of illusion of the Mīmāṃsists, which form the two chief points of discussion between later Mīmāṃsā and later Nyāya, are never alluded to in the *Nyāya sūtras*. The advocacy of Yoga methods (*Nyāya sūtras*, IV. ii. 38–42 and 46) seems also to be an alien element; these are not found in Vaiśeṣika and are not in keeping with the general tendency of the *Nyāya sūtras*, and the Japanese tradition that Mirok added them later on as Mahāmahopādhyāya Haraprasāda Śāstrī has pointed out[1] is not improbable.

The *Vaiśeṣika sūtras*, III. i. 18 and III. ii. 1, describe perceptional knowledge as produced by the close proximity of the self (ātman), the senses and the objects of sense, and they also adhere to the doctrine, that colour can only be perceived under special conditions of *saṃskāra* (conglomeration etc.). The reason for inferring the existence of manas from the non-simultaneity (*ayaugapadya*) of knowledge and efforts is almost the same with Vaiśeṣika as with Nyāya. The *Nyāya sūtras* give a more technical definition of perception, but do not bring in the questions of saṃskāra or udbhūtarūpavattva which Vaiśeṣika does. On the question of inference Nyāya gives three classifications as pūrvavat, śeṣavat and sāmānyatodṛṣṭa, but no definition. The *Vaiśeṣika sūtras* do not know of these classifications, and give only particular types or instances of inference (V. S. III. i. 7–17, IX. ii. 1–2, 4–5). Inference is said to be made when a thing is in contact with another, or when it is in a relation of inherence in it, or when it inheres in a third thing; one kind of effect may lead to the inference of another kind of effect, and so on. These are but mere collections of specific instances of inference without reaching a general theory. The doctrine of vyāpti (concomitance of *hetu* (reason) and *sādhya* (probandum)) which became so important in later Nyāya has never been properly formulated either in the *Nyāya sūtras* or in the Vaiśeṣika. *Vaiśeṣika sūtra*, III. i. 24, no doubt assumes the knowledge of concomitance between hetu and sādhya (*prasiddhipūrvakatvāt apadeśasya*),

[1] *J.A.S.B.* 1905.

but the technical vyāpti is not known, and the connotation of the term *prasiddhipūrvakatva* of Vaiśeṣika seems to be more loose than the term *vyāpti* as we know it in the later Nyāya. The *Vaiśeṣika sūtras* do not count scriptures (*śabda*) as a separate pramāṇa, but they tacitly admit the great validity of the Vedas. With *Nyāya sūtras* śabda as a pramāṇa applies not only to the Vedas, but to the testimony of any trustworthy person, and Vātsyāyana says that trustworthy persons may be of three kinds *ṛṣi*, *ārya* and *mleccha* (foreigners). Upamāna which is regarded as a means of right cognition in Nyāya is not even referred to in the *Vaiśeṣika sūtras.* The *Nyāya sūtras* know of other pramāṇas, such as *arthāpatti*, *sambhava* and *aitihya*, but include them within the pramāṇas admitted by them, but the *Vaiśeṣika sūtras* do not seem to know them at all[1]. The *Vaiśeṣika sūtras* believe in the perception of negation (abhāva) through the perception of the locus to which such negation refers (IX. i. 1–10). The *Nyāya sūtras* (II. ii. 1, 2, 7–12) consider that abhāva as non-existence or negation can be perceived; when one asks another to "bring the clothes which are not marked," he finds that marks are absent in some clothes and brings them ; so it is argued that absence or non-existence can be directly perceived[2]. Though there is thus an agreement between the Nyāya and the *Vaiśeṣika sūtras* about the acceptance of abhāva as being due to perception, yet their method of handling the matter is different. The *Nyāya sūtras* say nothing about the categories of *dravya*, *guṇa*, *karma*, *viśeṣa* and *samavāya* which form the main subjects of Vaiśeṣka discussions[3]. The *Nyāya sūtras* take much pains to prove the materiality of the senses. But this question does not seem to have been important with Vaiśeṣika. The slight reference to this question in VIII. ii. 5–6 can hardly be regarded as sufficient. The *Vaiśeṣika sūtras* do not mention the name of "Īśvara," whereas the *Nyāya sūtras* try to prove his existence on eschatological grounds. The reasons given in support of the existence of self in the *Nyāya sūtras* are mainly on the ground of the unity of sense-cognitions and the phenomenon of recognition, whereas the

[1] The only old authority which knows these pramāṇas is Caraka. But he also gives an interpretation of sambhava which is different from Nyāya and calls *arthāpatti* *arthaprāpti* (*Caraka* III. viii.).

[2] The details of this example are taken from Vātsyāyana's commentary.

[3] The *Nyāya sūtra* no doubt incidentally gives a definition of jāti as "*samānaprasavātmikā jātiḥ*" (II. ii. 71).

Vaiśeṣika lays its main emphasis on self-consciousness as a fact of knowledge. Both the Nyāya and the *Vaiśeṣika sūtras* admit the existence of atoms, but all the details of the doctrine of atomic structure in later Nyāya-Vaiśeṣika are absent there. The Vaiśeṣika calls salvation *niḥśreyasa* or *mokṣa* and the Nyāya *apavarga.* Mokṣa with Vaiśeṣika is the permanent cessation of connection with body; the apavarga with Nyāya is cessation of pain[1]. In later times the main points of difference between the Vaiśeṣika and Nyāya are said to lie with regard to theory of the notion of number, changes of colour in the molecules by heat, etc. Thus the former admitted a special procedure of the mind by which cognitions of number arose in the mind (e.g. at the first moment there is the sense contact with an object, then the notion of oneness, then from a sense of relativeness—apekṣābuddhi—notion of two, then a notion of two-ness, and then the notion of two things); again, the doctrine of pilupāka (changes of qualities by heat are produced in atoms and not in molecules as Nyāya held) was held by Vaiśeṣika, which the Naiyāyikas did not admit[2]. But as the *Nyāya sūtras* are silent on these points, it is not possible to say that such were really the differences between early Nyāya and early Vaiśeṣika. These differences may be said to hold between the later interpreters of Vaiśeṣika and the later interpreters of Nyāya. The Vaiśeṣika as we find it in the commentary of Praśastapāda (probably sixth century A.D.), and the Nyāya from the time of Udyotakara have come to be treated as almost the same system with slight variations only. I have therefore preferred to treat them together. The main presentation of the Nyāya-Vaiśeṣika philosophy in this chapter is that which is found from the sixth century onwards.

The Vaiśeṣika and Nyāya Literature.

It is difficult to ascertain definitely the date of the *Vaiśeṣika sūtras* by Kaṇāda, also called Aulūkya the son of Ulūka, though there is every reason to suppose it to be pre-Buddhistic. It

[1] Professor Vanamālī Vedāntatīrtha quotes a passage from *Saṃkṣepaśaṅkarajaya*, XVI. 68–69 in *J.A.S.B.*, 1905, and another passage from a Nyāya writer Bhāsarvajña, pp. 39–41, in *J.A.S.B.*, 1914, to show that the old Naiyāyikas considered that there was an element of happiness (*sukha*) in the state of mukti (salvation) which the Vaiśeṣikas denied. No evidence in support of this opinion is found in the Nyāya or the *Vaiśeṣika sūtras*, unless the cessation of pain with Nyāya is interpreted as meaning the presence of some sort of bliss or happiness.

[2] See Mādhava's *Sarvadarśanasaṃgraha-Aulūkyadarśana.*

appears from the *Vāyu purāna* that he was born in Prabhāsa near Dvārakā, and was the disciple of Somaśarmā. The time of Praśastapāda who wrote a bhāṣya (commentary) of the *Vaiśeṣika sūtras* cannot also unfortunately be ascertained. The peculiarity of Praśastapāda's bhāṣya is this that unlike other bhāṣyas (which first give brief explanations of the text of the sūtras and then continue to elaborate independent explanations by explaining the first brief comments), it does not follow the sūtras but is an independent dissertation based on their main contents[1]. There were two other bhāṣyas on the *Vaiśeṣika sūtras*, namely *Rāvaṇa-bhāṣya* and *Bharādvāja-vṛtti*, but these are now probably lost. References to the former are found in *Kiraṇāvalībhāskara* of Padmanābha Miśra and also in *Ratnaprabhā* 2. 2. 11. Four commentaries were written on this bhāṣya, namely *Vyomavatī* by Vyomaśekharācārya, *Nyāyakandalī* by Śrīdhara, *Kiraṇāvalī* by Udayana (984 A.D.) and *Līlāvatī* by Śrīvatsācārya. In addition to these Jagadīśa Bhaṭṭācārya of Navadvīpa and Śaṅkara Miśra wrote two other commentaries on the *Praśastapāda-bhāṣya*, namely *Bhāṣyasūkti* and *Kaṇāda-rahasya*. Śaṅkara Miśra (1425 A.D.) also wrote a commentary on the *Vaiśeṣika sūtras* called the *Upaskāra*. Of these *Nyāya-kandalī* of Śrīdhara on account of its simplicity of style and elaborate nature of exposition is probably the best for a modern student of Vaiśeṣika. Its author was a native of the village of Bhūrisṛṣṭi in Bengal (Rāḍha). His father's name was Baladeva and mother's name was Acchokā and he wrote his work in 913 Śaka era (990 A.D.) as he himself writes at the end of his work.

The *Nyāya sūtra* was written by Akṣapāda or Gautama, and the earliest commentary on it written by Vātsyāyana is known as the *Vātsyāyana-bhāṣya*. The date of Vātsyāyana has not

[1] The bhāṣya of Praśastapāda can hardly be called a bhāṣya (elaborate commentary). He himself makes no such claim and calls his work a compendium of the properties of the categories (*Padārthadharmasaṃgraha*). He takes the categories of *dravya*, *guṇa*, *karma*, *sāmānya*, *viśeṣa* and *samavāya* in order and without raising any discussions plainly narrates what he has got to say on them. Some of the doctrines which are important in later Nyāya-Vaiśeṣika discussions, such as the doctrine of creation and dissolution, doctrine of number, the theory that the number of atoms contributes to the atomic measure of the molecules, the doctrine of pilupāka in connection with the transformation of colours by heat occur in his narration for the first time as the *Vaiśeṣika sūtras* are silent on these points. It is difficult to ascertain his date definitely; he is the earliest writer on Vaiśeṣika available to us after Kaṇāda and it is not improbable that he lived in the 5th or 6th century A.D.

been definitely settled, but there is reason to believe that he lived some time in the beginning of the fourth century A.D. Jacobi places him in 300 A.D. Udyotakara (about 635 A.D.) wrote a *Vārttika* on Vātsyāyana's bhāṣya to establish the Nyāya views and to refute the criticisms of the Buddhist logician Diṅnāga (about 500 A.D.) in his *Pramāṇasamuccaya.* Vācaspatimiśra (840 A.D.) wrote a sub-commentary on the *Nyāyavārttika* of Udyotakara called *Nyāyavārttikatātparyaṭīkā* in order to make clear the right meanings of Udyotakara's *Vārttika* which was sinking in the mud as it were through numerous other bad writings (*dustarakunibandhapaṅkamagnānām*). Udayana (984 A.D.) wrote a sub-commentary on the *Tātparyaṭīkā* called *Tātparyaṭīkāpariśuddhi.* Varddhamāna (1225 A.D.) wrote a sub-commentary on that called the *Nyāyanibandhaprakāśa.* Padmanābha wrote a sub-commentary on that called *Varddhamānendu* and Śaṅkara Miśra (1425 A.D.) wrote a sub-commentary on that called the *Nyāydtātparyamaṇḍana.* In the seventeenth century Viśvanātha wrote an independent short commentary known as *Viśvanāthavṛtti*, on the *Nyāya sūtra*, and Rādhāmohana wrote a separate commentary on the *Nyāya sūtras* known as *Nyāyasūtravivaraṇa.* In addition to these works on the *Nyāya sūtras* many other independent works of great philosophical value have been written on the Nyāya system. The most important of these in medieval times is the *Nyāyamañjarī* of Jayanta (880 A.D.), who flourished shortly after Vācaspatimiśra. Jayanta chooses some of the *Nyāya sūtras* for interpretation, but he discusses the Nyāya views quite independently, and criticizes the views of other systems of Indian thought of his time. It is far more comprehensive than Vācaspati's *Tātparyaṭīkā*, and its style is most delightfully lucid. Another important work is Udayana's *Kusumāñjali* in which he tries to prove the existence of Īśvara (God). This work ought to be read with its commentary *Prakāśa* by Varddhamāna (1225 A.D.) and its sub-commentary *Makaranda* by Rucidatta (1275 A.D.). Udayana's *Ātmatattvaviveka* is a polemical work against the Buddhists, in which he tries to establish the Nyāya doctrine of soul. In addition to these we have a number of useful works on Nyāya in later times. Of these the following deserve special mention in connection with the present work. *Bhāṣāpariccheda* by Viśvanātha with its commentaries *Muktāvalī*, *Dinakarī* and *Rāmarudrī*, *Tarkasamgraha* with *Nyāyanirṇaya*, *Tarkabhāṣā* of Keśava Miśra with the commentary *Nyāyapradīpa*, *Saptapadārthī* of Śivāditya, *Tārkikarakṣā* of Varadarāja with the commentary *Niṣkaṇṭaka* of Mallinātha, *Nyāyasāra* of Mādhava Deva of the city of Dhāra and *Nyāyasiddhāntamañjarī* of Jānakīnātha Bhaṭṭācarya with the *Nyāyamañjarīsāra* by Yādavācārya, and *Nyāyasiddhāntadīpa* of Śaśadhara with *Prabhā* by Śeṣānantācārya.

The new school of Nyāya philosophy known as Navya-Nyāya began with Gaṅgeśa Upādhyāya of Mithilā, about 1200 A.D. Gaṅgeśa wrote only on the four pramāṇas admitted by the Nyāya, viz. pratyakṣa, anumāna, upamāna, and śabda, and not on any of the topics of Nyāya metaphysics. But it so happened that his discussions on anumāna (inference) attracted unusually great attention in Navadvīpa (Bengal), and large numbers of commentaries and commentaries of commentaries were written on the anumāna portion of his work *Tattvacintāmaṇi*, and many independent treatises on śabda and anumāna were also written by the scholars of Bengal, which became thenceforth for some centuries the home of Nyāya studies. The commentaries of Raghunātha Śiromaṇi (1500 A.D.), Mathurā Bhaṭṭācārya (1580 A.D.), Gadādhara Bhaṭṭācārya (1650 A.D.) and Jagadīśa Bhaṭṭācārya (1590 A.D.), commentaries on Śiromaṇi's commentary on *Tattvacintāmani*, had been very widely read in Bengal. The new school of Nyāya became the most important study in Navadvīpa and there appeared a series of thinkers who produced an extensive literature on the subject[1]. The contribution was not in the direction of metaphysics, theology, ethics, or religion, but consisted mainly in developing a system of linguistic notations to specify accurately and precisely any concept or its relation with other concepts[2].

Thus for example when they wished to define precisely the nature of the concomitance of one concept with another (e.g. smoke and fire), they would so specify the relation that the exact nature of the concomitance should be clearly expressed, and that there should be no confusion or ambiguity. Close subtle analytic thinking and the development of a system of highly technical

[1] From the latter half of the twelfth century to the third quarter of the sixteenth century the new school of Nyāya was started in Mithilā (Behar); but from the fifteenth to the seventeenth century Bengal became pre-eminently the home of Nyāya studies. See Mr Cakravarttī's paper, *J. A. S. B.* 1915. I am indebted to it for some of the dates mentioned in this section.

[2] *Īśvarānumāna* of Raghunātha as well as his *Padārthatattvanirūpaṇa* are, however, notable exceptions.

expressions mark the development of this literature. The technical expressions invented by this school were thus generally accepted even by other systems of thought, wherever the need of accurate and subtle thinking was felt. But from the time that Sanskrit ceased to be the vehicle of philosophical thinking in India the importance of this literature has gradually lost ground, and it can hardly be hoped that it will ever regain its old position by attracting enthusiastic students in large numbers.

I cannot close this chapter without mentioning the fact that so far as the logical portion of the Nyāya system is concerned, though Akṣapāda was the first to write a comprehensive account of it, the Jains and Buddhists in medieval times had independently worked at this subject and had criticized the Nyāya account of logic and made valuable contributions. In Jaina logic *Daśavaikālikaniryukti* of Bhadrabāhu (357 B.C.), Umāsvāti's *Tattvārthādhigama sūtra*, *Nyāyāvatāra* of Siddhasena Divākara (533 A.D.) Māṇikya Nandī's (800 A.D.) *Parīkṣāmukha sūtra*, and *Pramāṇanayatattvālokālaṃkāra* of Deva Sūri (1159 A.D.) and *Prameyakamalamārtaṇḍa* of Prabhācandra deserve special notice. *Pramāṇasamuccaya* and *Nyāyapraveśa* of Diṅnāga (500 A.D.), *Pramāṇavārttika kārikā* and *Nyāyabindu* of Dharmakīrtti (650 A.D.) with the commentary of Dharmottara are the most interesting of the Buddhist works on systematic logic[1]. The diverse points of difference between the Hindu, Jain and Buddhist logic require to be dealt with in a separate work on Indian logic and can hardly be treated within the compass of the present volume.

It is interesting to notice that between the *Vātsyāyana bhāṣya* and the Udyotakara's *Vārttika* no Hindu work on logic of importance seems to have been written: it appears that the science of logic in this period was in the hands of the Jains and the Buddhists; and it was Diṅnāga's criticism of Hindu Nyāya that roused Udyotakara to write the *Vārttika*. The Buddhist and the Jain method of treating logic separately from metaphysics as an independent study was not accepted by the Hindus till we come to Gaṅgeśa, and there is probably only one Hindu work of importance on Nyāya in the Buddhist style namely *Nyāyasāra* of Bhāsarvajña. Other older Hindu works generally treated of

[1] See *Indian Logic Medieval School*, by Dr S. C. Vidyābhūṣaṇa, for a bibliography of Jain and Buddhist Logic.

inference only along with metaphysical and other points of Nyāya interest[1].

The main doctrine of the Nyaya-Vaiśeṣika Philosophy[2].

The Nyāya-Vaiśeṣika having dismissed the doctrine of momentariness took a common-sense view of things, and held that things remain permanent until suitable collocations so arrange themselves that the thing can be destroyed. Thus the jug continues to remain a jug unless or until it is broken to pieces by the stroke of a stick. Things exist not because they can produce an impression on us, or serve my purposes either directly or through knowledge, as the Buddhists suppose, but because existence is one of their characteristics. If I or you or any other perceiver did not exist, the things would continue to exist all the same. Whether they produce any effect on us or on their surrounding environments is immaterial. Existence is the most general characteristic of things, and it is on account of this that things are testified by experience to be existing.

As the Nyāya-Vaiśeṣikas depended solely on experience and on valid reasons, they dismissed the Sāṃkhya cosmology, but accepted the atomic doctrine of the four elements (*bhūtas*), earth (*kṣiti*), water (*ap*), fire (*tejas*), and air (*marut*). These atoms are eternal; the fifth substance (*ākāsa*) is all pervasive and eternal. It is regarded as the cause of propagating sound; though all-pervading and thus in touch with the ears of all persons, it manifests sound only in the ear-drum, as it is only there that it shows itself as a sense-organ and manifests such sounds as the man deserves to hear by reason of his merit and demerit. Thus a deaf man though he has the ākāśa as his sense of hearing, cannot hear on account of his demerit which impedes the faculty of that sense organ[3]. In addition to these they admitted the existence of time (*kāla*) as extending from the past through the present to the

[1] Almost all the books on Nyāya and Vaiśeṣika referred to have been consulted in the writing of this chapter. Those who want to be acquainted with a fuller bibliography of the new school of logic should refer to the paper called "The History of Navya Nyāya in Bengal," by Mr Cakravarttī in *J. A. S. B.* 1915.

[2] I have treated Nyāya and Vaiśeṣika as the same system. Whatever may have been their original differences, they are regarded since about 600 A.D. as being in complete agreement except in some minor points. The views of one system are often supplemented by those of the other. The original character of the two systems has already been treated.

[3] See *Nyāyakandalī*, pp. 59–64.

endless futurity before us. Had there been no time we could have no knowledge of it and there would be nothing to account for our time-notions associated with all changes. The Sāṃkhya did not admit the existence of any real time; to them the unit of kāla is regarded as the time taken by an atom to traverse its own unit of space. It has no existence separate from the atoms and their movements. The appearance of kāla as a separate entity is a creation of our buddhi (*buddhinirmāṇa*) as it represents the order or mode in which the buddhi records its perceptions. But kāla in Nyaya-Vaiśeṣika is regarded as a substance existing by itself. In accordance with the changes of things it reveals itself as past, present, and future. Sāṃkhya regarded it as past, present, and future, as being the modes of the constitution of the things in its different manifesting stages of evolution (*adhvan*). The astronomers regarded it as being due to the motion of the planets. These must all be contrasted with the Nyāya-Vaiśeṣika conception of kāla which is regarded as an all-pervading, partless substance which appears as many in association with the changes related to it[1].

The seventh substance is relative space (*dik*). It is that substance by virtue of which things are perceived as being on the right, left, east, west, upwards and downwards; kāla like dik is also one. But yet tradition has given us varieties of it in the eight directions and in the upper and lower[2]. The eighth substance is the soul (*ātman*) which is all-pervading. There are separate ātmans for each person; the qualities of knowledge, feelings of pleasure and pain, desire, etc. belong to *ātman*. Manas (mind) is the ninth substance. It is atomic in size and the vehicle of memory; all affections of the soul such as knowing, feeling, and willing, are generated by the connection of manas with soul, the senses and the objects. It is the intermediate link which connects the soul with the senses, and thereby produces the affections of knowledge, feeling, or willing. With each single connection of soul with manas we have a separate affection of the soul, and thus our intellectual experience is conducted in a series, one coming after another and not simultaneously. Over and above all these we have Īśvara. The definition

[1] See *Nyāyakandalī*, pp. 64–66, and *Nyāyamañjarī*, pp. 136–139. The *Vaiśeṣika sūtras* regarded time as the cause of things which suffer change but denied it of things which are eternal.

[2] See *Nyāyakandalī*, pp. 66–69, and *Nyāyamañjarī*, p. 140.

of substance consists in this, that it is independent by itself, whereas the other things such as quality (*guṇa*), action (*karma*), sameness or generality (*sāmānya*), speciality or specific individuality (*viśeṣa*) and the relation of inherence (*samavāya*) cannot show themselves without the help of substance (*dravya*). Dravya is thus the place of rest (*āśraya*) on which all the others depend (*āśṛta*). Dravya, guṇa, karma, sāmānya, viśeṣa, and samavāya are the six original entities of which all things in the world are made up[1]. When a man through some special merit, by the cultivation of reason and a thorough knowledge of the fallacies and pitfalls in the way of right thinking, comes to know the respective characteristics and differences of the above entities, he ceases to have any passions and to work in accordance with their promptings and attains a conviction of the nature of self, and is liberated[2]. The Nyāya-Vaiśeṣika is a pluralistic system which neither tries to reduce the diversity of experience to any universal principle, nor dismisses patent facts of experience on the strength of the demands of the logical coherence of mere abstract thought. The entities it admits are taken directly from experience. The underlying principle is that at the root of each kind of perception there must be something to which the perception is due. It classified the percepts and concepts of experience into several ultimate types or categories (*padārtha*), and held that the notion of each type was due to the presence of that entity. These types are six in number—dravya, guṇa, etc. If we take a percept "I see a red book," the book appears to be an independent entity on which rests the concept of "redness" and "oneness," and we thus call the book a substance (*dravya*); dravya is thus defined as that which has the characteristic of a dravya (*dravyatva*). So also guṇa and karma. In the subdivision of different kinds of dravya also the same principle of classification is followed. In contrasting it with Sāṃkhya or Buddhism we see that for each unit of sensation (say

[1] *Abhāva* (negation) as dependent on bhāva (position) is mentioned in the *Vaiśeṣika sūtras*. Later Nyāya writers such as Udayana include *abhāva* as a separate category, but Śrīdhara a contemporary of Udayana rightly remarks that abhāva was not counted by Praśastapāda as it was dependent on bhāva—"*abhāvasya pṛthaganupadeśaḥ bhāvapāratantryāt na tvabhāvāt.*" *Nyāyakandalī*, p. 6, and *Lakṣaṇāvalī*, p. 2.

[2] "*Tattvato jñāteṣu bāhyādhyātmikeṣu viṣayeṣu doṣadarśanāt viraktasya samīhānivṛttau ātmajñasya tadarthāni karmāṇyakurvataḥ tatparityāgasādhanāni śrutismṛtyuditāni asaṅkalpitaphalāni upādadānasya ātmajñānamabhyasyataḥ prakṛṣṭanivarttakadharmopacaye sati paripakvātmajñānasyātyantikaśarīraviyogasya bhāvāt.*" *Ibid.* p. 7.

whiteness) the latter would admit a corresponding real, but Nyāya-Vaiśeṣika would collect "all whiteness" under the name of "the quality of white colour" which the atom possessed[1]. They only regarded as a separate entity what represented an ultimate mode of thought. They did not enquire whether such notions could be regarded as the modification of some other notion or not; but whenever they found that there were some experiences which were similar and universal, they classed them as separate entities or categories.

The six Padārthas: Dravya, Guṇa, Karma, Sāmānya, Viśeṣa, Samavāya.

Of the six classes of entities or categories (*padārtha*) we have already given some account of dravya[2]. Let us now turn to the others. Of the qualities (*guṇa*) the first one called *rūpa* (colour) is that which can be apprehended by the eye alone and not by any other sense. The colours are white, blue, yellow, red, green, brown and variegated (*citra*). Colours are found only in kṣiti, ap and tejas. The colours of ap and tejas are permanent (*nitya*), but the colour of kṣiti changes when heat is applied, and this, Śrīdhara holds, is due to the fact that heat changes the atomic structure of kṣiti (earth) and thus the old constitution of the substance being destroyed, its old colour is also destroyed, and a new one is generated. Rūpa is the general name for the specific individual colours. There is the genus *rūpatva* (colourness), and the rūpa guṇa (quality) is that on which rests this genus; rūpa is not itself a genus and can be apprehended by the eye.

The second is *rasa* (taste), that quality of things which can be apprehended only by the tongue; these are sweet, sour, pungent (*kaṭu*), astringent (*kaṣāya*) and bitter (*tikta*). Only kṣiti and ap have taste. The natural taste of ap is sweetness. Rasa like rūpa also denotes the genus rasatva, and rasa as quality must be distinguished from rasa as genus, though both of them are apprehended by the tongue.

The third is *gandha* (odour), that quality which can be apprehended by the nose alone. It belongs to kṣiti alone. Water

[1] The reference is to Sautrāntika Buddhism, "*yo yo viruddhādhyāsavān nāsāvekaḥ.*" See Paṇḍitāśoka's *Avayavinirākaraṇa*, *Six Buddhist Nyāya tracts*.

[2] The word "*padārtha*" literally means denotations of words.

or air is apprehended as having odour on account of the presence of earth materials.

The fourth is *sparśa* (touch), that quality which can be apprehended only by the skin. There are three kinds of touch, cold, hot, neither hot nor cold. Sparśa belongs to kṣiti; ap, tejas, and vāyu. The fifth *śabda* (sound) is an attribute of ākāśa. Had there been no ākāśa there would have been no sound.

The sixth is saṃkhyā (number), that entity of quality belonging to things by virtue of which we can count them as one, two, three, etc. The conception of numbers two, three, etc. is due to a relative oscillatory state of the mind (*apekṣābuddhi*); thus when there are two jugs before my eyes, I have the notion—This is one jug and that is another jug. This is called apekṣābuddhi; then in the two jugs there arises the quality of twoness (*dvitva*) and then an indeterminate perception (*nirvikalpa-dvitva-guṇa*) of dvitva in us and then the determinate perceptions that there are the two jugs. The conceptions of other numbers as well as of many arise in a similar manner[1].

The seventh is *parimiti* (measure), that entity of quality in things by virtue of which we perceive them as great or small and speak of them as such. The measure of the partless atoms is called *parimaṇḍala parimāṇa*; it is eternal, and it cannot generate the measure of any other thing. Its measure is its own absolutely; when two atoms generate a dyad (*dvyaṇuka*) it is not the measure of the atom that generates the aṇu (atomic) and the *hrasva* (small) measure of the dyad molecule (*dvyaṇuka*), for then the size (*parimāṇa*) of it would have been still smaller than the measure of the atom (*parimaṇḍala*), whereas the measure of the dyaṇuka is of a different kind, namely the small (*hrasva*)[2]. Of course two atoms generate a dyad, but then the number (saṃkhyā) of the atom should be regarded as bringing forth a new kind of measure, namely the small (*hrasva*) measure in the dyads. So again when three dyads (dyaṇuka) compose a tryaṇuka the number and not the measure "small"

[1] This is distinctively a Vaiśeṣika view introduced by Praśastapāda. Nyāya seems to be silent on this matter. See Śaṅkara Miśra's *Upaskāra*, VII. ii. 8.

[2] It should be noted that the atomic measure appears in two forms as eternal as in "paramāṇus" and non-eternal as in the dvyaṇuka. The parimaṇḍala parimāṇa is thus a variety of aṇuparimāṇa. The aṇuparimāṇa and the hrasvaparimāṇa represent the two dimensions of the measure of dvyaṇukas as mahat and dīrgha are with reference to tryaṇukas. See *Nyāyakandalī*, p. 133.

(*hrasva*) of the dyad is the cause of the measure "great" (*mahat*) of the tryaṇuka. But when we come to the region of these gross tryaṇukas we find that the "great" measure of the tryaṇukas is the cause of the measure of other grosser bodies composed by them. For as many tryaṇukas constitute a gross body, so much bigger does the thing become. Thus the cumulation of the tryaṇukas of mahat parimāṇa makes things of still more mahat parimāṇa. The measure of tryaṇukas is not only regarded as mahat but also as dīrgha (long) and this dīrgha parimāṇa has to be admitted as coexisting with mahat parimāṇa but not identical, for things not only appear as great but also as long (*dīrgha*). Here we find that the accumulation of tryaṇukas means the accumulation of "great" (*mahat*) and "long" (*dīrgha*) parimāṇa, and hence the thing generated happens to possess a measure which is greater and longer than the individual atoms which composed them. Now the hrasva parimāṇa of the dyads is not regarded as having a lower degree of greatness or length but as a separate and distinct type of measure which is called small (*hrasva*). As accumulation of grossness, greatness or length, generates still more greatness, grossness and length in its effect, so an accumulation of the hrasva (small) parimāṇa ought to generate still more hrasva parimāṇa, and we should expect that if the hrasva measure of the dyads was the cause of the measure of the tryaṇukas, the tryaṇukas should be even smaller than the dyaṇukas. So also if the atomic and circular (*parimaṇḍala*) size of the atoms is regarded as generating by their measure the measure of the dyaṇukas, then the measure of the dyaṇukas ought to be more atomic than the atoms. The atomic, small, and great measures should not be regarded as representing successively bigger measures produced by the mere cumulation of measures, but each should be regarded as a measure absolutely distinct, different from or foreign to the other measure. It is therefore held that if grossness in the cause generates still more greatness in the effect, the smallness and the parimaṇḍala measure of the dyads and atoms ought to generate still more smallness and subtleness in their effect. But since the dyads and the tryaṇuka molecules are seen to be constituted of atoms and dyads respectively, and yet are not found to share the measure of their causes, it is to be argued that the measures of the atoms and dyads do not generate the measure of their effects, but it is their *number* which is the cause of the measure of the latter. This explains aṇuparimāṇa, hrasva parimāṇa, mahat parimāṇa, and dīrgha parimāṇa. The parimāṇa of ākāśa, kāla, dik and ātman which are regarded as all-pervasive, is said to be paramamahat (absolutely large). The parimāṇas of the atoms, ākāśa, kāla, dik, manas, and ātman are regarded as eternal (*nitya*). All other kinds of parimāṇas as belonging to non-eternal things are regarded as non-eternal.

The eighth is *pṛthaktva* (mutual difference or separateness of things), that entity or quality in things by virtue of which things appear as different (e.g. this is different from that). Difference is perceived by us as a positive notion and not as a mere negation such as this jug is not this pot.

The ninth is *saṃyoga* (connection), that entity of guṇa by virtue of which things appear to us as connected.

The tenth is *vibhāga* (separation), that entity of guṇa which destroys the connection or contact of things.

The eleventh and twelfth guṇas, *paratva* and *aparatva*, give rise in us to the perceptions of long time and short time, remote and near.

The other guṇas such as *buddhi* (knowledge), *sukha* (happiness), *duḥkha* (sorrow), *icchā* (will), *dveṣa* (antipathy or hatred) and *yatna* (effort) can occur only with reference to soul.

The characteristic of *gurutva* (heaviness) is that by virtue of which things fall to the ground. The guṇa of *sneha* (oiliness) belongs to water. The guṇa of *saṃskāra* is of three kinds, (1) *vega* (velocity) which keeps a thing moving in different directions, (2) *sthiti-sthāpaka* (elasticity) on account of which a gross thing tries to get back its old state even though disturbed, (3) *bhāvanā* is that quality of ātman by which things are constantly practised or by which things experienced are remembered and recognized[1]. *Dharma* is the quality the presence of which enables the soul to enjoy happiness or to attain salvation[2]. *Adharma* is

[1] Praśastapāda says that bhāvanā is a special characteristic of the soul, contrary to intoxication, sorrow and knowledge, by which things seen, heard and felt are remembered and recognized. Through unexpectedness (as the sight of a camel for a man of South India), repetition (as in studies, art etc.) and intensity of interest, the saṃskāra becomes particularly strong. See *Nyāyakandalī*, p. 267. Kaṇāda however is silent on these points. He only says that by a special kind of contact of the mind with soul and also by the saṃskāra, memory (smṛti) is produced (IX. 2. 6).

[2] Praśastapāda speaks of *dharma* (merit) as being a quality of the soul. Thereupon Śrīdhara points out that this view does not admit that dharma is a power of karma (*na karmasāmarthyam*). Sacrifice etc. cannot be dharma for these actions being momentary

the opposite quality, the presence of which in the soul leads a man to suffer. *Adṛṣṭa* or destiny is that unknown quality of things and of the soul which brings about the cosmic order, and arranges it for the experience of the souls in accordance with their merits or demerits.

Karma means movement; it is the third thing which must be held to be as irreducible a reality as dravya or guṇa. There are five kinds of movement, (1) upward, (2) downward, (3) contraction, (4) expansion, (5) movement in general. All kinds of karmas rest on substances just as the guṇas do, and cause the things to which they belong to move.

Sāmānya is the fourth category. It means the genus, or aspect of generality or sameness that we notice in things. Thus in spite of the difference of colour between one cow and another, both of them are found to have such a sameness that we call them cows. In spite of all diversity in all objects around us, they are all perceived as *sat* or existing. This *sat* or existence is thus a sameness, which is found to exist in all the three things, dravya, guṇa, and karma. This sameness is called *sāmānya* or *jāti*, and it is regarded as a separate thing which rests on dravya, guṇa, or karma. This highest genus *sattā* (being) is called *parajāti* (highest universal), the other intermediate jātis are called *aparajāti* (lower universals), such as the genus of dravya, of karma, or of guṇa, or still more intermediate jātis such as *gotvajāti* (the genus cow), *nīlatvajāti* (the genus blue). The intermediate jātis or genera sometimes appear to have a special aspect as a species, such as *paśutva* (animal jāti) and *gotva* (the cow jāti); here however gotva appears as a species, yet it is in reality nothing but a jāti. The aspect as species has no separate existence. It is jāti which from one aspect appears as genus and from another as species.

they cannot generate the effects which are only to be reaped at a future time. If the action is destroyed its power (*sāmarthya*) cannot last. So dharma is to be admitted as a quality generated in the self by certain courses of conduct which produce happiness for him when helped by certain other conditions of time, place, etc. Faith (*śraddhā*), non-injury, doing good to all beings, truthfulness, non-stealing, sex-control, sincerity, control of anger, ablutions, taking of pure food, devotion to particular gods, fasting, strict adherence to scriptural duties, and the performance of duties assigned to each caste and stage of life, are enumerated by Praśastapāda as producing dharma. The person who strictly adheres to these duties and the *yamas* and *niyamas* (cf. Patañjali's Yoga) and attains Yoga by a meditation on the six padārthas attains a dharma which brings liberation (*mokṣa*). Śrīdhara refers to the Sāṃkhya-Yoga account of the method of attaining salvation (*Nyāyakandalī*, pp. 272–280). See also Vallabha's *Nyāyalīlāvatī*, pp. 74–75. (Bombay, 1915.)

This jāti or *sāmānya* thus must be regarded as having a separate independent reality though it is existent in dravya, guṇa and karma. The Buddhists denied the existence of any independent reality of sāmānya, but said that the sameness as cow was really but the negation of all non-cows (*apoha*). The perception of cow realizes the negation of all non-cows and this is represented in consciousness as the sameness as cow. He who should regard this sameness to be a separate and independent reality perceived in experience might also discover two horns on his own head[1]. The Nyāya-Vaiśeṣika said that negation of non-cows is a negative perception, whereas the sameness perceived as cow is a positive perception, which cannot be explained by the aforesaid negation theory of the Buddhists. Sāmānya has thus to be admitted to have a separate reality. All perception as sameness of a thing is due to the presence of this thing in that object[1]. This jāti is eternal or non-destructible; for even with the destruction of individuals comprehended within the jāti, the latter is not destroyed[2].

Through *viśeṣa* things are perceived as diverse. No single sensation that we receive from the external world probably agrees with any other sensation, and this difference must be due to the existence of some specific differences amongst the atoms themselves. The specific difference existing in the atoms, emancipated souls and minds must be regarded as eternally existing, and it

[1] The Buddhist Paṇḍitāśoka says that there is no single thing running through different individuals (e.g. cooks) by virtue of which the sāmānya could be established. For if it did exist then we could have known it simply by seeing any cook without any reference to his action of cooking by virtue of which the notion of generality is formed. If there is a similarity between the action of cooks that cannot establish jāti in the cooks, for the similarity applies to other things, viz. the action of the cooks. If the specific individualities of a cow should require one common factor to hold them together, then these should require another and that another, and we have a regressus ad infinitum. Whatever being perceptible is not perceived is non-existent (*yadyadupalabdhilakṣaṇaprāptam sannopalabhyate tattadasat*). Sāmānya is such, therefore sāmānya is non-existent. No sāmānya can be admitted to exist as an entity. But it is only as a result of the impressions of past experiences of existence and non-existence that this notion is formed and transferred erroneously to external objects. Apart from this no sāmānya can be pointed out as being externally perceptible—*Sāmānyadūṣaṇadikprasāritā*—in *Six Buddhist Nyāya Tracts*. The Vedānta also does not think that either by perception or by inference we can know jāti as a separate substance. So it discards jāti. See *Vedāntaparibhāṣā*, *Śikhāmaṇi* and *Maṇiprabhā*, pp. 69–71. See also Śrīharṣa's *Khaṇḍanakhaṇḍakhādya*, pp. 1079–1086.

[2] Similarity (*sādṛśya*) is not regarded as a separate category, for it is defined as identity in difference (*tadbhinnatve sati tadgatabhūyodharmavattvam*).

is on account of its presence that atoms appear as different to the yogins who can perceive them.

Samavāya, the inseparable relation of inherence, is a relation by virtue of which two different things such as substance and attribute, substance and karma, substance and sāmānya, kāraṇa (cause) and kārya (effect), atoms and viśeṣa, appear so unified that they represent one whole, or one identical inseparable reality. This peculiar relation of inseparable inherence is the cause why substance, action, and attribute, cause and effect, and jāti in substance and attribute appear as indissolubly connected as if they are one and the same thing. Saṃyoga or contact may take place between two things of the same nature which exist as disconnected and may later on be connected (*yutasiddha*), such as when I put my pen on the table. The pen and the table are both substances and were disconnected; the saṃyoga relation is the guṇa by virtue of which they appear to be connected for a while. Samavāya however makes absolutely different things such as dravya and guṇa and karma or kāraṇa and kārya (clay and jug) appear as one inseparable whole (*ayutasiddha*). This relation is thus a separate and independent category. This is not regarded as many like saṃyogas (contact) but as one and eternal because it has no cause. This or that object (e.g. jug) may be destroyed but the samavāya relation which was never brought into being by anybody always remains[1].

These six things are called the six padārthas or independent realities experienced in perception and expressed in language.

The Theory of Causation.

The Nyāya-Vaiśeṣika in most of its speculations took that view of things which finds expression in our language, and which we tacitly assume as true in all our ordinary experience. Thus

[1] The Vedānta does not admit the existence of the relation of samavāya as subsisting between two different entities (e.g. substance and qualities). Thus Śaṅkara says (*Brahma-sūtrabhāṣya* II. ii. 13) that if a samavāya relation is to be admitted to connect two different things, then another samavāya would be necessary to connect it with either of the two entities that it intended to connect, and that another, and so there will be a vicious infinite (*anavasthā*). Nyāya, however, would not regard it as vicious at all. It is well to remember that the Indian systems acknowledge two kinds of anavasthā—*prāmāṇikī* (valid infinite, as in case of the question of the seed and the tree, or of the avidyā and the passions), and another *aprāmāṇikī anavasthā* (vicious infinite) as when the admission of anything involves an infinite chain before it can be completed.

they admitted dravya, guṇa, karma and sāmānya. Viśeṣa they had to admit as the ultimate peculiarities of atoms, for they did not admit that things were continually changing their qualities, and that everything could be produced out of everything by a change of the collocation or arrangement of the constituting atoms. In the production of the effect too they did not admit that the effect was potentially pre-existent in the cause. They held that the material cause (e.g. clay) had some power within it, and the accessory and other instrumental causes (such as the stick, the wheel etc.) had other powers; the collocation of these two destroyed the cause, and produced the effect which was not existent before but was newly produced. This is what is called the doctrine of *asatkāryavāda*. This is just the opposite of the Sāṃkhya axiom, that what is existent cannot be destroyed (*nābhāvo vidyate sataḥ*) and that the non-existent could never be produced (*nāsato vidyate bhāvaḥ*). The objection to this view is that if what is non-existent is produced, then even such impossible things as the hare's horn could also be produced. The Nyāya-Vaiśeṣika answer is that the view is not that anything that is non-existent can be produced, but that which is produced was non-existent[1].

It is held by Mīmāṃsā that an unseen power resides in the cause which produces the effect. To this Nyāya objects that this is neither a matter of observation nor of legitimate hypothesis, for there is no reason to suppose that there is any transcendental operation in causal movement as this can be satisfactorily explained by molecular movement (*parispanda*). There is nothing except the invariable time relation (antecedence and sequence) between the cause and the effect, but the mere invariableness of an antecedent does not suffice to make it the cause of what succeeds; it must be an unconditional antecedent as well (*anyathāsiddhiśūnyasya niyatāpūrvavarttitā*). Unconditionality and invariability are indispensable for *kāryakāraṇa-bhāva* or cause and effect relation. For example, the non-essential or adventitious accompaniments of an invariable antecedent may also be invariable antecedents; but they are not unconditional, only collateral or indirect. In other words their antecedence is conditional upon something else (*na svātantryeṇa*). The potter's stick is an unconditional invariable antecedent of the jar; but the colour

[1] *Nyāyamañjari*, p. 494.

of a stick or its texture or size, or any other accompaniment or accident which does not contribute to the work done, is not an unconditional antecedent, and must not therefore be regarded as a cause. Similarly the co-effects of the invariable antecedents or what enters into the production of their co-effects may themselves be invariable antecedents; but they are not unconditional, being themselves conditioned by those of the antecedents of which they are effects. For example, the sound produced by the stick or by the potter's wheel invariably precedes the jar but it is a co-effect; and ākāśa (ether) as the substrate and vāyu (air) as the vehicle of the sound enter into the production of this co-effect, but these are no unconditional antecedents, and must therefore be rejected in an enumeration of conditions or causes of the jar. The conditions of the conditions should also be rejected; the invariable antecedent of the potter (who is an invariable antecedent of the jar), the potter's father, does not stand in a causal relation to the potter's handiwork. In fact the antecedence must not only be unconditionally invariable, but must also be immediate. Finally all seemingly invariable antecedents which may be dispensed with or left out are not unconditional and cannot therefore be regarded as causal conditions. Thus Dr Seal in describing it rightly remarks, "In the end, the discrimination of what is necessary to complete the sum of causes from what is dependent, collateral, secondary, superfluous, or inert (i.e. of the relevant from the irrelevant factors), must depend on the test of expenditure of energy This test the Nyāya would accept only in the sense of an operation analysable into molar or molecular motion (*parispanda eva bhautiko vyāpāraḥ karotyarthaḥ atīndriyastu vyāparo nāsti.* Jayanta's Mañjarī Āhnika I), but would emphatically reject, if it is advanced in support of the notion of a mysterious causal power or efficiency (*śakti*)[1]." With Nyāya all energy is necessarily kinetic. This is a peculiarity of Nyāya—its insisting that the effect is only the sum or resultant of the operations of the different causal conditions—that these operations are of the nature of motion or kinetic, in other words it firmly holds to the view that causation is a case of expenditure of energy, i.e. a redistribution of motion, but at the same time absolutely repudiates the Sāṃkhya conception of power or productive

[1] Dr P. C. Ray's *Hindu Chemistry*, 1909, pp. 249–250.

efficiency as metaphysical or transcendental (*atīndriya*) and finds nothing in the cause other than unconditional invariable complements of operative conditions (*kāraṇa-sāmagrī*), and nothing in the effect other than the consequent phenomenon which results from the joint operations of the antecedent conditions[1]. Certain general conditions such as relative space (*dik*), time (*kāla*), the will of Īśvara, destiny (*adṛṣṭa*) are regarded as the common cause of all effects (*kāryatva-prayojaka*). Those are called *sādhāraṇa-kāraṇa* (common cause) as distinguished from the specific causes which determine the specific effects which are called *asādhāraṇa kāraṇa*. It may not be out of place here to notice that Nyāya while repudiating transcendental power (*śakti*) in the mechanism of nature and natural causation, does not deny the existence of metaphysical conditions like merit (*dharma*), which constitutes a system of moral ends that fulfil themselves through the mechanical systems and order of nature.

The causal relation then like the relation of genus to species, is a natural relation of concomitance, which can be ascertained only by the uniform and uninterrupted experience of agreement in presence and agreement in absence, and not by a deduction from a certain *a priori* principle like that of causality or identity of essence[2].

The material cause such as the clay is technically called the *samavāyi-kāraṇa* of the jug. *Samavāya* means as we have seen an intimate, inseparable relation of inherence. A kāraṇa is called *samavāyi* when its materials are found inseparably connected with the materials of the effect. Asamavāyi-kāraṇa is that which produces its characteristics in the effect through the medium of the samavāyi or material cause, e.g. the clay is not the cause of the colour of the jug but the colour of the clay is the cause of the colour of the jug. The colour of the clay which exists in the clay in inseparable relation is the cause of the colour of the jug. This colour of the clay is thus called the asamavāyi cause of the jug. Any quality (*guṇa*) or movement which existing in the samavāya cause in the samavāya relation determines the characteristics of the effect is called the asamavāyi-kāraṇa. The instrumental

[1] Dr P. C. Ray's *Hindu Chemistry*, 1909, pp. 249–250.

[2] See for this portion Dr B. N. Seal's *Positive Sciences of the Ancient Hindus*, pp. 263–266. *Sarvadarśanasaṃgraha* on Buddhism. *Nyāyamañjarī*, *Bhāṣā-pariccheda*, with *Muktāvalī* and *Dinakarī*, and *Tarkasaṃgraha*. The doctrine of Anyathāsiddhi was systematically developed from the time of Gaṅgeśa.

nimitta and accessory (*sahakāri*) causes are those which help the material cause to produce the effect. Thus the potter, the wheel and the stick may be regarded as the nimitta and the sahakāri causes of the effect.

We know that the Nyāya-Vaiśeṣika regards the effect as non-existent, before the operation of the cause in producing it, but it holds that the guṇas in the cause are the causes of the guṇas in the effect, e.g. the black colour of the clay is the cause of the black colour of the effect, except in cases where heat comes as an extraneous cause to generate other qualities; thus when a clay jug is burnt, on account of the heat we get red colour, though the colour of the original clay and the jug was black. Another important exception is to be found in the case of the production of the parimāṇas of dvyaṇukas and trasareṇus which are not produced by the parimāṇas of an aṇu or a dyaṇuka, but by their number as we have already seen.

Dissolution (Pralaya) and Creation (Sṛṣṭi).

The docrine of pralaya is accepted by all the Hindu systems except the Mīmāṃsā[1]. According to the Nyāya-Vaiśeṣika view Īśvara wishing to give some respite or rest to all living beings desires to bring about dissolution (*saṃhārecchо bhavati*). Simultaneously with it the adṛṣṭa force residing in all the souls and forming bodies, senses, and the gross elements, ceases to act (*śakti-pratibandha*). As a result of this no further bodies, senses, or other products come into being. Then for the bringing about of the dissolution of all produced things (by the desire of Īśvara) the separation of the atoms commences and thus all combinations as bodies or senses are disintegrated; so all earth is reduced to the disintegrated atomic state, then all ap, then all tejas and then all vāyu. These disintegrated atoms and the souls associated with dharma, adharma and past impressions (*saṃskāra*) remain suspended in their own inanimate condition. For we know that souls in their natural condition are lifeless and knowledgeless, non-intelligent entities. It is only when these are connected with bodies that they possess knowledge through the activity of manas. In the state of pralaya owing to the adṛṣṭa of souls the

[1] The doctrine of pralaya and sṛṣṭi is found only in later Nyāya-Vaiśeṣika works, but the sūtras of both the systems seem to be silent on the matter.

atoms do not conglomerate. It is not an act of cruelty on the part of Īśvara that he brings about dissolution, for he does it to give some rest to the sufferings of the living beings.

At the time of creation, Īśvara wishes to create and this desire of Īśvara works in all the souls as adṛṣṭa. This one eternal desire of Īśvara under certain conditions of time (e.g. of pralaya) as accessory causes (*sahakāri*) helps the disintegration of atoms and at other times (e.g. that of creation) the constructive process of integration and unification of atoms for the world-creation. When it acts in a specific capacity in the diverse souls it is called adṛṣṭa. At the time of dissolution the creative function of this adṛṣṭa is suspended and at the time of creation it finds full play. At the time of creation action first begins in the vāyu atoms by the kinetic function of this adṛṣṭa, by the contact of the souls with the atoms. By such action the air atoms come in contact with one another and the dvyaṇukas are formed and then in a similar way the tryaṇukas are formed, and thus vāyu originates. After vāyu, the ap is formed by the conglomeration of water atoms, and then the tejas atoms conglomerate and then the earth atoms. When the four elements are thus conglomerated in the gross form, the god Brahmā and all the worlds are created by Īśvara and Brahmā is directed by Īśvara to do the rest of the work. Brahmā thus arranges for the enjoyment and suffering of the fruits of diverse kinds of karma, good or bad. Īśvara brings about this creation not for any selfish purpose but for the good of all beings. Even here sorrows have their place that they may lead men to turn from worldly attachment and try for the attainment of the highest good, mukti. Moreover Īśvara arranges for the enjoyment of pleasures and the suffering of pains according to the merits and demerits of men, just as in our ordinary experience we find that a master awards prizes or punishments according to good or bad deeds[1]. Many Nyāya books do not speak of the appointment of a Brahmā as deputy for supervision of the due disposal of the fruits of karma according to merit or demerit. It is also held that pralaya and creation were brought about in accordance with the karma of men, or that it may be due to a mere play (*līlā*) of Īśvara. Īśvara is one, for if there were many Īśvaras they might quarrel. The will of Īśvara not only brings about dissolution and creation,

[1] See *Nyāyakandalī*, pp. 48–54.

but also acts always among us in a general way, for without it our karmas could not ripen, and the consequent disposal of pleasures and sorrows to us and a corresponding change in the exterior world in the form of order or harmony could not happen. The exterior world is in perfect harmony with men's actions. Their merits and demerits and all its changes and modifications take place in accordance with merits and demerits. This desire (*icchā*) of Īśvara may thus be compared with the *icchā* of Īśvara as we find it in the Yoga system.

Proof of the Existence of Īśvara.

Sāṃkhya asserts that the teleology of the prakṛti is sufficient to explain all order and arrangement of the cosmos. The Mīmāṃsakas, the Cārvākas, the Buddhists and the Jains all deny the existence of Īśvara (God). Nyāya believes that Īśvara has fashioned this universe by his will out of the ever-existing atoms. For every effect (e.g. a jug) must have its cause. If this be so, then this world with all its order and arrangement must also be due to the agency of some cause, and this cause is Īśvara. This world is not momentary as the Buddhists suppose, but is permanent as atoms, is also an effect so far as it is a collocation of atoms and is made up of parts like all other individual objects (e.g. jug, etc.), which we call effects. The world being an effect like any other effect must have a cause like any other effect. The objection made against this view is that such effects as we ordinarily perceive may be said to have agents as their causes but this manifest world with mountains, rivers, oceans etc. is so utterly different in form from ordinary effects that we notice every day, that the law that every effect must have a cause cannot be said to hold good in the present case. The answer that Nyāya gives is that the concomitance between two things must be taken in its general aspect neglecting the specific peculiarities of each case of observed concomitance. Thus I had seen many cases of the concomitance of smoke with fire, and had thence formed the notion that "wherever there is smoke there is fire"; but if I had only observed small puffs of smoke and small fires, could I say that only small quantities of smoke could lead us to the inference of fire, and could I hold that therefore large volumes of smoke from the burning of a forest should not be sufficient reason for us to infer the existence of fire in the forest?

Thus our conclusion should not be that only smaller effects are preceded by their causes, but that all effects are invariably and unconditionally preceded by causes. This world therefore being an effect must be preceded by a cause, and this cause is Īśvara. This cause we cannot see, because Īśvara has no visible body, not because he does not exist. It is sometimes said that we see every day that shoots come out of seeds and they are not produced by any agent. To such an objection the Nyāya answer is that even they are created by God, for they are also effects. That we do not see any one to fashion them is not because there is no maker of them, but because the creator cannot be seen. If the objector could distinctly prove that there was no invisible maker shaping these shoots, then only could he point to it as a case of contradiction. But so long as this is not done it is still only a doubtful case of enquiry and it is therefore legitimate for us to infer that since all effects have a cause, the shoots as well as the manifest world being effects must have a cause. This cause is Īśvara. He has infinite knowledge and is all merciful. At the beginning of creation He created the Vedas. He is like our father who is always engaged in doing us good[1].

The Nyāya-Vaiśeṣika Physics.

The four kinds of atoms are earth, water, fire, and air atoms. These have mass, number, weight, fluidity (or hardness), viscosity (or its opposite), velocity, characteristic potential colour, taste, smell, or touch, not produced by the chemical operation of heat. Ākāśa (space) is absolutely inert and structure-less being only as the substratum of sound, which is supposed to travel wave-like in the manifesting medium of air. Atomic combination is only possible with the four elements. Atoms cannot exist in an uncombined condition in the creation stage; atmospheric air however consists of atoms in an uncombined state.

Two atoms combine to form a binary molecule (*dvyaṇuka*). Two, three, four, or five dvyaṇukas form themselves into grosser molecules of tryaṇuka, caturaṇuka, etc.[2] Though this was the generally current view, there was also another view as has been pointed out by Dr B. N. Seal in his *Positive Sciences of the Ancient Hindus*, that the "atoms have also an inherent tendency to unite," and that

[1] See Jayanta's *Nyāyamañjarī*, pp. 190–204, and Udayana's *Kusumāñjali* with *Prakāśa* and *Īśvarānumāna* of Raghunātha.

[2] *Kadācit tribhirārabhyate iti tryaṇukamityucyate, kadācit caturbhirārabhyate kadācit pañcabhiriti yatheṣṭaṃ kalpanā. Nyāyakandalī*, p. 32.

they do so in twos, threes, or fours, "either by the atoms falling into groups of threes, fours, etc. directly, or by the successive addition of one atom to each preceding aggregate[1]." Of course the atoms are regarded as possessed of an incessant vibratory motion. It must however be noted in this connection that behind this physical explanation of the union of atoms there is the adṛṣṭa, the will of Īśvara, which gives the direction of all such unions in harmony with the principle of a "moral government of the universe," so that only such things are produced as can be arranged for the due disposal of the effects of karma. "An elementary substance thus produced by primary atomic combination may however suffer qualitative changes under the influence of heat (*pākajotpatti*)." The impact of heat corpuscles decomposes a dvyaṇuka into the atoms and transforms the characters of the atoms determining them all in the same way. The heat particles continuing to impinge reunite the atoms so transformed to form binary or other molecules in different orders or arrangements, which account for the specific characters or qualities finally produced. The Vaiśeṣika holds that there is first a disintegration into simple atoms, then change of atomic qualities, and then the final re-combination, under the influence of heat. This doctrine is called the doctrine of *pīlupāka* (heating of atoms). Nyāya on the other hand thinks that no disintegration into atoms is necessary for change of qualities, but it is the molecules which assume new characters under the influence of heat. Heat thus according to Nyāya directly affects the characters of the molecules and changes their qualities without effecting a change in the atoms. Nyāya holds that the heat-corpuscles penetrate into the porous body of the object and thereby produce the change of colour. The object as a whole is not disintegrated into atoms and then reconstituted again, for such a procedure is never experienced by observation. This is called the doctrine of *piṭharapāka* (heating of molecules). This is one of the few points of difference between the later Nyāya and Vaiśeṣika systems[2].

Chemical compounds of atoms may take place between the

[1] Utpala's commentary on *Bṛhatsamhitā* I. 7.

[2] See Dr B. N. Seal in P. C. Ray's *Hindu Chemistry*, pp. 190–191, *Nyāyamañjarī*, p. 438, and Udyotakara's *Vārttika*. There is very little indication in the Nyāya and *Vaiśeṣika sūtras* that they had any of those differences indicated here. Though there are slight indications of these matters in the *Vaiśeṣika sūtras* (VII. 1), the *Nyāya sūtras* are almost silent upon the matter. A systematic development of the theory of creation and atomic combinations appear to have taken place after Vātsyāyana.

atoms of the same bhūta or of many bhūtas. According to the Nyāya view there are no differences in the atoms of the same bhūta, and all differences of quality and characteristics of the compound of the same bhūta are due only to diverse collocations of those atoms. Thus Udyotakara says (III. i. 4) that there is no difference between the atom of a barley seed and paddy seed, since these are all but atoms of earth. Under the continued impact of heat particles the atoms take new characters. It is heat and heat alone that can cause the transformations of colours, tastes etc. in the original bhūta atoms. The change of these physical characters depends on the colours etc. of the constituent substances in contact, on the intensity or degree of heat and also on the species of tejas corpuscles that impinge on the atoms. Heat breaks bodies in contact into atoms, transforms their qualities, and forms separate bodies with them.

Praśastapāda (the commentator of Vaiśeṣika) holds that in the higher compounds of the same bhūta the transformation takes place (under internal heat) in the constituent atoms of the compound molecules, atoms specially determined as the compound and not in the original atoms of the bhūta entering into the composition of the compound. Thus when milk is turned into curd, the transformation as curd takes place in the atoms determined as milk in the milk molecule, and it is not necessary that the milk molecule should be disintegrated into the atoms of the original bhūta of which the milk is a modification. The change as curd thus takes place in the milk atom, and the milk molecule has not to be disintegrated into kṣiti or ap atoms. So again in the fertilized ovum, the germ and the ovum substances, which in the Vaiśeṣika view are both isomeric modes of earth (with accompaniments of other bhūtas) are broken up into homogeneous earth atoms, and it is these that chemically combine under the animal heat and biomotor force vāyu to form the germ (*kalala*). But when the germ plasm develops, deriving its nutrition from the blood of the mother, the animal heat breaks up the molecules of the germ plasm into its constituent atoms, i.e. atoms specifically determined which by their grouping formed the germ plasm. These germ-plasm atoms chemically combine with the atoms of the food constituents and thus produce cells and tissues[1]. This atomic contact is called *ārambhaka-saṃyoga*.

[1] See Dr B. N. Seal's *Positive Sciences*, pp. 104–108, and *Nyāyakandalī*, pp. 33–34, "*Śarīrārambhe paramāṇava eva kāraṇam na śukra-śonitasannipātaḥ kriyāvibhāgā-*

In the case of poly-bhautik or bi-bhautik compounds there is another kind of contact called *upaṣṭambha.* Thus in the case of such compounds as oils, fats, and fruit juices, the earth atoms cannot combine with one another unless they are surrounded by the water atoms which congregate round the former, and by the infra-atomic forces thus set up the earth atoms take peculiar qualities under the impact of heat corpuscles. Other compounds are also possible where the ap, tejas, or the vāyu atoms form the inner radicle and earth atoms dynamically surround them (e.g. gold, which is the tejas atom with the earth atoms as the surrounding upaṣṭambhaka). Solutions (of earth substances in ap) are regarded as physical mixtures.

Udayana points out that the solar heat is the source of all the stores of heat required for chemical change. But there are differences in the modes of the action of heat; and the kind of contact with heat-corpuscles, or the kind of heat with chemical action which transforms colours, is supposed to differ from what transforms flavour or taste.

Heat and light rays are supposed to consist of indefinitely small particles which dart forth or radiate in all directions rectilineally with inconceivable velocity. Heat may penetrate through the interatomic space as in the case of the conduction of heat, as when water boils in a pot put on the fire; in cases of transparency light rays penetrate through the inter-atomic spaces with *parispanda* of the nature of deflection or refraction (*tiryag-gamana*). In other cases heat rays may impinge on the atoms and rebound back—which explains reflection. Lastly heat may strike the atoms in a peculiar way, so as to break up their grouping, transform the physico-chemical characters of the atoms, and again recombine them, all by means of continual impact with inconceivable velocity, an operation which explains all cases of chemical combination[1]. Govardhana a later Nyāya writer says that pāka means the combination of different kinds of heat. The heat that

dinyāyena tayorvināśe sati utpannapākajaiḥ paramāṇubhirārambhāt, na ca śukraśonita-paramāṇūnāṃ kaścidviśeṣaḥ pārthivatvāviśeṣāt....Pituḥ śukraṃ mātuḥ śonitaṃ tayos sannipātānantaraṃ jaṭharānalasambandhāt śukra-śonitārambhakeṣu paramāṇuṣu pūrvarūpādivināśe samāṇaguṇāntarotpattau dvyaṇukādikrameṇa kalalaśarīrotpattiḥ tatrāntaḥkaraṇapraveśo...tatra māturāhāraraso mātrayā saṃkrāmate, adṛṣṭavaśāttatra punarjaṭharānalasambandhāt kalalārambhakaparamāṇuṣu kriyāvibhāgādinyāyena kalalaśarīre naṣṭe samutpannapākajaiḥ kalalārambhakaparamāṇubhiradṛṣṭavaśād upajātakriyairāhāraparamāṇubhiḥ saha sambhūya śarīrāntaramārabhyate."

[1] See Dr Seal's *Positive Sciences of the Hindus.*

changes the colour of a fruit is different from that which generates or changes the taste. Even when the colour and taste remain the same a particular kind of heat may change the smell. When grass eaten by cows is broken up into atoms special kinds of heat-light rays change its old taste, colour, touch and smell into such forms as those that belong to milk[1].

In the Nyāya-Vaiśeṣika system all action of matter on matter is thus resolved into motion. Conscious activity (*prayatna*) is distinguished from all forms of motion as against the Sāṃkhya doctrine which considered everything other than puruṣa (intelligence) to arise in the course of cosmic evolution and therefore to be subject to vibratory motion.

The Origin of Knowledge (Pramāṇa).

The manner in which knowledge originates is one of the most favourite topics of discussion in Indian philosophy. We have already seen that Sāṃkhya-Yoga explained it by supposing that the buddhi (place of consciousness) assumed the form of the object of perception, and that the buddhi so transformed was then intelligized by the reflection of the pure intelligence or puruṣa. The Jains regarded the origin of any knowledge as being due to a withdrawal of a veil of karma which was covering the all-intelligence of the self.

Nyāya-Vaiśeṣika regarded all effects as being due to the assemblage of certain collocations which unconditionally, invariably, and immediately preceded these effects. That collocation (*sāmagrī*) which produced knowlege involved certain non-intelligent as well as intelligent elements and through their conjoint action uncontradicted and determinate knowledge was produced, and this collocation is thus called pramāṇa or the determining cause of the origin of knowledge[2]. None of the separate elements composing

[1] Govardhana's *Nyāyabodhinī* on *Tarkasaṃgraha*, pp. 9, 10.

[2] "*Avyabhicāriṇīmasandigdhārthopalabdhiṃ vidadhatī bodhābodhasvabhāvā sāmagrī pramāṇam.*" *Nyāyamañjarī*, p. 12. Udyotakara however defined "pramāṇa" as upalabdhihetu (cause of knowledge). This view does not go against Jayanta's view which I have followed, but it emphasizes the side of vyāpāra or movement of the senses, etc. by virtue of which the objects come in contact with them and knowledge is produced. Thus Vācaspati says: "*siddhamindriyādi, asiddhañca tatsannikarṣādi vyāpārayannutpādayan karaṇa eva caritārthaḥ karṇaṃ tvindriyādi tatsannikarṣādi vā nānyatra caritarthamiti sākṣādupalabdhāveva phale vyāprīyate.*" *Tātparyaṭīkā*, p. 15. Thus it is the action of the senses as pramāṇa which is the direct cause of the production of knowledge, but as this production could not have taken place without the

the causal collocation can be called the primary cause; it is only their joint collocation that can be said to determine the effect, for sometimes the absence of a single element composing the causal collocation is sufficient to stop the production of the effect. Of course the collocation or combination is not an entity separated from the collocated or combined things. But in any case it is the preceding collocations that combine to produce the effect jointly. These involve not only intellectual elements (e.g. indeterminate cognition as qualification (viśeṣaṇa) in determinate perceptions, the knowledge of liṅga in inference, the seeing of similar things in upamāna, the hearing of sound in śabda) but also the assemblage of such physical things (e.g. proximity of the object of perception, capacity of the sense, light, etc.), which are all indispensable for the origin of knowledge. The cognitive and physical elements all co-operate in the same plane, combine together and produce further determinate knowledge. It is this capacity of the collocations that is called pramāṇa.

Nyāya argues that in the Sāṃkhya view knowledge originates by the transcendent influence of puruṣa on a particular state of buddhi; this is quite unintelligible, for knowledge does not belong to buddhi as it is non-intelligent, though it contains within it the content and the form of the concept or the percept (knowledge). The puruṣa to whom the knowledge belongs, however, neither knows, nor feels, neither conceives nor perceives, as it always remains in its own transcendental purity. If the transcendental contact of the puruṣa with buddhi is but a mere semblance or appearance or illusion, then the Sāṃkhya has to admit that there is no real knowledge according to them. All knowledge is false. And since all knowledge is false, the Sāṃkhyists have precious little wherewith to explain the origin of right knowledge.

There are again some Buddhists who advocate the doctrine that simultaneously with the generation of an object there is the knowledge corresponding to it, and that corresponding to the rise of any knowledge there is the rise of the object of it. Neither is the knowledge generated by the object nor the object by the knowledge; but there is a sort of simultaneous parallelism. It is evident that this view does not explain why knowledge should

subject and the object, they also are to be regarded as causes in some sense. "*Pramātṛprameyayoḥ pramāṇe caritārthatvamacaritārthatvaṃ pramāṇasya tasmāt tadeva phalahetuḥ. Pramātṛprameye tu phaloddeśena pravṛtte iti taddhetū kathañcit.*" *Ibid. p.* 16.

express or manifest its object. If knowledge and the object are both but corresponding points in a parallel series, whence comes this correspondence? Why should knowledge illuminate the object. The doctrine of the Vijñāna vādins, that it is knowledge alone that shows itself both as knowledge and as its object, is also irrational, for how can knowledge divide itself as subject and object in such a manner that knowledge as object should require the knowledge as subject to illuminate it? If this be the case we might again expect that knowledge as knowledge should also require another knowledge to manifest it and this another, and so on *ad infinitum*. Again if pramāṇa be defined as *prāpaṇa* (capacity of being realized) then also it would not hold, for all things being momentary according to the Buddhists, the thing known cannot be realized, so there would be nothing which could be called pramāna. These views moreover do not explain the origin of knowledge. Knowledge is thus to be regarded as an effect like any other effect, and its origin or production occurs in the same way as any other effect, namely by the joint collocation of causes intellectual and physical[1]. There is no transcendent element involved in the production of knowledge, but it is a production on the same plane as that in which many physical phenomena are produced[2].

The four Pramāṇas of Nyāya.

We know that the Cārvākas admitted perception (*pratyakṣa*) alone as the valid source of knowledge. The Buddhists and the Vaiśeṣika admitted two sources, pratyakṣa and inference (*anumāna*). Sāṃkhya added *śabda* (testimony) as the third source;

[1] See *Nyāyamañjarī*, pp. 12–26.

[2] Discussing the question of the validity of knowledge Gaṅgeśa, a later naiyāyika of great fame, says that it is derived as a result of our inference from the correspondence of the perception of a thing with the activity which prompted us to realize it. That which leads us to successful activity is valid and the opposite invalid. When I am sure that if I work in accordance with the perception of an object I shall be successful, I call it valid knowledge. *Tattvacintāmaṇi*, K. Tarkavāgīśa's edition, *Prāmāṇyavāda*.

[3] The *Vaiśeṣika sūtras* tacitly admit the Vedas as a pramāṇa. The view that Vaiśeṣika only admitted two pramāṇas, perception and inference, is traditionally accepted, "*pratyakṣamekaṃcārvākāḥ kaṇādasugatau punaḥ anumānañca taccāpi*, etc." Praśastapāda divides all cognition (*buddhi*) as *vidyā* (right knowledge) and *avidyā* (ignorance). Under *avidyā* he counts *saṃśaya* (doubt or uncertainty), *viparyaya* (illusion or error), *anadhyavasāya* (want of definite knowledge, thus when a man who had never seen a mango, sees it for the first time, he wonders what it may be) and *svapna* (dream). Right knowledge (*vidyā*) is of four kinds, perception, inference, memory and the supernatural knowledge of the sages (*ārṣa*). Interpreting the *Vaiśeṣika sūtras* I. i. 3,

Nyāya adds a fourth, *upamāna* (analogy). The principle on which the four-fold division of pramāṇas depends is that the causal collocation which generates the knowledge as well as the nature or characteristic kind of knowledge in each of the four cases is different. The same thing which appears to us as the object of our perception, may become the object of inference or śabda (testimony), but the manner or mode of manifestation of knowledge being different in each case, and the manner or conditions producing knowledge being different in each case, it is to be admitted that inference and śabda are different pramāṇas, though they point to the same object indicated by the perception. Nyāya thus objects to the incorporation of śabda (testimony) or upamāna within inference, on the ground that since the mode of production of knowledge is different, these are to be held as different pramāṇas[1].

Perception (Pratyakṣa).

The naiyāyikas admitted only the five cognitive senses which they believed to be composed of one or other of the five elements. These senses could each come in contact with the special characteristic of that element of which they were composed. Thus the ear could perceive sound, because sound was the attribute of ākāśa, of which the auditory sense, the ear, was made up. The eye could send forth rays to receive the colour, etc., of things. Thus the cognitive senses can only manifest their specific objects by going over to them and thereby coming in contact with them. The conative senses (*vāk*, *pāṇi*, *pāda*, *pāyu*, and *upastha*) recognized in Sāṃkhya as separate senses are not recognized here as such for the functions of these so-called senses are discharged by the general motor functions of the body.

Perception is defined as that right knowledge generated by the contact of the senses with the object, devoid of doubt and error not associated with any other simultaneous sound cognition (such

VI. i. 1, and VI. i. 3, to mean that the validity of the Vedas depends upon the trustworthy character of their author, he does not consider scriptures as valid in themselves. Their validity is only derived by inference from the trustworthy character of their author. *Arthāpatti* (implication) and *anupalabdhi* (non-perception) are also classed as inference and *upamāna* (analogy) and *aitihya* (tradition) are regarded as being the same as faith in trustworthy persons and hence cases of inference.

1 *Sāmagrībhedāt phalabhedācca pramāṇabhedaḥ*
Anye eva hi sāmagrīphale pratyakṣaliṅgayoḥ
Anye eva ca sāmagrīphale śabdopamānayoḥ. *Nyāyamañjarī*, p. 33.

as the name of the object as heard from a person uttering it, just at the time when the object is seen) or name association, and determinate[1]. If when we see a cow, a man says here is a cow, the knowledge of the sound as associated with the percept cannot be counted as perception but as sound-knowledge (*śabda-pramāṇa*). That right knowledge which is generated directly by the contact of the senses with the object is said to be the product of the perceptual process. Perception may be divided as indeterminate (*nirvikalpa*) and (*savikalpa*) determinate. Indeterminate perception is that in which the thing is taken at the very first moment of perception in which it appears without any association with name. Determinate perception takes place after the indeterminate stage is just passed; it reveals things as being endowed with all characteristics and qualities and names just as we find in all our concrete experience. Indeterminate perception reveals the things with their characteristics and universals, but at this stage there being no association of name it is more or less indistinct. When once the names are connected with the percept it forms the determinate perception of a thing called savikalpa-pratyakṣa. If at the time of having the perception of a thing of which the name is not known to me anybody utters its name then the hearing of that should be regarded as a separate auditory name perception. Only that product is said to constitute nirvikalpa perception which results from the perceiving process of the contact of the senses with the object. Of this nirvikalpa (indeterminate) perception it is held by the later naiyāyikas that we are not conscious of it directly, but yet it has to be admitted as a necessary first stage without which the determinate consciousness could not arise. The indeterminate perception is regarded as the first stage in the process of perception. At the second stage it joins the other conditions of perception in producing the determinate perception. The contact of the sense with the object is regarded as being of six kinds: (1) contact with the dravya (thing) called saṃyoga, (2) contact with the guṇas (qualities) through the thing (*saṃyukta-samavāya*) in which they inhere in samavāya (inseparable) relation, (3) contact with the guṇas (such as colour etc.) in the generic character as universals of those qualities, e.g. colourness (rūpatva), which inhere in the guṇas in the samavāya relation.

[1] Gaṅgeśa, a later naiyāyika of great reputation, describes perception as immediate awareness (*pratyakṣasya sākṣātkāritvam lakṣaṇam*).

This species of contact is called saṃyukta-samaveta-samavāya, for the eye is in contact with the thing, in the thing the colour is in samavāya relation, and in the specific colour there is the colour universal or the generic character of colour in samavāya relation. (4) There is another kind of contact called samavāya by which sounds are said to be perceived by the ear. The auditory sense is ākāśa and the sound exists in ākāśa in the samavāya relation, and thus the auditory sense can perceive sound in a peculiar kind of contact called samaveta-samavāya. (5) The generic character of sound as the universal of sound (śabdatva) is perceived by the kind of contact known as samaveta-samavāya. (6) There is another kind of contact by which negation (*abhāva*) is perceived, namely saṃyukta viśeṣaṇa (as qualifying contact). This is so called because the eye perceives only the empty space which is qualified by the absence of an object and through it the negation. Thus I see that there is no jug here on the ground. My eye in this case is in touch with the ground and the absence of the jug is only a kind of quality of the ground which is perceived along with the perception of the empty ground. It will thus be seen that Nyāya admits not only the substances and qualities but all kinds of relations as real and existing and as being directly apprehended by perception (so far as they are directly presented).

The most important thing about the Nyāya-Vaiśeṣika theory of perception is this that the whole process beginning from the contact of the sense with the object to the distinct and clear perception of the thing, sometimes involving the appreciation of its usefulness or harmfulness, is regarded as the process of perception and its result perception. The self, the mind, the senses and the objects are the main factors by the particular kinds of contact between which perceptual knowledge is produced. All knowledge is indeed *arthaprakāśa*, revelation of objects, and it is called perception when the sense factors are the instruments of its production and the knowledge produced is of the objects with which the senses are in contact. The contact of the senses with the objects is not in any sense metaphorical but actual. Not only in the case of touch and taste are the senses in contact with the objects, but in the cases of sight, hearing and smell as well. The senses according to Nyāya-Vaiśeṣika are material and we have seen that the system does not admit of any other kind of transcendental (*atīndriya*) power (*śakti*) than that of actual vibratory movement which is within the purview of sense-cognition[1]. The production of knowledge is thus no transcendental occurrence, but is one which is similar to the effects produced by the conglomeration and movements of physical causes. When I perceive an orange, my visual or the tactual sense is in touch not only with its specific colour, or hardness, but also with the universals associated with them in a relation of inherence and also with the object itself of which the colour etc. are predicated. The result of this sense-contact at the first stage is called *ālocana-jñāna* (sense-cognition) and as a result of that there is roused the memory of its previous taste and a sense of pleasurable character (*sukhasādhanatvasmṛti*) and as a result of that I perceive the orange before me to have a certain pleasure-giving character[2]. It is urged that this appreciation of the orange as a pleasurable object should also be regarded as a direct result of perception through the action of the memory operating as a concomitant cause (sahakāri). I perceive the orange with the eye and understand the pleasure it will give, by the mind, and thereupon understand by the mind that it is a pleasurable object. So though this perception results immediately by the operation of the mind, yet since it could only happen in association with sense-contact, it must be considered as a subsidiary effect of sense-contact and hence regarded as visual perception. Whatever may be the successive intermediary processes, if the knowledge is a result of sense-contact and if it appertains to the object with which the sense is in contact, we should regard it as a result of the perceptual process. Sense-contact with the object is thus the primary and indispensable condition of all perceptions and not only can the senses be in contact with the objects, their qualities, and the universals associated with them but also with negation. A perception is erroneous when it presents an object in a character which it does not possess (*atasmiṃstaditi*) and right knowledge (*pramā*) is that which presents an object with a character which it really has

[1] *Na khalvatīndriyā śaktirasmābhirupagamyate*
yayā saha na kāryyasya sambandhajñānasambhavaḥ.
Nyāyamañjarī, p. 69.

[2] *Sukhādi manasā buddhvā kapitthādi ca cakṣuṣā*
tasya karaṇatā tatra manasaivāvagamyate...
...Saṃbandhagrahaṇakāle yattatkapitthādiviṣayamakṣajam
jñānam tadupādeyādijñānaphalamiti bhāṣyakṛtaścetasi sthitam
sukhasādhanatvajñānamupādeyajñānam.
Nyāyamañjarī, pp. 69–70; see also pp. 66–71.

(*tadvati tatprakārakānubhava*)[1]. In all cases of perceptual illusion the sense is in real contact with the right object, but it is only on account of the presence of certain other conditions that it is associated with wrong characteristics or misapprehended as a different object. Thus when the sun's rays are perceived in a desert and misapprehended as a stream, at the first indeterminate stage the visual sense is in real contact with the rays and thus far there is no illusion so far as the contact with a real object is concerned, but at the second determinate stage it is owing to the similarity of certain of its characteristics with those of a stream that it is misapprehended as a stream[2]. Jayanta observes that on account of the presence of the defect of the organs or the rousing of the memory of similar objects, the object with which the sense is in contact hides its own characteristics and appears with the characteristics of other objects and this is what is meant by illusion[3]. In the case of mental delusions however there is no sense-contact with any object and the rousing of irrelevant memories is sufficient to produce illusory notions[4]. This doctrine of illusion is known as *viparītakhyāti* or *anyathākhyāti*. What existed in the mind appeared as the object before us (*hṛdaye parisphurato'rthasya bahiravabhāsanam*)[5]. Later Vaiśeṣika as interpreted by Praśastapāda and Śrīdhara is in full agreement with Nyāya in this doctrine of illusion (*bhrama* or as Vaiśeṣika calls it *viparyaya*) that the object of illusion is always the right thing with which the sense is in contact and that the illusion consists in the imposition of wrong characteristics[6].

I have pointed out above that Nyāya divided perception into two classes as nirvikalpa (indeterminate) and savikalpa (determinate) according as it is an earlier or a later stage. Vācaspati says, that at the first stage perception reveals an object as a particular; the perception of an orange at this *avikalpika* or *nirvikalpika* stage gives us indeed all its colour, form, and also the universal of orangeness associated with it, but it does not reveal

[1] See Udyotakara's *Nyāyavārttika*, p. 37, and Gaṅgeśa's *Tattvacintāmaṇi*, p. 401, *Bibliotheca Indica*.

[2] "*Indriyeṇālocya marīcīn uccāvacamuccalato nirvikalpena gṛhītvā paścāttatropaghātadoṣāt viparyyeti, savikalpako'sya pratyayo bhrānto jāyate tasmādvijñānasya vyabhicāro nārthasya*, Vācaspati's *Tātparyaṭīkā*," p. 87.

[3] *Nyāyamañjarī*, p. 88. [4] *Ibid.* pp. 89 and 184. [5] *Ibid.* p. 184.

[6] *Nyāyakandalī*, pp. 177–181, "*Śuktisaṃyuktenendriyeṇa doṣasahakāriṇā rajatasaṃskārasacivena sādṛśyamanurundhatā śuktikāviṣayo rajatādhyavasāyaḥ kṛtaḥ*."

it in a subject-predicate relation as when I say "this is an orange." The avikalpika stage thus reveals the universal associated with the particular, but as there is no association of name at this stage, the universal and the particular are taken in one sweep and not as terms of relation as subject and predicate or substance and attribute (*jātyādisvarūpāvagāhi na tu jātyādīnāṃ mitho viśeṣaṇa-viśeṣyabhāvāvagāhīti yāvat*)[1]. He thinks that such a stage, when the object is only seen but not associated with name or a subject-predicate relation, can be distinguished in perception not only in the case of infants or dumb persons that do not know the names of things, but also in the case of all ordinary persons, for the association of the names and relations could be distinguished as occurring at a succeeding stage[2]. Śrīdhara, in explaining the Vaiśeṣika view, seems to be largely in agreement with the above view of Vācaspati. Thus Śrīdhara says that in the nirvikalpa stage not only the universals were perceived but the differences as well. But as at this stage there is no memory of other things, there is no manifest differentiation and unification such as can only result by comparison. But the differences and the universals as they are in the thing are perceived, only they are not consciously ordered as "different from this" or "similar to this," which can only take place at the savikalpa stage[3]. Vācaspati did not bring in the question of comparison with others, but had only spoken of the determinate notion of the thing in definite subject-predicate relation in association with names. The later Nyāya writers however, following Gaṅgeśa, hold an altogether different opinion on the subject. With them nirvikalpa knowledge means the knowledge of mere predication without any association with the subject or the thing to which the predicate refers. But such a knowledge is never testified by experience. The nirvikalpa stage is thus a logical stage in the development of perceptual cognition and not a psychological stage. They would

[1] *Tātparyaṭīkā*, p. 82, also *ibid.* p. 91, "*prathamamālocito'rthaḥ sāmānyaviśeṣavān.*"

[2] *Ibid.* p. 84, "*tasmādvyutpannasyāpi nāmadheyasmaraṇāya pūrvameṣitavyo vinaiva nāmadheyamarthapratyayaḥ.*"

[3] *Nyāyakandalī*, p. 189 ff., "*ataḥ savikalpakamicchatā nirvikalpakamapyeṣitavyam, tacca na sāmānyamātram gṛhṇāti bhedasyāpi pratibhāsanāt nāpi svalakṣaṇamātram sāmānyākārasyāpi saṃvedanāt vyaktyantaradarśane pratisandhānācca, kintu sāmānyam viśeṣañcobhayamapi gṛhṇāti yadi paramidaṃ sāmānyamayam viśeṣaḥ ityevaṃ vivicya na pratyeti vastvantarānusandhānavirahāt, piṇḍāntarānuvṛttigrahaṇāddhi sāmānyaṃ vivicyate, vyāvṛttigrahaṇādviśeṣoyamiti vivekaḥ.*"

not like to dispense with it for they think that it is impossible to have the knowledge of a thing as qualified by a predicate or a quality, without previously knowing the quality or the predicate (*viśiṣṭavaiśiṣṭyajñānam prati hi viśeṣaṇatāvacchedakaprakāraṃ jñānaṃ kāraṇaṃ*)[1]. So, before any determinate knowledge such as "I see a cow," "this is a cow" or "a cow" can arise it must be preceded by an indeterminate stage presenting only the indeterminate, unrelated, predicative quality as nirvikalpa, unconnected with universality or any other relations (*jātyādiyojanārahitaṃ vaiśiṣṭyānavagāhi niṣprakārakam nirvikalpakaṃ*)[2]. But this stage is never psychologically experienced (*atīndriya*) and it is only a logical necessity arising out of their synthetic conception of a proposition as being the relationing of a predicate with a subject. Thus Viśvanātha says in his Siddhāntamuktāvalī, "the cognition which does not involve relationing cannot be perceptual for the perception is of the form 'I know the jug'; here the knowledge is related to the self, the knower, the jug again is related to knowledge and the definite content of jugness is related to the jug. It is this content which forms the predicative quality (*viśeṣaṇatāvacchedaka*) of the predicate 'jug' which is related to knowledge. We cannot therefore have the knowledge of the jug without having the knowledge of the predicative quality, the content[3]." But in order that the knowledge of the jug could be rendered possible, there must be a stage at which the universal or the pure predication should be known and this is the nirvikalpa stage, the admission of which though not testified by experience is after all logically indispensably necessary. In the proposition "It is a cow," the cow is an universal, and this must be intuited directly before it could be related to the particular with which it is associated.

But both the old and the new schools of Nyāya and Vaiśeṣika admitted the validity of the savikalpa perception which the Buddhists denied. Things are not of the nature of momentary particulars, but they are endowed with class-characters or universals and thus our knowledge of universals as revealed by the perception of objects is not erroneous and is directly produced by objects. The Buddhists hold that the error of savikalpa perception consists in the attribution of jāti (universal), guṇa (quality),

[1] *Tattvacintāmaṇi*, p. 812. [2] *Ibid.* p. 809.

[3] *Siddhāntamuktāvalī* on *Bhāṣāpariccheda kārikā*, 58.

kriyā (action), nāma (name), and dravya (substance) to things[1]. The universal and that of which the universal is predicated are not different but are the same identical entity. Thus the predication of an universal in the savikalpa perception involves the false creation of a difference where there was none. So also the quality is not different from the substance and to speak of a thing as qualified is thus an error similar to the former. The same remark applies to action, for motion is not something different from that which moves. But name is completely different from the thing and yet the name and the thing are identified, and again the percept "man with a stick" is regarded as if it was a single thing or substance, though "man" and "stick" are altogether different and there is no unity between them. Now as regards the first three objections it is a question of the difference of the Nyāya ontological position with that of the Buddhists, for we know that Nyāya and Vaiśeṣika believe jāti, guṇa and kriyā to be different from substance and therefore the predicating of them of substance as different categories related to it at the determinate stage of perception cannot be regarded as erroneous. As to the fourth objection Vācaspati replies that the memory of the name of the thing roused by its sight cannot make the perception erroneous. The fact that memory operates cannot in any way vitiate perception. The fact that name is not associated until the second stage through the joint action of memory is easily explained, for the operation of memory was necessary in order to bring about the association. But so long as it is borne in mind that the name is not identical with the thing but is only associated with it as being the same as was previously acquired, there cannot be any objection to the association of the name. But the Buddhists further object that there is no reason why one should identify a thing seen at the present moment as being that which was seen before, for this identity is never the object of visual perception. To this Vācaspati says that through the help of memory or past impressions (*saṃskāra*) this can be considered as being directly the object of perception, for whatever may be the concomitant causes when the main cause of sense-contact is

[1] *Nyāyamañjarī*, pp. 93–100, "*Pañca caite kalpanā bhavanti jātikalpanā, guṇakalpanā, kriyākalpanā, nāmakalpanā dravyakalpanā ceti, tāśca kvacidabhede'pi bhedakalpanāt kvacicca bhede'pyabhedakalpanāt kalpanā ucyante.*" See Dharmakīrtti's theory of Perception, pp. 151–4. See also pp. 409–410 of this book.

present, this perception of identity should be regarded as an effect of it. But the Buddhists still emphasize the point that an object of past experience refers to a past time and place and is not experienced now and cannot therefore be identified with an object which is experienced at the present moment. It has to be admitted that Vācaspati's answer is not very satisfactory for it leads ultimately to the testimony of direct perception which was challenged by the Buddhists[1]. It is easy to see that early Nyāya-Vaiśeṣika could not dismiss the savikalpa perception as invalid for it was the same as the nirvikalpa and differed from it only in this, that a name was associated with the thing of perception at this stage. As it admits a gradual development of perception as the progressive effects of causal operations continued through the contacts of the mind with the self and the object under the influence of various intellectual (e.g. memory) and physical (e.g. light rays) concomitant causes, it does not, like Vedānta, require that right perception should only give knowledge which was not previously acquired. The variation as well as production of knowledge in the soul depends upon the variety of causal collocations.

Mind according to Nyāya is regarded as a separate sense and can come in contact with pleasure, pain, desire, antipathy and will. The later Nyāya writers speak of three other kinds of contact of a transcendental nature called *sāmānyalakṣaṇa*, *jñānalakṣaṇa* and *yogaja* (miraculous). The contact sāmānyalakṣaṇa is that by virtue of which by coming in contact with a particular we are transcendentally (*alaukika*) in contact with all the particulars (in a general way) of which the corresponding universal may be predicated. Thus when I see smoke and through it my sense is in contact with the universal associated with smoke my visual sense is in transcendental contact with all smoke in general. Jñānalakṣaṇa contact is that by virtue of which we can associate the perceptions of other senses when perceiving by any one sense. Thus when we are looking at a piece of sandal wood our visual sense is in touch with its colour only, but still we perceive it to be fragrant without any direct contact of the object with the organ of smell. The sort of transcendental contact (*alaukika sannikarṣa*) by virtue of which this is rendered

[1] *Tātparyaṭīkā*, pp. 88–95.

possible is called jñānalakṣaṇa. But the knowledge acquired by these two contacts is not counted as perception[1].

Pleasures and pains (*sukha* and *duḥkha*) are held by Nyāya to be different from knowledge (jñāna). For knowledge interprets, conceives or illumines things, but sukha etc. are never found to appear as behaving in that character. On the other hand we feel that we grasp them after having some knowledge. They cannot be self-revealing, for even knowledge is not so; if it were so, then that experience which generates sukha in one should have generated the same kind of feeling in others, or in other words it should have manifested its nature as sukha to all; and this does not happen, for the same thing which generates sukha in one might not do so in others. Moreover even admitting for argument's sake that it is knowledge itself that appears as pleasure and pain, it is evident that there must be some differences between the pleasurable and painful experiences that make them so different, and this difference is due to the fact that knowledge in one case was associated with sukha and in another case with duḥkha. This shows that sukha and duḥkha are not themselves knowledge. Such is the course of things that sukha and duḥkha are generated by the collocation of certain conditions, and are manifested through or in association with other objects either in direct perception or in memory. They are thus the qualities which are generated in the self as a result of causal operation. It should however be remembered that merit and demerit act as concomitant causes in their production.

The yogins are believed to have the pratyakṣa of the most distant things beyond our senses; they can acquire this power by gradually increasing their powers of concentration and perceive the subtlest and most distant objects directly by their mind. Even we ourselves may at some time have the notions of future events which come to be true, e.g. sometimes I may have the intuition that "To-morrow my brother will come,"

[1] *Siddhāntamuktāvalī* on *Kārikā* 63 and 64. We must remember that Gaṅgeśa discarded the definition of perception as given in the *Nyāya sūtra* which we have discussed above, and held that perception should be defined as that cognition which has the special class-character of direct apprehension. He thinks that the old definition of perception as the cognition generated by sense-contact involves a vicious circle (*Tattvacintāmaṇi*, pp. 538–546). Sense-contact is still regarded by him as the cause of perception, but it should not be included in the definition. He agrees to the six kinds of contact described first by Udyotakara as mentioned above.

and this may happen to be true. This is called pratibhāna-jñāna, which is also to be regarded as a pratyakṣa directly by the mind. This is of course different from the other form of perception called mānasa-pratyakṣa, by which memories of past perceptions by other senses are associated with a percept visualized at the present moment; thus we see a rose and perceive that it is fragrant; the fragrance is not perceived by the eye, but the manas perceives it directly and associates the visual percept with it. According to Vedānta this acquired perception is only a case of inference. The prātibha-pratyakṣa however is that which is with reference to the happening of a future event. When a cognition is produced, it is produced only as an objective cognition, e.g. This is a pot, but after this it is again related to the self by the mind as "I know this pot." This is effected by the mind again coming in contact for reperception of the cognition which had already been generated in the soul. This second reperception is called anuvyavasāya, and all practical work can proceed as a result of this anuvyavasāya[1].

Inference.

Inference (*anumāna*) is the second means of proof (pramāṇa) and the most valuable contribution that Nyāya has made has been on this subject. It consists in making an assertion about a thing on the strength of the mark or liṅga which is associated with it, as when finding smoke rising from a hill we remember that since smoke cannot be without fire, there must also be fire in yonder hill. In an example like this smoke is technically called liṅga, or hetu. That about which the assertion has been made (the hill in this example) is called pakṣa, and the term "fire" is called sādhya. To make a correct inference it is necessary that the hetu or liṅga must be present in the pakṣa,

[1] This later Nyāya doctrine that the cognition of self in association with cognition is produced at a later moment must be contrasted with the *triputīpratyakṣa* doctrine of Prabhākara, which holds that the object, knower and knowledge are all given simultaneously in knowledge. Vyavasāya (determinate cognition), according to Gaṅgeśa, gives us only the cognition of the object, but the cognition that I am aware of this object or cognition is a different functioning succeeding the former one and is called anu (after) vyavasāya (cognition), "*idamahaṃ jānāmīti vyavasāye na bhāsate tadbodhakendriyasannikarṣābhāvāt kintvidaṃviṣayakajñānatvaviśiṣṭasya jñānasya vaiśiṣṭyamātmani bhāsate; na ca svaprakāśe vyavasāye tādṛśaṃ svasya vaiśiṣṭyaṃ bhāsitumarhati, pūrvaṃ viśeṣaṇasya tasyājñānāt, tasmādidamahaṃ jānāmīti na vyavasāyaḥ kintu anuvyavasāyaḥ.*" *Tattvacintāmaṇi*, p. 795.

and in all other known objects similar to the pakṣa in having the sādhya in it (sapakṣa-sattā), i.e., which are known to possess the sādhya (possessing fire in the present example). The liṅga must not be present in any such object as does not possess the sādhya (*vipakṣa-vyāvṛtti* absent from vipakṣa or that which does not possess the sādhya). The inferred assertion should not be such that it is invalidated by direct perception (*pratyakṣa*) or the testimony of the śāstra (*abādhita-viṣayatva*). The liṅga should not be such that by it an inference in the opposite way could also be possible (*asat-pratipakṣa*). The violation of any one of these conditions would spoil the certitude of the hetu as determining the inference, and thus would only make the hetu fallacious, or what is technically called hetvābhāsa or seeming hetu by which no correct inference could be made. Thus the inference that sound is eternal because it is visible is fallacious, for visibility is a quality which sound (here the pakṣa) does not possess[1]. This hetvābhāsa is technically called *asiddha-hetu*. Again, hetvābhāsa of the second type, technically called *viruddha-hetu*, may be exemplified in the case that sound is eternal, since it is created; the hetu "being created" is present in the opposite of sādhya (*vipakṣa*), namely non-eternality, for we know that non-eternality is a quality which belongs to all created things. A fallacy of the third type, technically called *anaikāntika-hetu*, is found in the case that sound is eternal, since it is an object of knowledge. Now "being an object of knowledge" (*prameyatva*) is here the hetu, but it is present in things eternal (i.e. things possessing sādhya), as well as in things that are not eternal (i.e. which do not possess the sādhya), and therefore the concomitance of the hetu with the sādhya is not absolute (*anaikāntika*). A fallacy of the fourth type, technically called *kālātyayāpadiṣṭa*, may be found in the example—fire is not hot, since it is created like a jug, etc. Here pratyakṣa shows that fire is hot, and hence the hetu is fallacious. The fifth fallacy, called *prakaraṇasama*, is to be found in cases where opposite hetus are available at the same time for opposite conclusions, e.g. sound like a jug is non-

[1] It should be borne in mind that Nyāya did not believe in the doctrine of the eternality of sound, which the Mīmāṃsā did. Eternality of sound meant with Mīmāṃsā the theory that sounds existed as eternal indestructible entities, and they were only manifested in our ears under certain conditions, e.g. the stroke of a drum or a particular kind of movement of the vocal muscles.

eternal, since no eternal qualities are found in it, and sound like ākāśa is eternal, since no non-eternal qualities are found in it.

The Buddhists held in answer to the objections raised against inference by the Cārvākas, that inferential arguments are valid, because they are arguments on the principle of the uniformity of nature in two relations, viz. *tādātmya* (essential identity) and *tadutpatti* (succession in a relation of cause and effect). Tādātmya is a relation of genus and species and not of causation; thus we know that all pines are trees, and infer that this is a tree since it is a pine; tree and pine are related to each other as genus and species, and the co-inherence of the generic qualities of a tree with the specific characters of a pine tree may be viewed as a relation of essential identity (*tādātmya*). The relation of tadutpatti is that of uniformity of succession of cause and effect, e.g. of smoke to fire.

Nyāya holds that inference is made because of the invariable association (*niyama*) of the liṅga or hetu (the concomitance of which with the sādhya has been safeguarded by the five conditions noted above) with the sādhya, and not because of such specific relations as tādātmya or tadutpatti. If it is held that the inference that it is a tree because it is a pine is due to the essential identity of tree and pine, then the opposite argument that it is a pine because it is a tree ought to be valid as well; for if it were a case of identity it ought to be the same both ways. If in answer to this it is said that the characteristics of a pine are associated with those of a tree and not those of a tree with those of a pine, then certainly the argument is not due to essential identity, but to the invariable association of the liṅga (mark) with the liṅgin (the possessor of liṅga), otherwise called niyama. The argument from tadutpatti (association as cause and effect) is also really due to invariable association, for it explains the case of the inference of the type of cause and effect as well as of other types of inference, where the association as cause and effect is not available (e.g. from sunset the rise of stars is inferred). Thus it is that the invariable concomitance of the liṅga with the liṅgin, as safeguarded by the conditions noted above, is what leads us to make a valid inference[1].

We perceived in many cases that a liṅga (e.g. smoke) was associated with a liṅgin (fire), and had thence formed the notion

[1] See *Nyāyamañjarī* on anumāna.

that wherever there was smoke there was fire. Now when we perceived that there was smoke in yonder hill, we remembered the concomitance (*vyāpti*) of smoke and fire which we had observed before, and then since there was smoke in the hill, which was known to us to be inseparably connected with fire, we concluded that there was fire in the hill. The discovery of the liṅga (smoke) in the hill as associated with the memory of its concomitance with fire (*tṛtīya-liṅga-parāmarśa*) is thus the cause (*anumitikaraṇa* or *anumāna*) of the inference (*anumiti*). The concomitance of smoke with fire is technically called *vyāpti*. When this refers to the concomitance of cases containing smoke with those having fire, it is called *bahirvyāpti*; and when it refers to the conviction of the concomitance of smoke with fire, without any relation to the circumstances under which the concomitance was observed, it is called *antarvyāpti*. The Buddhists since they did not admit the notions of generality, etc. preferred antarvyāpti view of concomitance to bahirvyāpti as a means of inference[1].

Now the question arises that since the validity of an inference will depend mainly on the validity of the concomitance of sign (*hetu*) with the signate (*sādhya*), how are we to assure ourselves in each case that the process of ascertaining the concomitance (*vyāptigraha*) had been correct, and the observation of concomitance had been valid. The Mīmāṃsā school held, as we shall see in the next chapter, that if we had no knowledge of any such case in which there was smoke but no fire, and if in all the cases I knew I had perceived that wherever there was smoke there was fire, I could enunciate the concomitance of smoke with fire. But Nyāya holds that it is not enough that in all cases where there is smoke there should be fire, but it is necessary that in all those cases where there is no fire there should not be any smoke, i.e. not only every case of the existence of smoke should be a case of the existence of fire, but every case of absence of fire should be a case of absence of smoke. The former is technically called *anvayavyāpti* and the latter *vyatirekavyāpti*. But even this is not enough. Thus there may have been an ass sitting, in a hundred cases where I had seen smoke, and there might have been a hundred cases where there was neither ass nor smoke, but it cannot be asserted from it that there is any relation of concomi-

[1] See *Antarvyāptisamarthana*, by Ratnākaraśānti in the *Six Buddhist Nyāya Tracts*, *Bibliotheca Indica*, 1910.

tance, or of cause and effect between the ass and the smoke. It may be that one might never have observed smoke without an antecedent ass, or an ass without the smoke following it, but even that is not enough. If it were such that we had so experienced in a very large number of cases that the introduction of the ass produced the smoke, and that even when all the antecedents remained the same, the disappearance of the ass was immediately followed by the disappearance of smoke (*yasmin sati bhavanam yato vinā na bhavanam iti bhūyodarśanaṃ*, *Nyāyamañjarī*, p. 122), then only could we say that there was any relation of concomitance (*vyāpti*) between the ass and the smoke[1]. But of course it might be that what we concluded to be the hetu by the above observations of anvaya-vyatireka might not be a real hetu, and there might be some other condition (*upādhi*) associated with the hetu which was the real hetu. Thus we know that fire in green wood (*ārdrendhana*) produced smoke, but one might doubt that it was not the fire in the green wood that produced smoke, but there was some hidden demon who did it. But there would be no end of such doubts, and if we indulged in them, all our work endeavour and practical activities would have to be dispensed with (*vyāghāta*). Thus such doubts as lead us to the suspension of all work should not disturb or unsettle the notion of vyāpti or concomitance at which we had arrived by careful observation and consideration[2]. The Buddhists and the naiyāyikas generally agreed as to the method of forming the notion of concomitance or vyāpti (*vyāptigraha*), but the former tried to assert that the validity of such a concomitance always depended on a relation of cause and effect or of identity of essence, whereas Nyāya held that neither the relations of cause and effect, nor that of essential identity of genus and species, exhausted the field of inference, and there was quite a number of other types of inference which could not be brought under either of them (e.g. the rise of the moon and the tide of the ocean). A natural fixed order that certain things happening other things would happen could certainly exist, even without the supposition of an identity of essence.

But sometimes it happens that different kinds of causes often have the same kind of effect, and in such cases it is difficult to

[1] See *Tātparyaṭīkā* on anumāna and vyāptigraha.

[2] *Tātparyaṭīkā* on vyāptigraha, and *Tattvacintāmaṇi* of Gaṅgeśa on vyāptigraha.

infer the particular cause from the effect. Nyāya holds however that though different causes are often found to produce the same effect, yet there must be some difference between one effect and another. If each effect is taken by itself with its other attendant circumstances and peculiarities, it will be found that it may then be possible to distinguish it from similar other effects. Thus a flood in the street may be due either to a heavy downpour of rain immediately before, or to the rise in the water of the river close by, but if observed carefully the flooding of the street due to rain will be found to have such special traits that it could be distinguished from a similar flooding due to the rise of water in the river. Thus from the flooding of the street of a special type, as demonstrated by its other attendant circumstances, the special manner in which the water flows by small rivulets or in sheets, will enable us to infer that the flood was due to rains and not to the rise of water in the river. Thus we see that Nyāya relied on empirical induction based on uniform and uninterrupted agreement in nature, whereas the Buddhists assumed *a priori* principles of causality or identity of essence. It may not be out of place here to mention that in later Nyāya works great emphasis is laid on the necessity of getting ourselves assured that there was no such upādhi (condition) associated with the hetu on account of which the concomitance happened, but that the hetu was unconditionally associated with the sādhya in a relation of inseparable concomitance. Thus all fire does not produce smoke; fire must be associated with green wood in order to produce smoke. Green wood is thus the necessary condition (*upādhi*) without which no smoke could be produced. It is on account of this condition that fire is associated with smoke; and so we cannot say that there is smoke because there is fire. But in the concomitance of smoke with fire there is no condition, and so in every case of smoke there is fire. In order to be assured of the validity of vyāpti, it is necessary that we must be assured that there should be nothing associated with the hetu which conditioned the concomitance, and this must be settled by wide experience (*bhūyodarśana*).

Praśastapāda in defining inference as the "knowledge of that (e.g. fire) associated with the reason (e.g. smoke) by the sight of the reason" described a valid reason (*liṅga*) as that which is connected with the object of inference (*anumeya*) and which exists wherever the object of inference exists and is absent in all cases where it does not exist. This is indeed the same as the Nyāya qualifications of *pakṣasattva*, *sapakṣasattva* and *vipakṣāsattva* of a valid reason (hetu). Praśastapāda further quotes a verse to say that this is the same as what Kāśyapa (believed to be the family name of Kaṇāda) said. Kaṇāda says that we can infer a cause from the effect, the effect from the cause, or we can infer one thing by another when they are mutually connected, or in opposition or in a relation of inherence (IX. ii. 1 and III. i. 9). We can infer by a reason because it is duly associated (*prasiddhipūrvakatva*) with the object of inference. What this association was according to Kaṇāda can also be understood for he tells us (III. i. 15) that where there is no proper association, the reason (hetu) is either non-existent in the object to be inferred or it has no concomitance with it (*aprasiddha*) or it has a doubtful existence (*sandigdha*). Thus if I say this ass is a horse because it has horns it is fallacious, for neither the horse nor the ass has horns. Again if I say it is a cow because it has horns, it is fallacious, for there is no concomitance between horns and a cow, and though a cow may have a horn, all that have horns are not cows. The first fallacy is a combination of pakṣāsattva and sapakṣāsattva, for not only the present pakṣa (the ass) had no horns, but no horses had any horns, and the second is a case of vipakṣasattva, for those which are not cows (e.g. buffaloes) have also horns. Thus, it seems that when Praśastapāda says that he is giving us the view of Kaṇāda he is faithful to it. Praśastapāda says that wherever there is smoke there is fire, if there is no fire there is no smoke. When one knows this concomitance and unerringly perceives the smoke, he remembers the concomitance and feels certain that there is fire. But with regard to Kaṇāda's enumeration of types of inference such as "a cause is inferred from its effect, or an effect from the cause," etc., Praśastapāda holds that these are not the only types of inference, but are only some examples for showing the general nature of inference. Inference merely shows a connection such that from this that can be inferred. He then divides inference into two classes, dṛṣṭa (from the experienced characteristics of one member of a class to another member of the same class), and sāmānyato dṛṣṭa. Dṛṣṭa (perceived resemblance) is that where the previously known case and the inferred case is exactly of the same class. Thus as an example of it we can point out that by perceiving that only a cow has a hanging mass of flesh on its neck (sāsnā), I can whenever I see the same hanging mass of flesh at the neck of an animal infer that it is a cow. But when on the strength of a common quality the inference is extended to a different class of objects, it is called sāmānyato dṛṣṭa. Thus on perceiving that the work of the peasants is rewarded with a good harvest I may infer that the work of the priests, namely the performance of sacrifices, will also be rewarded with the objects for which they are performed (i.e. the attainment of heaven). When the conclusion to which one has arrived (*svaniścitārtha*) is expressed in five premisses for convincing others who are either in doubt, or in error or are simply ignorant, then the inference is called parārthānumāna. We know that the distinction of svārthānumāna (inference for oneself) and parārthānumāna (inference for others) was made by the Jains and Buddhists. Praśastapāda does not make a sharp distinction of two classes of inference, but he seems to mean that what one infers, it can be conveyed to others by means of five premisses in which case it is called parārthānumāna. But this need not be considered as an entirely new innovation of Praśastapāda, for in IX. 2, Kaṇāda himself definitely alludes to this distinction (*asyedaṃ kāryyakāraṇasambandhaścāvayavādbhavati*). The five premisses which are called in Nyāya *pratijñā*, *hetu dṛṣṭānta*, *upanaya*, and *nigamana* are called in Vaiśeṣika *pratijñā*, *apadeśa*, *nidarśana*, *anusandhāna*, and *pratyāmnāya*. Kaṇāda however does not mention the name of any of these premisses excepting the second "apadeśa." Pratijñā is of course the same as we have in Nyāya, and the term nidarśana is very similar to Nyāya dṛṣṭānta, but the last two are entirely different. Nidarśana may be of two kinds, (1) agreement in presence (e.g. that which has motion is a substance as is seen in the case of an arrow), (2) agreement in absence (e.g. what is not a substance has no motion as is seen in the case of the universal being[1]). He also points out cases of the fallacy of the example

[1] Dr Vidyābhūṣaṇa says that "An example before the time of Dignāga served as a mere familiar case which was cited to help the understanding of the listener, e.g. The hill is fiery; because it has smoke; like a kitchen (example). Asaṅga made the example more serviceable to reasoning, but Dignāga converted it into a universal proposition, that is a proposition expressive of the universal or inseparable connection between the middle term and the major term, e.g. The hill is fiery; because it has smoke; all that has smoke is fiery as a kitchen" (*Indian Logic*, pp. 95, 96). It is of course true that Vatsyāyana had an imperfect example as "like a kitchen" (*śabdaḥ utpattidharmakatvādanityaḥ sthālyādivat*, I. i. 36), but Praśastapāda has it in the proper form. Whether Praśastapāda borrowed it from Diṅnāga or Diṅnāga from Praśastapāda cannot be easily settled.

(*nidarśanābhāsa*). Praśastapāda's contribution thus seems to consist of the enumeration of the five premisses and the fallacy of the nidarśana, but the names of the last two premisses are so different from what are current in other systems that it is reasonable to suppose that he collected them from some other traditional Vaiśeṣika work which is now lost to us. It however definitely indicates that the study of the problem of inference was being pursued in Vaiśeṣika circles independently of Nyāya. There is no reason however to suppose that Praśastapāda borrowed anything from Diṅnāga as Professor Stcherbatsky or Keith supposes, for, as I have shown above, most of Praśastapāda's apparent innovations are all definitely alluded to by Kaṇāda himself, and Professor Keith has not discussed this alternative. On the question of the fallacies of nidarśana, unless it is definitely proved that Diṅnāga preceded Praśastapāda, there is no reason whatever to suppose that the latter borrowed it from the former[1].

The nature and ascertainment of concomitance is the most important part of inference. Vātsyāyana says that an inference can be made by the sight of the liṅga (reason or middle) through the memory of the connection between the middle and the major previously perceived. Udyotakara raises the question whether it is the present perception of the middle or the memory of the connection of the middle with the major that should be regarded as leading to inference. His answer is that both these lead to inference, but that which immediately leads to inference is *liṅga-parāmarśa*, i.e. the present perception of the middle in the minor associated with the memory of its connection with the major, for inference does not immediately follow the memory of the connection, but the present perception of the middle associated with the memory of the connection (*smṛtyanugṛhīto liṅgaparāmarśo*). But he is silent with regard to the nature of concomitance. Udyotakara's criticisms of Diṅnāga as shown by Vācaspati have no reference to this point. The doctrine of *tādātmya* and *tadutpatti* was therefore in all probability a new contribution to Buddhist logic by Dharmakīrtti. Dharmakīrtti's contention was that the root principle of the connection between the middle and the major was that the former was either identical in essence with the latter or its effect and that unless this was grasped a mere collection of positive or negative instances will not give us

[1] Praśastapāda's bhāṣya with *Nyāyakandalī*, pp. 200–255.

the desired connection[1]. Vācaspati in his refutation of this view says that the cause-effect relation cannot be determined as a separate relation. If causality means invariable immediate antecedence such that there being fire there is smoke and there being no fire there is no smoke, then it cannot be ascertained with perfect satisfaction, for there is no proof that in each case the smoke was caused by fire and not by an invisible demon. Unless it can be ascertained that there was no invisible element associated, it cannot be said that the smoke was immediately preceded by fire and fire alone. Again accepting for the sake of argument that causality can be determined, then also cause is known to precede the effect and therefore the perception of smoke can only lead us to infer the presence of fire at a preceding time and not contemporaneously with it. Moreover there are many cases where inference is possible, but there is no relation of cause and effect or of identity of essence (e.g. the sunrise of this morning by the sunrise of yesterday morning). In the case of identity of essence (*tādātmya* as in the case of the pine and the tree) also there cannot be any inference, for one thing has to be inferred by another, but if they are identical there cannot be any inference. The nature of concomitance therefore cannot be described in either of these ways. Some things (e.g. smoke) are naturally connected with some other things (e.g. fire) and when such is the case, though we may not know any further about the nature of this connection, we may infer the latter from the former and not vice versa, for fire is connected with smoke only under certain conditions (e.g. green wood). It may be argued that there may always be certain unknown conditions which may vitiate the validity of inference. To this Vācaspati's answer is that if even after observing a large number of cases and careful search such conditions (*upādhi*) cannot be discovered, we have to take it for granted that they do not exist and that there is a natural connection between the middle and the major. The later Buddhists introduced the method of *Pañcakāraṇī* in order to determine effectively the causal relation. These five conditions determining the causal relation are (1) neither the cause nor the effect is perceived, (2) the cause is perceived, (3) in immediate succession the effect is perceived, (4) the cause disappears, (5) in

[1] *Kāryyakāraṇabhāvādvā svabhāvādva niyāmakāt avinābhāvaniyamo' darśanānna na darśanāt. Tātparyaṭīkā*, p. 105.

immediate succession the effect disappears. But this method cannot guarantee the infallibility of the determination of cause and effect relation; and if by the assumption of a cause-effect relation no higher degree of certainty is available, it is better to accept a natural relation without limiting it to a cause-effect relation[1].

In early Nyāya books three kinds of inference are described, namely pūrvavat, śeṣavat, and sāmānyato-dṛṣṭa. Pūrvavat is the inference of effects from causes, e.g. that of impending rain from heavy dark clouds; śeṣavat is the inference of causes from effects, e.g. that of rain from the rise of water in the river; sāmānyato-dṛṣṭa refers to the inference in all cases other than those of cause and effect, e.g. the inference of the sour taste of the tamarind from its form and colour. *Nyāyamañjarī* mentions another form of anumāna, namely pariśeṣamāna (*reductio ad absurdum*), which consists in asserting anything (e.g. consciousness) of any other thing (e.g. ātman), because it was already definitely found out that consciousness was not produced in any other part of man. Since consciousness could not belong to anything else, it must belong to soul of necessity. In spite of these variant forms they are all however of one kind, namely that of the inference of the probandum (*sādhya*) by virtue of the unconditional and invariable concomitance of the hetu, called the vyāpti-niyama. In the new school of Nyāya (Navya-Nyāya) a formal distinction of three kinds of inference occupies an important place, namely anvayavyatireki, kevalānvayi, and kevalavyatireki. Anvayavyatireki is that inference where the vyāpti has been observed by a combination of a large number of instances of agreement in presence and agreement in absence, as in the case of the concomitance of smoke and fire (wherever there is smoke there is fire (*anvaya*), and where there is no fire, there is no smoke (*vyatireka*)). An inference could be for one's own self (*svārthānumāna*) or for the sake of convincing others (*parārthānumāna*). In the latter case, when it was necessary that an inference should be put explicitly in an unambiguous manner, five propositions (*avayavas*) were regarded as necessary, namely pratijña (e.g. the hill is fiery), hetu (since it has smoke), udāharaṇa (where there is smoke there is fire, as in the kitchen), upanaya (this hill has smoke), nigamana (therefore it has got

[1] Vātsyāyana's bhāṣya, Udyotakara's *Vārttika* and *Tātparyyaṭīkā*, I. i. 5.

fire). Kevalānvayi is that type of inference, the vyāpti of which could not be based on any negative instance, as in the case "this object has a name, since it is an object of knowledge (*idaṃ, vācyam prameyatvāt*)." Now no such case is known which is not an object of knowledge; we cannot therefore know of any case where there was no object of knowledge (*prameyatva*) and no name (*vācyatva*); the vyāpti here has therefore to be based necessarily on cases of agreement—wherever there is prameyatva or an object of knowledge, there is vācyatva or name. The third form of kevalavyatireki is that where positive instances in agreement cannot be found, such as in the case of the inference that earth differs from other elements in possessing the specific quality of smell, since all that does not differ from other elements is not earth, such as water; here it is evident that there cannot be any positive instance of agreement and the concomitance has to be taken from negative instances. There is only one instance, which is exactly the proposition of our inference—earth differs from other elements, since it has the special qualities of earth. This inference could be of use only in those cases where we had to infer anything by reason of such special traits of it as was possessed by it and it alone.

Upamāna and Śabda.

The third pramāṇa, which is admitted by Nyāya and not by Vaiśeṣika, is *upamāna*, and consists in associating a thing unknown before with its name by virtue of its similarity with some other known thing. Thus a man of the city who has never seen a wild ox (*gavaya*) goes to the forest, asks a forester—"what is gavaya?" and the forester replies—"oh, you do not know it, it is just like a cow"; after hearing this from the forester he travels on, and on seeing a gavaya and finding it to be similar to a cow he forms the opinion that this is a gavaya. This knowing an hitherto unknown thing by virtue of its similarity to a known thing is called *upamāna*. If some forester had pointed out a gavaya to a man of the city and had told him that it was called a gavaya, then also the man would have known the animal by the name gavaya, but then this would have been due to testimony (*śabda-pramāṇa*). The knowledge is said to be generated by the upamāna process when the association of the unknown animal with its name is made by the observer on the strength of the experience of the similarity of the unknown animal to a known one. The naiyāyikas are thorough realists, and as such they do not regard the observation of similarity as being due to any subjective process of the mind. Similarity is indeed perceived by the visual sense but yet the association of the name in accordance with the perception of similarity and the instruction received is a separate act and is called *upamāna*[1].

Śabda-pramāṇa or testimony is the right knowledge which we derive from the utterances of infallible and absolutely truthful persons. All knowledge derived from the Vedas is valid, for the Vedas were uttered by Īśvara himself. The Vedas give us right knowledge not of itself, but because they came out as the utterances of the infallible Īśvara. The Vaiśeṣikas did not admit śabda as a separate pramāṇa, but they sought to establish the validity of testimony (*śabda*) on the strength of inference (*anumiti*) on the ground of its being the utterance of an infallible person. But as I have said before, this explanation is hardly corroborated by the Vaiśeṣika sūtras, which tacitly admit the validity of the scriptures on its own authority. But anyhow this was how Vaiśeṣika was interpreted in later times.

Negation in Nyāya-Vaiśeṣika.

The problem of negation or non-existence (*abhāva*) is of great interest in Indian philosophy. In this section we can describe its nature only from the point of view of perceptibility. Kumārila[2]

[1] See *Nyāyamañjarī* on upamāna. The oldest Nyāya view was that the instruction given by the forester by virtue of which the association of the name "wild ox" to the strange animal was possible was itself "upamāna." When Praśastapāda held that upamāna should be treated as a case of testimony (*āptavacana*), he had probably this interpretation in view. But Udyotakara and Vācaspati hold that it was not by the instruction alone of the forester that the association of the name "wild ox" was made, but there was the perception of similarity, and the memory of the instruction of the forester too. So it is the perception of similarity with the other two factors as accessories that lead us to this association called upamāna. What Vātsyāyana meant is not very clear, but Diṅnāga supposes that according to him the result of upamāna was the knowledge of similarity or the knowledge of a thing having similarity. Vācaspati of course holds that he has correctly interpreted Vātsyāyana's intention. It is however definite that upamāna means the associating of a name to a new object (*samākhyāsambandhapratipattirupamānārthaḥ*, Vātsyāyana). Jayanta points out that it is the preception of similarity which directly leads to the association of the name and hence the instruction of the forester cannot be regarded as the direct cause and consequently it cannot be classed under testimony (*śabda*). See Praśastapāda and *Nyāyakandalī*, pp. 220–22, Vātsyāyana, Udyotakara, Vācaspati and Jayanta on *Upamāna*.

[2] See Kumārila's treatment of abhāva in the *Ślokavārttika*, pp. 473–492.

and his followers, whose philosophy we shall deal with in the next chapter, hold that negation (*abhāva*) appears as an intuition (*mānam*) with reference to the object negated where there are no means of ordinary cognition (*pramāṇa*) leading to prove the existence (*satparicchedakam*) of that thing. They held that the notion "it is not existent" cannot be due to perception, for there is no contact here with sense and object. It is true indeed that when we turn our eyes (e.g. in the case of the perception of the non-existence of a jug) to the ground, we see both the ground and the non-existence of a jug, and when we shut them we can see neither the jug nor the ground, and therefore it could be urged that if we called the ground visually perceptible, we could say the same with regard to the non-existence of the jug. But even then since in the case of the perception of the jug there is sense-contact, which is absent in the other case, we could never say that both are grasped by perception. We see the ground and remember the jug (which is absent) and thus in the mind rises the notion of non-existence which has no reference at all to visual perception. A man may be sitting in a place where there were no tigers, but he might not then be aware of their non-existence at the time, since he did not think of them, but when later on he is asked in the evening if there were any tigers at the place where he was sitting in the morning, he then thinks and becomes aware of the non-existence of tigers there in the morning, even without perceiving the place and without any operation of the memory of the non-existence of tigers. There is no question of there being any inference in the rise of our notion of non-existence, for it is not preceded by any notion of concomitance of any kind, and neither the ground nor the non-perception of the jug could be regarded as a reason (*liṅga*), for the non-perception of the jug is related to the jug and not to the negation of the jug, and no concomitance is known between the non-perception of the jug and its non-existence, and when the question of the concomitance of non-perception with non-existence is brought in, the same difficulty about the notion of non-existence (*abhāva*) which was sought to be explained will recur again. Negation is therefore to be admitted as cognized by a separate and independent process of knowledge. Nyāya however says that the perception of non-existence (e.g. there is no jug here) is a unitary perception of one whole, just as any perception of positive existence (e.g.

there is a jug on the ground) is. Both the knowledge of the ground as well as the knowledge of the non-existence of the jug arise there by the same kind of action of the visual organ, and there is therefore no reason why the knowledge of the ground should be said to be due to perception, whereas the knowledge of the negation of the jug on the ground should be said to be due to a separate process of knowledge. The non-existence of the jug is taken in the same act as the ground is perceived. The principle that in order to perceive a thing one should have sense-contact with it, applies only to positive existents and not to negation or non-existence. Negation or non-existence can be cognized even without any sense-contact. Non-existence is not a positive substance, and hence there cannot be any question here of sense-contact. It may be urged that if no sense-contact is required in apprehending negation, one could as well apprehend negation or non-existence of other places which are far away from him. To this the reply is that to apprehend negation it is necessary that the place where it exists must be perceived. We know a thing and its quality to be different, and yet the quality can only be taken in association with the thing and it is so in this case as well. We can apprehend non-existence only through the apprehension of its locus. In the case when non-existence is said to be apprehended later on it is really no later apprehension of non-existence but a memory of non-existence (e.g. of jug) perceived before along with the perception of the locus of non-existence (e.g. ground). Negation or non-existence (*abhāva*) can thus, according to Nyāya, generate its cognition just as any positive existence can do. Negation is not mere negativity or mere vacuous absence, but is what generates the cognition "is not," as position (*bhāva*) is what generates the cognition "it is."

The Buddhists deny the existence of negation. They hold that when a negation is apprehended, it is apprehended with specific time and space conditions (e.g. this is not here now); but in spite of such an apprehension, we could never think that negation could thus be associated with them in any relation. There is also no relation between the negation and its *pratiyogi* (thing negated—e.g. jug in the negation of jug), for when there is the pratiyogi there is no negation, and when there is the negation there is no pratiyogi. There is not even the relation of opposition (*virodha*), for we could have admitted it, if the negation of the jug existed before and opposed the jug, for how can the negation of the jug oppose the jug, without effecting anything at all? Again, it may be asked whether negation is to be regarded as a positive being or becoming or of the nature of not becoming or non-being. In the first alternative it will be like any other positive existents, and in the second case it will be permanent and eternal, and it cannot be related to this or that particular negation. There are however many kinds of non-perception, e.g. (1) svabhāvānupalabdhi (natural non-perception—there is no jug because none is perceived); (2) kāraṇānupalabdhi (non-perception of cause—there is no smoke here, since there is no fire); (3) vyāpakānupalabdhi (non-perception of the species—there is no pine here, since there is no tree); (4) kāryānupalabdhi (non-perception of effects—there are not the causes of smoke here, since there is no smoke); (5) svabhāvaviruddhopalabdhi (perception of contradictory natures—there is no cold touch here because of fire); (6) viruddhakāryopalabdhi (perception of contradictory effects—there is no cold touch here because of smoke); (7) viruddhavyāptopalabdhi (opposite concomitance—past is not of necessity destructible, since it depends on other causes); (8) kāryyaviruddhopalabdhi (opposition of effects—there is not here the causes which can give cold since there is fire); (9) vyāpakaviruddhopalabdhi (opposite concomitants—there is no touch of snow here, because of fire); (10) kāraṇaviruddhopalabdhi (opposite causes—there is no shivering through cold here, since he is near the fire); (11) kāraṇaviruddhakāryyopalabdhi (effects of opposite causes—this place is not occupied by men of shivering sensations for it is full of smoke[1]).

There is no doubt that in the above ways we speak of negation, but that does not prove that there is any reason for the cognition of negation (*heturnābhāvasamvidaḥ*). All that we can say is this that there are certain situations which justify the use (*yogyatā*) of negative appellations. But this situation or yogyatā is positive in character. What we all speak of in ordinary usage as non-perception is of the nature of perception of some sort. Perception of negation thus does not prove the existence of negation, but only shows that there are certain positive perceptions which are only interpreted in that way. It is the positive perception of the ground where the visible jug is absent that

[1] See *Nyāyabindu*, p. 11, and *Nyāyamañjarī*, pp. 53–7.

leads us to speak of having perceived the negation of the jug (*anupalambhaḥ abhāvaṃ vyavahārayati*)[1].

The Nyāya reply against this is that the perception of positive existents is as much a fact as the perception of negation, and we have no right to say that the former alone is valid. It is said that the non-perception of jug on the ground is but the perception of the ground without the jug. But is this being without the jug identical with the ground or different? If identical then it is the same as the ground, and we shall expect to have it even when the jug is there. If different then the quarrel is only over the name, for whatever you may call it, it is admitted to be a distinct category. If some difference is noted between the ground with the jug, and the ground without it, then call it "ground, without the jugness" or "the negation of jug," it does not matter much, for a distinct category has anyhow been admitted. Negation is apprehended by perception as much as any positive existent is; the nature of the objects of perception only are different; just as even in the perception of positive sense-objects there are such diversities as colour, taste, etc. The relation of negation with space and time with which it appears associated is the relation that subsists between the qualified and the quality (*viśeṣya viśeṣaṇa*). The relation between the negation and its pratiyogi is one of opposition, in the sense that where the one is the other is not. The *Vaiśeṣika sūtra* (IX. i. 6) seems to take abhāva in a similar way as Kumārila the Mīmaṃsist does, though the commentators have tried to explain it away[2]. In Vaiśeṣika the four kinds of negation are enumerated as (1) *prāgabhāva* (the negation preceding the production of an object—e.g. of the jug before it is made by the potter); (2) *dhvaṃsābhāva* (the negation following the destruction of an object—as of the jug after it is destroyed by the stroke of a stick); (3) *anyonyābhāva* (mutual negation—e.g. in the cow there is the negation of the horse and

[1] See *Nyāyabinduṭīkā*, pp. 34 ff., and also *Nyāyamañjarī*, pp. 48–63.

[2] Praśastapāda says that as the production of an effect is the sign of the existence of the cause, so the non-production of it is the sign of its non-existence. Śrīdhara in commenting upon it says that the non-preception of a sensible object is the sign (*liṅga*) of its non-existence. But evidently he is not satisfied with the view for he says that non-existence is also directly perceived by the senses (*bhāvavad abhāvo'pīndriyagrahaṇayogyaḥ*) and that there is an actual sense-contact with non-existence which is the collocating cause of the preception of non-existence (*abhāvendriyasannikarṣo'pi abhāvagrahaṇasāmagrī*), *Nyāyakandalī*, pp. 225–30.

in the horse that of the cow); (4) *atyantābhāva* (a negation which always exists—e.g. even when there is a jug here, its negation in other places is not destroyed)[1].

The necessity of the Acquirement of debating devices for the seeker of Salvation.

It is probable that the Nyāya philosophy arose in an atmosphere of continued disputes and debates; as a consequence of this we find here many terms related to debates which we do not notice in any other system of Indian philosophy. These are *tarka*, *nirṇaya*, *vāda*, *jalpa*, *vitaṇḍā*, *hetvābhāsa*, *chala*, *jāti* and *nigrahasthāna*.

Tarka means deliberation on an unknown thing to discern its real nature; it thus consists of seeking reasons in favour of some supposition to the exclusion of other suppositions; it is not inference, but merely an oscillation of the mind to come to a right conclusion. When there is doubt (*saṃśaya*) about the specific nature of anything we have to take to tarka. Nirṇaya means the conclusion to which we arrive as a result of tarka. When two opposite parties dispute over their respective theses, such as the doctrines that there is or is not an ātman, in which each of them tries to prove his own thesis with reasons, each of the theses is called a *vāda*. Jalpa means a dispute in which the disputants give wrangling rejoinders in order to defeat their respective opponents. A jalpa is called a *vitaṇḍā* when it is only a destructive criticism which seeks to refute the opponent's doctrine without seeking to establish or formulate any new doctrine. Hetvābhāsas are those which appear as hetus but are really not so. *Nyāya sūtras* enumerate five fallacies (*hetvābhāsas*) of the middle (hetu): *savyabhicāra* (erratic), *viruddha* (contradictory), *prakaraṇasama* (tautology), *sādhyasama* (unproved reason) and *kālātīta* (inopportune). Savyabhicāra is that where the same reason may prove opposite conclusions (e.g. sound is eternal because it is intangible like the atoms which are eternal, and sound is non-eternal because it is intangible like cognitions which are non-eternal); viruddha is that where the reason opposes the premiss to be proved (e.g. a jug is eternal, because it is produced); prakaraṇasama is that

[1] The doctrine of negation, its function and value with reference to diverse logical problems, have many diverse aspects, and it is impossible to do them justice in a small section like this.

where the reason repeats the thesis to be proved in another form (e.g. sound is non-eternal because it has not the quality of eternality); sādhyasama is that where the reason itself requires to be proved (e.g. shadow is a substance because it has motion, but it remains to be proved whether shadows have motion or not); kālātīta is a false analogy where the reason fails because it does not tally with the example in point of time. Thus one may argue that sound is eternal because it is the result of contact (stick and the drum) like colour which is also a result of contact of light and the object and is eternal. Here the fallacy lies in this, that colour is simultaneous with the contact of light which shows what was already there and only manifested by the light, whereas in the case of sound it is produced immediately after the contact of the stick and drum and is hence a product and hence non-eternal. The later Nyāya works divide savyabhicāra into three classes, (1) sādhāraṇa or common (e.g. the mountain is fiery because it is an object of knowledge, but even a lake which is opposed to fire is also an object of knowledge), (2) asādhāraṇa or too restricted (e.g. sound is eternal because it has the nature of sound; this cannot be a reason for the nature of sound exists only in the sound and nowhere else), and (3) anupasaṃhārin or unsubsuming (e.g. everything is non-eternal, because they are all objects of knowledge; here the fallacy lies in this, that no instance can be found which is not an object of knowledge and an opposite conclusion may also be drawn). The fallacy *satpratipakṣa* is that in which there is a contrary reason which may prove the opposite conclusion (e.g. sound is eternal because it is audible, sound is non-eternal because it is an effect). The fallacy *asiddha* (unreal) is of three kinds (1) *āśrayāsiddha* (the lotus of the sky is fragrant because it is like other lotuses; now there cannot be any lotus in the sky), (2) *svarūpāsiddha* (sound is a quality because it is visible; but sound has no visibility), (3) *vyāpyatvāsiddha* is that where the concomitance between the middle and the consequence is not invariable and inevitable; there is smoke in the hill because there is fire; but there may be fire without the smoke as in a red hot iron ball, it is only green-wood fire that is invariably associated with smoke. The fallacy *bādhita* is that which pretends to prove a thesis which is against direct experience, e.g. fire is not hot because it is a substance. We have already enumerated the fallacies counted by Vaiśeṣika. Contrary to Nyāya practice

Praśastapāda counts the fallacies of the example. Diṅnāga also counted fallacies of example (e.g. sound is eternal, because it is incorporeal, that which is incorporeal is eternal as the atoms; but atoms are not incorporeal) and Dharmakīrtti counted also the fallacies of the pakṣa (minor); but Nyāya rightly considers that the fallacies of the middle if avoided will completely safeguard inference and that these are mere repetitions. Chala means the intentional misinterpretation of the opponent's arguments for the purpose of defeating him. Jāti consists in the drawing of contradictory conclusions, the raising of false issues or the like with the deliberate intention of defeating an opponent. Nigrahasthāna means the exposure of the opponent's argument as involving self-contradiction, inconsistency or the like, by which his defeat is conclusively proved before the people to the glory of the victorious opponent. As to the utility of the description of so many debating tricks by which an opponent might be defeated in a metaphysical work, the aim of which ought to be to direct the ways that lead to emancipation, it is said by Jayanta in his *Nyāyamañjarī* that these had to be resorted to as a protective measure against arrogant disputants who often tried to humiliate a teacher before his pupils. If the teacher could not silence the opponent, the faith of the pupils in him would be shaken and great disorder would follow, and it was therefore deemed necessary that he who was plodding onward for the attainment of mokṣa should acquire these devices for the protection of his own faith and that of his pupils. A knowledge of these has therefore been enjoined in the *Nyāya sūtra* as being necessary for the attainment of salvation[1].

The doctrine of Soul.

Dhūrtta Cārvākas denied the existence of soul and regarded consciousness and life as products of bodily changes; there were other Cārvākas called Suśikṣita Cārvākas who admitted the existence of soul but thought that it was destroyed at death. The Buddhists also denied the existence of any permanent self. The naiyāyikas ascertained all the categories of metaphysics mainly by such inference as was corroborated by experience. They argued that since consciousness, pleasures, pains, willing, etc. could not belong to our body or the senses, there must be

[1] See *Nyāyamañjarī*, pp. 586–659, and *Tārkikarakṣā* of Varadarāja and *Niṣkaṇṭaka* of Mallinātha, pp. 185 ff.

some entity to which they belonged; the existence of the self is not proved according to Nyāya merely by the notion of our self-consciousness, as in the case of Mīmāṃsā, for Nyāya holds that we cannot depend upon such a perception, for it may be erroneous. It often happens that I say that I am white or I am black, but it is evident that such a perception cannot be relied upon, for the self cannot have any colour. So we cannot safely depend on our self-consciousness as upon the inference that the self has to be admitted as that entity to which consciousness, emotion, etc. adhere when they are produced as a result of collocations. Never has the production of ātman been experienced, nor has it been found to suffer any destruction like the body, so the soul must be eternal. It is not located in any part of the body, but is all-pervading, i.e. exists at the same time in all places (*vibhu*), and does not travel with the body but exists everywhere at the same time. But though ātman is thus disconnected from the body, yet its actions are seen in the body because it is with the help of the collocation of bodily limbs, etc. that action in the self can be manifested or produced. It is unconscious in itself and acquires consciousness as a result of suitable collocations[1].

Even at birth children show signs of pleasure by their different facial features, and this could not be due to anything else than the memory of the past experiences in past lives of pleasures and pains. Moreover the inequalities in the distribution of pleasures and pains and of successes and failures prove that these must be due to the different kinds of good and bad action that men performed in their past lives. Since the inequality of the world must have some reasons behind it, it is better to admit karma as the determining factor than to leave it to irresponsible chance.

Īśvara and Salvation.

Nyāya seeks to establish the existence of Īśvara on the basis of inference. We know that the Jains, the Sāṃkhya and the Buddhists did not believe in the existence of Īśvara and offered many antitheistic arguments. Nyāya wanted to refute these and prove the existence of Īśvara by an inference of the sāmānyato-dṛṣṭa type.

[1] *Jñānasamavāyanibandhanamevātmanaścetayitṛtvam*, &c. See *Nyāyamañjarī*, pp. 432 ff.

The Jains and other atheists held that though things in the world have production and decay, the world as a whole was never produced, and it was never therefore an effect. In contrast to this view the Nyāya holds that the world as a whole is also an effect like any other effect. Many geological changes and landslips occur, and from these destructive operations proceeding in nature it may be assumed that this world is not eternal but a result of production. But even if this is not admitted by the atheists they can in no way deny the arrangement and order of the universe. But they would argue that there was certainly a difference between the order and arrangement of human productions (e.g. a jug) and the order and arrangement of the universe; and therefore from the order and arrangement (*sanniveśa-viśiṣṭatā*) of the universe it could not be argued that the universe was produced by a creator; for, it is from the sort of order and arrangement that is found in human productions that a creator or producer could be inferred. To this, Nyāya answers that the concomitance is to be taken between the "order and arrangement" in a general sense and "the existence of a creator" and not with specific cases of "order and arrangement," for each specific case may have some such peculiarity in which it differs from similar other specific cases; thus the fire in the kitchen is not the same kind of fire as we find in a forest fire, but yet we are to disregard the specific individual peculiarities of fire in each case and consider the concomitance of fire in general with smoke in general. So here, we have to consider the concomitance of "order and arrangement" in general with "the existence of a creator," and thus though the order and arrangement of the world may be different from the order and arrangement of things produced by man, yet an inference from it for the existence of a creator would not be inadmissible. The objection that even now we see many effects (e.g. trees) which are daily shooting forth from the ground without any creator being found to produce them, does not hold, for it can never be proved that the plants are not actually created by a creator. The inference therefore stands that the world has a creator, since it is an effect and has order and arrangement in its construction. Everything that is an effect and has an order and arrangement has a creator, like the jug. The world is an effect and has order and arrangement and has therefore a creator. Just as the potter knows all the purposes of the jug that he makes, so Īśvara knows all the purposes of this wide universe and is thus omniscient. He knows all things always and therefore does not require memory; all things are perceived by him directly without any intervention of any internal sense such as manas, etc. He is always happy. His will is eternal, and in accordance with the karma of men the same will produces dissolution, creates, or protects the world, in the order by which each man reaps the results of his own deeds. As our self which is in itself bodiless can by its will produce changes in our body and through it in the external world, so Īśvara also can by his will create the universe though he has no body. Some, however, say that if any association of body with Īśvara is indispensable for our conception of him, the atoms may as well be regarded as his body, so that just as by the will of our self changes and movement of our body take place, so also by his will changes and movements are produced in the atoms[1].

The naiyāyikas in common with most other systems of Indian philosophy believed that the world was full of sorrow and that the small bits of pleasure only served to intensify the force of sorrow. To a wise person therefore everything is sorrow (*sarvaṃ duḥkhaṃ vivekinaḥ*); the wise therefore is never attached to the so-called pleasures of life which only lead us to further sorrows.

The bondage of the world is due to false knowledge (*mithyā-jñāna*) which consists in thinking as my own self that which is not my self, namely body, senses, manas, feelings and knowledge; when once the true knowledge of the six padārthas and as Nyāya says, of the proofs (*pramāṇa*), the objects of knowledge (*prameya*), and of the other logical categories of inference is attained, false knowledge is destroyed. False knowledge can be removed by constant thinking of its opposite (*pratipakṣa-bhāvanā*), namely the true estimates of things. Thus when any pleasure attracts us, we are to think that this is in reality but pain, and thus the right knowledge about it will dawn and it will never attract us again. Thus it is that with the destruction of false knowledge our attachment or antipathy to things and ignorance about them (collectively called *doṣa*, cf. the *kleśa* of Patañjali) are also destroyed.

With the destruction of attachment actions (*pravṛtti*) for the

[1] See *Nyāyamañjarī*, pp. 190–204, *Īśvarānumāna* of Raghunātha Śiromaṇi and Udayana's *Kusumāñjalī*.

fulfilment of desires cease and with it rebirth ceases and with it sorrow ceases. Without false knowledge and attachment, actions cannot produce the bondage of karma that leads to the production of body and its experiences. With the cessation of sorrow there is emancipation in which the self is divested of all its qualities (consciousness, feeling, willing, etc.) and remains in its own inert state. The state of mukti according to Nyāya-Vaiśeṣika is neither a state of pure knowledge nor of bliss but a state of perfect qualitilessness, in which the self remains in itself in its own purity. It is the negative state of absolute painlessness in mukti that is sometimes spoken of as being a state of absolute happiness (*ānanda*), though really speaking the state of mukti can never be a state of happiness. It is a passive state of self in its original and natural purity unassociated with pleasure, pain, knowledge, willing, etc.[1].

[1] *Nyāyamañjarī*, pp. 499–533.

CHAPTER IX

MĪMĀṂSĀ PHILOSOPHY[1]

A Comparative Review.

THE Nyāya-Vaiśeṣika philosophy looked at experience from a purely common sense point of view and did not work with any such monistic tendency that the ultimate conceptions of our common sense experience should be considered as coming out of an original universal (e.g. prakṛti of the Sāṃkhya). Space, time, the four elements, soul, etc. convey the impression that they are substantive entities or substances. What is perceived of the material things as qualities such as colour, taste, etc. is regarded as so many entities which have distinct and separate existence but which manifest themselves in connection with the substances. So also karma or action is supposed to be a separate entity, and even the class notions are perceived as separate entities inhering in substances. Knowledge (*jñāna*) which illuminates all things is regarded only as a quality belonging to soul, just as there are other qualities of material objects. Causation is viewed merely as the collocation of conditions. The genesis of knowledge is also viewed as similar in nature to the production of any other physical event. Thus just as by the collocation of certain physical circumstances a jug and its qualities are produced, so by the combination and respective contacts of the soul, mind, sense, and the objects of sense, knowledge (*jñāna*) is produced. Soul with Nyāya is an inert unconscious entity in which knowledge, etc. inhere. The relation between a substance and its quality, action, class notion, etc. has also to be admitted as a separate entity, as without it the different entities being without any principle of relation would naturally fail to give us a philosophic construction.

Sāṃkhya had conceived of a principle which consisted of an infinite number of reals of three different types, which by their combination were conceived to be able to produce all substances, qualities, actions, etc. No difference was acknowledged to exist between substances, qualities and actions, and it was conceived

[1] On the meaning of the word Mīmāṃsā see Chapter IV.

that these were but so many aspects of a combination of the three types of reals in different proportions. The reals contained within them the rudiments of all developments of matter, knowledge, willing, feelings, etc. As combinations of reals changed incessantly and new phenomena of matter and mind were manifested, collocations did not bring about any new thing but brought about a phenomenon which was already there in its causes in another form. What we call knowledge or thought ordinarily, is with them merely a form of subtle illuminating matter-stuff. Sāṃkhya holds however that there is a transcendent entity as pure consciousness and that by some kind of transcendent reflection or contact this pure consciousness transforms the bare translucent thought-matter into conscious thought or experience of a person.

But this hypothesis of a pure self, as essentially distinct and separate from knowledge as ordinarily understood, can hardly be demonstrated in our common sense experience; and this has been pointed out by the Nyāya school in a very strong and emphatic manner. Even Sāṃkhya did not try to prove that the existence of its transcendent puruṣa could be demonstrated in experience, and it had to attempt to support its hypothesis of the existence of a transcendent self on the ground of the need of a permanent entity as a fixed object, to which the passing states of knowledge could cling, and on grounds of moral struggle towards virtue and emancipation. Sāṃkhya had first supposed knowledge to be merely a combination of changing reals, and then had as a matter of necessity to admit a fixed principle as puruṣa (pure transcendent consciousness). The self is thus here in some sense an object of inference to fill up the gap left by the inadequate analysis of consciousness (*buddhi*) as being non-intelligent and incessantly changing.

Nyāya fared no better, for it also had to demonstrate self on the ground that since knowledge existed it was a quality, and therefore must inhere in some substance. This hypothesis is again based upon another uncritical assumption that substances and attributes were entirely separate, and that it was the nature of the latter to inhere in the former, and also that knowledge was a quality requiring (similarly with other attributes) a substance in which to inhere. None of them could take their stand upon the self-conscious nature of our ordinary thought and draw their conclusions on the strength of the direct evidence of this self-conscious thought. Of course it is true that Sāṃkhya had approached nearer to this view than Nyāya, but it had separated the content of knowledge and its essence so irrevocably that it threatened to break the integrity of thought in a manner quite unwarranted by common sense experience, which does not seem to reveal this dual element in thought. Anyhow the unification of the content of thought and its essence had to be made, and this could not be done except by what may be regarded as a makeshift—a transcendent illusion running on from beginningless time. These difficulties occurred because Sāṃkhya soared to a region which was not directly illuminated by the light of common sense experience. The Nyāya position is of course much worse as a metaphysical solution, for it did not indeed try to solve anything, but only gave us a schedule of inferential results which could not be tested by experience, and which were based ultimately on a one-sided and uncritical assumption. It is an uncritical common sense experience that substances are different from qualities and actions, and that the latter inhere in the former. To base the whole of metaphysics on such a tender and fragile experience is, to say the least, building on a weak foundation. It was necessary that the importance of the self-revealing thought must be brought to the forefront, its evidence should be collected and trusted, and an account of experience should be given according to its verdict. No construction of metaphysics can ever satisfy us which ignores the direct immediate convictions of self-conscious thought. It is a relief to find that a movement of philosophy in this direction is ushered in by the Mīmāṃsā system. The *Mīmāṃsā sūtras* were written by Jaimini and the commentary (*bhāṣya*) on it was written by Śabara. But the systematic elaboration of it was made by Kumārila, who preceded the great Śaṅkarācārya, and a disciple of Kumārila, Prabhākara.

The Mīmāṃsā Literature.

It is difficult to say how the sacrificial system of worship grew in India in the Brāhmaṇas. This system once set up gradually began to develop into a net-work of elaborate rituals, the details of which were probably taken note of by the priests. As some generations passed and the sacrifices spread over larger tracts of India and grew up into more and more elaborate details, the old rules and regulations began to be collected probably as tradition had it, and this it seems gave rise to the smṛti literature. Discussions and doubts became more common about the many intricacies of the sacrificial rituals, and regular rational enquiries into them were begun in different circles by different scholars and priests. These represent the beginnings of Mīmāṃsā (lit. attempts at rational enquiry), and it is probable that there were different schools of this thought. That Jaimini's *Mīmāṃsā sūtras* (which are with us the foundations of Mīmāṃsā) are only a comprehensive and systematic compilation of one school is evident from the references he gives to the views in different matters of other preceding writers who dealt with the subject. These works are not available now, and we cannot say how much of what Jaimini has written is his original work and how much of it borrowed. But it may be said with some degree of confidence that it was deemed so masterly a work at least of one school that it has survived all other attempts that were made before him. Jaimini's *Mīmāṃsā sūtras* were probably written about 200 B.C. and are now the ground work of the Mīmāṃsā system. Commentaries were written on it by various persons such as Bhartṛmitra (alluded to in *Nyāyaratnākara* verse 10 of *Ślokavārttika*), Bhavadāsa (*Pratijñasūtra* 63), Hari and Upavarṣa (mentioned in *Śāstradīpikā*). It is probable that at least some of these preceded Śabara, the writer of the famous commentary known as the *Śabara-bhāṣya*. It is difficult to say anything about the time in which he flourished. Dr Gaṅgānātha Jhā would have him about 57 B.C. on the evidence of a current verse which speaks of King Vikramāditya as being the son of Śabarasvāmin by a Kṣattriya wife. This bhāṣya of Śabara is the basis of the later Mīmāṃsā works. It was commented upon by an unknown person alluded to as Vārttikakāra by Prabhākara and merely referred to as "yathāhuḥ" (as they say) by Kumārila. Dr Gaṅgānātha Jhā says that Prabhākara's commentary *Bṛhatī* on the *Śabara-bhāṣya* was based upon the work of this Vārttikakāra. This *Bṛhatī* of Prabhākara had another commentary on it—*Ṛjuvimālā* by Śālikanātha Miśra, who also wrote a compendium on the Prabhākara interpretation of Mīmāṃsā called *Prakaraṇapañcikā*. Tradition says that Prabhākara (often referred to as Nibandhakāra), whose views are often alluded to as "gurumata," was a pupil of Kumārila. Kumārila Bhaṭṭa, who is traditionally believed to be the senior contemporary of Śaṅkara (788 A.D.), wrote his celebrated independent exposition of Śabara's bhāṣya in three parts known as *Śloka-vārttika* (dealing only with the philosophical portion of Śabara's work as contained in the first chapter of the first book known as Tarkapāda), *Tantravārttika* (dealing with the remaining three chapters of the first book, the second and the third book) and *Ṭupṭīkā* (containing brief notes on the remaining nine books)[1]. Kumārila is referred to by his later followers as Bhaṭṭa, Bhaṭṭa-pāda, and Vārttikakāra. The next great Mīmāṃsā scholar and follower of Kumārila was Maṇḍana Miśra, the author of *Vidhi-viveka*, *Mīmāṃsānukramaṇī* and the commentator of *Tantra-vārttika*, who became later on converted by Śaṅkara to Vedantism. Pārthasārathi Miśra (about ninth century A.D.) wrote his *Śāstradī-pikā*, *Tantraratna*, and *Nyāyaratnamālā* following the footprints of Kumārila. Amongst the numerous other followers of Kumārila, the names of Sucarita Miśra the author of *Kāśikā* and Someśvara the author of *Nyāyasudhā* deserve special notice. Rāmakṛṣṇa Bhaṭṭa wrote an excellent commentary on the *Tarkapāda* of *Śās-tradīpikā* called the *Yuktisnehapūraṇī-siddhānta-candrikā* and Somanātha wrote his *Mayūkhamālikā* on the remaining chapters of *Śāstradīpikā*. Other important current Mīmāṃsā works which deserve notice are such as *Nyāyamālāvistara* of Mādhava, *Subo-dhinī*, *Mīmāṃsābālaprakāśa* of Śaṅkara Bhaṭṭa, *Nyāyakaṇikā* of Vācaspati Miśra, *Mīmāṃsāparibhāṣa* by Kṛṣṇayajvan, *Mīmāṃsā-nyāyaprakāśa* by Anantadeva, Gāgā Bhaṭṭa's *Bhaṭṭacintāmaṇi*, etc. Most of the books mentioned here have been consulted in the writing of this chapter. The importance of the Mīmāṃsā litera-ture for a Hindu is indeed great. For not only are all Vedic duties to be performed according to its maxims, but even the smṛti literatures which regulate the daily duties, ceremonials and rituals of Hindus even at the present day are all guided and explained by them. The legal side of the smṛtis consisting of inheritance, proprietory rights, adoption, etc. which guide Hindu civil life even under the British administration is explained according to the Mīmāṃsā maxims. Its relations to the Vedānta philosophy will be briefly indicated in the next chapter. Its relations with Nyāya-Vaiśeṣika have also been pointed out in various places of this chapter. The views of the two schools of Mīmāṃsā as propounded by Prabhākara and Kumārila on all the important topics have

[1] Mahāmahopādhyāya Haraprasāda Śāstrī says, in his introduction to *Six Buddhist Nyāya Tracts*, that "Kumārila preceded Saṅkara by two generations."

also been pointed out. Prabhākara's views however could not win many followers in later times, but while living it is said that he was regarded by Kumārila as a very strong rival[1]. Hardly any new contribution has been made to the Mīmāṃsā philosophy after Kumārila and Prabhākara. The *Mīmāṃsā sūtras* deal mostly with the principles of the interpretation of the Vedic texts in connection with sacrifices, and very little of philosophy can be gleaned out of them. Śabara's contributions are also slight and vague. Vārttikakāra's views also can only be gathered from the references to them by Kumārila and Prabhākara. What we know of Mīmāṃsā philosophy consists of their views and theirs alone. It did not develop any further after them. Works written on the subject in later times were but of a purely expository nature. I do not know of any work on Mīmāṃsā written in English except the excellent one by Dr Gaṅgānātha Jhā on the Prabhākara Mīmāṃsā to which I have frequently referred.

The Parataḥ-prāmāṇya doctrine of Nyāya and the Svataḥ-prāmāṇya doctrine of Mīmāṃsā.

The doctrine of the self-validity of knowledge (*svataḥ-prāmāṇya*) forms the cornerstone on which the whole structure of the Mīmāṃsā philosophy is based. Validity means the certitude of truth. The Mīmāṃsā philosophy asserts that all knowledge excepting the action of remembering (*smṛti*) or memory is valid in itself, for it itself certifies its own truth, and neither depends on any other extraneous condition nor on any other knowledge for its validity. But Nyāya holds that this self-validity of knowledge is a question which requires an explanation. It is true that under certain conditions a piece of knowledge is produced in us, but what is meant by saying that this knowledge is a proof of its own truth? When we perceive anything as blue, it is the direct result of visual contact, and this visual contact cannot certify that the knowledge generated is true, as the visual contact is not in any touch with the knowledge

[1] There is a story that Kumārila, not being able to convert Prabhākara, his own pupil, to his views, attempted a trick and pretended that he was dead. His disciples then asked Prabhākara whether his burial rites should be performed according to Kumārila's views or Prabhākara's. Prabhākara said that his own views were erroneous, but these were held by him only to rouse up Kumārila's pointed attacks, whereas Kumārila's views were the right ones. Kumārila then rose up and said that Prabhākara was defeated, but the latter said he was not defeated so long as he was alive. But this has of course no historic value.

it has conditioned. Moreover, knowledge is a mental affair and how can it certify the objective truth of its representation? In other words, how can my perception "a blue thing" guarantee that what is subjectively perceived as blue is really so objectively as well? After my perception of anything as blue we do not have any such perception that what I have perceived as blue is really so. So this so-called self-validity of knowledge cannot be testified or justified by any perception. We can only be certain that knowledge has been produced by the perceptual act, but there is nothing in this knowledge or its revelation of its object from which we can infer that the perception is also objectively valid or true. If the production of any knowledge should certify its validity then there would be no invalidity, no illusory knowledge, and following our perception of even a mirage we should never come to grief. But we are disappointed often in our perceptions, and this proves that when we practically follow the directions of our perception we are undecided as to its validity, which can only be ascertained by the correspondence of the perception with what we find later on in practical experience. Again, every piece of knowledge is the result of certain causal collocations, and as such depends upon them for its production, and hence cannot be said to rise without depending on anything else. It is meaningless to speak of the validity of knowledge, for validity always refers to objective realization of our desires and attempts proceeding in accordance with our knowledge. People only declare their knowledge invalid when proceeding practically in accordance with it they are disappointed. The perception of a mirage is called invalid when proceeding in accordance with our perception we do not find anything that can serve the purposes of water (e.g. drinking, bathing). The validity or truth of knowledge is thus the attainment by practical experience of the object and the fulfilment of all our purposes from it (*arthakriyā-jñāna* or *phalajñāna*) just as perception or knowledge represented them to the perceiver. There is thus no self-validity of knowledge (*svataḥ-prāmāṇya*), but validity is ascertained by *saṃvāda* or agreement with the objective facts of experience[1].

It is easy to see that this Nyāya objection is based on the supposition that knowledge is generated by certain objective collocations of conditions, and that knowledge so produced can

[1] See *Nyāyamañjarī*, pp. 160–173.

only be tested by its agreement with objective facts. But this theory of knowledge is merely an hypothesis; for it can never be experienced that knowledge is the product of any collocations; we have a perception and immediately we become aware of certain objective things; knowledge reveals to us the facts of the objective world and this is experienced by us always. But that the objective world generates knowledge in us is only an hypothesis which can hardly be demonstrated by experience. It is the supreme prerogative of knowledge that it reveals all other things. It is not a phenomenon like any other phenomenon of the world. When we say that knowledge has been produced in us by the external collocations, we just take a perverse point of view which is unwarranted by experience; knowledge only photographs the objective phenomena for us; but there is nothing to show that knowledge has been generated by these phenomena. This is only a theory which applies the ordinary conceptions of causation to knowledge and this is evidently unwarrantable. Knowledge is not like any other phenomena for it stands above them and interprets or illumines them all. There can be no validity in things, for truth applies to knowledge and knowledge alone. What we call agreement with facts by practical experience is but the agreement of previous knowledge with later knowledge; for objective facts never come to us directly, they are always taken on the evidence of knowledge, and they have no other certainty than what is bestowed on them by knowledge. There arise indeed different kinds of knowledge revealing different things, but these latter do not on that account generate the former, for this is never experienced; we are never aware of any objective fact before it is revealed by knowledge. Why knowledge makes different kinds of revelations is indeed more than we can say, for experience only shows that knowledge reveals objective facts and not why it does so. The rise of knowledge is never perceived by us to be dependent on any objective fact, for all objective facts are dependent on it for its revelation or illumination. This is what is said to be the self-validity (*svataḥ-prāmāṇya*) of knowledge in its production (*utpatti*). As soon as knowledge is produced, objects are revealed to us; there is no intermediate link between the rise of knowledge and the revelation of objects on which knowledge depends for producing its action of revealing or illuminating them. Thus knowledge is not only independent of anything else in its own rise but in its own action as well (*svakāryakaraṇe svataḥ prāmāṇyaṃ jñānasya*). Whenever there is any knowledge it carries with it the impression that it is certain and valid, and we are naturally thus prompted to work (*pravṛtti*) according to its direction. There is no indecision in our mind at the time of the rise of knowledge as to the correctness of knowledge; but just as knowledge rises, it carries with it the certainty of its revelation, presence, or action. But in cases of illusory perception other perceptions or cognitions dawn which carry with them the notion that our original knowledge was not valid. Thus though the invalidity of any knowledge may appear to us by later experience, and in accordance with which we reject our former knowledge, yet when the knowledge first revealed itself to us it carried with it the conviction of certainty which goaded us on to work according to its indication. Whenever a man works according to his knowledge, he does so with the conviction that his knowledge is valid, and not in a passive or uncertain temper of mind. This is what Mīmāṃsā means when it says that the validity of knowledge appears immediately with its rise, though its invalidity may be derived from later experience or some other data (*jñānasya prāmāṇyam svataḥ aprāmāṇyaṃ parataḥ*). Knowledge attained is proved invalid when later on a contradictory experience (*bādhakajñāna*) comes in or when our organs etc. are known to be faulty and defective (*karaṇadoṣajñāna*). It is from these that knowledge appearing as valid is invalidated; when we take all necessary care to look for these and yet find them not, we must think that they do not exist. Thus the validity of knowledge certified at the moment of its production need not be doubted unnecessarily when even after enquiry we do not find any defect in sense or any contradiction in later experience. All knowledge except memory is thus regarded as valid independently by itself as a general rule, unless it is invalidated later on. Memory is excluded because the phenomenon of memory depends upon a previous experience, and its existing latent impressions, and cannot thus be regarded as arising independently by itself.

The place of sense organs in perception.

We have just said that knowledge arises by itself and that it could not have been generated by sense-contact. If this be so, the diversity of perceptions is however left unexplained. But in face of the Nyāya philosophy explaining all perceptions on the ground of diverse sense-contact the Mīmāṃsā probably could not afford to remain silent on such an important point. It therefore accepted the Nyāya view of sense-contact as a condition of knowledge with slight modifications, and yet held their doctrine of svataḥ-prāmāṇya. It does not appear to have been conscious of a conflict between these two different principles of the production of knowledge. Evidently the point of view from which it looked at it was that the fact that there were the senses and contacts of them with the objects, or such special capacities in them by virtue of which the things could be perceived, was with us a matter of inference. Their actions in producing the knowledge are never experienced at the time of the rise of knowledge, but when the knowledge arises we argue that such and such senses must have acted. The only case where knowledge is found to be dependent on anything else seems to be the case where one knowledge is found to depend on a previous experience or knowledge as in the case of memory. In other cases the dependence of the rise of knowledge on anything else cannot be felt, for the physical collocations conditioning knowledge are not felt to be operating before the rise of knowledge, and these are only inferred later on in accordance with the nature and characteristic of knowledge. We always have our first start in knowledge which is directly experienced from which we may proceed later on to the operation and nature of objective facts in relation to it. Thus it is that though contact of the senses with the objects may later on be imagined to be the conditioning factor, yet the rise of knowledge as well as our notion of its validity strikes us as original, underived, immediate, and first-hand.

Prabhākara gives us a sketch as to how the existence of the senses may be inferred. Thus our cognitions of objects are phenomena which are not all the same, and do not happen always in the same manner, for these vary differently at different moments; the cognitions of course take place in the soul which may thus be regarded as the material cause (*samavāyikāraṇa*); but there must be some such movements or other specific associations (*asamavāyikāraṇa*) which render the production of this or that specific cognition possible. The immaterial causes subsist either in the cause of the material cause (e.g. in the case of the colouring of a white piece of cloth, the colour of the yarns which is the cause of the colour in the cloth subsists in the yarns which form the material cause of the cloth) or in the material cause itself (e.g. in the case of a new form of smell being produced in a substance by fire-contact, this contact, which is the immaterial cause of the smell, subsists in that substance itself which is put in the fire and which the smell is produced). The soul is eternal and has no other cause, and it has to be assumed that the immaterial cause required for the rise of a cognition must inhere in the soul, and hence must be a quality. Then again accepting the Nyāya conclusions we know that the rise of qualities in an eternal thing can only take place by contact with some other substances. Now cognition being a quality which the soul acquires would naturally require the contact of such substances. Since there is nothing to show that such substances inhere in other substances they are also to be taken as eternal. There are three eternal substances, time, space, and atoms. But time and space being all-pervasive the soul is always in contact with them. Contact with these therefore cannot explain the occasional rise of different cognitions. This contact must then be of some kind of atom which resides in the body ensouled by the cognizing soul. This atom may be called *manas* (mind). This manas alone by itself brings about cognitions, pleasure, pain, desire, aversion, effort, etc. The manas however by itself is found to be devoid of any such qualities as colour, smell, etc., and as such cannot lead the soul to experience or cognize these qualities; hence it stands in need of such other organs as may be characterized by these qualities; for the cognition of colour, the mind will need the aid of an organ of which colour is the characteristic quality; for the cognition of smell, an organ having the odorous characteristic and so on with touch, taste, vision. Now we know that the organ which has colour for its distinctive feature must be one composed of tejas or light, as colour is a feature of light, and this proves the existence of the organ, the eye—for the cognition of colour; in a similar manner the existence of the earthly organ (organ of smell), the aqueous organ (organ of taste), the ākāśic organ (organ of sound) and the airy organ (organ of touch) may be demonstrated. But without manas none of these organs is found to be effective. Four necessary contacts have to be admitted, (1) of the sense organs with the object, (2) of the sense organs with the qualities of the object, (3) of the manas with the sense organs, and (4) of the manas with the soul. The objects of perception are of three kinds, (1) substances, (2) qualities, (3) jāti or class. The material substances are tangible objects of earth, fire, water, air in large dimensions (for in their fine atomic states they cannot be perceived). The qualities are colour, taste, smell, touch, number, dimension, separateness, conjunction, disjunction, priority, posteriority, pleasure, pain, desire, aversion, and effort[1].

It may not be out of place here to mention in conclusion that Kumārila Bhaṭṭa was rather undecided as to the nature of the senses or of their contact with the objects. Thus he says that the senses may be conceived either as certain functions or activities, or as entities having the capacity of revealing things without coming into actual contact with them, or that they might be entities which actually come in contact with their objects[2], and he prefers this last view as being more satisfactory.

Indeterminate and determinate perception.

There are two kinds of perception in two stages, the first stage is called *nirvikalpa* (indeterminate) and the second *savikalpa* (determinate). The nirvikalpa perception of a thing is its perception at the first moment of the association of the senses and their objects. Thus Kumārila says that the cognition that appears first is a mere *ālocana* or simple perception, called non-determinate pertaining to the object itself pure and simple, and resembling the cognitions that the new-born infant has of things around himself. In this cognition neither the genus nor the differentia is presented to consciousness; all that is present there is the individual wherein these two subsist. This view of indeterminate perception may seem in some sense to resemble the Buddhist view which defines it as being merely the specific individuality (*svalakṣaṇa*) and regards it as being the only valid element in perception, whereas all the rest are conceived as being imaginary

[1] See *Prakaraṇapañcikā*, pp. 52 etc., and Dr Gaṅgānātha Jhā's *Prabhākaramīmāṃsā*, pp. 35 etc.

[2] *Ślokavārttika*, see *Pratyakṣasūtra*, 40 etc., and *Nyāyaratnākara* on it. It may be noted in this connection that Sāṃkhya-Yoga did not think like Nyāya that the senses actually went out to meet the objects (*prāpyakāritva*) but held that there was a special kind of functioning (*vṛtti*) by virtue of which the senses could grasp even such distant objects as the sun and the stars. It is the functioning of the sense that reached the objects. The nature of this vṛtti is not further clearly explained and Pārthasārathi objects to it as being almost a different category (*tattvāntara*).

impositions. But both Kumārila and Prabhākara think that both the genus and the differentia are perceived in the indeterminate stage, but these do not manifest themselves to us only because we do not remember the other things in relation to which, or in contrast to which, the percept has to show its character as genus or differentia; a thing can be cognized as an "individual" only in comparison with other things from which it differs in certain well-defined characters; and it can be apprehended as belonging to a class only when it is found to possess certain characteristic features in common with some other things; so we see that as other things are not presented to consciousness through memory, the percept at the indeterminate stage cannot be fully apprehended as an individual belonging to a class, though the data constituting the characteristic of the thing as a genus and its differentia are perceived at the indeterminate stage[1]. So long as other things are not remembered these data cannot manifest themselves properly, and hence the perception of the thing remains indeterminate at the first stage of perception. At the second stage the self by its past impressions brings the present perception in relation to past ones and realizes its character as involving universal and particular. It is thus apparent that the difference between the indeterminate and the determinate perception is this, that in the latter case memory of other things creeps in, but this association of memory in the determinate perception refers to those other objects of memory and not to the percept. It is also held that though the determinate perception is based upon the indeterminate one, yet since the former also apprehends certain such factors as did not enter into the indeterminate perception, it is to be regarded as a valid cognition. Kumārila also agrees with Prabhākara in holding both the indeterminate and the determinate perception valid[2].

Some Ontological Problems connected with the Doctrine of Perception.

The perception of the class (*jāti*) of a percept in relation to other things may thus be regarded in the main as a difference between determinate and indeterminate perceptions. The problems of jāti and avayavāvayavī (part and whole notion) were

[1] Compare this with the Vaiśeṣika view as interpreted by Śrīdhara.

[2] See *Prakaraṇapañcikā* and *Śāstradīpikā*.

the subjects of hot dispute in Indian philosophy. Before entering into discussion about jāti, Prabhākara first introduced the problem of *avayava* (part) and *avayavī* (whole). He argues as an exponent of svataḥ-prāmāṇyavāda that the proof of the true existence of anything must ultimately rest on our own consciousness, and what is distinctly recognized in consciousness must be admitted to have its existence established. Following this canon Prabhākara says that gross objects as a whole exist, since they are so perceived. The subtle atoms are the material cause and their connection (*saṃyoga*) is the immaterial cause (*asamavāyikāraṇa*), and it is the latter which renders the whole altogether different from the parts of which it is composed; and it is not necessary that all the parts should be perceived before the whole is perceived. Kumārila holds that it is due to the point of view from which we look at a thing that we call it a separate whole or only a conglomeration of parts. In reality they are identical, but when we lay stress on the notion of parts, the thing appears to be a conglomeration of them, and when we look at it from the point of view of the unity appearing as a whole, the thing appears to be a whole of which there are parts (see *Ślokavārttika, Vanavāda*)[1].

Jāti, though incorporating the idea of having many units within one, is different from the conception of whole in this, that it resides in its entirety in each individual constituting that jāti (*vyāśajya-*

[1] According to Sāṃkhya-Yoga a thing is regarded as the unity of the universal and the particular (*sāmānyaviśeṣasamudāyo dravyam*, *Vyāsabhāṣya*, III. 44); for there is no other separate entity which is different from them both in which they would inhere as Nyāya holds. Conglomerations can be of two kinds, namely those in which the parts exist at a distance from one another (e.g. a forest), and those in which they exist close together (*nirantarā hi tadavayavāḥ*), and it is this latter combination (*ayutasiddhāvayava*) which is called a dravya, but here also there is no separate whole distinct from the parts; it is the parts connected in a particular way and having no perceptible space between them that is called a thing or a whole. The Buddhists as Paṇḍitāśoka has shown did not believe in any whole (*avayavī*); it is the atoms which in connection with one another appeared as a whole occupying space (*paramāṇava eva hi pararūpadeśaparihāreṇotpannāḥ parasparasahitā avabhāsamānā deśavitānavanto bhavanti*). The whole is thus a mere appearance and not a reality (see *Avayavinirākaraṇa*, *Six Buddhist Nyāya Tracts*). Nyāya however held that the atoms were partless (*niravayava*) and hence it would be wrong to say that when we see an object we see the atoms. The existence of a whole as different from the parts which belong to it is directly experienced and there is no valid reason against it:

"*aduṣṭakaraṇodbhūtamanāvirbhūtabādhakam*
asandigdañca vijñānaṃ katham mithyeti kathyate."

Nyāyamañjarī, pp. 550 ff.

vṛtti), but the establishment of the existence of wholes refutes the argument that jāti should be denied, because it involves the conception of a whole (class) consisting of many parts (individuals). The class character or jāti exists because it is distinctly perceived by us in the individuals included in any particular class. It is eternal in the sense that it continues to exist in other individuals, even when one of the individuals ceases to exist. When a new individual of that class (e.g. cow class) comes into being, a new relation of inherence is generated by which the individual is brought into relation with the class-character existing in other individuals; for inherence (*samavāya*) according to Prabhākara is not an eternal entity but an entity which is both produced and not produced according as the thing in which it exists is non-eternal or eternal, and it is not regarded as one as Nyāya holds, but as many, according as there is the infinite number of things in which it exists. When any individual is destroyed, the class-character does not go elsewhere, nor subsist in that individual, nor is itself destroyed, but it is only the inherence of class-character with that individual that ceases to exist. With the destruction of an individual or its production it is a new relation of inherence that is destroyed or produced. But the class-character or jāti has no separate existence apart from the individuals as Nyāya supposes. Apprehension of jāti is essentially the apprehension of the class-character of a thing in relation to other similar things of that class by the perception of the common characteristics. But Prabhākara would not admit the existence of a highest genus sattā (being) as acknowledged by Nyāya. He argues that the existence of class-character is apprehended because we find that the individuals of a class possess some common characteristic possessed by all the heterogeneous and disparate things of the world as can give rise to the conception of a separate jāti as sattā, as demanded by the naiyāyikas. That all things are said to be *sat* (existing) is more or less a word or a name without the corresponding apprehension of a common quality. Our experience always gives us concrete existing individuals, but we can never experience such a highest genus as pure existence or being, as it has no concrete form which may be perceived. When we speak of a thing as *sat*, we do not mean that it is possessed of any such class-characters as sattā (being); what we mean is simply that the individual has its specific existence or *svarū-*

pasattā. Thus the Nyāya view of perception as taking only the thing in its pure being apart from qualities, etc. (*sanmātra-viṣayam pratyakṣaṃ*) is made untenable by Prabhākara, as according to him the thing is perceived direct with all its qualities. According to Kumārila however jāti is not something different from the individuals comprehended by it and it is directly perceived. Kumārila's view of jāti is thus similar to that held by Sāṃkhya, namely that when we look at an individual from one point of view (jāti as identical with the individual), it is the individual that lays its stress upon our consciousness and the notion of jāti becomes latent, but when we look at it from another point of view (the individual as identical with jāti) it is the jāti which presents itself to consciousness, and the aspect as individual becomes latent. The apprehension as jāti or as individual is thus only a matter of different points of view or angles of vision from which we look at a thing. Quite in harmony with the conception of jāti, Kumārila holds that the relation of inherence is not anything which is distinct from the things themselves in which it is supposed to exist, but only a particular aspect or phase of the things themselves (*Ślokavārttika, Pratyakṣasūtra*, 149, 150, *abhedāt samavāyo'stu svarūpam dharmadharmiṇoḥ*), Kumārila agrees with Prabhākara that jāti is perceived by the senses (*tatraikabuddhinirgrāhyā jātirindriyagocarā*).

It is not out of place to mention that on the evidence of Prabhākara we find that the category of viśeṣa admitted by the Kaṇāda school is not accepted as a separate category by the Mīmāṃsā on the ground that the differentiation of eternal things from one another, for which the category of viśeṣa is admitted, may very well be effected on the basis of the ordinary qualities of these things. The quality of pṛthaktva or specific differences in atoms, as inferred by the difference of things they constitute, can very well serve the purposes of viśeṣa.

The nature of knowledge.

All knowledge involves the knower, the known object, and the knowledge at the same identical moment. All knowledge whether perceptual, inferential or of any other kind must necessarily reveal the self or the knower directly. Thus as in all knowledge the self is directly and immediately perceived, all knowledge may be regarded as perception from the point of view of self. The division of the pramāṇas as pratyakṣa (perception), anumāna (inference), etc. is from the point of view of the objects of knowledge with reference to the varying modes in which they are brought within the purview of knowledge. The self itself however has no illumining or revealing powers, for then even in deep sleep we could have knowledge, for the self is present even then, as is proved by the remembrance of dreams. It is knowledge (*saṃvid*) that reveals by its very appearance both the self, the knower, and the objects. It is generally argued against the self-illuminative character of knowledge that all cognitions are of the forms of the objects they are said to reveal; and if they have the same form we may rather say that they have the same identical reality too. The Mīmāṃsā answer to these objections is this, that if the cognition and the cognized were not different from one another, they could not have been felt as such, and we could not have felt that it is by cognition that we apprehend the cognized objects. The cognition (*saṃvedana*) of a person simply means that such a special kind of quality (*dharma*) has been manifested in the self by virtue of which his active operation with reference to a certain object is favoured or determined, and the object of cognition is that with reference to which the active operation of the self has been induced. Cognitions are not indeed absolutely formless, for they have the cognitional character by which things are illumined and manifested. Cognition has no other character than this, that it illumines and reveals objects. The things only are believed to have forms and only such forms as knowledge reveal to us about them. Even the dream cognition is with reference to objects that were perceived previously, and of which the impressions were left in the mind and were aroused by the unseen agency (*adṛṣṭa*). Dream cognition is thus only a kind of remembrance of that which was previously experienced. Only such of the impressions of cognized objects are roused in dreams as can beget just that amount of pleasurable or painful experience, in accordance with the operation of adṛṣṭa, as the person deserves to have in accordance with his previous merit or demerit.

The Prabhākara Mīmāṃsā, in refuting the arguments of those who hold that our cognitions of objects are themselves cognized by some other cognition, says that this is not possible, since we do not experience any such double cognition and also because it would lead us to a *regressus ad infinitum*, for if a second cognition is necessary to interpret the first, then that would require a third and so on. If a cognition could be the object of another cognition, then it could not be self-valid. The cognition is not of course unknown to us, but that is of course because it is self-cognized, and reveals itself to us the moment it reveals its objects. From the illumination of objects also we can infer the presence of this self-cognizing knowledge. But it is only its presence that is inferred and not the cognition itself, for inference can only indicate the presence of an object and not in the form in which it can be apprehended by perception (*pratyakṣa*). Prabhākara draws a subtle distinction between perceptuality (*saṃvedyatva*) and being object of knowledge (*prameyatva*). A thing can only be apprehended (*saṃvedyate*) by perception, whereas inference can only indicate the presence of an object without apprehending the object itself. Our cognition cannot be apprehended by any other cognition. Inference can only indicate the presence or existence of knowledge but cannot apprehend the cognition itself[1].

Kumārila also agrees with Prabhākara in holding that perception is never the object of another perception and that it ends in the direct apprehensibility of the object of perception. But he says that every perception involves a relationship between the perceiver and the perceived, wherein the perceiver behaves as the agent whose activity in grasping the object is known as cognition. This is indeed different from the Prabhākara view, that in one manifestation of knowledge the knower, the known, and the knowledge, are simultaneously illuminated (the doctrine of *tripuṭīpratyakṣa*)[2].

The Psychology of Illusion.

The question however arises that if all apprehensions are valid, how are we to account for illusory perceptions which cannot be regarded as valid? The problem of illusory perception and its psychology is a very favourite topic of discussion in Indian philosophy. Omitting the theory of illusion of the Jains called *satkhyāti* which we have described before, and of the Vedāntists, which we shall describe in the next chapter, there are three different theories of illusion, viz. (1) *ātmakhyāti*, (2) *viparītakhyāti* or *anyathākhyāti*, and (3) *akhyāti* of the Mīmāṃsā school. The

[1] See *Prabhākaramīmāṃsā*, by Dr Gaṅgānātha Jhā.

[2] *loc. cit.* pp. 26–28.

viparītākhyāti or anyathākhyāti theory of illusion is accepted by the Nyāya, Vaiśeṣika and the Yoga, the ākhyāti theory by Mīmāṃsā and Sāṃkhya and the ātmakhyāti by the Buddhists.

The commonest example of illusion in Indian philosophy is the illusory appearance of a piece of broken conch-shell as a piece of silver. That such an illusion occurs is a fact which is experienced by all and agreed to by all. The differences of view are with regard to its cause or its psychology. The idealistic Buddhists who deny the existence of the external world and think that there are only the forms of knowledge, generated by the accumulated karma of past lives, hold that just as in the case of a correct perception, so also in the case of illusory perception it is the flow of knowledge which must be held responsible. The flow of knowledge on account of the peculiarities of its own collocating conditions generates sometimes what we call right perception and sometimes wrong perception or illusion. On this view nothing depends upon the so-called external data. For they do not exist, and even if they did exist, why should the same data sometimes bring about the right perception and sometimes the illusion? The flow of knowledge creates both the percept and the perceiver and unites them. This is true both in the case of correct perception and illusory perception. Nyāya objects to the above view, and says that if knowledge irrespective of any external condition imposes upon itself the knower and the illusory percept, then the perception ought to be of the form "I am silver" and not "this is silver." Moreover this theory stands refuted, as it is based upon a false hypothesis that it is the inner knowledge which appears as coming from outside and that the external as such does not exist.

The viparītakhyāti or the anyathākhyāti theory supposes that the illusion takes place because on account of malobservation we do not note the peculiar traits of the conch-shell as distinguished from the silver, and at the same time by the glow etc. of the conch-shell unconsciously the silver which I had seen elsewhere is remembered and the object before me is taken as silver. In illusion the object before us with which our eye is associated is not conch-shell, for the traits peculiar to it not being grasped, it is merely an object. The silver is not utterly non-existent, for it exists elsewhere and it is the memory of it as experienced before that creates confusion and leads us to think of the conch-shell as silver. This school agrees with the ākhyāti school that the fact that I remember silver is not taken note of at the time of illusion. But it holds that the mere non-distinction is not enough to account for the phenomenon of illusion, for there is a definite positive aspect associated with it, viz. the false identification of silver (seen elsewhere) with the conch-shell before us.

The akhyāti theory of Mīmāṃsā holds that since the special peculiarities of the conch-shell are not noticed, it is erroneous to say that we identify or cognize positively the conch-shell as the silver (perceived elsewhere), for the conch-shell is not cognized at all. What happens here is simply this, that only the features common to conch-shell and silver being noticed, the perceiver fails to apprehend the difference between these two things, and this gives rise to the cognition of silver. Owing to a certain weakness of the mind the remembrance of silver roused by the common features of the conch-shell and silver is not apprehended, and the fact that it is only a memory of silver seen in some past time that has appeared before him is not perceived; and it is as a result of this non-apprehension of the difference between the silver remembered and the present conch-shell that the illusion takes place. Thus, though the illusory perception partakes of a dual character of remembrance and apprehension, and as such is different from the ordinary valid perception (which is wholly a matter of direct apprehension) of real silver before us, yet as the difference between the remembrance of silver and the sight of the present object is not apprehended, the illusory perception appears at the moment of its production to be as valid as a real valid perception. Both give rise to the same kind of activity on the part of the agent, for in illusory perception the perceiver would be as eager to stoop and pick up the thing as in the case of a real perception. Kumārila agrees with this view as expounded by Prabhākara, and further says that the illusory judgment is as valid to the cognizor at the time that he has the cognition as any real judgment could be. If subsequent experience rejects it, that does not matter, for it is admitted in Mīmāṃsā that when later experience finds out the defects of any perception it can invalidate the original perception which was self-valid at the time of its production[1]. It is easy to see that the Mīmāṃsā had to adopt this view of illusion to maintain the doctrine that all cognition at the moment of its production is valid. The ākhyāti theory

[1] See *Prakaraṇapañcikā*, *Śāstradīpikā*, and *Ślokavārttika*, sūtra 2.

tries to establish the view that the illusion is not due to any positive wrong knowledge, but to a mere negative factor of non-apprehension due to certain weakness of mind. So it is that though illusion is the result, yet the cognition so far as it is cognition, is made up of two elements, the present perception and memory, both of which are true so far as they are individually present to us, and the cognition itself has all the characteristics of any other valid knowledge, for the mark of the validity of a cognition is its power to prompt us to action. In doubtful cognitions also, as in the case "Is this a post or a man?" what is actually perceived is some tall object and thus far it is valid too. But when this perception gives rise to two different kinds of remembrance (of the pillar and the man), doubt comes in. So the element of apprehension involved in doubtful cognitions should be regarded as self-valid as any other cognition.

Inference.

Śabara says that when a certain fixed or permanent relation has been known to exist between two things, we can have the idea of one thing when the other one is perceived, and this kind of knowledge is called inference. Kumārila on the basis of this tries to show that inference is only possible when we notice that in a large number of cases two things (e.g. smoke and fire) subsist together in a third thing (e.g. kitchen, etc.) in some independent relation, i.e. when their coexistence does not depend upon any other eliminable condition or factor. It is also necessary that the two things (smoke and fire) coexisting in a third thing should be so experienced that all cases of the existence of one thing should also be cases involving the existence of the other, but the cases of the existence of one thing (e.g. fire), though including all the cases of the existence of the other (smoke), may have yet a more extensive sphere where the latter (smoke) may not exist. When once a permanent relation, whether it be a case of coexistence (as in the case of the contiguity of the constellation of Kṛttikā with Rohiṇī, where, by the rise of the former the early rise of the latter may be inferred), or a case of identity (as in the relation between a genus and its species), or a case of cause and effect or otherwise between two things and a third thing which had been apprehended in a large number of cases, is perceived, they fuse together in the mind as forming one whole, and as a result of that when the existence of the one (e.g. smoke) in a thing (hill) is noticed, we can infer the existence of the thing (hill) with its counterpart (fire). In all such cases the thing (e.g. fire) which has a sphere extending beyond that in which the other (e.g. smoke) can exist is called *gamya* or *vyāpaka* and the other (e.g. smoke) *vyāpya* or *gamaka* and it is only by the presence of gamaka in a thing (e.g. hill, the pakṣa) that the other counterpart the gamya (fire) may be inferred. The general proposition, universal coexistence of the gamaka with the gamya (e.g. wherever there is smoke there is fire) cannot be the cause of inference, for it is itself a case of inference. Inference involves the memory of a permanent relation subsisting between two things (e.g. smoke and fire) in a third thing (e.g. kitchen); but the third thing is remembered only in a general way that the coexisting things must have a place where they are found associated. It is by virtue of such a memory that the direct perception of a basis (e.g. hill) with the gamaka thing (e.g. smoke) in it would naturally bring to my mind that the same basis (hill) must contain the gamya (i.e. fire) also. Every case of inference thus proceeds directly from a perception and not from any universal general proposition. Kumārila holds that the inference gives us the minor as associated with the major and not of the major alone, i.e. of the fiery mountain and not of fire. Thus inference gives us a new knowledge, for though it was known in a general way that the possessor of smoke is the possessor of fire, yet the case of the mountain was not anticipated and the inference of the fiery mountain is thus a distinctly new knowledge (*deśakālādhikyādyuktamagṛhītagrāhitvam anumānasya, Nyāyaratnākara*, p. 363)[1]. It should also be noted that in forming the notion of the permanent relation between two things, a third thing in which these two subsist is always remembered and for the conception of this permanent relation it is enough that in the large number of cases where the concomitance was noted there was no knowledge of any case where the concomitance failed, and it is not indispensable that the negative instances in which the absence of the gamya or vyāpaka was marked by an

[1] It is important to note that it is not unlikely that Kumārila was indebted to Diṅnāga for this; for Diṅnāga's main contention is that "it is not fire, nor the connection between it and the hill, but it is the fiery hill that is inferred" for otherwise inference would give us no new knowledge (see Vidyābhūṣaṇa's *Indian Logic*, p. 87 and *Tātparyaṭīkā*, p. 120.

absence of the gamaka or vyāpya, should also be noted, for a knowledge of such a negative relation is not indispensable for the forming of the notion of the permanent relation[1]. The experience of a large number of particular cases in which any two things were found to coexist together in another thing in some relation associated with the non-perception of any case of failure creates an expectancy in us of inferring the presence of the gamya in that thing in which the gamaka is perceived to exist in exactly the same relation[2]. In those cases where the circle of the existence of the gamya coincides with the circle of the existence of the gamaka, each of them becomes a gamaka for the other. It is clear that this form of inference not only includes all cases of cause and effect, of genus and species but also all cases of coexistence as well.

The question arises that if no inference is possible without a memory of the permanent relation, is not the self-validity of inference destroyed on that account, for memory is not regarded as self-valid. To this Kumārila's answer is that memory is not invalid, but it has not the status of pramāṇa, as it does not bring to us a new knowledge. But inference involves the acquirement of a new knowledge in this, that though the coexistence of two things in another was known in a number of cases, yet in the present case a new case of the existence of the gamya in a thing is known from the perception of the existence of the gamaka and this knowledge is gained by a means which is not perception, for it is only the gamaka that is seen and not the gamya. If the gamya is also seen it is no inference at all.

As regards the number of propositions necessary for the explicit statement of the process of inference for convincing others (*pārārthānumāna*) both Kumārila and Prabhākara hold that three premisses are quite sufficient for inference. Thus the first three premisses pratijñā, hetu and dṛṣṭānta may quite serve the purpose of an anumāna.

There are two kinds of anumāna according to Kumārila viz. pratyakṣatodṛṣṭasambandha and sāmānyatodṛṣṭasambandha. The former is that kind of inference where the permanent

[1] Kumārila strongly opposes a Buddhist view that concomitance (*vyāpti*) is ascertained only by the negative instances and not by the positive ones.

[2] "*tasmādanavagate'pi sarvatrānvaye sarvataśca vyatireke bahuśaḥ sāhityāvagamamātrādeva vyabhicārādarśanasanāthādanumānotpattiraṅgīkartavyaḥ.*" *Nyāyaratnākara*, p. 288.

relation between two concrete things, as in the case of smoke and fire, has been noticed. The latter is that kind of inference where the permanent relation is observed not between two concrete things but between two general notions, as in the case of movement and change of place, e.g. the perceived cases where there is change of place there is also motion involved with it; so from the change of place of the sun its motion is inferred and it is held that this general notion is directly perceived like all universals[1].

Prabhākara recognizes the need of forming the notion of the permanent relation, but he does not lay any stress on the fact that this permanent relation between two things (fire and smoke) is taken in connection with a third thing in which they both subsist. He says that the notion of the permanent relation between two things is the main point, whereas in all other associations of time and place the things in which these two subsist together are taken only as adjuncts to qualify the two things (e.g. fire and smoke). It is also necessary to recognize the fact that though the concomitance of smoke in fire is only conditional, the concomitance of the fire in smoke is unconditional and absolute[2]. When such a conviction is firmly rooted in the mind that the concept of the presence of smoke involves the concept of the presence of fire, the inference of fire is made as soon as any smoke is seen. Prabhākara counts separately the fallacies of the minor (*pakṣābhāsa*), of the enunciation (*pratijñābhāsa*) and of the example (*dṛṣṭāntābhāsa*) along with the fallacies of the middle and this seems to indicate that the Mīmāṃsā logic was not altogether free from Buddhist influence. The cognition of smoke includes within itself the cognition of fire also, and thus there would be nothing left unknown to be cognized by the inferential cognition. But this objection has little force with Prabhākara, for he does not admit that a pramāṇa should necessarily bring us any new knowledge, for pramāṇa is simply defined as "apprehension." So though the inferential cognition always pertains to things already known it is yet regarded by him as a pramāṇa, since it is in any case no doubt an apprehension.

[1] See *Ślokavārttika*, *Nyāyaratnākara*, *Śāstradīpikā*, *Yuktisnehapūraṇī*, *Siddhāntacandrikā* on anumāna.

[2] On the subject of the means of assuring oneself that there is no condition (*upādhi*) which may vitiate the inference, Prabhākara has nothing new to tell us. He says that where even after careful enquiry in a large number of cases the condition cannot be discovered we must say that it does not exist (*prayatnenānviṣyamāṇe aupādhikatvānavagamāt*, see *Prakaraṇapañcikā*, p. 71).

Upamāna, Arthāpatti.

Analogy (*upamāna*) is accepted by Mīmāṃsā in a sense which is different from that in which Nyāya took it. The man who has seen a cow (*go*) goes to the forest and sees a wild ox (*gavaya*), and apprehends the similarity of the gavaya with the *go*, and then cognizes the similarity of the *go* (which is not within the limits of his perception then) with the *gavaya*. The cognition of this similarity of the *gavaya* in the *go*, as it follows directly from the perception of the similarity of the *go* in the *gavaya*, is called upamāna (analogy). It is regarded as a separate pramāṇa, because by it we can apprehend the similarity existing in a thing which is not perceived at the moment. It is not mere remembrance, for at the time the *go* was seen the *gavaya* was not seen, and hence the similarity also was not seen, and what was not seen could not be remembered. The difference of Prabhākara and Kumārila on this point is that while the latter regards similarity as only a quality consisting in the fact of more than one object having the same set of qualities, the former regards it as a distinct category.

Arthāpatti (implication) is a new pramāṇa which is admitted by the Mīmāṃsā. Thus when we know that a person Devadatta is alive and perceive that he is not in the house, we cannot reconcile these two facts, viz. his remaining alive and his not being in the house without presuming his existence somewhere outside the house, and this method of cognizing the existence of Devadatta outside the house is called *arthāpatti* (presumption or implication).

The exact psychological analysis of the mind in this arthāpatti cognition is a matter on which Prabhākara and Kumārila disagree. Prabhākara holds that when a man knows that Devadatta habitually resides in his house but yet does not find him there, his knowledge that Devadatta is living (though acquired previously by some other means of proof) is made doubtful, and the cause of this doubt is that he does not find Devadatta at his house. The absence of Devadatta from the house is not the cause of implication, but it throws into doubt the very existence of Devadatta, and thus forces us to imagine that Devadatta must remain somewhere outside. That can only be found by implication, without the hypothesis of which the doubt cannot be removed. The mere absence of Devadatta from the house is not enough for making the presumption that he is outside the house, for he might also be dead. But I know that Devadatta was living and also that he was not at home; this perception of his absence from home creates a doubt as regards my first knowledge that he is living, and it is for the removal of this doubt that there creeps in the presumption that he must be living somewhere else. The perception of the absence of Devadatta through the intermediate link of a doubt passes into the notion of a presumption that he must then remain somewhere else. In inference there is no element of doubt, for it is only when the smoke is perceived to exist beyond the least element of doubt that the inference of the fire is possible, but in presumption the perceived non-existence in the house leads to the presumption of an external existence only when it has thrown the fact of the man's being alive into doubt and uncertainty[1].

Kumārila however objects to this explanation of Prabhākara, and says that if the fact that Devadatta is living is made doubtful by the absence of Devadatta at his house, then the doubt may as well be removed by the supposition that Devadatta is dead, for it does not follow that the doubt with regard to the life of Devadatta should necessarily be resolved by the supposition of his being outside the house. Doubt can only be removed when the cause or the root of doubt is removed, and it does not follow that because Devadatta is not in the house therefore he is living. If it was already known that Devadatta was living and his absence from the house creates the doubt, how then can the very fact which created the doubt remove the doubt? The cause of doubt cannot be the cause of its removal too. The real procedure of the presumption is quite the other way. The doubt about the life of Devadatta being removed by previous knowledge or by some other means, we may presume that he must be outside the house when he is found absent from the house. So there cannot be any doubt about the life of Devadatta. It is the certainty of his life associated with the perception of his absence from the house that leads us to the presumption of his external existence. There is an opposition between the life of Devadatta and his absence from the house, and the mind cannot come to rest without the presumption of his external existence. The mind oscillates between two contradictory poles both of which it accepts but

[1] See *Prakaraṇapañcikā*, pp. 113–115.

cannot reconcile, and as a result of that finds an outlet and a reconciliation in the presumption that the existence of Devadatta must be found outside the house.

Well then, if that be so, inference may as well be interpreted as presumption. For if we say that we know that wherever there is smoke there is fire, and then perceive that there is smoke in the hill, but no fire, then the existence of the smoke becomes irreconcilable, or the universal proposition of the concomitance of smoke with fire becomes false, and hence the presumption that there is fire in the hill. This would have been all right if the universal concomitance of smoke with fire could be known otherwise than by inference. But this is not so, for the concomitance was seen only in individual cases, and from that came the inference that wherever there is smoke there is fire. It cannot be said that the concomitance perceived in individual cases suffered any contradiction without the presumption of the universal proposition (wherever there is smoke there is fire); thus arthāpatti is of no avail here and inference has to be accepted. Now when it is proved that there are cases where the purpose of inference cannot be served by arthāpatti, the validity of inference as a means of proof becomes established. That being done we admit that the knowledge of the fire in the hill may come to us either by inference or by arthāpatti.

So inference also cannot serve the purpose of arthāpatti, for in inference also it is the hetu (reason) which is known first, and later on from that the sādhya (what is to be proved); both of them however cannot be apprehended at the same moment, and it is exactly this that distinguishes arthāpatti from anumāna. For arthāpatti takes place where, without the presumption of Devadatta's external existence, the absence from the house of Devadatta who is living cannot be comprehended. If Devadatta is living he must exist inside or outside the house. The mind cannot swallow a contradiction, and hence without presuming the external existence of Devadatta even the perceived non-existence cannot be comprehended. It is thus that the contradiction is resolved by presuming his existence outside the house. Arthāpatti is thus the result of arthānupapatti or the contradiction of the present perception with a previously acquired certain knowledge.

It is by this arthāpattipramāṇa that we have to admit that there is a special potency in seeds by which they produce the shoots, and that a special potency is believed to exist in sacrifices by which these can lead the sacrificer to Heaven or some such beneficent state of existence.

Śabda pramāṇa.

Śabda or word is regarded as a separate means of proof by most of the recognized Indian systems of thought excepting the Jaina, Buddhist, Cārvāka and Vaiśeṣika. A discussion on this topic however has but little philosophical value and I have therefore omitted to give any attention to it in connection with the Nyāya, and the Sāṃkhya-Yoga systems. The validity and authority of the Vedas were acknowledged by all Hindu writers and they had wordy battles over it with the Buddhists who denied it. Some sought to establish this authority on the supposition that they were the word of God, while others, particularly the Mīmāṃsists strove to prove that they were not written by anyone, and had no beginning in time nor end and were eternal. Their authority was not derived from the authority of any trustworthy person or God. Their words are valid in themselves. Evidently a discussion on these matters has but little value with us, though it was a very favourite theme of debate in the old days of India. It was in fact the most important subject for Mīmāṃsā, for the *Mīmāṃsā sūtras* were written for the purpose of laying down canons for a right interpretation of the Vedas. The slight extent to which it has dealt with its own epistemological doctrines has been due solely to their laying the foundation of its structure of interpretative maxims, and not to writing philosophy for its own sake. It does not dwell so much upon salvation as other systems do, but seeks to serve as a rational compendium of maxims with the help of which the Vedas may be rightly understood and the sacrifices rightly performed. But a brief examination of the doctrine of word (*śabda*) as a means of proof cannot be dispensed with in connection with Mīmāṃsa as it is its very soul.

Śabda (word) as a pramāṇa means the knowledge that we get about things (not within the purview of our perception) from relevant sentences by understanding the meaning of the words of which they are made up. These sentences may be of two kinds, viz. those uttered by men and those which belong to the Vedas. The first becomes a valid means of knowledge when it is not uttered by untrustworthy persons and the second is valid in itself. The meanings of words are of course known to us before, and cannot therefore be counted as a means of proof; but the meanings of sentences involving a knowledge of the relations of words cannot be known by any other acknowledged means of proof, and it is for this that we have to accept śabda as a separate means of proof. Even if it is admitted that the validity of any sentence may be inferred on the ground of its being uttered by a trustworthy person, yet that would not explain how we understand the meanings of sentences, for when even the name or person of a writer or speaker is not known, we have no difficulty in understanding the meaning of any sentence.

Prabhākara thinks that all sounds are in the form of letters, or are understandable as combinations of letters. The constituent letters of a word however cannot yield any meaning, and are thus to be regarded as elements of auditory perception which serve as a means for understanding the meaning of a word. The reason of our apprehension of the meaning of any word is to be found in a separate potency existing in the letters by which the denotation of the word may be comprehended. The perception of each letter-sound vanishes the moment it is uttered, but leaves behind an impression which combines with the impressions of the successively dying perceptions of letters, and this brings about the whole word which contains the potency of bringing about the comprehension of a certain meaning. If even on hearing a word the meaning cannot be comprehended, it has to be admitted that the hearer lacks certain auxiliaries necessary for the purpose. As the potency of the word originates from the separate potencies of the letters, it has to be admitted that the latter is the direct cause of verbal cognition. Both Prabhākara and Kumārila agree on this point.

Another peculiar doctrine expounded here is that all words have natural denotative powers by which they themselves out of their own nature refer to certain objects irrespective of their comprehension or non-comprehension by the hearer. The hearer will not understand the meaning unless it is known to him that the word in question is expressive of such and such a meaning, but the word was all along competent to denote that meaning and it is the hearer's knowledge of that fact that helps him to understand the meaning of a word. Mīmāṃsā does not think that the association of a particular meaning with a word is due to conventions among people who introduce and give meanings to the words[1]. Words are thus acknowledged to be denotative of themselves. It is only about proper names that convention is admitted to be the cause of denotation. It is easy to see the bearing of this doctrine on the self-validity of the Vedic commandments, by the performance of which such results would arise as could not have been predicted by any other person. Again all words are believed to be eternally existent; but though they are ever present some manifestive agency is required by which they are manifested to us. This manifestive agency consists of the effort put forth by the man who pronounces the word. Nyāya thinks that this effort of pronouncing is the cause that produces the word while Mīmāṃsā thinks that it only manifests to the hearer the ever-existing word.

The process by which according to Prabhākara the meanings of words are acquired may be exemplified thus: a senior commands a junior to bring a cow and to bind a horse, and the child on noticing the action of the junior in obedience to the senior's commands comes to understand the meaning of "cow" and "horse." Thus according to him the meanings of words can only be known from words occuring in injunctive sentences; he deduces from this the conclusion that words must denote things only as related to the other factors of the injunction (*anvitābhidhāna vāda*), and no word can be comprehended as having any denotation when taken apart from such a sentence. This doctrine holds that each word yields its meaning only as being generally related to other factors or only as a part of an injunctive sentence, thus the word *gām* accusative case of *go* (cow) means that it is intended that something is to be done with the cow or the bovine genus, and it appears only as connected with a specific kind of action, viz. bringing in the sentence *gām ānaya*—bring the cow. Kumārila however thinks that words independently express separate meanings which are subsequently combined into a sentence expressing one connected idea (*abhihitānvayavāda*). Thus in *gām ānaya*, according to Kumārila, *gām* means the bovine class in the accusative character and *ānaya* independently means

[1] According to Nyāya God created all words and associated them with their meanings.

bring; these two are then combined into the meaning "bring the cow." But on the former theory the word *gām* means that it is connected with some kind of action, and the particular sentence only shows what the special kind of action is, as in the above sentence it appears as associated with bringing, but it cannot have any meaning separately by itself. This theory of Kumārila which is also the Nyāya theory is called abhihitānvayavāda[1].

Lastly according to Prabhākara it is only the Veda that can be called śabda-pramāṇa, and only those sentences of it which contain injunctions (such as, perform this sacrifice in this way with these things). In all other cases the validity of words is only inferred on the ground of the trustworthy character of the speaker. But Kumārila considers the words of all trustworthy persons as śabda-pramāṇa.

The Pramāṇa of Non-perception (anupalabdhi).

In addition to the above pramāṇas Kumārila admits a fifth kind of pramāṇa, viz. *anupalabdhi* for the perception of the non-existence of a thing. Kumārila argues that the non-existence of a thing (e.g. there is no jug in this room) cannot be perceived by the senses, for there is nothing with which the senses could come into contact in order to perceive the non-existence. Some people prefer to explain this non-perception as a case of anumāna. They say that wherever there is the existence of a visible object there is the vision of it by a perceiver. When there is no vision of a visible object, there is no existence of it also. But it is easy to see that such an inference presupposes the perception of want of vision and want of existence, but how these non-perceptions are to be accounted for is exactly the point to be solved. How can the perception of want of vision or want of existence be grasped? It is for this that we have to admit a separate mode of pramāṇa namely anupalabdhi.

All things exist in places either in a positive (*sadrūpa*) or in a negative relation (*asadrūpa*), and it is only in the former case

[1] See *Prabhākaramīmāṃsā* by Dr Gaṅgānātha Jhā and S. N. Dasgupta's *Study of Patanjali*, appendix. It may be noted in this connection that Mīmāṃsā did not favour the Sphoṭa doctrine of sound which consists in the belief that apart from the momentary sounds of letters composing a word, there was a complete word form which was manifested (sphoṭa) but not created by the passing sounds of the syllables. The work of the syllable sounds is only to project this word-manifestation. See Vācaspati's *Tattvabindu*, *Ślokavārttika* and *Prakaraṇapañcikā*. For the doctrine of anvitābhidhāna see Śālikanātha's *Vākyārthamātṛkāvṛtti*.

that they come within the purview of the senses, while in the latter case the perception of the negative existence can only be had by a separate mode of the movement of the mind which we designate as a separate pramāṇa as anupalabdhi. Prabhākara holds that non-perception of a visible object in a place is only the perception of the empty place, and that therefore there is no need of admitting a separate pramāṇa as anupalabdhi. For what is meant by empty space? If it is necessary that for the perception of the non-existence of jug there should be absolutely empty space before us, then if the place be occupied by a stone we ought not to perceive the non-existence of the jug, inasmuch as the place is not absolutely empty. If empty space is defined as that which is not associated with the jug, then the category of negation is practically admitted as a separate entity. If the perception of empty space is defined as the perception of space at the moment which we associated with a want of knowledge about the jug, then also want of knowledge as a separate entity has to be accepted, which amounts to the same thing as the admission of the want or negation of the jug. Whatever attempt may be made to explain the notion of negation by any positive conception, it will at best be an attempt to shift negation from the objective field to knowledge, or in other words to substitute for the place of the external absence of a thing an associated want of knowledge about the thing (in spite of its being a visible object) and this naturally ends in failure, for negation as a separate category has to be admitted either in the field of knowledge or in the external world. Negation or abhāva as a separate category has anyhow to be admitted. It is said that at the first moment only the ground is seen without any knowledge of the jug or its negation, and then at the next moment comes the comprehension of the non-existence of the jug But this also means that the moment of the perception of the ground is associated with the want of knowledge of the jug or its negation. But this comes to the same thing as the admission of negation as a separate category, for what other meaning can there be in the perception of "only the ground" if it is not meant that it (the perception of the ground) is associated with or qualified by the want of knowledge of the jug? For the perception of the ground cannot generate the notion of the non-existence of the jug, since even where there is a jug the ground is perceived. The qualifying phrase that "only the ground is perceived" becomes meaningless, if things whose presence is excluded are not specified as negative conditions qualifying the perception of the ground. And this would require that we had already the notion of negation in us, which appeared to us of itself in a special manner unaccountable by other means of proof. It should also be noted that non-perception of a sensible object generates the notion of negation immediately and not through other negations, and this is true not only of things of the present moment but also of the memory of past perceptions of non-existence, as when we remember that there was no jug here. Anupalabdhi is thus a separate pramāṇa by which the absence or want of a sensible object—the negation of a thing—can be comprehended.

Self, Salvation, God.

Mīmāṃsā has to accept the existence of soul, for without it who would perform the Vedic commandments, and what would be the meaning of those Vedic texts which speak of men as performing sacrifices and going to Heaven thereby? The soul is thus regarded as something entirely distinct from the body, the sense organs, and buddhi; it is eternal, omnipresent, and many, one in each body. Prabhākara thinks that it is manifested to us in all cognitions. Indeed he makes this also a proof for the existence of self as a separate entity from the body, for had it not been so, why should we have the notion of self-persistence in all our cognitions—even in those where there is no perception of the body? Kumārila however differs from Prabhākara about this analysis of the consciousness of self in our cognitions, and says that even though we may not have any notion of the parts of our body or their specific combination, yet the notion of ourselves as embodied beings always appears in all our cognitions. Moreover in our cognitions of external objects we are not always conscious of the self as the knower; so it is not correct to say that self is different from the body on the ground that the consciousness of self is present in all our cognitions, and that the body is not cognized in many of our cognitions. But the true reason for admitting that the self is different from the body is this, that movement or willing, knowledge, pleasure, pain, etc., cannot be attributed to the body, for though the body exists at death these cannot then be found. So it has to be admitted that they must belong to some other entity owing to the association with which the body appears to be endowed with movement etc. Moreover knowledge, feeling, etc. though apparent to the perceiver, are not yet perceived by others as other qualities of the body, as colour etc., are perceived by other men. It is a general law of causation that the qualities of the constituent elements (in the cause) impart themselves to the effect, but the earth atoms of which the body is made up do not contain the qualities of knowledge etc., and this also corroborates the inference of a separate entity as the vehicle of knowledge etc. The objection is sometimes raised that if the soul is omnipresent how can it be called an agent or a mover? But Mīmāṃsā does not admit that movement means atomic motion, for the principle of movement is the energy which moves the atoms, and this is possessed by the omnipresent soul. It is by the energy imparted by it to the body that the latter moves. So it is that though the soul does not move it is called an agent on account of the fact that it causes the movement of the body. The self must also be understood as being different from the senses, for even when one loses some of the senses he continues to perceive his self all the same as persisting all through.

The question now arises, how is self cognized? Prabhākara holds that the self as cognizor is never cognized apart from the cognized object, nor is the object ever cognized without the cognizor entering into the cognition as a necessary factor. Both the self and the object shine forth in the self-luminous knowledge in what we have already described as tripuṭī-pratyakṣa (perception as three-together). It is not the soul which is self-illumined but knowledge; so it is knowledge which illumines both the self and the object in one operation. But just as in the case of a man who walks, the action of walking rests upon the walker, yet he is regarded as the agent of the work and not as the object, so in the case of the operation of knowledge, though it affects the self, yet it appears as the agent and not as the object. Cognition is not soul, but the soul is manifested in cognition as its substratum, and appears in it as the cognitive element "I" which is inseparable from all cognitions. In deep sleep therefore when no object is cognized the self also is not cognized.

Kumārila however thinks that the soul which is distinct from the body is perceived by a mental perception (*mānasa-pratyakṣa*) as the substratum of the notion of "I," or in other words the self perceives itself by mental perception, and the perception of its own nature shines forth in consciousness as the "I." The objection that the self cannot itself be both subject and object to its own operation does not hold, for it applies equally to Prabhākara's theory in which knowledge reveals the self as its object and yet considers it as the subject of the operation. The analogy of linguistic usage that though the walking affects the walker yet he is the agent, cannot be regarded as an escape from this charge, for the usage of language is not philosophical analysis. Though at the time of the cognition of objects the self is cognized, yet it does not appear as the knower of the knowledge of objects, but reveals itself as an object of a separate mental perception which is distinct from the knowledge of objects. The self is no doubt known as the substratum of "I," but the knowledge of this self does not reveal itself necessarily with the cognition of objects, nor does the self show itself as the knower of all knowledge of objects, but the self is apprehended by a separate mental intuition which we represent as the "I." The self does not reveal itself as the knower but as an object of a separate intuitive process of the mind. This is indeed different from Prabhākara's analysis, who regarded the cognition of self as inseparable from the object-cognition, both being the result of the illumination of knowledge. Kumārila agrees with Prabhākara however in holding that soul is not self-illuminating (*svayamprakāśa*), for then even in deep sleep the soul should have manifested itself; but there is no such manifestation then, and the state of deep sleep appears as an unconscious state. There is also no bliss in deep sleep, for had it been so people would not have regretted that they had missed sensual enjoyments by untimely sleep. The expression that "I slept in bliss" signifies only that no misery was felt. Moreover the opposite representation of the deep sleep state is also found when a man on rising from sleep says "I slept so long without knowing anything not even my own self." The self is not atomic, since we can simultaneously feel a sensation in the head as well as in the leg. The Jaina theory that it is of the size of the body which contracts and expands according to the body it occupies is unacceptable. It is better therefore that the soul should be regarded as all-pervading as described in the Vedas. This self must also be different in different persons for otherwise their individual experiences of objects and of pleasure and pain cannot be expiained[1].

[1] See *Ślokavārttika*, ātmavāda *Śāstra-dīpikā*, ātmavāda and mokṣavāda.

Kumārila considered the self to be merely the potency of knowledge (*jñānaśakti*)[1]. Cognitions of things were generated by the activity of the manas and the other senses. This self itself can only be cognized by mental perception. Or at the time of salvation there being none of the senses nor the manas the self remains in pure existence as the potency of knowledge without any actual expression or manifestation. So the state of salvation is the state in which the self remains devoid of any of its characteristic qualities such as pleasure, pain, knowledge, willing, etc., for the self itself is not knowledge nor is it bliss or ānanda as Vedānta supposes; but these are generated in it by its energy and the operation of the senses. The self being divested of all its senses at that time, remains as a mere potency of the energy of knowledge, a mere existence. This view of salvation is accepted in the main by Prabhākara also.

Salvation is brought about when a man enjoys and suffers the fruits of his good and bad actions and thereby exhausts them and stops the further generation of new effects by refraining from the performance of kāmya-karmas (sacrifices etc. performed for the attainment of certain beneficent results) and guarantees himself against the evil effects of sin by assiduously performing the nitya-karmas (such as the sandhyā prayers etc., by the performance of which there is no benefit but the non-performance of which produces sins). This state is characterized by the dissolution of the body and the non-production of any further body or rebirth.

Mīmāṃsā does not admit the existence of any God as the creator and destroyer of the universe. Though the universe is made up of parts, yet there is no reason to suppose that the universe had ever any beginning in time, or that any God created it. Every day animals and men are coming into being by the action of the parents without the operation of any God. Neither is it necessary as Nyāya supposes that dharma and adharma should have a supervisor, for these belong to the performer and

[1] It may be mentioned in this connection that unlike Nyāyā Mīmāṃsā did not consider all activity as being only of the nature of molecular vibration (*parispanda*). It admitted the existence of energy (*śakti*) as a separate category which manifested itself in actual movements. The self being considered as a śakti can move the body and yet remain unmoved itself. Manifestation of action only means the relationing of the energy with a thing. Nyāyā strongly opposes this doctrine of a non-sensible (atīndriya) energy and seeks to explain all action by actual molecular motion.

no one can have any knowledge of them. Moreover there cannot be any contact (*saṃyoga*) or inherence (*samavāya*) of dharma and adharma with God that he might supervise them; he cannot have any tools or body wherewith to fashion the world like the carpenter. Moreover he could have no motive to create the world either as a merciful or as a cruel act. For when in the beginning there were no beings towards whom should he be actuated with a feeling of mercy? Moreover he would himself require a creator to create him. So there is no God, no creator, no creation, no dissolution or pralaya. The world has ever been running the same, without any new creation or dissolution, sṛṣṭi or pralaya.

Mīmāṃsā as philosophy and Mīmāṃsā as ritualism.

From what we have said before it will be easy to see that Mīmāṃsā agrees in the main with Vaiśeṣika about the existence of the categories of things such as the five elements, the qualities, rūpa, rasa, etc. Kumārila's differences on the points of jāti, samavāya, etc. and Prabhākara's peculiarities have also been mentioned before. On some of these points it appears that Kumārila was influenced by Sāṃkhya thought rather than by Nyāya. Sāṃkhya and Vaiśeṣika are the only Hindu systems which have tried to construct a physics as a part of their metaphysics; other systems have generally followed them or have differed from them only on minor matters. The physics of Prabhākara and Kumārila have thus but little importance, as they agree in general with the Vaiśeṣika view. In fact they were justified in not laying any special stress on this part, because for the performance of sacrifices the common-sense view of Nyāya-Vaiśeṣika about the world was most suitable.

The main difference of Mīmāṃsā with Nyāya consists of the theory of knowledge. The former was required to prove that the Veda was self-valid and that it did not derive its validity from God, and also that it was not necessary to test its validity by any other means. To do this it began by trying to establish the self-validity of all knowledge. This would secure for the Veda the advantage that as soon as its orders or injunctions were communicated to us they would appear to us as valid knowledge, and there being nothing to contradict them later on there would be nothing in the world which could render the Vedic injunctions invalid. The other pramāṇas such as perception, inference, etc. were described, firstly to indicate that they could not show to us how dharma could be acquired, for dharma was not an existing thing which could be perceived by the other pramāṇas, but a thing which could only be produced by acting according to the injunctions of the Vedas. For the knowledge of dharma and adharma therefore the śabdapramāṇa of the Veda was our only source. Secondly it was necessary that we should have a knowledge of the different means of cognition, as without them it would be difficult to discuss and verify the meanings of debatable Vedic sentences. The doctrine of creation and dissolution which is recognized by all other Hindu systems could not be acknowledged by the Mīmāṃsā as it would have endangered the eternality of the Vedas. Even God had to be dispensed with on that account.

The Veda is defined as the collection of Mantras and Brāhmaṇas (also called the *vidhis* or injunctive sentences). There are three classes of injunctions (1) apūrva-vidhi, (2) niyama-vidhi, and (3) parisaṅkhyā-vidhi. Apūrva-vidhi is an order which enjoins something not otherwise known, e.g. the grains should be washed (we could not know that this part of the duty was necessary for the sacrifice except by the above injunction). Niyama-vidhi is that where when a thing could have been done in a number of ways, an order is made by the Veda which restricts us to following some definite alternative (e.g. though the chaff from the corn could be separated even by the nails, the order that "corn should be threshed" restricts us to the alternative of threshing as the only course acceptable for the sacrifice). In the niyama-vidhi that which is ordered is already known as possible but only as an alternative, and the vidhi insists upon one of these methods as the only one. In apūrva-vidhi the thing to be done would have remained undone and unknown had it not been for the vidhi. In parisaṅkhyā-vidhi all that is enjoined is already known but not necessarily as possible alternatives. A certain mantra "I take up the rein" (*imām agṛbhnāṃ raśanāṃ*) which could be used in a number of cases should not however be used at the time of holding the reins of an ass.

There are three main principles of interpreting the Vedic sentences. (1) When some sentences are such that connectively they yield a meaning but not individually, then they should be taken together connectively as a whole. (2) If the separate sentences can however yield meanings separately by themselves they should not be connected together. (3) In the case of certain sentences which are incomplete suitable words from the context of immediately preceding sentences are to be supplied.

The vidhis properly interpreted are the main source of dharma. The mantras which are generally hymns in praise of some deities or powers are to be taken as being for the specification of the deity to whom the libation is to be offered. It should be remembered that as dharma can only be acquired by following the injunctions of the Vedas they should all be interpreted as giving us injunctions. Anything therefore found in the Vedas which cannot be connected with the injunctive orders as forming part of them is to be regarded as untrustworthy or at best inexpressive. Thus it is that those sentences in the Vedas which describe existing things merely or praise some deed of injunction (called the *arthavādas*) should be interpreted as forming part of a vidhi-vākya (injunction) or be rejected altogether. Even those expressions which give reasons for the performance of certain actions are to be treated as mere arthavādas and interpreted as praising injunctions. For Vedas have value only as mandates by the performance of which dharma may be acquired.

When a sacrifice is performed according to the injunctions of the Vedas, a capacity which did not exist before and whose existence is proved by the authority of the scriptures is generated either in the action or in the agent. This capacity or positive force called *apūrva* produces in time the beneficient results of the sacrifice (e.g. leads the performer to Heaven). This apūrva is like a potency or faculty in the agent which abides in him until the desired results follow[1].

It is needless to dilate upon these, for the voluminous works of Śabara and Kumārila make an elaborate research into the nature of sacrifices, rituals, and other relevant matters in great detail, which anyhow can have but little interest for a student of philosophy.

[1] See Dr Gaṅgānātha Jhā's *Prabhākaramīmāṃsā* and Mādhava's *Nyāyamālāvistara*.

CHAPTER X

THE ŚAṄKARA SCHOOL OF VEDĀNTA

Comprehension of the philosophical Issues more essential than the Dialectic of controversy.

PRAMĀṆA in Sanskrit signifies the means and the movement by which knowledge is acquired, *pramātā* means the subject or the knower who cognizes, *pramā* the result of pramāṇa—right knowledge, *prameya* the object of knowedge, and *prāmāṇya* the validity of knowledge acquired. The validity of knowledge is sometimes used in the sense of the faithfulness of knowledge to its object, and sometimes in the sense of an inner notion of validity in the mind of the subject—the knower (that his perceptions are true), which moves him to work in accordance with his perceptions to adapt himself to his environment for the attainment of pleasurable and the avoidance of painful things. The question wherein consists the prāmāṇya of knowledge has not only an epistemological and psychological bearing but a metaphysical one also. It contains on one side a theory of knowledge based on an analysis of psychological experience, and on the other indicates a metaphysical situation consistent with the theory of knowledge. All the different schools tried to justify a theory of knowledge by an appeal to the analysis and interpretation of experience which the others sometimes ignored or sometimes regarded as unimportant. The thinkers of different schools were accustomed often to meet together and defeat one another in actual debates, and the result of these debates was frequently very important in determining the prestige of any school of thought. If a Buddhist for example could defeat a great Nyāya or Mīmāṃsā thinker in a great public debate attended by many learned scholars from different parts of the country, his fame at once spread all over the country and he could probably secure a large number of followers on the spot. Extensive tours of disputation were often undertaken by great masters all over the country for the purpose of defeating the teachers of the opposite schools and of securing adherents to their own. These debates were therefore not generally conducted merely in a passionless philosophical mood with the object of arriving at the truth but in order to inflict a defeat on opponents and to establish the ascendency of some particular school of thought. It was often a sense of personal victory and of the victory of the school of thought to which the debater adhered that led him to pursue the debate. Advanced Sanskrit philosophical works give us a picture of the attitude of mind of these debaters and we find that most of these debates attempt to criticize the different schools of thinkers by exposing their inconsistencies and self-contradictions by close dialectical reasoning, anticipating the answers of the opponent, asking him to define his statements, and ultimately proving that his theory was inconsistent, led to contradictions, and was opposed to the testimony of experience. In reading an advanced work on Indian philosophy in the original, a student has to pass through an interminable series of dialectic arguments, and negative criticisms (to thwart opponents) sometimes called *vitaṇḍā*, before he can come to the root of the quarrel, the real philosophical divergence. All the resources of the arts of controversy find full play for silencing the opponent before the final philosophical answer is given. But to a modern student of philosophy, who belongs to no party and is consequently indifferent to the respective victory of either side, the most important thing is the comprehension of the different aspects from which the problem of the theory of knowledge and its associated metaphysical theory was looked at by the philosophers, and also a clear understanding of the deficiency of each view, the value of the mutual criticisms, the speculations on the experience of each school, their analysis, and their net contribution to philosophy. With Vedānta we come to an end of the present volume, and it may not be out of place here to make a brief survey of the main conflicting theories from the point of view of the theory of knowledge, in order to indicate the position of the Vedānta of the Śaṅkara school in the field of Indian philosophy so far as we have traversed it. I shall therefore now try to lay before my readers the solution of the theory of knowledge (*pramāṇavāda*) reached by some of the main schools of thought. Their relations to the solution offered by the Śaṅkara Vedānta will also be dealt with, as we shall attempt to sketch the views of the Vedānta later on in this chapter.

The philosophical situation. A Review.

Before dealing with the Vedānta system it seems advisable to review the general attitude of the schools already discussed to the main philosophical and epistemological questions which determine the position of the Vedānta as taught by Śaṅkara and his school.

The Sautrāntika Buddhist says that in all his affairs man is concerned with the fulfilment of his ends and desires (*puruṣārtha*). This however cannot be done without right knowledge (*samyagjñāna*) which rightly represents things to men. Knowledge is said to be right when we can get things just as we perceived them. So far as mere representation or illumination of objects is concerned, it is a patent fact that we all have knowledge, and therefore this does not deserve criticism or examination. Our enquiry about knowledge is thus restricted to its aspect of later verification or contradiction in experience, for we are all concerned to know how far our perceptions of things which invariably precede all our actions can be trusted as rightly indicating what we want to get in our practical experience (*arthaprāpakatva*). The perception is right (*abhrānta* non-illusory) when following its representation we can get in the external world such things as were represented by it (*saṃvādakatva*). That perception alone can be right which is generated by the object and not merely supplied by our imagination. When I say "this is the cow I had seen," what I see is the object with the brown colour, horns, feet, etc., but the fact that this is called cow, or that this is existing from a past time, is not perceived by the visual sense, as this is not generated by the visual object. For all things are momentary, and that which I see now never existed before so as to be invested with this or that permanent name. This association of name and permanence to objects perceived is called *kalpanā* or *abhilāpa*. Our perception is correct only so far as it is without the abhilāpa association (*kalpanāpoḍha*), for though this is taken as a part of our perceptual experience it is not derived from the object, and hence its association with the object is an evident error. The object as unassociated with name—the nirvikalpa—is thus what is perceived. As a result of the pratyakṣa the manovijñāna or thought and mental perception of pleasure and pain is also determined. At one moment perception reveals the object as an object of knowledge (*grāhya*), and by the fact of the rise of such a percept, at another moment it appears as a thing realizable or attainable in the external world. The special features of the object undefinable in themselves as being what they are in themselves (*svalakṣaṇa*) are what is actually perceived (*pratyakṣaviṣaya*)[1]. The *pramāṇaphala* (result of perception) is the

[1] There is a difference of opinion about the meaning of the word "svalakṣaṇa" of Dharmakīrtti between my esteemed friend Professor Stcherbatsky of Petrograd and myself. He maintains that Dharmakīrtti held that the content of the presentative element at the moment of perception was almost totally empty. Thus he writes to me, "According to your interpretation svalakṣaṇa means—the object (or idea with Vijñānavādin) *from which everything past and everything future has been eliminated*, this I do not deny at all. But I maintain that if everything past and future has been taken away, what remains? *The present* and the present is a *kṣaṇa* i.e. nothing....The reverse of kṣaṇa is a kṣaṇasaṃtāna or simply saṃtāna and in every saṃtāna there is a synthesis ekībhāva of moments past and future, produced by the intellect (buddhi = niścaya = kalpanā = adhyavasāya)....There is in the perception of a jug *something* (a kṣaṇa of sense knowledge) which we must distinguish from the *idea* of a jug (which is always a saṃtāna, always vikalpita), and if you take the idea away in a strict unconditional sense, no knowledge remains: kṣanasya jñānena prāpayitumaśakyatvāt. This is absolutely the Kantian teaching about *Synthesis of Apprehension*. Accordingly pratyakṣa is a *transcendental* source of knowledge, because practically speaking it gives no knowledge at all. This *pramāṇa* is *asatkalpa*. Kant says that without the elements of intuition (= sense-knowledge = pratyakṣa = kalpanāpoḍha) our cognitions would be empty and without the elements of intellect (kalpanā = buddhi = synthesis = ekībhāva) they would be blind. Empirically both are always combined. This is exactly the theory of Dharmakīrtti. He is a Vijñānavādī as I understand, because he maintains the cognizability of ideas (vijñāna) alone, but the reality is an incognizable foundation of our knowledge; he admits, it is bāhya, it is artha, it is arthakriyākṣaṇa = svalakṣaṇa; that is the reason for which he sometimes is called Sautrāntika and this school is sometimes called Sautrānta-vijñānavāda, as opposed to the Vijñānavāda of Aśvaghoṣa and Āryāsaṅga, which had no elaborate theory of cognition. If the jug as it exists in our representation were the svalakṣaṇa and paramārthasat, what would remain of Vijñānavāda? But there is the perception of the jug as opposed to the *pure idea* of a jug (śuddhā kalpanā), an element of reality, the sensational kṣaṇa, which is communicated to us by sense knowledge. Kant's 'thing in itself' is also a kṣaṇa and also an element of sense knowledge of pure sense as opposed to *pure reason*, Dharmakīrtti has also *śuddhā kalpanā* and *śuddham pratyakṣam*....And very interesting is the opposition between pratyakṣa and anumāna, the first moves from kṣaṇa to saṃtāna and the second from saṃtāna to kṣaṇa, that is the reason that although bhrānta the anumāna is nevertheless pramāṇa because through it we indirectly also reach kṣaṇa, the arthakriyākṣaṇa. It is bhrānta directly and pramāṇa indirectly; pratyakṣa is pramāṇa directly and bhrānta (asatkalpa) indirectly...." So far as the passages to which Professor Stcherbatsky refers are concerned, I am in full agreement with him. But I think that he pushes the interpretation too far on Kantian lines. When I perceive "this is blue," the perception consists of two parts, the actual presentative element of sense-knowledge (*svalakṣaṇa*) and the affirmation (*niścaya*). So far we are in complete agreement. But Professor Stcherbatsky says that this sense-knowledge is a kṣaṇa (moment) and is nothing. I also hold that it is a kṣaṇa, but it is nothing only in the sense that it is not the same as the notion involving affirmation such as "this is blue." The affirmative process occurring at the succeeding moments is determined by the presentative element of the

ideational concept and power that such knowledge has of showing the means which being followed the thing can be got (*yena kṛtena arthaḥ prāpito bhavati*). Pramāṇa then is the similarity of the knowledge with the object by which it is generated, by which we assure ourselves that this is our knowledge of the object as it is perceived, and are thus led to attain it by practical experience. Yet this later stage is pramāṇaphala and not pramāṇa which consists merely in the vision of the thing (devoid of other associations), and which determines the attitude of the perceiver towards the perceived object. The pramāṇa therefore only refers to the newly-acquired knowledge (*anadhigatādhigantṛ*) as this is of use to the perceiver in determining his relations with the objective world. This account of perception leaves out the real epistemological question as to how the knowledge is generated by the external world, or what it is in itself. It only looks to the correctness or faithfulness of the perception to the object and its value for us in the practical realization of our ends. The question of the relation of the external world with knowledge as determining the latter is regarded as unimportant.

first moment (*pratyakṣabalotpanna* N. T., p. 20) but this presentative element divested from the product of the affirmative process of the succeeding moments is not characterless, though we cannot express its character; as soon as we try to express it, names and other ideas consisting of affirmation are associated and these did not form a part of the presentative element. Its own character is said to be its own specific nature (*svalakṣaṇa*). But what is this specific nature? Dharmakīrtti's answer on this point is that by specific nature he means those specific characteristics of the object which appear clear when the object is near and hazy when it is at a distance (*yasyārthasya sannidhānāsannidhānābhyām jñānapratibhāsabhedastat svalakṣaṇam* N., p. 1 and N. T., p. 16). Sense-knowledge thus gives us the specific characteristics of the object, and this has the same form as the object itself; it is the appearance of the "blue" in its specific character in the mind and when this is associated by the affirmative or ideational process, the result is the concept or idea "this is blue" (*nīlasarūpaṃ pratyakṣamanubhūyamānaṃ nīlabodharūpamavasthāpyate ... nīlasārūpyamasya pramāṇam nīlavikalpanarūpaṃ tvasya pramāṇaphalam*, N. T. p. 22). At the first moment there is the appearance of the blue (*nīlanirbhāsaṃ hi vijñānam*, N. T. 19) and this is direct acquaintance (*yatkiñcit arthasya sākṣātkārijñānam tatpratyakṣamucyate*, N. T. 7) and this is real (*paramārthasat*) and valid. This blue sensation is different from the idea "this is blue" (*nīlabodha*, N. T. 22) which is the result of the former (pramāṇaphala) through the association of the affirmative process (*adhyavasāya*) and is regarded as invalid for it contains elements other than what were presented to the sense, and is a *vikalpapratyaya*. In my opinion *svalakṣaṇa* therefore means pure sensation of the moment presenting the specific features of the object and with Dharmakīrtti this is the only thing which is valid in perception and vikalpapratyaya or pramānaphala is the idea or concept which follows it. But though the latter is a product of the former, yet, being the construction of succeeding moments, it cannot give us the pure stage of the first moment of sensation-presentation (*kṣaṇasya prāpayitumaśakyatvāt*, N. T. 16). N. T. = *Nyāyabinduṭīkā*, N = *Nyāyabindu* (Peterson's edition).

The Yogācāras or idealistic Buddhists take their cue from the above-mentioned Sautrāntika Buddhists, and say that since we can come into touch with knowledge and knowledge alone, what is the use of admitting an external world of objects as the data of sensation determining our knowledge? You say that sensations are copies of the external world, but why should you say that they copy, and not that they alone exist? We never come into touch with objects in themselves; these can only be grasped by us simultaneously with knowledge of them, they must therefore be the same as knowledge (*sahopalambhaniyamāt abhedo nīlataddhiyoḥ*); for it is in and through knowledge that external objects can appear to us, and without knowledge we are not in touch with the so-called external objects. So it is knowledge which is self-apparent in itself, that projects itself in such a manner as to appear as referring to other external objects. We all acknowledge that in dreams there are no external objects, but even there we have knowledge. The question why then if there are no external objects, there should be so much diversity in the forms of knowledge, is not better solved by the assumption of an external world; for in such an assumption, the external objects have to be admitted as possessing the infinitely diverse powers of diversely affecting and determining our knowledge; that being so, it may rather be said that in the beginningless series of flowing knowledge, preceding knowledge-moments by virtue of their inherent specific qualities determine the succeeding knowledge-moments. Thus knowledge alone exists; the projection of an external word is an illusion of knowledge brought about by beginningless potencies of desire (*vāsanā*) associated with it. The preceding knowledge determines the succeeding one and that another and so on. Knowledge, pleasure, pain, etc. are not qualities requiring a permanent entity as soul in which they may inhere, but are the various forms in which knowledge appears. Even the cognition, "I perceive a blue thing," is but a form of knowledge, and this is often erroneously interpreted as referring to a permanent knower. Though the cognitions are all passing and momentary, yet so long as the series continues to be the same, as in the case of one person, say Devadatta, the phenomena of memory, recognition, etc. can happen in the succeeding moments, for these are evidently illusory cognitions, so far as they refer to the permanence of the objects believed to have been perceived before, for things or knowledge-moments, whatever they may be, are destroyed the next moment after their birth. There is no permanent entity as perceiver or knower, but the knowledge-moments are at once the knowledge, the knower and the known. This thoroughgoing idealism brushes off all references to an objective field of experience, interprets the verdict of knowledge as involving a knower and the known as mere illusory appearance, and considers the flow of knowledge as a self-determining series in successive objective forms as the only truth. The Hindu schools of thought, Nyāya, Sāṃkhya, and the Mīmāṃsā, accept the duality of soul and matter, and attempt to explain the relation between the two. With the Hindu writers it was not the practical utility of knowledge that was the only important thing, but the nature of knowledge and the manner in which it came into being were also enquired after and considered important.

Pramāṇa is defined by Nyāya as the collocation of instruments by which unerring and indubitable knowledge comes into being. The collocation of instruments which brings about definite knowledge consists partly of consciousness (*bodha*) and partly of material factors (*bodhābodhasvabhāva*). Thus in perception the proper contact of the visual sense with the object (e.g. jug) first brings about a non-intelligent, non-apprehensible indeterminate consciousness (*nirvikalpa*) as the jugness (*ghaṭatva*) and this later on combining with the remaining other collocations of sense-contact etc. produces the determinate consciousness: this is a jug. The existence of this indeterminate state of consciousness as a factor in bringing about the determinate consciousness, cannot of course be perceived, but its existence can be inferred from the fact that if the perceiver were not already in possession of the qualifying factor (*viśeṣanajñāna* as jugness) he could not have comprehended the qualified object (*viśiṣṭabuddhi*) the jug (i.e. the object which possesses jugness). In inference (*anumāṇa*) knowledge of the liṅga takes part, and in upamāna the sight of similarity with other material conglomerations. In the case of the Buddhists knowledge itself was regarded as pramāṇa; even by those who admitted the existence of the objective world, right knowledge was called pramāṇa, because it was of the same form as the external objects it represented, and it was by the form of the knowledge (e.g. blue) that we could apprehend that the external object was also blue. Knowledge does not determine the external world but simply enforces our convictions about the external world. So far as knowledge leads us to form our convictions of the external world it is pramāṇa, and so far as it determines our attitude towards the external world it is pramāṇaphala. The question how knowledge is generated had little importance with them, but how with knowledge we could form convictions of the external world was the most important thing. Knowledge was called pramāṇa, because it was the means by which we could form convictions (*adhyavasāya*) about the external world. Nyāya sought to answer the question how knowledge was generated in us, but could not understand that knowledge was not a mere phenomenon like any other objective phenomenon, but thought that though as a guṇa (quality) it was external like other guṇas, yet it was associated with our self as a result of collocations like any other happening in the material world. Pramāṇa does not necessarily bring to us new knowledge (*anadhigatādhigantṛ*) as the Buddhists demanded, but whensoever there were collocations of pramāṇa, knowledge was produced, no matter whether the object was previously unknown or known. Even the knowledge of known things may be repeated if there be suitable collocations. Knowledge like any other physical effect is produced whenever the cause of it namely the pramāṇa collocation is present. Categories which are merely mental such as class (*sāmānya*), inherence (*samavāya*), etc., were considered as having as much independent existence as the atoms of the four elements. The phenomenon of the rise of knowledge in the soul was thus conceived to be as much a phenomenon as the turning of the colour of the jug by fire from black to red. The element of indeterminate consciousness was believed to be combining with the sense contact, the object, etc. to produce the determinate consciousness. There was no other subtler form of movement than the molecular. Such a movement brought about by a certain collocation of things ended in a certain result (*phala*). Jñāna (knowledge) was thus the result of certain united collocations (*sāmagrī*) and their movements (e.g. contact of manas with soul, of manas with the senses, of the senses with the object, etc.). This confusion renders it impossible to understand the real philosophical distinction between knowledge and an external event of the objective world. Nyāya thus fails to explain the cause of the origin of knowledge, and its true relations with the objective world. Pleasure, pain, willing, etc. were regarded as qualities which belonged to the soul, and the soul itself was regarded as a qualitiless entity which could not be apprehended directly but was inferred as that in which the qualities of jñāna, sukha (pleasure), etc. inhered. Qualities had independent existence as much as substances, but when any new substances were produced, the qualities rushed forward and inhered in them. It is very probable that in Nyāya the cultivation of the art of inference was originally pre-eminent and metaphysics was deduced later by an application of the inferential method which gave the introspective method but little scope for its application, so that inference came in to explain even perception (e.g. this is a jug since it has jugness) and the testimony of personal psychological experience was taken only as a supplement to corroborate the results arrived at by inference and was not used to criticize it[1].

Sāṃkhya understood the difference between knowledge and material events. But so far as knowledge consisted in being the copy of external things, it could not be absolutely different from the objects themselves; it was even then an invisible translucent sort of thing, devoid of weight and grossness such as the external objects possessed. But the fact that it copies those gross objects makes it evident that knowledge had essentially the same substances though in a subtler form as that of which the objects were made. But though the matter of knowledge, which assumed the form of the objects with which it came in touch, was probably thus a subtler combination of the same elementary substances of which matter was made up, yet there was in it another element, viz. intelligence, which at once distinguished it as utterly different from material combinations. This element of intelligence is indeed different from the substances or content of the knowledge itself, for the element of intelligence is like a stationary light, "the self," which illuminates the crowding, bustling knowledge which is incessantly changing its form in accordance with the objects with which it comes in touch. This light of intelligence is the same that finds its manifestation in consciousness as the "I," the changeless entity amidst all the fluctuations of the changeful procession of knowledge. How this element of light which is foreign to the substance of knowledge

[1] See *Nyāyamañjarī* on pramāṇa.

relates itself to knowledge, and how knowledge itself takes it up into itself and appears as conscious, is the most difficult point of the Sāmkhya epistemology and metaphysics. The substance of knowledge copies the external world, and this copy-shape of knowledge is again intelligized by the pure intelligence (*puruṣa*) when it appears as conscious. The forming of the buddhi-shape of knowledge is thus the pramāṇa (instrument and process of knowledge) and the validity or invalidity of any of these shapes is criticized by the later shapes of knowledge and not by the external objects (*svataḥ-prāmāṇya* and *svataḥ-aprāmāṇya*). The pramāṇa however can lead to a pramā or right knowledge only when it is intelligized by the puruṣa. The puruṣa comes in touch with buddhi not by the ordinary means of physical contact but by what may be called an inexplicable transcendental contact. It is the transcendental influence of puruṣa that sets in motion the original prakṛti in Sāṃkhya metaphysics, and it is the same transcendent touch (call it yogyatā according to Vācaspati or samyoga according to Bhiksu) of the transcendent entity of purusa that transforms the non-intelligent states of buddhi into consciousness. The Vijñānavādin Buddhist did not make any distinction between the pure consciousness and its forms (*ākāra*) and did not therefore agree that the ākāra of knowledge was due to its copying the objects. Sāṃkhya was however a realist who admitted the external world and regarded the forms as all due to copying, all stamped as such upon a translucent substance (*sattva*) which could assume the shape of the objects. But Sāṃkhya was also transcendentalist in this, that it did not think like Nyāya that the ākāra of knowledge was all that knowledge had to show; it held that there was a transcendent element which shone forth in knowledge and made it conscious. With Nyāya there was no distinction between the shaped buddhi and the intelligence, and that being so consciousness was almost like a physical event. With Sāṃkhya however so far as the content and the shape manifested in consciousness were concerned it was indeed a physical event, but so far as the pure intelligizing element of consciousness was concerned it was a wholly transcendent affair beyond the scope and province of physics. The rise of consciousness was thus at once both transcendent and physical.

The Mīmāṃsist Prabhākara agreed with Nyāya in general as regards the way in which the objective world and sense contact induced knowledge in us. But it regarded knowledge as a unique phenomenon which at once revealed itself, the knower and the known. We are not concerned with physical collocations, for whatever these may be it is knowledge which reveals things—the direct apprehension that should be called the pramāṇa. Pramāṇa in this sense is the same as pramiti or pramā, the phenomenon of apprehension. Pramāṇa may also indeed mean the collocations so far as they induce the pramā. For pramā or right knowledge is never produced, it always exists, but it manifests itself differently under different circumstances. The validity of knowledge means the conviction or the specific attitude that is generated in us with reference to the objective world. This validity is manifested with the rise of knowledge, and it does not await the verdict of any later experience in the objective field (*saṃvādin*). Knowledge as nirvikalpa (indeterminate) means the whole knowledge of the object and not merely a non-sensible hypothetical indeterminate class-notion as Nyāya holds. The savikalpa (determinate) knowledge only re-establishes the knowledge thus formed by relating it with other objects as represented by memory[1].

Prabhākara rejected the Sāṃkhya conception of a dual element in consciousness as involving a transcendent intelligence (*cit*) and a material part, the buddhi; but it regarded consciousness as an unique thing which by itself in one flash represented both the knower and the known. The validity of knowledge did not depend upon its faithfulness in reproducing or indicating (*pradarśakatva*) external objects, but upon the force that all direct apprehension (*anubhūti*) has of prompting us to action in the external world; knowledge is thus a complete and independent unit in all its self-revealing aspects. But what the knowledge was in itself apart from its self-revealing character Prabhākara did not enquire.

Kumārila declared that jñāna (knowledge) was a movement brought about by the activity of the self which resulted in producing consciousness (*jñātatā*) of objective things. Jñāna itself cannot be perceived, but can only be inferred as the movement necessary for producing the jñātatā or consciousness of things. Movement with Kumārila was not a mere atomic vibration, but was a non-sensuous transcendent operation of which vibration

[1] Sāṃkhya considered nirvikalpa as the dim knowledge of the first moment of consciousness, which, when it became clear at the next moment, was called savikalpa.

was sometimes the result. Jñāna was a movement and not the result of causal operation as Nyāya supposed. Nyāya would not also admit any movement on the part of the self, but it would hold that when the self is possessed of certain qualities, such as desire, etc., it becomes an instrument for the accomplishment of a physical movement. Kumārila accords the same self-validity to knowledge that Prabhākara gives. Later knowledge by experience is not endowed with any special quality which should decide as to the validity of the knowledge of the previous movement. For what is called saṃvādi or later testimony of experience is but later knowledge and nothing more[1]. The self is not revealed in the knowledge of external objects, but we can know it by a mental perception of self-consciousness. It is the movement of this self in presence of certain collocating circumstances leading to cognition of things that is called jñāna[2]. Here Kumārila distinguishes knowledge as movement from knowledge as objective consciousness. Knowledge as movement was beyond sense perception and could only be inferred.

The idealistic tendency of Vijñānavāda Buddhism, Sāṃkhya, and Mīmāṃsā was manifest in its attempt at establishing the unique character of knowledge as being that with which alone we are in touch. But Vijñānavāda denied the external world, and thereby did violence to the testimony of knowledge. Sāṃkhya admitted the external world but created a gulf between the content of knowledge and pure intelligence; Prabhākara ignored this difference, and was satisfied with the introspective assertion that knowledge was such a unique thing that it revealed with itself, the knower and the known; Kumārila however admitted a transcendent element of movement as being the cause of our objective consciousness, but regarded this as being separate from self. But the question remained unsolved as to why, in spite of the unique character of knowledge, knowledge could relate itself to the world of objects, how far the world of external objects or of knowledge could be regarded as absolutely true. Hitherto judgments were only relative, either referring to one's being prompted to the objective world, to the faithfulness of the representation of objects, the suitability of fulfilling our requirements, or to verification by later

[1] See *Nyāyaratnamālā*, svataḥ-prāmāṇya-nirṇaya.

[2] See *Nyāyamañjarī* on Pramāṇa, *Ślokavārttika* on Pratyakṣa, and Gāgā Bhaṭṭa's *Bhaṭṭacintāmaṇi* on Pratyakṣa.

uncontradicted experience. But no enquiry was made whether any absolute judgments about the ultimate truth of knowledge and matter could be made at all. That which appeared was regarded as the real. But the question was not asked, whether there was anything which could be regarded as absolute truth, the basis of all appearance, and the unchangeable reality. This philosophical enquiry had the most wonderful charm for the Hindu mind.

Vedānta Literature.

It is difficult to ascertain the time when the *Brahma-sūtras* were written, but since they contain a refutation of almost all the other Indian systems, even of the Śūnyavāda Buddhism (of course according to Śaṅkara's interpretation), they cannot have been written very early. I think it may not be far from the truth in supposing that they were written some time in the second century B.C. About the period 780 A.D. Gauḍapāda revived the monistic teaching of the Upaniṣads by his commentary on the Māṇḍūkya Upaniṣad in verse called *Māṇḍūkyakārikā*. His disciple Govinda was the teacher of Śaṅkara (788—820 A.D.). Śaṅkara's commentary on the *Brahma-sūtras* is the root from which sprang forth a host of commentaries and studies on Vedāntism of great originality, vigour, and philosophic insight. Thus Ānandagiri, a disciple of Śaṅkara, wrote a commentary called *Nyāyanirṇaya*, and Govindānanda wrote another commentary named *Ratnaprabhā*. Vācaspati Miśra, who flourished about 841 A.D., wrote another commentary on it called the *Bhāmatī*. Amalānanda (1247—1260 A.D.) wrote his *Kalpataru* on it, and Apyayadīkṣita (1550 A.D.) son of Raṅgarājādhvarīndra of Kāñcī wrote his *Kalpataruparimala* on the *Kalpataru*. Another disciple of Śaṅkara, Padmapāda, also called Sanandana, wrote a commentary on it known as *Pañcapādikā*. From the manner in which the book is begun one would expect that it was to be a running commentary on the whole of Śankara's bhāṣya, but it ends abruptly at the end of the fourth sūtra. Mādhava (1350), in his *Śaṅkaravijaya*, recites an interesting story about it. He says that Sureśvara received Śaṅkara's permission to write a *vārttika* on the bhāṣya. But other pupils objected to Śaṅkara that since Sureśvara was formerly a great Mīmāṃsist (Maṇḍana Miśra was called Sureśvara after his conversion to Vedāntism) he was not competent to write a good *vārttika* on the bhāṣya. Sureśvara, disappointed, wrote a treatise called *Naiṣkarmyasiddhi.* Padmapāda wrote a ṭīkā but this was burnt in his uncle's house. Śaṅkara, who had once seen it, recited it from memory and Padmapāda wrote it down. Prakāśātman (1200) wrote a commentary on Padmapāda's *Pañcapādikā* known as *Pañcapādikāvivaraṇa.* Akhaṇḍānanda wrote his *Tattvadīpana*, and the famous Nṛsiṃhāśrama Muni (1500) wrote his *Vivaraṇabhāvaprakāśikā* on it. Amalānanda and Vidyāsāgara also wrote commentaries on *Pañcapādikā*, named *Pañcapādikādarpaṇa* and *Pañcapādikāṭīkā* respectively, but the *Pañcapādikāvivaraṇa* had by far the greatest reputation. Vidyāraṇya who is generally identified by some with Mādhava (1350) wrote his famous work *Vivaraṇaprameyasaṃgraha*[1], elaborating the ideas of *Pañcapādikāvivaraṇa*; Vidyāraṇya wrote also another excellent work named *Jīvanmuktiviveka* on the Vedānta doctrine of emancipation. Sureśvara's (800 A.D.) excellent work *Naiṣkarmyasiddhi* is probably the earliest independent treatise on Śaṅkara's philosophy as expressed in his bhāṣya. It has been commented upon by Jñānottama Miśra. Vidyāraṇya also wrote another work of great merit known as *Pañcadaśī*, which is a very popular and illuminating treatise in verse on Vedānta. Another important work written in verse on the main teachings of Śaṅkara's bhāṣya is *Saṃkṣepaśārīraka*, written by Sarvajñātma Muni (900 A.D.). This has also been commented upon by Rāmatīrtha. Śrīharṣa (1190 A.D.) wrote his *Khaṇḍanakhaṇḍakhādya*, the most celebrated work on the Vedānta dialectic. Citsukha, who probably flourished shortly after Śrīharṣa, wrote a commentary on it, and also wrote an independent work on Vedānta dialectic known as *Tattvadīpikā* which has also a commentary called *Nayanaprasādinī* written by Pratyagrūpa. Śaṅkara Miśra and Raghunātha also wrote commentaries on *Khaṇḍanakhaṇḍakhādya.* A work on Vedānta epistemology and the principal topics of Vedānta of great originality and merit known as *Vedāntaparibhāṣā* was written by Dharmarājādhvarīndra (about 1550 A.D.). His son Rāmakṛṣṇādhvarin wrote his *Śikhāmaṇi* on it and Amaradāsa his *Maṇiprabhā.* The *Vedāntaparibhāṣā* with these two commentaries forms an excellent exposition of some of the fundamental principles of Vedānta. Another work of supreme importance

[1] See Narasiṃhācārya's article in the *Indian Antiquary*, 1916.

(though probably the last great work on Vedānta) is the *Advaitasiddhi* of Madhusūdana Sarasvatī who followed Dharmarājādhvarīndra. This has three commentaries known as *Gauḍabrahmānandī*, *Viṭṭhaleśopadhyāyī* and *Siddhivyākhyā*. Sadānanda Vyāsa wrote also a summary of it known as *Advaitasiddhisiddhāntasāra*. Sadānanda wrote also an excellent elementary work named *Vedāntasāra* which has also two commentaries *Subodhinī* and *Vidvanmanorañjinī*. The *Advaitabrahmasiddhi* of Sadānanda Yati though much inferior to *Advaitasiddhi* is important, as it touches on many points of Vedānta interest which are not dealt with in other Vedānta works. The *Nyāyamakaranda* of Ānandabodha Bhaṭṭārakācāryya treats of the doctrines of illusion very well, as also some other important points of Vedānta interest. *Vedāntasiddhāntamuktāvalī* of Prakāśānanda discusses many of the subtle points regarding the nature of ajñāna and its relations to cit, the doctrine of *dṛṣṭisṛṣṭivāda*, etc., with great clearness. *Siddhāntaleśa* by Apyayadīkṣita is very important as a summary of the divergent views of different writers on many points of interest. *Vedāntatattvadīpikā* and *Siddhāntatattva* are also good as well as deep in their general summary of the Vedānta system. *Bhedadhikkāra* of Nṛsiṃhāśrama Muni also is to be regarded as an important work on the Vedānta dialectic.

The above is only a list of some of the most important Vedānta works on which the present chapter has been based.

Vedānta in Gauḍapāda.

It is useless I think to attempt to bring out the meaning of the Vedānta thought as contained in the *Brahma-sūtras* without making any reference to the commentary of Śaṅkara or any other commentator. There is reason to believe that the *Brahma-sūtras* were first commented upon by some Vaiṣṇava writers who held some form of modified dualism[1]. There have been more than a half dozen Vaiṣṇava commentators of the *Brahma-sūtras* who not only differed from Śaṅkara's interpretation, but also differed largely amongst themselves in accordance with the different degrees of stress they laid on the different aspects of their dualistic creeds. Every one of them claimed that his interpretation was the only one that was faithful to the sūtras and to

[1] This point will be dealt with in the 2nd volume, when I shall deal with the systems expounded by the Vaiṣṇava commentators of the *Brahma-sūtras*.

the Upaniṣads. Should I attempt to give an interpretation myself and claim that to be the right one, it would be only just one additional view. But however that may be, I am myself inclined to believe that the dualistic interpretations of the *Brahma-sūtras* were probably more faithful to the sūtras than the interpretations of Śaṅkara.

The *Śrīmadbhagavadgītā*, which itself was a work of the Ekānti (singularistic) Vaiṣṇavas, mentions the *Brahma-sūtras* as having the same purport as its own, giving cogent reasons[1]. Professor Jacobi in discussing the date of the philosophical sūtras of the Hindus has shown that the references to Buddhism found in the *Brahma-sūtras* are not with regard to the Vijñānavāda of Vasubandhu, but with regard to the Śūnyavāda, but he regards the composition of the *Brahma-sūtras* to be later than Nāgārjuna. I agree with the late Dr S. C. Vidyābhūṣhana in holding that both the Yogācāra system and the system of Nāgārjuna evolved from the *Prajñāpāramitā*[2]. Nāgārjuna's merit consisted in the dialectical form of his arguments in support of Śūnyavāda; but so far as the essentials of Śūnyavāda are concerned I believe that the Tathatā philosophy of Aśvaghoṣa and the philosophy of the *Prajñāpāramitā* contained no less. There is no reason to suppose that the works of Nāgārjuna were better known to the Hindu writers than the *Mahāyāna sūtras*. Even in such later times as that of Vācaspati Miśra, we find him quoting a passage of the *Śālistambha sūtra* to give an account of the Buddhist doctrine of pratītyasamutpāda[3]. We could interpret any reference to Śūnyavāda as pointing to Nāgārjuna only if his special phraseology or dialectical methods were referred to in any way. On the other hand, the reference in the *Bhagavadgītā* to the *Brahma-sūtras* clearly points out a date prior to that of Nāgārjuna; though we may be slow to believe such an early date as has been assigned to the *Bhagavadgītā* by Telang, yet I suppose that its date could safely be placed so far back as the first half of the first century B.C. or the last part of the second century B.C. The *Brahma-sūtras* could thus be placed slightly earlier than the date of the *Bhagavadgītā*.

[1] "Brahmasūtrapadaiścaiva hetumadbhirviniścitaḥ" *Bhagavadgītā*. The proofs in support of the view that the *Bhagavadgītā* is a Vaiṣṇava work will be discussed in the 2nd volume of the present work in the section on *Bhagavadgītā* and its philosophy.

[2] *Indian Antiquary*, 1915.

[3] See Vācaspati Miśra's *Bhāmatī* on Śaṅkara's bhāsya on *Brahma-sūtra*, II. ii.

I do not know of any evidence that would come in conflict with this supposition. The fact that we do not know of any Hindu writer who held such monistic views as Gauḍapāda or Śaṅkara, and who interpreted the *Brahma-sūtras* in accordance with those monistic ideas, when combined with the fact that the dualists had been writing commentaries on the *Brahma-sūtras*, goes to show that the *Brahma-sūtras* were originally regarded as an authoritative work of the dualists. This also explains the fact that the *Bhagavadgītā*, the canonical work of the Ekānti Vaiṣṇavas, should refer to it. I do not know of any Hindu writer previous to Gauḍapāda who attempted to give an exposition of the monistic doctrine (apart from the Upaniṣads), either by writing a commentary as did Śaṅkara, or by writing an independent work as did Gauḍapāda. I am inclined to think therefore that as the pure monism of the Upaniṣads was not worked out in a coherent manner for the formation of a monistic system, it was dealt with by people who had sympathies with some form of dualism which was already developing in the later days of the Upaniṣads, as evidenced by the dualistic tendencies of such Upaniṣads as the Śvetāśvatara, and the like. The epic Sāṃkhya was also the result of this dualistic development.

It seems that Bādarāyaṇa, the writer of the *Brahma-sūtras*, was probably more a theist, than an absolutist like his commentator Śaṅkara. Gauḍapāda seems to be the most important man, after the Upaniṣad sages, who revived the monistic tendencies of the Upaniṣads in a bold and clear form and tried to formulate them in a systematic manner. It seems very significant that no other kārikās on the Upaniṣads were interpreted, except the *Māṇḍūkyakārikā* by Gauḍapāda, who did not himself make any reference to any other writer of the monistic school, not even Bādarāyaṇa. Śaṅkara himself makes the confession that the absolutist (*advaita*) creed was recovered from the Vedas by Gauḍapāda. Thus at the conclusion of his commentary on Gauḍapāda's kārikā, he says that "he adores by falling at the feet of that great guru (teacher) the adored of his adored, who on finding all the people sinking in the ocean made dreadful by the crocodiles of rebirth, out of kindness for all people, by churning the great ocean of the Veda by his great churning rod of wisdom recovered what lay deep in the heart of the Veda, and is hardly attainable even by the immortal gods[1]." It seems particularly significant that Śaṅkara should credit Gauḍapāda and not Bādarāyaṇa with recovering the Upaniṣad creed. Gauḍapāda was the teacher of Govinda, the teacher of Śaṅkara; but he was probably living when Śaṅkara was a student, for Śaṅkara says that he was directly influenced by his great wisdom, and also speaks of the learning, self-control and modesty of the other pupils of Gauḍapāda[2]. There is some dispute about the date of Śaṅkara, but accepting the date proposed by Bhaṇḍarkar, Paṭhak and Deussen, we may consider it to be 788 A.D.[3], and suppose that in order to be able to teach Śaṅkara, Gauḍapāda must have been living till at least 800 A.D.

Gauḍapāda thus flourished after all the great Buddhist teachers Aśvaghoṣa, Nāgārjuna, Asaṅga and Vasubandhu; and I believe that there is sufficient evidence in his kārikās for thinking that he was possibly himself a Buddhist, and considered that the teachings of the Upaniṣads tallied with those of Buddha. Thus at the beginning of the fourth chapter of his kārikās he says that he adores that great man (*dvipadām varam*) who by knowledge as wide as the sky realized (*sambuddha*) that all appearances (*dharma*) were like the vacuous sky (*gaganopamam*[4]). He then goes on to say that he adores him who has dictated (*deśita*) that the touch of untouch (*asparśayoga*—probably referring to Nirvāṇa) was the good that produced happiness to all beings, and that he was neither in disagreement with this doctrine nor found any contradiction in it (*avivādaḥ aviruddhaśca*). Some disputants hold that coming into being is of existents, whereas others quarrelling with them hold that being (*jāta*) is of non-existents (*abhūtasya*); there are others who quarrel with them and say that neither the existents nor non-existents are liable to being and there is one non-coming-into-being (*advayamajātim*). He agrees with those who hold that there is no coming into being[5]. In IV. 19 of his kārikā he again says that the Buddhas have shown that there was no coming into being in any way (*sarvathā Buddhairajātiḥ paridīpitaḥ*).

[1] Śaṅkara's bhāṣya on Gauḍapāda's kārikā, Ānandāśrama edition, p. 214.

[2] Ānandāśrama edition of Śaṅkara's bhāṣya on Gauḍapāda's kārikā, p. 21.

[3] Telang wishes to put Śaṅkara's date somewhere in the 8th century, and Veṅkateśvara would have him in 805 A.D.–897 A.D., as he did not believe that Śaṅkara could have lived only for 32 years. *J. R. A. S.* 1916.

[4] Compare *Laṅkāvatāra*, p. 29, *Kathaṃ ca gaganopamam*.

[5] Gauḍapāda's kārikā, IV. 2, 4.

Again, in IV. 42 he says that it was for those realists (*vastuvādi*), who since they found things and could deal with them and were afraid of non-being, that the Buddhas had spoken of origination (*jāti*). In IV. 90 he refers to *agrayāna* which we know to be a name of *Mahāyāna*. Again, in IV. 98 and 99 he says that all appearances are pure and vacuous by nature. These the Buddhas, the emancipated one (*mukta*) and the leaders know first. It was not said by the Buddha that all appearances (*dharma*) were knowledge. He then closes the kārikās with an adoration which in all probability also refers to the Buddha[1].

Gauḍapāda's work is divided into four chapters: (1) Āgama (scripture), (2) Vaitathya (unreality), (3) Advaita (unity), (4) Alātaśānti (the extinction of the burning coal). The first chapter is more in the way of explaining the Māṇḍūkya Upaniṣad by virtue of which the entire work is known as *Māṇḍūkyakārikā*. The second, third, and fourth chapters are the constructive parts of Gauḍapāda's work, not particularly connected with the Māṇḍūkya Upaniṣad.

In the first chapter Gauḍapāda begins with the three apparent manifestations of the self: (1) as the experiencer of the external world while we are awake (*viśva* or *vaiśvānara ātmā*), (2) as the experiencer in the dream state (*taijasa ātmā*), (3) as the experiencer in deep sleep (*suṣupti*), called the *prājña* when there is no determinate knowledge, but pure consciousness and pure bliss (*ānanda*). He who knows these three as one is never attached to his experiences. Gauḍapāda then enumerates some theories of creation: some think that the world has proceeded as a creation from the prāṇa (vital activity), others consider creation as an expansion (*vibhūti*) of that cause from which it has proceeded; others imagine that creation is like dream (*svapna*) and magic (*māyā*); others, that creation proceeds simply by the will of the Lord; others that it proceeds from time; others that it is for the enjoyment of the Lord (*bhogārtham*) or for his play only (*krīḍārtham*), for such is the nature (*svabhāva*) of the Lord, that he creates, but he cannot have any longing, as all his desires are in a state of fulfilment.

[1] Gauḍapāda's kārikā, IV. 100. In my translation I have not followed Śaṅkara, for he has I think tried his level best to explain away even the most obvious references to Buddha and Buddhism in Gauḍapāda's kārikā. I have, therefore, drawn my meaning directly as Gauḍapāda's kārikās seemed to indicate. I have followed the same principle in giving the short exposition of Gauḍapāda's philosophy below.

Gauḍapāda does not indicate his preference one way or the other, but describes the fourth state of the self as unseen (*adṛṣṭa*), unrelationable (*avyavahāryam*), ungraspable (*agrāhyam*), indefinable (*alakṣaṇa*), unthinkable (*acintyam*), unspeakable (*avyapadeśya*), the essence as oneness with the self (*ekātmapratyayasāra*), as the extinction of the appearance (*prapañcopaśama*), the quiescent (*śāntam*), the good (*śivam*), the one (*advaita*)[1]. The world-appearance (*prapañca*) would have ceased if it had existed, but all this duality is mere māyā (magic or illusion), the one is the ultimately real (*paramārthataḥ*). In the second chapter Gauḍapāda says that what is meant by calling the world a dream is that all existence is unreal. That which neither exists in the beginning nor in the end cannot be said to exist in the present. Being like unreal it appears as real. The appearance has a beginning and an end and is therefore false. In dreams things are imagined internally, and in the experience that we have when we are awake things are imagined as if existing outside, but both of them are but illusory creations of the self. What is perceived in the mind is perceived as existing at the moment of perception only; external objects are supposed to have two moments of existence (namely before they are perceived, and when they begin to be perceived), but this is all mere imagination. That which is unmanifested in the mind and that which appears as distinct and manifest outside are all imaginary productions in association with the sense faculties. There is first the imagination of a perceiver or soul (*jīva*) and then along with it the imaginary creations of diverse inner states and the external world. Just as in darkness the rope is imagined to be a snake, so the self is also imagined by its own illusion in diverse forms. There is neither any production nor any destruction (*na nirodho, na cotpattiḥ*), there is no one who is enchained, no one who is striving, no one who wants to be released[2]. Imagination finds itself realized in the non-existent existents and also in the sense

[1] Compare in Nāgārjuna's first kārikā the idea of *prapañcopaśamam śivam. Anirodhamanutpādamanucchedamaśāśvatam anekārthamanānārthamanāgamamanirgamam yaḥ pratītyasamutpādam prapañcopaśamam śivam deśayāmāsa sambuddhastam vande vadatāmvaram.* Compare also Nāgārjuna's Chapter on *Nirvāṇaparīkṣā*, *Pūrvopalambhopaśamaḥ prapañcopaśamaḥ śivaḥ na kvacit kasyacit kaścit dharmmo buddhenadeśitaḥ.* So far as I know the Buddhists were the first to use the words *prapañcopaśaman śivam.*

[2] Compare Nāgārjuna's kārikā, "anirodhamanutpādam" in *Mādhyamikavṛtti*, *B. T. S.*, p. 3.

of unity; all imagination either as the many or the one (*advaya*) is false; it is only the oneness (*advayatā*) that is good. There is no many, nor are things different or non-different (*na nānedam ...na pṛthag nāpṛthak*)[1]. The sages who have transcended attachment, fear, and anger and have gone beyond the depths of the Vedas have perceived it as the imaginationless cessation of all appearance (*nirvikalpaḥ prapañcopaśamaḥ*), the one[2].

In the third chapter Gauḍapāda says that truth is like the void (*ākāśa*) which is falsely conceived as taking part in birth and death, coming and going and as existing in all bodies; but howsoever it be conceived, it is all the while not different from ākāśa. All things that appear as compounded are but dreams (*svapna*) and māyā (magic). Duality is a distinction imposed upon the one (*advaita*) by māyā. The truth is immortal, it cannot therefore by its own nature suffer change. It has no birth. All birth and death, all this manifold is but the result of an imposition of māyā upon it[3]. One mind appears as many in the dream, so also in the waking state one appears as many, but when the mind activity of the Togins (sages) is stopped arises this fearless state, the extinction of all sorrow, final cessation. Thinking everything to be misery (*duḥkham sarvam anusmṛtya*) one should stop all desires and enjoyments, and thinking that nothing has any birth he should not see any production at all. He should awaken the mind (*citta*) into its final dissolution (*laya*) and pacify it when distracted; he should not move it towards diverse objects when it stops. He should not taste any pleasure (*sukham*) and by wisdom remain unattached, by strong effort making it motionless and still. When he neither passes into dissolution nor into distraction; when there is no sign, no appearance that is the perfect Brahman. When there is no object of knowledge to come into being, the unproduced is then called the omniscent (*sarvajña*).

In the fourth chapter, called the Alātaśānti, Gauḍapāda further

[1] Compare *Mādhyamikakārikā*, *B. T. S.*, p. 3, *anekārtham anānārtham*, etc.

[2] Compare *Laṅkāvatārasūtra*, p. 78, *Advayāsamsāraparinirvāṇavatsarvadharmāḥ tasmāt tarhi mahāmate Śunyatānutpādādvayaniḥsvabhāvalakṣaṇe yogaḥ karaṇiyaḥ*; also 8, 46, *Yaduta svacittaviṣayavikalpadṛṣṭyānavabodhanāt vijñānānām svacittadṛśyamātrānavatāreṇa mahāmate vālapṛthagjanāḥ bhāvābhāvasvabhāvaparamārthadṛṣṭidvayavādino bhavanti.*

[3] Compare Nāgārjuna's kārikā, *B. T. S.*, p. 196, *Ākāśam śaśaśṛṅgañca bandhyāyāḥ putra eva ca asantaścābhivyajyante tathābhāvena kalpanā*, with Gauḍapāda's kārikā, III. 28, *Asato māyayā janma tatvato naiva jāyate bandhyāputro na tattvena māyāya vāpi jāyate.*

describes this final state[1]. All the dharmas (appearances) are without death or decay[2]. Gauḍapāda then follows a dialectical form of argument which reminds us of Nāgārjuna. Gauḍapāda continues thus: Those who regard kāraṇa (cause) as the kāryya (effect in a potential form) cannot consider the cause as truly unproduced (*aja*), for it suffers production; how can it be called eternal and yet changing? If it is said that things come into being from that which has no production, there is no example with which such a case may be illustrated. Nor can we consider that anything is born from that which has itself suffered production. How again can one come to a right conclusion about the *regressus ad infinitum* of cause and effect (*hetu* and *phala*)? Without reference to the effect there is no cause, and without reference to cause there is no effect. Nothing is born either by itself or through others; call it either being, non-being, or being-non-being, nothing suffers any birth, neither the cause nor the effect is produced out of its own nature (*svabhāvataḥ*), and thus that which has no beginning anywhere cannot be said to have a production. All experience (*prajñapti*) is dependent on reasons, for otherwise both would vanish, and there would be none of the afflictions (*saṃkleśa*) that we suffer. When we look at all things in a connected manner they seem to be dependent, but when we look at them from the point of view of reality or truth the reasons cease to be reasons. The mind (*citta*) does not come in touch with objects and thereby manifest them, for since things do not exist they are not different from their manifestations in knowledge. It is not in any particular case that the mind produces the manifestations of objects while they do not exist so that it could be said to be an error, for in present, past, and future the mind never comes in touch with objects which only appear by reason of their diverse manifestations. Therefore neither the mind nor the objects seen by it are ever produced. Those who perceive them to suffer production are really traversing the reason of vacuity (*khe*), for all production is but false imposition on the vacuity. Since the unborn is perceived as being born, the essence then is the absence of

[1] The very name Alātaśānti is absolutely Buddhistic. Compare Nāgārjuna's kārikā, *B. T. S.*, p. 206, where he quotes a verse from the *Śataka*.

[2] The use of the word dharma in the sense of appearance or entity is peculiarly Buddhistic. The Hindu sense is that given by Jaimini, "Codanālakṣaṇah arthah, dharmah." Dharma is determined by the injunctions of the Vedas.

production, for it being of the nature of absence of production it could never change its nature. Everything has a beginning and an end and is therefore false. The existence of all things is like a magical or illusory elephant (*māyāhastī*) and exists only as far as it merely appears or is related to experience. There is thus the appearance of production, movement and things, but the one knowledge (*vijñāna*) is the unborn, unmoved, the unthingness (*avastutva*), the cessation (*śāntam*). As the movement of burning charcoal is perceived as straight or curved, so it is the movement (*spandita*) of consciousness that appears as the perceiving and the perceived. All the attributes (e.g. straight or curved) are imposed upon the charcoal fire, though in reality it does not possess them; so also all the appearances are imposed upon consciousness, though in reality they do not possess them. We could never indicate any kind of causal relation between the consciousness and its appearance, which are therefore to be demonstrated as unthinkable (*acintya*). A thing (*dravya*) is the cause of a thing (*dravya*), and that which is not a thing may be the cause of that which is not a thing, but all the appearances are neither things nor those which are not things, so neither are appearances produced from the mind (*citta*), nor is the mind produced by appearances. So long as one thinks of cause and effect he has to suffer the cycle of existence (*saṃsāra*), but when that notion ceases there is no saṃsāra. All things are regarded as being produced from a relative point of view only (*saṃvṛti*), there is therefore nothing permanent (*śāśvata*). Again, no existent things are produced, hence there cannot be any destruction (*uccheda*). Appearances (*dharma*) are produced only apparently, not in reality; their coming into being is like māyā, and that māyā again does not exist. All appearances are like shoots of magic coming out of seeds of magic and are not therefore neither eternal nor destructible. As in dreams, or in magic, men are born and die, so are all appearances. That which appears as existing from an imaginary relative point of view (*kalpita saṃvṛti*) is not so in reality (*paramārtha*), for the existence depending on others, as shown in all relative appearance, is after all not a real existence. That things exist, do not exist, do exist and not exist, and neither exist nor not exist; that they are moving or steady, or none of those, are but thoughts with which fools are deluded.

It is so obvious that these doctrines are borrowed from the Mādhyamika doctrines, as found in the Nāgārjuna's kārikās and the Vijñānavāda doctrines, as found in *Laṅkāvatāra*, that it is needless to attempt to prove it. Gauḍapāda assimilated all the Buddhist Śūnyavāda and Vijñānavāda teachings, and thought that these held good of the ultimate truth preached by the Upaniṣads. It is immaterial whether he was a Hindu or a Buddhist, so long as we are sure that he had the highest respect for the Buddha and for the teachings which he believed to be his. Gauḍapāda took the smallest Upaniṣads to comment upon, probably because he wished to give his opinions unrestricted by the textual limitations of the bigger ones. His main emphasis is on the truth that he realized to be perfect. He only incidentally suggested that the great Buddhist truth of indefinable and unspeakable vijñāna or vacuity would hold good of the highest ātman of the Upaniṣads, and thus laid the foundation of a revival of the Upaniṣad studies on Buddhist lines. How far the Upaniṣads guaranteed in detail the truth of Gauḍapāda's views it was left for his disciple, the great Śaṅkara, to examine and explain.

Vedānta and Śaṅkara (788–820 A.D.).

Vedānta philosophy is the philosophy which claims to be the exposition of the philosophy taught in the Upaniṣads and summarized in the *Brahma-sūtras* of Bādarāyaṇa. The Upaniṣads form the last part of the Veda literature, and its philosophy is therefore also called sometimes the Uttara-Mīmāṃsā or the Mīmāṃsā (decision) of the later part of the Vedas as distinguished from the Mīmāṃsā of the previous part of the Vedas and the Brāhmaṇas as incorporated in the *Pūrvamīmāṃsā sūtras* of Jaimini. Though these *Brahma-sūtras* were differently interpreted by different exponents, the views expressed in the earliest commentary on them now available, written by Śaṅkarācārya, have attained wonderful celebrity, both on account of the subtle and deep ideas it contains, and also on account of the association of the illustrious personality of Śaṅkara. So great is the influence of the philosophy propounded by Śaṅkara and elaborated by his illustrious followers, that whenever we speak of the Vedānta philosophy we mean the philosophy that was propounded by Śaṅkara. If other expositions are intended the names of the exponents have to be mentioned (e.g. Rāmānuja-mata, Vallabha-mata, etc.). In this chapter we shall limit ourselves to the exposition of the Vedānta philosophy as elaborated by Śaṅkara and his followers. In Śaṅkara's work (the commentaries on the *Brahma-sūtra* and the ten Upaniṣads) many ideas have been briefly incorporated which as found in Śaṅkara do not appear to be sufficiently clear, but are more intelligible as elaborated by his followers. It is therefore better to take up the Vedānta system, not as we find it in Śaṅkara, but as elaborated by his followers, all of whom openly declare that they are true to their master's philosophy.

For the other Hindu systems of thought, the sūtras (*Jaimini sūtra*, *Nyāya sūtra*, etc.) are the only original treatises, and no foundation other than these is available. In the case of the Vedānta however the original source is the Upaniṣads, and the sūtras are but an extremely condensed summary in a systematic form. Śaṅkara did not claim to be the inventor or expounder of an original system, but interpreted the sūtras and the Upaniṣads in order to show that there existed a connected and systematic philosophy in the Upaniṣads which was also enunciated in the sūtras of Bādarāyaṇa. The Upaniṣads were a part of the Vedas and were thus regarded as infallible by the Hindus. If Śaṅkara could only show that his exposition of them was the right one, then his philosophy being founded upon the highest authority would be accepted by all Hindus. The most formidable opponents in the way of accomplishing his task were the Mīmāṃsists, who held that the Vedas did not preach any philosophy, for whatever there was in the Vedas was to be interpreted as issuing commands to us for performing this or that action. They held that if the Upaniṣads spoke of Brahman and demonstrated the nature of its pure essence, these were mere exaggerations intended to put the commandment of performing some kind of worship of Brahman into a more attractive form. Śaṅkara could not deny that the purport of the Vedas as found in the Brāhmaṇas was explicitly of a mandatory nature as declared by the Mīmāṃsā, but he sought to prove that such could not be the purport of the Upaniṣads, which spoke of the truest and the highest knowledge of the Absolute by which the wise could attain salvation. He said that in the karmakāṇḍa—the (sacrificial injunctions) Brāhmaṇas of the Vedas—the purport of the Vedas was certainly of a mandatory nature, as it was intended for ordinary people who were anxious for this or that pleasure, and were never actuated by any desire of knowing the absolute truth, but the Upaniṣads, which were intended for the wise who had controlled their senses and become disinclined to all earthly joys, demonstrated the one Absolute, Unchangeable, Brahman as the only Truth of the universe. The two parts of the Vedas were intended for two classes of persons. Śaṅkara thus did not begin by formulating a philosophy of his own by logical and psychological analysis, induction, and deduction. He tried to show by textual comparison of the different Upaniṣads, and by reference to the content of passages in the Upaniṣads, that they were concerned in demonstrating the nature of Brahman (as he understood it) as their ultimate end. He had thus to show that the uncontradicted testimony of all the Upaniṣads was in favour of the view which he held. He had to explain all doubtful and apparently conflicting texts, and also to show that none of the texts referred to the doctrines of mahat, prakṛti, etc. of the Sāṃkhya. He had also to interpret the few scattered ideas about physics, cosmology, eschatology, etc. that are found in the Upaniṣads consistently with the Brahman philosophy. In order to show that the philosophy of the Upaniṣads as he expounded it was a consistent system, he had to remove all the objections that his opponents could make regarding the Brahman philosophy, to criticize the philosophies of all other schools, to prove them to be self-contradictory, and to show that any interpretation of the Upaniṣads, other than that which he gave, was inconsistent and wrong. This he did not only in his bhāṣya on the *Brahma-sūtras* but also in his commentaries on the Upaniṣads. Logic with him had a subordinate place, as its main value for us was the aid which it lent to consistent interpretations of the purport of the Upaniṣad texts, and to persuading the mind to accept the uncontradicted testimony of the Upaniṣads as the absolute truth. His disciples followed him in all, and moreover showed in great detail that the Brahman philosophy was never contradicted either in perceptual experience or in rational thought, and that all the realistic categories which Nyāya and other systems had put forth were self-contradictory and erroneous. They also supplemented his philosophy by constructing a Vedānta epistemology, and by rethinking elaborately the relation of the māyā, the Brahman, and the world of appearance and other relevant topics. Many problems of great philosophical interest which had been left out or slightly touched by Śaṅkara were discussed fully by his followers. But it should always be remembered that philosophical reasonings and criticisms are always to be taken as but aids for convincing our intellect and strengthening our faith in the truth revealed in the Upaniṣads. The true work of logic is to adapt the mind to accept them. Logic used for upsetting the instructions of the Upaniṣads is logic gone astray. Many lives of Śaṅkarācārya were written in Sanskrit such as the *Śaṅkara-digvijaya*, *Śaṅkara-vijaya-vilāsa*, *Śaṅkara-jaya*, etc. It is regarded as almost certain that he was born between 700 and 800 A.D. in the Malabar country in the Deccan. His father Śivaguru was a Yajurvedi Brāhmin of the Taittirīya branch. Many miracles are related of Śaṅkara, and he is believed to have been the incarnation of Śiva. He turned ascetic in his eighth year and became the disciple of Govinda, a renowned sage then residing in a mountain cell on the banks of the Narbuda. He then came over to Benares and thence went to Badarikāśrama. It is said that he wrote his illustrious bhāṣya on the *Brahma-sūtra* in his twelfth year. Later on he also wrote his commentaries on ten Upaniṣads. He returned to Benares, and from this time forth he decided to travel all over India in order to defeat the adherents of other schools of thought in open debate. It is said that he first went to meet Kumārila, but Kumārila was then at the point of death, and he advised him to meet Kumārila's disciple. He defeated Maṇḍana and converted him into an ascetic follower of his own. He then travelled in various places, and defeating his opponents everywhere he established his Vedānta philosophy, which from that time forth acquired a dominant influence in moulding the religious life of India.

Śaṅkara carried on the work of his teacher Gauḍapāda and by writing commentaries on the ten Upaniṣads and the *Brahma-sūtras* tried to prove, that the absolutist creed was the one which was intended to be preached in the Upaniṣads and the *Brahma-sūtras*[1]. Throughout his commentary on the *Brahma-sūtras*, there is ample evidence that he was contending against some other rival interpretations of a dualistic tendency which held that the Upaniṣads partly favoured the Sāṃkhya cosmology

[1] The main works of Śaṅkara are his commentaries (bhāṣya) on the ten Upaniṣads (Īśa, Kena, Kaṭha, Praśna, Muṇḍaka, Māṇḍūkya, Aitareya, Taittirīya, Bṛhadāraṇyaka, and Chāndogya), and on the *Brahma-sūtra*.

of the existence of prakṛti. That these were actual textual interpretations of the *Brahma-sūtras* is proved by the fact that Śaṅkara in some places tries to show that these textual constructions were faulty[1]. In one place he says that others (referring according to Vācaspati to the Mīmāṃsā) and some of us (referring probably to those who interpreted the sūtras and the Upaniṣads from the Vedānta point of view) think that the soul is permanent. It is to refute all those who were opposed to the right doctrine of perceiving everything as the unity of the self (*ātmaikatva*) that this Śārīraka commentary of mine is being attempted[2]. Rāmānuja, in the introductory portion of his bhāṣya on the *Brahma-sūtra*, says that the views of Bodhāyana who wrote an elaborate commentary on the *Brahma-sūtra* were summarized by previous teachers, and that he was following this Bodhāyana bhāṣya in writing his commentary. In the *Vedārthasaṃgraha* of Rāmānuja mention is made of Bodhāyana, Ṭaṅka, Guhadeva, Kapardin, Bhāruci as Vedāntic authorities, and Draviḍācāryya is referred to as the "bhāṣyakāra" commentator. In Chāndogya III. x. 4, where the Upaniṣad cosmology appeared to be different from the *Viṣṇupurāṇa* cosmology, Śaṅkara refers to an explanation offered on the point by one whom he calls "ācāryya" (*atroktaḥ parihāraḥ ācāryyaiḥ*) and Ānandagiri says that "ācāryya" there refers to Draviḍācāryya. This Draviḍācāryya is known to us from Rāmānuja's statement as being a commentator of the dualistic school, and we have evidence here that he had written a commentary on the Chāndogya Upaniṣad.

A study of the extant commentaries on the *Brahma-sūtras* of Bādarāyaṇa by the adherents of different schools of thought leaves us convinced that these sūtras were regarded by all as condensations of the teachings of the Upaniṣads. The differences of opinion were with regard to the meaning of these sūtras and the Upaniṣad texts to which references were made by them in each particular case. The *Brahma-sūtra* is divided into four adhyāyas or books, and each of these is divided into four chapters or pādas. Each of these contains a number of topics of discussion (*adhikaraṇa*) which are composed of a number of sūtras, which raise the point at issue, the points that lead to doubt and uncertainty, and the considerations that should lead one to favour

[1] See note on p. 432.
[2] Śaṅkara's bhāṣya on the *Brahma-sūtras*, I. iii. 19.

a particular conclusion. As explained by Śaṅkara, most of these sūtras except the first four and the first two chapters of the second book are devoted to the textual interpretations of the Upaniṣad passages. Śaṅkara's method of explaining the absolutist Vedānta creed does not consist in proving the Vedānta to be a consistent system of metaphysics, complete in all parts, but in so interpreting the Upaniṣad texts as to show that they all agree in holding the Brahman to be the self and that alone to be the only truth. In Chapter I of Book II Śaṅkara tries to answer some of the objections that may be made from the Sāṃkhya point of view against his absolutist creed and to show that some apparent difficulties of the absolutist doctrine did not present any real difficulty. In Chapter II of Book II he tries to refute the Sāṃkhya, Yoga, Nyāya-Vaiśeṣika, the Buddhist, Jaina, Bhāgavata and Śaiva systems of thought. These two chapters and his commentaries on the first four sūtras contain the main points of his system. The rest of the work is mainly occupied in showing that the conclusion of the sūtras was always in strict agreement with the Upaniṣad doctrines. Reason with Śaṅkara never occupied the premier position; its value was considered only secondary, only so far as it helped one to the right understanding of the revealed scriptures, the Upaniṣads. The ultimate truth cannot be known by reason alone. What one debater shows to be reasonable a more expert debater shows to be false, and what he shows to be right is again proved to be false by another debater. So there is no final certainty to which we can arrive by logic and argument alone. The ultimate truth can thus only be found in the Upaniṣads; reason, discrimination and judgment are all to be used only with a view to the discovery of the real purport of the Upaniṣads. From his own position Śaṅkara was not thus bound to vindicate the position of the Vedānta as a thoroughly rational system of metaphysics. For its truth did not depend on its rationality but on the authority of the Upaniṣads. But what was true could not contradict experience. If therefore Śaṅkara's interpretation of the Upaniṣads was true, then it would not contradict experience. Śaṅkara was therefore bound to show that his interpretation was rational and did not contradict experience. If he could show that his interpretation was the only interpretation that was faithful to the Upaniṣads, and that its apparent contradictions with experience could in some way be explained, he considered that he had nothing more to do. He was not writing a philosophy in the modern sense of the term, but giving us the whole truth as taught and revealed in the Upaniṣads and not simply a system spun by a clever thinker, which may erroneously appear to be quite reasonable. Ultimate validity does not belong to reason but to the scriptures.

He started with the premise that whatever may be the reason it is a fact that all experience starts and moves in an error which identifies the self with the body, the senses, or the objects of the senses. All cognitive acts presuppose this illusory identification, for without it the pure self can never behave as a phenomenal knower or perceiver, and without such a perceiver there would be no cognitive act. Śaṅkara does not try to prove philosophically the existence of the pure self as distinct from all other things, for he is satisfied in showing that the Upaniṣads describe the pure self unattached to any kind of impurity as the ultimate truth. This with him is a matter to which no exception can be taken, for it is so revealed in the Upaniṣads. This point being granted, the next point is that our experience is always based upon an identification of the self with the body, the senses, etc. and the imposition of all phenomenal qualities of pleasure, pain, etc. upon the self; and this with Śaṅkara is a beginningless illusion. All this had been said by Gauḍapāda. Śaṅkara accepted Gauḍapāda's conclusions, but did not develop his dialectic for a positive proof of his thesis. He made use of the dialectic only for the refutation of other systems of thought. This being done he thought that he had nothing more to do than to show that his idea was in agreement with the teachings of the Upaniṣads. He showed that the Upaniṣads held that the pure self as pure being, pure intelligence and pure bliss was the ultimate truth. This being accepted the world as it appears could not be real. It must be a mere magic show of illusion or māyā. Śaṅkara never tries to prove that the world is māyā, but accepts it as indisputable. For, if the self is what is ultimately real, the necessary conclusion is that all else is mere illusion or māyā. He had thus to quarrel on one side with the Mīmāṃsā realists and on the other with the Sāṃkhya realists, both of whom accepted the validity of the scriptures, but interpreted them in their own way. The Mīmāṃsists held that everything that is said in the Vedas is to be interpreted as requiring us to perform particular kinds of action, or to desist from doing certain other kinds. This would mean that the Upaniṣads being a part of the Veda should also be interpreted as containing injunctions for the performance of certain kinds of actions. The description of Brahman in the Upaniṣads does not therefore represent a simple statement of the nature of Brahman, but it implies that the Brahman should be meditated upon as possessing the particular nature described there, i.e. Brahman should be meditated upon as being an entity which possesses a nature which is identical with our self; such a procedure would then lead to beneficial results to the man who so meditates. Śaṅkara could not agree to such a view. For his main point was that the Upaniṣads revealed the highest truth as the Brahman. No meditation or worship or action of any kind was required; but one reached absolute wisdom and emancipation when the truth dawned on him that the Brahman or self was the ultimate reality. The teachings of the other parts of the Vedas, the karmakāṇḍa (those dealing with the injunctions relating to the performance of duties and actions), were intended for inferior types of aspirants, whereas the teachings of the Upaniṣads, the jñānakāṇḍa (those which declare the nature of ultimate truth and reality), were intended only for superior aspirants who had transcended the limits of sacrificial duties and actions, and who had no desire for any earthly blessing or for any heavenly joy. Throughout his commentary on the *Bhagavadgītā* Śaṅkara tried to demonstrate that those who should follow the injunctions of the Veda and perform Vedic deeds, such as sacrifices, etc., belonged to a lower order. So long as they remained in that order they had no right to follow the higher teachings of the Upaniṣads. They were but karmins (performers of scriptural duties). When they succeeded in purging their minds of all desires which led them to the performance of the Vedic injunctions, the field of karmamārga (the path of duties), and wanted to know the truth alone, they entered the jñānamārga (the way of wisdom) and had no duties to perform. The study of Vedānta was thus reserved for advanced persons who were no longer inclined to the ordinary joys of life but wanted complete emancipation. The qualifications necessary for a man intending to study the Vedānta are (1) discerning knowledge about what is eternal and what is transitory (*nityānityavastuviveka*), (2) disinclination to the enjoyment of the pleasures of this world or of the after world (*ihāmutraphalabhogavirāga*), (3) attainment of peace, self-restraint, renunciation, patience, deep concentration and faith (*śamadamādisādhanasampat*) and desire for salvation (*mumukṣutva*). The person who had these qualifications should study the Upaniṣads, and as soon as he became convinced of the truth about the identity of the self and the Brahman he attained emancipation. When once a man realized that the self alone was the reality and all else was māyā, all injunctions ceased to have any force with him. Thus, the path of duties (*karma*) and the path of wisdom (*jñāna*) were intended for different classes of persons or adhikārins. There could be no joint performance of Vedic duties and the seeking of the highest truth as taught in the Upaniṣads (*jñāna-karma-samuccayābhāvaḥ*). As against the dualists he tried to show that the Upaniṣads never favoured any kind of dualistic interpretations. The main difference between the Vedānta as expounded by Gauḍapāda and as explained by Śaṅkara consists in this, that Śaṅkara tried as best he could to dissociate the distinctive Buddhist traits found in the exposition of the former and to formulate the philosophy as a direct interpretation of the older Upaniṣad texts. In this he achieved remarkable success. He was no doubt regarded by some as a hidden Buddhist (*pracchanna Bauddha*), but his influence on Hindu thought and religion became so great that he was regarded in later times as being almost a divine person or an incarnation. His immediate disciples, the disciples of his disciples, and those who adhered to his doctrine in the succeeding generations, tried to build a rational basis for his system in a much stronger way than Śaṅkara did. Our treatment of Śaṅkara's philosophy has been based on the interpretations of Vedānta thought, as offered by these followers of Śaṅkara. These interpretations are nowhere in conflict with Śaṅkara's doctrines, but the questions and problems which Śaṅkara did not raise have been raised and discussed by his followers, and without these one could not treat Vedānta as a complete and coherent system of metaphysics. As these will be discussed in the later sections, we may close this with a short description of some of the main features of the Vedānta thought as explained by Śaṅkara.

Brahman according to Śaṅkara is "the cause from which (proceeds) the origin or subsistence and dissolution of this world which is extended in names and forms, which includes many agents and enjoyers, which contains the fruit of works specially determined according to space, time, and cause, a world which is formed after an arrangement inconceivable even by the (imagination of the) mind[1]." The reasons that Śaṅkara adduces for the existence of Brahman may be considered to be threefold: (1) The world must have been produced as the modification of something, but in the Upaniṣads all other things have been spoken of as having been originated from something other than Brahman, so Brahman is the cause from which the world has sprung into being, but we could not think that Brahman itself originated from something else, for then we should have a *regressus ad infinitum* (*anavasthā*). (2) The world is so orderly that it could not have come forth from a non-intelligent source. The intelligent source then from which this world has come into being is Brahman. (3) This Brahman is the immediate consciousness (*sākṣi*) which shines as the self, as well as through the objects of cognition which the self knows. It is thus the essence of us all, the self, and hence it remains undenied even when one tries to deny it, for even in the denial it shows itself forth. It is the self of us all and is hence ever present to us in all our cognitions.

Brahman according to Śaṅkara is the identity of pure intelligence, pure being, and pure blessedness. Brahman is the self of us all. So long as we are in our ordinary waking life, we are identifying the self with thousands of illusory things, with all that we call "I" or mine, but when in dreamless sleep we are absolutely without any touch of these phenomenal notions the nature of our true state as pure blessedness is partially realized. The individual self as it appears is but an appearance only, while the real truth is the true self which is one for all, as pure intelligence, pure blessedness, and pure being.

All creation is illusory māyā. But accepting it as māyā, it may be conceived that God (Īśvara) created the world as a mere sport; from the true point of view there is no Īśvara who creates the world, but in the sense in which the world exists, and we all exist as separate individuals, we can affirm the existence of Īśvara, as engaged in creating and maintaining the world. In reality all creation is illusory and so the creator also is illusory. Brahman, the self, is at once the material cause (*upādāna-kāraṇa*) as well as the efficient cause (*nimitta-kāraṇa*) of the world.

[1] Śaṅkara's commentary, I. i. 2. See also Deussen's *System of the Vedānta*.

There is no difference between the cause and the effect, and the effect is but an illusory imposition on the cause—a mere illusion of name and form. We may mould clay into plates and jugs and call them by so many different names, but it cannot be admitted that they are by that fact anything more than clay; their transformations as plates and jugs are only appearances of name and form (*nāmarūpa*). This world, inasmuch as it is but an effect imposed upon the Brahman, is only phenomenally existent (*vyavahārika*) as mere objects of name and form (*nāmarūpa*), but the cause, the Brahman, is alone the true reality (*pāramārthika*)[1].

The main idea of the Vedānta philosophy.

The main idea of the advaita (non-dualistic) Vedānta philosophy as taught by the Śaṅkara school is this, that the ultimate and absolute truth is the self, which is one, though appearing as many in different individuals. The world also as apart from us the individuals has no reality and has no other truth to show than this self. All other events, mental or physical, are but passing appearances, while the only absolute and unchangeable truth underlying them all is the self. While other systems investigated the pramāṇas only to examine how far they could determine the objective truth of things or our attitude in practical life towards them, Vedānta sought to reach beneath the surface of appearances, and enquired after the final and ultimate truth underlying the microcosm and the macrocosm, the subject and the object. The famous instruction of Śvetaketu, the most important Vedānta text (*mahāvākya*) says, "That art thou, O Śvetaketu." This comprehension of my self as the ultimate truth is the highest knowledge, for when this knowledge is once produced, our cognition of world-appearances will automatically cease. Unless the mind is chastened and purged of all passions and desires, the soul cannot comprehend this truth; but when this is once done, and the soul is anxious for salvation by a knowledge of the highest truth, the preceptor instructs him, "That art thou." At once he becomes the truth itself, which is at once identical with pure bliss and pure intelligence; all ordinary notions and cognitions of diversity and of the

[1] All that is important in Śaṅkara's commentary of the *Brahma-sūtras* has been excellently systematised by Deussen in his *System of the Vedānta*; it is therefore unnecessary for me to give any long account of this part. Most of what follows has been taken from the writings of his followers.

many cease; there is no duality, no notion of mine and thine; the vast illusion of this world process is extinct in him, and he shines forth as the one, the truth, the Brahman. All Hindu systems believed that when man attained salvation, he became divested of all world-consciousness, or of all consciousness of himself and his interests, and was thus reduced to his own original purity untouched by all sensations, perceptions, feelings and willing, but there the idea was this that when man had no bonds of karma and no desire and attachment with the world and had known the nature of his self as absolutely free and unattached to the world and his own psychosis, he became emancipated from the world and all his connections with the world ceased, though the world continued as ever the same with others. The external world was a reality with them; the unreality or illusion consisted in want of true knowledge about the real nature of the self, on account of which the self foolishly identified itself with world-experiences, worldly joys and world-events, and performed good and bad works accordingly. The force of accumulated karmas led him to undergo the experiences brought about by them. While reaping the fruits of past karmas he, as ignorant as ever of his own self, worked again under the delusion of a false relationship between himself and the world, and so the world process ran on. Mukti (salvation) meant the dissociation of the self from the subjective psychosis and the world. This condition of the pure state of self was regarded as an unconscious one by Nyāya-Vaiśeṣika and Mīmāṃsā, and as a state of pure intelligence by Sāṃkhya and Yoga. But with Vedānta the case is different, for it held that the world as such has no real existence at all, but is only an illusory imagination which lasts till the moment when true knowledge is acquired. As soon as we come to know that the one truth is the self, the Brahman, all our illusory perceptions representing the world as a field of experience cease. This happens not because the connections of the self with the world cease, but because the appearance of the world process does not represent the ultimate and highest truth about it. All our notions about the abiding diversified world (lasting though they may be from beginningless time) are false in the sense that they do not represent the real truth about it. We not only do not know what we ourselves really are, but do not also know what the world about us is. We take our ordinary experiences of the world as representing it correctly, and proceed on our career of daily activity. It is no doubt true that these experiences show us an established order having its own laws, but this does not represent the real truth. They are true only in a relative sense, so long as they appear to be so; for the moment the real truth about them and the self is comprehended all world-appearances become unreal, and that one truth, the Brahman, pure being, bliss, intelligence, shines forth as the absolute—the only truth in world and man. The world-appearance as experienced by us is thus often likened to the illusory perception of silver in a conch-shell; for the moment the perception appears to be true and the man runs to pick it up, as if the conch-shell were a real piece of silver; but as soon as he finds out the truth that this is only a piece of conch-shell, he turns his back on it and is no longer deluded by the appearance or again attracted towards it. The illusion of silver is inexplicable in itself, for it was true for all purposes so long as it persisted, but when true knowledge was acquired, it forthwith vanished. This world-appearance will also vanish when the true knowledge of reality dawns. When false knowledge is once found to be false it cannot return again. The Upaniṣads tell us that he who sees the many here is doomed. The one, the Brahman, alone is true; all else is but delusion of name and form. Other systems believed that even after emancipation, the world would continue as it is, that there was nothing illusory in it, but I could not have any knowledge of it because of the absence of the instruments by the processes of which knowledge was generated. The Sāṃkhya puruṣa cannot know the world when the buddhi-stuff is dissociated from it and merged in the prakṛti, the Mīmāṃsā and the Nyāya soul is also incapable of knowing the world after emancipation, as it is then dissociated from manas. But the Vedānta position is quite distinct here. We cannot know the world, for when the right knowledge dawns, the perception of this world-appearance proves itself to be false to the person who has witnessed the truth, the Brahman. An illusion cannot last when the truth is known; what is truth is known to us, but what is illusion is undemonstrable, unspeakable, and indefinite. The illusion runs on from beginningless time; we do not know how it is related to truth, the Brahman, but we know that when the truth is once known the false knowledge of this world-appearance disappears once for all. No intermediate link is necessary to effect it, no mechanical dissociation of buddhi or manas, but just as by finding out the glittering piece to be a conch-shell the illusory perception of silver is destroyed, so this illusory perception of world-appearance is also destroyed by a true knowledge of the reality, the Brahman. The Upaniṣads held that reality or truth was one, and there was "no many" anywhere, and Śaṅkara explained it by adding that the "many" was merely an illusion, and hence did not exist in reality and was bound to disappear when the truth was known. The world-appearance is māyā (illusion). This is what Śaṅkara emphasizes in expounding his constructive system of the Upaniṣad doctrine. The question is sometimes asked, how the māyā becomes associated with Brahman. But Vedānta thinks this question illegitimate, for this association did not begin in time either with reference to the cosmos or with reference to individual persons. In fact there is no real association, for the creation of illusion does not affect the unchangeable truth. Māyā or illusion is no real entity, it is only false knowledge (*avidyā*) that makes the appearance, which vanishes when the reality is grasped and found. Māyā or avidyā has an apparent existence only so long as it lasts, but the moment the truth is known it is dissolved. It is not a real entity in association with which a real world-appearance has been brought into permanent existence, for it only has existence so long as we are deluded by it (*prātītika-sattā*). Māyā therefore is a category which baffles the ordinary logical division of existence and non-existence and the principle of excluded middle. For the māyā can neither be said to be "is" nor "is not" (*tattvānyatvābhyām anirvacanīyā*). It cannot be said that such a logical category does not exist, for all our dream and illusory cognitions demonstrate it to us. They exist as they are perceived, but they do not exist since they have no other independent existence than the fact of their perception. If it has any creative function, that function is as illusive as its own nature, for the creation only lasts so long as the error lasts. Brahman, the truth, is not in any way sullied or affected by association with māyā, for there can be no association of the real with the empty, the māyā, the illusory. It is no real association but a mere appearance.

In what sense is the world-appearance false?

The world is said to be false—a mere product of māyā. The falsehood of this world-appearance has been explained as involved in the category of the indefinite which is neither *sat* "is" nor *asat* "is not." Here the opposition of the "is" and "is not" is solved by the category of time. The world-appearance is "is not," since it does not continue to manifest itself in all times, and has its manifestation up to the moment that the right knowledge dawns. It is not therefore "is not" in the sense that a "castle in the air" or a hare's horn is "is not," for these are called *tuccha*, the absolutely non-existent. The world-appearance is said to be "is" or existing, since it appears to be so for the time the state of ignorance persists in us. Since it exists for a time it is *sat* (is), but since it does not exist for all times it is *asat* (is not). This is the appearance, the falsehood of the world-appearance (*jagat-prapañca*) that it is neither *sat* nor *asat* in an absolute sense. Or rather it may also be said in another way that the falsehood of the world-appearance consists in this, that though it appears to be the reality or an expression or manifestation of the reality, the being, *sat*, yet when the reality is once rightly comprehended, it will be manifest that the world never existed, does not exist, and will never exist again. This is just what we find in an illusory perception; when once the truth is found out that it is a conch-shell, we say that the silver, though it appeared at the time of illusory perception to be what we saw before us as "this" (this is silver), yet it never existed before, does not now exist, and will never exist again. In the case of the illusory perception of silver, the "this" (pointing to a thing before me) appeared as silver; in the case of the world-appearance, it is the being (*sat*), the Brahman, that appears as the world; but as in the case when the "this" before us is found to be a piece of conch-shell, the silver is at once dismissed as having had no existence in the "this" before us, so when the Brahman, the being, the reality, is once directly realized, the conviction comes that the world never existed. The negation of the world-appearance however has no separate existence other than the comprehension of the identity of the real. The fact that the real is realized is the same as that the world-appearance is negated. The negation here involved refers both to the thing negated (the world-appearance) and the negation itself, and hence it cannot be contended that when the conviction of the negation of the world is also regarded as false (for if the negation is not false then it remains as an entity different from Brahman and hence the unqualified monism fails), then this reinstates the reality of the world-appearance; for negation of the world-appearance is as much false as the world-appearance itself, and hence on the realization of the truth the negative thesis, that the world-appearance does not exist, includes the negation also as a manifestation of world-appearance, and hence the only thing left is the realized identity of the truth, the being. The peculiarity of this illusion of world-appearance is this, that it appears as consistent with or inlaid in the being (*sat*) though it is not there. This of course is dissolved when right knowledge dawns. This indeed brings home to us the truth that the world-appearance is an appearance which is different from what we know as real (*sadvilakṣaṇa*); for the real is known to us as that which is proved by the pramāṇas, and which will never again be falsified by later experience or other means of proof. A thing is said to be true only so long as it is not contradicted; but since at the dawn of right knowledge this world-appearance will be found to be false and non-existing, it cannot be regarded as real[1]. Thus Brahman alone is true, and the world-appearance is false; falsehood and truth are not contrary entities such that the negation or the falsehood of falsehood will mean truth. The world-appearance is a whole and in referring to it the negation refers also to itself as a part of the world-appearance and hence not only is the positive world-appearance false, but the falsehood itself is also false; when the world-appearance is contradicted at the dawn of right knowledge, the falsehood itself is also contradicted.

Brahman differs from all other things in this that it is self-luminous (*svaprakāśa*) and has no form; it cannot therefore be the object of any other consciousness that grasps it. All other things, ideas, emotions, etc., in contrast to it are called *dṛśya* (objects of consciousness), while it is the *draṣṭā* (the pure consciousness comprehending all objects). As soon as anything is comprehended as an expression of a mental state (*vṛtti*), it is said to have a form and it becomes dṛśya, and this is the characteristic of all objects of consciousness that they cannot reveal themselves apart from being manifested as objects of consciousness through a mental state.

[1] See *Advaitasiddhi*, *Mithyātvanirukti*.

Brahman also, so long as it is understood as a meaning of the Upaniṣad text, is not in its true nature; it is only when it shines forth as apart from the associations of any form that it is svaprakāśa and draṣṭā. The knowledge of the pure Brahman is devoid of any form or mode. The notion of *dṛśyatva* (objectivity) carries with it also the notion of *jaḍatva* (materiality) or its nature as non-consciousness (*ajñānatva*) and non-selfness (*anātmatva*) which consists in the want of self-luminosity of objects of consciousness. The relation of consciousness (*jñāna*) to its objects cannot be regarded as real but as mere illusory impositions, for as we shall see later, it is not possible to determine the relation between knowledge and its forms. Just as the silver-appearance of the conch-shell is not its own natural appearance, so the forms in which consciousness shows itself are not its own natural essence. In the state of emancipation when supreme bliss (*ānanda*) shines forth, the ānanda is not an object or form of the illuminating consciousness, but it is the illumination itself. Whenever there is a form associated with consciousness, it is an extraneous illusory imposition on the pure consciousness. These forms are different from the essence of consciousness, not only in this that they depend on consciousness for their expression and are themselves but objects of consciousness, but also in this that they are all finite determinations (*paricchinna*), whereas consciousness, the abiding essence, is everywhere present without any limit whatsoever. The forms of the object such as cow, jug, etc. are limited in themselves in what they are, but through them all the pure being runs by virtue of which we say that the cow is, the jug is, the pot is. Apart from this pure being running through all the individual appearances, there is no other class (*jāti*) such as cowness or jugness, but it is on this pure being that different individual forms are illusorily imposed (*ghaṭādīkam sadarthe-kalpitam, pratyekam tadanubiddhatvena pratīyamānatvāt*). So this world-appearance which is essentially different from the Brahman, the being which forms the material cause on which it is imposed, is false (*upādānaniṣṭhātyantābhāvapratiyogitvalakṣaṇamithyātvasiddhiḥ*—as Citsukha has it).

The nature of the world-appearance, phenomena.

The world-appearance is not however so illusory as the perception of silver in the conch-shell, for the latter type of worldly illusions is called *prātibhāsika*, as they are contradicted by other later experiences, whereas the illusion of world-appearance is never contradicted in this worldly stage and is thus called *vyavahārika* (from *vyavahāra*, practice, i.e. that on which is based all our practical movements). So long as the right knowledge of the Brahman as the only reality does not dawn, the world-appearance runs on in an orderly manner uncontradicted by the accumulated experience of all men, and as such it must be held to be true. It is only because there comes such a stage in which the world-appearance ceases to manifest itself that we have to say that from the ultimate and absolute point of view the world-appearance is false and unreal. As against this doctrine of the Vedānta it is sometimes asked how, as we see the reality (*sattva*) before us, we can deny that it has truth. To this the Vedānta answers that the notion of reality cannot be derived from the senses, nor can it be defined as that which is the content of right knowledge, for we cannot have any conception of right knowledge without a conception of reality, and no conception of reality without a conception of right knowledge. The conception of reality comprehends within it the notions of unalterability, absoluteness, and independence, which cannot be had directly from experience, as this gives only an appearance but cannot certify its truth. Judged from this point of view it will be evident that the true reality in all our experience is the one self-luminous flash of consciousness which is all through identical with itself in all its manifestations of appearance. Our present experience of the world-appearance cannot in any way guarantee that it will not be contradicted at some later stage. What really persists in all experience is the being (*sat*) and not its forms. This being that is associated with all our experience is not a universal genus nor merely the individual appearance of the moment, but it is the being, the truth which forms the substratum of all objective events and appearances (*ekenaiva sarvānugatena sarvatra satpratītiḥ*). Things are not existent because they possess the genus of being (*sat*) as Nyāya supposes, but they are so because they are themselves but appearance imposed on one identical being as the basis and ground of all experience. Being is thus said to be the basis (*adhiṣṭhāna*) on which the illusions appear. This being is not different with different things but one in all appearances. Our perceptions of the world-appearance could have been taken as a guarantee of their reality, if the reality which is supposed of them could be perceived by the senses, and if inference and śruti (scriptures) did not point the other way. Perception can of course invalidate inference, but it can do so only when its own validity has been ascertained in an undoubted and uncontested manner. But this is not the case with our perceptions of the world-appearance, for our present perceptions cannot prove that these will never be contradicted in future, and inference and śruti are also against it. The mere fact that I perceive the world-appearance cannot prove that what I perceive is true or real, if it is contradicted by inference. We all perceive the sun to be small, but our perception in this case is contradicted by inference and we have hence to admit that our perceptions are erroneous. We depend (*upajīvya*) indeed for all our transactions on perception, but such dependence cannot prove that that on which we depend is absolutely valid. Validity or reality can only be ascertained by proper examination and enquiry (*parīkṣā*), which may convince us that there is no error in it. True it is that by the universal testimony of our contemporaries and by the practical fruition and realization of our endeavours in the external world, it is proved beyond doubt that the world-appearance before us is a reality. But this sort of examination and enquiry cannot prove to us with any degree of satisfaction that the world-appearance will never be contradicted at any time or at any stage. The Vedānta also admits that our examination and enquiry prove to us that the world-appearance now exists as it appears; it only denies that it cannot continue to exist for all times, and a time will come when to the emancipated person the world-appearance will cease to exist. The experience, observation, and practical utility of the objects as perceived by us cannot prove to us that these will never be contradicted at any future time. Our perception of the world-appearance cannot therefore disprove the Vedānta inference that the world-appearance is false, and it will demonstrate itself to be so at the time when the right knowledge of Brahman as one dawns in us. The testimony of the Upaniṣads also contradicts the perception which grasps the world-appearance in its manifold aspect.

Moreover we are led to think that the world-appearance is false, for it is not possible for us to discover any true relation between the consciousness (*dṛk*) and the objects of consciousness (*dṛśya*). Consciousness must be admitted to have some kind of connection with the objects which it illumines, for had it not been so there could be any knowledge at any time irrespective of its connections with the objects. But it is not possible to imagine any kind of connection between consciousness and its objects, for it can neither be contact (*saṃyoga*) nor inherence (*samavāya*); and apart from these two kinds of connections we know of no other. We say that things are the objects of our consciousness, but what is meant by it is indeed difficult to define. It cannot be that objectivity of consciousness means that a special effect like the jñātatā of Mīmāṃsā is produced upon the object, for such an effect is not admissible or perceivable in any way; nor can objectivity also mean any practical purpose (of being useful to us) associated with the object as Prabhākara thinks, for there are many things which are the objects of our consciousness but not considered as useful (e.g. the sky). Objectivity also cannot mean that the thing is the object of the thought-movement (*jñāna-kāraṇa*) involved in knowledge, for this can only be with reference to objects present to the perceiver, and cannot apply to objects of past time about which one may be conscious, for if the thing is not present how can it be made an object of thought-movement? Objectivity further cannot mean that the things project their own forms on the knowledge and are hence called objects, for though this may apply in the case of perception, it cannot be true of inference, where the object of consciousness is far away and does not mould consciousness after its own form. Thus in whatever way we may try to conceive manifold things existing separately and becoming objects of consciousness we fail. We have also seen that it is difficult to conceive of any kind of relation subsisting between objects and consciousness, and hence it has to be admitted that the imposition of the world-appearance is after all nothing but illusory.

Now though all things are but illusory impositions on consciousness yet for the illumination of specific objects it is admitted even by Vedānta that this can only take place through specific sense-contact and particular mental states (*vṛtti*) or modes; but if that be so why not rather admit that this can take place even on the assumption of the absolute reality of the manifold external world without? The answer that the Vedānta gives to such a question is this, that the phenomenon of illumination has not to undergo any gradual process, for it is the work of one flash like the work of the light of a lamp in removing darkness; so it is not possible that the external reality should have to pass through any process before consciousness could arise; what happens is simply this, that the reality (*sat*) which subsists in all things as the same identical one reveals the object as soon as its veil is removed by association with the vṛtti (mental mould or state). It is like a light which directly and immediately illuminates everything with which it comes into relation. Such an illumination of objects by its underlying reality would have been continuous if there were no veils or covers, but that is not so as the reality is hidden by the veil of ajñāna (nescience). This veil is removed as soon as the light of consciousness shines through a mental mould or vṛtti, and as soon as it is removed the thing shines forth. Even before the formation of the vṛtti the illusory impositions on the reality had still been continuing objectively, but it could not be revealed as it was hidden by ajñāna which is removed by the action of the corresponding vṛtti; and as soon as the veil is removed the thing shines forth in its true light. The action of the senses, eye, etc. serves but to modify the vṛtti of the mind, and the vṛtti of the mind once formed, the corresponding ajñāna veil which was covering the corresponding specific part of the world-appearance is removed, and the illumination of the object which was already present, being divested of the veil, shows itself forth. The illusory creations were there, but they could not be manifested on account of the veil of nescience. As soon as the veil is removed by the action of the vṛtti the light of reality shows the corresponding illusory creations. So consciousness in itself is the ever-shining light of reality which is never generated but ever exists; errors of perception (e.g. silver in the conch-shell) take place not because the doṣa consisting of the defect of the eye, the glaze of the object and such other elements that contributed to the illusion, generated the knowledge, but because it generated a wrong vṛtti. It is because of the generation of the wrong vṛtti that the manifestation is illusory. In the illusion "this is silver" as when we mistake the conch-shell for the silver, it is the *cit*, consciousness or reality as underlying the object represented to us by "this" or "*idam*" that is the basis (*adhiṣṭhāna*) of the illusion of silver. The cause of error is our nescience or non-cognition (*ajñāna*) of it in the form of the conch-shell, whereas the right knowledge is the cognition of it as conch-shell. The basis is not in the content of my knowledge as manifested in my mental state (*vṛtti*), so that the illusion is not of the form that the "knowledge is silver" but of "this is silver." Objective phenomena as such have reality as their basis, whereas the expression of illumination of them as states of knowledge is made through the *cit* being manifested through the mental mould or states. Without the vṛtti there is no illuminating knowledge. Phenomenal creations are there in the world moving about as shadowy forms on the unchangeable basis of one cit or reality, but this basis, this light of reality, can only manifest these forms when the veil of nescience covering them is temporarily removed by their coming in touch with a mental mould or mind-modification (*vṛtti*). It is sometimes said that since all illumination of knowledge must be through the mental states there is no other entity of pure consciousness apart from what is manifested through the states. This Vedānta does not admit, for it holds that it is necessary that before the operation of the mental states can begin to interpret reality, reality must already be there and this reality is nothing but pure consciousness. Had there been no reality apart from the manifesting states of knowledge, the validity of knowledge would also cease; so it has to be admitted that there is the one eternal self-luminous reality untouched by the characteristics of the mental states, which are material and suffer origination and destruction. It is this self-luminous consciousness that seems to assume diverse forms in connection with diverse kinds of associations or limitations (*upādhi*). It manifests *ajñāna* (nescience) and hence does not by itself remove the ajñāna, except when it is reflected through any specific kind of vṛtti. There is of course no difference, no inner and outer varieties between the reality, the pure consciousness which is the essence, the basis and the ground of all phenomenal appearances of the objective world, and the consciousness that manifests itself through the mental states. There is only one identical pure consciousness or reality, which is at once the basis of the phenomena as well as their interpreter by a reflection through the mental states or vṛttis.

The phenomena or objects called the dṛśya can only be determined in their various forms and manifestations but not as to their ultimate reality; there is no existence as an entity of any relation such as saṃyoga (contact) or samavāya (inherence) between them and the pure consciousness called the dṛk; for the truth is this, that the dṛk (perceiver) and the dṛśya (perceived) have one identical reality; the forms of phenomena are but illusory creations on it.

It is sometimes objected that in the ordinary psychological illusion such as "this is silver," the knowledge of "this" as a thing is only of a general and indefinite nature, for it is perceived as a thing but its special characteristics as a conch-shell are not noticed, and thus the illusion is possible. But in Brahman or pure consciousness there are neither definite nor indefinite characteristics of any kind, and hence it cannot be the ground of any illusion as the piece of conch-shell perceived indefinitely as a mere "this" can be. The answer of Vedānta is that when the Brahman stands as the ground (*adhiṣṭhāna*) of the world-appearance its characteristic as sat or real only is manifested, whereas its special character as pure and infinite bliss is never noticed; or rather it may be said that the illusion of world-appearance is possible because the Brahman in its true and correct nature is never revealed to us in our objective consciousness; when I say "the jug is," the "isness," or "being," does not shine in its purity, but only as a characteristic of the jug-form, and this is the root of the illusion. In all our experiences only the aspect of Brahman as real shines forth in association with the manifold objects, and therefore the Brahman in its true nature being unknown the illusion is made possible. It is again objected that since the world-appearance can serve all practical purposes, it must be considered as real and not illusory. But the Vedānta points out that even by illusory perceptions practical effects are seen to take place; the illusory perception of a snake in a rope causes all the fear that a real snake could do; even in dreams we feel happy and sad, and dreams may be so bad as to affect or incapacitate the actual physical functions and organs of a man. So it is that the past impressions imbedded in us continuing from beginningless time are sufficient to account for our illusory notions, just as the impressions produced in actual waking life account for the dream creations. According to the good or bad deeds that a man has done in previous lives and according to the impressions or potencies (*saṃskāra*) of his past lives each man has a particular kind of world-experience for himself and the impressions of one cannot affect the formation of the illusory experience of the other. But the experience of the world-appearance is not wholly a subjective creation for each individual, for even before his cognition the phenomena of world-appearance were running in some unknowable state of existence (*svena adhyastasya saṃskārasya viyadād-yadhyāsajanakatvopapatteḥ tatpratītyabhāvepi tadadhyāsasya pūrvam sattvāt kṛtsnasyāpi vyavahārikapadārthasya ajñātasattvābhyupagamāt*). It is again sometimes objected that illusion is produced by malobserved similarity between the ground (*adhiṣṭhāna*) and the illusory notion as silver in "this is silver," but no such similarity is found between the Brahman and the world-appearance. To this Vedānta says that similarity is not an indispensable factor in the production of an illusion (e.g. when a white conch is perceived as yellow owing to the defect of the eye through the influence of bile or *pitta*). Similarity helps the production of illusion by rousing up the potencies of past impressions or memories; but this rousing of past memories may as well be done by *adṛṣṭa*—the unseen power of our past good or bad deeds. In ordinary illusion some defect is necessary but the illusion of this world-appearance is beginningless, and hence it awaits no other doṣa (defect) than the avidyā (nescience) which constitutes the appearance. Here avidyā is the only doṣa and Brahman is the only adhiṣṭhāna or ground. Had there not been the Brahman, the self-luminous as the adhiṣṭhāna, the illusory creations could not have been manifested at all. The cause of the direct perception of illusion is the direct but indefinite perception of the adhiṣṭhāna. Hence where the adhiṣṭhāna is hidden by the veil of avidyā, the association with mental states becomes necessary for removing the veil and manifesting thereby the self-luminous adhiṣṭhāna. As soon as the adhiṣṭhāna, the ground, the reality, the blissful self-luminous Brahman is completely realized the illusions disappear. The disappearance of the phenomena means nothing more than the realization of the self-luminous Brahman.

The Definition of Ajñāna (nescience).

Ajñāna the cause of all illusions is defined as that which is beginningless, yet positive and removable by knowledge (*anādi-bhāvarūpatve sati jñānanivartyatvam*). Though it manifests itself in all ordinary things (veiled by it before they become objects of perception) which have a beginning in time, yet it itself has no beginning, for it is associated with the pure consciousness which is beginningless. Again though it has been described as positive (*bhāvarūpa*) it can very well constitute the essence of negation (*abhāva*) too, for the positivity (*bhāvatva*) does not mean here the opposite of abhāva (negation) but notes merely its difference from abhāva (*abhāva-vilakṣaṇatvamātram vivakṣitam*). Ajñāna is not a positive entity (*bhāva*) like any other positive entity, but it is called positive simply because it is not a mere negation (*abhāva*). It is a category which is believed neither to be positive in the ordinary sense nor negative, but a third one which is different both from position as well as from negation. It is sometimes objected that ajñāna is a mere illusory imagination of the moment caused by defect (*doṣa*) and hence it cannot be beginningless (*anādi*); but Vedānta holds that the fact that it is an imagination or rather imposition, does not necessarily mean that it is merely a temporary notion produced by the defects; for it could have been said to be a temporary product of the moment if the ground as well as the illusory creation associated with it came into being for the moment, but this is not the case here, as the cit, the ground of illusion, is ever-present and the ajñāna therefore being ever associated with it is also beginningless. The ajñāna is the indefinite which is veiling everything, and as such is different from the definite or the positive and the negative. Though it is beginningless yet it can be removed by knowledge, for to have a beginning or not to have it does not in any way determine whether the thing is subject to dissolution or not for the dissolution of a thing depends upon the presence of the thing which can cause it; and it is a fact that when knowledge comes the illusion is destroyed; it does not matter whether the cause which produced the illusion was beginningless or not. Some Vedāntists however define ajñāna as the substance constituting illusion, and say that though it is not a positive entity yet it may be regarded as forming the substance of the illusion; it is not necessary that only a positive entity should be the matter of any thing, for what is necessary for the notion of a material cause (*upādāna*) is this, that it should continue or persist as the same in all changes of effects. It is not true that only what is positive can persist in and through the effects which are produced in the time process. Illusion is unreal and it is not unnatural that the ajñāna which also is unreal should be the cause of it.

Ajñāna established by Perception and Inference.

Ajñāna defined as the indefinite which is neither positive nor negative is also directly experienced by us in such perceptions as "I do not know, or I do not know myself or anybody else," or "I do not know what you say," or more particularly "I had been sleeping so long happily and did not know anything." Such perceptions point to an object which has no definite characteristics, and which cannot properly be said to be either positive or negative. It may be objected that the perception "I do not know" is not the perception of the indefinite, the ajñāna, but merely the negation of knowledge. To this Vedānta says that had it been the perception of a negation merely, then the negation must have been associated with the specific object to which it applied. A negation must imply the thing negatived; in fact negation generally appears as a substantive with the object of negation as a qualifying character specifying the nature of the negation. But the perception "I do not know or I had no knowledge" does not involve the negation of any particular knowledge of any specific object, but the knowledge of an indefinite objectless ignorance. Such an indefinite ajñāna is positive in the sense that it is certainly not negative, but this positive indefinite is not positive in the same sense in which other definite entities are called positive, for it is merely the characterless, passive indefinite showing itself in our experience. If negation meant only a general negation, and if the perception of negation meant in each case the perception of a general negation, then even where there is a jug on the ground, one should perceive the negation of the jug on the ground, for the general negation in relation to other things is there. Thus negation of a thing cannot mean the general notion of the negation of all specific things; similarly a general negation without any specific object to which it might apply cannot manifest itself to consciousness; the notion of a general negation of knowledge is thus opposed to any and every knowledge, so that if the latter is present the former cannot be, but the perception "I do not know" can persist, even though many individual objects be known to us. Thus instead of saying that the perception of "I do not know" is the perception of a special kind of negation, it is rather better to say that it is the perception of a different category namely the indefinite, the ajñāna. It is our common experience that after experiencing the indefinite (*ajñāna*) of a specific type we launch forth in our endeavours to remove it. So it has to be admitted that the perception of the indefinite is different from the perception of mere negation. The character of our perceiving consciousness (*sākṣi*) is such that both the root ajñāna as well as its diverse forms with reference to particular objects as represented in mental states (*vṛtti-jñāna*), are comprehended by it. Of course when the vṛttijñāna about a thing as in ordinary perceptions of objects comes in, the ajñāna with regard to it is temporarily removed, for the vṛttijñāna is opposed to the ajñāna. But so far as our own perceiving consciousness (*sākṣi-caitanya*) is conceived it can comprehend both the ajñāna and the jñāna (knowledge) of things. It is thus often said that all things show themselves to the perceiving consciousness either as known or as unknown. Thus the perceiving consciousness comprehends all positives either as indefinite ajñāna or as states of knowledge or as specific kinds of ajñāna or ignorance, but it is unable to comprehend a negation, for negation (*abhāva*) is not a perception, but merely the absence of perception (*anupalabdhi*). Thus when I say I do not know this, I perceive the indefinite in consciousness with reference to that thing, and this is not the perception of a negation of the thing. An objection is sometimes raised from the Nyāya point of view that since without the knowledge of a qualification (*viśeṣana*) the qualified thing (*viśiṣṭa*) cannot be known, the indefinite about an object cannot be present in consciousness without the object being known first. To this Vedānta replies that the maxim that the qualification must be known before the qualified thing is known is groundless, for we can as well perceive the thing first and then its qualification. It is not out of place here to say that negation is not a separate entity, but is only a peculiar mode of the manifestation of the positive. Even the naiyāyikas would agree that in the expression "there is no negation of a jug here," no separate negation can be accepted, for the jug is already present before us. As there are distinctions and differences in positive entities by illusory impositions, so negations are also distinguished by similar illusory impositions and appear as the negation of jug, negation of cloth, etc.; so all distinctions between negations are unnecessary, and it may be accepted that negation like position is one which appears as many on account of illusory distinctions and impositions. Thus the content of negation being itself positive, there is no reason to object that such perceptions as "I do not know" refer to the perception of an indefinite ajñāna in consciousness. So also the perception "I do not know what you say" is not the perception of negation, for this would require that the hearer should know first what was said by the speaker, and if this is so then it is impossible to say "I do not know what you say."

So also the cognition "I was sleeping long and did not know anything" has to be admitted as referring to the perception of the indefinite during sleep. It is not true as some say that during sleep there is no perception, but what appears to the awakened man as "I did not know anything so long" is only an inference; for, it is not possible to infer from the pleasant and active state of the senses in the awakened state that the activity had ceased in the sleep state and that since he had no object of knowledge then, he could not know anything; for there is no invariable concomitance between the pleasant and active state of the senses and the absence of objects of knowledge in the immediately preceding state. During sleep there is a mental state of the form of the indefinite, and during the awakened state it is by the impression (*saṃskāra*) of the aforesaid mental state of ajñāna that one remembers that state and says that "I did not perceive anything so long." The indefinite (*ajñāna*) perceived in consciousness is more fundamental and general than the mere negation of knowledge (*jñānābhāva*) and the two are so connected that though the latter may not be felt, yet it can be inferred from the perception of the indefinite. The indefinite though not definite is thus a positive content different from negation and is perceived as such in direct and immediate consciousness both in the awakened state as well as in the sleeping state.

The presence of this ajñāna may also be inferred from the manner in which knowledge of objects is revealed in consciousness, as this always takes place in bringing a thing into consciousness which was not known or rather known as indefinite before we say "I did not know it before, but I know it now." My present knowledge of the thing thus involves the removal of an indefinite which was veiling it before and positing it in consciousness, just as the first streak of light in utter darkness manifests itself by removing the darkness[1]. Apart from such an inference its exist-

[1] See *Pañcapādikāvivaraṇa*, *Tattvadīpana*, and *Advaitasiddhi*.

ence is also indicated by the fact that the infinite bliss of Brahman does not show itself in its complete and limitless aspect. If there was no ajñāna to obstruct, it would surely have manifested itself in its fullness. Again had it not been for this ajñāna there would have been no illusion. It is the ajñāna that constitutes the substance of the illusion; for there is nothing else that can be regarded as constituting its substance; certainly Brahman could not, as it is unchangeable. This ajñāna is manifested by the perceiving consciousness (*sākṣi*) and not by the pure consciousness. The perceiving consciousness is nothing but pure intelligence which reflects itself in the states of avidyā (ignorance).

Locus and Object of Ajñāna, Ahaṃkāra, and Antaḥkaraṇa.

This ajñāna rests on the pure *cit* or intelligence. This cit or Brahman is of the nature of pure illumination, but yet it is not opposed to the ajñāna or the indefinite. The cit becomes opposed to the ajñāna and destroys it only when it is reflected through the mental states (*vṛtti*). The ajñāna thus rests on the pure cit and not on the cit as associated with such illusory impositions as go to produce the notion of ego "*aham*" or the individual soul. Vācaspati Miśra however holds that the ajñāna does not rest on the pure cit but on the jīva (individual soul). Mādhava reconciles this view of Vācaspati with the above view, and says that the ajñāna may be regarded as resting on the jīva or individual soul from this point of view that the obstruction of the pure cit is with reference to the jīva (*Cinmātrāśritam ajñānam jīvapakṣapātitvāt jīvāśritam ucyate* Vivaraṇaprameya, p. 48). The feeling "I do not know" seems however to indicate that the ajñāna is with reference to the perceiving self in association with its feeling as ego or "I"; but this is not so; such an appearance however is caused on account of the close association of ajñāna with antaḥkaraṇa (mind) both of which are in essence the same (see Vivaraṇaprameyasaṃgraha, p. 48).

The ajñāna however does not only rest on the cit, but it has the cit as its viṣaya or object too, i.e. its manifestations are with reference to the self-luminous cit. The self-luminous cit is thus the entity on which the veiling action of the ajñāna is noticed; the veiling action is manifested not by destroying the self-luminous character, nor by stopping a future course of luminous career on the part of the cit, nor by stopping its relations with the viṣaya, but by causing such an appearance that the self-luminous cit seems so to behave that we seem to think that it is not or it does not shine (*nāsti na prakāśate iti vyavahāraḥ*) or rather there is no appearance of its shining or luminosity. To say that Brahman is hidden by the ajñāna means nothing more than this, that it is such (*tadyogyatā*) that the ajñāna can so relate itself with it that it appears to be hidden as in the state of deep sleep and other states of ajñāna-consciousness in experience. Ajñāna is thus considered to have both its locus and object in the pure cit. It is opposed to the states of consciousness, for these at once dispel it. The action of this ajñāna is thus on the light of the reality which it obstructs for us, so long as the obstruction is not dissolved by the states of consciousness. This obstruction of the cit is not only with regard to its character as pure limitless consciousness but also with regard to its character as pure and infinite bliss; so it is that though we do not experience the indefinite in our pleasurable feelings, yet its presence as obstructing the pure cit is indicated by the fact that the full infinite bliss constituting the essence of Brahman is obstructed; and as a result of that there is only an incomplete manifestation of the bliss in our phenomenal experiences of pleasure. The ajñāna is one, but it seems to obstruct the pure cit in various aspects or modes, with regard to which it may be said that the ajñāna has many states as constituting the individual experiences of the indefinite with reference to the diverse individual objects of experience. These states of ajñāna are technically called tulājñāna or avasthājñāna. Any state of consciousness (vṛttijñāna) removes a manifestation of the ajñāna as tulājñāna and reveals itself as the knowledge of an object.

The most important action of this ajñāna as obstructing the pure cit, and as creating an illusory phenomenon is demonstrated in the notion of the ego or ahaṃkāra. This notion of ahaṃkāra is a union of the true self, the pure consciousness and other associations, such as the body, the continued past experiences, etc.; it is the self-luminous characterless Brahman that is found obstructed in the notion of the ego as the repository of a thousand limitations, characters, and associations. This illusory creation of the notion of the ego runs on from beginningless time, each set of previous false impositions determining the succeeding set of impositions and so on. This blending of the unreal associations held up in the mind (*antaḥkaraṇa*) with the real, the false with the true, that is at the root of illusion. It is the antaḥkaraṇa taken as the self-luminous self that reflects itself in the cit as the notion of the ego. Just as when we say that the iron ball (red hot) burns, there are two entities of the ball and the fire fused into one, so here also when I say "I perceive" there are two distinct elements of the self as consciousness and the mind or antaḥkaraṇa fused into one. The part or aspect associated with sorrow, materiality, and changefulness represents the antaḥkaraṇa, whereas that which appears as the unchangeable perceiving consciousness is the self. Thus the notion of ego contains two parts, one real and the other unreal.

We remember that this is distinctly that which Prabhākara sought to repudiate. Prabhākara did not consider the self to be self-luminous, and held that such is the threefold nature of thought (*tripuṭī*), that it at once reveals the knowledge, the object of knowledge, and the self. He further said that the analogy of the red-hot iron ball did not hold, for the iron ball and the fire are separately experienced, but the self and the antaḥkaraṇa are never separately experienced, and we can never say that these two are really different and only have an illusory appearance of a seeming unity. Perception (*anubhava*) is like a light which illuminates both the object and the self, and like it does not require the assistance of anything else for the fulfilling of its purpose. But the Vedānta objects to this saying that according to Prabhākara's supposition it is impossible to discover any relation between the self and the knowledge. If knowledge can be regarded as revealing itself, the self may as well be held to be self-luminous; the self and the knowledge are indeed one and the same. Kumārila thinks this thought (*anubhava*) to be a movement, Nyāya and Prabhākara as a quality of the self[1]. But if it were a movement like other movements, it could not affect itself as illumination. If it were a substance and atomic in size, it would only manifest a small portion of a thing, if all-pervasive then it would illuminate everything, if of medium size it would depend on its parts for its own

[1] According to Nyāya the *ātman* is conscious only through association with consciousness, but it is not consciousness (*cit*). Consciousness is associated with it only as a result of suitable collocations. Thus *Nyāyamañjarī* in refuting the doctrine of self-luminosity (*svdprakāśa*) says (p. 432)

sacetanaścitā yogāttadyogena vinā jaḍaḥ
nārthāvabhāsādanyaddhi caitanyaṃ nāma manmahe.

constitution and not on the self. If it is regarded as a quality of the self as the light is of the lamp, then also it has necessarily to be supposed that it was produced by the self, for from what else could it be produced? Thus it is to be admitted that the self, the ātman, is the self-luminous entity. No one doubts any of his knowledge, whether it is he who sees or anybody else. The self is thus the same as vijñāna, the pure consciousness, which is always of itself self-luminous[1].

Again, though consciousness is continuous in all stages, waking or sleeping, yet ahaṃkāra is absent during deep sleep. It is true that on waking from deep sleep one feels "I slept happily and did not know anything": yet what happens is this, that during deep sleep the antaḥkaraṇa and the ahaṃkāra are altogether submerged in the ajñāna, and there are only the ajñāna and the self; on waking, this ahaṃkāra as a state of antaḥkarṇa is again generated, and then it associates the perception of the ajñāna in the sleep and originates the perception "I did not know anything." This ahaṃkāra which is a mode (*vṛtti*) of the antaḥkaraṇa is thus constituted by avidyā, and is manifested as jñānaśakti (power of knowledge) and kriyāśakti (power of work). This kriyāśakti of the ahaṃkāra is illusorily imposed upon the self, and as a result of that the self appears to be an active agent in knowing and willing. The ahaṃkāra itself is regarded, as we have already seen, as a mode or vṛtti of the antaḥkaraṇa, and as such the ahaṃkāra of a past period can now be associated; but even then the vṛtti of antaḥkaraṇa, ahaṃkāra, may be regarded as only the active side or aspect of the antaḥkaraṇa. The same antaḥkaraṇa is called manas in its capacity as doubt, buddhi in its capacity as achieving certainty of knowledge, and citta in its capacity as remembering[2]. When the pure cit shines forth in association with this antaḥkaraṇa, it is called a jīva. It is clear from the above account that the ajñāna is not a mere nothing, but is the principle of the phenomena. But it cannot stand alone, without the principle of the real to support it (*āśraya*); its own nature as the ajñāna or indefinite is perceived directly by the pure consciousness; its movements as originating the phenomena remain indefinite in themselves, the real as under-

[1] See *Nyāyamakaranda*, pp. 130–140, *Citsukha* and *Vivaraṇaprameyasaṃgraha*, pp. 53–58.

[2] See *Vedānta-paribhāṣā*, p. 88, Bombay edition.

lying these phenomenal movements can only manifest itself through these which hide it, when corresponding states arise in the antaḥkaraṇa, and the light of the real shines forth through these states. The antaḥkaraṇa of which ahaṃkāra is a moment, is itself a beginningless system of ajñāna-phenomena containing within it the associations and impressions of past phenomena as merit, demerit, instincts, etc. from a beginningless time when the jīva or individual soul began his career.

Anirvācyavāda and the Vedānta Dialectic.

We have already seen that the indefinite ajñāna could be experienced in direct perception and according to Vedānta there are only two categories. The category of the real, the self-luminous Brahman, and the category of the indefinite. The latter has for its ground the world-appearance, and is the principle by which the one unchangeable Brahman is falsely manifested in all the diversity of the manifold world. But this indefinite which is different from the category of the positive and the negative, has only a relative existence and will ultimately vanish, when the true knowledge of the Brahman dawns. Nothing however can be known about the nature of this indefinite except its character as indefinite. That all the phenomena of the world, the fixed order of events, the infinite variety of world-forms and names, all these are originated by this avidyā, ajñāna or māyā is indeed hardly comprehensible. If it is indefinite nescience, how can all these well-defined forms of world-existence come out of it? It is said to exist only relatively, and to have only a temporary existence beside the permanent infinite reality. To take such a principle and to derive from it the mind, matter, and indeed everything else except the pure self-luminous Brahman, would hardly appeal to our reason. If this system of world-order were only seeming appearance, with no other element of truth in it except pure being, then it would be indefensible in the light of reason. It has been proved that whatever notions we have about the objective world are all self-contradictory, and thus groundless and false. If they have all proceeded from the indefinite they must show this character when exposed to discerning criticism. All categories have to be shown to be so hopelessly confused and to be without any conceivable notion that though apparent before us yet they crumble into indefiniteness as soon as they are examined, and one cannot make any such assertion about them as that they are or that they are not. Such negative criticisms of our fundamental notions about the world-order were undertaken by Śrīharṣa and his commentator and follower Citsukha. It is impossible within the limits of this chapter to give a complete account of their criticisms of our various notions of reality. I shall give here only one example.

Let us take the examination of the notion of difference (*bheda*) from *Khaṇḍanakhaṇḍakhādya*. Four explanations are possible of the notion of difference: (1) the difference may be perceived as appearing in its own characteristics in our experience (*svarūpa-bheda*) as Prabhākara thinks; (2) the difference between two things is nothing but the absence of one in the other (*anyonyābhāva*), as some Naiyāyikas and Bhāṭṭas think; (3) difference means divergence of characteristics (*vaidharmya*) as the Vaiśeṣikas speak of it; (4) difference may be a separate quality in itself like the pṛthaktva quality of Nyāya. Taking the first alternative, we see that it is said that the jug and the cloth represent in themselves by their very form and existence their mutual difference from each other. But if by perceiving the cloth we perceive only its difference from the jug as the characteristic of the cloth, then the jug also must have penetrated into the form of the cloth, otherwise how could we perceive in the cloth its characteristics as the difference from the jug? i.e. if difference is a thing which can be directly perceived by the senses, then as difference would naturally mean difference from something else, it is expected that something else such as jug, etc. from which the difference is perceived must also be perceived directly in the perception of the cloth. But if the perception of difference between two things has penetrated together in the same identical perception, then the self-contradiction becomes apparent. Difference as an entity is not what we perceive in the cloth, for difference means difference from something else, and if that thing from which the difference is perceived is not perceived, then how can the difference as an entity be perceived? If it is said that the cloth itself represents its difference from the jug, and that this is indicated by the jug, then we may ask, what is the nature of the jug? If the difference from the cloth be the very nature of the jug, then the cloth itself is also involved in the nature of the jug. If it is said that the jug only indicates that it is a term from which difference is intended to be conveyed, then that also becomes impossible, for how can we imagine that there is a term which is independent of any association of its difference from other things, and is yet a term which establishes the notion of difference? If it is a term of difference, it cannot be independent of its relation to other things from which it is differentiated. If its difference from the cloth is a quality of the jug, then also the old difficulty comes in, for its difference from the cloth would involve the cloth also in itself; and if the cloth is involved in the nature of the jug as its quality, then by the same manner the jug would also be the character of the cloth, and hence not difference but identity results. Moreover, if a cloth is perceived as a character of the jug, the two will appear to be hanging one over the other, but this is never so experienced by us. Moreover, it is difficult to ascertain if qualities have any relation with things; if they have not, then absence of relation being the same everywhere everything might be the quality of everything. If there is a relation between these two, then that relation would require another relation to relate itself with that relation, and that would again require another relation and that another, and so on. Again, it may be said that when the jug, etc. are seen without reference to other things, they appear as jug, etc., but when they are viewed with reference to cloth, etc. they appear as difference. But this cannot be so, for the perception as jug is entirely different from the perception of difference. It should also be noted that the notion of difference is also different from the notions of both the jug and the cloth. It is one thing to say that there are jug and cloth, and quite another thing to say that the jug is different from the cloth. Thus a jug cannot appear as difference, though it may be viewed with reference to cloth. The notion of a jug does not require the notions of other things for its manifestation. Moreover, when I say the jug is different from the cloth, I never mean that difference is an entity which is the same as the jug or the cloth; what I mean is that the difference of the cloth from the jug has its limits in the jug, and not merely that the notion of cloth has a reference to jug. This shows that difference cannot be the characteristic nature of the thing perceived.

Again, in the second alternative where difference of two

things is defined as the absence of each thing in the other, we find that if difference in jug and cloth means that the jug is not in the cloth or that cloth is not in jug, then also the same difficulty arises; for when I say that the absence or negation of jug in the cloth is its difference from the jug, then also the residence of the absence of jug in the cloth would require that the jug also resides in the cloth, and this would reduce difference to identity. If it is said that the absence of jug in the cloth is not a separate thing, but is rather the identical cloth itself, then also their difference as mutual exclusion cannot be explained. If this mutual negation (*anyonyabhāva*) is explained as the mere absence of jugness in the cloth and of clothness in the jug, then also a difficulty arises; for there is no such quality in jugness or clothness that they may be mutually excluded; and there is no such quality in them that they can be treated as identical, and so when it is said that there is no jugness in cloth we might as well say that there is no clothness in cloth, for clothness and jugness are one and the same, and hence absence of jugness in the cloth would amount to the absence of clothness in the cloth which is self-contradictory. Taking again the third alternative we see that if difference means divergence of characteristics (*vaidharmya*), then the question arises whether the vaidharmya or divergence as existing in jug has such a divergence as can distinguish it from the divergence existing in the cloth; if the answer is in the affirmative then we require a series of endless vaidharmyas progressing *ad infinitum*. If the answer is in the negative then there being no divergence between the two divergences they become identical, and hence divergence of characteristics as such ceases to exist. If it is said that the natural forms of things are difference in themselves, for each of them excludes the other, then apart from the differences—the natural forms—the things are reduced to formlessness (*niḥsvarūpatā*). If natural forms (*svarūpa*) mean special natural forms (*svarūpa-viśeṣa*) then as the special natural forms or characteristics only represent difference, the natural forms of the things as apart from the special ones would appear to be identical. So also it may be proved that there is no such quality as pṛthaktva (separateness) which can explain differences of things, for there also the questions would arise as to whether separateness exists in different things or similar ones or whether separateness is identical with the thing in which it exists or not, and so forth.

The earliest beginnings of this method of subtle analysis and dialectic in Indian philosophy are found in the opening chapters of *Kathāvatthu.* In the great *Mahābhaṣya* on Pāṇini by Patañjali also we find some traces of it. But Nāgārjuna was the man who took it up in right earnest and systematically cultivated it in all its subtle and abstruse issues and counter-issues in order to prove that everything that appeared as a fixed order or system was non-existent, for all were unspeakable, indescribable and self-contradictory, and thus everything being discarded there was only the void (*śūnya*). Śaṅkara partially utilized this method in his refutations of Nyāya and the Buddhist systems; but Śrīharṣa again revived and developed it in a striking manner, and after having criticized the most important notions and concepts of our everyday life, which are often backed by the Nyāya system, sought to prove that nothing in the world can be defined, and that we cannot ascertain whether a thing is or is not. The refutations of all possible definitions that the Nyāya could give necessarily led to the conclusion that the things sought to be defined did not exist though they appeared to do so; the Vedāntic contention was that this is exactly as it should be, for the indefinite ajñāna produces only appearances which when exposed to reason show that no consistent notions of them can be formed, or in other words the world-appearance, the phenomena of māyā or ajñāna, are indefinable or anirvacanīya. This great work of Śrīharṣa was followed by *Tattvadīpikā* of Citsukha, in which he generally followed Śrīharṣa and sometimes supplemented him with the addition of criticisms of certain new concepts. The method of Vedānta thus followed on one side the method of Śūnyavāda in annulling all the concepts of world-appearance and on the other Vijñānavāda Buddhism in proving the self-illuminating character of knowledge and ultimately established the self as the only self-luminous ultimate reality.

The Theory of Causation.

The Vedānta philosophy looked at the constantly changing phenomena of the world-appearance and sought to discover the root whence proceeded the endless series of events and effects. The theory that effects were altogether new productions caused by the invariable unconditional and immediately preceding antecedents, as well as the theory that it was the cause which evolved and by its transformations produced the effect, are considered insufficient to explain the problem which the Vedānta had before it. Certain collocations invariably and unconditionally preceded certain effects, but this cannot explain how the previous set of phenomena could be regarded as producing the succeeding set. In fact the concept of causation and production had in it something quite undefinable and inexplicable. Our enquiry after the cause is an enquiry after a more fundamental and primary form of the truth of a thing than what appears at the present moment when we wished to know what was the cause of the jug, what we sought was a simpler form of which the effect was only a more complex form of manifestation, what is the ground, the root, out of which the effect has come forth? If apart from such an enquiry we take the pictorial representation of the causal phenomena in which some collocations being invariably present at an antecedent point of time, the effect springs forth into being, we find that we are just where we were before, and are unable to penetrate into the logic of the affair. The Nyāya definition of cause and effect may be of use to us in a general way in associating certain groups of things of a particular kind with certain other phenomena happening at a succeeding moment as being relevant pairs of which one being present the other also has a probability of being present, but can do nothing more than this. It does not answer our question as to the nature of cause. Antecedence in time is regarded in this view as an indispensable condition for the cause. But time, according to Nyāya, is one continuous entity; succession of time can only be conceived as antecedence and consequence of phenomena, and these again involve succession; thus the notions of succession of time and of the antecedence and consequence of time being mutually dependent upon each other (*anyonyāśraya*) neither of these can be conceived independently. Another important condition is invariability. But what does that mean? If it means invariable antecedence, then even an ass which is invariably present as an antecedent to the smoke rising from the washerman's house, must be regarded as the cause of the smoke[1]. If it means such an antecedence as contributes to the happening of the effect, it becomes again difficult to understand anything about its contri-

[1] Asses are used in carrying soiled linen in India. Asses are always present when water is boiled for washing in the laundry.

buting to the effect, for the only intelligible thing is the antecedence and nothing more. If invariability means the existence of that at the presence of which the effect comes into being, then also it fails, for there may be the seed but no shoot, for the mere presence of the seed will not suffice to produce the effect, the shoot. If it is said that a cause can produce an effect only when it is associated with its accessory factors, then also the question remains the same, for we have not understood what is meant by cause. Again when the same effect is often seen to be produced by a plurality of causes, the cause cannot be defined as that which happening the effect happens and failing the effect fails. It cannot also be said that in spite of the plurality of causes, each particular cause is so associated with its own particular kind of effect that from a special kind of cause we can without fail get a special kind of effect (cf. Vātsyāyana and *Nyāyamañjarī*), for out of the same clay different effects come forth namely the jug, the plate, etc. Again if cause is defined as the collocation of factors, then the question arises as to what is meant by this collocation; does it mean the factors themselves or something else above them? On the former supposition the scattered factors being always present in the universe there should always be the effect; if it means something else above the specific factors, then that something always existing, there should always be the effect. Nor can collocation (*sāmagrī*) be defined as the last movement of the causes immediately succeeding which the effect comes into being, for the relation of movement with the collocating cause is incomprehensible. Moreover if movement is defined as that which produces the effect, the very conception of causation which was required to be proved is taken for granted. The idea of necessity involved in the causal conception that a cause is that which must produce its effect is also equally undefinable, inexplicable, and logically inconceivable. Thus in whatsoever way we may seek to find out the real nature of the causal principle from the interminable series of cause-effect phenomena we fail. All the characteristics of the effects are indescribable and indefinable ajñāna of māyā, and in whatever way we may try to conceive these phenomena in themselves or in relation to one another we fail, for they are all carved out of the indefinite and are illogical and illusory, and some day will vanish for ever. The true cause is thus the pure being, the reality which is unshakable in itself, the ground upon which all appearances being imposed they appear as real. The true cause is thus the unchangeable being which persists through all experience, and the effect-phenomena are but impositions upon it of ajñāna or avidyā. It is thus the clay, the permanent, that is regarded as the cause of all clay-phenomena as jug, plates, etc. All the various modes in which the clay appears are mere appearances, unreal, indefinable, and so illusory. The one truth is the clay. So in all world-phenomena the one truth is being, the Brahman, and all the phenomena that are being imposed on it are but illusory forms and names. This is what is called the *satkāryavāda* or more properly the *satkāraṇavāda* of the Vedānta, that the cause alone is true and ever existing, and phenomena in themselves are false. There is only this much truth in them, that all are imposed on the reality or being which alone is true. This appearance of the one cause the being, as the unreal many of the phenomena is what is called the *vivarttavāda* as distinguished from the *sāṃkhyayogapariṇāmavāda*, in which the effect is regarded as the real development of the cause in its potential state. When the effect has a different kind of being from the cause it is called *vivartta* but when the effect has the same kind of being as the cause it is called *pariṇāma* (*kāraṇasvalakṣaṇānyathābhāvaḥ pariṇāmaḥ tadvilakṣaṇo vivarttaḥ* or *vastunastatsamattāko'nyathābhāvaḥ pariṇāmaḥ tadviṣamasattākaḥ vivarttaḥ*). Vedānta has as much to object against the Nyāya as against the pariṇāma theory of causation of the Sāṃkhya; for movement, development, form, potentiality, and actuality—all these are indefinable and inconceivable in the light of reason; they cannot explain causation but only restate things and phenomena as they appear in the world. In reality however though phenomena are not identical with the cause, they can never be defined except in terms of the cause (*Tadabhedam vinaiva tadvyatirekeṇa durvacam kāryyam vivarttaḥ*).

This being the relation of cause and effect or Brahman and the world, the different followers of Śaṅkara Vedānta in explaining the cause of the world-appearance sometimes lay stress on the māyā, ajñāna or avidyā, sometimes on the Brahman, and sometimes on them both. Thus Sarvajñātmamuni, the writer of *Saṅkṣepa-śārīraka* and his followers think that the pure Brahman should be regarded as the causal substance (*upādāna*) of the world-appearance, whereas Prakāśātman Akhaṇḍānanda, and

Mādhava hold that Brahman in association with māyā, i.e. the māyā-reflected form of Brahman as Īśvara should be regarded as the cause of the world-appearance. The world-appearance is an evolution or pariṇāma of the māyā as located in Īśvara, whereas Īśvara (God) is the vivartta causal matter. Others however make a distinction between māyā as the cosmical factor of illusion and avidyā as the manifestation of the same entity in the individual or jīva. They hold that though the world-appearance may be said to be produced by the māyā yet the mind etc. associated with the individual are produced by the avidyā with the jīva or the individual as the causal matter (*upādāna*). Others hold that since it is the individual to whom both Īśvara and the world-appearance are manifested, it is better rather to think that these are all manifestations of the jīva in association with his avidyā or ajñāna. Others however hold that since in the world-appearance we find in one aspect pure being and in another materiality etc., both Brahman and māyā are to be regarded as the cause, Brahman as the permanent causal matter, upādāna and māyā as the entity evolving in pariṇāma. Vācaspati Miśra thinks that Brahman is the permanent cause of the world-appearance through māyā as associated with jīva. Māyā is thus only a sahakāri or instrument as it were, by which the one Brahman appears in the eye of the jīva as the manifold world of appearance. Prakāśānanda holds however in his *Siddhānta Muktāvalī* that Brahman itself is pure and absolutely unaffected even as illusory appearance, and is not even the causal matter of the world-appearance. Everything that we see in the phenomenal world, the whole field of world-appearance, is the product of māyā, which is both the instrumental and the upādāna (causal matter) of the world-illusion. But whatever these divergences of view may be, it is clear that they do not in any way affect the principal Vedānta text that the only unchangeable cause is the Brahman, whereas all else, the effect-phenomena, have only a temporary existence as indefinable illusion. The word māyā was used in the Ṛg-Veda in the sense of supernatural power and wonderful skill, and the idea of an inherent mystery underlying it was gradually emphasized in the Atharva Veda, and it began to be used in the sense of magic or illusion. In the Bṛhadāraṇyaka, Praśna, and Svetāśvatara Upaniṣads the word means magic. It is not out of place here to mention that in the older Upaniṣads the word māyā occurs only once in the Bṛhadāraṇyaka and once only in the Praśna. In early Pāli Buddhist writings it occurs only in the sense of deception or deceitful conduct. Buddhaghoṣa uses it in the sense of magical power. In Nāgārjuna and the *Laṅkāvatāra* it has acquired the sense of illusion. In Śaṅkara the word māyā is used in the sense of illusion, both as a principle of creation as a śakti (power) or accessory cause, and as the phenomenal creation itself, as the illusion of world-appearance.

It may also be mentioned here that Gauḍapāda the teacher of Śaṅkara's teacher Govinda worked out a system with the help of the māyā doctrine. The Upaniṣads are permeated with the spirit of an earnest enquiry after absolute truth. They do not pay any attention towards explaining the world-appearance or enquiring into its relations with absolute truth. Gauḍapāda asserts clearly and probably for the first time among Hindu thinkers, that the world does not exist in reality, that it is māyā, and not reality. When the highest truth is realized māyā is not removed, for it is not a thing, but the whole world-illusion is dissolved into its own airy nothing never to recur again. It was Gauḍapāda who compared the world-appearance with dream appearances, and held that objects seen in the waking world are unreal, because they are capable of being seen like objects seen in a dream, which are false and unreal. The ātman says Gauḍapāda is at once the cognizer and the cognized, the world subsists in the ātman through māyā. As ātman alone is real and all duality an illusion, it necessarily follows that all experience is also illusory. Śaṅkara expounded this doctrine in his elaborate commentaries on the Upaniṣads and the Brahma-sūtra, but he seems to me to have done little more than making explicit the doctrine of māyā. Some of his followers however examined and thought over the concept of māyā and brought out in bold relief its character as the indefinable thereby substantially contributing to the development of the Vedānta philosophy.

Vedānta theory of Perception and Inference[1].

Pramāṇa is the means that leads to right knowledge. If memory is intended to be excluded from the definition then

[1] Dharmarājādhvarīndra and his son Rāmakṛṣṇa worked out a complete scheme of the theory of Vedantic perception and inference. This is in complete agreement with the general Vedānta metaphysics. The early Vedantists were more interested in

pramāṇa is to be defined as the means that leads to such right knowledge as has not already been acquired. Right knowledge (*pramā*) in Vedānta is the knowledge of an object which has not been found contradicted (*abādhitārthaviṣayajñānatva*). Except when specially expressed otherwise, pramā is generally considered as being excludent of memory and applies to previously unacquired (*anadhigata*) and uncontradicted knowledge. Objections are sometimes raised that when we are looking at a thing for a few minutes, the perception of the thing in all the successive moments after the first refers to the image of the thing acquired in the previous moments. To this the reply is that the Vedānta considers that so long as a different mental state does not arise, any mental state is not to be considered as momentary but as remaining ever the same. So long as we continue to perceive one thing there is no reason to suppose that there has been a series of mental states. So there is no question as to the knowledge of the succeeding moments being referred to the knowledge of the preceding moments, for so long as any mental state has any one thing for its object it is to be considered as having remained unchanged all through the series of moments. There is of course this difference between the same percept of a previous and a later moment following in succession, that fresh elements of time are being perceived as prior and later, though the content of the mental state so far as the object is concerned remains unchanged. This time element is perceived by the senses though the content of the mental state may remain undisturbed. When I see the same book for two seconds, my mental state representing the book is not changed every second, and hence there can be no *such supposition* that I am having separate mental states in succession each of which is a repetition of the previous one, for so long as the general content of the mental state remains the same there is no reason for supposing that there has been any change in the mental state. The mental state thus remains the same so long as the content is not changed, but though it remains the same it can note the change in the time elements as extraneous

demonstrating the illusory nature of the world of appearance, and did not work out a logical theory. It may be incidentally mentioned that in the theory of inference as worked out by Dharmarājādhvarīndra he was largely indebted to the Mīmāṃsā school of thought. In recognizing arthapatti, upamāna śabda and anupalabdhi also Dharmarājādhvarīndra accepted the Mīmāṃsā view. The Vedantins, previous to Dharmarājādhvarīndra, had also tacitly followed the Mīmāṃsā in these matters.

addition. All our uncontradicted knowledge of the objects of the external world should be regarded as right knowledge until the absolute is realized.

When the antaḥkaraṇa (mind) comes in contact with the external objects through the senses and becomes transformed as it were into their forms, it is said that the antaḥkaraṇa has been transformed into a state (*vṛtti*)[1]. As soon as the antaḥkaraṇa has assumed the shape or form of the object of its knowledge, the ignorance (*ajñāna*) with reference to that object is removed, and thereupon the steady light of the pure consciousness (*cit*) shows the object which was so long hidden by ignorance. The appearance or the perception of an object is thus the self-shining of the cit through a vṛtti of a form resembling an object of knowledge. This therefore pre-supposes that by the action of ajñāna, pure consciousness or being is in a state of diverse kinds of modifications. In spite of the cit underlying all this diversified objective world which is but the transformation of ignorance (ajñāna), the former cannot manifest itself by itself, for the creations being of ignorance they are but sustained by modifications of ignorance. The diversified objects of the world are but transformations of the principle of ajñāna which is neither real nor unreal. It is the nature of ajñāna that it veils its own creations. Thus on each of the objects created by the ajñāna by its creating (*vikṣepa*) capacity there is a veil by its veiling (*āvaraṇa*) capacity. But when any object comes in direct touch with antaḥkaraṇa through the senses the antaḥkaraṇa becomes transformed into the form of the object, and this leads to the removal of the veil on that particular ajñāna form—the object, and as the self-shining cit is shining through the particular ajñāna state, we have what is called the perception of the thing. Though there is in reality no such distinction as the inner and the outer yet the ajñāna has created such illusory distinctions as individual souls and the external world of objects the distinctions of time, space,

[1] Vedānta does not regard manas (mind) as a sense (indriya). The same antaḥkaraṇa, according to its diverse functions, is called manas, buddhi, ahaṃkāra, and citta. In its functions as doubt it is called manas, as originating definite cognitions it is called buddhi. As presenting the notion of an ego in consciousness ahaṃkāra, and as producing memory citta. These four represent the different modifications or states (vṛtti) of the same entity (which in itself is but a special kind of modification of ajñāna as antaḥkaraṇa).

etc. and veiled these forms. Perception leads to the temporary and the partial breaking of the veil over specific ajñāna forms so that there is a temporary union of the cit as underlying the subject and the object through the broken veil. Perception on the subjective side is thus defined as the union or undifferentiation (*abheda*) of the subjective consciousness with the objective consciousness comprehending the sensible objects through the specific mental states (*tattadindriyayogyaviṣayāvacchinnacaitanyābhinnatvam tattadākāraviṣayāvacchinnajñānasya tattadaṃśe pratyakṣatvam*). This union in perception means that the objective has at that moment no separate existence from the subjective consciousness of the perceiver. The consciousness manifesting through the antaḥkaraṇa is called jīvasākṣi.

Inference (*anumāna*), according to Vedānta, is made by our notion of concomitance (*vyāptijñāna*) between two things, acting through specific past impressions (*saṃskāra*). Thus when I see smoke on a hill, my previous notion of the concomitance of smoke with fire becomes roused as a subconscious impression, and I infer that there is fire on the hill. My knowledge of the hill and the smoke is by direct perception. The notion of concomitance revived in the subconscious only establishes the connection between the smoke and the fire. The notion of concomitance is generated by the perception of two things together, when no case of the failure of concomitance is known (*vyabhicārājñāna*) regarding the subject. The notion of concomitance being altogether subjective, the Vedantist does not emphasize the necessity of perceiving the concomitance in a large number of cases (*bhūyodarśanam sakṛddarśanam veti viśeṣo nādaraṇīyaḥ*). Vedānta is not anxious to establish any material validity for the inference, but only subjective and formal validity. A single perception of concomitance may in certain cases generate the notion of the concomitance of one thing with another when no contradictory instance is known. It is immaterial with the Vedānta whether this concomitance is experienced in one case or in hundreds of cases. The method of agreement in presence is the only form of concomitance (*anvayavyāpti*) that the Vedānta allows. So the Vedānta discards all the other kinds of inference that Nyāya supported, viz. *anvayavyatireki* (by joining agreement in presence with agreement in absence), *kevalānvayi* (by universal agreement where no test could be applied of agreement in absence) and *kevalavyatireki* (by universal agreement in absence). Vedānta advocates three premisses, viz. (1) *pratijña* (the hill is fiery); (2) *hetu* (because it has smoke) and (3) *dṛṣṭānta* (as in the kitchen) instead of the five propositions that Nyāya maintained[1]. Since one case of concomitance is regarded by Vedānta as being sufficient for making an inference it holds that seeing the one case of appearance (silver in the conch-shell) to be false, we can infer that all things (except Brahman) are false (*Brahmabhinnam sarvam mithyā Brahmabhinnatvāt yedevam tadevam yathā śuktirūpyam*). First premiss (*pratijñā*) all else excepting Brahman is false; second premiss (*hetu*) since all is different from Brahman; third premiss (*dṛṣṭānta*) whatever is so is so as the silver in the conch[2].

Ātman, Jīva, Īśvara, Ekajīvavāda and Dṛṣṭisṛṣṭivāda.

We have many times spoken of truth or reality as self-luminous (*svayaṃprakāśa*). But what does this mean? Vedānta defines it as that which is never the object of a knowing act but is yet immediate and direct with us (*avedyatve sati aparokṣavyavahārayogyatvam*). Self-luminosity thus means the capacity of being ever present in all our acts of consciousness without in any way being an object of consciousness. Whenever anything is described as an object of consciousness, its character as constituting its knowability is a quality, which may or may not be present in it, or may be present at one time and absent at another. This makes it dependent on some other such entity which can produce it or manifest it. Pure consciousness differs from all its objects in this that it is never dependent on anything else for its manifestation, but manifests all other objects such as the jug, the cloth, etc. If consciousness should require another consciousness to manifest it, then that might again require another, and that another, and so on *ad infinitum* (*anavasthā*). If consciousness did not manifest itself at the time of the object-manifestation, then even on seeing or knowing a thing one might doubt if he had seen or known it. It is thus to be admitted that consciousness (*anubhūti*) manifests itself and thereby maintains the ap-

[1] Vedānta would have either pratijñā, hetu and udāharaṇa, or udāharaṇa, upanaya and nigamana, and not all the five of Nyāya, viz. pratijñā, hetu, udāharaṇa, upanaya and nigamana.

[2] Vedantic notions of the pramāṇa of upamāna, arthāpatti, śabda and anupalabdhi, being similar to the mīmāṃsā view, do not require to be treated here separately.

pearance of all our world experience. This goes directly against the jñātatā theory of Kumārila that consciousness was not immediate but was only inferable from the manifesting quality (*jñātatā*) of objects when they are known in consciousness.

Now Vedānta says that this self-luminous pure consciousness is the same as the self. For it is only self which is not the object of any knowledge and is yet immediate and ever present in consciousness. No one doubts about his own self, because it is of itself manifested along with all states of knowledge. The self itself is the revealer of all objects of knowledge, but is never itself the object of knowledge, for what appears as the perceiving of self as object of knowledge is but association comprehended under the term ahaṃkāra (ego). The real self is identical with the pure manifesting unity of all consciousness. This real self called the ātman is not the same as the jīva or individual soul, which passes through the diverse experiences of worldly life. Īśvara also must be distinguished from this highest ātman or Brahman. We have already seen that many Vedāntists draw a distinction between māyā and avidyā. Māyā is that aspect of ajñāna by which only the best attributes are projected, whereas avidyā is that aspect by which impure qualities are projected. In the former aspect the functions are more of a creative, generative (*vikṣepa*) type, whereas in the latter veiling (*āvaraṇa*) characteristics are most prominent. The relation of the cit or pure intelligence, the highest self, with māyā and avidyā (also called ajñāna) was believed respectively to explain the phenomenal Īśvara and the phenomenal jīva or individual. This relation is conceived in two ways, namely as upādhi or pratibimba, and avaccheda. The conception of pratibimba or reflection is like the reflection of the sun in the water where the image, though it has the same brilliance as the sun, yet undergoes the effect of the impurity and movements of the water. The sun remains ever the same in its purity untouched by the impurities from which the image sun suffers. The sun may be the same but it may be reflected in different kinds of water and yield different kinds of images possessing different characteristics and changes which though unreal yet phenomenally have all the appearance of reality. The other conception of the relation is that when we speak of ākāsa (space) in the jug or of ākāśa in the room. The ākāśa in reality does not suffer any modification in being within the jug or within the room. In reality it is all-pervasive and is neither limited (*avachinna*) within the jug or the room, but is yet conceived as being limited by the jug or by the room. So long as the jug remains, the ākāśa limited within it will remain as separate from the ākāśa limited within the room.

Of the Vedantists who accept the reflection analogy the followers of Nṛsiṃhāśrama think that when the pure cit is reflected in the māyā, Īśvara is phenomenally produced, and when in the avidyā the individual or jīva. Sarvajñātmā however does not distinguish between the māyā and the avidyā, and thinks that when the cit is reflected in the avidyā in its total aspect as cause, we get Īśvara, and when reflected in the antaḥkaraṇa—a product of the avidyā—we have jīva or individual soul.

Jīva or individual means the self in association with the ego and other personal experiences, i.e. phenomenal self, which feels, suffers and is affected by world-experiences. In jīva also three stages are distinguished; thus when during deep sleep the antaḥkaraṇa is submerged, the self perceives merely the ajñāna and the jīva in this state is called prājña or ānandamaya. In the dream-state the self is in association with a subtle body and is called taijasa. In the awakened state the self as associated with a subtle and gross body is called viśva. So also the self in its pure state is called Brahman, when associated with māyā it is called Īśvara, when associated with the fine subtle element of matter as controlling them, it is called hiraṇyagarbha; when with the gross elements as the ruler or controller of them it is called virāṭ puruṣa.

The jīva in itself as limited by its avidyā is often spoken of as pāramarthika (real), when manifested through the sense and the ego in the waking states as vyavahārika (phenomenal), and when in the dream states as dream-self, prātibhāṣika (illusory).

Prakāśātmā and his followers think that since ajñāna is one there cannot be two separate reflections such as jīva and Īśvara; but it is better to admit that jīva is the image of Īśvara in the ajñāna. The totality of Brahma-cit in association with māyā is Īśvara, and this when again reflected through the ajñāna gives us the jīva. The manifestation of the jīva is in the antaḥkaraṇa as states of knowledge. The jīva thus in reality is Īśvara and apart from jīva and Īśvara there is no other separate existence of

Brahma-caitanya. Jīva being the image of Īśvara is thus dependent on him, but when the limitations of jīva are removed by right knowledge, the jīva is the same Brahman it always was.

Those who prefer to conceive the relation as being of the avaccheda type hold that reflection (pratibimba) is only possible of things which have colour, and therefore jīva is cit limited (avacchinna) by the antaḥkaraṇa (mind). Īśvara is that which is beyond it; the diversity of antaḥkaraṇas accounts for the diversity of the jīvas. It is easy however to see that these discussions are not of much fruit from the point of view of philosophy in determining or comprehending the relation of Īśvara and jīva. In the Vedānta system Īśvara has but little importance, for he is but a phenomenal being; he may be better, purer, and much more powerful than we, but yet he is as much phenomenal as any of us. The highest truth is the self, the reality, the Brahman, and both jīva and Īśvara are but illusory impositions on it. Some Vedantists hold that there is but one jīva and one body, and that all the world as well as all the jīvas in it are merely his imaginings. These dream jīvas and the dream world will continue so long as that super-jīva continues to undergo his experiences; the world-appearance and all of us imaginary individuals, run our course and salvation is as much imaginary salvation as our world-experience is an imaginary experience of the imaginary jīvas. The cosmic jīva is alone the awakened jīva and all the rest are but his imaginings. This is known as the doctrine of ekajīva (one-soul).

The opposite of this doctrine is the theory held by some Vedantists that there are many individuals and the world-appearance has no permanent illusion for all people, but each person creates for himself his own illusion, and there is no objective datum which forms the common ground for the illusory perception of all people; just as when ten persons see in the darkness a rope and having the illusion of a snake there, run away, and agree in their individual perceptions that they have all seen the same snake, though each really had his own illusion and there was no snake at all. According to this view the illusory perception of each happens for him subjectively and has no corresponding objective phenomena as its ground. This must be distinguished from the normal Vedānta view which holds that objectively phenomena are also happening, but that these are illusory only in the sense that they will not last permanently and have thus only a temporary and relative existence in comparison with the truth or reality which is ever the same constant and unchangeable entity in all our perceptions and in all world-appearance. According to the other view phenomena are not objectively existent but are only subjectively imagined; so that the jug I see had no existence before I happened to have the perception that there was the jug; as soon as the jug illusion occurred to me I said that there was the jug, but it did not exist before. As soon as I had the perception there was the illusion, and there was no other reality apart from the illusion. It is therefore called the theory of dṛṣṭisṛṣṭivāda, i.e. the theory that the subjective perception is the creating of the objects and that there are no other objective phenomena apart from subjective perceptions. In the normal Vedānta view however the objects of the world are existent as phenomena by the sense-contact with which the subjective perceptions are created. The objective phenomena in themselves are of course but modifications of ajñāna, but still these phenomena of the ajñāna are there as the common ground for the experience of all. This therefore has an objective epistemology whereas the dṛṣṭisṛṣṭivāda has no proper epistemology, for the experiences of each person are determined by his own subjective avidyā and previous impressions as modifications of the avidyā. The dṛṣṭisṛṣṭivāda theory approaches nearest to the Vijñānavāda Buddhism, only with this difference that while Buddhism does not admit of any permanent being Vedānta admits the Brahman, the permanent unchangeable reality as the only truth, whereas the illusory and momentary perceptions are but impositions on it.

The mental and physical phenomena are alike in this, that both are modifications of ajñāna. It is indeed difficult to comprehend the nature of ajñāna, though its presence in consciousness can be perceived, and though by dialectic criticism all our most well-founded notions seem to vanish away and become self-contradictory and indefinable. Vedānta explains the reason of this difficulty as due to the fact that all these indefinable forms and names can only be experienced as modes of the real, the self-luminous. Our innate error which we continue from beginningless time consists in this, that the real in its full complete light is ever hidden from us, and the glimpse that we get of it is always through manifestations of forms and names; these phenomenal forms and names are undefinable, incomprehensible, and unknowable in themselves, but under certain conditions they are manifested by the self-luminous real, and at the time they are so manifested they seem to have a positive being which is undeniable. This positive being is only the highest being, the real which appears as the being of those forms and names. A lump of clay may be moulded into a plate or a cup, but the plate-form or the cup-form has no existence or being apart from the being of the clay; it is the being of the clay that is imposed on the diverse forms which also then seem to have being in themselves. Our illusion thus consists in mutually misattributing the characteristics of the unreal forms—the modes of ajñāna and the real being. As this illusion is the mode of all our experience and its very essence, it is indeed difficult for us to conceive of the Brahman as apart from the modes of ajñāna. Moreover such is the nature of ajñānas that they are knowable only by a false identification of them with the self-luminous Brahman or ātman. Being as such is the highest truth, the Brahman. The ajñāna states are not non-being in the sense of nothing of pure negation (*abhāva*), but in the sense that they are not being. Being that is the self-luminous illuminates non-being, the ajñāna, and this illumination means nothing more than a false identification of being with non-being. The forms of ajñāna if they are to be known must be associated with pure consciousness, and this association means an illusion, superimposition, and mutual misattribution. But apart from pure consciousness these cannot be manifested or known, for it is pure consciousness alone that is self-luminous. Thus when we try to know the ajñāna states in themselves as apart from the ātman we fall in a dilemma, for knowledge means illusory superimposition or illusion, and when it is not knowledge they evidently cannot be known. Thus apart from its being a factor in our illusory experience no other kind of its existence is known to us. If ajñāna had been a non-entity altogether it could never come at all, if it were a positive entity then it would never cease to be; the ajñāna thus is a mysterious category midway between being and non-being and indefinable in every way; and it is on account of this that it is called *tattvānyatvābhyām anirvācya* or undefinable and undeterminable either as real or unreal. It is real in the sense that it is a necessary postulate of our phenomenal experience and unreal in its own nature, for apart from its connection with consciousness it is incomprehensible and undefinable. Its forms even while they are manifested in consciousness are self-contradictory and incomprehensible as to their real nature or mutual relation, and comprehensible only so far as they are manifested in consciousness, but apart from these no rational conception of them can be formed. Thus it is impossible to say anything about the ajñāna (for no knowledge of it is possible) save so far as manifested in consciousness and depending on this the Dṛṣṭisṛṣṭivādins asserted that our experience was inexplicably produced under the influence of avidyā and that beyond that no objective common ground could be admitted. But though this has the general assent of Vedānta and is irrefutable in itself, still for the sake of explaining our common sense view (*pratikarmavyavasathā*) we may think that we have an objective world before us as the common field of experience. We can also imagine a scheme of things and operations by which the phenomenon of our experience may be interpreted in the light of the Vedānta metaphysics.

The subject can be conceived in three forms: firstly as the ātman, the one highest reality, secondly as jīva or the ātman as limited by its psychosis, when the psychosis is not differentiated from the ātman, but ātman is regarded as identical with the psychosis thus appearing as a living and knowing being, as *jīvasākṣi* or perceiving consciousness, or the aspect in which the jīva comprehends, knows, or experiences; thirdly the antaḥkaraṇa psychosis or mind which is an inner centre or bundle of avidyā manifestations, just as the outer world objects are exterior centres of avidyā phenomena or objective entities. The antaḥkaraṇa is not only the avidyā capable of supplying all forms to our present experiences, but it also contains all the tendencies and modes of past impressions of experience in this life or in past lives. The antaḥkaraṇa is always turning the various avidyā modes of it into the jīvasākṣi (jīva in its aspect as illuminating mental states), and these are also immediately manifested, made known, and transformed into experience. These avidyā states of the antaḥkaraṇa are called its vṛttis or states. The specific peculiarity of the vṛtti-ajñānas is this that only in these forms can they be superimposed upon pure consciousness, and thus be interpreted as states of consciousness and have their indefiniteness or cover removed. The forms of ajñāna remain as indefinite and hidden or veiled only so long as they do not come into relation to these vṛttis of antaḥkaraṇa, for the ajñāna can be destroyed by the cit only in the form of a vṛtti, while in all other forms the ajñāna veils the cit from manifestation. The removal of ajñāna-vṛttis of the antaḥkaraṇa or the manifestation of vṛtti-jñāna is nothing but this, that the antaḥkaraṇa states of avidyā are the only states of ajñāna which can be superimposed upon the self-luminous ātman (*adhyāsa*, false attribution). The objective world consists of the avidyā phenomena with the self as its background. Its objectivity consists in this that avidyā in this form cannot be superimposed on the self-luminous cit but exists only as veiling the cit. These avidyā phenomena may be regarded as many and diverse, but in all these forms they serve only to veil the cit and are beyond consciousness. It is only when they come in contact with the avidyā phenomena as antaḥkaraṇa states that they coalesce with the avidyā states and render themselves objects of consciousness or have their veil of āvaraṇa removed. It is thus assumed that in ordinary perceptions of objects such as jug, etc. the antaḥkaraṇa goes out of the man's body (*śarīramadhyāt*) and coming in touch with the jug becomes transformed into the same form, and as soon as this transformation takes place the cit which is always steadily shining illuminates the jug-form or the jug. The jug phenomena in the objective world could not be manifested (though these were taking place on the background of the same self-luminous Brahman or ātman as forms of the highest truth of my subjective consciousness) because the ajñāna phenomena in these forms serve to veil their illuminator, the self-luminous. It was only by coming into contact with these phenomena that the antaḥkaraṇa could be transformed into corresponding states and that the illumination dawned which at once revealed the antaḥkaraṇa states and the objects with which these states or vṛttis had coalesced. The consciousness manifested through the vṛttis alone has the power of removing the ajñāna veiling the cit. Of course there are no actual distinctions of inner or outer, or the cit within me and the cit without me. These are only of appearance and due to avidyā. And it is only from the point of view of appearance that we suppose that knowledge of objects can only dawn when the inner cit and the outer cit unite together through the antaḥkaraṇavṛtti, which makes the external objects translucent as it were by its own translucence, removes the ajñāna which was veiling the external self-luminous cit and reveals the object phenomena by the very union of the cit as reflected through it and the cit as underlying the object phenomena. The pratyakṣa-pramā or right knowledge by perception is the cit, the pure consciousness, reflected through the vṛtti and identical with the cit as the background of the object phenomena revealed by it. From the relative point of view we may thus distinguish three consciousnesses: (1) consciousness as the background of objective phenomena, (2) consciousness as the background of the jīva or pramātā, the individual, (3) consciousness reflected in the vṛtti of the antaḥkaraṇa; when these three unite perception is effected.

Pramā or right knowledge means in Vedānta the acquirement of such new knowledge as has not been contradicted by experience (*abādhita*). There is thus no absolute definition of truth. A knowledge acquired can be said to be true only so long as it is not contradicted. Thus the world appearance though it is very true now, may be rendered false, when this is contradicted by right knowledge of Brahman as the one reality. Thus the knowledge of the world appearance is true now, but not true absolutely. The only absolute truth is the pure consciousness which is never contradicted in any experience at any time. The truth of our world-knowledge is thus to be tested by finding out whether it will be contradicted at any stage of world experience or not. That which is not contradicted by later experience is to be regarded as true, for all world knowledge as a whole will be contradicted when Brahma-knowledge is realized.

The inner experiences of pleasure and pain also are generated by a false identification of antaḥkaraṇa transformations as pleasure or pain with the self, by virtue of which are generated the perceptions, "I am happy," or "I am sorry." In continuous perception of anything for a certain time as an object or as pleasure, etc. the mental state or vṛtti is said to last in the same way all the while so long as any other new form is not taken up by the antaḥkaraṇa for the acquirement of any new knowledge. In such cases when I infer that there is fire on the hill that I see, the hill is an object of perception, for the antaḥkaraṇa vṛtti is one with it, but that there is fire in it is a matter of inference, for the antaḥkarana vṛtti cannot be in touch with the fire; so in the same experience there may be two modes of mental modification, as perception in seeing the hill, and as inference in inferring the fire in the hill. In cases of acquired perception, as when on seeing sandal wood I think that it is odoriferous sandal wood, it is pure perception so far as the sandal wood is concerned, it is inference or memory so far as I assert it to be odoriferous. Vedānta does not admit the existence of the relation called *samavāya* (inherence) or *jāti* (class notion); and so does not distinguish perception as a class as distinct from the other class called inference, and holds that both perception and inference are but different modes of the transformations of the antaḥkaraṇa reflecting the cit in the corresponding vṛttis. The perception is thus nothing but the cit manifestation in the antaḥkaraṇa vṛtti transformed into the form of an object with which it is in contact. Perception in its objective aspect is the identity of the cit underlying the object with the subject, and perception in the subjective aspect is regarded as the identity of the subjective cit with the objective cit. This identity of course means that through the vṛtti the same reality subsisting in the object and the subject is realized, whereas in inference the thing to be inferred, being away from contact with antaḥkaraṇa, has apparently a different reality from that manifested in the states of consciousness. Thus perception is regarded as the mental state representing the same identical reality in the object and the subject by antaḥkaraṇa contact, and it is held that the knowledge produced by words (e.g. this is the same Devadatta) referring identically to the same thing which is seen (e.g. when I see Devadatta before me another man says this is Devadatta, and the knowledge produced by "this is Devadatta" though a verbal (*śābda*) knowledge is to be regarded as perception, for the antaḥkaraṇa vṛtti is the same) is to be regarded as perception or pratyakṣa. The content of these words (this is Devadatta) being the same as the perception, and there being no new relationing knowledge as represented in the proposition "this is Devadatta" involving the unity of two terms "this" and "Devadatta" with a copula, but only the indication of one whole as Devadatta under visual perception already experienced, the knowledge proceeding from "this is Devadatta" is regarded as an example of nirvikalpa knowledge. So on the occasion of the rise of Brahma-consciousness when the preceptor instructs "thou art Brahman" the knowledge proceeding from the sentence is not savikalpa, for though grammatically there are two ideas and a copula, yet from the point of view of intrinsic significance (*tātparya*) one identical reality only is indicated. Vedānta does not distinguish nirvikalpa and savikalpa in visual perception, but only in śābda perception as in cases referred to above. In all such cases the condition for nirvikalpa is that the notion conveyed by the sentence should be one whole or one identical reality, whereas in savikalpa perception we have a combination of different ideas as in the sentence, "the king's man is coming" (*rājapuruṣa āgacchati*). Here no identical reality is signified, but what is signified is the combination of two or three different concepts[1].

It is not out of place to mention in this connection that Vedānta admits all the six pramāṇas of Kumārila and considers like Mīmāṃsā that all knowledge is self-valid (*svataḥ-pramāṇa*). But pramā has not the same meaning in Vedānta as in Mīmāṃsā. There as we remember pramā meant the knowledge which goaded one to practical action and as such all knowledge was pramā, until practical experience showed the course of action in accordance with which it was found to be contradicted. In Vedānta however there is no reference to action, but pramā means only uncontradicted cognition. To the definition of self-validity as given by Mīmāṃsā Vedānta adds another objective qualification, that such knowledge can have svataḥ-prāmāṇya as is not vitiated by the presence of any doṣa (cause of error, such as defect of senses or the like). Vedānta of course does not think like Nyāya that positive conditions (e.g. correspondence, etc.) are necessary for the validity of knowledge, nor does it divest knowledge of all qualifications like the Mīmāṃsists, for whom all knowledge is self-valid as such. It adopts a middle course and holds that absence of doṣa is a necessary condition for the self-validity of knowledge. It is clear that this is a compromise, for whenever an external condition has to be admitted, the knowledge cannot be regarded as self-valid, but Vedānta says that as it requires only a negative condition for the absence of doṣa, the objection does not apply to it, and it holds that if it depended on the presence of any positive condition for proving the validity of knowledge like the Nyāya, then only its theory of self-validity would have been damaged. But since it wants only a negative condition, no blame can be

[1] See *Vedāntaparibhāṣā* and *Śikhāmaṇi*.

attributed to its theory of self-validity. Vedānta was bound to follow this slippery middle course, for it could not say that the pure cit reflected in consciousness could require anything else for establishing its validity, nor could it say that all phenomenal forms of knowledge were also all valid, for then the world-appearance would come to be valid; so it held that knowledge could be regarded as valid only when there was no doṣa present; thus from the absolute point of view all world-knowledge was false and had no validity, because there was the avidyā-doṣa, and in the ordinary sphere also that knowledge was valid in which there was no doṣa. Validity (prāmāṇya) with Mīmāṃsā meant the capacity that knowledge has to goad us to practical action in accordance with it, but with Vedānta it meant correctness to facts and want of contradiction. The absence of doṣa being guaranteed there is nothing which can vitiate the correctness of knowledge[1].

Vedānta Theory of Illusion.

We have already seen that the Mīmāṃsists had asserted that all knowledge was true simply because it was knowledge (*yathārthāḥ sarve vivādaspadībhūtāḥ pratyayāḥ pratyayatvāt*). Even illusions were explained by them as being non-perception of the distinction between the thing perceived (e.g. the conch-shell), and the thing remembered (e.g. silver). But Vedānta objects to this, and asks how there can be non-distinction between a thing which is clearly perceived and a thing which is remembered? If it is said that it is merely a non-perception of the non-association (i.e. non-perception of the fact that this is not connected with silver), then also it cannot be, for then it is on either side mere negation, and negation with Mīmāṃsā is nothing but the bare presence of the locus of negation (e.g. negation of jug on the ground is nothing but the bare presence of the ground), or in other words non-perception of the non-association of "silver" and "this" means barely and merely the "silver" and "this." Even admitting for argument's sake that the distinction between two things or two ideas is not perceived, yet merely from such a negative aspect no one could be tempted to move forward to action (such as stooping down to pick up a piece of illusory silver). It is positive

[1] See *Vedāntaparibhāṣā*, *Śikhāmaṇi*, *Maṇiprabhā* and Citsukha on svataḥprāmāṇya.

conviction or perception that can lead a man to actual practical movement. If again it is said that it is the general and imperfect perception of a thing (which has not been properly differentiated and comprehended) before me, which by the memory of silver appears to be like true silver before me and this generates the movement for picking it up, then this also is objectionable. For the appearance of the similarity with real silver cannot lead us to behave with the thing before me as if it were real silver. Thus I may perceive that gavaya (wild ox) is similar to cow, but despite this similarity I am not tempted to behave with the gavaya as if it were a cow. Thus in whatever way the Mīmāṃsā position may be defined it fails[1]. Vedānta thinks that the illusion is not merely subjective, but that there is actually a phenomenon of illusion as there are phenomena of actual external objects; the difference in the two cases consists in this, that the illusion is generated by the doṣa or defect of the senses etc., whereas the phenomena of external objects are not due to such specific doṣas. The process of illusory perception in Vedānta may be described thus. First by the contact of the senses vitiated by doṣas a mental state as "thisness" with reference to the thing before me is generated; then in the thing as "this" and in the mental state of the form of that "this" the cit is reflected. Then the avidyā (nescience) associated with the cit is disturbed by the presence of the doṣa, and this disturbance along with the impression of silver remembered through similarity is transformed into the appearance of silver. There is thus an objective illusory silver appearance, as well as a similar transformation of the mental state generated by its contact with the illusory silver. These two transformations, the silver state of the mind and external phenomenal illusory silver state, are manifested by the perceiving consciousness (*sākṣicaitanya*). There are thus here two phenomenal transformations, one in the avidyā states forming the illusory objective silver phenomenon, and another in the antaḥkaraṇa-vṛtti or mind state. But in spite of there being two distinct and separate phenomena, their object being the same as the "this" in perception, we have one knowledge of illusion. The special feature of this theory of illusion is that an indefinable (*anirvacanīya-khyāti*) illusory silver is created in every case where an illusory perception of silver occurs. There are three orders of reality in Vedānta, namely the

[1] See *Vivaraṇa-prameya-saṃgraha* and *Nyāyamakaranda* on akhyāti refutation.

pāramārthika or absolute, *vyavahārika* or practical ordinary experience, and *prātibhāsika*, illusory. The first one represents the absolute truth; the other two are false impressions due to doṣa. The difference between vyavahārika and prātibhāsika is that the doṣa of the vyavahārika perception is neither discovered nor removed until salvation, whereas the doṣa of the prātibhāsika reality which occurs in many extraneous forms (such as defect of the senses, sleep, etc.) is perceived in the world of our ordinary experience, and thus the prātibhāsika experience lasts for a much shorter period than the vyavahārika. But just as the vyavahārika world is regarded as phenomenal modifications of the ajñāna, as apart from our subjective experience and even before it, so the illusion (e.g. of silver in the conch-shell) is also regarded as a modification of avidyā, an undefinable creation of the object of illusion, by the agency of the doṣa. Thus in the case of the illusion of silver in the conch-shell, indefinable silver is created by the doṣa in association with the senses, which is called the creation of an indefinable (*anirvacanīya*) silver of illusion. Here the cit underlying the conch-shell remains the same but the avidyā of antaḥkaraṇa suffers modifications (*pariṇāma*) on account of doṣa, and thus gives rise to the illusory creation. The illusory silver is thus *vivartta* (appearance) from the point of view of the cit and pariṇāma from the point of view of avidyā, for the difference between vivartta and pariṇāma is, that in the former the transformations have a different reality from the cause (cit is different from the appearance imposed on it), while in the latter case the transformations have the same reality as the transforming entity (appearance of silver has the same stuff as the avidyā whose transformations it is). But now a difficulty arises that if the illusory perception of silver is due to a coalescing of the cit underlying the antaḥkaraṇa-vṛtti as modified by doṣa and the object—cit as underlying the "this" before me (in the illusion of "this is silver"), then I ought to have the experience that "I am silver" like "I am happy" and not that "this is silver"; the answer is, that as the coalescing takes place in connection with my previous notion as "this," the form of the knowledge also is "this is silver," whereas in the notion "I am happy," the notion of happiness takes place in connection with a previous vṛtti of "I." Thus though the coalescing of the two "cits" is the same in both cases, yet in one case the knowledge takes the form of "I am," and in another as "this is" according as the previous impression is "I" or "this." In dreams also the dream perceptions are the same as the illusory perception of silver in the conch-shell. There the illusory creations are generated through the defects of sleep, and these creations are imposed upon the cit. The dream experiences cannot be regarded merely as memory-products, for the perception in dream is in the form that "I see that I ride in the air on chariots, etc." and not that "I remember the chariots." In the dream state all the senses are inactive, and therefore there is no separate objective cit there, but the whole dream experience with all characteristics of space, time, objects, etc. is imposed upon the cit. The objection that since the imposition is on the pure cit the imposition ought to last even in waking stages, and that the dream experiences ought to continue even in waking life, does not hold; for in the waking stages the antaḥkaraṇa is being constantly transformed into different states on the expiry of the defects of sleep, etc., which were causing the dream cognitions. This is called *nivṛtti* (negation) as distinguished from *bādha* (cessation). The illusory creation of dream experiences may still be there on the pure cit, but these cannot be experienced any longer, for there being no doṣa of sleep the antaḥkaraṇa is active and suffering modifications in accordance with the objects presented before us. This is what is called nivṛtti, for though the illusion is there I cannot experience it, whereas bādha or cessation occurs when the illusory creation ceases, as when on finding out the real nature of the conch-shell the illusion of silver ceases, and we feel that this is not silver, this was not and will not be silver. When the conch-shell is perceived as silver, the silver is felt as a reality, but this feeling of reality was not an illusory creation, though the silver was an objective illusory creation; for the reality in the śukti (conch-shell) is transferred and felt as belonging to the illusion of silver imposed upon it. Here we see that the illusion of silver has two different kinds of illusion comprehended in it. One is the creation of an indefinable silver (*anirvacanīya-rajatotpatti*) and the other is the attribution of the reality belonging to the conch-shell to the illusory silver imposed upon it, by which we feel at the time of the illusion that it is a reality. This is no doubt the *anyathākhyāti* form of illusion as advocated by Nyāya. Vedānta admits that when two things (e.g. red flower and crystal) are both present before my senses, and I attribute the quality of one to the other by illusion (e.g. the illusion that the crystal is red), then the illusion is of the form of anyathākhyāti; but if one of the things is not present before my senses and the other is, then the illusion is not of the anyathākhyāti type, but of the anirvacanīyakhyāti type. Vedānta could not avoid the former type of illusion, for it believed that all appearance of reality in the world-appearance was really derived from the reality of Brahman, which was self-luminous in all our experiences. The world appearance is an illusory creation, but the sense of reality that it carries with it is a misattribution (*anyathākhyāti*) of the characteristic of the Brahman to it, for Brahman alone is the true and the real, which manifests itself as the reality of all our illusory world-experience, just as it is the reality of śukti that gives to the appearance of silver its reality.

Vedānta Ethics and Vedānta Emancipation.

Vedānta says that when a duly qualified man takes to the study of Vedānta and is instructed by the preceptor—"Thou art that (Brahman)," he attains the emancipating knowledge, and the world-appearance becomes for him false and illusory. The qualifications necessary for the study of Vedānta are (1) that the person having studied all the Vedas with the proper accessories, such as grammar, lexicon etc. is in full possession of the knowledge of the Vedas, (2) that either in this life or in another, he must have performed only the obligatory Vedic duties (such as daily prayer, etc. called *nitya-karma*) and occasionally obligatory duty (such as the birth ceremony at the birth of a son, called *naimittika-karma*) and must have avoided all actions for the fulfilment of selfish desires (*kāmya-karmas*, such as the performance of sacrifices for going to Heaven) and all prohibited actions (e.g. murder, etc. *niṣiddha-karma*) in such a way that his mind is purged of all good and bad actions (no karma is generated by the *nitya* and *naimittika-karma*, and as he has not performed the *kāmya* and prohibited karmas, he has acquired no new karma). When he has thus properly purified his mind and is in possession of the four virtues or means of fitting the mind for Vedānta instruction (called *sādhana*) he can regard himself as properly qualified for the Vedānta instruction. These virtues are (1) knowledge of what is eternal and what is transient, (2) disinclination to enjoyments of this life and of the heavenly life after death, (3) extreme distaste for all enjoyments, and anxiety for attaining the means of right knowledge, (4) control over the senses by which these are restrained from everything but that which aids the attainment of right knowledge (*dama*), (*a*) having restrained them, the attainment of such power that these senses may not again be tempted towards worldly enjoyments (*uparati*), (*b*) power of bearing extremes of heat, cold, etc., (*c*) employment of mind towards the attainment of right knowledge, (*d*) faith in the instructor and Upaniṣads; (5) strong desire to attain salvation. A man possessing the above qualities should try to understand correctly the true purport of the Upaniṣads (called *śravaṇa*), and by arguments in favour of the purport of the Upaniṣads to strengthen his conviction as stated in the Upaniṣads (called *manana*) and then by *nididhyāsana* (meditation) which includes all the Yoga processes of concentration, try to realize the truth as one. Vedānta therefore in ethics covers the ground of Yoga; but while for Yoga emancipation proceeds from understanding the difference between puruṣa and prakṛti, with Vedānta salvation comes by the dawn of right knowledge that Brahman alone is the true reality, his own self[1]. Mīmāṃsā asserts that the Vedas do not declare the knowledge of one Brahman to be the supreme goal, but holds that all persons should act in accordance with the Vedic injunctions for the attainment of good and the removal of evil. But Vedānta holds that though the purport of the earlier Vedas is as Mīmāṃsā has it, yet this is meant only for ordinary people, whereas for the elect the goal is clearly as the Upaniṣads indicate it, namely the attainment of the highest knowledge. The performance of Vedic duties is intended only for ordinary men, but yet it was believed by many (e.g. Vācaspati Miśra and his followers) that due performance of Vedic duties helped a man to acquire a great keenness for the attainment of right knowledge; others believed (e.g. Prakāśātmā and his followers) that it served to bring about suitable opportunities by securing good preceptors, etc. and to remove many obstacles from the way so that it became easier for a person to attain the desired right knowledge.

In the acquirement of ordinary knowledge the ajñānas re-

[1] See *Vedāntasāra* and *Advaitabrahmasiddhi*.

moved are only smaller states of ajñāna, whereas when the Brahma-knowledge dawns the ajñāna as a whole is removed. Brahma-knowledge at the stage of its first rise is itself also a state of knowledge, but such is its special strength that when this knowledge once dawns, even the state of knowledge which at first reflects it (and which being a state is itself ajñāna modification) is destroyed by it. The state itself being destroyed, only the pure infinite and unlimited Brahman shines forth in its own true light. Thus it is said that just as fire riding on a piece of wood would burn the whole city and after that would burn the very same wood, so in the last state of mind the Brahma-knowledge would destroy all the illusory world-appearance and at last destroy even that final state[1].

The mukti stage is one in which the pure light of Brahman as the identity of pure intelligence, being and complete bliss shines forth in its unique glory, and all the rest vanishes as illusory nothing. As all being of the world-appearance is but limited manifestations of that one being, so all pleasures also are but limited manifestations of that supreme bliss, a taste of which we all can get in deep dreamless sleep. The being of Brahman however is not an abstraction from all existent beings as the *sattā* (being as class notion) of the naiyāyika, but the concrete, the real, which in its aspect as pure consciousness and pure bliss is always identical with itself. Being (*sat*) is pure bliss and pure consciousness. What becomes of the avidyā during mukti (emancipation) is as difficult for one to answer as the question, how the avidyā came forth and stayed during the world-appearance. It is best to remember that the category of the indefinite avidyā is indefinite as regards its origin, manifestation and destruction. Vedānta however believes that even when the true knowledge has once been attained, the body may last for a while, if the individual's previously ripened karmas demand it. Thus the emancipated person may walk about and behave like an ordinary sage, but yet he is emancipated and can no longer acquire any new karma. As soon as the fruits due to his ripe karmas are enjoyed and exhausted, the sage loses his body and there will never be any other birth for him, for the dawn of perfect knowledge has burnt up for him all budding karmas of beginningless previous lives, and he is no longer subject to any

[1] *Siddhāntaleśa*.

of the illusions subjective or objective which could make any knowledge, action, or feeling possible for him. Such a man is called *jīvanmukta*, i.e. emancipated while living. For him all world-appearance has ceased. He is the one light burning alone in himself where everything else has vanished for ever from the stage[1].

Vedānta and other Indian Systems.

Vedānta is distinctly antagonistic to Nyāya, and most of its powerful dialectic criticism is generally directed against it. Śaṅkara himself had begun it by showing contradictions and inconsistencies in many of the Nyāya conceptions, such as the theory of causation, conception of the atom, the relation of samavāya, the conception of jāti, etc.[2] His followers carried it to still greater lengths as is fully demonstrated by the labours of Śrīharṣa, Citsukha, Madhusūdana, etc. It was opposed to Mīmāṃsā so far as this admitted the Nyāya-Vaiśeṣika categories, but agreed with it generally as regards the pramāṇas of anumāna, upamiti, arthāpatti, śabda, and anupalabdhi. It also found a great supporter in Mīmāṃsā with its doctrine of the self-validity and self-manifesting power of knowledge. But it differed from Mīmāṃsā in the field of practical duties and entered into many elaborate discussions to prove that the duties of the Vedas referred only to ordinary men, whereas men of higher order had no Vedic duties to perform but were to rise above them and attain the highest knowledge, and that a man should perform the Vedic duties only so long as he was not fit for Vedānta instruction and studies.

With Sāṃkhya and Yoga the relation of Vedānta seems to be very close. We have already seen that Vedānta had accepted all the special means of self-purification, meditation, etc., that were advocated by Yoga. The main difference between Vedānta and Sāṃkhya was this that Sāṃkhya believed that the stuff of which the world consisted was a reality side by side with the puruṣas. In later times Vedānta had compromised so far with Sāṃkhya that it also sometimes described māyā as being made up of sattva, rajas, and tamas. Vedānta also held that according to these three characteristics were formed diverse modifications

[1] See *Pañcadaśī*.

[2] See Śaṅkara's refutation of Nyāya, *Śaṅkara-bhāṣya*, II. ii.

of the māyā. Thus Īśvara is believed to possess a mind of pure sattva alone. But sattva, rajas and tamas were accepted in Vedānta in the sense of tendencies and not as reals as Sāṃkhya held it. Moreover, in spite of all modifications that māyā was believed to pass through as the stuff of the world-appearance, it was indefinable and indefinite, and in its nature different from what we understand as positive or negative. It was an unsubstantial nothing, a magic entity which had its being only so long as it appeared. Prakṛti also was indefinable or rather undemonstrable as regards its own essential nature apart from its manifestation, but even then it was believed to be a combination of positive reals. It was undefinable because so long as the reals composing it did not combine, no demonstrable qualities belonged to it with which it could be defined. Māyā however was undemonstrable, indefinite, and indefinable in all forms; it was a separate category of the indefinite. Sāṃkhya believed in the personal individuality of souls, while for Vedānta there was only one soul or self, which appeared as many by virtue of the māyā transformations. There was an adhyāsa or illusion in Sāṃkhya as well as in Vedānta; but in the former the illusion was due to a mere non-distinction between prakṛti and puruṣa or mere misattribution of characters or identities, but in Vedānta there was not only misattribution, but a false and altogether indefinable creation. Causation with Sāṃkhya meant real transformation, but with Vedānta all transformation was mere appearance. Though there were so many differences, it is however easy to see that probably at the time of the origin of the two systems during the Upaniṣad period each was built up from very similar ideas which differed only in tendencies that gradually manifested themselves into the present divergences of the two systems. Though Śaṅkara laboured hard to prove that the Sāṃkhya view could not be found in the Upaniṣads, we can hardly be convinced by his interpretations and arguments. The more he argues, the more we are led to suspect that the Sāṃkhya thought had its origin in the Upaniṣads. Śaṅkara and his followers borrowed much of their dialectic form of criticism from the Buddhists. His Brahman was very much like the śūnya of Nāgārjuna. It is difficult indeed to distinguish between pure being and pure non-being as a category. The debts of Śaṅkara to the self-luminosity of the Vijñānavāda Buddhism can hardly be overestimated. There seems to be much truth in the accusations against Śaṅkara by Vijñāna Bhikṣu and others that he was a hidden Buddhist himself. I am led to think that Śaṅkara's philosophy is largely a compound of Vijñānavāda and Śūnyavāda Buddhism with the Upaniṣad notion of the permanence of self superadded.

INDEX[1]

[1] The words are arranged in the order of the English alphabet. Sanskrit and Pāli technical terms and words are in small italics; names of books are in italics with a capital. English words and other names are in Roman with a capital. Letters with diacritical marks come after ordinary ones. But throughout the body of the book the names of Vedic works are in Roman with a capital, as a mark of respect for their supposed revealed character.

self, 161 ff.; doctrine of momentariness and the doctrine of causal efficiency, 163 ff.; doctrine of *pañcakāraṇī* as determining cause-effect relation, refuted by Vācaspati, 352; doctrine of *tādātmya* and *tadutpatti* as grounds of inference refuted by Vācaspati, 352; epistemology of the Sautrāntikas, 408 ff.; evolution of thought in, 166; heretical schools prior to, 79; identity and recognition, 162; influence on Mīmāṃsā logic, 388, 390; nature of existence, 163; no-soul doctrine in, 93; ontological problems, 164 ff.; relation of substance and quality, 164; relation of universals and particulars, 164; relation of the whole and the part, 164; relation of cause and effect, 164; relation of inherence, 165; relation of power to the power-possessor, 165; relation to Upaniṣads, 80; schools, rise of, 112; sense-data and sensations in, 95; state of philosophy prior to, 78; the *khandha*-doctrine, 93; Theravāda schools, 112; views on *sāmānya*, 318 *n.*; *vyāpti* by negative instances, 389 *n.*; Yogācāra epistemology, 411 ff.

Buddhism (early), *avijjā* in, 99; causal connection, 84; definition of samādhi, 101; four noble truths, 101; importance of feeling, 97; *kamma*, classification of, 108; *kamma*, the doctrine of, 106; *karma* and desire, 108; *khandhas* as "I," 98; *kilesas* in, 100; meditation in, stages of, 105; meditation of human body as impure, 103; meditation of universal friendship, pity etc., 103; *nivvāṇa* and heresy in, 109; *nivvāṇa*, theory of, 108; no-self doctrine, contrasted with Upaniṣad self-doctrine, 110; objects of concentration, 104; pessimism in, 102 *n.*; preparatory measures for meditation, 102; science of breath, 103; sense-contact theory in, 97; *sīla* and *samādhi* in, 100; theory of cognition in, 96; Upaniṣads, relation with, 109; volition in, 98

Buddhism in Translations, 88 *n.*, 89 *n.*, 90 *n.*, 99 *n.*, 107 *n.*, 108 *n.*, 111 *n.*

Buddhismus, 218 *n.*

Buddhist, 130 *n.*, 161, 163, 169, 177, 178, 230, 233, 237, 278, 299, 300, 378, 389 *n.*, 390, 394, 406, 423, 429, 434, 437, 465; canonical works, 82; council, 129; doctrines, 281; literature, 78, 82, 92; logic, 120, 155, 157, 309; missionaries, 301 *n.*; philosophy, 3, 7, 84, 145, 164, 210; psychology, 96, 96 *n.*

Buddhistic, 81, 427 *n.*; doctrines, 82, 100; texts, 109

Buddhists, 7, 68, 68 *n.*, 75, 112, 129, 147, 167, 173, 174, 182, 185, 186, 187, 196, 203, 229, 240 *n.*, 257, 274, 279, 296, 301, 307, 309, 310, 318, 325, 331, 332, 339, 340, 341, 345, 346, 347, 348, 350, 352, 357, 362, 363, 380 *n.*, 385, 411, 413

buddhitattva, 249, 250

Bulletin de l'Académie des Sciences de Russie, 119 *n.*

Burgess, J., 170 *n.*

Bühler, 170 *n.*, 276

caitasikakarma, 123

caitta, 121

caittadharma, 121

caittasaṃskṛta dharmas, 124

caittikas, 112

cakrabhramivaddhṛtaśarīraḥ, 268

Cakradatta, 231

cakraka, 205

Cakrapāṇi, 213 *n.*, 231, 235, 236

Cakrapāṇidatta, 230

cakravarttī, 91 *n.*

Cakravarttī, Mr, 308 *n.*

Calcutta, 165 *n.*, 168

Calcutta University, 121, 208 *n.*, 213

Cambridge, 155 *n.*

Candrakānta Tarkālaṃkāra, 279

Candrakīrti, 85 *n.*, 86 *n.*, 87, 90 *n.*, 109, 125 *n.*, 128, 129, 138, 140, 166; his interpretation of nāma, 88 *n.*

Candraprajñapti, 171 *n.*

Candrikā, 212

Caṇḍāvīja, 171 *n.*

Capacity, 159, 160

Caraka, 91 *n.*, 212, 213, 216, 217, 218, 219, 224, 231, 280, 281, 287 *n.*, 302, 304 *n.*; his view of soul, 91 *n.*; system of Sāṃkhya in, 214

Caraka kārikā, 280

Caraka saṃhitā, 302

Caraka, śārīra, 280 *n.*

Carake Patañjaliḥ, 235

carv, 79

Caryāpiṭaka, 83

Categories, 281, 283, 287, 312, 313, 365, 413, 461, 492

Category, 317, 378 *n.*, 398, 442, 443, 493

catudhātuvavatthānabhāvanā, 102

catuḥsūtrī, 70

catuḥśaraṇa, 171 *n.*

catuḥśataka, 129

caturaṇuka, 326

cauryya, 193

Causal activity, 165; collocations, 341; efficiency, 163, 168; movement, 320

Causation, 466, 468; as real change, 53

Cause, 326

Cause-collocation, 274, 275

cāgānussati, 102

cāmara, 172

cāritra, 195, 199

Cārvāka, 68, 71, 87, 302

Cārvākas, 78, 79, 325, 332, 345, 362, 394; philosophy of, 79

Central India, 172

M0200201 200 00 Set of 5 vols.